ISLAND HISTORICAL ECOLOGY

ISLAND HISTORICAL ECOLOGY

Socionatural Landscapes of
the Eastern and Southern Caribbean

Edited by
Peter E. Siegel

berghahn
NEW YORK • OXFORD
www.berghahnbooks.com

First published in 2018 by
Berghahn Books
www.berghahnbooks.com

© 2018, 2025 Peter E. Siegel
First paperback edition published in 2025

All rights reserved. Except for the quotation of short passages for the purposes of criticism and review, no part of this book may be reproduced in any form or by any means, electronic or mechanical, including photocopying, recording, or any information storage and retrieval system now known or to be invented, without written permission of the publisher.

Library of Congress Cataloging-in-Publication Data

Names: Siegel, Peter E., editor.
Title: Island historical ecology : socionatural landscapes of the eastern and southern Caribbean / edited by Peter E. Siegel.
Description: New York, NY : Berghahn Books, 2018. | Includes bibliographical references and index.
Identifiers: LCCN 2017050582 (print) | LCCN 2017053546 (ebook) | ISBN 9781785337642 (eBook) | ISBN 9781785337635 (hardback : alk. paper)
Subjects: LCSH: Human ecology—Caribbean Area—History. | Nature—Effect of human beings on—Caribbean Area—History. | Landscape changes—Caribbean Area—History.
Classification: LCC GF524 (ebook) | LCC GF524 .I75 2018 (print) | DDC 304.209729—dc23
LC record available at https://lccn.loc.gov/2017050582

British Library Cataloguing in Publication Data

A catalogue record for this book is available from the British Library

ISBN 978-1-78533-763-5 hardback
ISBN 978-1-83695-058-5 paperback
ISBN 978-1-83695-180-3 epub
ISBN 978-1-78533-764-2 web pdf

https://doi.org/10.3167/9781785337635

Contents

	Figures	viii
	Tables	xii
	Acknowledgments	xv
	Foreword: A Prelude to Island Historical Ecology *William Balée*	xvi
	Preface *Peter E. Siegel*	xix

Part I: Method, Theory, and Applications of Island Historical Ecology

Chapter 1.	Migrations, Colonization Processes, and Landscape Learning *Peter E. Siegel*	3
Chapter 2.	Unique Challenges in Archipelagoes: Examples from the Mediterranean and Pacific Islands *Thomas P. Leppard*	15
Chapter 3.	A Cultural Framework for Caribbean Island Historical Ecology Across the Lesser Antilles *Corinne L. Hofman and Menno L. P. Hoogland*	34
Chapter 4.	Methods for Addressing Island Historical Ecology *Deborah M. Pearsall, John G. Jones, Nicholas P. Dunning, Peter E. Siegel, Pat Farrell, Jason H. Curtis, and Neil A. Duncan*	57

Part II: West Indian Island Historical Ecology

Chapter 5.	Trinidad *Pat Farrell, Neil A. Duncan, John G. Jones, Nicholas P. Dunning, Deborah M. Pearsall, and Peter E. Siegel*	75

Chapter 6.	Grenada *John G. Jones, Deborah M. Pearsall, Pat Farrell, Nicholas P. Dunning, Jason H. Curtis, Neil A. Duncan, and Peter E. Siegel*	129
Chapter 7.	Curaçao *Nicholas P. Dunning, John G. Jones, Neil A. Duncan, Deborah M. Pearsall, and Peter E. Siegel*	155
Chapter 8.	Barbados *Nicholas P. Dunning, John G. Jones, Deborah M. Pearsall, and Peter E. Siegel*	182
Chapter 9.	Martinique *Neil A. Duncan, Nicholas P. Dunning, John G. Jones, Deborah M. Pearsall, and Peter E. Siegel*	203
Chapter 10.	Marie-Galante *John G. Jones, Nicholas P. Dunning, Deborah M. Pearsall, and Peter E. Siegel*	226
Chapter 11.	Antigua *John G. Jones, Nicholas P. Dunning, Deborah M. Pearsall, Neil A. Duncan, and Peter E. Siegel*	239
Chapter 12.	Barbuda *John G. Jones, Nicholas P. Dunning, Neil A. Duncan, Deborah M. Pearsall, and Peter E. Siegel*	270
Chapter 13.	St. Croix *Deborah M. Pearsall, Nicholas P. Dunning, John G. Jones, Neil A. Duncan, and Peter E. Siegel*	285

**PART III: SYNTHESIS AND FUTURE DIRECTIONS
IN ISLAND HISTORICAL ECOLOGY**

Chapter 14.	Assessing Colonization, Landscape Learning, and Socionatural Changes in the Caribbean *Peter E. Siegel, Deborah M. Pearsall, Nicholas P. Dunning, John G. Jones, Pat Farrell, Neil A. Duncan, and Jason H. Curtis*	299

Chapter 15. Insights from the Outside: Some Wider
Perspectives and Future Directions in
Caribbean Island Historical Ecology 345
John F. Cherry

References 367

Glossary 412

Notes on Contributors 416

Index 420

Figures

1.1.	Map of the Caribbean Basin.	9
2.1.	Map of the Pacific Islands.	17
2.2.	Map of the Mediterranean Sea.	18
3.1.	Early Archaic Age sites on Curaçao.	39
3.2.	Archaic Age sites on Saba and Curaçao.	42
3.3.	Multicomponent Early to Late Ceramic Age sites on Grande-Terre, Guadeloupe.	50
3.4.	Late Ceramic Age sites on Saba and La Désirade and early colonial Kalinago site on St. Vincent.	54
4.1a.	The modified Livingstone rod-piston corer used in this project.	61
4.1b.	Initiating a core drive.	61
4.1c.	Core in progress.	61
4.1d.	Extracting a core drive.	61
4.1e.	Filled and labeled core tubes.	61
4.2.	Portion of bisected core showing aspects of its stratigraphy.	62
4.3.	Core sampling diagram.	63
5.1.	Map of Trinidad showing the surface geology and coring locations.	76
5.2a.	St. John wetland 1, Trinidad, core phytolith diagram: resolved.	85
5.2b.	St. John wetland 1, Trinidad, core phytolith diagram: composite.	86
5.3.	St. John wetland 2, Trinidad, core pollen-percentage diagram.	90
5.4a.	St. John wetland 2, Trinidad, core phytolith diagram: resolved.	96
5.4b.	St. John wetland 2, Trinidad, core phytolith diagram: composite.	97
5.5a.	Cedros wetland, Trinidad, core phytolith diagram: resolved.	102

5.5b.	Cedros wetland, Trinidad, core phytolith diagram: composite.	103
5.6.	Nariva Swamp, Trinidad, Core 1 pollen-percentage diagram.	107
5.7a.	Nariva Swamp, Trinidad, Core 1 phytolith diagram: resolved.	108
5.7b.	Nariva Swamp, Trinidad, Core 1 phytolith diagram: composite.	109
5.8.	Nariva Swamp, Trinidad, Core 3 pollen-percentage diagram.	115
5.9a.	Nariva Swamp, Trinidad, Core 3 phytolith diagram: resolved.	117
5.9b.	Nariva Swamp, Trinidad, Core 3 phytolith diagram: composite.	118
5.10.	Nariva Swamp, Trinidad, Core 4 pollen-percentage diagram.	122
5.11a.	Nariva Swamp, Trinidad, Core 4 phytolith diagram: resolved.	124
5.11b.	Nariva Swamp, Trinidad, Core 4 phytolith diagram: composite.	125
6.1.	Map of Grenada showing the surface geology and coring locations.	131
6.2.	Cleaning ourselves and coring equipment of mangrove muck fronting the Meadow Beach, Grenada coring location.	135
6.3.	Meadow Beach, Grenada, core pollen-percentage diagram.	141
6.4a.	Meadow Beach, Grenada, core phytolith diagram: resolved.	142
6.4b.	Meadow Beach, Grenada, core phytolith diagram: composite.	143
6.5.	Lake Antoine, Grenada, core pollen-percentage diagram.	147
6.6a.	Lake Antoine, Grenada, core phytolith diagram: resolved.	149
6.6b.	Lake Antoine, Grenada, core phytolith diagram: composite.	150
6.7.	Total phosphorous values in the Lake Antoine core sediments.	151
7.1.	Map of Curaçao showing the surface geology and coring locations.	156
7.2.	San Juan Bay, Curaçao.	159

7.3.	San Juan Bay, Curaçao, core pollen-percentage diagram.	166
7.4a.	San Juan Bay, Curaçao, core phytolith diagram: resolved.	170
7.4b.	San Juan Bay, Curaçao, core phytolith diagram: composite.	171
7.5.	Spaanse Water, Curaçao, core pollen-percentage diagram.	176
7.6a.	Spaanse Water, Curaçao, core phytolith diagram: resolved.	178
7.6b.	Spaanse Water, Curaçao, core phytolith diagram: composite.	179
8.1.	Map of Barbados showing the surface geology and coring location.	183
8.2.	Marine terrace near Graeme Hall wetland, Barbados.	186
8.3.	Graeme Hall, Barbados, core pollen-percentage diagram.	199
9.1.	Map of Martinique showing the surface geology and coring locations.	204
9.2.	Baie de Fort-de-France, Martinique, core pollen-percentage diagram.	211
9.3a.	Baie de Fort-de-France, Martinique, core phytolith diagram: resolved.	216
9.3b.	Baie de Fort-de-France, Martinique, core phytolith diagram: composite.	217
9.4.	Pointe Figuier, Martinique, core pollen-percentage diagram.	220
9.5a.	Pointe Figuier, Martinique, core phytolith diagram: resolved.	222
9.5b.	Pointe Figuier, Martinique, core phytolith diagram: composite.	223
10.1.	Map of Marie-Galante showing the surface geology and coring location.	227
10.2.	Vieux Fort, Marie-Galante, core pollen-percentage diagram.	235
11.1.	Map of Antigua showing the surface geology and coring locations.	240
11.2.	Cross-section of two soil profiles exposed on a hillslope in the Ayres Creek watershed, Antigua.	244
11.3.	Nonsuch Bay, Antigua, core pollen-percentage diagram.	254
11.4a.	Nonsuch Bay, Antigua, core phytolith diagram: resolved.	259
11.4b.	Nonsuch Bay, Antigua, core phytolith diagram: composite.	260
11.5.	Cross-section of the terrain between Betty's Hope plantation and Nonsuch Bay.	262
11.6.	Jolly Beach, Antigua, core pollen-percentage diagram.	266

12.1.	Map of Barbuda showing the surface geology and coring locations.	271
12.2.	Low Pond, Barbuda, core pollen-percentage diagram.	276
12.3.	Grassy Island, Barbuda, core pollen-percentage diagram.	279
12.4.	Grassy Island, Barbuda, core phytolith diagram: resolved.	280
13.1.	Map of St. Croix showing the surface geology and coring locations.	286
13.2a.	Coakley Bay, St. Croix, core phytolith diagram: resolved.	294
13.2b.	Coakley Bay, St. Croix, core phytolith diagram: composite.	295
14.1.	Paleoclimatic reconstructions for the circum-Caribbean region.	316

Tables

4.1.	Locations of All Cores.	58
4.2.	Overview of Phytolith Sampling and Recovery.	66
4.3.	Marantaceae Species Collected on Project Islands.	69
5.1.	Sediment Descriptions of the St. John, Trinidad Core.	86
5.2.	Radiocarbon Dates from Trinidad Cores.	88
5.3.	Sedimentation Rates for the Trinidad Cores.	89
5.4.	Plant Taxa Identified in the Trinidad Cores with No Documented Ethnobotanical or Anthropogenic Correlates.	91
5.5.	Ethnobotanical Associations and Disturbance Indicators Represented in the Trinidad Cores.	92
5.6.	Sediment Descriptions of the Cedros, Trinidad Core.	101
5.7.	Sediment Descriptions of the Nariva Swamp, Trinidad Core 1.	105
5.8.	Sediment Descriptions of the Nariva Swamp, Trinidad Core 2.	111
5.9.	Sediment Descriptions of the Nariva Swamp, Trinidad Core 3.	113
5.10.	Sediment Descriptions of the Nariva Swamp, Trinidad Core 4.	120
6.1.	Pollen Taxa Identified in the Grenada Cores.	133
6.2.	Radiocarbon Dates from the Grenada Cores.	136
6.3.	Sediment Descriptions of the Meadow Beach, Grenada Core.	137
6.4.	Particle Size Percentages from the Meadow Beach, Grenada Core.	138
6.5.	Loss-on-Ignition Results from the Meadow Beach, Grenada Core Sediments.	139
6.6.	Sedimentation Rates for the Grenada Cores.	140
6.7.	Ethnobotanical Associations and Disturbance Indicators Represented in the Grenada Cores.	144
6.8.	Plant Taxa Identified in the Grenada Cores with No Documented Ethnobotanical or Anthropogenic Correlates.	145

7.1.	Sediment Descriptions of the San Juan, Curaçao Core.	161
7.2.	Radiocarbon Dates from the Curaçao Cores.	165
7.3.	Ethnobotanical Associations and Disturbance Indicators Represented in the Curaçao Cores.	167
7.4.	Plant Taxa Identified in the Curaçao Cores with No Documented Ethnobotanical or Anthropogenic Correlates.	169
7.5.	Sedimentation Rates for the Curaçao Cores.	170
7.6.	Sediment Descriptions of the Spaanse Water, Curaçao Core.	174
8.1.	Description of Low Slope Soils in the Graeme Hall, Barbados Watershed.	187
8.2.	Description of Bordering Side Slope Soils that are Geomorphically Unstable in the Graeme Hall, Barbados Watershed.	187
8.3.	Sediment Descriptions of the Graeme Hall, Barbados Core.	195
8.4.	Radiocarbon Dates from the Graeme Hall, Barbados Core.	196
8.5.	Sedimentation Rates for the Graeme Hall, Barbados Core.	199
8.6.	Ethnobotanical Associations and Disturbance Indicators Represented in the Graeme Hall, Barbados Core.	200
8.7.	Plant Taxa Identified in the Graeme Hall, Barbados Core with No Documented Ethnobotanical or Anthropogenic Correlates.	202
9.1.	Radiocarbon Dates from the Martinique Cores.	208
9.2.	Sediment Descriptions of the Baie de Fort-de-France, Martinique Core.	209
9.3.	Plant Taxa Identified in the Martinique Cores with No Documented Ethnobotanical or Anthropogenic Correlates.	212
9.4.	Ethnobotanical Associations and Disturbance Indicators Represented in the Martinique Cores.	214
9.5.	Sediment Descriptions of the Pointe Figuier, Martinique Core.	219
9.6.	Sedimentation Rates for the Martinique Cores.	223
10.1.	Sediment Descriptions of the Vieux Forte, Marie-Galante Core.	230
10.2.	Radiocarbon Dates from the Vieux Fort, Marie-Galante Core.	233
10.3.	Sedimentation Rates for the Vieux Fort, Marie-Galante Core.	233

10.4.	Ethnobotanical Associations and Disturbance Indicators Represented in the Marie-Galante Core.	236
10.5.	Plant Taxa Identified in the Marie-Galante Core Samples with No Documented Ethnobotanical or Anthropogenic Correlates.	237
11.1.	Radiocarbon Dates from the Antigua Cores.	247
11.2.	Pollen Taxa Identified in the Nonsuch Bay and Jolly Beach, Antigua Cores.	248
11.3.	Sediment Descriptions of the Nonsuch Bay, Antigua Core.	250
11.4.	Sedimentation Rates for the Antigua Cores.	255
11.5.	Ethnobotanical Associations and Disturbance Indicators Represented in the Antigua Cores.	256
11.6.	Plant Taxa Identified in the Antigua Cores with No Documented Ethnobotanical or Anthropogenic Correlates.	258
11.7.	Sediment Descriptions of the Jolly Beach, Antigua Core.	263
12.1.	Barbuda Dates Reported by Watters et al. (1992).	273
12.2.	Radiocarbon Dates from the Barbuda Cores.	274
12.3.	Pollen Taxa Identified in the Barbuda Cores.	275
12.4.	Ethnobotanical Associations and Disturbance Indicators Represented in the Barbuda Cores.	282
12.5.	Plant Taxa Identified in the Barbuda Cores with No Documented Ethnobotanical or Anthropogenic Correlates.	284
13.1.	Sediment Descriptions of the Coakley Bay, St. Croix Core.	291
13.2.	Radiocarbon Dates from the Coakley Bay, St. Croix Core.	292
13.3.	Coakley Bay, St. Croix Core Charcoal Counts.	293
13.4.	Coakley Bay, St. Croix Core Sedimentation Rates.	296
14.1.	Summary of Ethnobotanically Useful Plant Taxa Identified in Project Core Sections Dating to the Archaic and Ceramic Ages.	306
14.2.	Summary of Disturbance Indicators Identified in Project Core Sections Dating to the Archaic and Ceramic Ages.	312
14.3.	Early Radiometric Dates from the Eastern and Southern Caribbean Associated with Archaeological Deposits or Sediments with Evidence of Human Activities.	321
14.4.	Earliest Single Radiometric Dates Per Island from the Eastern and Southern Caribbean Associated with Archaeological Deposits or Sediments with Evidence of Human Activities.	340

Acknowledgments

Primary data included in the book were collected through grants awarded to Principal Investigator Peter E. Siegel. Siegel assembled a team of interdisciplinary senior environmental scientists and archaeologists to carry out the research. He appreciates the crucial input of Jason Curtis, Nick Dunning, John Jones, and Debby Pearsall in preparing the research design. We were fortunate to have Neil Duncan and Pat Farrell join the team. Bill Balée, John Cherry, Corinne Hofman, Menno Hoogland, and Tom Leppard graciously agreed to author sections of the book, thus providing external and comparative perspectives on our Caribbean island historical ecology research. One undergraduate and four graduate students participated in the project. Two major grants from the National Science Foundation (BCS-0718819, BCS-0818372) and one from the National Geographic Society (8438-08) supported fieldwork and follow-up analyses. In addition, Siegel was awarded a grant from the School for Advanced Research (Santa Fe, New Mexico) to convene the team in Santa Fe to discuss results and implications of the project (Research Team Short Seminar).

The Antoinette C. Bigel Endowment fund in the anthropology department at Montclair State University provided support for a student to participate in one round of fieldwork. The dean's office in the College of Humanities and Social Sciences at Montclair State University provided additional funds for shipping of field equipment and graphics production. Many people provided information and assistance in field logistics and expedited government approvals: the late Peter O'Brien Harris, the late Keith O. Laurence, and David Maharaj (Trinidad); Corinne L. Hofman and Menno L.P. Hoogland (Curaçao); Alissandra Cummins, Kevin Farmer, and Harry Roberts (Barbados); Benoît Bérard and Olivier Kayser (Martinique); Christian Stouvenot and Michel Grandguillotte (Marie-Galante); Reg and Nikki Murphy (Antigua); Reg Murphy, Cory Look, and Sophia Perdikaris (Barbuda); and Michael A. Evans, Richard S. Kanaski, and Patton Mulford (St. Croix). Kathryn Carlson (Geography, Urban, Environment & Sustainability Studies, University of Minnesota, Duluth) prepared the maps in the book. Sushant Singh assisted in the preparation of Fig. 4.3. Paula J. Reimer in the School of Geography, Archaeology and Palaeoecology at Queen's University, Belfast, provided Siegel with valuable input regarding the use of calibrated median dates.

🌿 Foreword

A Prelude to Island Historical Ecology

William Balée

One of the most significant challenges in the development of historical ecology as a field is rooted in rigid academic structures. These need to be traversed and perhaps even reorganized and rebuilt, because several disciplines concerned with phenomena that undergo change (unlike geometry, for example, wherein the formula for a right triangle is and always will be the same), including archaeology, history, soil science, biology, ecology, and in fact all other evolutionary and historical sciences, cannot grapple with every reality that comes under their umbrella or into their academic territory without considering human footprints, and even signatures. The book before you now is a promising step forward in unification of knowledge pertinent to the origins and transformations of land- and seascapes in the Caribbean, but it is much more than that. The historical ecologists who wrote the following chapters are actively navigating new frontiers of knowledge between events and artifacts of history (and prehistory), on the one hand, and geological and biological phenomena on the other. They are helping to break down walls or structures of academia that are not delivering on resolving comprehensive understanding of the historical interaction of cultures and environments in specific locales over particular periods of time, and for that reason they have embraced the research program of historical ecology. I can only endorse the book heartily, and encourage you to read on in these remarkably lucid and instructive pages.

This tightly organized collection of essays takes the reader past those academic structures that impede explorations of historical ecology, and into their interstices, by incorporating a notion of socionatural reality, as noted in the subtitle and scattered throughout the papers of the volume. Most of the professoriate in today's universities still wears nineteenth-century garb, because the system of rewards (tenure, salary, office space) is keyed to the cyclical repetition of the same fields that saw their permanence borne of accepting the walls and structures that divided one field of knowledge from another. Socionatural phenomena don't have a specific office or territory in the university but research is leading to the conclusion that we need to bring the empiricism deriving from the study of these phenomena together in a more coherent, logical, and yes, scientific way. The rewards of scholarship are important; without them we would not have much advancement of knowledge in the university, or in the books produced by the researchers and teachers of the university. We can appreciate those advances, but we need to supersede the sharp distinction that originated during the age of positivism between natural and ethnographic (or social) sciences, and that became fixed across Western academia shortly thereafter. The disciplines of today originated in that division. Another way of saying this is that the university, like the emperor, needs a perspicacious and curious mind of youth, or a new age of innocence, replete with empirical curiosity and fearlessness to state the obvious when it is encountered in situ. Given what we already know about climate change and anthropogenic forcing agents of global warming—and much of the most dire aspects of that seems obvious even to nonscientists—it might be opportune to recognize the human impacts that predate such dramatic transformation of every land- and seascape on the planet. I'm not talking about an anthropocene that might be another word for all that is negative about human influence on earth's environments, and particularly on that environment consisting of the atmosphere, nor am I addressing whether the anthropocene should be dated 150 years ago or 15,000 years ago, which are controversies at an analytically higher (and more abstract) level than the essays in the volume before you now. The empiricism you will find herein impresses me greatly: the book is hard to put down.

Island Historical Ecology is written, for the most part, by a team of researchers who are on the same page regarding human and natural history, at least as these histories pertain to a distinct region—the Caribbean. In chapter 14 the authors denote the region as consisting of a superhighway of flora, fauna, and people linking the numerous small dots of islands in the Caribbean archipelago into a larger and more consistently realistic historical–ecological whole. It really is a region in the historical–ecological sense (Marquardt and Crumley 1987); in many ways, it is a sort of laboratory for understanding insular historical ecology. That has to be different from continental historical ecology for reasons similar to those cited in all time-sensitive sciences, like landscape ecology, which the authors specifically cite as akin to historical ecology— I agree. And there is a lot that could be done institutionally, by the way, to link these fields more systematically together, for the purpose of educating the next generation of historical and landscape ecologists, who could be keys to helping local populations and small-scale societies manage more fruitfully and carefully their landscape legacies, regardless of what might be out of their control anyway, such as climate change.

To me, the book instantiates a rapid maturation of historical ecology in the past twenty or so years. The book is rather narrowly—but, to be sure, deeply—focused on the smaller islands of the Lesser Antilles and with even a sharper eye to the Windward Islands. A good reason for this focus is that all the evidence thus far collected suggests that the first humans in the Caribbean came from that direction, and even farther south, of course, from northern South America. The book is concerned with the early arrival of humanity, a concern of the editor and a subject he and his colleagues have advanced greatly (Siegel et al. 2015), as it should be, into this new lifeworld of islands. What the book reveals in the new research presented herein is that human arrival seems to be much earlier than received wisdom by Caribbeanist archaeologists of the recent past had retrodicted. In addition, the changes made in land and seascapes since that time are arguably based on the movements (migrations) of societies with distinctive cultures back and forth across these islands. Useful comparison is made between other insular regions, such as the Mediterranean and Oceania; though the scale and local issues differ, the idea of insularity in a historical–ecological context is well preserved, and cognized by the authors instructively. The book is highly beneficial for our collective knowledge as historical ecologists for it exhibits vast erudition built up on several islands here presented together in a single treatise. I see this treatise as a landmark volume that will lead to further research into the Greater Antilles, and to more-incisive probing and unraveling of continuing prehistoric mysteries that in their essence can be approached and resolved via the lens and toolkit of historical ecology, as is so well exemplified in the pages of this book.

# Preface

Peter E. Siegel

Islands are ideal settings for investigating linked historical processes of colonization, human-induced habitat modifications, effects of plant and animal introductions on native landscapes, and socionatural landscapes as evolving systems (Broodbank 2000; Burney 1997a; Clark, Leach, and O'Connor 2008; Fitzhugh and Hunt 1997; Fitzpatrick and Keegan 2007; Keegan and Diamond 1987; Kirch 2011; Kirch and Hunt 1997; Newsom and Wing 2004; Patton 1996; Terrell 1997). Why and how people migrate are questions that transcend the boundaries of anthropology, sociology, political science, economics, geography, and history. Numerous pushes and pulls have been cited as causal, depending on interrelated factors of demography, environment, economy, politics, ideology, and historical circumstance (Anthony 1990, 1997; Chapman and Hamerow 1997; Fix 1999; King 2007; Manning 2005; Rockman and Steele 2003). Do people move because they want to or because they must? Do they go in large groups, entire villages, family groups, or in age-grade cohorts? In cases of expanding or colonizing populations, to what extent did people modify landscapes, and, perhaps introduce new species of plants or animals? In establishing new colonies, people brought knowledge of previous environments and ways of coping with them. This background information undoubtedly was a resource and filter through which colonists viewed characteristics of new territories. Do people try to reproduce their homelands in new places? Are colonization processes different for people moving across expanses of mainland compared to islands? Finally, what are the dynamics of people moving into places already occupied by others, compared to situations of first settlers?

Human–environment relations have been the subject of inquiry in the social and natural sciences for decades (Bennett 1976; Butzer 1982; Claiborne 1970; Colten 1998; Goudie 2000; Norwine 1978; Redman 1999; Tickell 1977). Over the years, the theoretical pendulum has swung from viewing the environment as the passive recipient of human activities to one where environment molds the nature of social formations (Butzer 1996; Kidder 2006; Meggers 1954, 1995). Viewpoints are diverse in a number of arenas, ranging from basic research on climate to governmental policy statements; this is attested by opening almost any recent issue of *Science* or *Nature*. A more realistic perspective sees the relationship between environment and culture in a synergistic context (Balée 2006; Balée and Erickson 2006a; Crumley 1994a; Gunn 1994; McIntosh et al. 2000; Redman 1999, 2005; Russell 1997; Scarry and Steponaitis 1997; van der Leeuw and Redman 2002). That is, humans have in the past and continue today to modify the environment, whether by design or not (Roberts et al. 2017). Environmental settings are very real physical contexts at given moments in history that people consider when making large or small decisions, at scales ranging from the individual to the family to the nation. Debates in archaeology, climatology, and public policy center on the nature of the synergy between humans and environment. It is this synergy that we are addressing over eight millennia of human occupations in the Caribbean.

We are building on the principles of historical ecology as they have been applied most prominently in continental settings (Balée 1998a, 2006, 2013; Balée and Erickson 2006b; Crumley 1994b). As such, our interdisciplinary project has been explicitly directed to identifying and characterizing "human-mediated disturbance[s] as a [form] of landscape transformation" (Balée 2006: 75) across a broad range of tropical and subtropical island settings in the Caribbean archipelago. Approximately eighty years of archaeological research in the Caribbean reveals continuous human occupations over the past four thousand to eight thousand years, depending on which portion of the archipelago is under consideration. Within this temporal range, it is crucial to consider multiple colonization events, and their underlying processes, in regard to one or more surrounding mainland areas.

Organization of the Book

We address island ecologies from the perspective of social and cultural interventions over the full range of human occupations. The case study centers on the islands between Venezuela and Puerto Rico, the locus of the West Indies that experienced the longest continuous series of occupations, spanning eight thousand years. The book is divided into three parts. Part I addresses the larger theoretical issues of human migrations, colonization processes, and notions of landscape learning. These issues will be considered in the context of archipelago settings and the unique challenges faced by humans in colonizing islands. To provide a comparative perspective, a chapter is included that reviews the Pacific and Mediterranean islands in terms of colonization processes and cultural developments. The archaeological framework for the current case study is then presented. Part I closes with a chapter detailing the methods used in our fieldwork and analysis.

The West Indian case study is presented in part II in a series of chapters authored by project members. Each island selected for research receives a single chapter detailing project results and implications, which are integrated with other relevant paleoecological and archaeological investigations. These chapters are organized consistently, thus allowing for comparisons across the broad range of island ecologies.

Finally, part III begins with a synthesis of the case study results and contributions made to Caribbean archaeology and historical ecology. The first chapter in part III includes a discussion addressing larger issues of colonization and landscape learning illuminated by the case study. A model for human–environment relations in an archipelago setting is offered, articulating with other seminal studies in the field (e.g., Kirch 2000, 2011; Kirch and Hunt 1997; Patton 1996). The book closes with a chapter by John Cherry, a senior scholar who has devoted decades to a career in Mediterranean island archaeology, colonization, and interisland interactions. More recently he has been working on Montserrat, one of the islands in the Lesser Antilles. As such, Professor Cherry brings the perspective of an outsider and insider to the issues and findings discussed in the preceding chapters and addresses future lines of research in island historical ecologies.

Audience

There are very few synthetic book-length case studies available in island historical ecology. A number of books have been published with single-chapter case studies and general overviews of island archaeology (Clark, Leach, and O'Connor 2008; Kirch and Hunt 1997; Papadopoulos and Leventhal 2003; Rainbird 2007). Patrick Kirch and his Biocomplexity in the Environment team have "sought to move beyond" what they call "a narrowly descriptive, qualitative 'historical ecology' (Kirch and Hunt 1997) toward testable, dynamic, quantitative models that incorporate feedback processes, thresholds and nonlinearities, selection, risk, uncertainty, and vulnerability" (Hawai'i Biocomplexity Project Team 2010: 164). Kirch (2010b) and his team certainly have been conducting a magnificent well-controlled investigation into the interdependent dynamics of the physical environment, human demography, agricultural intensification, and social complexity over thousands of years of human occupations in the Hawai'ian Islands. However, I would not level the charge that the perspective from historical ecology is "narrowly descriptive" or necessarily and solely "qualitative." There are many historical ecology studies that are expansively analytic and quantitative in addressing a range of issues, including biodiversity (Balée 1998b, 2013), fire and vegetation histories (Athens 1997; Parkes 1997; Pyne 1998), food production (Zent 1998), landscape changes (Allen 1997; Kirch 1997a), and animal exploitation and extinction patterns (Anderson 1997; Orliac 1997; Steadman 1997). (See also studies in Balée and Erickson 2006a.)

We are building on the insights and approaches pioneered by others in the field of island historical ecology by presenting a strategically organized book-length case study, which allows for broad global comparisons and the generation of new insights and hypotheses. The book will be of broad appeal to scholars, graduate students, and advanced undergraduates with interests in historical ecology, environmental studies, historical geography, human impacts to landscapes, synergistic approaches to environmental research, island ecology, island archaeology, processes of human colonization and migration, pollen and phytolith analysis, soil science and geoarchaeology, and Caribbean archaeology and ecology.

PART I
Method, Theory, and Applications of Island Historical Ecology

1

MIGRATIONS, COLONIZATION PROCESSES, AND LANDSCAPE LEARNING

Peter E. Siegel

From the beginnings of human history people have been on the move, sometimes as individuals or small exploratory parties followed by larger subgroups and other times as large mission-directed groups. As people moved into and settled new places, legacies of their actions have been preserved in the forms of archaeological and paleoecological records. Clues concerning motivating circumstances, group composition, and interactions between colonizing and resident populations are sometimes embedded in these records.

When investigating human occupations within regions over hundreds or thousands of years, it is important to assess the relative roles of new immigrants or colonists as agents of change versus in-place evolutionary trajectories of resident populations. However, as Alan Fix (1999: 185) emphasized, "Polar hypotheses of waves of migration versus *in situ* differentiation allows a wide spectrum of intermediate positions." In addressing trajectories of cultural change, it is crucial to consider sources and circulation of people, ideas, and objects and resources. The focus on colonization processes and subsequent circulation of people becomes particularly sharp in island settings because there is constant trafficking in a wide variety of things, ranging from ideas to objects to people, between adjacent islands, across island groups, and with surrounding mainland areas (Anderson 2003; Broodbank 2000; Kirch 1984, 1990, 1997b, 2011; Rainbird 2007). Colonization, interaction, and interregional connections are important to consider in the context of shifting social formations and emergent complexity (e.g., Curet and Hauser 2011; Hofman et al. 2007; Kirch 2010a).

Colonization of the Caribbean islands has long been the center of archaeological and historical research (Chanlatte Baik 1991; Farnsworth 2001; Keegan 1995; Rainey 1940; Rouse 1958, 1986, 1992; Siegel 1991a; Wilson 2007; Wilson, Iceland, and Hester 1998). Much of this research has been descriptive and colonization events or migrations have been viewed rather monolithically, with little concern for underlying processes or historical circumstances. We still see references to distinct migratory waves of cultures: Archaic waves of migration, Early Ceramic Age wave, Late Ceramic Age wave (Chanlatte Baik 2013; Chanlatte Baik and Narganes Storde 1990; Coppa et al. 2008; Keegan 1995). This perspective may not be surprising, especially for the Early Ceramic Age Saladoid cultures, for which there is remarkable consistency in artifact assemblages, cosmology, and social organization from Venezuela through Puerto Rico (Rouse 1992; Siegel 1989, 2010; Wilson 1997, 2007). However, there is great diversity in the island ecologies, ranging from desert to low-coral to high-volcanic tropical-island settings (Woods 1989; Woods and Sergile 2001). It is crucial that this diversity be addressed in the context of understanding colonizing strategies, variability in human–land relations, and interregional connections (Boomert 2001; Fitzpatrick and Keegan 2007; Hofman et al. 2007).

In terms of underlying processes, especially in preindustrial settings, it makes more sense to view migration as a series of non-mutually exclusive pulses, or small-scale excursions, rather than as distinct population waves riding on the backs of big directional arrows. That is, in the band- and tribal-based social context of the Archaic and Saladoid settling of the Caribbean, exploratory forays by small groups of people into the islands were made as additive processes of "land [and sea] scape learning" (Meltzer 2003; Rockman 2003). As camps and settlements were established by these pioneers or scouts, lines of communication were maintained with homeland communities. In the Caribbean lines of communication between pioneering settlements and homelands were reinforced through social and economic exchange networks (Hofman et al. 2007; Mol 2014; Mol and Mans 2013). Measuring colonization pulses archaeologically is a challenge, given the small numbers of people that may have been involved. The paleoecological record may provide a more-reliable or -observable view of otherwise nearly indiscernible traces. As people set foot on new landscapes, modifications were made to those landscapes if for no other reason than people had to clear vegetation for shelters. These modifications are likely to show up in microbotanical records, with qualitative and quantitative shifts in pollen and phytolith assemblages and concentrations of charcoal microparticulates. Paleoecological investigations have been successful in identifying human modifications to landscapes that were nearly invisible archaeologically (Burney 1997a, 1997b; Burney, Pigott Burney, and MacPhee 1994; Burney et al. 1995; Jones 1994; Neff et al. 2006; Pohl et al. 1996; Pope et al. 2001).

In their analysis of the Neolithic colonization of Europe, Stuart Fiedel and David Anthony (2003) suggested that colonists followed a two-stage strategy. First, small groups of scouts started out from Anatolia, investigating landforms, soils, and other people and reporting back to home communities. This was followed by some portion of the home community making the journey to the new place. Fiedel and Anthony (2003: 145) "introduced the concept of 'leap-frog' migration. ... Initial migrants moved long distances to colonize selected locations that met specific ecological and social criteria [, leaving] uninhabited areas that were filled in only after population increase within the initial settlements." Anthony suggested that people following a focal subsistence economy (see Cleland 1976) are more likely to leapfrog great distances when searching for "particular types of terrain ... where a variety of crops and farming econiches are exploited" (Anthony 1990: 901). Some recent discussions of Saladoid migrants possibly skipping much of the Lesser Antilles in settling the Caribbean are consistent with Anthony and Fiedel's leapfrog model (Fitzpatrick, Kappers, and Giovas 2010).

In discussing patterns of migration, Patrick Manning distinguished colonization, whole-community migration, and cross-community migration (Manning 2005: 4–10). Colonization is defined as individuals leaving one community and establishing a new one outside the original home range, more or less replicating the home community (Manning 2005: 5). Whole-community migration refers to entire communities picking up and reestablishing themselves elsewhere (Manning 2005: 5–6). Cross-community migration consists of some individuals departing one community and joining another (Manning 2005: 6). Some combination of colonization and cross-community migration probably characterized the entry of Saladoid people into the Caribbean islands. However, we would modify Manning's definition of colonization by not requiring replication of the home community. In regard to the European Neolithic, Fiedel and Anthony observed that "we should be able to recognize the Anatolian origin of immigrant material culture [and] we should not expect to find an exact reproduction of Anatolian material culture in Greece, because long-distance migration usually has a transforming effect on social identities. Colonists do not represent a random sample of all parts of their homeland, but instead tend to recruit from quite specific places and social segments, so they depart carrying just a subset of the homeland's dialects and material culture" (Fiedel and Anthony 2003: 150).

In the case of the island Saladoid cultures of the Caribbean, we see replication and modification of home-community patterns, depending on local circumstances (Boomert 2000; Roosevelt 1980; Rouse 1992; Siegel 1996). Saladoid people certainly had a model for how they viewed village organization and they adapted that model to the islands as appropriate (Siegel 2010). And we would add the expectation, especially in an archipelago setting, for the two-stage process described by Fiedel and Anthony (2003): small groups of scouts followed by subsets of larger communities. "Within specific historical contexts, migration can be understood as a behavior that is typically performed by defined subgroups with specific goals, targeted on known destinations and likely to use familiar routes" (Anthony 1990: 895–896). Anthony (1990: 908) concluded, "'Cultures' do not migrate ... [but] goal-oriented subgroup[s]" do. We should start considering small-scale migration or colonization pulses when addressing preindustrial dispersal patterns into island settings.

The Current Study

The Caribbean archipelago was the last region of the New World to be settled by people prior to the arrival of Europeans and the first to be settled by Europeans. Current landscapes of the Caribbean islands are products of human engagements over the past four thousand to eight thousand years, depending on which portion of the archipelago is under consideration. Over the past twenty to thirty years archaeologists working in the Caribbean have increasingly been studying the nature of human–environment relations and the effects of these relations on the structure, organization, and biotic composition of landscapes. These studies were a direct outgrowth of the post-1960s interests in subsistence and settlement patterns, although in many cases those interests in the Caribbean were secondary to other issues, most notably time–space systematics (Siegel 2013).

It has been within only the past ten years at best that some archaeologists in the Caribbean have engaged in truly interdisciplinary approaches to human–environment relations from the very inception of a project in developing the research design, carrying out appropriate fieldwork and analysis, through publication. There is growing awareness that pre-Columbian people in the Caribbean transformed, manipulated, and managed landscapes and biota to a great extent. Knowingly or not, they accomplished these transformations through a variety of actions resulting in transporting of landscapes, extinctions of some species and introductions of others, and alterations of some microenvironments and the creation of others (deFrance 2013; Newsom and Pearsall 2003; Newsom and Wing 2004; Pagán-Jiménez 2013; Siegel et al. 2005).

We have been studying colonization history and consequent socionatural landscapes in the eastern Caribbean over a period from approximately 6000 B.C. through early European occupations. Within this context of colonization events, we are addressing the origins, evolution, and dispersal of agriculture in the region and how the transition to agriculture in the Caribbean is related to hemispheric-wide patterns, especially in South and Central America (Jones 1994; Neff et al. 2006; Newsom and Pearsall 2003; Newsom and Wing 2004; Pearsall 1995, 1997, 2003; Piperno and Pearsall 1998; Piperno et al. 2000; Roosevelt 1980, 1989). The origins and elaboration of agriculture in the Caribbean were likely a combination of influences and introductions from elsewhere and autochthonous developments within the islands (deFrance and Newsom 2005; Newsom and Wing 2004; Siegel et al. 2005). Newsom and Wing (2004: 189) observed, "Biological information from archaeological sites and the ecology of the settled islands is fundamental to interpretations of human colonization and adaptations for life on tropical island archipelagos. ... The introduction of organisms into island ecosystems adds to the number and kinds of resources available for human use but also changes the endemic flora and fauna in subtle or sometimes overwhelming ways." Comparing how agriculture and managed landscapes developed in archipelago versus continental settings will enhance our understanding of the context of domestication and the broad range of conditions under which it occurred.

Embedded within the framework of shared culture, especially in the Early Ceramic Age, there is evidence for flexibility and opportunism as fundamental features of island adaptations (Siegel 1993; Wilson 1997). Investigating varied topographical contexts and strategies of early and later colonists to the Caribbean, including Europeans, will inform on issues relating to the conditions under which horticulture is adopted and adapted, landscapes are modified and perhaps managed, and shared cultural patterns are negotiated, accommodated, and ultimately changed.

The current research articulates with and builds on other investigations addressing human–land relations; agricultural origins, production, and dispersal; and historical ecology (Balée 1998a; Balée and Erickson 2006a; Bellwood 2001; Crumley 1994b; Piperno and Pearsall 1998; Redman 1999). Intensification of plant use in the Caribbean has recently become the focus of considerable research using multiple lines of evidence, including charred macrobotanical remains from occupation sites, microfossils (pollen, phytoliths, charcoal particulates) in environmental cores, starch grains embedded in the surfaces of artifacts and human teeth, and land-use histories (Berman and Pearsall 2000, 2008; Burney, Pigott Burney, and MacPhee 1994; deFrance and Newsom 2005; deFrance, Keegan, and Newsom 1996; Mickleburgh and Pagán-

Jiménez 2012; Newsom 1993; Newsom and Pearsall 2003; Newsom and Wing 2004; Pagán-Jiménez et al. 2005; Pagán-Jiménez et al. 2015; Perry et al. 2007; Siegel et al. 2005; Siegel et al. 2015). Combining studies of ancient plant residues with Holocene climatic reconstructions is allowing for more-nuanced views of human–land interactions (e.g., Brenner and Binford 1988; Burney, Pigott Burney, and MacPhee 1994; Curtis and Hodell 1993; Higuera-Gundy et al. 1999; Hodell et al. 1991; Kjellmark 1996; Nyberg, Kuijpers, et al. 2001a; Nyberg, Winter, et al. 2001b; Peros 2004; Siegel et al. 2005). Prior to these systematic studies, and frankly still appearing in the archaeological literature today, conventional thinking was that Early Ceramic Age cultures, or subsets of them, migrated into the West Indies from South America and introduced the first plant cultigens. And, based on the presence of enormous quantities of thick ceramic griddle fragments and chipped-stone microflakes, it has been assumed that manioc (*Manihot esculenta*) was the crop of choice brought from Amazonia. DeBoer's (1975) cautionary tale about these assumptions has been addressed within the past fifteen years in the Caribbean and South America, and results of these studies clearly show the fallacy of conventional wisdom (Pagán-Jiménez et al. 2005; Perry 2005).

Recent studies suggest that pre-Columbian agriculture and land use was considerably more complex than heretofore thought (Neff et al. 2006; Newsom and Wing 2004; Piperno and Pearsall 1998). Tantalizing new data hint at Archaic landscape management, perhaps linked to horticultural activities (Ayes Suárez 1988; Burney, Pigott Burney, and MacPhee 1994; Siegel et al. 2005). Ideas about managed landscapes, home-garden production, and origins and dispersals of cultigens (and some animals) articulate with issues being addressed more broadly in the neotropics (e.g., Balée and Erickson 2006a; Neff et al. 2006; Newsom and Wing 2004; Piperno and Pearsall 1998; Piperno et al. 2000; Pope et al. 2001; Wing 2001; Wing et al. 2002).

We selected locations for environmental fieldwork on nine islands between Venezuela and Puerto Rico (fig. 1.1). These islands encompass the range of geologic and topographic variability in the eastern and southern Caribbean, the setting for some of the Early and Late Archaic occupations and the Early Neolithic colonization of the West Indies. The islands were Trinidad, Curaçao, Grenada, Barbados, Martinique, Marie-Galante (Guadeloupe), Antigua, Barbuda, and St. Croix. Coring locations were selected near known archaeological sites, allowing us to assess human impacts on and adjustments to local and supralocal environmental settings. Paleoecological data are viewed against known human occupations in each area. In doing so, we envision culture and

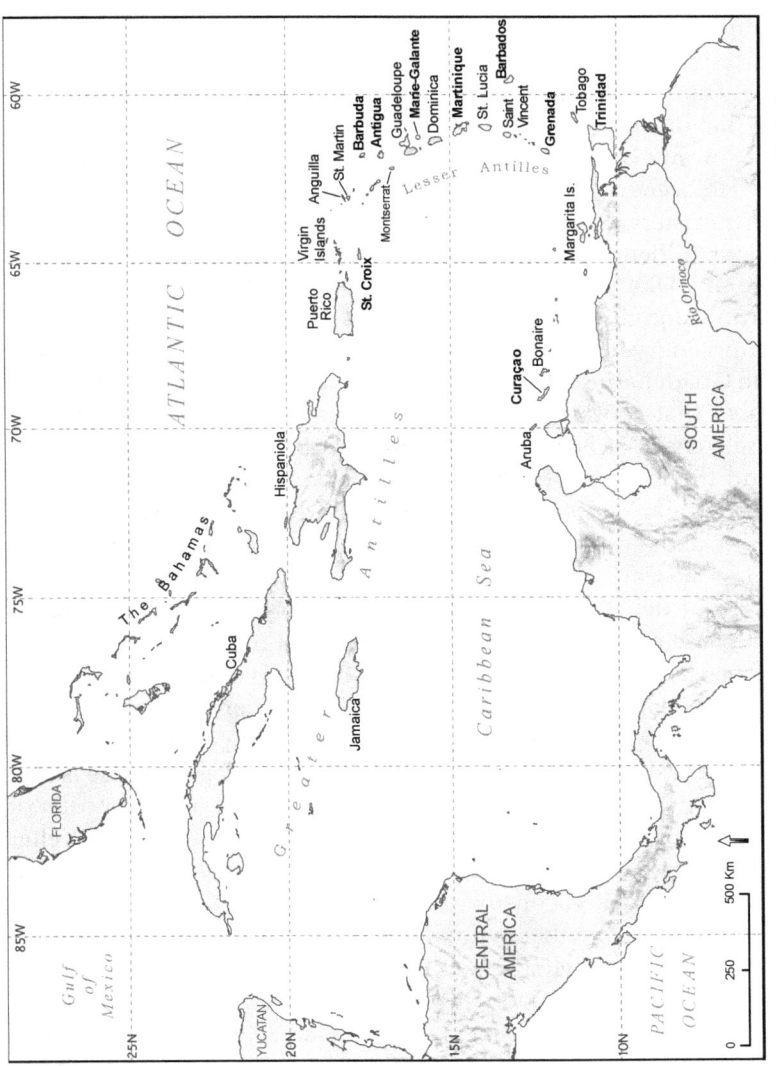

Figure 1.1. Map of the Caribbean Basin. Environmental cores were collected from Trinidad, Curaçao, Grenada, Barbados, Martinique, Marie-Galante (Guadeloupe), Antigua, Barbuda, and St. Croix.

environment in an interactive context. Environmental data reflect the physical settings available to human groups as well as changes people made to those settings.

Most of the islands between Puerto Rico and Venezuela are included in the Lesser Antilles. Geologically, Puerto Rico and the Virgin Islands are grouped together within the Greater Antilles (Lewis et al. 1990). The islands to the south and east of St. Croix are referred to as the Lesser Antilles. The southern portion of the Lesser Antilles consists of a single row of islands and islets, from Grenada to Martinique. These islands contain volcanic and sedimentary rocks, ranging in age from Mid Eocene to Holocene. North of Martinique, two arcs of islands continue: (1) a northeastern or outer arc consisting of low-lying islands covered by Eocene to Pleistocene calcareous deposits (Marie-Galante, Grande-Terre de Guadeloupe, La Désirade, Antigua, Barbuda, St. Bartholomew, St. Martin, Anguilla, Dog, Sombrero) and (2) a northwestern or inner arc comprising young volcanic islands (Dominica, les Saintes, Basse-Terre de Guadeloupe, Montserrat, Redonda, Nevis, St. Kitts, St. Eustatius, Saba) that continues from the line of southern volcanic islands. The single chain of islands in the southern portion of the Lesser Antilles and the inner arc of the northern islands are collectively called the Volcanic Caribbees or the Lesser Antilles Volcanic Arc. The outer arc (low islands) of the northern portion of the chain is referred to as the Limestone Caribbees (Case et al. 1984; Maury et al. 1990: 141–143). There is some debate regarding the geological origins and age of the La Désirade basement complex, although it is still mapped as one of the Limestone Caribbees (Maury et al. 1990: fig. 1). Based on tectonic history, others consider La Désirade to be "a dismembered fragment of the Greater Antilles" (Montgomery, Pessagno, and Muñoz 1992: 1431). Barbados is the easternmost of the Lesser Antilles. Geologically, the island is distinguished from the volcanic islands to the west by deposits of fossiliferous marls, tuffs, and clasts (Case et al. 1984; Speed and Keller 1993). Trinidad is the largest of the Caribbean islands south of Puerto Rico. Geologically, it is considered part of the South American mainland; it separated from that mainland only in the early post-Pleistocene with rising sea level (Bellizzia and Dengo 1990).

Our research is subsumed within the interpretive framework of historical ecology (Balée 1998a; Balée and Erickson 2006a; Crumley 1994a). There is increasing acceptance by anthropologists, ecologists, earth scientists, and archaeologists that human activities throughout the Holocene most likely had an impact on the structure and composition of biomes, ecozones, forest types, and habitats (Colinvaux 1987, 1993; Jones 1994; Moran 1993; Moran and Ostrom 2005; Piperno and Pearsall

1998; Piperno et al. 2000; Roosevelt 1980, 1989, 1991). Specifically, we hypothesize that the Caribbean islands may be thought of as cognized landscapes, beginning with the earliest human occupations. However, we reject notions of necessary landscape degradation with the arrival of humans; in some cases, plant biodiversity increased following landscape modification by humans, especially in the context of horticultural practices (Balée 1998b: 19–22; Newsom and Wing 2004: 189–190). Over the long term, landscapes undergo changes in relation to climatic and ethological factors. With the onset of human occupations, history is introduced as a contingent aspect of the landscape. Historical ecology provides a framework in which such seemingly disparate domains of culture as belief systems, economic systems, social and political organization, and technology may be integrated (e.g., Balée 1998b; Rival 1998, 2002). Laura Rival (1998: 245) observed, "History, which is about the production and reproduction of collectivities, must therefore also be about the social relations that have developed between human collectivities and other living organisms. As such, history is inscribed in the environment, in the knowledge of the environment, and in its symbolic representation." Evaluating shifts in observable and measurable dimensions of landscapes in the context of human behavior promotes an explicitly anthropological, multidisciplinary, and integrative perspective to the study of human–environmental relations (Redman 1999, 2005). It is this explicitly integrative perspective that is appropriate to apply at the current stage of research in Caribbean archaeology and environmental studies. Careful and systematic collection, analysis, and dating of microfossils preserved in sediments will enable us to evaluate anthropogenic landscapes in the context of environmental and cultural factors.

One of the challenges in historical ecology is to distinguish natural environmental perturbations from "the effects of direct [and indirect] human action" (Stevens 1999: 2). In discussing East African paleoecology, David Burney observed, "The fundamental problem … is to separate in the fossil and historical record the purely background-level environmental change from that which is caused by humans" (Burney 1996b: 19). He found that "wetter areas … with a shorter dry season … and arid … regions lacking enough litter to burn easily, show a much less frequent occurrence of prehuman fire and a marked increase in fire after human colonization. This is also the same trend found in a wet site with low seasonality in Puerto Rico. Here the sudden appearance of charcoal in the sediments apparently signals the arrival of the first indigenous peoples of the West Indies about 5 kya" (Burney 1996a: 30; see also Burney 1993; Burney, Pigott Burney, and MacPhee 1994). Kjellmark (1996: 143) made a similar observation for an island in the Bahamas: "The increase in charcoal and transition to a pyrogenic vegetation type on Andros begins shortly after human colonization of the Bahamas and is probably a result of human alterations in fire frequency." Weng et al. (2002) studied two sediment cores in lowland Ecuador, in portions of the country where very little human occupation was identified. Although they documented vegetational and climatic changes through the Holocene, "almost no charcoal fragments were found in either core" (Weng et al. 2002: 84).

Global environmental parameters provide a context for the initial most-ancient occupations (ca. 6000 B.C.) and subsequent dispersals through the Caribbean Basin. Regional and local topographic variability were undoubtedly evaluated and acted on differently by groups, depending on perceived and fundamental needs. As the earliest Archaic populations occupied places we expect some degree of landscape modification to have occurred, related to settlements and economic and social pursuits. Likewise, the ensuing Ceramic Age groups built on previously wrought landscape changes. This form of analysis is based on before-and-after comparisons of plant microfossils, soil-formation factors, and regional environmental indicators documented within each core sequence. Before-and-after comparisons are based on observable changes in lithostratigraphic units, biozones, radiocarbon/cultural chronologies, or some combination of these (Burney 1997a: 446–447). The baseline for this analysis is derived from Early to Mid Holocene contexts in the deepest strata of the cores that clearly predate the earliest human occupations of the region.

Genesis of the Study

In an earlier pilot study, we conducted paleoenvironmental research in connection with Maisabel, a large Ceramic Age site located on the north coast of Puerto Rico (Jones and Pearsall 1999; Siegel et al. 2001; Siegel et al. 2005). Sediment cores extracted from a small pond defining one edge of the site and from a mangrove located to the east of the site provided data enabling us to address shifting patterns of land use by Archaic- and Ceramic Age groups, potential interactions between groups, and environmental changes that occurred naturally as well as those wrought by humans at various times in pre-Columbian history. Based on the success of that study, we proposed to follow the same strategy in a series of island settings across the eastern and southern Caribbean.

Archaeological evidence for Archaic occupations on most islands of the Caribbean is slim and it has been generally assumed that these people were sparsely distributed and that they trod lightly on the landscape. However, recent studies suggest a more active role on the part of Archaic occupants in manipulating landscapes, and these first modified landscapes were undoubtedly of significance for later migrants (Burney 1997a; Burney, Pigott Burney, and MacPhee 1994; Jones and Pearsall 1999; Moscoso et al. 1999; Newsom 1993; Newsom and Pearsall 2003; Newsom and Wing 2004; Siegel et al. 2001; Siegel et al. 2005). In addition, there is evidence in some areas that Archaic groups could have been somewhat more settled than has been commonly believed, with established villages (Rodríguez 1999; Versteeg, Tacoma, and van de Velde 1990) and central-base camps (Boomert 2000: 54–65). There is suggestive evidence for cultivated plants in Archaic contexts, based on starch-grain and phytolith studies (Jones and Pearsall 1999; Pagán-Jiménez 2013; Pagán-Jiménez et al. 2005; Pagán-Jiménez et al. 2015; Siegel et al. 2001; Siegel et al. 2005). Although studies are few and far between, clearly it is time to rethink the nature of Archaic subsistence and adaptations in the Caribbean from a fresh perspective, especially given the evidence for early agriculture in Belize (Jones 1994) and the likelihood that the first Archaic colonists to the northern Caribbean originated in the Yucatán Peninsula approximately 4000 B.C. (Wilson, Iceland, and Hester 1998).

General goals of the current research were to investigate variability in human–environment interactions in relation to a range of topographic and geological settings; to Holocene climate change; to social, political, and economic changes in Archaic, Saladoid, and post-Saladoid cultures; and to early European colonial activities. Contexts were selected based on the likely presence of intact sediments with preserved plant microfossils and charcoal particulates. One challenge was to document subtle yet potentially important indicators of human modifications to landscapes, especially during early periods of occupation. Frequently, microfossils preserved in sediments within or near archaeological sites are the only records of anthropogenic landscapes (Burney 1997a; Iriarte et al. 2004; Pohl et al. 1996; Pope et al. 2001). Archaeological deposits themselves often are not conducive for preserving the very evidence needed in reconstructing past environmental conditions, especially those associated with food collectors or early food producers, early plant domestication, and less-than-intensive landscape modifications. Mary Pohl and her colleagues lamented that "macrobotanical remains are rarely preserved in humid tropical environments" and emphasized that "paleoecological investigations can detect human occupation even in the absence of sites. Such evidence comes in the form of vegetation disturbance including charcoal from burning for forest clearance and the pollen and phytoliths of domesticated plants" (Pohl et al. 1996: 356). Likewise, in discussing Archaic occupations in the Caribbean, Burney (1997a: 446–447) indicated that "low human population densities" resulted in a thin archaeological record compared to "that for sedentary agriculturalists" and that pollen and charcoal-particulate analysis may be a better way "to detect human arrival and impacts" to landscapes.

In the next chapter, Thomas Leppard reviews colonization processes in two well-documented island settings of the world: the Mediterranean and Pacific Islands. In doing so, he provides us with a comparative framework when assessing the data presented in part II of the book.

2

UNIQUE CHALLENGES IN ARCHIPELAGOES
Examples from the Mediterranean and Pacific Islands
Thomas P. Leppard

Islands have strange effects on people, animals, and the imagination. There is a well-developed and well-studied Western trope that islands are alien, potentially hostile, liminal, and transformative (Baldacchino 2008; Boomert and Bright 2007; Broodbank 1999, 2000: 6–21; Irwin 1999; Keegan 1999; Rainbird 1999, 2007; Terrell 1999). That said, islands are biogeographically transformative in a real and quantifiable sense (Losos and Ricklefs 2010; MacArthur and Wilson 1967; Whittaker and Fernández-Palacios 2007)—the challenges and opportunities posed by getting to islands, then successfully living and reproducing on them, result in new behaviors, new ecological dynamics, and ultimately new taxa. Human colonizing populations are similarly exposed to the transformative properties of insular living; varying isolation (depending on geographic or cultural metrics), ecological heterogeneity, and the sheer liminality of islands open new vistas of opportunity in human action while simultaneously foreclosing on others. Island environments may circumscribe human behavior, then, in comparable ways. Does this potentially parallel circumscription drive or encourage broadly comparable types of response? That is, do the parameters of island physiography promote parallel types of adaptation? The purpose of this chapter is to consider the profound challenges posed to human colonists practicing mixed horticultural and agropastoral regimes by two diverse island contexts: the insular Pacific and Mediterranean. It explores whether common challenges resulted—or did not result—in comparable modes of adaptation regarding sociopolitical organization, subsistence regimes, demographic and kinship structures, and so on. In doing so, it aims to provide a comparative framework for key questions in Caribbean prehistory, and highlight issues and challenges addressed by the researchers in this book on Caribbean island historical ecology.

Prospero's Cell: Lessons from Similarity and Diversity

> You are three men of sin, whom Destiny,
> That hath to instrument this lower world
> And what is in't, the never-surfeited sea
> Hath caused to belch up you, and on this island
> Where man doth not inhabit—you 'mongst men
> Being most unfit to live.
> Shakespeare, *The Tempest*, 3.3

The Pacific spans half of the surface of the planet, ranging from polar to equatorial and back to polar latitudes; the world's largest and deepest ocean, its scale arguably conditions human behaviors and processes (fig. 2.1). As well as containing some of the most densely spaced archipelagoes on earth, extremely isolated fragments of land—Rapa Nui (Easter Island), Hawai'i—find their home in this immense space. Its oceanic and terrestrial ecologies range from tropical and subtropical reef systems to the titanic plankton blooms and associated trophic pyramids of the subpolar Pacific. The Mediterranean, by contrast, is land-girt, a peninsula reversed, sandwiched between 35 and 40 degrees north (fig. 2.2). More than half of this 2.5 million km² sea is visible from neighboring land. Parched, and with only its major rivers and the Strait of Gibraltar to feed it, evaporation rates in the Mediterranean render it highly saline, oligotrophic, and, as such, relatively fish-free. Its geotectonic origins mean land and sea are interlocked to such an extent that Mediterranean isolation implied something starkly different to Pacific isolation, with the Iberian, Italian, and Balkan Peninsulas stretching across the great divide toward North Africa.

Such divergent *longue durée* histories of the development in terms of geology and ecological composition might provide reasons for us to be pessimistic that there are common lessons to be learned from the human histories of the Mediterranean and the Pacific. Indeed, human experience of these seas seems, at first blush, to have been very different. Even if we retain a skeptical stance toward claims that premodern hominins constituted the first Cretans and Sardinians, the Mediterranean in the terminal Pleistocene and Early Holocene was an increasingly busy space; the eastern Mediterranean in particular witnessed a dramatic increase in seagoing activity in the millennia either side of 10,000 B.C., with Mesolithic communities in the Aegean and probably on Cyprus (e.g., Sampson, Kaczanowska, and Kozłowski 2010; Simmons 2011). The immensity of the Pacific, by contrast, has proved to be intimidating to human navigators. The first successful colonization of remote Oceania appears to have occurred no earlier than the second

Unique Challenges in Archipelagoes • 17

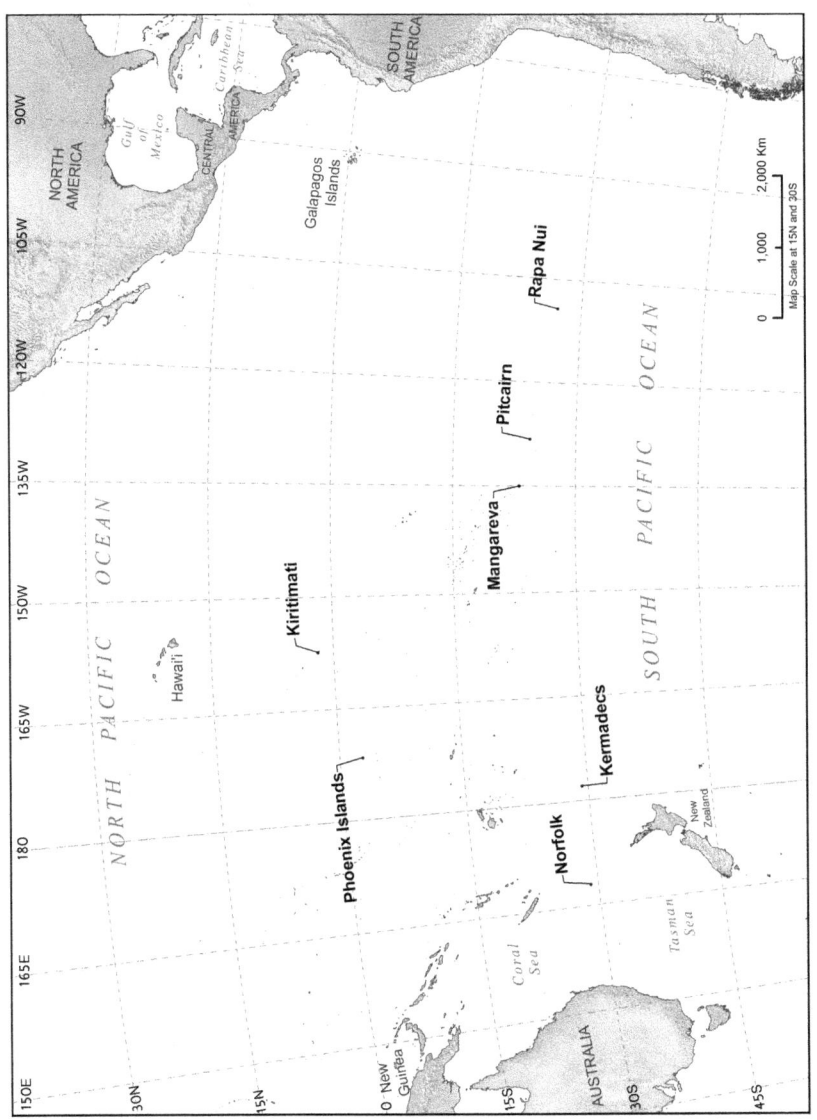

Figure 2.1. Map of the Pacific Islands

18 • Chapter 2

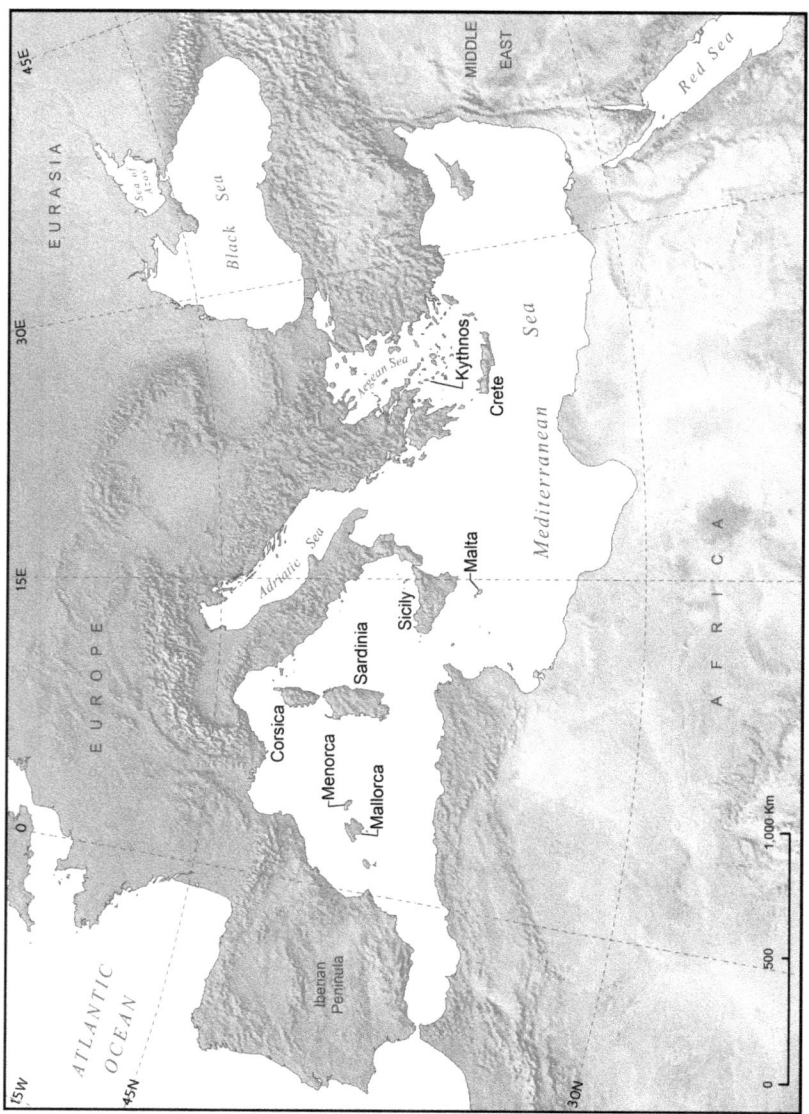

Figure 2.2. Map of the Mediterranean Sea.

millennium B.C. The three corners of Polynesia were reached around a thousand years ago (e.g., Hunt and Lipo 2006; Wilmshurst et al. 2008; Wilmshurst et al. 2011), at a time when the islands of the Mediterranean were objects of contestation between the terrestrial empires of the emperor in Constantinople and the caliph in Baghdad. There seems, then, to be little common ground between the islands of the two seas and the human experience of their insularity. Demonstrating that this is not the case occupies the remainder of this chapter.

Challenges of Colonization

The islands of the Pacific and the Mediterranean were colonized at different times, in different manners, by colonists using different modes of marine transport. The act of colonization itself, however, and a raft of associated logistical issues and processes—organization of population, navigation, demographic viability, technological capacity—presented profound challenges to would-be islanders in both seas.

The challenges of distance and of establishing viable breeding populations were anticipated in island biogeography; the work of Losos and Ricklefs (2010), MacArthur and Wilson (1963, 1967), and Whittaker and Fernández-Palacios (2007) offered a quantification of the effects of distance and isolation in terms of taxonomic turnover. One theme of this work was the degree to which insularity corresponds not only to endemism (separation facilitating allopatric speciation), but also, conversely, to islands possessing relatively depauperate faunas and floras in comparison with mainlands. Clearly, humans can escape the limitations imposed on animals and plants in processes of dispersal. Distance and remoteness remain, however, conditioning factors in human behaviors—it is undeniable that the most remote islands with pre- or protohistoric populations (e.g., Hawai'i, Rapa Nui, New Zealand, Iceland) were colonized more recently than other human niches; islands more remote than these (e.g., Kerguelen, Tristan da Cunha, the Falklands) were not colonized until the modern era.

Isolation is, in addition, a conditioning factor in long-term or cross-generational aggregate behaviors and community structure, as it is in nonhuman species; the development of insular creole languages is an excellent illustration of this effect. An example is the Nor'fuk language, a curious blend of Tahitian and eighteenth-century English spoken on Norfolk Island. Derived intermediately from Pitkern or Pitcairnese, itself the creole language of the HMS *Bounty* mutineers and their Tahitian companions (Buffett and Laycock 1988), Nor'fuk and other insular creoles demonstrate the tendency for island living to encourage novel cultural change. Isolation also retains the capacity to promote maladaptive or nonnormative behaviors in modern populations. The arrest and imprisonment of a significant proportion of the adult male population of Pitcairn itself for repeated and systematic sexual assaults on young girls hints at the extent to which lack of contact can encourage unique subsets of behavior, with the culture of sexual assault having developed in situ over two centuries (Marks 2009). Isolation can also have physiological impacts. The unusually high occurrence of asthma among modern Tristanians (Soodyall et al. 2003) is attributable to endogamous practices deriving from the sheer remoteness of Tristan da Cunha; three of the first settlers were asthmatic, and this condition now affects 50 percent of the population some eight generations after settlement. This hints again at the capacity of insularity to promote diversity, both culturally, but also perhaps in the physical constitution and structure of populations.[1]

These and other observations suggest that the logic underlying island biogeography (which has advanced considerably since MacArthur and Wilson's work, and now comprises a diverse body of theory that should be treated seriously by island archaeologists; e.g., Losos and Ricklefs 2010) still has a fundamental relevance, if not perhaps predictive capacity, for understanding the dynamics of diachronic colonization processes (Cherry 1981, 1984, 1990; Dawson 2011). Islands are, in short, hard to get to, both before colonization and after a population has been established. The combination of outrigger technology and sidereal navigation in the Pacific, perhaps assisted by cyclical reversals in the El Niño Southern Oscillation (Anderson et al. 2006), was, for example, an effective means of conquering oceanic distance. It does not follow that this conquest was simple, facile, or often attempted. Similarly, the Mediterranean's basins and subdivisions posed significant challenges to the oceangoing technologies available to terminal Pleistocene and Early-Mid Holocene colonists. With no evidence for the sail in the Aegean or points west until the early second millennium (at which time there first appears the proxy evidence of seal stone and hieroglyphic representations from Crete in contexts dated to ca. 1850 B.C.), and no evidence for stabilizing technologies, paddled dugouts or other canoes probably provided the only means of seagoing. Comparatively short-range technologies such as this would have rendered the seemingly cramped Mediterranean a much more daunting space (e.g., Broodbank 2010). In that vein, new information may well suggest that Mediterranean human island histories go deeper into time than previously imagined (e.g., Efstratiou et al. 2013; Strasser et al. 2010; Strasser et al. 2011); we should be very skeptical, however, of attempts to construct elaborate scenarios from these patchy data. A lower Palaeolithic Mediterranean populated by seagoing hominins of various stripes and species is inherently unlikely (Leppard 2014a). For the vast majority of the duration of the ongoing encounter between humans and the Mediterranean, the latter was an effective barrier to the former's movement.

Sheer distance was and is not the only challenge presented to colonizing populations. Getting to a Crete or a New Zealand was perhaps slightly less than half the battle. A detailed consideration of the logistics required in the Neolithic colonization of Crete, for example, provides food for thought. Broodbank and Strasser (1991) laid out, in detail, the necessary level of organization and tonnage of vessels and supplies in a viable, targeted movement from the Anatolian seaboard to the north coast of the island (where Knossos provided earliest evidence for Neolithic settlement; Evans et al. 1964). A viable breeding population of settlers quickly fills several small dugout canoes; viable breeding populations of cattle, sheep, goat, and pigs (all evidenced at Knossos) several more. Fodder for humans and beasts would take up further space, space that required propulsion through the water from additional bodies, even before considering the necessary supplies to get through a first winter, with an island harvest not yet planted. Following this through to its natural conclusion leads to the realization that the necessary size of a colonizing flotilla of this sort would have been impressive (forgetting, for the moment, initial scouting activities, and two-way flow between the new foundation and the founder). Considering the scale of individual Early and Middle Neolithic settlements across the Mediterranean, the capacity to organize movements on this scale would have challenged structures of decision making and labor organization. We should explore in more detail how—globally—colonizing events were articulated at the social level. Coercion, ritualized sanction, and cost-benefit logics were all surely implicated in these moments of profound schism within the community.

For a variety of reasons, colonization events in the Late Holocene Pacific may not have been as large-scale as their Mediterranean equivalents. Heavier reliance on lagoonal and pelagic resources, and richer foraging prospects in tropical and subtropical forest than in Mediterranean maquis and garrigue woodland, meant that the colonists of remote Oceania were not starting entirely from scratch. Dietary evidence, however, does indicate the extent to which Lapita populations and their successors were utilizing terrestrial foodstuffs (Kennett, Anderson, and Winterhalder 2006; Nunn et al. 2007; Valentin et al. 2010). Taro, coconut, breadfruit, and the Oceanic domesticates—dog, chicken, and pig—all required passage and space. The transported landscapes of the Pacific (Kirch 1982; Kirch and Hunt 1997) did not transport themselves, and colonization events likely constituted notable gatherings of vessels, resources, and people, extra-mundane occurrences in their own right. Ethnographic evidence from the Pacific in turn sheds some light on the social aspects of these events, and their challenging and potentially tense nature. Communities may have cleaved along kin lines, junior lineages losing out in the struggle for space and wealth, both material and symbolic.

Frequently, the challenge of distance—when better options for expansion of settlement existed—was too great. The Balearic islands of Mallorca, Menorca, Ibiza, and Formentera are visible from the Spanish mainland. While certainly remote by prehistoric Mediterranean standards (Cherry 1984, 1990), their existence must have been known to Neolithic and Early Chalcolithic communities. It is all the more surprising, then, that there is an approximately three-thousand-year lag between the Neolithicization of the Iberian coast (Tarrus 2008; Zilhão 2000) and indisputable evidence for the colonization of Mallorca by agropastoral communities, with permanent settlement of Mallorca best dated to circa 2400 B.C., and Menorca slightly later (Alcover 2008). This is perhaps best explained by the unattractive combination of small (compared to Crete, Sicily, or Sardinia) islands that are also some distance from the mainland. A Neolithic assessment of the challenges presented by an effective colonization of the Balearics rendered the return not worth the outlay until very late in the third millennium, and even then the expectations of biogeography hold good, with the largest island in the group the target for colonization. This is contemporary with both the "collapse" of stratified Millaran societies in Andalucía and Murcia (e.g., Chapman 1990), and a short-term period of Mediterranean-wide desiccation, either of which could conceivably have functioned to render island living or new niche colonization comparatively more attractive. The Balearic archipelago provides an example in which deliberate choices were made about the benefits and disadvantages of island colonization; for the Pacific super-remotes, such as Lord Howe Island or the Galapagos, the insurmountable challenge of discovery precluded even nonpermanent settlement.

Challenges of Adaptation

Islands are unlike mainlands, not only in their physical separation from contiguous landmasses, but also in their environmental and ecological composition. For a variety of reasons, they tend toward ecological heterogeneity. Geological and pedological patchiness, combined with changing oceanographic and meteorological rhythms, make small islands in particular very challenging from the perspective of subsistence strategies developed on mainlands. Fragility accompanies this heterogeneity. While the lack of resilience of islands in contrast to mainland systems can be overstated, high rates of endemism on islands and general poverty in terms of higher-tier predators (due to insular restrictions on subsistence base, range, and breeding populations) can render island faunas—and by extension wider ecosystems—unstable in the face of newly arrived mainland competition. Establishing viable strategies of long-term landscape exploitation was, then, a challenge common to the Pacific and Mediterranean, and this challenge was not always met successfully. The expression of and response to these challenges in the prehistory of the Mediterranean and Pacific were, of course, different; heuristic interest lies in the existence of the challenges, and in the nature of the adaptive response.

The arrival of human settlers in the Pacific and Mediterranean was accompanied by the arrival of commensal species, both domesticates and hitchhikers. In the Mediterranean, ovicaprids in particular, but also cattle and pigs, transformed the grazing landscapes of the islands, out-competing endemic ungulates. In the Pacific, domesticates such as the pig, and commensals such as the Pacific rat, had deleterious effects on native island species, especially endemic birds. This ecological collision was accompanied by opportunistic human predation, with both sets of colonizing populations supplementing food-producing lifeways with exploitation of island faunas. The colonization of the small groups of the southeast Pacific, and also of the super-remote Rapa Nui, seems to have involved massive realignments in ecosystemic dynamics, associated with permanent settlement by Polynesian voyagers. On Mangareva—colonized perhaps circa A.D. 1000—anthropogenic deposits contain skeletal remains of seabirds, and doves and pigeons now extinct on the island (Kirch et al. 2010). Notwithstanding the extinction of the short-range endemics, it is likely that the size of the breeding colonies of seabirds were severely impacted by human predation, accompanied by Pacific rats raiding nests (as well as eating endocarps of endemic palms, e.g., *Pritchardia* in Hawai'i and *Jubaea* in Rapa Nui). This, in turn, would have had a pronounced effect on the nutrient cycle on the island. Mangareva is today severely deforested, and this process has been argued to derive from the absence of nutrients entering the soil from seabird guano (Kirch 2005; also Rolett 2007). Deforestation, in turn, has implications for the retention of soil, hydrological dynamics, and the organization of horticultural activity, presenting fresh challenges to received traditions of Polynesian subsistence. Deforestation on Rapa Nui is also anthropogenically derived, whether directly through felling and burning, or via similar chains of ecological causation as on Mangareva.

Catastrophic, short-term realignments of island ecosystems are harder to trace in the deep time of Mediterranean colonization. That said, endemic fragility was certainly present, with all the major islands retaining descendants of populations stranded on them during the Messinian salinity event (5.96–5.33 million years ago), during which time the geotectonic closing of the Strait of Gibraltar resulted in the desiccation of the entire basin. These survivors of the Miocene radiated into endemic forms, with the Mediterranean on the eve of Neolithic colonization possessing many dwarf (e.g., *Elephas falconeri, Myotragus balearicus*) and gigantized (e.g., *Cygnus falconeri*) species. It is unclear what large-scale ecological effects the extinction of these island endemics had. This extirpation may have been caused by humans—the extinction of the Balearic, Maltese, and Cypriot island faunas aligns suspiciously well with evidence for Neolithic (Chalcolithic, in the Balearics) colonization, although it is worth noting that both eustatic sea-level rise and changing climatic conditions would have stressed island faunas. It could be that the grazing niches the Mediterranean ungulates occupied were filled by introduced ovicaprids, although overgrazing by domesticated ungulates probably had a deleterious effect on Mediterranean oak forest (as did the Younger Dryas, a brief regression to Pleistocene conditions that seems to correlate well with the first Epipalaeolithic/Mesolithic and Early Neolithic interest in islands; Broodbank 2006). A firmer grasp of Mediterranean colonization would perhaps help clarify these issues, although data are now plentiful (Dawson 2011). Of more benefit would be modeling of the different impact signatures of agropastoral as opposed to hunter–gatherer populations, and comparative studies of the anthropogenic extinction of island endemics.

Occasionally, the relationships between colonizing and island faunas were not so one-sided, with resulting human behaviors running counter to the general tendencies of colonizing human populations. Cyprus was colonized precociously early by Mediterranean standards, possibly with short-term visits in the Epipalaeolithic, and was certainly settled permanently by farmers by the Pre-Pottery Neolithic (PPN) B (Belfer-Cohen and Goring-Morris 2009; Knapp 2010; Manning et al. 2010). Presumably deriving from the Levantine coast, these agropastoralists transported with them ovicaprids, cattle, and pig, representing the earliest Mediterranean example of colonization of an oceanic (i.e., having been separated from Eurasia since the Zanclean Flood, not having a classically oceanic geology) island by a Neolithic community. Following the Cypro PPN, however, adaptive strategies on the island took a bizarre turn, possibly reflecting the joint challenges of isolation, environmental fragility, and individual subsistence choices aggregated over the long term. By the start of the Khirokitia phase—named for the type-site—at around 7000 b.c., domestic *Bos* disappears from the zooarchaeological record (Knapp 2013: 43–119). Pottery, apparently, remained entirely unknown, and instead of cattle husbandry there is continued evidence for the large-scale exploitation of fallow deer. These deer, clearly not domesticated, were themselves introduced to the island during the PPN, so should perhaps be regarded less as an insular wild species than as an introduced feral one.

It is difficult to pick apart this odd series of developments, not least because they represent starkly different trajectories of landscape exploitation than witnessed in the other Mediterranean islands. A clue may lie in the very early introduction of cattle, and in the types of ecological niche that they occupy. While the "secondary products revolution" (Sherratt 1981) now appears to be a series of events that do not cluster as tightly as had been supposed (e.g., Greenfield 2010), it is unclear how extensively or which secondary products were being utilized systematically in the PPNB. If cattle were introduced to Cyprus during a period in which they were culturally framed as solely a source of meat (and not of milk or, perhaps more importantly, of traction), then it becomes possible to see how, over the long term, they may have become much less attractive than other mobile larders. Fallow deer, requiring no input of labor or calories, provided a relatively accessible source of meat in an ecological niche that was otherwise unexploited by islanders. By contrast, cattle were large and expensive (particularly as regards their water consumption in a dry Mediterranean environment), bringing no other tangible benefit, and extracting large amounts of energy from the island system. The inappropriateness of these animals in an isolated and fragile island context may have resulted in a lack of interest in maintaining a viable breeding population. Despite hunting, ungulates thrived in the woody hinterland of the mountainous island.

This isolated case is nonetheless an excellent example of how, in general terms, island landscapes were differently challenging depending on the relationships between sets of dynamics, not least various human strategies of food production, and the geological and climatic contexts into which these strategies were introduced. Cyprus posed different challenges to an Epipalaeolithic population (if the mass dying of dwarf hippopotami at Aetokremnos can be blamed on humans) than to PPN farmers, and both responded to these challenges with different adaptive techniques. PPNB communities altered their lifeways in substantial ways to fit with insular fragility and environmental rhythms; hunter–gatherer communities, by contrast, seem to have abandoned the island or become locally extinct. The rhetoric of ecocide (Diamond 2005) as regards these massive ecological changes arguably overstates the case, and fails to recognize the adaptive capacity of island populations. Yet in both the Mediterranean and the Pacific, bodies of evidence suggest that some islands underwent either repeated episodes of colonization, or were abandoned after a period of settlement, as seems to have been the case with hunter–gatherer communities on Cyprus (and indeed on other Mediterranean islands). Cyclical or permanent abandonment, or even local microextinctions of human populations, is a feature of island prehistory in both the Mediterranean and the Pacific.

At Contact many of the innumerable dots scattered across the Pacific were occupied. Having expanded across half the globe, Austronesian populations had colonized islands as environmentally diverse as temperate New Zealand and tropical Hawai'i, and as different in scale as Viti Levu and the tiny atolls of Micronesia. The massive ecological ramifications of Contact have been explored at the human level (Kirch and Rallu 2007); yet despite the transmission of pathogens between previously separate populations, no Pacific communities were totally eradicated. Europeans noted, however, that some of the unoccupied islands that they visited or settled had clear indicators of prior human presence, most obviously in the form of material culture, structures, and anthropogenic deposits. The so-called mystery islands included some very small isolates, such as Pitcairn, and groups of small and ecologically depauperate islands, such as the Phoenix Islands and the Kermadec group (Higham and Johnson 1997; Irwin 1990; Kirch 1988). Kiritimati Island (Christmas), though, is larger, and today supports a substantial population, yet was found deserted by the first European arrivals. The only viable explanation is that these populations failed to overcome the challenges of insular living, either abandoning their islands or undergoing localized extinction. The central question is why these processes occurred on some Pacific islands, but not on others.

The situation in the Mediterranean is not as clear-cut; today, all the major islands are inhabited, with very few exceptions. (Palagruža has probably always only been a stopping point between Croatia and Italy [Forenbaher and Kaiser 2011].) Even the tiny Isole Tremiti (in total 3.13 km^2) maintain a permanent population. Yet in prehistory there appear to be cases in which islands were initially colonized, only for this colonization to be followed by a period of ominous silence before human traces reappear. An example comes from Kythnos, an island in the Cycladic archipelago in the Aegean. Extensive excavation, accompanied by radiocarbon dates, gives the site at Maroula a secure Epipalaeolithic/Mesolithic date (Sampson, Kaczanowska, and Kozłowski 2010). This community—not the only one of Mesolithic date in the Aegean (Efstratiou et al. 2013)—was clearly exploiting maritime resources, as well as the nearby obsidian flows on Melos. This population is hard to trace farther forward in time, however; there is no Neolithic settlement on Kythnos, and humans are evident again only in the third millennium B.C., separated from Maroula by the best part of five thousand years. This could be for a series of reasons; notably, Mesolithic populations in the Aegean were mobile (although not as mobile as Upper Palaeolithic equivalents), moving seasonally between niches. That said, clearly this mode of living did not last much beyond 7000 B.C., with agropastoralists colonizing the Cyclades in the fifth millennium.

In both the Mediterranean and the Pacific, islands—attractive enough to be settled for extended periods of time—either were abandoned, or their properties encouraged the localized extinction of isolated human populations. What is needed is a means to choose between these two alternatives: Did people leave willingly to found further colonies, or are these prehistoric remains indexing the challenges of small-island living? It is hard to imagine the processes involved in these outcomes—specifically, what pressures a nonetheless isolated population experiences to promote such drastic results. Thinking about the effects of island spaces on human demography provides one way to model these processes at a general level.

Small islands promote ecological fragility in one further noteworthy respect. As MacArthur and Wilson recognized, the size of small islands relative to mainland point of origin can have severe effects on population dynamics for island taxa (Hanski 2010). For taxa in the higher levels of trophic pyramids, small initial colonizing populations and scarcity of resources brought about by insular ecological poverty keep populations relatively low, hovering closer to the threshold of reproductive unviability. Proximity to this threshold makes it more likely to be crossed, if total numbers are forced down by some other stressor, and this is a driving force behind island extinctions. The same constraints also render human populations on islands more vulnerable than equivalent mainland populations (Weiss and Smouse 1976; Williamson and Sabath 1982; also Keegan 2010). In particular, the *stability* of human populations seems to be reduced, with both increases and decreases seemingly much more random than in mainland contexts (Demetrius, Gundlach, and Ochs 2004). This stability derives from the increased impact of stochastic effects on smaller populations compared with larger.

Clearly, and as discussed in some detail below, human populations are rarely true isolates; degree of isolation or connectivity, if this can be measured, will impact demographic dynamics through the inflow of new reproductive partners. Consequently, a highly connected small population will be much more resilient than a weakly connected equivalent.[2] On this basis, the prime candidates for localized extinction—in the abstract—would be isolated, very small populations. We can assume in this case a general positive correlation between island size and population in both the Mediterranean and the Pacific, and this matches well with the data on so-called mystery islands in the Pacific. The Phoenix Islands are small atolls, with a total land area for the whole archipelago no more than 30 km². The Kermadecs, while not as small, are profoundly isolated, situated halfway between Fiji and the North Island of New Zealand. Both demographic crash and abandonment could be occurring in unison in this instance, with the remnants of small populations abandoning the archipelago for New Zealand while in the midst of a population crunch (the evidence for New Zealand obsidian on Raoul Island is relevant in this regard; Higham and Johnson 1997: 217). Pitcairn, of course, is both very small and very remote. The current population is only a few dozen, and it is unclear whether this population would be viable without modern systems of communication and subsistence.

The situation is less obvious with cases such as Kythnos and Kiritimati. Kythnos is not unusually small by Cycladic standards, nor is it especially remote. We might note that the population density for Epipalaeolithic/Mesolithic populations was probably less than that for equivalent Neolithic populations. Because smaller communities are more exposed to irreversible crash, the potential fragility of island living shifts, depending on the mode of subsistence in question. This raises a fascinating set of questions—which cannot be addressed here, but Leppard (2015) attempts to chart the problem in more detail— about changing definitions of insularity, demographic viability, and in particular about varying degrees of adaptability within human populations and the associated ecological dynamics. The shift from hunter–gatherer to food-producing strategies essentially reconfigures trophic structures; humans as hunter–gatherers exist as apex predators, which are notoriously rare in island settings because of issues of range size and associated reproductive problems. As agropastoralists, however, humans move lower down (or even outside) the pyramid, either no longer relying on the same configuration of food webs or creating their own. It could be this lesson from biogeography, rather than issues of island geography and configuration (distance-area effects), that explains the very late colonization of islands in general (Gamble 1996: 203–240): island living may become feasible only with the trophic shift associated with the transition to food production. Whether or not this is correct, we need in general to pay more attention to the ecological dynamics of human populations, and how these both foreclose on and generate opportunities and long-term strategies.

In possible cases of localized extinction, lack of interaction with or access to other populations is largely to blame. This recognition suggests a final set of challenges for Pacific and Mediterranean island living, the importance of retaining meaningful social links and systems of communication across many miles of ocean. These last hurdles—best thought of as challenges of connectivity—and the failure to overcome them can represent important drivers of social and cultural change, both in the Pacific and in the Mediterranean.

Challenges of Connectivity

The temptation to draw parallels where none exist is best resisted, and the human and cultural trajectories of the prehistoric Pacific and Mediterranean are unique. The last set of challenges considered here, though, were present for early islanders in both seas and, in both, the challenges were not fully overcome. In the Pacific and Mediterranean, prehistoric populations gained previously inaccessible islands, and established viable communities. The extent to which these communities were able to or interested in maintaining contact with the wider world has a significant bearing on our understanding of the development of insular cultures in comparative perspective.

The initial, coastwise colonization of the central and western Mediterranean by Neolithic communities seems to have been very rapid (Zilhão 2001); the most acceptable current model is of agropastoral populations fissioning, with subsets of these populations undertaking targeted niche-colonization of favorable coastal patches. This process was comparatively rapid, completed in perhaps less than a millennium. Colonization involved the retention of a distinct suite of materials, and in particular a style of potting known as Cardial-Impressed. Variations of this tradition spread from the Adriatic and the Tyrrhenian to the Atlantic coast of Iberia (Barnett 2000; Guilaine and Manen 2007). There are certainly spatial and chronological distinctions in this pottery and its decoration, but the basic technique and decorative schemes—walking a cardium shell across the vessel when leather-hard to produce complex designs—remain the same. This broad homogeneity suggests a cultural, if not genetic, relationship; despite not knowing how traditions of potting were transmitted—horizontally, vertically, endogamously, exogamously—this shared material tradition indexes shared technological practice, and perhaps shared ideological systems, in a gross way. The retention of homogeneity is probably derived from founder effects, as communities budded off in pulses of coastwise migration.

The well-known example of a large, coherent sphere of stylistic continuity in the Pacific is also associated with the first colonization by food-producing populations. Lapita pottery—massive-walled red-slipped vessels, incised and infilled with white paint—is found in the Bismarck archipelago, Sāmoa, and points in between, occurring in domestic and mortuary contexts of the first settlers (e.g., Anderson and Clark 1999; Kirch 2000; Sheppard 2011). The spatial extent of Lapita greatly exceeds that of the Cardial-Impressed phenomenon, but the rate of spread, and the retention of coherent sets of decorative techniques across very large areas, suggest that both cases represent material and cultural signatures that have peculiar associations with episodes of long-range niche colonization. Tellingly, in both cases these broadly homogenous cultural entities are subsequently replaced by diversity. In the fifth to late fourth millennia western and central Mediterranean, a bewildering array of ceramic styles develops in place of ancestral types; for example, Diana and Stentinello traditions on Sicily, Skorba on Malta, and Ozieri on Sardinia (e.g., Malone 2003; Webster 1996). These changes are accompanied by increased diversity in mortuary and ritual practices, culminating in the monumentalism of the third and second millennia. A broadly approximate pattern is witnessed in the Pacific, with the Lapita tradition being replaced with a ceramic craft production. This transition appears to accompany the development of Polynesian societies in situ in remote Oceania, prior to the final expansion into the corners of the Polynesian triangle.

As the existence of large areas of broadly homogeneous craft traditions must index an underlying social situation, so the breakdown of these homogeneities must index a change in this situation; it is not the goal, though, to explore this in detail here (Leppard 2014b). It is simply interesting to note that early, rapid maritime colonization events could derive their coherence from these shared craft traditions; very swift expansion leaves little time for cultural innovation. Moreover, these colonizing populations would have been small. As we have seen, inflow of new genetic material tends to make small populations more robust, and we might expect such exchanges to have occurred in the Lapita or

Cardial-Impressed expansions. It is unclear whether either tradition of potting was explicitly gendered or otherwise socially delineated, but large-scale exogamy would contribute to the retention of craft similarity across broad areas (either expanses of Mediterranean coast, or Pacific open ocean). By that token, it is possible to model how demographic expansion and the ebb of colonization could have rendered endogamy, or shorter-range exogamy, more readily acceptable (Leppard 2015). While Mediterranean and Pacific islanders could clearly still traverse substantial distances, the necessity of doing so may have receded as demographic stability increased. The challenge becomes not so much one of distance, but rather one of connectivity. With the breakdown in kin and cultural ties between separate populations, social storage and recursive obligations would have faded, exposing socially isolated communities to sporadic ecological crunches. Happily, this approach may hint that social isolation and geographic isolation can be mutually reinforcing processes, depending on context. Malta, for example, was consistently geographically isolated, but as the ecological position and demographic dynamics of its population altered over the long term, this geographic isolation encouraged exaggerated social isolation (which seems to come to an end in the last centuries of the third millennium B.C., a time of Mediterranean-wide upheavals).

The observation that there may be a relationship between the isolation of island societies and cultural change is both stimulating and problematic. Clearly, cultural behaviors do not speciate, and are created actively by individuals rather than representing chance mutations that may or may not be adaptively advantageous. If we propose, however, that the mode of transmission of cultural practices may in some general sense be analogous to genetic flow, then lessons from biogeography and community ecology could shed light on the long-term development of island societies. The reduction of flow of ideas, people, materials, and genes between insular societies as a motor of cultural change opens new vistas of research, not least as regards the reintegration of previously isolated societies into wider networks and the implications of this for endemic cultural forms.

Concluding Thoughts

> All parts of the earth's surface and all prehistoric situations are obviously in the final analysis unique, but it is by examining the similarities that we are likely to arrive at non-trivial conclusions.
>
> Lewthwaite 1982: 316

The Mediterranean Sea and the Pacific Ocean are divided by scale and environmental composition. They are united by the problems they and their islands present to communities of animals and plants. Humans, as animals uniquely adapted to overcoming environmental constraints, were nonetheless subject to the limitations as well as the opportunities afforded by islands. The sheer physical separation of islands from continents and from each other, their unique ecological properties, and their tendency to be both environmentally fragmented and fragile rendered island living challenging. The responses to these challenges varied immensely from the small atolls of the Pacific to the large karstic islands of the Mediterranean, but on a fundamental level they served to promote the emergence of highly individual and esoteric societies and cultural forms.

The Caribbean in some ways occupies an interstitial space between the Mediterranean and the Pacific. A subdivision of the Atlantic, equivalent in size to the Mediterranean, it is nonetheless situated within subtropical and tropical latitudes, permitting the development of both reef and tropical forest systems. Its location, however, also exposes it to the capriciousness of the ITCZ (the Intertropical Convergence Zone, the dynamics of which govern equatorial rainfall). A central set of questions clusters around whether the challenges of insular living extended to the Greater and Lesser Antilles, and whether any patterns in human social and spatial organization in Caribbean prehistory can be understood in terms of adaptive responses to these challenges. The degree to which we can answer these questions in the affirmative or negative will have profound implications for the viability of a comparative island archaeology (and comparative archaeology more broadly, if we remain interested in the utility of attempting to generalize about human behavior). In the chapters that follow, the research team addresses these issues within the analytic framework offered by island historical ecology.

Acknowledgments

I would like to thank Peter Siegel for inviting me to contribute to this volume, and for his forbearance. Elizabeth Murphy and John Cherry offered constructive comments on the first and the last drafts of this chapter, drafts separated by half a decade in which, inevitably, my thinking has evolved. Comments from two anonymous reviewers were encouraging and helpful in equal measure. My debt to the work of John Cherry and of Cyprian Broodbank should be obvious.

Notes

1. Insularity writ large may also have transformative effects in terms of human evolution; witness the dwarfism of *Homo floresiensis,* and the possible role of the Mediterranean in separating breeding populations of premodern humans.
2. The resilience and fragility of prehistoric systems of settlement from the perspective of complex network studies is fascinating, particularly in terms of how human spatial organization responds to growth and stress; archipelagoes represent ideal contexts in which to explore degrees of connectivity, and the social impacts of the breakdown of connectivity, e.g., Knappett, Evans, and Rivers 2008, 2011.

3

A Cultural Framework for Caribbean Island Historical Ecology across the Lesser Antilles

Corinne L. Hofman and Menno L. P. Hoogland

The Lesser Antillean Islandscape

The islands of the precolonial Lesser Antilles are characterized by a distinctly maritime orientation of its first settlers who adapted to a great variety of natural environments and social circumstances. The discontinuous resource distributions across the archipelago and the urge for social engagement and bonding stimulated craft specialization on the part of the Amerindian communities, human mobility, and the formation of regionwide social networks (Hofman and Bright 2010; Hofman et al. 2007; Hofman and Hoogland 2011). The Caribbean Sea is a semi-enclosed basin of the western Atlantic Ocean, surrounded by the Central and South American coastal areas and by the Lesser and Greater Antilles. It stretches over an area of 2.754 million km^2, comprising thousands of islands, islets, reefs, and cays of rock, sand, or coral. General processes underlie the formation of the Lesser Antillean archipelago, but individual limestone, composite, or volcanic islands are extremely varied in their geologies and ecologies (Knippenberg 2006; Van Soest 2000). Within and across the islands great habitat diversity is linked to variations in latitude, elevation, climate, rainfall, and salinity. The Lesser Antilles include Trinidad and Tobago, the Leeward Antilles or Venezuelan offshore islands, as well as the Windward and Leeward Islands, which form the eastern boundary of the Caribbean Sea with the Atlantic Ocean. Trinidad and Tobago are continental islands related to the South American mainland. Trinidad and the mainland were connected by a land bridge until about 7000–6000 cal B.C. when sea-level rise separated them. The island is characterized by diverse ecosystems and greater biodiversity than neighboring Tobago. The flora and fauna of both islands, however, are more diverse than the rest of the Antilles and clearly reflect the mainland connection. The east–west island chain from Margarita, Coche, and Cubagua to Aruba is situated offshore from the north coast of Venezuela and is included with the Lesser Antilles. Margarita and Aruba at both ends of the 900-km-long offshore chain are part of the South American continental shelf, as are other major islands including Los Monjes (situated off the Guajira Peninsula), La Tortuga, La Sola, Los Testigos, and Los Frailes. Patos Island, Los Roques archipelago, Blanquilla, Los Hermanos archipelago, La Orchila, Bonaire, and Curaçao are located outside the continental shelf. They are oceanic islands and separated from the mainland by the Bonaire Trench (Newsom and Wing 2004). The islands are characterized by xeric environments and large salt deposits. Extensive mangroves border most of the islands. A continuous chain of volcanic islands extends from Grenada in the south to Saba in the north, forming a visual line via the Virgin Islands toward the Greater Antilles. Halfway up the volcanic chain from Marie-Galante begins a series of flat limestone islands stretching to Anguilla and forming a striking contrast to the mountainous volcanic islands.

The insular world would probably have had an exotic appearance to mainland communities upon their arrival. It is obvious from the archaeological record, however, that adaptation to and domestication of these new island regions took place rapidly, reflecting flexible and opportunistic human behavioral strategies (deFrance, Keegan, and Newsom 1996; Fitzpatrick and Keegan 2007; Hofman and Hoogland 2011; Siegel 1991a). The coastal regions of the Caribbean islands and associated mainland areas are characterized by large marine ecosystems comprising coral reefs, mangrove areas, seagrass beds, rocky shores, and sandy beaches. Endemic fauna could easily be captured in the mangroves, coastal reefs, and estuaries (Wilson 2007). A wealth of marine resources characterized the insular environments, in contrast to terrestrial fauna, which was less abundant and diverse compared to the continental homeland regions (Newsom and Wing 2004). Over time, new animal and plant species were intentionally or accidentally transported from the mainland or from island to island (Terrell et al. 2003; Fitzpatrick and Keegan 2007; Hofman et al. 2011; Pagán-Jiménez et al. 2015). Animals including agoutis, hutias, monkeys, guinea pigs, birds, and dogs were introduced from the mainland as additional food resources, for hunting, or for ritual purposes (Crock and Carder 2011; Grouard 2001; Grouard, Perdikaris, and Debue 2013; Keegan and Hofman 2017; Kimura et al. 2016; Laffoon et al. 2014; Newsom and Wing 2004). A variety of wild and domesticated plants were introduced to the islands, some of which have been managed or cultivated from circa 7800 B.P. on Trinidad. Exogenous plants include papaya, peanut, pepper, *cupey*, sapodilla, yellow sapote, wild avocado, mastic-bully, sweet potato, manioc, maize, and tobacco (Keegan and Hofman 2017; Newsom 1993; Newsom and Wing 2004; Pagán-Jiménez 2011; Pagán-Jiménez et al. 2015; Pearsall 1989; Rodríguez Ramos, Pagán-Jiménez, and Hofman 2013).

Centuries of slash-and-burn, slope cultivation, and other landscape modifications have resulted in deforestation, thereby tremendously impacting the islands' original biotopes and richness of species (Fitzpatrick and Keegan 2007). Alternating wet and dry periods have characterized the Early to Mid Holocene climates (Beets et al. 2006; Curtis and Hodell 1993; Curtis, Brenner, and Hodell 2001; Higuera-Gundy et al. 1999; Hodell et al. 1991; Malaizé et al. 2011; Siegel et al. 2005). Palaeoenvironmental records for Guadeloupe and St. Martin show periods of drought and frequent hurricanes during the entire Archaic Age (from ca. 4300 cal B.C.), followed by a more humid era and fewer hurricanes during the Ceramic Age (Beets et al. 2006; Malaizé et al. 2011). Droughts have been recorded for the period between cal A.D. 800 and 1000 concomitantly with such conditions in other parts of the Americas (see Maya region) and corresponding to the transition between the Early and Late Ceramic episodes in the Antilles (Hofman and Hoogland 2015; Keegan and Hofman 2017; Lane, Horn, and Kerr 2014). Substantial differences in values of snail-shell carbon isotopes from the Lesser Antilles showed responses in vegetation to wetter conditions after A.D. 1000. Caribbean islanders adapted to climatological fluctuations and other natural events, including storms, hurricanes, tsunamis, volcanic eruptions, earthquakes, sea-level changes, and severe droughts (Cooper 2010, 2013; Cooper and Boothroyd 2011; Davis 2003; Delpuech 2004; Hofman and Hoogland 2015). The Leeward Islands have been particularly vulnerable to destructive hurricanes, most of which originate in the Central Atlantic, because the main hurricane track passes through these islands. Tsunamis dating to circa 4200 B.P., 3100 B.P., 1500 B.P., and 500 B.P. probably impacted the islands of Curaçao and Bonaire (Scheffers et al. 2009). These extreme wave events altered the islands' ecosystems and coastal mangroves (Engel et al. 2012) with serious repercussions to human survival strategies as well as to the visibility of archaeological sites today. People adapted house structures to protect themselves from such environmental hazards as hurricanes, earthquakes, storms, rains, and heat (Hofman and Hoogland 2015; Samson et al. 2015). During severe droughts in extremely arid environments, such as some of the limestone islands, water procurement and management systems have been put in place (Hofman and Hoogland 2015). These included ditches (*rooi* is a small natural gully that fills with water during periods of rain) for irrigation on Aruba; pot stacks for water procurement on Barbados and Grande-Terre, Guadeloupe; or rainwater containers of *Lobatus gigas* in the Los Roques archipelago (Hofman and Hoogland 2015). Environmental processes combined with natural catastrophes must have impacted the agricultural potential and resource availability of the islands. This would have resulted in periods of population stress influencing the indigenous lifeways and socioeconomic strategies, as, for example, suggested for the Saladoid–Troumassoid transition (cal A.D. 600–800) in the Lesser Antilles, which coincides with the onset of a drought period (Blancaneaux 2009; Fitzpatrick and Keegan 2007; Hofman and Hoogland 2015; Petitjean Roget 2005).

A Cultural Framework for the Lesser Antilles

The pre-Columbian history of the Leeward and Windward islands is divided into an Archaic Age (ca. 6000–4000 B.C. to A.D. 100), an Early Ceramic Age (ca. 800/400 B.C. to A.D. 600/800) and a Late Ceramic Age (ca. A.D. 600/800–1500) (Keegan and Hofman 2017; Petersen, Hofman, and Curet 2004). The archaeological record of the Leeward Antilles, in particular that of the ABC (Aruba, Bonaire, Curaçao) islands, relevant to the present volume, has been divided into an Archaic (starting at 2900 B.C.) and a Ceramic Age (from around A.D. 470). Peoples and cultures are classified according to series, styles, and complexes (see Rouse 1992), while the heterogeneity and complexity of the Caribbean indigenous landscape is emphasized (see also Keegan and Hofman 2017). Traditionally the region has been divided into a Caribbean Cultural Area and an Intermediate Cultural Area and therefore rarely is considered as an interconnected space (Rouse 1986, 1992; see also Hofman and Hoogland 2011; but Newsom and Wing 2004).

Exploring Insular Territories

The earliest evidence for human occupation in the islands comes from Trinidad. An isolated find of a Joboid-like spearhead recovered near Biche suggests that there was a human presence during Paleo-Indian times or the Lithic Age (ca. 10,000 years ago or earlier) at a time when Trinidad was not separated from the mainland prior to when sea-level increases created the island (Boomert 2000; Harris 1993). However, more-solid evidence comes from Archaic Age sites such as St. John and Banwari Trace—ranging between approximately eight thousand and six thousand years ago (Boomert 2000; Pagán-Jiménez et al. 2015). In total, nearly thirty Archaic Age sites have been recorded in Trinidad and Tobago, including eleven midden sites (Boomert 2000: 49, 54–55). Previously these sites were associated with the so-called Ortoiroid tradition, which includes the Banwarian and Ortoiran subseries (Rouse 1992). The sites of St. John and Banwari are located in the southwest of the island on hillocks at the edge of a major lagoon, characterized by an extensive mangrove stand (Boomert 2000: 53–68; Boomert, Faber-Morse, and Rouse 2013: 10–16, 59–67; Pagán-Jiménez et al. 2015). Stone and bone projectile points and peccary-tooth fishhooks, clearly associated with hunting and fishing activities, as well as ground stone tools for plant processing, make up the toolkits. At St. John proof for early cultivation of maize and other plants has been documented from starch grain analyses on several of the stone tools (Pagán-Jiménez et al. 2015). These very early sites are separated by a temporal gap of at least 2,500 to 3,000 years from the earliest human occupation in the Leeward and Windward Islands and the Leeward Antilles ABC islands (Siegel et al. 2015). On the coast of present-day Venezuela, the earliest ^{14}C dates associated with Archaic Age populations (5550±100 B.P., 5190±120 B.P.) have been obtained from the Cerro Iguanas shell midden of the Tucacas area. Although these mainland developments may have been influential to the offshore islands, the earliest documented occupation on Curaçao is no earlier than approximately 2600 B.C. (Haviser 2001a; Hoogland and Hofman 2015; Kraan et al. 2016). To date, evidence is lacking for Archaic occupations on the Las Aves and Los Roques archipelagos and the La Orchila group. Margarita and Cubagua have yielded several Archaic sites generally ranging in age between 7,000 and 2,000 years ago.

The ABC islands were first visited by communities of hunter–fisher–foragers, presumably on a temporary basis, between ca. 2600 B.C. (Curaçao), ca. 1500 B.C. (Aruba), and 1000 B.C. (Bonaire) (Haviser 1987; Haviser and Hofman 2015; Hoogland and Hofman 2015; Harold Kelly and Corinne Hofman, personal communication 2017). On Curaçao, Bonaire and Aruba campsites were located in mangrove settings, near lagoons, or along the banks of gullies (so-called *rooien*). Shell deposits were found at Spaanse Water and St. Joris on Curaçao, at Lagun and Goto Lake on Bonaire and at Spaans Lagoen and Rooi Bingamosa on Aruba (Hoogland and Hofman 2015; Harold Kelly and Corinne Hofman personal communication 2017). Campsites were used by mainland communities (present-day Venezuela, and Colombia in the case of Aruba) (Dijkhoff and Linville 2004: 5; Harold Kelly personal communication 2012) to exploit sea-grass beds in the shallow waters and inside the lagoons (Hoogland and Hofman 2015). They prepared conch shells, mangrove clams, and oysters. A number of hearth features with burned conchs at Spaanse Water suggest that shells were heated in order to extract meat. The meat was dried and prepared, probably for export to the mainland home settlements located some 100 km from Curaçao (Hoogland and Hofman 2015). The Lagun site assemblage comprises ground shell and stone tools, hammerstones, grinding stones, and shell gouges. The somewhat later Goto Lake shell deposits include hammerstones and ground shell and coral tools, but no ground stone implements, nor the typical shell gouges (Haviser 1991a: 60, 2015). The Bonaire assemblages are characterized by unifacial and bifacial flakes, showing similarities to the material of the El Heneal complex in the western part of the central Venezuelan coast, dating to 1400 cal B.C. (Haviser 2001a). However, the ground shell material resembles the Manicuaroid series from Cubagua and Margarita (Rouse and Allaire 1978), except for the shell gouges.

Rockshelters or caves were found at Seru Boca, Tomasitu, and Rooi Rincón on Curaçao (fig. 3.1). Rooi Rincón is radiocarbon dated to 4490±60 B.P. and is associated with the largest freshwater source on

Figure 3.1. Early Archaic Age sites on Curaçao. Clockwise from left: (a) Rock shelter at the Seru Boca site. (b) Rock paintings at the Seru Boca site. (c) Rock shelters located in the drainage system of Rooi Rincon. (d) Shell deposits on the slope of St. Michielsberg.

the island (Haviser 1987: 48). The toolkit is characterized by unifacial and bifacial flakes. Flake/pebble tools and shell gouges characterize the toolkits in these sites (Haviser 1987: 47–48). Pictographs or red and occasionally white and red (only on Aruba) paintings embellish the walls of some of these rockshelters and caves. Their dating is not confirmed, however, and they could well belong to the much later Ceramic Age occupations. Regionally, similar rock paintings have been documented in southern Cuba. The hill site of St. Michielsberg on Curaçao has revealed a number of Archaic Age burials (Haviser 1987).

In the Windward Islands, south of the Guadeloupe Passage, not many Archaic Age sites have been documented (Callaghan 2010), with the exception of Barbados and Martinique, which have yielded potential Archaic Age remains. Reported ^{14}C dates on *Lobatus* shells from the Heywoods site on Barbados are 4360±40 B.P., 4230±50 B.P., and 3980±100 B.P. (Fitzpatrick 2011). The lithics from Heywoods, however, are not typical for the Archaic Age compared to other contemporaneous assemblages.

The reliability of Le Godinot and Boutbois as Archaic Age sites on Martinique, reported by Allaire and Mattioni (1983), has lately been questioned by Benoît Bérard (personal communication 2012) on the basis of poor artifact and contextual evidence. The near absence of Archaic Age sites in the Windward Islands could be caused by various problems related to site preservation and visibility as a result of sea-level rise, local tectonics (e.g., subduction and uplift), volcanic activity, and hurricanes or other storm events. These may have affected shorelines by submerging, covering, or erasing coastal sites (e.g., Cooper 2011, 2013; Davis 2003; Delpuech 2004; Delpuech, Hofman, and Hoogland 2001; Fitzpatrick 2012; Hofman and Hoogland 2015; Hofman et al. 2012; Siegel et al. 2015; Watters, Donahue, and Stuckenrath 1992). It is possible that entire islands are now submerged or covered by mangrove mud or other sediments. The Amerindian sites of the Cul-de-Sac Marin in Guadeloupe, for example, are now under water and the Late Ceramic Age site of Anse Trabaud on Martinique was found to be buried under 2 m of mangrove deposit due to similar processes (Delpuech, Hofman, and Hoogland 2001; Hoogland et al. 2015). The paucity of Archaic sites has on the other hand been related to cultural phenomena: it is possible that the earliest South American colonists bypassed the southern Lesser Antilles in order to head straight for the northern islands where there is sufficient evidence for Archaic Age settlement from around four thousand years ago (Callaghan 2010). Alternatively, the northern Lesser Antilles could have been colonized from the Greater Antilles by people in search for resources such as flint; the Lesser Antilles were settled from around five thousand years ago (Hofman et al. 2011; Hofman et al. 2014; Rodríguez Ramos et al. 2013).

Archaic Age groups between 3300 B.C. and A.D. 100 occupied the Leeward Islands, from Guadeloupe northward. Antigua and St. Martin have been the most intensively investigated in this region and also present the majority of Archaic sites. These occupations may be divided into three phases based on a series of radiocarbon dates (Hofman et al. 2011; Hofman et al. 2014;).

Early Archaic (ca. 3300–2600 B.C.) sites are typically located along coastlines with communities relying heavily on fish and shellfish (Newsom and Wing 2004: 80; Nokkert et al. 1995; Reitz 1989). On Antigua, such sites are generally situated on the low-lying limestone plain along the northeastern coast of the island (Davis 2000). Mangroves, shallow muddy and sandy bottoms, and shallow rocky areas provided good marine food resources. The Long Island area (Flinty Bay) offered easy access to the flint quarries. These factors influenced the decisions for establishing early campsites (Davis 2000: 91, 101). Toolkits include abundant flint artifacts representing all stages of reduction. Long Island flint, characterized by an expedient technology based on flake production, is widely known from contemporary sites across the Leeward Islands (Crock, Petersen, and Douglas 1995; Hofman et al. 2011; Hofman et al. 2014; Knippenberg 1999). Large flint blades have been found only at Jolly Beach (Antigua), and on the high-altitude sites of The Level (Saba), Upper Blake's (Montserrat) and Capesterre Belle Eau (Basse Terre, Guadeloupe) (Cherry, Ryzewski, Leppard, and Bocancea 2012; Hofman, Bright, and Hoogland 2006; Hofman and Hoogland 2003; Stouvenot and Casagrande 2015; van Gijn 1993). The latter three sites are located in the interior parts of the islands. Jolly Beach is located on Antigua's west coast overlooking an extensive offshore marine zone rich in fish, shellfish, turtle, and manatee (Davis 2000). Marine flint nodules present at the western edge of the site may have been a reason for communities to settle at Jolly Beach. The site's toolkit is very similar to that from the Archaic Age Dominican and Cuban sites of Barrera-Mordan and Cayo Redondo (Davis 2000: 99).

During the main phase of Archaic Age occupations in the Leeward Islands (ca. 2600–800 B.C.), Antigua continued to be intensively occupied. The flint sources at Jolly Beach and those on Long Island were then also exploited by communities residing on Guadeloupe, Barbuda, St. Kitts, Saba, Anguilla, St. Martin, St. Thomas, and Puerto Rico (Hofman, Bright, and Hoogland 2006;). Many of the Archaic Age sites in the region evidence multiple episodes of occupation, abandonment, and reoccupation, sometimes spanning several centuries. Campsites, mostly located on the islands' shores, in mangrove areas, or as seen in Plum Piece, in the forested interiors of Saba at an altitude of 400 m above mean sea level (fig. 3.2). This site was likely occupied during specific seasons and activities may have alternated with other islands (Hofman, Bright, and Hoogland 2006; Lundberg 1989). A burial recently found in the Morne Rita cave on Marie-Galante was dated to the Archaic Age (Fouéré et al. 2015). Fish and shellfish were exploited at the coastal sites while mountain crabs and birds were the preferred food in the tropical forest at Plum Piece. The presence of Antiguan flint in many of these sites (except Krum Bay, St. Thomas, and most of the Puerto Rican sites) highlights the importance of this raw material from the onset of island settlement and the quarries may have been the major impetus for groups from the Greater Antilles and elsewhere to venture into the northern Lesser Antilles (Hofman and Hoogland 2011; Hofman et al. 2011; Hofman et al. 2014).

The Leeward Islands also host several Late Archaic sites: Baie Orientale (St. Martin), Fort Bay (Saba), Corre Corre and Smith Gut (St. Eustatius), and Hitchman's (Nevis). These sites (or components thereof)

Figure 3.2. Archaic Age sites on Saba and Curaçao. Clockwise from top left: (a) View of the northwestern coast of Saba. Location of the Archaic Age site of Plum Piece is indicated by the ellipse. (b) Excavations at the site of Plum Piece. (c) View from the Tafelberg on the southern shore of Spaanse Water. Location of the shell deposits is indicated by the ellipses. (d) Excavations at the Archaic Age site of Spaanse Water.

were occupied between 800 B.C. and A.D. 100, making them contemporaneous with the earliest Ceramic Age settlements on these islands. The camp areas at Baie Orientale have been associated with shellfish cooking and the manufacture of shell and stone tools (Bonnissent et al. 2001). Based on the available radiocarbon dates for St. Martin, the site would have been occupied simultaneously with the Huecoid/Saladoid Hope Estate site.

Archaic–Ceramic Age Interactions

The continuous exploratory expeditions, transmission of ideas and information, and population movements from various parts of the continent would have favored intercultural relationships among Archaic Age and later between Archaic and incoming Ceramic Age communities, downplaying the idea of a cultural replacement concomitant with the Archaic-Ceramic interface (Hofman, Bright, and Hoogland 2006). The Early Ceramic Age in the Lesser Antilles is characterized by the Huecoid and Saladoid peoples and cultures who entered the archipelago from continental South America (Rouse 1992). The origins of the Huecoid ceramic tradition, however, have long been contested (see the so-called La Hueca problem in Oliver 1999) but could also have been an in situ development reflecting Archaic-Ceramic Age interactions with links to the continent, particularly the Isthmo-Colombian area (Hofman, Bright, and Rodríguez Ramos 2010; Laffoon et al. 2014; Rodríguez Ramos and Pagán-Jiménez 2005).

Starch grains analysis on several Archaic Age tools from Puerto Rico and the Lesser Antilles evidence early plant management (Pagán-Jiménez 2011). In Puerto Rico, the Dominican Republic, and Cuba, semipermanent and permanent settlements with dense midden deposits and a typical Archaic Age toolkit also evidence plant processing during this period. These sites have equally revealed the first occurrences of pottery (Rivera-Callazo 2011; Ulloa Hung and Valcárcel Rojas 2002; Veloz Maggiolo 1976, 1977), which has led some to question the proposed single colonization movement by Saladoid horticulturalists and bringers of pottery from northeastern Venezuela (e.g., Curet 2005; Fitzpatrick 2013; Fitzpatrick and Callaghan 2009; Hofman et al. 2007; Hofman, Bright, and Rodríguez Ramos 2010; Keegan 2004, 2009; Keegan and Rodríguez Ramos 2004; Rodríguez Ramos and Pagán-Jiménez 2005; Rodríguez Ramos, Pagán-Jiménez, and Hofman 2013).

Flint sources on Antigua and Long Island may have been a pivotal node in the Archaic-Ceramic Age interactions and an impetus for peoples from different backgrounds and origins to establish social relationships (Hofman et al. 2011; Hofman et al., 2014). Between 800 B.C. and A.D. 100, the first Huecoid and Saladoid settlements appear side by side between Grenada and Puerto Rico, while Archaic sites are still present on some of the Leeward Islands. Other lithic materials like radiolarian greenstone and numerous semiprecious stones as serpentinite, amethyst, carnelian, diorite, turquoise, and jadeite began to circulate between the Huecoid and Saladoid settlements. Access to or even monopoly of these materials was acquired by establishing major settlements in the vicinity of quarries (Hofman et al. 2011, 2014). The wealth of material culture remains associated with Early Ceramic Age settlements has been tentatively interpreted by Arie Boomert (2000) to be the product of a kind of "Big Man" society whereby public ceremonies of competitive emulation was the social process through which large quantities of social valuables were buried in the middens of Huecoid and Saladoid settlement/workshop sites (Hofman et al. 2007). Increased interest in specific resources known and exploited for many centuries was probably foundational for the sociocultural, political, and economic dynamics at play during the Late Archaic and Early Ceramic episodes in the Lesser Antilles (Hofman et al. 2007; Hofman et al. 2014; Keegan and Hofman 2017). Circulation of semiprecious stones, beads, and amulets, as well as the exchange of axes, adzes, celts, and sharp tools from flint and greenstone, have dominated the social relationships across the archipelago. Trants on Montserrat, for example, was an important Saladoid settlement and workshop for carnelian beads. This raw material was probably procured on Antigua and then traded across the region as raw material and as finished beads. Huecoid and Saladoid communities at Hope Estate on St. Martin exploited the greenstone quarries at Hope Hill, located less than half a mile from the settlement. The raw material was distributed to communities on the surrounding islands and finished adzes, axes, and celts circulated through down-the-line exchange as far south as Grenada (Knippenberg 2006). People at La Hueca/Sorcé, Vieques and Punta Candelero, Puerto Rico had access to sources of serpentinite on Puerto Rico. The La Hueca/Sorcé site has a Huecoid and a Saladoid component; the wealth of lapidary objects in all stages of manufacture suggest that this was an important settlement/workshop site with a probable ceremonial role serving a larger region (Chanlatte Baik 1981, 1983, 2013; Oliver 1999; Rodríguez López 1989). The Pearls site on the east coast of Grenada at the south end of the interaction sphere is known for its production of amethyst beads (Cody 1991a, 1991b). Pearls also has a Huecoid and a Saladoid component and the tremendous amounts of semiprecious stonework next to elaborate ceramics suggests that this settlement had a similar ceremonial function as La Hueca/Sorcé (Hofman, personal observation 2012–2017).

Between Puerto Rico/Vieques and Grenada, Huecoid materials have been recovered on St. Croix, St. Martin, Montserrat, Marie-Galante, and Grande-Terre and Basse-Terre of Guadeloupe. Huecoid assemblages are characterized by extremely thin earthenwares with curvilinear zoned-incised decorations, filled either with punctations or with crosshatching (Chanlatte Baik 1981, 1983, 2013; Hofman 1999; Keegan and Hofman 2017). A typical Huecoid vessel is an oval dish or shallow bowl shaped like the body of an aquatic animal (fish or turtle), with the tail decorated with curvilinear incised motifs. On top of the head a zoomorphic figure was added as a sort of alter ego (Hofman and Jacobs 2000/2001). The site of Trants on Montserrat yielded one of the earliest dates for the Saladoid series in the northeastern Caribbean and Pearls on Grenada for the Windward Islands. Grenada was probably one of the most densely populated islands during Saladoid times. The eastern part of Grenada is extremely rich in Saladoid occupations, in both coastal and inland environments. On Martinique the site of Vivé, partly buried under volcanic ash, marked the onset of Saladoid occupations on the island (Bérard 2004). Two main wares characterize the Saladoid series on the basis of differences in material, shape, and decoration: white-on-red painted (WOR) ware and zoned-incised crosshatched (ZIC) ware (Rouse 1989; Rouse and Alegría 1990; Rouse and Morse 1999;). However, when closely examining the variety of styles across the archipelago, the Saladoid series appears to be much more heterogeneous than previously documented, possibly reflecting the complexity of kinship ties and social connectedness across the region (Hofman 1993; Hofman and Hoogland 2004; Keegan 2004, and see his notion of Saladoid veneer). The Saladoid phenomenon can be considered one of the most important phases of precolonial Caribbean history (Bérard 2013: 94). The Early Ceramic Age horticulturalists exploited a variety of environments in the interior of the islands as well as near rivers, beaches, mangrove areas, and reefs. Subsistence practices included the cultivation of ground provisions, fishing, and collecting. A multitude of root crops were increasingly cultivated, processed, and baked, evidenced by the multitude of clay griddles, sometimes with extremely elaborate fiber patterns on their bases, found in Early Ceramic Age assemblages. Habitation areas are surrounded by dense middens with tons of shell, fish, and crab remains. The deceased were buried in the habitation area or in a central plaza (Siegel 1989, 2010). Dogs were buried together with humans, sometimes accompanied by grave goods (Grouard, Perdikaris, and Debue 2013; Hoogland and Hofman 2013; Rodríguez López 2007).

On the ABC islands, the Archaic-Ceramic Age transition is less well understood. However, small amounts of pottery have been found at the Archaic Age shell heaps on Curaçao and Aruba dating between 200 B.C. and A.D. 600 (Hoogland and Hofman 2015; Harold Kelly and Corinne Hofman, personal communication 2017) (fig. 3.2). This pottery is coarse and brittle and totally different in paste and texture from the later Ocumaroid and Dabajuroid ceramics found in these islands. The earliest ceramic assemblages on Bonaire, Curaçao were previously dated to ca. A.D. 470 (Haviser 1987, 1991a;). On Aruba, Canashitu (100 B.C.–A.D. 100), Boca Urirama (A.D. 600), and Malmok (occupied until A.D. 900) are much later Archaic burial sites (Dijkhoff 1997: 25). Malmok's dates are contemporaneous with the earliest Dabajuroid sites on Aruba and Malmok also has a later ceramic component (Versteeg, Tacoma, and van de Velde 1990).

Early Ceramic Age Expansions

Around A.D. 200 the Saladoid series is known from the east coast of Venezuela, the coastal zone of the Guianas where it was identified at the site of Wonotobo Falls in Western Suriname, Margarita island and Los Testigos, many of the Lesser Antilles and Puerto Rico, and tentatively the eastern Dominican Republic (Boomert 1983; Rouse 1989, 1992; Rouse, Allaire, and Boomert 1985). On the ABC islands there is sparse evidence of Saladoid ceramics. ZIC-decorated sherds have been found intermingled with later materials at the Santa Cruz II site on Aruba, which according to Boomert (2000: 230) would eventually represent the western tip of Saladoid expansion. On Trinidad, Saladoid presence is manifested as the Cedros and Palo Seco complexes. Cedros-style ceramics have been found only in two sites (Boomert 2000: 129). Palo Seco pottery is considered to be Saladoid with Barrancoid influences and is much more common on the island. Pottery of the Barrancoid series of the lower Orinoco is characterized by thick-walled vessels with red or black designs and modeled-incised anthropomorphic and zoomorphic head lugs. These influences gradually infiltrated the Trinidadian Saladoid assemblages around the time of Christ (Boomert 2006: 160). By A.D. 300 the increase in interaction and regional trade relationships between the island and the Orinoco valley is exemplified in the Erin complex on Trinidad (Boomert 2000: 160–161). Around A.D. 500, the Arauquinoid series, which developed in the middle Orinoco, first influenced only the south coast of Trinidad, resulting in a combined Barrancoid/Arauquinoid ceramic style known as St. Catherine's (Boomert 2006: 162).

Most of the Windward Islands have archaeological deposits dating between A.D. 200 and A.D. 600. Saladoid wares were replaced by Troumassoid pottery around A.D. 600, whereas in the northern Lesser Antilles Saladoid ceramics persisted until ca. A.D. 850–900. From about the fifth century A.D., pottery became thicker, heavier, and softer, and distinctive Saladoid features like painting and ZIC were emphasized by areal painting, heavy modeling, and deep broad-line incisions (Petersen, Hofman, and Curet 2004; Rouse 1992; Wilson 2007: 66). Rims were often thickened, triangular, or flanged, sometimes painted red; surfaces were frequently polished and of a buff-pinkish color (Drewett 1991). On the Windward Islands these ceramic styles are known as modified Saladoid (Mattioni and Bullen 1970) or Troumassée A (McKusick 1960). Barrancoid influences have been found in the Leeward Islands, albeit in a very attenuated form (Petersen, Hofman, and Curet 2004; Wilson 2007).

The social landscape between A.D. 400 and 600/800 offers a quite dynamic picture with settlements located in very diverse settings, the colonization of yet uninhabited islands, and the appearance of ceremonial sites, many of which include petroglyphs (Dubelaar 1992: 27; Fitzpatrick 2013; Hofman and Hoogland 2004). These are located along creeks, rivers, or coastlines; in river valleys or ravines; on the tops of low wooded hills; in rock shelters; and sometimes in caves. Saladoid middens are rich in shellfish, fish, and small land animals, reflecting a broad-spectrum subsistence economy. The faunal assemblage of the Late Saladoid Golden Rock site on St. Eustatius indicates that coral reefs and rocky banks were exploited (van der Klift 1992: 77). Small mammals such as rice rats and agoutis have been found, together with sea turtles and iguanid lizards (van der Klift 1992: 77–79). Of the more than fifty different shell species recorded from this site, most are *Cittarium pica*. Isotope studies confirm that the major part of the diet was based on marine resources (Taverne and Versteeg 1992: 91–92).

Sizeable villages were aligned along the coasts or interior of the islands. Social activities took place at the village level, similar to what has been proposed for south-central Puerto Rico in this period (Torres 2010). The large, round Golden Rock *maloca* structure with a diameter of 19 m may reflect such communal happenings (Versteeg and Schinkel 1992). The deceased were buried in the habitation area, outside the houses. The production and macroregional circulation of semiprecious materials and ornaments, as proposed for the first Ceramic Age settlers, shifted toward a more localized exploitation, procurement and use of resources, and intensification of local networks (Hofman et al. 2007). The presence of jadeitite artifacts, however, also indicates that long-distance exchange relationships persisted (Garcia-Casco et al. 2013).

Late Ceramic Age

The islands of the Lesser Antilles were affected by periods of severe drought between A.D. 700 and 900 (Beets et al. 2006; Malaizé et al. 2011) reflected in significant changes in settlement locations, settlement density, and exploitation strategies. Late Ceramic Age settlements are located in both coastal and inland settings and a great variety of habitats were exploited (Allaire 1997; Bradford 2001; Bright 2011; Haviser 1997; Hofman et al. 2004). Local artifact styles developed and the northern Lesser Antilles formed one interaction sphere with the Virgin Islands, Puerto Rico, and the Greater Antilles. The Windward Islands show enduring influences from Venezuela and the Guianas (Hofman 2013). The post-Saladoid landscape reflects a dynamic social environment, whereby intra-island and interisland communities formed social networks based on kin and trade relationships and sociopolitical restructuring. Quite a few settlements formed pairs, on the same island or with neighboring islands, with social and economic implications, including spousal exchanges (Bright 2011; Keegan 1985, 1992). There is an increase noticeable in inland settlements and an optimal use of natural environments with villages and hamlets located near and along rivers (Bright 2011; de Waal 2006). Large villages were inhabited over long periods of time, evidenced by a palimpsest of residential and burial structures and by thick deposits of Late Saladoid, Troumassoid, and Suazoid cultural remains (Bradford 2001; Bright 2011; Hofman, Hoogland, and Delpuech 2001). Many habitats and eco-niches were exploited; activities were more evenly spread across the landscape and less centralized in a few large settlements (de Waal 2006; Hofman et al. 2004; Hofman and Hoogland 2011). Islets, cays, and promontories were regularly visited and exploited for the procurement of specific raw materials and food sources as well as for the performance of particular ceremonies (Bright 2011; Hofman et al. 2004). Site assemblages in the Leeward Islands are characterized by Mamoran Troumassoid ceramics, influenced by the Ostionoid series (Elenan Ostionoid subseries) from the Virgin Islands and Puerto Rico (Rouse 1992). They typically included vessels with red-slipped surfaces and broad-line incised designs and zoomorphic pelican bowls were characteristic. In the Windward Islands pottery has been classified as the Troumassoid and Suazoid series (Troumassan and Suazan Troumassoid subseries) (Hofman 2013; Rouse 1992; Wilson 2007).

The shift from Saladoid to Troumassoid cultural traditions is contemporaneous with the decline of the Barrancoid series and its replacement by the Arauquinoid series on Trinidad, in the Orinoco Valley, and along the littoral of the Guianas. On Barbados, Grenada, the Grenadines, Saint Vincent, Saint Lucia, and Martinique, and in small amounts on Guadeloupe, Caliviny-style pottery shows up in early Suazoid (Suazan Troumassoid) assemblages with red-painted scroll motifs on buff surfaces (Boomert 1987; Boomert and Kameneff 2005; Bullen 1964; Hofman 2013; Hofman and Branford 2011; Sutty 1983). Caliviny pottery also distinguishes itself by a series of very characteristic *adornos* representing human faces. The Suazoid ceramics are distinguished by specific anthropomorphic *adornos,* red slipped and/or scratched surfaces, female figurines, and footed griddles. Pottery production probably took place at the household level and clays were procured close to the settlements if available and/or accessible (Hofman, Hoogland, and van Gijn 2008). Clay sources on nearby islands were also exploited and clay and pottery vessels were transported or exchanged over short or longer distances (Descantes et al. 2008; Isendoorn, Hofman, and Booden 2008)

Late Ceramic Age communities in the Lesser Antilles had a mixed subsistence economy targeting a variety of food sources, mostly available in the local environment of the settlements (Hofman 2013). Stable isotope analyses from sites in Guadeloupe and Saint Lucia indicate that a large percentage of the human diet was marine based, with fish and shellfish as the predominant components (Laffoon et al. 2016; Laffoon and de Vos 2011). At the site of Anse à la Gourde, Guadeloupe and several sites in southern Martinique, it was found that contrary to the diffuse subsistence economy during the Saladoid, when all major ecozones (deep water reefs, river mouths, lagoons and mangroves, sandy sea bottoms, vegetated terrestrial zones, estuaries) were exploited, post-Saladoid procurement strategies were focused more on the vicinity of the settlement and primarily targeted lagoons, coral reefs, and estuaries (Grouard 2001: 246–247, 2013) (fig. 3.3). The heavily marine-based diet was supplemented with maize, root crops (manioc, sweet potatoes, yams, zamia), beans, and fruits (Hoogland et al. 2015; Mickleburgh and Pagán-Jiménez 2012; Newsom and Wing 2004; Jaime Pagán-Jiménez personal communication, 2012). Refuse deposits also typically contain the remains of rice rats, agoutis, peccaries, guinea pigs, and armadillos (Boomert 2000; Fitzpatrick et al. 2009; Grouard 2001). Some of these species were brought in from the mainland (Keegan and Hofman 2017; Kimura et al. 2016).

Figure 3.3. Multicomponent Early to Late Ceramic Age sites on Grande-Terre, Guadeloupe. Clockwise from top left: (a) Aerial view of the Morel site with test trenches excavated in 1993. (b) The seashore at the Morel site in the late 1990s after severe storm events. (c) Aerial view of the Anse à la Gourde site. The ellipse marks the site location. (d) Excavations near the dunes at the Anse à la Gourde site in 1996.

On Barbados, small villages were located around most of the marine inlets on the island. On the more barren northern and southeastern parts of the island, outlying hamlets from the larger settlements grew cotton and processed salt (Drewett 2004: 221). Cotton and salt were also important for communities in southern Martinique, notably in the area of the Savane des Pétrifications and the Late Ceramic Age sites of Macabou, Anse Trabaud, and Salines (Allaire 1991; Hoogland et al. 2015).

The multicomponent settlement of Anse à la Gourde comprises a habitation area and a plaza surrounded by thick midden deposits reflecting the disposal of garbage over many centuries (A.D. 400–1400). The post-Saladoid component revealed a number of round and oval houses of various sizes with human burials under the floors and outside the structures (Hofman 2013; Hofman, Hoogland, and Delpuech 2001; Hofman et al. 2014). The mortuary behavior is similar to that documented for other sites of the period including Pointe de Grande Anse (Basse-Terre, Guadeloupe), Anse Lavoutte (Saint Lucia), and Grand Bay (Carriacou) (Hofman et al. 2012; Hoogland and Hofman 2013; van den Bel and Romon 2010). In the case of Anse à la Gourde, the deceased were often wrapped in perishable containers, possibly hammocks or baskets; in some cases ceramic vessels covered the face, head, or other parts of the body. Taphonomic evidence shows that burial pits were left open until the soft tissues had decomposed (Hoogland and Hofman 2013).

Distribution patterns of nonperishable objects and materials suggest that local and microregional interaction spheres were created through monopolizing and manipulating the manufacture and/or exchange of goods and marriage partners (Crock 2000; Haviser 1991b; Hofman 2013; Hofman and Hoogland 2011; Hofman et al. 2007; Hofman, Bright, and Rodríguez Ramos 2010; Hofman, Hoogland, and van Gijn 2008; Hoogland 1996; Rodríguez Ramos 2010), possibly out of the need to establish elaborate alliance networks among neighbors in order to form larger local sociopolitical units. In Trinidad, Saladoid and later Arauquinoid settlements reveal similar subsistence strategies comprising root-crop and maize horticulture, hunting, fishing, and the collection of shellfish and wild plants (Boomert 2000). The Manzanilla settlement on Trinidad shows an Arauquinoid habitation, consisting of two houses and a small midden, associated with at least twenty burials (Dorst 2008: 5). The Arauquinoid series is characterized by the Bontour complex, the pottery of which is tempered with crushed shell and rarely freshwater sponge spicules (*cauixí*). Vessels include jars with inflected contours and punctuated appliqué fillets at the base of the neck and open bowls with very few decorations (Boomert 2006: 163). The sequence of ceramic styles on Trinidad is similar to that of the neighboring South American mainland, suggesting continuous interaction between the inhabitants of both regions (Boomert 2006: 165–166).

On the ABC islands, the first Dabajuroid settlements were established between A.D. 800 and A.D. 1000. Major villages on Bonaire are Wanapa, Amboina, and Put Bronswinkel (Haviser 1991a: 56). The Wanapa ceramic style from Bonaire is typically associated with the Savaan style on Curaçao. Several traits at Wanapa, such as dotted painting and alternate-color parallel lines on buff, reflecting Ocumaroid traits, distinguish the ceramics from the mainland Dabajuroid (Haviser 1991b: 61). Dabajuroid ceramics are also found in small quantities on Los Aves, to the west of Bonaire, which seems to be the boundary of the Dabajuroid/Valencioid interaction sphere (Antczak and Antczak 2015). The nearby Los Roques archipelago, however, is related to the Valencioid cultural tradition of central Venezuela (Antczak and Antczak 2006). On Curaçao, major Dabajuroid sites are Knip, San Juan, Santa Barbara, and De Savaan. Next to Dabajuroid pottery, the cultural remains at these sites include shell discs, celts and gouges, ornamental carved objects of shell and bone, bone projectile points, and ground turtle bone plates (Haviser 1987: 51–52). The preferred raw material for stone tools was chert, as opposed to basalt, shale, and limestone, which were common during the Archaic Age. Microflakes have been considered a proxy for the processing of manioc and the presence of *metates* as an indication for the preparation of maize (Haviser 1987: 52; although see Perry 2005). However, to date no microbotanical analysis has been carried out on these tools to justify these interpretations.

Most Dabajuroid settlements are located inland or on coastal bays on the south coast of Curaçao. They cluster mainly in the western half of the island, which corresponds with the location of its lithic sources (Haviser 1987: 139). Exploitation of the *Pinctata radiata* oyster and *Lobatus gigas* intensified in comparison to what was found in Archaic Age sites. *Cittarium pica* and chitons were also major constituents of the diet. *Melongena melongena* is rare in Ceramic Age assemblages and the specimens found are smaller than those from Archaic Age sites. Exploitation of bivalves diminished significantly over time and *Pecten zic-zac* disappeared from Dabajuroid assemblages.

On Aruba, three major settlements—Tanki Flip, Santa Cruz, and Savaneta—and a number of smaller sites were occupied from A.D. 900/1000 (Dijkhoff and Linville 2004: 6). Tanki Flip, located in the northwestern part of the island, was abandoned by A.D. 1400 (Bartone and Versteeg 1997: 110–113). Ceramic Age settlements tend to be located near one or more gullies, which were used as natural irrigation channels. Furthermore, the gullies facilitated travel and communication across the island. At Tanki Flip, several human-made gullies oriented north–south are connected to the natural west–east oriented *rooien* (Raymundo Dijkhoff, personal communication 2010). Several round and oval structures suggest houses of varying sizes (Versteeg 1997: 448–449). Fish bones account for about 70 percent of the faunal assemblage, indicating the importance of marine resources in the diet (Versteeg 1997: 451). The majority of fish were caught in shallow water and coral reef areas (Grouard 1997: 264). Shells were gathered from both the leeward and windward coasts of the island (Versteeg 1997: 450). Corrugated rims characterize the Dabajuroid ceramics of Aruba. Vessels display relatively frequent ornamental appliqués, lugs, and ears, as well as flat, annular, and low-stand ring bases. Temper consists of crushed quartz particles; the vessel shapes include mainly open bowls, griddles, cazuelas, necked jars, and large urns with cylindrical necks (Dijkhoff 1997; Dijkhoff and Linville 2004; Haviser 1989). Ceramic styles and lithic production differ among the three islands. On Curaçao and Bonaire, ceramics and lithics share similar characteristics and seem to have been locally produced in contrast to the Aruban ones, which are clearly different (Niels Groot and Sebastiaan Knippenberg, personal communication 2010). On Aruba, the Dabajuroid Santa Cruz and Savaneta styles (Versteeg and Rostain 1997) show close stylistic affiliations to the mainland's Urumaco and Los Médanos styles (Oliver 1989, 1997). Archaeological and ethnohistoric data indicate close relationships between Aruba and coastal Falcón (Antczak and Antczak 2016; Oliver 1989).

Around the European Encounter

Archaeological evidence suggests that the sociopolitical landscape in the northern Lesser Antilles was disrupted and destabilized several centuries before European colonization due to the emergence of powerful elites in the Greater Antilles (Hofman 2013). In the Leeward Islands, there are few sites that postdate A.D. 1200. The Kelbey's Ridge site on Saba and the sites of Morne Cybèle and Morne Souffleur on La Désirade are rare exceptions and date to the period A.D. 1300–1480 (fig. 3.4). The Saba and La Désirade sites are located at a distance of 460 km from each other, but reflect a similar sort of settlement pattern. They are strategically situated on elevated landforms overlooking the sea and surrounding islands (de Waal 2006; Hofman 1995a). All three sites show affiliations with the Greater Antilles: Kelbey's Ridge has a presence of Chicoid style pottery whereas the La Désirade sites have shell masks or *guaizas,* reminiscent of the so-called Taíno culture (Hofman 1995a; Mol 2014). Chicoid pottery and paraphernalia have also been found on other sites in the Lesser Antilles but their dating is less clear (Allaire 1990; Hofman 2013; Hofman et al. 2007). The Morne Cybèle pottery is clearly different from other ceramic styles in the archipelago and is characterized by geometric modeling and animal or human *adornos,* often in combination with punctuations (de Waal 2006; Hofman 1995a; Hofman et al. 2004). In some aspects it presents common features with the Suazoid and Cayo pottery of the Windward Islands. Suazoid pottery dates between A.D. 1000 and A.D. 1500. Cayo pottery has been correlated with the Island Carib (Kalinago) in the islands and dated to around A.D. 1250 (Allaire 2013; Boomert 1986, 2011). To date, more than twenty Cayo sites have been recorded between Grenada and Basse-Terre of Guadeloupe, with a rare occurrence in Tobago (Bright 2011; Hofman 2013; Hofman and Hoogland 2012; Keegan and Hofman 2017). Cayo settlements were often located along the east coasts of islands (facing the Atlantic Ocean) and in proximity to rivers (fig. 3.4). In the villages of Argyle and La Poterie, postholes of a series of round houses

Figure 3.4. Late Ceramic Age sites on Saba and La Désirade and early colonial Kalinago site on St. Vincent. Clockwise from top left: (a) Test units in the Kelbey's Ridge 2 site, Saba. (b) View of the sea and islands from the Kelbey's Ridge 2 site. (c) View of the Late Ceramic Age Morne Cybèle site, La Désirade. (d) View to the south from the Kalinago Argyle site, St. Vincent.

(*manná*) were uncovered. The remains of two large oval structures (*taboüi*) were excavated in Argyle. The houses were arranged around a central plaza (Hofman and Hoogland 2012; Hofman, Hoogland, and Roux 2015). Cayo pottery is most abundant on Grenada, Saint Vincent, and Dominica (Allaire 2013; Boomert 1986, 2009; Bright 2011; Hofman 1995b; Hofman and Hoogland 2012; Kirby 1974; Petitjean Roget 2015). Characteristic features include incisions on a flat rim, cone-shaped necks and bodies, and typical appliqué decorations consisting of small figures made from clay balls, which were perforated with a hollow straw, often in combination with hands. Multiconvex vessels with appliquéd anthropomorphic faces are typical (Boomert 1986).

Recent excavations of two Kalinago sites on the islands of Grenada (La Poterie) and Saint Vincent (Argyle) have confirmed the presence of Carib or Kalinago communities in these islands until the early seventeenth century (Hofman 2013; Hofman and Hoogland 2012; Hofman, Hoogland, and Roux 2015; Keegan and Hofman 2017). Both sites have yielded Cayo ceramics mixed with European trade wares. The stylistic affiliation of the Cayo pottery with mainland Koriabo and Greater Antillean Chicoid and Meillacoid ceramics suggest either that Kalinago communities who produced this pottery maintained a multitude of ties with neighboring parties or that there were an amalgamation of peoples from various areas in a period of unrest and huge population displacement in the context of indigenous slavery following European colonization beginning in 1492 (Hofman 2013; Hofman et al. 2014) The presence of Taíno paraphernalia or copies thereof in many Late Ceramic Age sites as far south as Grenada point to the fact that tied relationships between the Greater and Lesser Antilles were already established before the arrival of Europeans (Hofman, Hoogland, and van Gijn 2008). Cayo and Suazoid pottery probably cooccurred during late precolonial and early colonial times and both styles influenced the Afro-Caribbean or folk pottery still manufactured on several islands of the Lesser Antilles, notably in southern Saint Lucia, in the area of Choiseul and Pointe Caraïbe (Boomert 2009; Hofman 2013; Hofman and Hoogland 2012; Hofman and Jacobs 2004; Hofman et al. 2004).

Mayoid is the last ceramic series on Trinidad and is characterized by *caraipé* temper, the burned bark of a particular savanna tree (Boomert 2006: 163–164). The Mayoid cultural assemblage is typical of the period of Amerindian–European interaction.

The large Dabajuroid settlements on the ABC islands were occupied until around A.D. 1500. By the time of conquest in 1499, the islands were reported to have been inhabited by Indios Curacaos, Arawakan-speaking Caquetío who also lived in the coastal area of Venezuela (Oliver 1989). Many of the indigenous peoples from the offshore islands were deported to the Hispaniolan goldmines in the Cibao Valley around 1514–1515 (Dijkhoff and Linville 2004: 6–7) or were under threat of the violent slave raids led by Spanish pearl fishery entrepreneurs from the east coast of Venezuela. This was the end of the intensive indigenous networks that were established for centuries between the islands and between the islands and the mainland (Antczak and Antczak 2016).

An early Spanish hunting camp for whales and dolphins was found at Spaanse Water lagoon on Curaçao dating to A.D. 1524–1558. Dozens of ear bones and vertebrae from the Antillean beaked whale and common dolphin were recovered from a hearth. The hunting of whales and dolphins was a common tradition in the Mediterranean, but not an indigenous custom in the Caribbean. The preparation technique, however, is clearly Amerindian (Hoogland and Hofman 2015) and the hearth represents a clear example of Indigenous–European intercultural dynamics in the first decennia of colonial encounters.

Cultural Overview as Context for the Current Investigation

The cultural overview that we presented in this chapter is based on decades of archaeological, ethnohistorical, ethnographic, ethnobiological, and environmental research in the Caribbean islands and adjacent sections of the mainland. As demonstrated in a number of investigations in the neotropics and elsewhere, including several recent ones in the Caribbean, carefully conducted paleoecological research with an explicit focus on past human action helps to provide more-nuanced insights into how and when people not only colonized and moved across, but also interacted with, landscapes (Mandryk 2003). These kinds of studies promote integrative and realistic perspectives on what happened in history and on the intimate relations between humans and the biophysical environment, resulting in everchanging blends of socionatural landscapes. Thus begins a study of island historical ecology in the Caribbean Sea.

Acknowledgments

We would like to acknowledge the Netherlands Organisation for Scientific Research (NWO) and the European Research Council under the European Union's Seventh Framework Programme (FP7/2007-2013) / ERC-NEXUS1492 grant agreement n° 319209 for the financial support granted during the 30 years of our archaeological research in the Caribbean region. We thank Arie Boomert and Alvaro Castilla-Beltrán for their help with copy editing the text and references.

4

METHODS FOR ADDRESSING ISLAND HISTORICAL ECOLOGY

Deborah M. Pearsall, John G. Jones, Nicholas P. Dunning, Peter E. Siegel, Pat Farrell, Jason H. Curtis, and Neil A. Duncan

Introduction

The foundation of this investigation was the collection of multiple independent proxies of environmental conditions and anthropogenic landscapes spanning and ideally predating the range of human occupations in the southern and eastern Caribbean. Proxies included plant microfossils (pollen, phytoliths, charcoal particulates) and sediment chemistry. These data were evaluated within the frameworks of available archaeological and paleoclimate records. Sediment cores were taken in places where the potential was good for the preservation of proxies.

At the core of the research design is the need to draw comparisons among environmental sequences from diverse islands. To achieve this goal, consistent field and laboratory methods were used throughout the project. In this chapter we describe the methods and approaches used during fieldwork and in the analysis and interpretation of pollen, phytoliths, and sediments from the cores.

Our research team conducted four rounds of environmental fieldwork, including coring and landscape characterization in selected locations on Trinidad (seven cores), Grenada (two cores), Barbados (one core), Martinique (two cores), Marie-Galante (Guadeloupe) (one core), Antigua (three cores), Barbuda (two cores), Curaçao (two cores), and St. Croix (three cores). Not all cores produced useful data. We present GPS coordinates for all cores in case future researchers are considering the same locations for similar studies (tab. 4.1). In general, coring locations were selected in wetlands or in a lake in proximity to known archaeological sites, allowing us to assess human impacts on, and adjustments to, local, supra-local, and regional environmental settings. It was important to select temporal and spatial scales of analysis that would enable us to identify, measure, and characterize sources of

Table 4.1. Locations of All Cores Collected in the Project.[a]

Island, Location, Year Core Collected	Core Number	Northing[b]	Westing[b]
Trinidad, Cedros site, 2007	CE07-1	1004.534	6150.401
Trinidad, Oropuche Lagoon, St. John site, 2007	SJ07-1	1012.338	6131.265
Trinidad, Oropuche Lagoon, St. John site, 2007	SJ07-2	1012.590	6131.446
Trinidad, Nariva Swamp, 2008	NV08-1	1031.035	6102.603
Trinidad, Nariva Swamp, 2008	NV08-2	1027.222	6104.723
Trinidad, Nariva Swamp, 2008	NV08-3	1031.222	6104.723
Trinidad, Nariva Swamp/Sand Hill, 2008	NV08-4	1026.790	6104.158
Grenada, Meadow Beach, 2008	MB08-1	1209.728	6136.403
Grenada, Lake Antoine, 2008	12-VII-08	1211.011	6136.393
Curaçao, Spanish Water, 2009	SW09-1	1205.0266	6850.2581
Curaçao, San Juan, 2009	CC09-1	1215.133	6906.104
Barbados, Graeme Hall, 2008	GH08-1	1304.281	5934.598
Antigua, Jolly Beach site, 2007	JB07-1	1703.745	6153.123
Antigua, Nonsuch Bay, 2007	NS07-1	1704.153	6142.959
Antigua, Nonsuch Bay, 2007	NS07-2	1704.150	6143.274
Antigua, Hermitage Bay, 2007	HB07-1	1704.919	6153.698
Antigua, Crosby Lagoon, 2009	CL09-1	1708.708	6151.258
Barbuda, Low Pond, 2009	LP09-2	1738.756	6149.479
Barbuda, Grassy Island, 2009	GI09-1	1742.037	6152.201
Martinique, Baie de Fort-de-France, 2008	KC08-1	1433.802	6059.677
Martinique, Pointe Figuier, 2008	PF08-1	1427.680	6054.558
Marie Galante, Vieux Fort, 2008	VF08-1	1558.697	6117.637
St. Croix, Coakley Bay, 2007	CB07-1	1745.303	6438.394
St. Croix, West End Pond, 2007	WE07-1	1741.127	6453.343
St. Croix, Salt River, 2007	SR07-1	1745.985	6445.702

a. Not all cores contained useful data, thus not all are analyzed.
b. Coordinates are in degrees, minutes, and seconds. Example: N1004.534 = N10 degrees, 04 minutes, 53.4 seconds.

variability in the environmental record and to assess causal links between the physical environment and cultural life (Gunn 1994: 68–70).

Except for some volcanic islands, natural lakes are absent in the Lesser Antilles. On most islands we targeted wetlands, typically coastal mangrove swamps with good potential for preserved plant microfossils. In some cases, intact wetlands suitable for microfossil preservation had been drained for modern agriculture or development projects. This was most extreme on Barbados, where remnants of only a single wetland remained on the island (Ramcharan 2005). Because the predominant mode of deposition of phytoliths in swamps and lakes is fluvial, we attempted to core on the landward side of depressions, where sedimentation from in-flowing streams was presumed to be greatest. Continuously saturated sediments were targeted to increase the likelihood of preserved pollen.

Reconnaissance surveys were conducted in the watersheds that potentially contributed sediment to each coring location. Watersheds were determined by analysis of topographic maps and field observations. Within each drainage, observations were made of current soil state (e.g., degree of anthropogenic degradation), current land use, and evidence of past land use. These data combined with soil surveys, current and historical records of land use, and archaeological inventories provided background information in assessing possible landscape dynamics over time. Disturbances to landscapes potentially impacting stratigraphic relations were assessed through radiocarbon chronologies.

At this stage of research in Caribbean archaeology, it is critical to explore systematically potential linkages between society, economy, and environment when discussing culture change. To what extent did Archaic groups modify landscapes and, perhaps, introduce cultigens, after which later Ceramic Age people imported their own plants and horticultural practices? What was the nature of interactions between Archaic and Ceramic Age groups? What was the timing and rate of introduction of new species of plants and animals to the West Indies by Native Americans? Based on our earlier study (Siegel et al. 2005), we might offer expectations in regard to these questions:

a. Periods of significant modifications of the landscape may be monitored by distinct spikes in charcoal microparticulate distributions and associated vegetational changes documented in pollen and phytolith assemblages (Burney 1997a; Burney, Pigott Burney, and MacPhee 1994; Burney et al. 1995; Kjellmark 1996; Neff et al. 2006; Piperno and Pearsall 1998; Pohl et al. 1996).
b. Introductions of new plant species may be identified by comparing pollen and phytolith assemblages before and after radiometrically

dated cultural occupations. To the extent possible, we viewed such comparisons against measures of environmental change, documented in earlier paleoclimate studies (Beets et al. 2006; Bertran et al. 2004; Brenner and Binford 1988; Curtis, Brenner, and Hodell 2001; Curtis and Hodell 1993; Higuera-Gundy et al. 1999; Hodell et al. 1991; Kjellmark 1996; Nyberg et al. 2001a, 2001b).
  c. Interactions between Archaic and Ceramic Age groups potentially can be documented by tracking the timing and locations of landscape modification/clearing in relation to known archaeological sites of each period.

In the current investigation, we sought data to address human impacts at three analytical levels: locally, supra-locally, and the larger catchment basin. Integrating lines of evidence within and across spatial scales of analysis and chronologically will maximize the potential for identifying subtle culturally induced landscape modifications and distinguishing natural from human perturbations.

Coring Technology and Collecting Methods

Cores were recovered using a modified Livingstone rod-piston corer built by Jason Curtis (fig. 4.1) (Colinvaux 2007; Myrbo and Wright 2008; Wright 1967). This device was used to collect successive 1-m drives into soft sediments of wetlands. The corer consists of 5.7-cm outside diameter polycarbonate core tubes (1.22 m long to collect 1-m core sections, sharpened at one end by beveling), a head to which the core tube is attached for a drive, a piston (attached to a cable) that locks and closes the core tube at its lower end while it is lowered into position then releases to begin the sediment drive, and drive rods used to lower the corer into position in the bore hole and to drive the sample. A pneumatic fitting on the head serves to hold the piston in position after a full drive so that when the corer is retrieved the piston does not slide downward and sediment does not fall out.

After a core section is collected and retrieved, the bottom of the tube is capped with a Caplug (from Caplugs, SC-2-1/4, www.caplugs.com), secured with duct tape, and labeled with depth of the section. The top of the tube is then capped, taped, and labeled "Up."

Prior to sampling, cores were split and described (fig. 4.2). Physical descriptions included color (Munsell), other visible attributes (e.g., large pieces of organic debris, charcoal, shells), and finger tests of texture. Sampling for physical/chemical analysis was conducted by natural strata.

Methods for Addressing Island Historical Ecology • 61

Figure 4.1a. The modified Livingstone rod-piston corer used in this project (St. John's wetland, Trinidad).

Figure 4.1b. Initiating a core drive (Nariva Swamp, Trinidad).

Figure 4.1c. Core in progress (Vieux Fort wetland, Marie-Galante).

Figure 4.1d. Extracting a core drive (Nariva Swamp, Trinidad).

Figure 4.1e. Filled and labeled core tubes (Baie de Fort-de-France mangrove, Martinique).

62 • Chapter 4

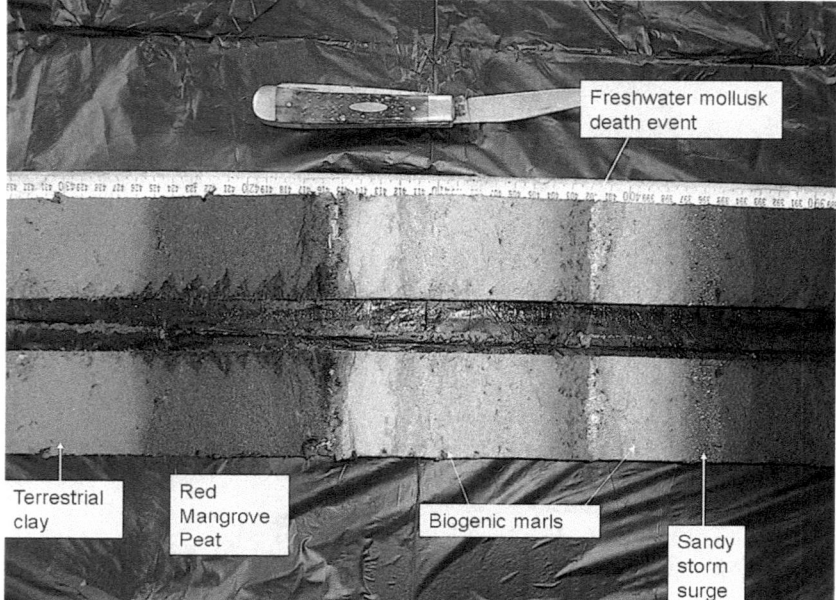

Figure 4.2. Portion of bisected core showing aspects of its stratigraphy (Vieux Fort, Marie-Galante core).

Phytolith samples were taken every 5 cm and pollen every 2 cm, thus embedding two pollen samples within each phytolith sample (fig. 4.3). In some cores pollen subsamples were taken at 5-cm intervals. Testing of the sediment subsamples was carried out in the laboratories of the Department of Geography, University of Cincinnati; Spectrum Analytic Inc., Washington Courthouse, Ohio; Department of Geography, University of Minnesota, Duluth; Department of Geological Sciences, University of Florida, Gainesville; Department of Anthropology, Washington State University, Pullman; and Department of Anthropology, University of Missouri, Columbia.

Two cores were collected from the deepest part of Lake Antoine on Grenada using two attached inflatable boats as a platform. One boat was anchored using three woven plastic bags (rice sacks) filled with rock. The other boat was used as a tender. The uppermost unconsolidated lake sediments were collected using a 7.6-cm mud-water interface sediment corer, specifically designed to retrieve those flocculate layers of sediment without disturbance. Next, the section of sediment from 50 to 150 cm was collected without casing pipe. Then casing pipe (10-cm PVC drain pipe) was lowered into the sediment and pushed

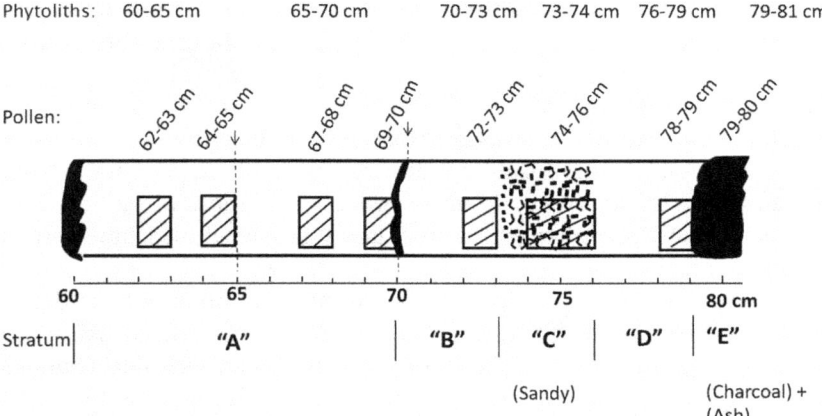

Figure 4.3. Core sampling diagram.

in approximately 1 m to hold it in position, and sediments from 1.5 to 8.5 m were collected through the casing. A backup parallel core was collected from the mud surface to 8.03 m. Lake sediments were transported in their plastic collecting tubes to the University of Florida Department of Geological Sciences for sampling and analysis of carbonate microfossils suitable for oxygen isotope analysis. Unfortunately, adequate microfossils for isotope analysis were discontinuously preserved, precluding their use for climate reconstruction.

One of the lake sediment cores was measured for magnetic susceptibility and density. This was done while the sediment was contained in the polycarbonate coring tubes using a Geotech Multisensor Core Logger (www.geotek.co.uk). After measurements were complete, the polycarbonate core tubes were split lengthwise with razor knives, a wire was run through the mud, and the sediment split lengthwise into working and archive halves. Samples were collected at 5-cm intervals for pollen and phytolith analysis, 25-cm intervals for organic matter analysis, and 25-cm intervals for carbonate microfossils. The only carbonate microfossils observed were tiny (less than 25 microns) ostracods that were too small for oxygen isotopic analysis.

Physical and Chemical Analyses of Sediments

All samples were air dried at 105° C for twenty-four hours to determine dry weight. Percentages of organic matter and organic carbon were determined by loss on ignition (LOI) (Dean 1974). Samples were then ground and the Bouyoucos hydrometer method was used to determine particle-size percentages of remaining inorganic material (Bouyoucos 1936). Laboratory analyses by the hydrometer method were used to confirm field finger tests of texture, which can be misleading in highly organic sediments because organic material can feel like clay to the finger. Particle size is important to measure, especially in sediments from dynamic coastal settings to identify processes of sandbar aggradation or degradation linked to shifts in relative sea level and brackish to freshwater ratios.

Chemical analyses provide additional information about the depositional environment. P, Ca, Mg, Na, and S were measured using the Mehlich-3 ICP method (Mehlich 1984). Na and Ca levels reflect changes in salinity, from brackish environments open to marine flow to closed freshwater lagoons. Elevated P values may indicate human activities within the watershed contributing to the depositional setting (Holliday and Gartner 2007; Lippi 1988; Sjöberg 1976).

Pollen Methods

Pollen samples were quantified (1–2 cm^3) using European *Lycopodium* spp. spores as exotic tracers, unlikely to be found in Caribbean fossil pollen assemblages (Stockmarr 1971). Tracer spores allow fossil pollen concentration values to be calculated and minimize processing error. In the event that no fossil pollen is observed in the sediment sample, the presence of *Lycopodium* tracer spores verifies that processor error was not a factor in the pollen loss.

Following the addition of the tracer spores, the samples were washed with 10 percent hydrochloric acid. This step removed carbonates and dissolved the bonding agent in the tracer spore tablets. Samples were then rinsed in distilled water, sieved through 150-μm mesh screens, and swirled to remove the heavier inorganic particles. Next, samples were consolidated, and 50 percent hydrofluoric acid was added to the residues to remove unwanted silicates. This step deflocculated the residues, effectively removing all colloidal material smaller than 2 microns. Samples were then washed in 1 percent KOH to remove any remaining humates, dehydrated in glacial acetic acid, and subjected to an acetolysis treatment (Erdtman 1960) consisting of nine parts acetic anhydride to one part concentrated sulfuric acid. During this process, the samples were placed in a heating block for a period not exceeding eight minutes. This step removed most unwanted organic materials, including cellulose, hemicellulose, lipids, and proteins, and converted these materials to water-soluble humates. The samples were then rinsed in distilled water until a neutral pH was achieved.

Samples were next subjected to a heavy density separation using zinc chloride or sodium polytungstate (2.00 specific gravity). After the lighter organic fraction was isolated from the heavier minerals, the lighter pollen and charcoal remains were collected. Residues were then dehydrated in absolute alcohol, and transferred to a glycerine medium for curation in glass vials. Permanent slides were prepared using glycerine as a mounting medium, and pollen and charcoal identifications and counts were made on a Nikon compound stereomicroscope at 400x magnification. Identifications were confirmed with the Washington State University Palynology Laboratory's pollen reference collection. With adequate preservation, minimum 200-grain counts were made for each sample (Barkeley 1934; Bryant and Hall 1993: 280).

Pollen and charcoal concentration values were calculated for all samples. Pollen concentration values below 2,500 grains/ml of sediment may not reflect past conditions and usually record a differentially preserved assemblage (Bryant and Hall 1993; Hall 1981). Counts with low concentration values should be viewed with caution. Pollen results were graphed as percentages of the total sum in Tiliagraph, a computer program designed for the presentation of plant microfossil data (Grimm 1988). Charcoal and total pollen concentrations were also graphed. Pollen zones were calculated by a constrained sum of squares analysis, although in all cases these zones were empirically obvious. Following standard palynological conventions, interpretations of each sequence were made from the base of the core upward and were based on appearance/disappearance of key indicator plants, shifts in relative abundance of taxa, and patterning and magnitude of charcoal concentrations.

Phytolith Methods

After samples were received in the lab, an initial set (typically eight samples to correspond to equipment capacities) was selected from each core. These samples were distributed among the major lithostratigraphic units in the core. If the core proved to be of interest based on dating, identified plant taxa, or nature of sediments and phytoliths were well represented then additional samples were processed to fill in the stratigraphy. Approximately twenty-four samples were processed from productive cores (tab. 4.2).

Table 4.2. Overview of Phytolith Sampling and Recovery.

Island/Core	Number Samples	Number with Phytoliths	Number with 200-ct	pH Range
Trinidad				
SJ07-1	24	20 (83%)	6 (25%)	1.5–3.9
SJ07-2	16	9 (56%)	1 (6%)	2.1–4.5
CE07-1	24	23 (96%)	8 (33%)	1.7–6.6
NV08-1	24	19 (79%)	5 (21%)	1.6–7.2
NV08-3	24	7 (29%)	1 (4%)	1.4–5.1
NV08-4	24/28	18 (75%)	9 (38%)	1.1–4.6
Curaçao				
SW09-1	8	5 (63%)	2 (25%)	3.5–7.6
CC09-1	8	8 (100%)	6 (75%)	7.8–8.6
Grenada				
MB08-1	24	12 (50%)	7 (29%)	1.5–6.2
Antoine	5	5 (100%)	1 (20%)	4.8–7.8
Barbados				
GH08-1	8	0	0	4.7–7.8
Martinique				
PF08-1	8	6 (75%)	4 (50%)	1.8–6.8
KC08-1	24	11 (46%)	5 (21%)	1.1–5.2
Marie-Galante				
VF08-1	18	1 (6%)	0	4.7–7.9
Antigua				
NS07-2	8	6 (75%)	2 (25%)	7.0–8.0
JB07-1	8	0	0	3.7–8.6
Barbuda				
GI09-1	4	3 (75%)	0	6.9–8.4
CL09-1	3	1 (33%)	0	8.2–8.3
LP09-1	4	1 (25%)	0	7.7–8.2
St. Croix				
CB07-1	24	18 (75%)	1 (4%)	7.7–8.6

Samples were processed following the standard University of Missouri (MU) phytolith processing procedure (Pearsall 2015). All steps involving chemicals were followed by repeated rinses in distilled water. Briefly, processing begins with initial preparation of samples, during which dried samples are crushed, sieved, and the quantity of sediment to be processed is weighed (generally 10 g) and pH is measured. The next steps remove carbonates and certain oxides using dilute HCl followed by mixed strong acid (concentrated HCl and concentrated nitric acid [HNO_3]). Organic matter is then removed through brief exposure of the sample to household bleach and extended treatment with full strength (35%) hydrogen peroxide (H_2O_2). Dispersion using 0.1 percent Na_2H_2EDTA follows. Dispersed samples are then sieved to remove particles greater than 250 μm. Using gravity sedimentation by centrifuge, clays are then removed from samples. At this point, phytoliths should be free from all chemical bonds to soil particles, and can be floated from the sample using a heavy liquid (2.3 specific gravity). We now recommend and use lithium metatungstate (LMT) for flotation, but for this project zinc iodide was used for most samples.

Following flotation, phytolith extracts were dried in a low temperature oven and a standard slide mount made for each sample in Canada balsam. Slides were examined until a 200-count of diagnostic phytoliths was reached, or the entire slide was scanned. Identifications were made using the MU phytolith comparative collection (http://phytolith.missouri.edu). Diatoms and sponge spicules were tallied outside the 200-count. Two Tilia graphs were produced for each core; a resolved diagram of all taxa and a composite diagram of grouped data.

Phytolith recovery was variable among the cores, most likely a result of low phytolith influx in some locations or periods. Phytoliths were recovered from all cores except GH08-1 and JB07-1, and VF08-1 had only 1 productive sample. In no core did all samples achieve a 200-count of diagnostic phytoliths. Rather than calculate proportions of phytoliths based on counts of less than two hundred per slide we presented all data as raw counts. For samples exceeding two hundred diagnostic phytoliths counting stopped at two hundred: the relative numbers of kinds of phytoliths can be compared for these samples. Counts below two hundred represent all diagnostics on a single slide and these data are treated as presence/absence.

The specifics of phytolith occurrences within cores will be discussed for each core in the chapters that follow. In general, phytolith recovery is related to three factors: phytolith deposition (influx), phytolith dissolution, and processing success. This creates a complex situation for trying to understand why phytoliths were/were not present in samples.

Phytoliths are silt-sized particles (with some fine sand-sized), and so silts must be deposited for phytoliths to be present. (See Pearsall 2015 and Piperno 2006 for general discussions of phytolith production, deposition, and recovery.) How great a proportion of silts (relative to clays, sands) leads to high phytolith counts is unknown. We graphed count versus proportion of silts for several cores, and did not observe any clear correlations. Silts deposited in mangrove swamp strata must be washed from lands with phytolith-producing plants to introduce phytoliths into cores. Nature and density of vegetation, size of watershed, and frequency of silt influx may be important variables for phytolith influx. Intuitively, less dense vegetation (drier islands) and vegetation with fewer phytolith producers (e.g., fewer grasses and palms, more legume trees and mangroves) should result in lower influx of diagnostic phytoliths. Samples dominated by peats, with relatively little mineral fraction, would logically contain fewer phytoliths, and be challenging to process (see below).

Phytoliths can dissolve in situations of high pH, but this does not seem to be a simple relationship, but one that is affected by temperature and water percolation. For example, we have processed archaeological samples with pH 8.5 and higher and recovered abundant phytoliths, and in other cases recovered nothing. In the case of the Caribbean cores, we graphed count versus pH for several cores, and found no clear correlations. The three cores that lacked phytoliths did have samples in the higher pH range, but not uniformly so: GH08-1, pH 4.7–7.8; VF08-1, pH 4.7–7.9; JB07-1, pH 3.7–8.6. Note that all cores from Trinidad were very acidic, and phytolith recovery was more even overall in those cores.

Good phytolith recovery depends on removing organics from samples, since phytoliths are bound up chemically and electronically with organic matter. As a rule of thumb, if one sees pollen in a sample, organic removal was incomplete. The core samples were challenging in this regard, as many were rich in peats. We extended processing times for organic removal, and added Schultze solution (concentrated nitric acid and potassium chlorate) and brief KOH exposure to organic removal for some cores. We graphed phytolith counts versus percentage organic matter for several cores, and found no clear relationship. While we did not tally organic matter, including pollen, observed in slide-mounts, informally there seemed to be no correlation between seeing pollen and the relative abundance of phytoliths: pollen and other organics were seen in samples with and without two hundred phytolith counts.

Considering everything, low phytolith influx is the likely predominant factor affecting recovery of phytoliths from the cores studied, rather than pH or processing issues. A multivariate analysis of factors potentially affecting deposition and recovery (% silt, % organic matter, pH, watershed size, stream flow, abundance of mangrove pollen, grass pollen [i.e., a proxy for high/low phytolith producing vegetation], depth/age, sample size, others?) might help identify the most important variables.

Phytolith Identification Notes

Nodular Spheres

This family-level phytolith diagnostic is produced both by cultivated Marantaceae species producing edible rhizomes, like arrowroot (*Maranta arundinacea*) and leren (*Calathea latifolia=C. allouia*), and by wild taxa in these genera and others. (Nodular spheres are also produced in several Bombacaceae taxa [MU laboratory documents], but in abundance only in *Pseudobombax*, not a likely source for any of the islands in the project.) We searched discoverlife.com and Tropicos (Missouri Botanical Garden database) for collections of Marantaceae species on the islands cored for the project (tab. 4.3). Wild Marantaceae species have been collected only on Trinidad and Tobago and Antigua. Arrowroot (*Maranta arundinacea*) has been collected on Grenada, Martinique, Antigua, Barbuda, and St. Croix. There are no specimens of Marantaceae in

Table 4.3. Marantaceae Species Collected on Project Islands.[a]

Island	Species
Trinidad	*Calathea lutea, C. casupito, C. latifolia, Donax striatus, Ischnosiphon arouma, Maranta gibba, M. tonckat, Monotogma sp., Stromanthe tonckat, Thalia geniculata*
Curaçao	none
Grenada	*Maranta arundinacea*
Barbados	None
Martinique	*Maranta arundinacea, Calathea lutea, C. latifolia (=C. allouia)*
Marie-Galante	none
Antigua	*Maranta arundinacea*
Barbuda	*Maranta arundinacea*
St. Croix	*Maranta arundinacea*

a. Compiled from www.discoverlife.org and Tropicos.

the databases for the other islands (Curaçao, Barbados, Marie-Galante). Based on these distributions, finding Marantaceae phytoliths on any island except Trinidad and Antigua might lead us to conclude (1) that arrowroot and/or leren was being cultivated, or (2) that a wild member of the family was present that has since disappeared (or has never been collected).

However, the Tropicos database also includes literature references to plant genera and species, which give a much different picture of Marantaceae distributions in the study area. The distribution of *Calathea lutea* is listed as Caribbean in several floras from Central and South America (e.g., by Kennedy 2003). The distribution of *Ischnosiphon arouma* is given as Leeward Islands (i.e., potentially Antigua, Barbuda, Marie Galante), Windward Islands (Martinique, Grenada, Barbados), and Trinidad and Tobago by Andersson (1977). Kennedy (2003) lists *Maranta gibba* for these island groups, as well as for the Netherlands Antilles (Curaçao) and the Virgin Islands (St. Croix).

Given the documented diversity of Marantaceae species on Trinidad, in common with the South American mainland, genus-level diagnostics are a more reliable indicator of potentially cultivated species in cores from that island. Nodular spheres are produced in great abundance in Marantaceae leaves. By contrast, genus and species-level diagnostic phytoliths, produced in seeds and roots rather than leaves, are much less abundant. This production pattern makes it likely that cultivated Marantaceae will contribute more nodular spheres than seed or root phytoliths to the environmental record, making identification of arrowroot or leren challenging. On all islands, finding Marantaceae phytoliths in association with indicators of human activity would lend increased confidence to a conclusion that arrowroot or leren cultivation was taking place.

Rugulose Spheres

Like nodular spheres, rugulose spheres (known as globular granulate in revised nomenclature) were described early in the history of phytolith research by Piperno (1988). We follow Iriarte and Paz (2009), among others, in dividing rugulose spheres into two size categories: small (< 10 μm) and large (10–30 μm). Small rugulose spheres are produced in leaves and wood of a wide range of woody dicots, and can be used as a generalized indicator of this kind of plant (along with sclerids). The robust herbs *Canna* (Cannaceae), members of the Marantaceae, and *Costus* (Zingiberaceae) also produce rugulose spheres in abundance, and these tend to be larger (10–30 microns) than those produced in woody dicots (some smaller rugulose spheres also occur in these herbs [MU lab documents]). We will use large rugulose spheres to indicate Marantaceae/Cannaceae/Zingiberaceae (robust forest herbs and cultivated plants) and small rugulose spheres to indicate woody dicots. We would expect small rugulose spheres to occur in strata dominated by mangrove vegetation.

Maize

At MU we identify maize in the lowland tropics two ways using phytoliths: by large (greater than 16 μm on smallest side) leaf cross-bodies of a three-dimensional morphology referred to as Variant 1, and by cob/glume bodies of several types. (See Pearsall 2015 and Pearsall, Chandler-Ezell, and Chandler-Ezell 2003 for detailed descriptions of methods.) Maize leaves tend to produce more crosses than wild grasses that also produce panicoid phytoliths (lobed bodies); in addition, more maize crosses, of all sizes, tend to be Variant 1 than crosses produced in wild grasses. As will be seen in the core discussions, while Variant 1 crosses did occur in relatively abundant quantities in some core contexts, few were large. Production of crosses is variable among maize varieties; for example, a number of common Mesoamerican varieties lack large crosses (Pearsall 2015), and some Andean varieties lack crosses altogether (Logan 2006). Finding Variant 1 crosses in association with indicators of human activity would lend increased confidence to a conclusion that maize cultivation was taking place.

PART II

WEST INDIAN ISLAND HISTORICAL ECOLOGY

5

TRINIDAD

*Pat Farrell, Neil A. Duncan, John G. Jones,
Nicholas P. Dunning, Deborah M. Pearsall, and Peter E. Siegel*

Background

Trinidad has long been considered the likely first stepping-stone for groups of people moving from mainland South America into the West Indies (Boomert 2013; Rouse 1992). This view was based in part on the earliest known site in the islands belonging to the Banwari Trace complex (ca. 6000 cal yr B.C.), located along the west coast of Trinidad, and on a mainlander bias that views nearest neighbors as the most logical paths of colonization within vast oceans. One emerging alternative view of island chronology is that maritime navigational ease and resource availability, rather than island proximity, could have determined the timing and direction of movement and colonization in the Caribbean. Rather than following a trail of island stepping-stones, some have been arguing that island inhabitants took giant leaps as they explored and moved (Callaghan 2003; Fitzpatrick 2013). This view makes the role of Trinidad and its chronological placement in the early island-hopping economy even more compelling. From the perspective of cultural interactions and adaptive strategies, Boomert suggested that throughout pre-Columbian human occupations, Trinidad was really "an extension of the mainland of South America, which in a physical sense indeed it once was" (Boomert 2006: 166). During the Ceramic Age, Trinidad played a key role as a hub in the cultural exchange between the Orinoco Valley, the Guiana coast, the Gulf of Paria, and the southern Lesser Antilles (Boomert 2000, 2006; Wilson 2007).

Trinidad is unique to the islands between Puerto Rico and Venezuela in a variety of ways. Its sheer size (4,828 km^2) is greater than all of the Lesser Antilles combined (fig. 5.1). This was significant in pre-Contact times when the central and southern portions of the island were more closely tied to South America than to Trinidad's own northern coast (Boomert 2006). Being the most southerly of the West Indies, Trinidad is buffeted by easterly waves and tropical depressions, but its near-

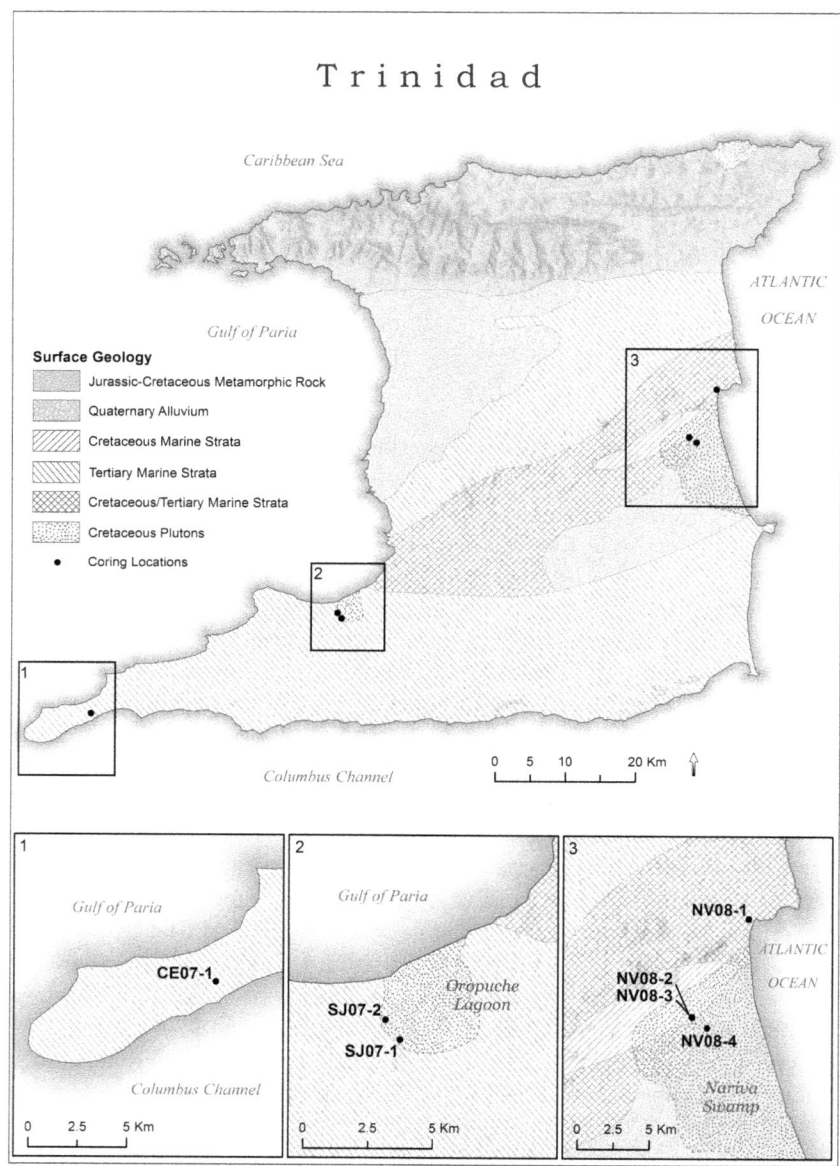

Figure 5.1. Map of Trinidad showing the surface geology and coring locations.

equatorial latitude places it outside the Atlantic hurricane belt. Trinidad's proximity to South America and recent land bridge connection are reflected in its geological structure and floral and faunal assemblages. Trinidad is close enough to the mainland to receive substantial inputs of sediment and freshwater from the massive Orinoco River system of South America, affecting the salinity and sediment load of Trinidad's coastal wetlands. Trinidad's colonial history is unique among the islands as well. While the other islands were transformed by the slave trade and colonial export economies in the sixteenth and seventeenth centuries, Trinidad remained sparsely settled by Europeans and produced only small quantities of tobacco and cacao; as a result the effects of plantation agriculture were not felt for some two hundred years later than on other islands in the Caribbean (Brereton 1981; Watts 1987).

The geology of Trinidad has more in common with mainland South America than with other islands in the Caribbean. Trinidad was part of South America until the Miocene, after which the landmasses separated (Donovan 1994). It was still connected to the mainland by land bridges, during periods of low sea level throughout the Pleistocene. These land bridges to the South American mainland were submerged with sea-level rise during the Early to Mid Holocene. Remnants of those bridges form the westward-extending peninsulas of Trinidad, less than 20 km from the east coast of Venezuela. Trinidad lies on the shallow continental shelf with ocean depth no more than 100 m (Snow 1985).

Trinidad is located outside of the Lesser Antilles island arc. The seismicity of the island is a result of a transform boundary between the South American and Caribbean plates (U.S. Geological Survey [USGS] 2010). Recent studies in Trinidad indicate that the El Pilar fault in northern Trinidad is currently not active and boundary motion is accommodated on the Central Range fault, where evidence points to active fault movement in the Late Holocene, most recently between 2,710 and 550 years ago (Prentice et al. 2010).

Trinidad comprises five distinct geologic regions, trending generally east to west (Day and Chenworth 2004; Donovan 1994; Liddle 1946). The Northern Range is a continuation of the Cordillera de la Costa Province, which is the eastern branch of the South American Andean chain, and achieves the highest elevations of the three ranges in Trinidad, averaging 460 m, with several peaks more than 600 m and one, Aripo, rising to 1,025 m. The Northern Range was a major barrier for pre-Contact population movement and inhibited intra-island travel and interaction (Boomert 2006). At the foothills of the Northern Range, the Northern Terraces are constituted by a sandy-terrace system with a llanos landscape. South of the El Pilar Fault, the terraces descend into the Northern Lowlands, also called the Caroni Lowlands, a structural trough. The region comprises detrital fans and terraces and is dissected by streams flowing out of the Northern Range. It is in this lowland that the extensive Caroni Swamp on the west coast is located. The lowland rises gently in the south, where another terrace system makes up the foothills of the Central Range. This range comprises northeast–southwest trending hills formed by anticlinal structure, and includes prominent limestone hills. The Southern Lowlands lie in a synclinal basin, filled with Cretaceous sediments; they are expressed as a low-lying landscape of undulating countryside, called Naparima. The Southern Lowlands include the extensive Nariva Swamp on the east coast and the Oropuche Lagoon and Roussillac Swamp on the west coast. At the southern margin of the lowlands is the Southern Range, a series of low hills produced by small anticlinal structures. The Southern Range, particularly in the west, has been extensively explored for oil (Ahmad 2011; Barr 1981; Donovan 1994; Jermy and Walker 1985).

High-energy streams course down the deeply dissected Northern Range, but most drainage on the island is in the form of low-gradient rivers following the east–west structural lowlands of the Northern and Southern basins. Six major rivers drain Trinidad: Caroni, Northern Oropuche, Guaracara, Nariva, Southern Oropuche, and Ortoire. Sea-level rise in the Holocene generated aggradation of the island's river systems and inundation of coastal embayments, creating a complex system of interfingered coastal and floodplain ecosystems (Ramcharan 2004). The northern drainages of the Caroni and Northern Oropuche Rivers are characterized by mature stream systems with broad, alluvial-filled valleys and meander belts. Extensive swamps, such as the Caroni tidal mangrove swamp, occupy the river mouths. Although karst landscapes cover only 1.6 percent of Trinidad's land area, well-developed karst in the Northern Range includes sinkholes, karren landforms, springs, caves and cockpit karst and the Tama caves, dolines, springs, and ephemeral valleys in the Central Range (Day and Chenworth 2004).

Today, Trinidad is separated from the South American mainland by the Gulf of Paria, a shallow semienclosed bay that joins the Caribbean Sea to the north through the Dragon's Mouths (Bocas del Dragón) channels and, to the south, meets the Columbus Channel via the narrow Serpent's Mouth. Discharge from the massive Orinoco River system on the South American mainland is carried to both the east and west coasts of Trinidad by the Guiana Current. This current is fed by the North Brazil current and is a major source of water flowing into the Caribbean (CIMAS 2008). Annual cycles of freshwater discharge from the Orinoco cause changes in salinity in the coastal swamps on the north and east coasts of Trinidad. The water in the Gulf of Paria has a lower salinity than the Tropical Atlantic surface water and seasonal variations in rainfall, both on the mainland and the island, causes seasonal salinity variations in the Caroni mangrove swamp (Wilson et al. 2008). These cycles also cause seasonal loading of coastal waters with sediment from the catchment areas of the South American continent.

Trinidad has a maritime, tropical monsoonal climate with a seasonal precipitation regime. The rainy season generally extends from June to December, with significant local variations. Temperature and humidity are high year-round due to the tropical maritime setting. Typical of tropical climates, the diurnal variation in temperature is greater than the seasonal variation. The diurnal range is 10–15°C and the seasonal range is 2–3°C (Ahmad 2011; Barker 1998; Berridge 1981; Potter et al. 2004).

Precipitation across the island is highly varied because the persistent northeast trade winds bring a disproportionate amount of moisture to the northeast shore and island topography governs rainfall patterns on the rest of the island. Precipitation decreases westward with maximum precipitation in the northeast. Average annual rainfall varies from more than 3,750 mm in parts of the Northern Range, to 2,750 mm in the highest portions of the Central Range, to 1,375 mm on the west coast (Ahmad 2011; Berridge 1981). Although the Coriolis effect is weak at Trinidad's near-equator latitude, positioning the island outside the Atlantic hurricane belt, hurricanes made landfall in Trinidad and Tobago in 1933 and 1963 (Berridge 1981).

Quaternary climate change and concomitant sea-level variation are critical to an understanding of Trinidad's land bridge connections to South America, the island's evolving shorelines and estuaries, and earliest signs of human activities on this and other islands in the Caribbean. Climate change during the Pleistocene–Holocene transition is coincident with adaptive changes evident in the resources used by the inhabitants of the South American lowlands who became increasingly dependent on estuaries and mangrove environments. Timing of the land bridge severance from the mainland is not agreed on and the range of published dates varies (Boomert 2006; Snow 1985). It is difficult to determine local sea-level rise; even a relatively small basin such as the Caribbean Sea does not follow a homogenous sea-level curve due to local variations in isostatic response, local tectonics, and changes in the earth's rotational state (Rull, Vegas-Vilarrúbia, and Espinoza de Pernía 1999; Toscano, Peltier, and Drummond 2011). In general terms, it is agreed that eustatic sea level was, on average, 121±5 m lower than present at the height of the last glacial maximum, 18,000 years ago, and that temperatures in the low latitudes were between 5–8°C lower than present (Burnham and Graham 1999; Curtis, Brenner, and Hodell 2001; Fairbanks 1989; Geophysics Study Committee 1990; Guilderson, Fairbanks, and Rubenstone 1994; Leyden 1985; Webb et al. 1997). Holocene data from the wider Caribbean indicate that sea level had reached its present height by approximately three thousand years ago (Gischler 2006; Ramcharan 2004; Rull 2000; Scheffers et al. 2009; Toscano and Macintyre 2006).

Evidence points to Late Pleistocene aridity associated with lower temperatures due to the feedback loop between atmospheric moisture and greenhouse effect (Brenner 1994; Curtis, Brenner, and Hodell 2001; Haug et al. 2001; Holmes et al. 1995; Leyden 1985). These Late Pleistocene and Early Holocene intervals of cooler, drier climate supported an array of moist forests, dry forests, and savannas (Burnham and Graham 1999). In the Early Holocene, climate became more mesic (Beets et al. 2004; Brenner et al. 2000; Caffrey 2011; Curtis 1997; Curtis, Brenner, and Hodell 2001; Haug et al. 2001; Higuera-Gundy et al. 1999; Hodell et al. 1991; Hodell et al. 2005; Leyden 1985, 1987; Mangini et al. 2007; Mayle and Power 2008; Vaughan, Deevey, and Garrett-Jones 1985). The timing of increased precipitation has been estimated to range between 10,000 and 8,500 years ago (Curtis, Brenner, and Hodell 2001). Reconstructions from Lakes Valencia, Venezuela, and Miragoâne in Haiti reveal dry conditions persisting until 6050–5050 B.C. (Curtis, Brenner, and Hodell 2001; Leyden 1985). Mesic conditions in Panama were present by 8550 B.C. and in Jamaica xeric conditions dominated until 7550 B.C. (Bush et al. 1992; Curtis, Brenner, and Hodell 2001; Street-Perrott et al. 1993). Rising sea level in the Early Holocene was suggested as causal in shifts from savannas to mangrove-dominated environments in coastal regions (Van der Hammen 1988) and cores from the current project support this reconstruction. Moist conditions prevailed during the Early to Mid Holocene for much of the Caribbean and evidence points to drying during the Late Holocene, although the timing of the drying episode is not consistent across the Caribbean region (Deevey, Brenner, and Binford 1983; Islebe et al. 1996; Piperno, Bush, and Colinvaux 1990). Data from Guadeloupe suggest a stormy dry period from 800 to 1000 A.D. (Beets et al. 2006). Lakes on the Yucatán Peninsula also indicate a series of droughts in the Late Holocene (Curtis, Hodell, and Brenner 1996; Whitmore et al. 1996). Closer to Trinidad, Curtis, Brenner, and Hodell (2001) examined a core from Lake Valencia in Venezuela and found that salinity increased in the lake after 1050 B.C., but oxygen isotope evidence was lacking. Rull, Vegas-Vilarrúbia, and Espinoza de Pernía (1999) analyzed a core from eastern Venezuela and a peat layer dated to 5050 B.C. was buried 9.2 m below the surface, suggesting an average sea-level rise of 13.2 cm every hundred years since that time. Studies of marine cores from the Cariaco Basin on the north coast of Venezuela also indicate Late Holocene aridity, including notably drier episodes in the fourth century B.C., and second, ninth, and eleventh centuries A.D. (Haug et al. 2001; Haug et al. 2003). Coring data from the present study are consistent with previous research, indicating that Trinidad, like the South American northern coast, did experience a period of aridity in the Late Holocene.

Trinidad has a wide variety of vegetation assemblages, whose distributions are controlled by latitude, precipitation regimes, edaphic variations, fire, topography, and biogeographical influences, from both the South American mainland and the Lesser Antilles. Until recent geological time, the land connection to the mainland created a strong division in species composition and morphology between the Caribbean islands to the north and Trinidad. Trinidad has strikingly high biodiversity; there are more species of woody plants in Trinidad rainforests than all woody flora of the United States (Eyre 1998). Lying outside the tropical hurricane belt, Trinidad forests are unique to the Caribbean (with the exception of the southern Caribbean ABC islands) in that they are not hurricane-modified rainforests and therefore do not undergo intermittent recovery cycles following hurricanes. Floral biodiversity, lack of hurricane destruction, and proximity to the mainland may explain Trinidad's early dates of occupation.

Beard (1946) divided the seasonal lowland rainforests of Trinidad into evergreen, semievergreen, and seasonal deciduous forests based on rainfall distribution, slope, and soil porosity and water retention. Evergreen seasonal rainforests occur in regions with greatest rainfall; semideciduous rainforests occur in regions with less rainfall and steeper slopes; seasonal deciduous forests occur in the northwest peninsula where rainfall values are the lowest. Additional forest types occur in limited fashion. These include the dry Evergreen Montane Rainforests and Elfin Woodlands, a thicket formation of tree ferns, small trees, and palms (Jermy and Walker 1985).

Savannas covered vast areas of the Caribbean in the past and were no doubt much more common during drier phases of the Late Pleistocene and Early Holocene (Beard 1946; Watts 1987). Trinidad still has vast expanses of savanna, the most extensive being the Aripo savannas in the east-central region of the Northern Terraces, situated between upper tributaries of the Caroni and Northern Oropuche Rivers. Soils are waterlogged in the wet season and very dry in the dry season. Vegetation is dominated by grasses, sedges, small herbs, and scattered shrubs.

Xerophytic plants are the most successful and the savannas have been modified by drainage and burning in historic times (Richardson 1963). The remaining savannas are probably refugia from drier climatic periods in the Holocene, when savannas were far more extensive. Coring data from the present study are consistent with this reconstruction.

Trinidad's shoreline is home to extensive swamps, some of which have been partly or completely drained for agriculture. Freshwater swamps range from small ones located at river mouths to the large Nariva Swamp in the east. Other, less-extensive, freshwater swamps are found along the Caroni and Southern Oropuche Rivers. On the Gulf of Paria coast, freshwater swamps extend inland from the brackish swamps in the tidal zone. Freshwater swamp vegetation in Trinidad includes grasses, sedges, aroids, and palm or swamp forest. Palm forests are predominantly palmist or moriche and swamp forest is predominantly swamp bloodroot (*Pterocarpus*) (Jermy and Walker 1985; Kenny 2008). Several intertidal swamps are found in Trinidad: in the west are the Caroni, Godineau, and Roussillac Swamps. In the east are the estuaries of the Nariva and the Northern Oropuche. On the southwest peninsula are the Los Blanquizales and Fullarton Swamps. Intertidal swamps comprise a continuum from freshwater to saltwater and all show pronounced seasonal changes in salinity. Plant communities follow this continuum and include sedges in the weakly brackish waters to mangrove in the brackish end of the spectrum, with red being the most common of the mangrove types in Trinidad. Extensive mud flats are exposed in some of the swamps at low tide and were important sources of shellfish throughout the Holocene.

Ahmad (2011) reclassified Trinidad's soils, updating earlier treatments (Chenery 1952; Hardy 1981). Soil types covering most of Trinidad are highly weathered Ultisols and clay Vertisols. Ahmad's classification divides Trinidad's soils into three categories: alluvial plain soils, terrace soils, and upland soils. Alluvial plain soils include cultivated beach sands (Entisols), hydromorphic soils (Histosols), and alluvial soils that are either freely drained or poorly drained. These alluvial plain soils are considered by Ahmad (2011) to have the greatest agricultural potential. The hydromorphic soils, found in saturated conditions, such as the large swamplands in Trinidad, have marine influence and high clay content with vertic properties, which cause them to swell when wet and shrink and crack when dry.

Terrace soils are classified by Ahmad (2011) as freely drained or poorly drained. Well-drained terrace soils include the soils developed in colluvial or alluvial sediments from the Northern Range. These are erodible soils with loam and clay loam textures and are generally acid and cation deficient. Poorly drained terrace soils are predominantly found on the Northern terraces.

Soils in the savanna regions of Trinidad have silty to fine sand topsoil horizons, an illuvial clay horizon that has been called a "clay pan" (Richardson 1963) and a densipan (Smith, Arya, and Stark 1975) due to its impenetrable nature and high bulk density (Ahmad 2011). Many of the savanna soils have plinthite development and are highly leached, and are acid and nutrient deficient (Ahmad 2011). These soils are waterlogged during the wet season and become very dry in the dry season (Richardson 1963).

Upland soils in Trinidad include intermediate and high upland soils, both with good or poor drainage. The well-drained and poorly drained high upland soils are found exclusively in the Northern Range. Well-drained intermediate upland soils are on sand and clay sediments in the south, and poorly drained intermediate upland soils are in the Central Range. Intermediate upland soils cover 42 percent of the land area of the island.

Environmental Coring on Trinidad

In total, seven cores were recovered from Trinidad: three in the west and four in the extensive Nariva Swamp region on the east coast.

Western Trinidad: St. John and Cedros

The coring locations of St. John and Cedros were chosen because of the well-known archaeological records for these sites. The St. John site is located between the Banwari Trace site and the Gulf of Paria in southwestern Trinidad. This Archaic site is contemporaneous with Banwari Trace (ca. 6000 cal yr B.C.) and contains an assemblage of stone and bone tools (Boomert 2000; Harris 1973; Pagán-Jiménez et al. 2015; Wilson 2007). The St. John site has been classified as Banwarian Ortoiroid. Based on environmental setting, comparable technologies, and diet, its occupants may have originated along the Venezuela Coast, the Orinoco Delta, and the Guiana coast (Boomert 2000, 2006; Wilson 2007).

The Southern Oropuche River is a large, low-gradient river flowing westward along a structural trough in south-central Trinidad. Large portions of its floodplain are occupied by wetlands, though many areas have been drained historically for cultivation. The entire drainage basin occupies an area of about 185 km^2. Soils within the low-lying portions of the Southern Oropuche drainage are deep, hydromorphic, and poorly drained: these soils include heaving clay (Vertisols), organic mucks (Histosols), and poorly developed alluvial soils (Inceptisols). Soils on the sloping terrain of the watershed are predominantly deeply weathered tropical Alfisols and Ultisols formed from saprolitic sedimentary rock. Two cores were extracted from wetlands near the St. John site, some 3 km inland from the Gulf of Paria.

St. John (Core SJ07-1)

A 2.82-m core was extracted from a small wetland lying within an embayment along the southern edge of the Southern Oropuche floodplain and below the ridge on which the St. John site is located. The majority of mineral sediment at this location is likely to have been produced by local sheetwash from immediately adjacent ridges covering a few hundred square meters. The wetland from which the core was extracted has evidently been extensively drained in historic times. Sediments recovered from the core revealed disturbance from clearing for farming and little potential for preserved pollen assemblages. Phytoliths are well preserved in the core, although their abundance is not consistent throughout (figs. 5.2a, 5.2b). The middle (about 140–105 cm) and upper (50–0 cm) portions of the core show a relatively strong influx of phytoliths. Deposition patterns are driven largely by arboreal and understory plants, with palms contributing heavily in the upper part of the core, and woody trees/shrubs represented by small rugulose spheres in the middle of the core. Marantaceae were present in most of the productive samples, occurring earliest at 204–206 cm. Sedge, a freshwater indicator, appears at the top of the sequence. Variant 1 crosses were identified in the uppermost three levels analyzed, and one cross, from level 26–32 cm, is large enough to be classified as maize. This sequence is not dated; it likely represents historic or modern phytolith influx associated with farming.

St. John (Core SJ07-2)

The second core near the St. John site was more productive. A 4.74-m core was collected from a red mangrove wetland adjacent to a small tributary of the Southern Oropuche River, which can be seasonally inundated by flooding from the main channel. Sediments in the core reflect the complex influxes of sediments from the larger Southern Oropuche watershed (tab. 5.1).

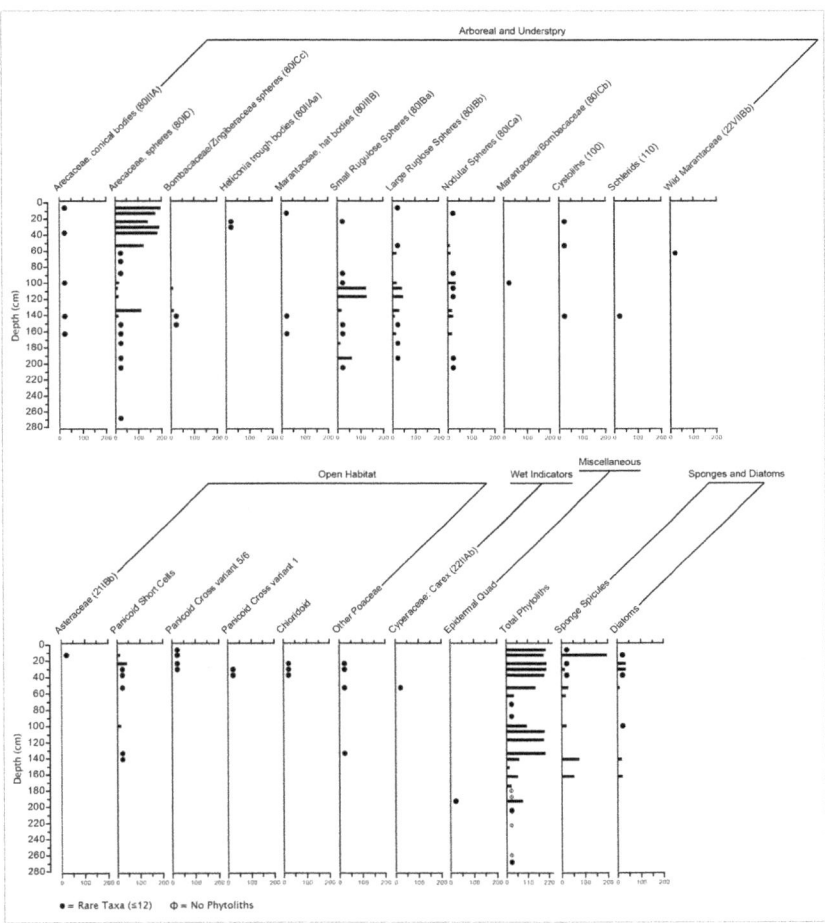

Figure 5.2a. St. John wetland 1, Trinidad, core phytolith diagram: resolved.

Two radiocarbon dates were obtained from this core: 3570 cal med B.C. from organic sediment at 464 cm and cal med A.D. 1225 from a depth of 165–170 cm (tab. 5.2). Sediments from 0 to 300 cm are highly organic clays and peats and become more notably mineral below 300 cm, though organic matter remains significant. Pulses of higher mineral clay inputs throughout the core are as likely to derive from overbank flooding of the Southern Oropuche as from local ridges. Phosphate levels show a notable upward spike several places in the core, typically in strata with charcoal concentrations: 403–440 cm, 386–387 cm, 355–360 cm,

86 • Chapter 5

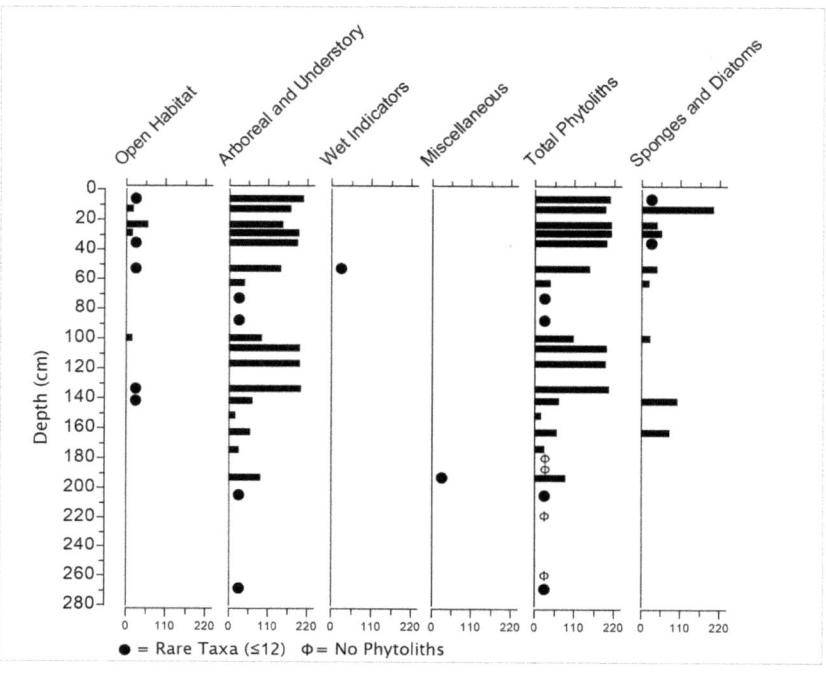

Figure 5.2b. St. John wetland 1, Trinidad, core phytolith diagram: composite.

Table 5.1. Sediment Descriptions of the St. John, Trinidad Core (Core SJ07-1).

Depth (cm)	Color	OM (LOI)	Total P (ppm)	Sand %	Silt %	Clay %	Notes
0–7	Black						Fibric muck
7–100	Dark olive gray (5Y 3/2)	22.5	468	5		51	Sapric peat
100–111							Fibric peat (palm root?)
111–175	Dark olive gray (5Y 3/2)	18.1	365	0	35	65	Sapric peaty clay
175–200	Dark green gray (Gley 10Y 4/1)	22.8	130	10	28	62	Banded sapric and fibric peat
200–220	Dark green gray (Gley 10Y 3/1)	19.5	119	2	31	67	Sapric peaty clay; light mottling

(continued)

Table 5.1. (continued)

Depth (cm)	Color	OM (LOI)	Total P (ppm)	Sand %	Silt %	Clay %	Notes
220–241	Dark green gray (Gley 10Y 3/1)	18.3	117	1	35	64	Sapric peaty clay; blue-gray mottles
241–250	Dark green gray (Gley 10Y 3/1)	17.4	95	5	29	66	Fibric peaty clay
250–279	Dark green gray (Gley 10Y 4/1)	16.0	102	2	28	70	Fibric peaty clay
279–281			245				Charcoal band within peat
281–286	Greenish gray (Gley 10Y 5/1)	14.7	158	6	27	67	Fibric peaty clay
286–287							Charcoal band
287–300	Greenish gray (Gley 10Y 6/1)	12.2	109	7	30	63	Fibric peaty clay
300–355	Dark gray (Gley N 4/N)	7.4	129	5	24	71	Organic clay
355–360			211				Organic clay with charcoal bands
360–386	Dark gray (Gley N 4/N)	7.1	140	4	23	73	Organic clay
386–387			195				Organic clay with charcoal bands
387–400	Dark gray (Gley N 4/N)	6.9	133	5	25	70	Organic clay
400–403							Hole slop
403–430	Dark gray (Gley N 4/N)	7.8	206	3	23	74	Organic clay with a few thin charcoal bands
430–440	Greenish gray (Gley 10Y 5/1)	5.6	118	1	23	76	Organic clay
440–454	Dark green gray (Gley 10Y 4/1)	6.0	138	2	24	74	Organic clay
454–455							Charcoal band
455–474	Very dark gray (Gley N 3/N)	7.7	122	2	19	79	Organic clay

Table 5.2. Radiocarbon Dates from Trinidad Cores.

Core Location	Lab Sample Number	Core Number/ Sample Depth	^{14}C Age (BP)[a]	^{13}C/^{12}C Ratio	2-Sigma Calibrated Date Range[b]	Median Cal Date
Cedros	AA82470	CE07-1, 128 cm, OS[c]	2490±40	-28.3	790–420 BC/2380–2740 BP	630 BC/2580 BP
Cedros	AA82469	CE07-1, 315 cm, OS	4280±40	-28.1	3020–2760 BC/4710–4970 BP	2900 BC/4850 BP
Cedros	AA77444	CE07-1, 433–436 cm, OS	4730±40	-27.9	3640–3380 BC/5330–5580 BP	3525 BC/5475 BP
St John (Oropuche Lagoon)	Beta-378826	SJ07-2, 165–170 cm, OS	820±30	-26.4	AD 1165–1265/685–785 BP	AD 1225/730 BP
St John (Oropuche Lagoon)	AA77388	SJ07-2, 464 cm, OS	4790±40	-28.4	3650–3380 BC/5330–5600 BP	3570 BC/5520 BP
Nariva Swamp	Beta-379162	NV08-1, 100–105 cm, PP[d]	1750±30	-26.5	AD 220–380/1570–1730 BP	AD 295/1660 BP
Nariva Swamp	Beta-378825	NV08-1, 100–105 cm, OS	3220±30	-27.4	1600–1430 BC/3370–3550 BP	1485 BC/3435 BP
Nariva Swamp	Beta-382069	NV08-1, 100–105 cm, OS	3260±30	-27.2	1620–1450 BC/3400–3570 BP	1540 BC/3490 BP
Nariva Swamp	Beta-343380	NV08-1, 208–210 cm, PW[e]	5900±30	-25.0	4840–4710 BC/6660–6790 BP	4765 BC/6715 BP
Nariva Swamp	AA82681	NV08-1, 250–251 cm, PW	6160±70	-30.4	5300–4940 BC/6890–7250 BP	5110 BC/7060 BP
Nariva Swamp	AA82679	NV08-2, 374 cm, PW	3260±50	-26.5	1640–1430 BC/3380–3590 BP	1540 BC/3490 BP
Nariva Swamp	Beta-343381	NV08-3, 196–204 cm, PW	2480±30	-27.0	770–420 BC/2380–2720 BP	635 BC/2585 BP
Nariva Swamp	AA84719	NV08-3, 445–447 cm, PW	3990±35	-29.2	2620–2410 BC/4360–4570 BP	2525 BC/4475 BP
Nariva Swamp	AA85864	NV08-4, 235 cm, PW	3575±45	-25.7	2030–1770 BC/3720–4060 BP	1925 BC/3885 BP
Nariva Swamp	AA85865	NV08-4, 280–281 cm, PW	3280±45	-29.3	1660–1450 BC/3400–3610 BP	1560 BC/3510 BP
Nariva Swamp	AA82680	NV08-4, 685–686 cm, PW	5910±50	-28.6	4930–4620 BC/6640–6880 BP	4780 BC/6730 BP

a. 1-sigma range.
b. Dates were calibrated using the IntCal13 method of CALIB ver. 7.0 (Reimer et al. 2013).
c. Organic sediment.
d. Preserved plant matter.
e. Preserved wood.

and 278–281 cm; these likely represent periods of human disturbance. Elevated phosphate levels may also be associated with modern agricultural inputs in upper sections of the core.

Three pollen zones are readily apparent in the profile (fig. 5.3). The basal zone (165/170–474 cm) is bracketed by radiocarbon dates of A.D. 1225 to 3570 B.C. This zone reflects a brackish or saline red mangrove–dominated environment. Charcoal is reduced in this zone and likely minimal human activity was taking place in the site vicinity during this period (tab. 5.3). Around A.D. 1225, a dramatic shift in the local environment resulted in a significant reduction in red mangrove pollen with a subsequent increase in Cyperaceae (sedge family), Asteraceae (aster or composite family), Poaceae (grass family), and Arecaceae (palm family) pollen. These taxa represent disturbance freshwater types and reflect landscape modifications in the immediate site area (tab. 5.4). Appreciable increases in particulate carbon support evidence for a nearby human settlement and sedimentation rate increased considerably (tab. 5.5). At the top of this zone, a single *Zea mays* (maize) pollen grain was noted, but the date of the cultivation of this taxon might be relatively recent. The upper zone is marked by a renewed presence of mangrove pollen and represents recent or historic activity in the site area.

This core was sampled for phytoliths from the base, representing a time before 3570 B.C. to around 100 cm, sometime after A.D. 1225. Phytolith recovery was low in most levels sampled, but somewhat higher

Table 5.3. Sedimentation Rates for the Trinidad Cores.

Core, ^{14}C sample depths	^{14}C Date Ranges (Median Cal Dates, BP)	Sedimentation Rate (cm/yr)
CE07-1, 0–128 cm	0–2580	.0496
CE07-1, 128–315 cm	2580–4850	.0823
CE07-1, 315–434 cm	4850–5475	.1904
SJ07-2, 0–167 cm	0–730	.2287
SJ07-2, 167–464 cm	730–5520	.0620
NV08-1, 0–103 cm	0–3490	.0295
NV08-1, 103–209 cm	3490–6720	.0328
NV08-1, 209–250 cm	6720–7060	.1205
NV08-2/NV08-3, 0–200 cm	0–2585	.0773
NV08-2/NV08-3, 200–374 cm	2585–3490	.1922
NV08-2/NV08-3, 374–446 cm	3490–4475	.0730

90 • Chapter 5

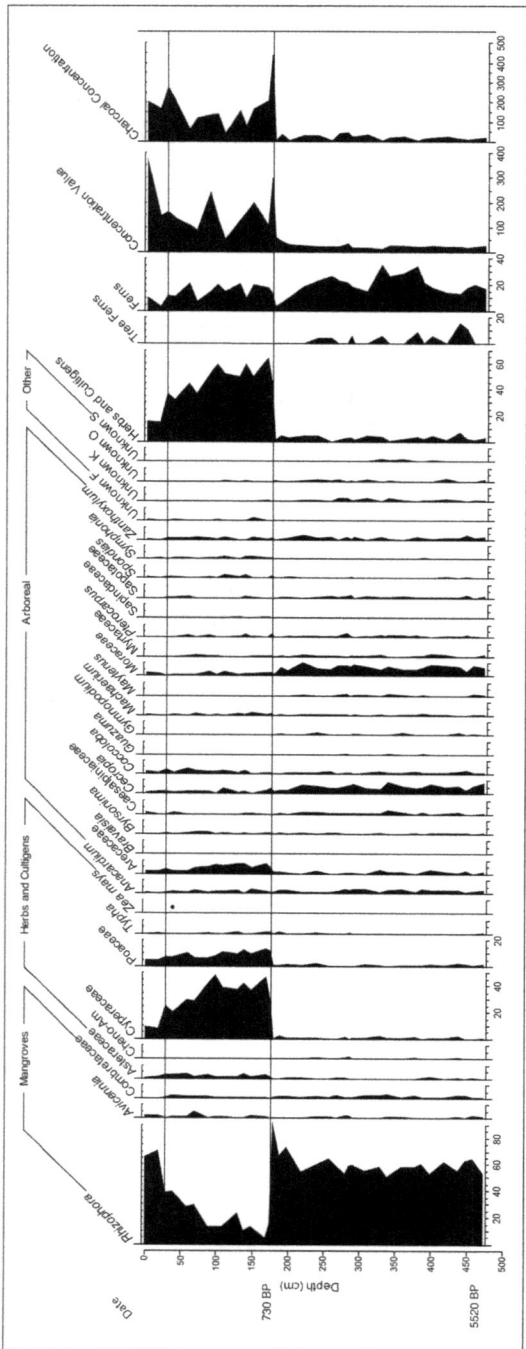

Figure 5.3. St. John wetland 2, Trinidad, core pollen-percentage diagram. Pollen and charcoal concentrations are expressed as grains and fragments, respectively, per cm³ of sediment.

Table 5.4. Plant Taxa Identified in the Trinidad Cores with No Documented Ethnobotanical or Anthropogenic Correlates other than Perhaps Fuel Wood, Especially Arboreal Taxa.

Taxon	Common Name	Core NV08-1	Core NV08-3	Core NV08-4	Core SJ07-2	Core CE07-1
HERBS/CULTIGENS						
Acalypha	Copperleaf, flowering shrub					
Lythraceae	Cigar plant	X				
Polygonaceae, *Gymnopodium*	Common sorrel	X			X	X
ARBOREAL						
Erythrina	Leguminosae family, cockspur, cockscomb coraltree					X
Hura	Sand box			X		
Ilex	Holly		X	X		X
Machaerium	Escambrón, spiny climbing shrub or small tree. Form thickets in mangrove swamps.		X	X	X	X
Maytenus	Caribbean Mayten, staff vine	X			X	
Pterocarpus	Swamp bloodwood tree. Grows in swamp forests, mainly on landward side of mangrove.		X	X	X	X
Quercus	Oak					
Trema	Elm trees. Small evergreens growing in open forests or clearings.					
Zanthoxylum	Prickly ash	X	X	X	X	X
FERNS						
Acrostichum	Leather swamp fern. High saltwater tolerance.			X	X	
Unknown ferns		X	X	X	X	X

Table 5.5. Ethnobotanical Associations and Disturbance Indicators Represented in the Trinidad Cores.[a]

Taxon	Ethnobotanical Association or Disturbance Indicator	Core NV08-1	Core NV08-3	Core NV08-4	Core SJ07-2	Core CE07-1
MANGROVE						
Avicennia	Black mangrove. Throat pains, incontinence.	X			X	
Combretaceae	White mangrove. Slows bleeding.	X	X	X	X	
Rhizophora	Red mangrove. Diarrhea, fever, malaria, excellent fuel wood.	X	X	X	X	
HERBS/CULTIGENS						
Asteraceae	Aster or Composite family. Herbs and shrubs. Many are invasive weed species of cleared open areas.	X	X	X	X	
Borreria	Weedy herb in Madder family. Alkaloid and iridoid extracts have medicinal properties.		X			
Cheno-Ams	Chenopod and amaranth families. Favor disturbed or open habitats. Young greens and mature seeds are edible. Includes seablite, saltwort, chenopod, amaranth.		X[b]		X[b]	
Cyperaceae, *Cladium*	Sedge family. Grasslike herbaceous plants, many are weeds that invade cleared open areas.	X	X	X	X	
Fabaceae, *Desmodium*	Wild herbaceous legumes. Includes cohoba, edible beans. Species include plants with medicinal uses and for producing narcotic snuff, edible fruit, and fish poison.	X	X			

(continued)

Table 5.5. (continued)

Taxon	Ethnobotanical Association or Disturbance Indicator	Core NV08-1	Core NV08-3	Core NV08-4	Core SJ07-2	Core CE07-1
Bombacaceae/ Malvaceae	Mallow family. Some have medicinal properties, others fruits and leaves are edible. Cotton (*Gossypium*) is in this family.					X
Marantaceae, *Calathea, Maranta*	Maranta family, starchy edible rhizomes. Includes West Indian arrowroot.	X		X		X
Nymphaeaceae, *Nymphaea*	Water lilies. Leaves, flower buds, and seeds are edible.	X[b]				
Onagraceae	Includes evening primrose, a mild narcotic.			X[b]		
Poaceae	Grass family. Often associated with areas frequently fired. Edible starchy grains.	X	X	X	X	X
Polygonaceae, *Polygonum*	Knotweed. Some species cooked and eaten.		X	X[b]		
Typha	Cattail. Colonizing plants to newly cleared wetlands. Edible rhizomes.	X	X	X[b]	X	
Zea mays	Maize. Edible grain.				X[b]	
ARBOREAL						
Acacia	Young spines used to relieve gum and tooth pain.		X			
Alchornea	Many species have medicinal properties.	X		X[b]		
Anacardiaceae, *Anacardium, Spondias* sp.	Cashew family. Edible fruit, Hogplum.	X	X	X		

(*continued*)

Table 5.5. (continued)

Taxon	Ethnobotanical Association or Disturbance Indicator	Core NV08-1	Core NV08-3	Core NV08-4	Core SJ07-2	Core CE07-1
Apocynaceae	Dogbane family. Golden trumpet vine. Fibers used for cordage. Some produce edible flowers.		X[b]	X		
Arecaceae	Palm family. Edible fruit, thatching, cordage, needles, posts.	X	X	X	X	X
Byrsonima	Edible fruit, nance.		X	X	X	
Bursera	Gumbo limbo. Resin has medicinal properties, leaves used for tea.		X	X	X	
Caesalpiniaceae, Cassia	Anthraquinone glycosides from the seeds and leaves used as a laxative and anti-inflammatory agent.		X	X		
Cecropia	Pumpwood. Fast-growing colonizing trees common to disturbed forest habitats and clearings.	X	X	X	X	
Celtis	Hackberry, edible fruit.			X		
Chrysobalanaceae	Coco-Plum family. Edible fruits.	X				X[b]
Coccoloba	Sea grape. Edible fruit, medicinal.	X	X[b]	X	X	
Guazuma	West Indian elm, pigeon wood. Seeds of some have medicinal properties and others are edible.				X	
Hippocratea	Medicine vine, medicinal, anti-inflammatory.		X[b]	X[b]		
Hirea	Liana. Used for rope.		X			

(continued)

Trinidad • 95

Table 5.5. (continued)

Taxon	Ethnobotanical Association or Disturbance Indicator	Core NV08-1	Core NV08-3	Core NV08-4	Core SJ07-2	Core CE07-1
Moraceae, *Ficus, Brosimum*	Mulberry family. Edible fruit, breadnut, medicinal. Often colonize open cleared areas.	X	X	X	X	
Myrtaceae, *Eugenia, Psidium*	Myrtle family. Edible fruit, medicinal. Frequently found in windbreak and secondary forest growth. Includes guava, Eugenia, allspice.	X		X	X	
Rhamnaceae	Buckthorn family. Edible berries.	X				
Sapindaceae	Soapberry family. Fruits and seeds of some are edible, others poisonous.	X	X	X	X[b]	
Sapotaceae, *Chrysophyllum, Sideroxylon*	Sapote family. Edible fruit, medicinal, latex in some species. Includes edible fruits of chicle, sapote, lucuma.	X	X	X	X	
Sebastiana	Flowers, leaves edible of some species.		X[b]			
Symphonia	Resin used for caulking in canoes and as a fastening agent for arrowpoints to spear shafts and stone flakes to wooden boards.		X	X	X	

a. Information drawn from Bandaranayake 1998; Carretero et al. 2008; deFrance and Newsom 2005; Instituto Nacional Indigenista 2009; Im Thurn 1883; Liogier and Martorell 2000; Little and Wadsworth 1964; Little et al. 1974; Maria Conserva and Costa Ferreira 2012; Milliken et al. 2009 onwards; Morton 1965; Newsom 2008; Newsom and Pearsall 2003; Newsom and Wing 2004; Nuñez Melendez 1992; Pearsall 2002; Piperno 2002; Piperno and Pearsall 1998; Taylor 1996 onwards.
b. Trace amounts.

96 • Chapter 5

from 140 to 200 cm, bracketing the A.D. 1225 date (figs. 5.4a, 5.4b). Arboreal and understory taxa account for most phytoliths recovered, especially palm and Marantaceae. Marantaceae (nodular spheres), in fact, dominated the single sample with a 200-count. Five Variant 1 crosses were identified in the 145–150 cm level. While none is large enough to be classified definitively as maize, this concentration is unusual and suggestive of maize.

A surface soil sample (MU 3480) was taken from a remnant swamp forest along the edge of the cored mangrove region. Plants identified by John Jones in the locality included coyol palm, *Mauritania* palm, *Bactris* palm, the trees *Coccoloba* and *Cecropia*, and plants in the Rutaceae, Sap-

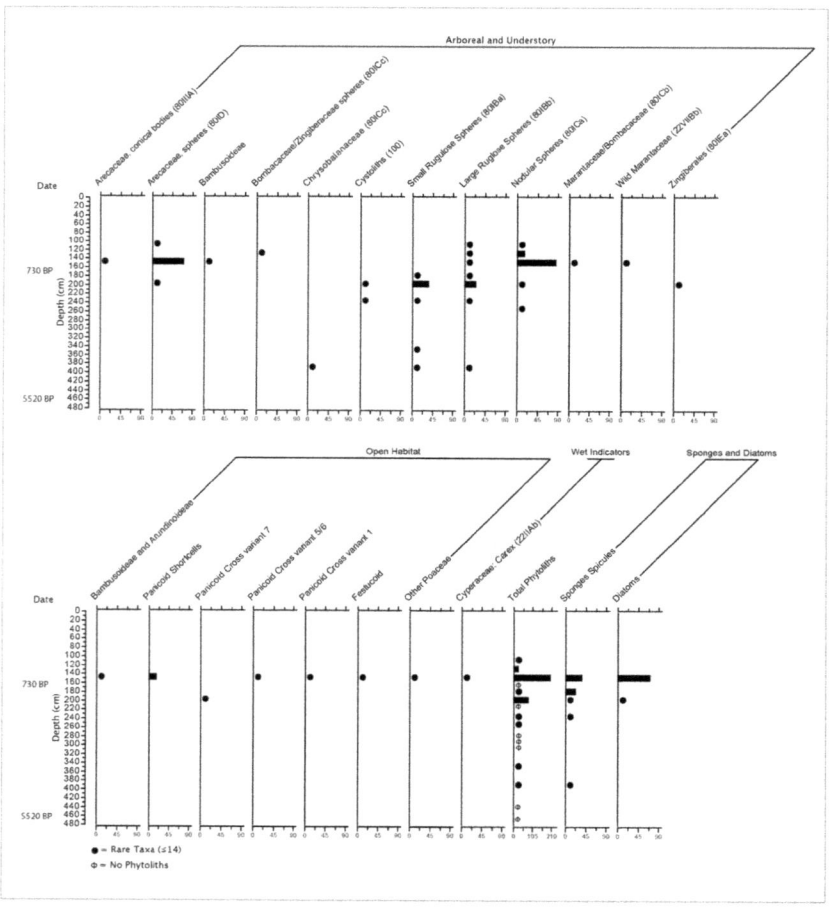

Figure 5.4a. St. John wetland 2, Trinidad, core phytolith diagram: resolved.

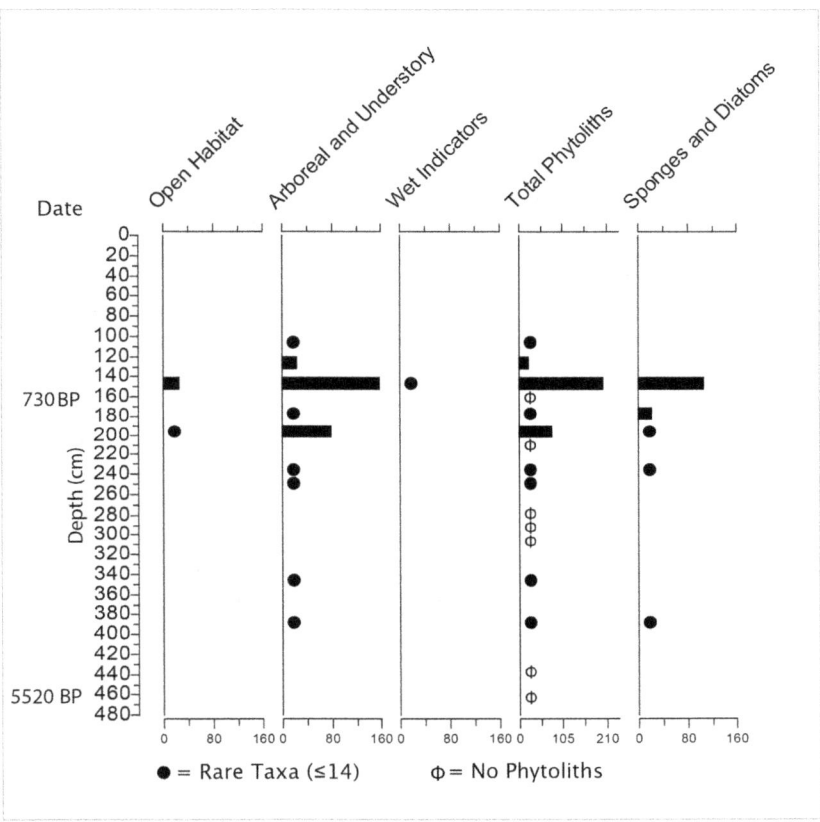

Figure 5.4b. St. John wetland 2, Trinidad, core phytolith diagram: composite.

indaceae, Melastomaceae, Araceae, Cyperaceae, and *Aechmea* (Bromiliaceae, piñuela) taxa (Pearsall field notes, 2007). The sample produced a 200-count, overwhelmingly dominated by palm phytoliths. *Heliconia,* Marantaceae, and grass phytoliths were also present. Palm phytoliths occurred only in the upper section of the core (100–200 cm), suggesting that a similar swamp forest occurred near the coring locality before A.D. 1225. While phytolith counts deeper in the core are too low to draw firm conclusions, it is interesting that the few phytoliths present are not palms, suggesting the swamp forest may have been farther from the coring locality earlier in time. This phytolith patterning is consistent with Jones's interpretation of the pollen data, a mangrove-dominated environment, in strata below 140 cm, suggesting that low phytolith influx affected recovery. In the strata above, dating after A.D. 1225, phytoliths suggestive of maize are associated with significant landscape change evident in the pollen fraction: a reduction in mangrove and increase in sedges, grasses, palms, and a maize pollen grain.

The nearby site of St. John is an Archaic shell midden site located atop a small hill, originally covered in tropical forest, that rose above the surrounding swamp (Boomert 2000; Wilson 2007). A date of 4920±50 B.C. was retrieved from marine shell (Boomert 2000: 516) and the site is contemporaneous with Early Banwari Trace (Boomert 2000: 57). The occupational duration is unclear, but Boomert suggests that it was similar to that of the Banwari Trace site (ca. 6060–4520 B.C.); a deposit of late-prehistoric Bontour complex pottery was found in the upper levels of Rouse's 1953 excavations in the St. John site, however (Boomert 2000: 57n2; Boomert, Faber-Morse, and Rouse 2013: 14). The bottom of the shell midden at St. John comprised freshwater pond snails and river conch and species found in brackish mudflats and estuaries. The upper part of the midden was made up of shells from mangrove-adapted species and the uppermost layer of the midden was exclusively oyster shells (Boomert 2000; Harris 1972b; Rouse 1953). Based on radiocarbon dates from the Banwari Trace excavation, the Oropuche shifted from a freshwater to slightly brackish-water lagoon to mangrove approximately 4250–4050 B.C., which corresponds with the date of full submergence of the Gulf of Paria by ca. 4250 B.C. (Boomert 2000; Van Andel and Sachs 1964). It is likely that sea level continued to rise, perhaps more slowly, after this date. In the Early Holocene, the coastal Guianas, most of the Gulf of Paria, and the Orinoco Delta were extensive mangrove wetlands. As sea level rose, peaty clay sediments were deposited in these mangroves. Due to isostatic subsidence in these areas, relative sea level continued to rise long after ca. 4250 B.C. (Boomert 2000; Krook 1979; Wong 1989). The core did not extend to the depth at which the freshwater environment changed to brackish mangrove (ca. 4250–4050 B.C.), an earlier change demonstrated by the midden contents of the St. John and Banwari Trace sites.

High levels of total phosphate associated with charcoal in the core profile, at depths of 403–440 cm and 386–387 cm, after 2845 B.C., are likely associated with the St. John occupation. The site was occupied when sea level was still rising (Scheffers et al. 2009; Wilson 2007), but after the Gulf of Paria had opened. The coring location would have been farther from the ocean at 3570 B.C. than it is at present, and was in a red mangrove wetland in saline, brackish waters in a tidal estuary. From ca. 3570 to 1050 B.C., the approximate time of eustatic sea-level stabilization for much of the Caribbean, the mangrove forest slowly adjusted to the encroaching sea and increasing sediment from the land. Our core clearly showed an environmental shift from brackish to freshwater swamp sometime around A.D. 1225. This scenario represents a period of succession of mangrove to freshwater swamp, after sea level stabilized. As mangroves trap silt and organics, the sediment surface slowly rises and makes the environment no longer favorable to mangrove vegetation (Chapman 1976). While this is a natural succession process, it would be greatly facilitated by increased sediment load from human activities such as forest clearing (tab. 5.3). Human activity is suggested by the presence of maize pollen and possible maize phytoliths and appreciable increase in charcoal concentration in the top of the profile.

The radiocarbon date of A.D. 1225, bracketed by the mangrove-to-freshwater transition, is consistent with the late Ceramic Age Bontour complex in Trinidad, a time of an increasingly vast network of trade and communication and growing population in Trinidad and the Lower Orinoco (Boomert 2000; Boomert, Faber-Morse, and Rouse 2013: 138–141; Harris 1978; Willey 1971), thus the anthropogenic contribution to this transition is plausible. Additionally, forest clearance arguably took place in the vicinity at this time because the inhabitants of early to late Ceramic Age settlements, in addition to their gathering, fishing, and hunting lifestyles were systematically engineering landscapes; their site locations in Trinidad show a preference for soils suited to horticulture (Boomert 2000).

Cedros (Core CE07-1)

Cedros is an Early Saladoid site located on Trinidad's southwestern peninsula, which affords access to freshwater and mangrove swamps. The site is situated on a low hill, approximately 200 m from the current coast. It is the closest to South America of all the Early Saladoid sites and is relatively small in size. The early component of the site dates to ca. 350–150 B.C. (Boomert 2000; Harris 1978; Wilson 2007).

Extensive wetlands exist along the coast of Columbus Bay near the southwestern point of Trinidad. A 448-cm core was extracted from a mixed mangrove wetland located several hundred meters inland from the southern coast of the southwest peninsula, behind a beach ridge, and not far from the Cedros site. The drainage basin containing this wetland covers about 6.5 km^2 with upland areas mantled by deeply weathered tropical Alfisols and Ultisols formed from saprolitic sedimentary rocks. However, sediment contributions from local bedrock ridges (catchment of about 500 m^2) and a nearby old beach ridge probably contribute the majority of mineral sediment at the coring location. Storm surges could also contribute marine sediment within the wetland. Soils within the Cedros wetland are deep, hydromorphic, and poorly drained, predominantly organic mucks (Histosols), but with higher elevation areas of deep clay Vertisols, and poorly developed alluvial soils (Inceptisols). Three samples from the core produced radiocarbon dates: ca. 3525 B.C. (organic sediment, 433–436 cm), ca. 2900 B.C. (wood, 315 cm), and ca. 630 B.C. (wood, 128 cm) (tab. 5.2). In total, twenty-four pollen samples were processed and prepared from this core, but low pollen concentration values and excessive amounts of extraneous detritus precluded further analysis.

From 0 to 30 cm, fibric and hemic muck predominated (tab. 5.6). The mineral component of the sediments increased progressively from 30 to 448 cm. Stratification within the sediments is suggestive of episodic but moderate energy colluvial and alluvial deposition. High sand content in many strata suggest contributions from the nearby beach ridge or in-washing marine sediments.

The Cedros core had fairly consistent phytolith deposition in the lower levels, from the base to around 280 cm, dating from ca. 3525 B.C. to somewhat after ca. 2900 B.C. (tab. 5.2, figs. 5.5a, 5.5b). This is followed by an interval of low deposition, from just below 150 cm to 280 cm. From 25 to 150 cm, phytolith recovery was good, after ca. 630 B.C. Arboreal and understory plants dominated the samples with good counts, with abundant Marantaceae (arrowroot family) indicators (nodular and rugulose spheres) in the lower zone, and large and small rugulose spheres in the upper zone. The Cedros phytolith assemblage is more diverse than that from the St. John core. Note the presence of *Celtis* (hackberry) and more common occurrence of Chrysobalanaceae (some taxa have edible fruits). Open indicators are absent until 265 cm, as are diatoms and sponge spicules. This pattern suggests opening and drying of the environment represented in levels above 265 cm, beginning at some time prior to ca. 630 B.C. At 55–60 cm a more diverse group of grasses was documented. (One Variant 1 cross was observed in this level, but was too small to be identified as maize.) A surface sample was analyzed near the coring locality (Surface Sample #11). It has almost equal quantities of *Marantaceae* (nodular spheres, large rugulose spheres) and palm phytoliths, and a few grasses. This sample documents a shift from the uppermost core level analyzed to increased palm growth and reduced grasses in the locality.

A single *Maranta* seed body phytolith occurred in the lowest level analyzed (444–448 cm) just below the stratum dated to ca. 3525 B.C. The phytolith is a good fit to the genus-level diagnostic found in both wild and cultivated *Maranta* species. Two wild species, *Maranta gibba* and *M. tonckat,* have been collected on Trinidad and may be the source of this phytolith. It is also possible that domesticated arrowroot (*Maranta*

Table 5.6. Sediment Descriptions of the Cedros, Trinidad Core (Core CE07-1).

Depth (cm)	Color	OM (LOI)	Total P (ppm)	Sand%	Silt%	Clay%	Notes
0–10	Black (7.5YR 2.5/1)	78.3					Fibric peat and root mat
10–30	Black (10YR 2/1)	71.7					Coarse hemic peat; roots; decomposing wood
30–68	Black (5Y 2.5/1)	56.4		34	55	11	Silty sapric peat
68–83	Black (10YR 2/1)	48		5	66	29	Silty hemic peat
83–98	Black (2.5Y 2.5/1)	39.1		53	15	32	Sandy hemic peat
100–110	Black (10YR 2/1)	42.6		4	64	32	
110–121							Mangrove wood and silt matrix
121–133	Very dark gray (10YR 3/1)	25.5		21	47	32	Silty hemic peat
133–149	Dark green gray (Gley 10Y 3/1)	18.3	213	55	31	14	Strongly mottled
149–175	Dark green gray (Gley 10Y 3/1)	10		52	28	20	Mangrove roots
175–198	Dark green gray (Gley 10Y 4/1)	8.4		42	39	19	
206–300	Dark blue gray (Gley 5B 4/1)	2.2		51	27	22	Weakly mottled; no laminations
300–327	Dark blue gray (Gley 5B 4/1)	4.2		38	22	40	Micro bands of sapric peat
327–330	Dark blue gray (Gley 5B 4/1)	2.5		29	41	30	Finely laminated bands
330–378	Dark blue gray (Gley 5B 4/1)	3.8		49	15	36	Weakly laminated
378–400	Dark blue gray (Gley 5B 4/1)	5.7		71	14	15	Micro bands of sapric peat
402–436	Dark green gray (Gley BG 3/1)	5.1		55	28	17	
436–448	Dark blue gray (Gley 5B 4/1)	3		46	34	20	Weakly laminated

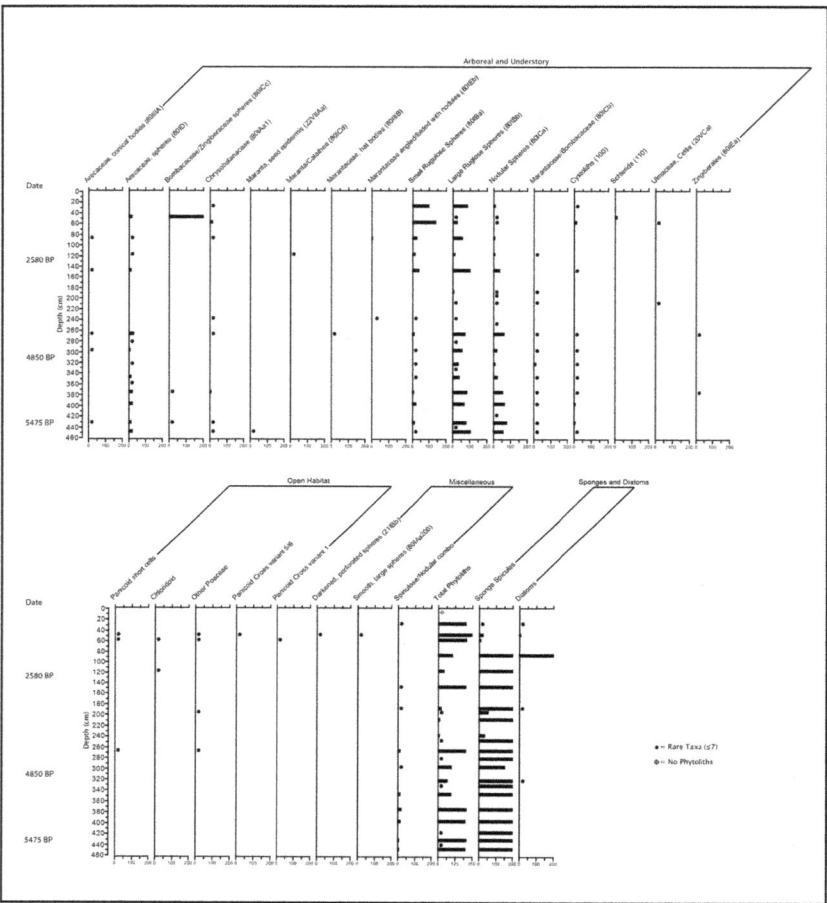

Figure 5.5a. Cedros wetland, Trinidad, core phytolith diagram: resolved.

arundinacea) was introduced into the island by early Archaic populations (see also Pagán-Jiménez et al. 2015).

The base of this core represents the environment of the peninsula in Archaic times. Although the Gulf of Paria is thought to have been fully submerged prior to the basal date of ca. 3525 B.C., sea level was still rising and the distance between the peninsula and the South American mainland would not have been great. The episodic introductions of sand in the lower core suggest that the area was impacted by storm surges and wave energy, although the location was farther from the coast than it is today (tab. 5.3). Although nomadic hunters and foragers may have visited Trinidad as early as ca. 8050 B.C., the first occupation was later, after Trinidad had become an island (Boomert 2006). Archaic midden sites, flint deposits, and individual finds have been

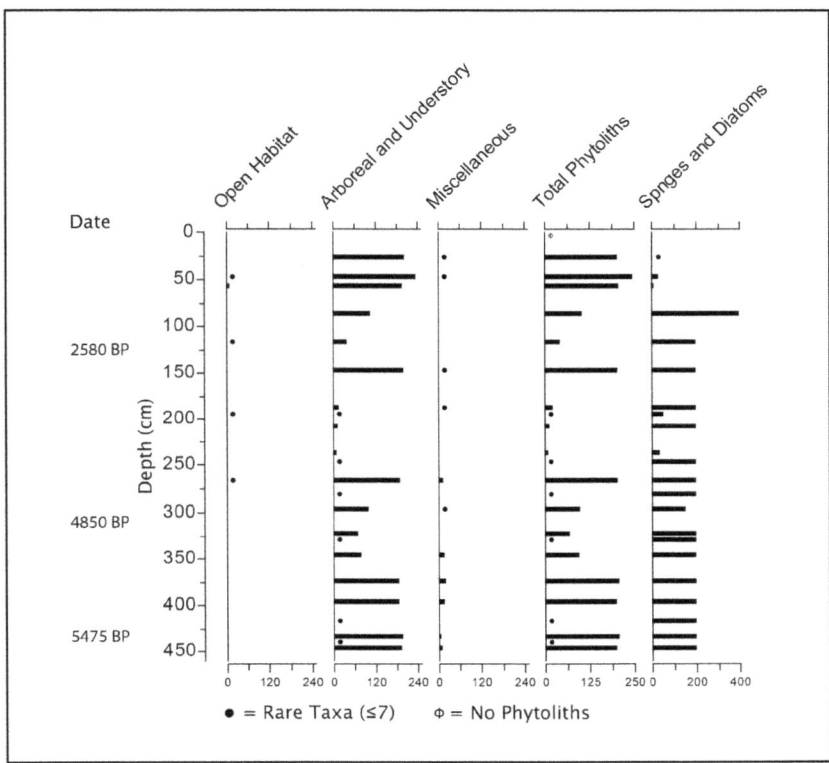

Figure 5.5b. Cedros wetland, Trinidad, core phytolith diagram: composite.

documented on the southwest peninsula and it was no doubt inhabited when the organic materials yielding our basal date were deposited. The presence of arboreal and understory taxa in the lower half of the core suggests that the site was in tropical forest from sometime before ca. 3525 B.C. to sometime after 2900 B.C. Archaic middens on the peninsula include the bones of forest-dwelling mammals, along with extensive shellfish. The *Maranta* phytolith is interesting in its suggestion of the introduction of arrowroot to the island since artifacts in the Banwari Trace and St. John sites included ground stone tools for vegetable food processing, with edible roots, palm starch, and seeds being the likely foods (Boomert 2006; Harris 1972b; Pagán-Jiménez et al. 2015). A gradual shift is evident in the Archaic middens of the southwest peninsula away from land/forest resources to marine (estuarine) resources. This may represent the effects of both rising sea level and a gradual retreat of the forest edge in response to Late Holocene drying. The phytolith and sediment records show the forest canopy opening and drying from sometime before 630 B.C., shortly before the early occupation of the Ceramic Age Cedros site. By the time the Cedros settlement was established, sea level would have reached its present height. Cedros, like other Early Saladoid sites, was located close to the coast on the top of a low rise, and was inhabited by pottery-making horticulturalists (Boomert 2000; Olsen 1974; Rouse 1947). Root crops were an important part of the Saladoid diet; the abundance of Marantaceae phytoliths in the core, and *Celtis* (hackberry) and Chrysobalanaceae (edible fruits) in the upper core suggest that the southwest peninsula was an ideal environment for these groups.

Eastern Trinidad: Nariva Swamp

Nariva Swamp is an extensive freshwater wetland in eastern Trinidad with a catchment area of about 450 km^2. Annual rainfall in the swamp is more than 2,000 mm with pronounced seasonal variation. The wetland receives alluvial sediment predominantly from rivers draining the gently sloping plain to the west, where streams drain the Central Range. Soils in the catchment area include hydromorphic Histosols in the low-lying poorly drained regions, Ultisols and Alfisols in the uplands, and poorly developed Inceptisols along stream channels. Alluvial sediments from the plain consist of silty clays. Nariva Swamp is separated from the Atlantic Ocean by a barrier island, the Cocal. Water drains from the swamp through the Nariva River, a tidal lagoon entering the ocean through a channel in the barrier island. During periods of heavy precipitation, the barrier island is breached, creating a second discharge to the Atlantic, several kilometers north of the Nariva River (Ramcharan 2004). Along the western margin of the swamp, river channels were dredged and straightened in the mid twentieth century to encourage rice and vegetable cultivation; extensive areas in the western margin are still used for cultivation (Brown 2000). Six vegetation types are found in the swamp: marsh forest, herbaceous swamp, palm forest, swamp forest, secondary forest, and mangrove forests that dominate the coastal portions (Kenny 2008).

Nariva Swamp 1 (Core NV08-1)

Core NV08-1 was extracted from a red and black mangrove estuary where the Le Branche River drains into the Atlantic (fig. 5.1). The core location was approximately 250 m from the river. This mangrove wetland is separated from the main body of Nariva Swamp to the south by the ridge on which the Eastern Main Highway is built and by low hills to the southwest. The estuary receives sediments from the clayey ridge on which the Eastern Highway is situated, and from the ridge to the north where the North Manzanilla road traverses the Manzanilla Windbelt Forest Reserve. Soils observed in the natural levee of the river near the coring location were silty clay Alfisols. Soils on the ridge slope were lateritic Ultisols, extensively bioturbated by crabs.

The NV08-1 core reached a total depth of 318 cm. Sediments were predominately organic silty clays, likely derived from low-energy alluvial deposition from the Le Branche drainage (tab. 5.7). The lower

Table 5.7. Sediment Descriptions of the Nariva Swamp, Trinidad Core 1 (Core NV08-1).

Depth (cm)	Organics	Color	Texture	Notes
0–17	Fibric	7.5YR 3/1	Silt loam	
17–32	Hemic	10YR 3/1	Silt	H_2S
32–40	Sapric	10YR 2/1	Clayey silt	H_2S
40–55	Sapric	Gley 1 2.5/N (few 7.5 YR 4/4 mottles)		
55–64	Sapric	Gley 1 2.5/N	Clayey silt	H_2S
64–85	Sapric	Gley 3/N	Silty Clay	Noticeably more clay; bottom of first tube
85–96				Slop; beginning of second tube
96–110	Sapric	Gley1 3/N	Silty clay	
110–140	Sapric	Gley1 6/N	Clayey silt	(some fibers, roots, pores); abrupt boundary
140–156	Sapric	Gley1 2.5/N	Silty clay loam	Abrupt boundary; black flecks (charcoal?); shell
156–176	Sapric		Silty clay loam	Few fibersGley1 3/N; charcoal flecks; bottom of second tube
176–183				Slop; top of second tube
183–193	Sapric	Gley1 2.5/N	Clayey silt	
193–207	Sapric	Gley1 2.5/N; 5Y 2.5/1	Silty clay loam	Abundant fibers and pores
207–213				Large piece of wood
216–235	Sapric	Mixed		Clay skins; slickensides; abundant fibers; black specks
235–267	Sapric	Gley1 5/N	Silty clay	Abundant black flecks
268–305	Sapric	Gley1 4/N	Silty clay	Clam burrow; charcoal
305–318	Sapric	Gley1 3/N	Silty clay	Clay skins; fibers; charcoal flecks; rocks @ 310–314

portion of the core, below 225 cm, contained almost no sand. Two levels of the core (40–50 cm, 96–110 cm) yielded higher sand percentages, suggesting periods when the Le Branche River overflowed its banks and higher-energy sediments were deposited, or when tropical storms carried sand into the estuary. The core contained two levels of unusually high organic carbon content at approximately the same levels as above (30–40 cm, 96–110 cm). A radiocarbon date of ca. 5110 B.C. was obtained at 250 cm (tab. 5.2).

Pollen preservation was good with moderate phytolith deposition and abundant particulate charcoal representation (figs. 5.6, 5.7a, 5.7b). From the base of the core to approximately 180 cm a combination of ethnobotanically significant and disturbance-indicator taxa are represented (tabs. 5.4, 5.5).

The core did not penetrate sediments deeper than 320 cm (beneath the basal charcoal spike), thus we did not obtain an unambiguous pre-anthropogenic landscape. The relatively high charcoal concentration at the core base underlies the deepest dated context, followed by sustained but somewhat lower charcoal concentrations, with two additional higher values at 160 cm and 80 cm. The charcoal particulate concentration values between 280 cm and 195 cm ranged from 250 to 500 fragments per cm^3, higher than the sustained charcoal concentrations in the other project cores for the same periods (fig. 5.6). In addition to frequency and magnitude of burning events, a number of other factors influence charcoal concentration values, including sedimentation rates, fuel types, fire temperature, and secondary transport mechanisms. This makes comparisons across coring locations difficult. The Nariva sequence is noteworthy, nonetheless, for the strength of the charcoal signature.

The stratigraphically lower two elevated charcoal concentrations (core base and 160 cm), separated by sustained charcoal presence, date to the Mid Holocene period of wet conditions (Banner et al. 1996; Higuera-Gundy et al. 1999; Mangini et al. 2007). Some have argued that sustained levels of charcoal values do not necessarily indicate human-induced burning, but may represent background charcoal influx between fire events. It has been further proposed that wet climate conditions may lead to greater abundance of vegetative fuel, increasing the likelihood of fire events (Caffrey and Horn 2015; Higuera et al. 2009; Higuera et al. 2010). We suggest that sustained charcoal during the mesic conditions of the Mid Holocene combined with somewhat elevated percentages of Poaceae and higher values of *Cecropia* and Moraceae below 195 cm indicate that local clearings were being maintained (Athens et al. 2014; Burney 1997a, 1997b; Burney, Pigott Burney, and MacPhee

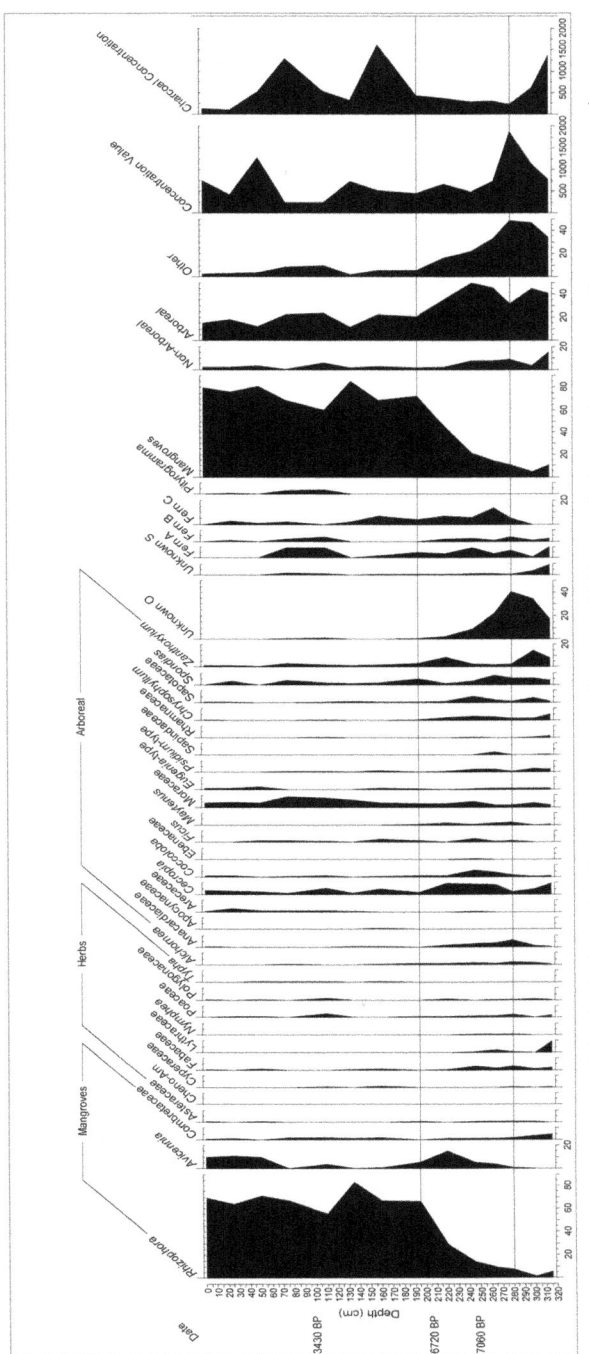

Figure 5.6. Nariva Swamp, Trinidad, Core 1 pollen-percentage diagram. Pollen and charcoal concentrations are expressed as grains and fragments, respectively, per cm³ of sediment.

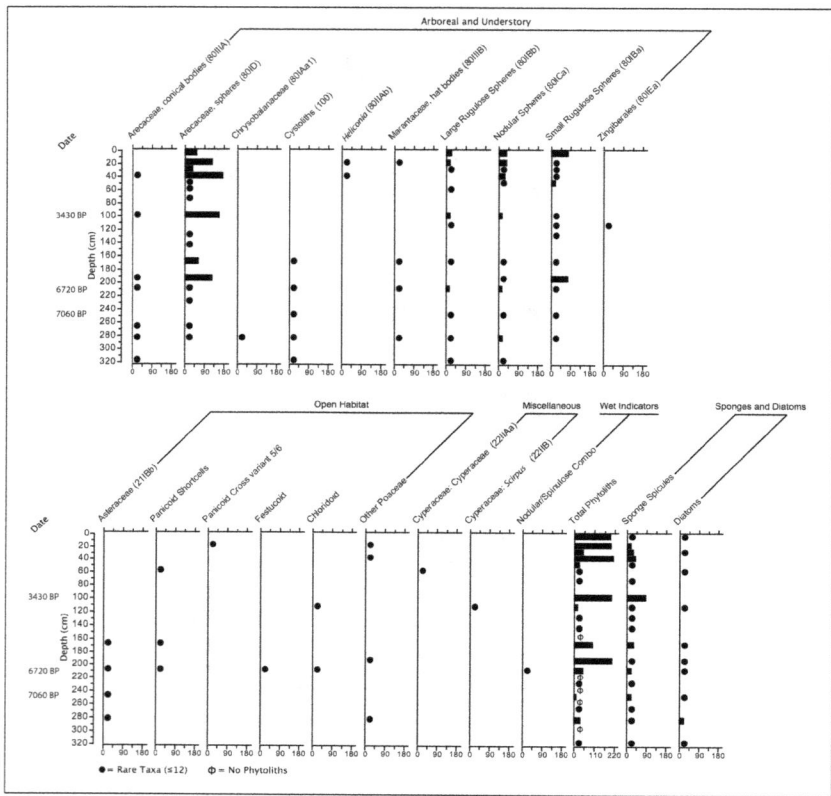

Figure 5.7a. Nariva Swamp, Trinidad, Core 1 phytolith diagram: resolved.

1994; Pyne 1998). The initial high value of *Cecropia* is associated with the basal spike in charcoal. Elevated percentages of Moraceae and *Cecropia* persist above 195 cm, along with high charcoal values, suggesting that this portion of Nariva Swamp was continuously occupied and managed by humans for millennia (fig. 5.6). Ethnobotanically useful taxa associated with the period below 195 cm (prior to ca. 4765 B.C.) include Fabaceae, Anacardiaceae, *Spondias, Coccoloba,* and Sapotaceae (tab. 5.5).

Sediment, phytolith, pollen, and charcoal data support a gradual shift in depositional environments and vegetation, and a strong transition by ca. 4765 B.C. Prior to this date, there was a notable absence of sand in the profile, representing a time when sea level was still slowly rising and the coring location was not yet estuarine. Phytolith and pollen evidence reveal open, mixed habitats with arboreal, understory, and open-habitat plants, including Poaceae, *Cecropia,* and Moraceae. Habitats may have been managed and maintained through sustained burn-

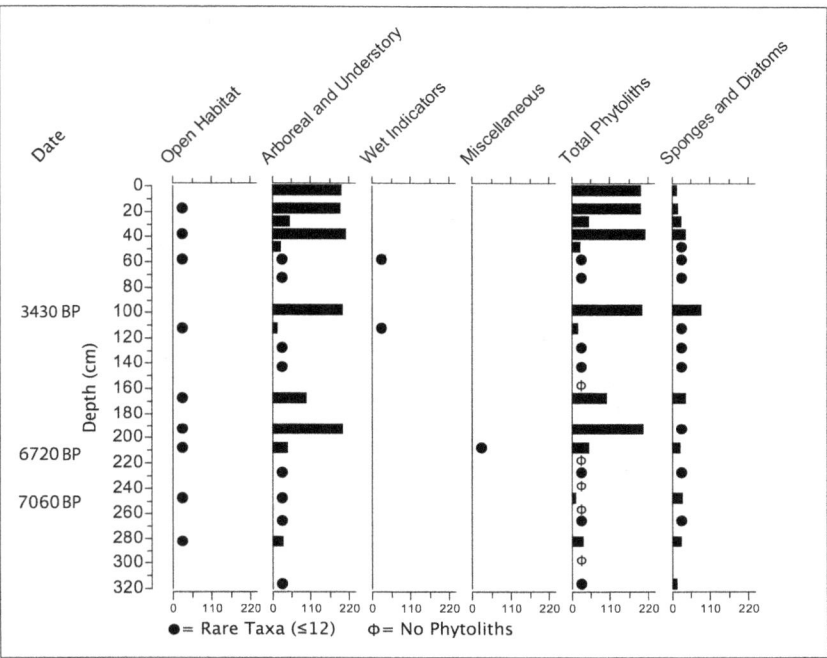

Figure 5.7b. Nariva Swamp, Trinidad, Core 1 phytolith diagram: composite.

ing. Subsequently, Asteraceae was absent, grass phytoliths decreased, and the location received sediments carried from the Central Range uplands including microfossils of savanna vegetation. As sea level encroached and the estuary was formed, storms on the windward coast contributed sand to the sediment profile. Phytolith evidence in the upper portion of the core, subsequent to ca. 4765 B.C., reflects a vegetation shift to freshwater swamp forest, with palm and sedges, and finally to reduced palm and increased woody dicots, probably representing mangrove and a shift to brackish conditions (figs. 5.7a, 5.7b). Likewise, pollen data show a marked shift by ca. 4765 B.C., with decreasing arboreal types (including Anacardiaceae, *Coccoloba, Psidium*-type, Sapindaceae, *Chrysophyllum,* Sapotaceae, and *Cecropia*) and increased and sustained *Rhizophora* (fig. 5.6).

While the NV08-1 core was quite productive for phytoliths, with nineteen of twenty-four samples producing phytoliths, counts tended to be low, with only five samples reaching a 200-count (figs. 5.7a, 5.7b). The lowest meter of the core (205 cm to base) had little to no phytolith influx; influx increased and decreased in the middle of the core, and was consistently higher in the top meter. The zone of low to no phytolith influx was characterized by a mix of arboreal, understory, and open-habitat taxa. Asteraceae (sunflower family), not commonly seen in this project, occurred in four samples. Strata with more-abundant phytoliths in the middle and upper parts of the core tended to be dominated by palms, but the uppermost strata showed a more even mix of palm, Marantaceae, and woody dicots. Open habitat indicators decreased in the upper portion of the core. These patterns suggest an open, mixed habitat early in the sequence, followed by higher influx in the coring locality from swamp forest with palm (also note the sedges), and then a shift to reduced palm/increased woody dicots (perhaps mangrove swamp). Marantaceae phytoliths occur consistently throughout the core, but no genus-level diagnostics were recovered.

The core profile provides a glimpse of environmental changes after ca. 5110 B.C. Sediment, phytolith, and pollen data support a gradual shift in depositional environments and vegetation, and a strong transition at approximately 160–225 cm. Below this depth there was a notable absence of sand in the profile. This represents a time when sea level was still slowly rising and the coring location was not yet estuarine. Phytolith evidence suggests that this was an open, mixed habitat with arboreal, understory, and open habitat plants, including Asteraceae. After this time, Asteraceae is absent and grass phytoliths decrease. At this time the site received sediment carried from the Central Range uplands, which likely included savanna vegetation. As sea level encroached and the estuary was formed, storms on the windward coast contributed sand to the sediment. The upper portion of the core shows a vegetation shift to freshwater swamp forest, with palm and sedges, and finally to reduced palm and woody dicots, probably representing mangrove and a shift to brackish conditions.

Nariva Swamp 2 and 3 (Cores NV08-2 and NV08-3)

Core NV08-2 was retrieved from an area along the western margin of Nariva Swamp that has been cleared, drained, and channeled in the past fifty years for commercial rice production, small-holder production of vegetables, and fish-raising. Sediment to a depth of 384 cm was recovered. The basal section of NV08-2 was lost during collection, so a second drive, 3 m to the south, was made and 517 cm were recovered in Core NV08-3 (fig. 5.1).

The upper 170 cm of sediments in NV08-2 and NV08-3 consisted of clay and silty clay mineral horizons with flecks and bands of charcoal, including pieces of intact burned vegetation (tabs. 5.8, 5.9). These mineral sediments are probably fluvial in origin from the Petit Poole and other streams draining the sloping plain to the west of Nariva. The top-

Table 5.8. Sediment Descriptions of the Nariva Swamp, Trinidad Core 2 (Core NV08-2).

Depth (cm)	Organics	Color	Texture	Notes
0–2				(top of Tube 1); black duff; charcoal
2–27		2.5Y 5/1 & gley1 2.5/N	Clay	
27–40		5Y 5/1	Clay	Fine black bands (bottom of Tube 1)
40–56		5Y 5/1	Silty clay	(top of Tube 2); oxidized root channels; very plastic; black flecks
56–66		2.5Y 5/1	Silty clay	Black flecks and discontinuous black bands; very plastic, stiff clay
66–76		2.5Y 4/1	Silty clay	Black bands; plastic, stiff clay
76–94		Gley1 2.5/N	Silty clay	Black, smeary layer
94–99		2.5Y 4/1, 3/1	Silty clay	Flecks of burnt wood
99–104		5Y 2.5/2	Silty clay	(bottom of Tube 2) Abundant charcoal
104–130				(top of Tube 3); slop
130–140		5Y 2.5/1	Silty clay	(same as 99–104?)
140–147		2.5Y 3/1	Silty clay	Charcoal-rich; platy
147–152				Charcoal-rich; blocky
152–155		2mm bands of black & tan 2.5Y 4/2	Slty clay	Platy
155–160		Marbled brown (10YR 2/2) and black	Clay	Weak blocky; thin hemic peaty band at 159; tan (2.5Y 4/2) band at 160
160–163				Burned vegetation (some intact branches)
163–175	Sapric	7.5YR 2.5/2	Silt	Thin bands of tan silt at 166–168; abundant black plates of charcoal
175–178		7.5YR 4/3	Silt	Pieces (3 mm x 2cm) of undecomposed reddish wood
178–181	Sapric	2.5YR 2.5/4		Peat
181–185	Hemic	2.5YR 2.5/4		Peat
185–198	Sapric	2.5YR 2.5/4		Peat
198–205	Fibric	2.5YR 2.5/4		Peat (bottom of Tube 3) (top of Tube 4)
205–213				Slop; (top of Tube 4)
213–230	Sapric (fibric stems?)	2.5Y 3/2		Few large pieces of undecomposed wood

(continued)

Table 5.8. *(continued)*

Depth (cm)	Organics	Color	Texture	Notes
230–241		2.5Y 5/1	Silty clay	Large pieces of fibric undecomposed peat
241–254	Fibric	2.5Y 3/1	Silty	Abundant fibric peat
254–260	Fibric	2.5Y 4/1	Silty	
260–287		2.5Y 4/1	Silty clay	Black flecks; some sapric fibers
287–304		2.5Y 3/1	Silty clay	Abundant fibers (bottom of Tube 4)
304–313		2.5 Y 3/1		(Top of Tube 5) Same as bottom of Tube 4; flecks of charcoal
313–330		2.5Y 4/1	Silty clay	Abundant fibers; abundant charcoal
330–338		2.5Y 5/1	Silty clay	Abundant charcoal flecks; abundant fibers
338–360		5Y 4/1	Silty clay	Abundant fibers; abundant charcoal flecks; platy
360–384		2.5Y 5/3	Silty clay	Abundant sapric fibers; abundant charcoal flecks

most sediments are the result of dredging and draining activities and charcoal and burnt fibers represent burning and clearing for cultivation and for cattle ranching. In both cores, sediments from the next lower 2 m consisted of a peat layer overlying peaty clay and silty clay horizons with charcoal flecks and bands. A sample of preserved wood from 374 cm dated to ca. 1540 B.C. In NV08-3 the peaty, silty clay and charcoal layers extended to a depth of 488 cm. From 488 to 501 cm the core consisted of dense, brittle, dark gray clay; the base of the core (501–517 cm) was dark gray silty clay containing woody fibers (tab. 5.9). These clays are comparable with the upland Ultisol soils in the catchment area. Preserved wood from 445 to 447 cm was dated to ca. 2525 B.C.

Pollen preservation was excellent throughout the NV08-3 sequence, indicating that the sediments had always remained wet, and the sequence likely represents a continuous record. Four zones were apparent. The basal section, from 380 to 527 cm, shows a generally red mangrove–dominated environment, indicating an appreciable amount of swamp-forest types (fig. 5.8). Savanna vegetation was also represented in the assemblage and includes *Byrsonima* (craboo, nance) and Asteraceae. Of particular significance is the abundance of unknown pollen type T (hereafter Unknown T). This grain is currently unidentified and may represent a different species of *Byrsonima*. It occurs solely in

Table 5.9. Sediment Descriptions of the Nariva Swamp, Trinidad Core 3 (Core NV08-3).

Depth (cm)	Organics	Color	Texture	Notes
0–2		black		(top of Tube 1) charcoal
2–7		2.5Y 4/1	Clay	Oxidation around roots
7–10		black	clay	charcoal
10–17		7.5 YR 5/1	clay	
17–19		Black	Clay	Charcoal
19–19.5		7.5YR 5/1	Clay	
19.5–22		Black	clay	charcoal
22–37		7.5YR 5/1	Silty clay	Red fibers
37–46			clay	Thin dark bands; abundant black flecks
46–50		2.5Y 3/2	Silty clay	Charcoal flecks (bottom of Tube 1)
50–70		2.5Y 5/1	Silty clay	Slop? (top of Tube 2); few red mottles
70–76		10YR 5/1	Silty clay	Thin bands of black flecks and thin bands of dark brown (10YR 4/1)
76–87		10YR 2/1	Silty clay	Abundant charcoal
87–94		Mottled 10YR 5/2, 10YR 4/3	Silty clay	Thin, discontinuous bands of charcoal flecks; some bands of burnt fibers
94–110	Hemic	2.5Y 5/2, 10YR 3/2	Silty clay	Alternating bands of light tan and dark peat; charcoal
110–111	sapric	5YR 3/2		(bottom of Tube 2)
111–155				Slop; (top of Tube 3)
155–165		10YR 4/2, 10YR 4/1	silt	Slop?
165–171	Sapric	5YR 3/4		Reddish brown peat
171–179		10YR 3/4	Silt	Abundant white flecks (CaCO$_3$?)
179–195	hemic	5YR 2.5/2		Reddish brown peat
195–207				Undecomposed wood
207–211	fibric	7.5YR 4/2		Peat; (bottom of Tube 3)
211–225				Slop; (top of Tube 4)
225–235	Sapric	10YR 5/2	Silty clay	
235–242		10YR 5/2	Silty clay	Abundant organic material
242–257	Sapric	Mottled 7.5YR 3/2, 10YR 5/2		Abundant organic material; one root

(continued)

Table 5.9. *(continued)*

Depth (cm)	Organics	Color	Texture	Notes
257–267	Sapric	2.5Y 5/2	Silty clay	Abundant organic material; some fibric wood
267–286	Sapric and fibric	2.5Y 5/2	Silty clay	
286–303	Hemic	2.5Y 5/1	Silty clay	Abundant organic material; (bottom of Tube 4)
303–330		2.5Y 4/2	Silty clay	Abundant black flecks; sapric fibers
330–383		2.5Y 5/2	Silty clay	Abundant sapric fibers; abundant charcoal flecks; increasing clay; (bottom of Tube 5)
383–428		10YR 3/2	Silty clay	(top of Tube 6); abundant fibric fibers and charcoal flecks; increasing clay
428–436	Fibric/sapric	10YR 3/3	Silty clay	
436–468		2.5Y 5/1	Silty clay	Palm root; abundant fibers: decomposed and undecomposed; (bottom of Tube 6)
468–475				Slop; (top of Tube 7)
475–488		10YR 4/2	Silty clay	Abundant sapric fibers; charcoal flecks
488–494		2.5Y 4/1	Silty clay	Dense, brittle clay (fragipan?)
494–498		2.5Y 4/2	Silty clay	Stiff clay; charcoal flecks; sapric fibers
498–501		2.5Y 5/1	Clay	Stiff clay
501–510		2.5Y 4/2	Silty clay	Includes gleyed (gley1 4/10 GY) pieces of wood; abundant sapric fibers
510–517		2.5Y 4/1	Silty clay	Abundant fibers (bottom of Tube 7)

the two basal zones and is clearly a significant environmental indicator. Overall, this zone represents what was probably a brackish-water environment, located very near a swamp forest (as indicated by significant numbers of Moraceae and *Pterocarpus* grains), in an area surrounded by savanna. The second zone, 200–380 cm, is similar to the basal zone, although there is a reduction in red mangrove pollen and a corresponding expansion of swamp-forest and savanna types, particularly *Byrsonima* and Unknown T. Human presence is not indicated by either cultivated plants or trees, or by high concentrations of particulate charcoal. Zone 3,

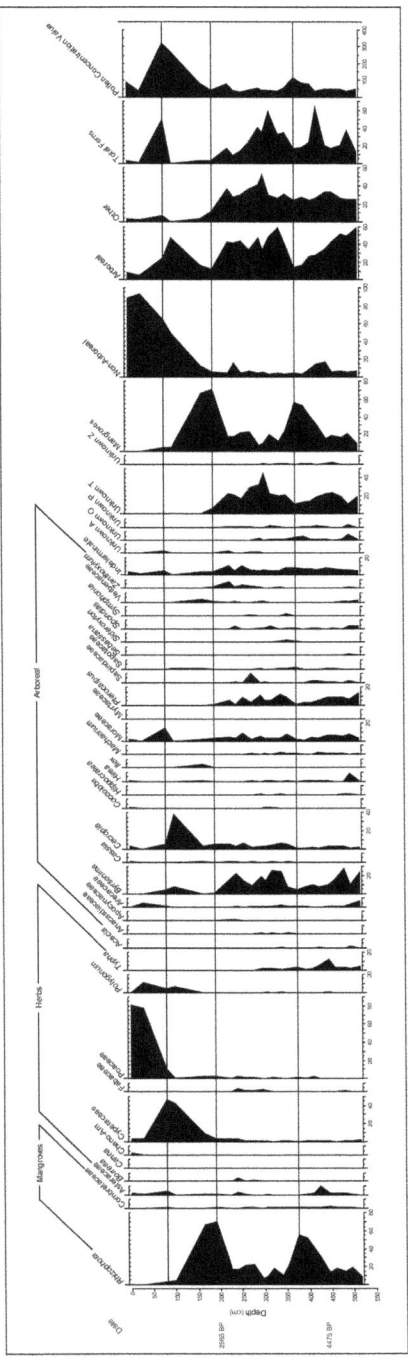

Figure 5.8. Nariva Swamp, Trinidad, Core 3 pollen-percentage diagram. Pollen and charcoal concentrations are expressed as grains and fragments, respectively, per cm³ of sediment.

200–80 cm, shows a significant change in environment from a brackish setting to a freshwater system. Red mangrove pollen is reduced in this zone and is replaced by freshwater-loving sedges. Unknown T is eliminated from the profile at this level. *Cecropia,* a quick-growing gap colonizer, becomes common in this zone and *Polygonum* (knotweed) also increased significantly, confirming the freshwater nature of the local environment. It is possible that this shift to a freshwater system made the region more appealing for habitation; in the middle of this section we see a significant increase in charcoal, marking the onset of human activity in the area. The uppermost zone, 0–80 cm, represents increased human activity and contains a tremendous quantity of charcoal as the field had recently been burned in preparation for rice agriculture. Grass pollen is dominant here and represents historic period rice cultivation. *Polygonum* is high in this zone because it is currently the dominant weed in the field area. Overall, the core represents an initially brackish environment, when the region was closer to the sea, with a gradual infilling of the system and a corresponding shift to a freshwater environment.

The NV08-3 core was not very productive for phytoliths, but shows some interesting trends (figs. 5.9a, 5.9b). Marantaceae is absent and there is very low palm occurrence (even in the productive top stratum), in combination with a scattering of grass phytoliths. Influx was very low, but there were open habitats contributing phytoliths to the sequence. Interestingly, Variant 1 crosses were recovered in four strata (very top of Pollen Zone 2 and in Pollen Zones 3 and 4), and in relatively large quantity (for this rare type) in the top level analyzed (top of Pollen Zone 4). One maize cob phytolith was recovered from the top level, confirming maize in association with historic-period rice production documented in the pollen record. Only three of the Variant 1 crosses from this level were large enough to be classified definitively as maize, which lends some support to the notion that maize varieties being grown were not depositing many large crosses. Variant 1 crosses first appear at 225–230 cm, after ca. 2525 B.C. and correspond to an expansion of swamp-forest and savanna pollen types (fig. 5.8). However this pollen zone does not show an increase in particulate carbon as might be expected if humans were clearing land for cultivation. Poaceae pollen is also low in this zone, suggesting that maize is a more likely source of the Variant 1 crosses than local wild grasses.

The sediment record in the NV08-2 and NV08-3 cores is consistent with a scenario of gradual shoreline encroachment with rising sea level. NV08-2 sediments were deposited after ca. 1540 B.C. While there are no pollen or phytolith data for this core, the sediments include silty clay derived from streams draining highly weathered soils in the uplands

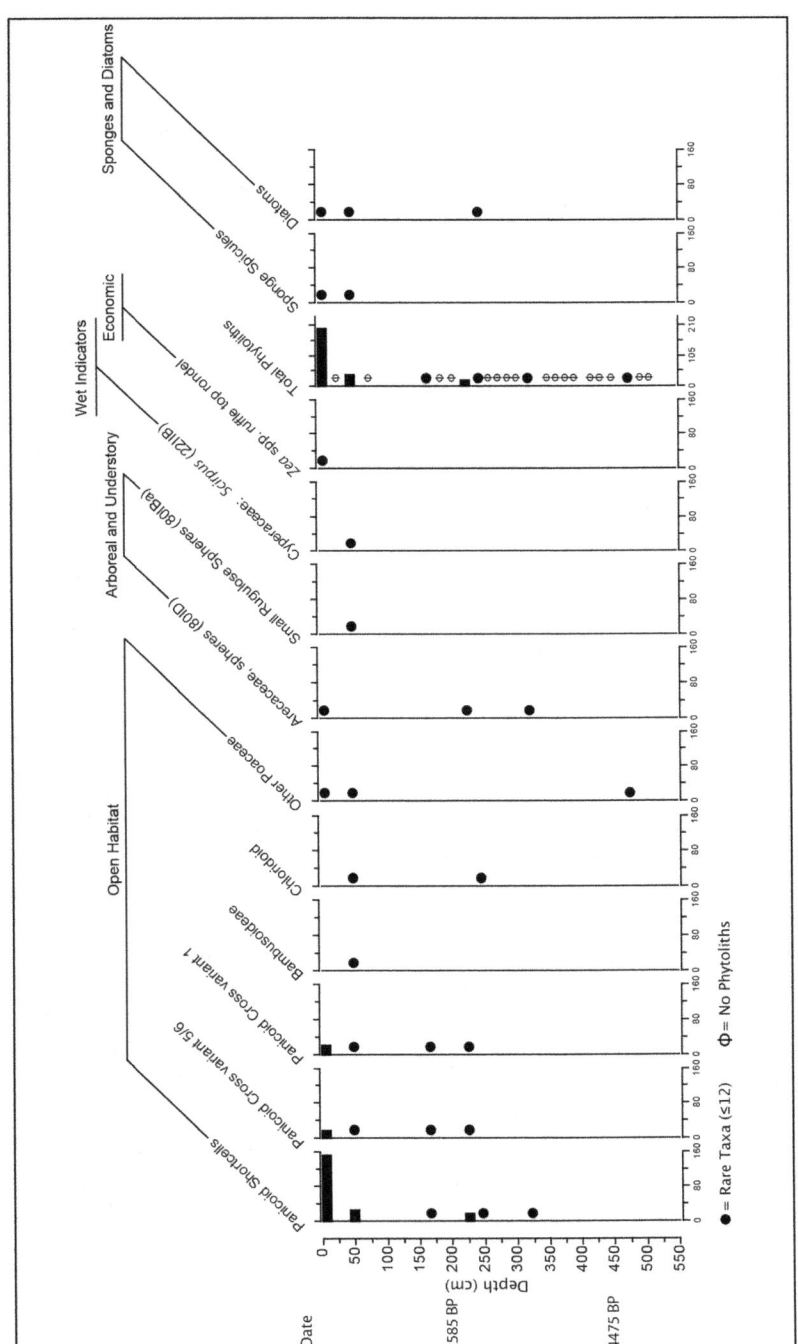

Figure 5.9a. Nariva Swamp, Trinidad, Core 3 phytolith diagram: resolved.

118 • Chapter 5

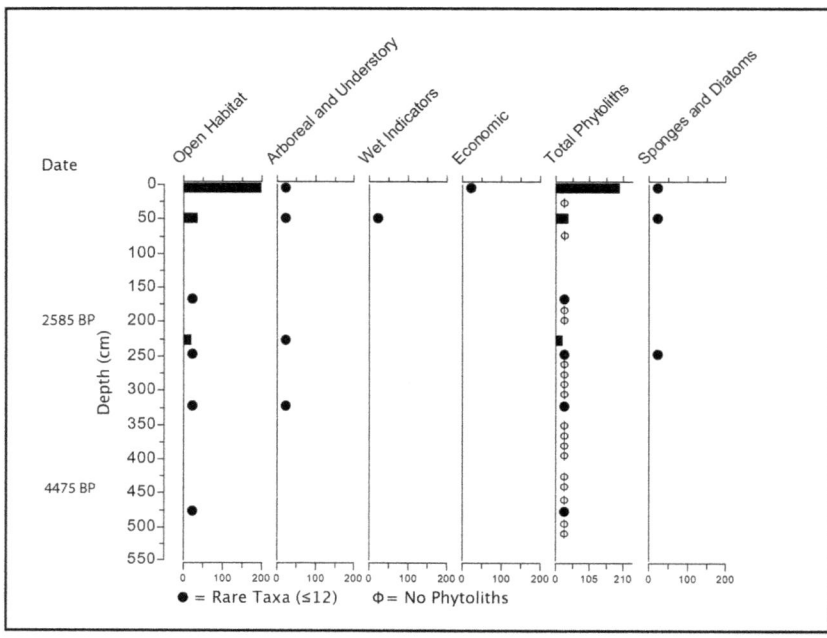

Figure 5.9b. Nariva Swamp, Trinidad, Core 3 phytolith diagram: composite.

and the sloping plain to the west. As the sea encroached, organic sediments were generated in saline estuaries and were incorporated in the silty clay alluvial sediment; the peat layer in the core from 178 to 313 cm reflects this environment. The upper sediments in NV08-2, 178 cm to surface, include clay and silty clay that were deposited as the streams draining the watershed aggraded and, in historic times, as clearing for agriculture accelerated erosion.

The upper section of the NV08-3 core, deposited after ca. 2525 B.C., shows a sediment sequence matching NV08-2: peaty, silty clay underlying a thick peat layer, buried by 165 cm of silty clay. In NV08-3 the core extended to 527 cm, with the lower 82 cm deposited prior to ca. 2525 B.C. Sediments in the lower 82 cm included silty clays with woody fibers covered by a cap of dense clay at 488–501 cm. The lower pollen zone represents a brackish red mangrove wetland with nearby swamp-forest and savanna vegetation contributing pollen. This environment was probably increasing in salinity as sea level rose. At the top of this zone, red mangrove pollen rapidly increased and swamp-forest species decreased. These changes at the top of the zone occur just after ca. 2525 B.C. The rate of sea-level rise slowed at about 2050 B.C. but continued until around 1050 B.C. (Ramcharan 2004). The pollen record after this point shows a clear shift to freshwater swamp forest and an increase in savanna indicators (fig. 5.8). As the mangrove trapped the silt and clay in the Nariva Swamp basin, the surface rose and the environment became less suitable for mangrove. At the same time, a barrier island was actively building at a seaward location from the coring site in the wetland, altering the brackish setting to a freshwater lagoon (see discussion for NV08-4). Late Holocene drying could account for the pulse of savanna indicators in the pollen record, such as *Byrsonima*. Mangrove increased at the beginning of the next pollen zone but was replaced by freshwater sedges and later by grass. Charcoal concentration values increased as well at this time, indicating burning and clearing activities.

Nariva Swamp 4 (Core NV08-4)

Core NV08-4 was extracted at the edge of a sandy island in Nariva Swamp. Soils on the island were yellowish brown sandy loam Inceptisols and Alfisols. These sand islands within the swamp have been identified by Ramcharan (2004) as remnants of a sandbar, now located well inland from the present coastline. The core was very peat-rich, with considerably more sand than the other Nariva cores (tab. 5.10). The upper 85 cm of the core comprised peaty silty clay with charcoal, the result of rapid sedimentation due to cultivation on adjacent upland slopes. From 85 to 145 cm, the core contained noticeably higher sand content, peat, and abundant charcoal. Large, undecomposed roots were found at 117–151 cm. Peaty silty clay with abundant, discontinuous bands of charcoal dominated the profile from 145 to 310 cm. A radiocarbon date of ca. 1935 B.C. was obtained at 235 cm. A second sample collected from 280 to 281 cm dated to ca. 1560 B.C. (tab. 5.2). This discrepancy in dates will be discussed later. The core consisted of peat from 310 to 538 cm. The top of this peat (310–350 cm) was high in sand content, with occasional pulses of extremely high sand content throughout the peat layer. Mineral sediments of silty clay texture containing charcoal layers and flecks lay beneath the peat deposit in the core. A date of ca. 4780 B.C. was obtained from preserved wood at 685 cm. The base of the core at 700 cm consisted of peat.

Coring took place in a *Montrichardia* swamp adjacent to an area of elevated swamp forest. Sediments throughout the sequence were made up exclusively of peat and organic detritus. Pollen preservation was superb and twenty-four samples were processed and counted. Overall, the sequence from NV08-4 represents one of the longest records from the Caribbean area. Five zones were apparent in the pollen sequence (fig. 5.10). The basal zone, dating to sometime prior to ca. 4780 B.C.,

Table 5.10. Sediment Descriptions of the Nariva Swamp, Trinidad Core 4 (Core NV08-4).

Depth (cm)	Organics	Color	Texture	Notes
0–4	Sapric			(top of Tube 1); peat
4–10	fibric			Peat; charcoal
10–12	sapric		muck	
12–21	Fibric			Peat
21–35	Sapric	10YR 4/2	Silty muck	
35–47	Sapric	2.5Y 2.5/1		Peat
47–62	Sapric	2.5Y 3/1	Silty clay	Charcoal
62–67		10YR 4/1	Silty clay	
67–85	Sapric	10YR 2/1		Peat
85–89	Hemic	Black		Peat, small amount of sand
89–94		10YR 3/3	Peaty sand	
94–100		10YR 2/2	Sapric peat	Abundant charcoal; (bottom of Tube 1)
100–110				Slop; (top of Tube 2)
110–114				Charcoal
114–123	Sapric	7.5YR 2.5/3		Pieces of charcoal
123–139	Sapric	10YR 2/2	Silty peat	
				(large undecomposed roots from 117–151; fewer roots from 150–172)
139–147	Sapric	5YR 4/2	Silty clay	
147–160	Sapric	7.5YR 3/2		Peat
160–170	Sapric	5YR 3/2	Silty clay	Charcoal flecks
170–175	Sapric	10YR 5/2, 10YR 3/2	Silty clay	Indistinct bands
175–198		10YR 3/2, 10YR 4/2	Silty clay	Indistinct bands; charcoal
198–200				Fibers; (bottom of Tube2)
200–208				Slop; (top of Tube 3)
208–215	Sapric	10YR 2/2		Peat
215–230	Sapric	7.5YR 3/2		peat; discontinuous lines of black charcoal
230–245	Sapric	10YR 4/2	Silty clay	Discontinuous bands of 10YR 5/3 and black charcoal
245–260	Hemic	10YR 2/1		Peat

(continued)

Table 5.10. *(continued)*

Depth (cm)	Organics	Color	Texture	Notes
260–270	Sapric	10YR 3/2	Silt	Indistinct bands
270–295	Hemic	10YR 2/1		Peat
295–300	Hemic	10YR 3/3		Peat; (bottom of Tube 3)
300–310				Slop; (top of Tube 4); large piece of wood
310–314	Hemic	5YR 2.5/1		peat
314–350	Fibric	5YR 2.5/2		Peat
350–370	Hemic	5YR 3/1		Peat
370–380	Sapric	5YR 2.5/2		Peat
380–400	Hemic	7.5YR 3/2		Peat (bottom of Tube 4)
400–408				Slop; (top of Tube 5)
408–420	Hemic	5YR 2.5/2		Peat
420–465	Fibric	Reddish		Peat
465–500	Sapric	5YR 3/1		Peat; (bottom of Tube 5)
500–505				Slop; (top of Tube 6)
505–510	Sapric	5YR 2.5/2		Peat
510–538	Hemic/sapric	7.5YR 3/2		Peat; some charcoal
538–557		2.5Y 4/1	Gleyed silt	Few fibers and black flecks
557–564	Hemic	7.5YR 4/6		Peat
564–595	Hemic/sapric	7.5YR 3/1	silt	Fibers throughout
595–600	Sapric	10YR 3/1		(bottom of Tube 6)
600–610				Slop; (top of Tube 7)
610–636		10YR 4/1	Silty clay	Few fibers
636–650		10YR 4/1, 2.5Y 4/1	Silty clay	Finely laminated; few fibers; charcoal
650–666		2.5Y 4/1	Silty clay	Abundant black flecks
666–667				Charcoal layer
667–680		2.5Y 3/1	Silty clay	Few fibers and charcoal
680–694		5Y 3/1	Silty clay	Few fibers and charcoal flecks
694–700	Hemic			Peat; (bottom of Tube 7)

122 • Chapter 5

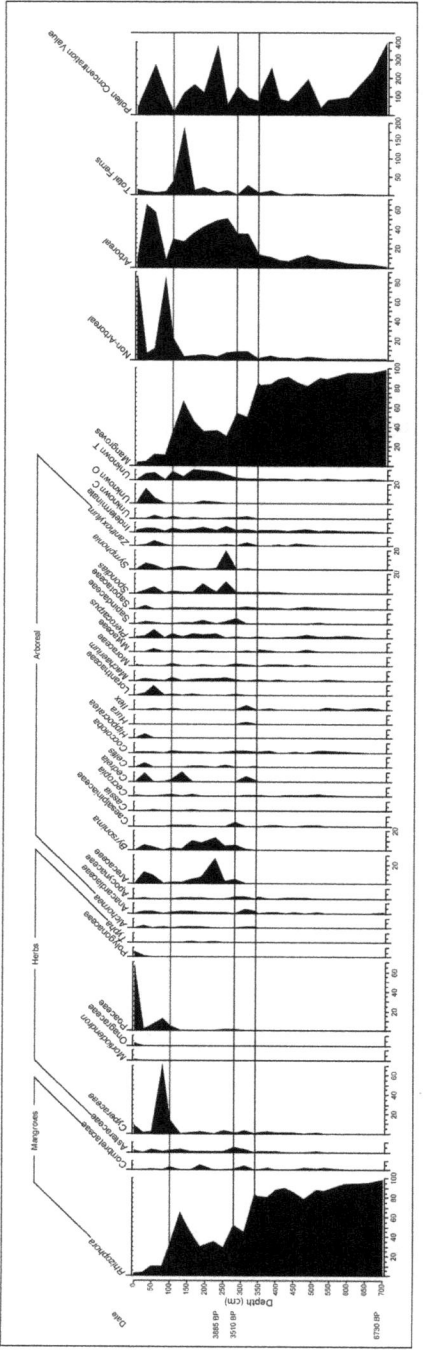

Figure 5.10. Nariva Swamp, Trinidad, Core 4 pollen-percentage diagram. Pollen and charcoal concentrations are expressed as grains and fragments, respectively, per cm³ of sediment.

extends from 701 to 660 cm. Here we see a mangrove-dominated environment, indicating that the area was significantly more brackish than today. Other taxa are almost completely lacking in this lowermost zone. There is an appreciable quantity of charcoal present in this portion of the core suggesting that fires, of possible human origin, occurred in the coring vicinity at that time. The second and largest zone (660–350 cm) represents a red mangrove environment. Through time, arboreal (mostly swamp-forest) taxa became more common, confirming the progradation of the area. Charcoal concentration values were reduced, perhaps suggesting that the environment was less favorable as a location for human activities.

Zone 3 (350–280 cm) is marked by a significant reduction in red mangrove pollen, along with a corresponding increase in swamp-forest taxa, including Anacardiaceae (cashew family), Arecaceae, *Cedrela* (cedar), *Hura* (sand box), *Ilex* (holly), Sapindaceae (soapberry family), and *Zanthoxylum* (prickly ash). Pollen from *Byrsonima*, most frequently encountered in savanna regions, became more common at this time as well. This short section recorded an environment that changed from brackish swamp to a less saline swamp-forest area. Additionally, charcoal concentrations were elevated, suggesting greater fire frequencies in the vicinity, which were possibly of human origin.

Zone 4 (280–100 cm) shows a continued reduction in red mangrove pollen as well as an increase in forest types. The potentially ethnobotanically significant taxa Arecaceae and *Spondias* (hogplum) are elevated during this time. Somewhat elevated concentrations of charcoal hint that there may be an association between these plants and human activity in the area. *Byrsonima* pollen as well as Unknown T also become much more common with expansion of savannas in the vicinity. The uppermost zone, occurring from 100 cm to the surface, was marked by dramatic fluctuations between sedges, arboreal types, and grasses. These changes likely signal historic activity at the coring location. Charcoal concentrations were high, probably reflecting the burning of fields for rice or cane production.

Overall, the NV08-4 sequence reflects the progradation of the region, from a brackish mangrove swamp, to a swamp-forest environment, to a region with more-extensive savannas. The presence of an appreciable and sustained quantity of charcoal around ca. 4780 B.C. suggests early human activity in the area.

The Nariva 4 core had relatively abundant phytoliths with good deposition in the top and bottom of the core, and a notable reduction in the middle (320–525 cm) (figs. 5.11a, 5.11b). The general pattern of the core is characterized by an arboreal signal with indicators of open

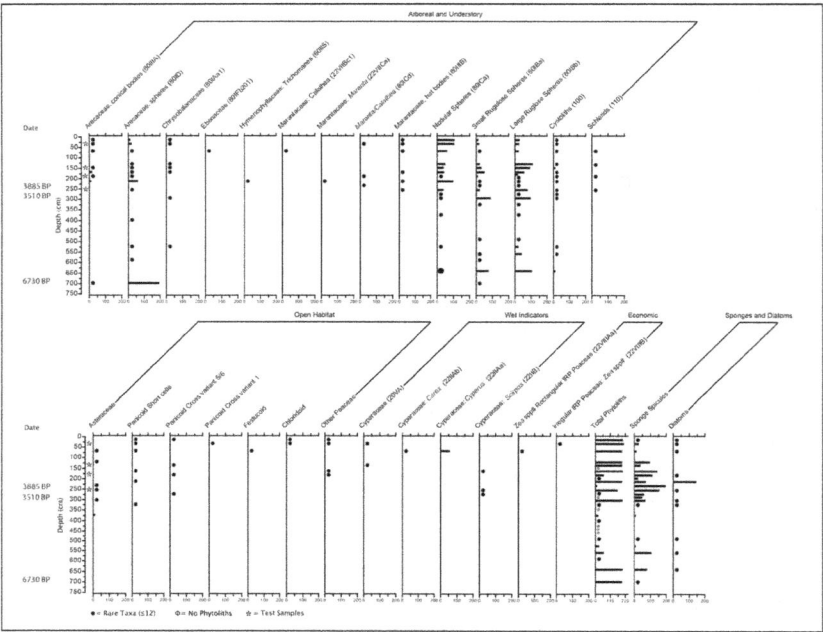

Figure 5.11a. Nariva Swamp, Trinidad, Core 4 phytolith diagram: resolved.

habitat in the uppermost zone. Of the twenty-eight samples analyzed, twenty-two produced phytoliths. The bottom zone of the core (635–700 cm) is characterized by high concentrations of phytoliths from arboreal and understory plants. In the very bottom of this zone, the assemblage is dominated by Arecaceae (palm) spheres, whereas the upper portion is dominated by both large and small rugulose spheres indicating a forested environment comprising woody dicots and forest herbs. Both samples had counts of two hundred phytoliths.

The mid zone (295–635 cm) is sparse in phytoliths, but the few that are present suggest an arboreal habitat indicated by rugulose spheres and Aracaceae and Chrysobalanaceae spheres. The top zone (0–295 cm) exhibited an abundance of phytoliths and provided the greatest diversity of taxa in the core. Only two samples yielded zero phytoliths and four samples had more than two hundred phytoliths. The marked difference in the phytolith assemblage of this zone is the presence of open habitat indicators. Phytoliths from Asteraceae and Poaceae are present in increasing diversity from the bottom to the top of the zone. Cyperaceae phytoliths are also present, indicating a wetland habitat. Nodular and rugulose spheres still dominate the phytolith assemblage,

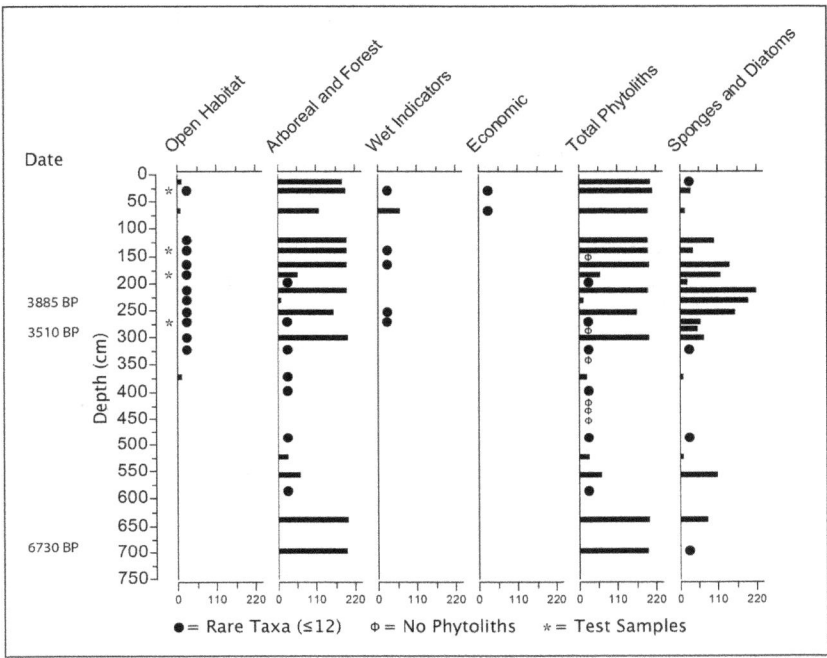

Figure 5.11b. Nariva Swamp, Trinidad, Core 4 phytolith diagram: composite.

and Chrysobalanaceae spheres indicate arboreal habitats are still quite common. Sponge spicule counts peak in this zone and gradually taper away at the top of the core.

Few economic indicators were present in the core, but there are some important signals. The uppermost samples of this highest zone (10–15 cm, 65–70 cm) yielded regular and irregular IRP (irregular with short projections) phytoliths, respectively. Both types of phytoliths indicate the presence of genus *Zea* and probably reflect the presence of maize in these uppermost strata. There was also one Variant 1 cross, although it was not large enough to be considered an indicator of maize. A general phytolith indicator of the plant family Marantaceae, nodular spheres, was present in much higher numbers in this upper zone. This zone contained multiple phytolith types, although in low abundances that specifically reveal the presence of *Calathea* and *Maranta*, both members of the *Marantaceae* family. Wild species of both genera have been identified on Trinidad. It is possible, however, that these phytoliths indicate the cultivation of leren (*C. allouia*) and/or arrowroot (*M. arundiacea*), especially considering their occurrence in a zone that is increasingly marked by open habitat.

The NV08-4 core indicates environmental changes in an intertidal zone during Mid to Late Holocene climate change. Pollen and phytoliths in the lower section of the core, deposited prior to ca. 4780 B.C., show a mangrove-dominated environment with abundant forest species in the watershed of the broadly sloping plain of the Southern Lowlands (figs. 5.10, 5.11a, 5.11b). The abundant arboreal and understory species reflect the mesic climate of the Mid Holocene. Sea-level rise in the Mid to Late Holocene fluctuated. In the Early Mid Holocene, when the lower part of the core sediments were deposited, sea level rose rapidly until ca. 4050 B.C., when the rate slowed by ca. 2050 B.C. at which time it continued to slow until it ceased rising around 1050 B.C. (Rull 1999; Van der Hammen 1974).

Charcoal concentration is unusually high in the basal zone of the core, indicating burning (fig. 5.10). An isolated stemmed point (Biche point) not found in an archaeological context about 7.5 km from the coring site is stylistically similar to stemmed points found in northern South America that have been dated to ca. 8600–6100 B.C. (Aceituno et al. 2013). At that time, sea level was 7 m below its present level and the land now inundated (forming Nariva Swamp) was a savanna or open forest environment (Boomert 2006; Harris 1991; Ramcharan 1980, 2004). Several later Archaic sites of the Ortoire complex have been documented along the margins of Nariva Swamp, near Manzanilla and Point Radix. It is conceivable that other Archaic sites in the center of the existing swamp have been inundated.

After ca. 4780 B.C., particle sizes of the sediments changed, becoming more sand-rich (Pollen Zone 2). The environment continued to be brackish, dominated by mangroves, but with the increasing presence of swamp-forest species. This pattern became more marked just prior to ca. 1560 B.C. (Pollen Zone 3), as mangrove decreased rapidly and swamp-forest species increased in the pollen record. At the same time, charcoal concentrations increased, as did savanna species indicators, signaling the end of the Mid Holocene and the beginning of a drying episode. This level in the core is the time of the beginning of sandbar development and a decline in the rate of sea-level rise.

Lying in a synclinal basin, the Nariva Swamp acts as a sediment sink, collecting material not only from the rivers draining the Central Range and the Southern Lowlands, but also from the Guiana Current, which carries an enormous sediment load off the nearby South American continent. This load allows sufficient sediment for sandbar and beach development on the gentle slope of the Nariva Basin. The sand hill at the coring site is a remnant of one of these old sandbars, developed as marine flooding was reduced and sea level continued to rise, allowing freshwater to accumulate landwards and mangrove environments to move seawards. These conditions are closely aligned with those indicated by Ramcharan's data in Nariva Swamp, where he documented a mangrove-dominated environment that began to decline by ca. 2000 B.C., and was transformed to a freshwater environment by ca. 800 B.C. (Ramcharan 1980, 2004).

Two radiocarbon dates from the core are in incorrect stratigraphic order: ca. 1935 B.C., 235 cm; and ca. 1560 B.C., 280 cm. This may be due to reworking of sediments as long shore drift was slowly building the sandbar, a dynamic process interrupted by storm events that breached the sand barrier. The sandbar near the coring site was formed in this dynamic building process, migrating for millennia, but it seems to have stabilized by Pollen Zone 3. Using the broadest bracket of the 2-sigma range, we can safely assume that the core zone above 235–280 cm was deposited sometime after ca. 2100–1500 B.C., placing it near the transition from Late Mid Holocene to Early to Late Holocene.

Pollen Zone 4 represents an arid environment with increases in savanna taxa and open habitat indicators dominating the phytolith samples. Forest species also increased, including ethnobotanically useful taxa. *Symphonia,* found in this upper zone, produces a resin when mixed with beeswax and powdered charcoal has been documented ethnographically in the Guianas for caulking canoes; it is also used as a fastener for arrowpoints to spear shafts and stone flakes to wooden grater boards (Boomert 2000: 87; Im Thurn 1883: 315; Roth 1924). Mangrove decreased except for resurgence near the top of the zone followed by another decline. This period shows a dynamically changing environment as the area prograded and sedimentation in the Nariva basin moved the shore (and mangrove communities) toward the sea. There was a general shift in the setting from a mangrove to a freshwater swamp environment of palm and swamp bloodroot (*Pterocarpus*), which can tolerate slightly brackish water. As the sandbar was repeatedly building and being breached, conditions varied along a salinity gradient, producing a complex pattern in the core sediments, as freshwater and mangrove species rotated. For example, the increase in mangrove at 150–200 cm corresponds with a low sand interval in the sediments and represents a period when the sand barrier was breached. Harris (1991) noted a similar pattern with alternating periods of brackish and freshwater conditions in Nariva between 12,600 and 2900 B.C. During regression periods sandbars were present, associated with freshwater swamps.

The zone after ca. 1560 B.C. corresponds with Ortoire complex midden sites along the margins of Nariva Swamp: Ortoire, Cocal 1, North Manzanilla 2, Kernahan Trace, and Chip Chip Hill. These midden sites, with the exception of Chip Chip Hill, are located on sandbars; the Ortoire midden yielded a date of ca. 900 B.C. (ca. 2890 cal yr B.P.) (Boomert 2000). All middens contain subsistence evidence of fishing, hunting, and plant collecting, and evidence of exploitation of brackish, freshwater, and forest resources. The most recent section of the core shows elevated sedge concentrations and fluctuations between sedges, arboreal taxa, and grasses resulting from historic activities related to cattle ranching, cacao production, vegetable and rice farming, and fishing.

Discussion

The landscapes of Trinidad underwent profound changes and shifts in resource availability through the Holocene. Sea level rose, temperatures increased, savannas and forests expanded and contracted as climatic moisture waxed and waned, and Archaic and Ceramic Age peoples occupied the entire island. Sea-level changes resulted in diminished land area and land bridges to the mainland were severed. Coastal wetlands formed, which represented crucially important resources for all human groups who occupied the island. These wetlands shifted between freshwater and saline, due to sediment trapping in mangrove environments enhanced by human activities, as in the case of the St. John setting; or by natural aggradation of sandbars, as in the case of Nariva Swamp. Archaeological middens contain both freshwater and saltwater shellfish, an important part of the paleodiets from Archaic through Ceramic Age times. Consistent with other locations in the Caribbean, several cores indicated Late Holocene xeric conditions and the expansion of once-significant savannas on Trinidad; relict Aripo savannas still exist in some of these areas. The stemmed Biche point (although of uncertain origin), potentially representing a Paleo-Indian presence and the oldest documented sites in the Caribbean are located in Trinidad, where one small step from the mainland initiated still-evolving regional human history.

6

GRENADA

John G. Jones, Deborah M. Pearsall, Pat Farrell, Nicholas P. Dunning, Jason H. Curtis, Neil A. Duncan, and Peter E. Siegel

Background

Grenada is the southernmost island in the Lesser Antilles volcanic island arc lying on the eastern margin of the Caribbean plate where the Atlantic oceanic crust subducts beneath the Caribbean plate (fig. 1.1). The Lesser Antilles arc is a double arc that coalesces to the south, forming a single row of islands, including Grenada, the Grenadines, St. Vincent, St. Lucia, and Martinique. These Southern Volcanic Caribeees include both active and dormant volcanoes. Volcanic island arc formation is taking place between Grenada and Carriacou, where the seamount, Kick 'Em Jenny, located 8 km north of Grenada, has erupted eleven times since it was first reported in 1939 (K. E. Bullen 1965; Maury et al. 1990; Potter et al. 2004). Volcanic activity in Grenada is predominantly Miocene and Pliocene-Quaternary in age.

Grenada is located 140 km north-northwest of Trinidad and the northeast coast of Venezuela. First noted by Columbus in 1498 on his third voyage to the New World, Grenada was not permanently occupied by European colonists until the early seventeenth century. Despite the island's size of 312 km^2, only fourteen prehistoric sites are documented for the island, dating to Saladoid or post-Saladoid occupations (Boomert 2000: 232–234; Bullen 1964: fig. 1). There are no documented Archaic occupations on the island, although this would have been an ideal stopping point for groups moving both north and south through the Lesser Antilles; the absence of known Archaic sites is probably due to sampling and taphonomic factors.

Paleoenvironmental studies on Grenada have been limited. John McAndrews (1996) reported on a core from Grand Etang and Levera National Parks, providing some data related to the changing environment of the island. McAndrews's study at Levera, which centers on a discussion of environmental change as a result of fluctuating sea level remains unpublished. A study of pollen from Lake Antoine was also conducted by McAndrews and Ramcharan (2008), while Benz (2010) reported on several additional environmental studies that have been conducted in the region in an effort to determine changing Holocene environments and sea-level fluctuations (Ellison and Stoddart 1991; Graham 1995; Parkinson, DeLaune, and White 1994; Rull, Vegas-Vilarrúbia, and Espinoza de Pernía 1999; Woodroffe 1981; Woodroffe and Grindrod 1991).

Grenada's terrain is characterized by rugged relief (fig. 6.1). A mountain chain made up of volcanic peaks of andesite and basalt runs the length of the island (Thomas 2000). Highest relief is located along the western side of the island while eastern slopes are gentler and extensive coastal plains extend to the sea. Low hills cover the northeastern and southwestern portions of the island. The southeastern coast is a deeply embayed ria coast of headlands and submerged valleys. The southern part of the island is covered by lahar deposits and reworked volcanic sediments, a result of high precipitation carrying unconsolidated ash and pyroclastic flow materials to low-lying terrain. Two unique characteristics of Grenada's geology are the presence of Si-undersaturated basalts and eight well-preserved explosion craters, including the depression occupied by Lake Antoine (Arculus 1976). Lake Antoine basin comprises tuff, scoria, and ash deposits. Soils observed in the basin were highly weathered Ultisols developed in volcanic ejecta.

Grenada is located in the northeast trade wind belt with a tropical, wet climate. Annual precipitation varies from more than 3,500 mm on the windward slopes to less than 1,500 mm in the lowlands. Greatest monthly totals occur from June through November when tropical storms and hurricanes are most prevalent. Rainfall is less pronounced from December through May when the ITCZ migrates south, however there are significant local variations in the length and intensity of seasonal differences. Given its location in the Atlantic hurricane belt, Grenada has been devastated by hurricanes, including Hurricanes Janet in 1955 and Ivan in 2004.

Vegetation communities in Grenada have been substantially altered by land clearing for colonial and recent agricultural pursuits and by the introduction of nonnative plant taxa. Additionally, hurricanes periodically alter vegetative cover (Beard 1944). Beard (1944) identified six natural vegetation types on the island, divided into seasonal, montane, and disturbance climax groups. Before Hurricane Janet in 1955, "the original lowland and montane rainforests, palm brakes, and elfin forest" occurred only as relic remnants (Ahmad 2011: 170; also Beard 1944). Hurricane Janet further eliminated native remnants of these forests (Wright 1959). Patches of stunted montane woodland still exist in some higher elevations and are characterized by evergreen seasonal

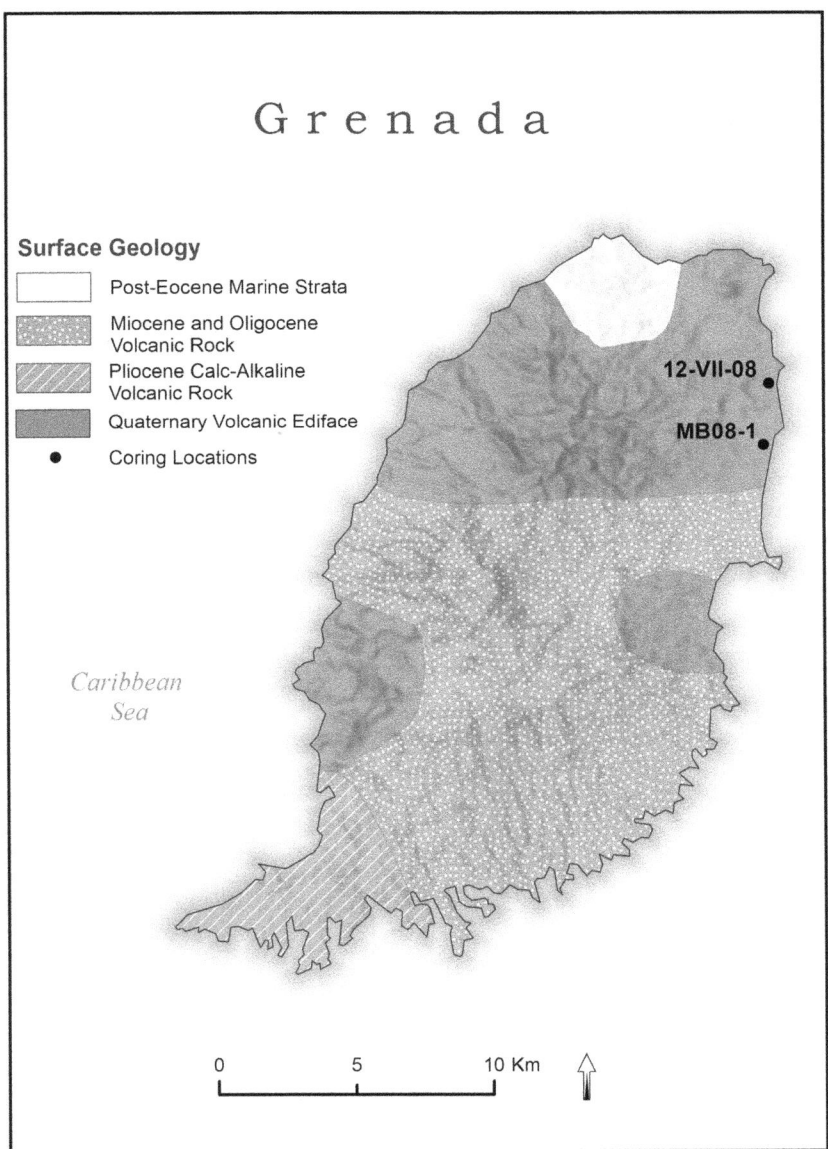

Figure 6.1. Map of Grenada showing the surface geology and coring locations.

forest. Human impacts on Grenada landscapes have been greatest in coastal areas, where few remnants of native vegetation remain (Ternan, Williams, and Francis 1989). The east coast includes some mangrove forests, and cactus thorn scrub is found in the southwest extent of the island, which has a long dry season. Most of the relatively drier areas of the northeast and southwest portions of the island are covered by secondary vegetation of thorn scrub, thorn savanna, and, frequently, acacia and logwood trees (Ahmad 2011). A wide variety of historically introduced plants include almond, bamboo, breadfruit, jackfruit, mango, cacao, nutmeg, banana, coconut, and sugarcane.

Rugged relief contributes to soil erosion, especially on extremely steep slopes and landslides; soil loss is a common hazard. This is particularly true when soils have been cleared of vegetation for cultivation or by severe storms and heavy rainfall. Land fragmentation has also contributed to soil loss on the island. Ahmad (2011) remarked that Grenada has suffered less soil erosion and fertility loss than many other Caribbean islands for a few reasons: the soils are derived from mineral-rich parent material and receive periodic input of nutrients from volcanic ash, the dominance of tree crop agriculture has provided good protection from erosion, and early colonial crops such as cotton and tobacco, which are very damaging to soil, were not important in Grenada.

Previous archaeological research completed on Grenada includes excavations at the Savanne Suazey site as well as stratigraphic tests and surface collections at the Salt Pond, Westerhall Point, Caliviny Island, and Pearls sites (R. P. Bullen 1964, 1965). The majority of information recovered from these sites relies on an interpretation of the ceramic sequences found on the island and radiocarbon dates are lacking. Most of the sites are located in the northeast section of the island, while the Caliviny Island site is situated just off of the southern coastline. Work at Pearls uncovered the Simon-Saline series (Pearls complex) of ceramics, believed to be the earliest pottery recovered from Grenada, and was followed chronologically by pottery of the Caliviny series, eventually being replaced by pottery from the Suazey series (Cruxent and Rouse 1961).

Environmental Coring on Grenada

Very little paleoecological work has been conducted on Grenada, hence the need for complete and well-dated sequences validated with pollen, phytolith, and charcoal spectra to establish past environmental conditions and the changing role of humans in the island's ecology. Two cores were collected on Grenada: one at Meadow Beach and another at Lake Antoine (fig. 6.1). Both are located in northeastern Grenada in the vicinity of six archaeological sites documented by Bullen (1964: fig. 1). Pollen preservation was generally excellent and approximately eighty-two pollen taxa were identified in both of the sequences (tab. 6.1).

Table 6.1. Pollen Taxa Identified in the Grenada Cores.

Taxon	Common Name	Taxon	Common Name
Avicennia	Black Mangrove	Arecaceae Type P	
Combretaceae	White Mangrove	Arecaceae *Sabal* Type	
Rhizophora	Red Mangrove	Bombacaceae	Bombax Family
Acalypha	Three-Seeded Mercury	*Bursera*	Gumbo limbo
Alternanthera	Joseph's Coat	*Byrsonima*	Nance
Asteraceae	Aster Family	Caesalpiniaceae	Fabaceae Subfamily
Cheno-Am	Goosefoot, Pigweed	*Cassia*	Cassia
Cladium	Sawgrass	*Cecropia*	Trumpet
Convolvulaceae	Morning Glory Family	*Cedrela*	Cedar
Croton	Croton	*Celtis*	Hackberry
Cucurbitaceae	Squash Family	*Coccoloba*	Sea Grape
Cyperaceae	Sedge Family	*Guazuma*	Bay Cedar
Desmodium	Tick Seed	*Gymnopodium*	Canelita
Euphorbiaceae	Spurge Family	*Haematoxylon*	Logwood
Fabaceae	Bean or Legume Family	*Hippocratea*	
Lamiaceae	Mint Family	*Hirea*	Barbados Cherry Type
Lythraceae	Loosestrife Family	*Hura*	Sandbox
Malvaceae	Mallow Family	*Ilex*	Holly
Montrichardia		Loranthaceae	Mistletoe Family
Nuphar	Water Lily	*Machaerium*	Rosewood
Nymphea	Water Lily	*Maytenus*	Maytenus
Onagraceae	Evening Primrose Family	*Mimosa*	
Passiflora	Passion Flower	Moraceae	Mulberry Family
Phaseolus	Bean	Moraceae Type F	
Poaceae	Grass Family	Moraceae Type T	
Polygonaceae	Knotweed Family	*Myrica*	Wax Myrtle
Portulaca	Purslane	Myrtaceae	Myrtle Family
Ranunculaceae	Crowfoot Familiy	*Pilocarpus*	
Rumex	Dock	*Piper*	Pepper
Solanaceae	Nightshade Family	*Protium*	Copal

(continued)

Table 6.1. *(continued)*

Taxon	Common Name	Taxon	Common Name
Verbenaceae	Vervain Family	*Pterocarpus*	
Zea mays	Maize	*Quercus*	Oak
Acacia	Acacia	Rhamnaceae	Buckthorn Family
Alchornea	Alchornea	Rubiaceae	Madder Family
Anacardiaceae	Cashew Family	Rutaceae	Rue Family
Anacardiaceae Type R		Sapindaceae	Soapberry Family
Anona	Soursop	Sapotaceae	Sapodilla Family
Apocynaceae	Dogbane Family	*Spondias*	Hogplum
Arecaceae	Palm Family	Tiliaceae	Basswood Family
Arecaceae Type G		*Trema*	Trema
Arecaceae Type H		*Zanthoxylum*	Prickly Ash
		Indeterminate	poor preservation

Meadow Beach (Core MB08-1)

Meadow Beach is located about 1.6 km north of the Pearls site in what is currently a red, black, and white mangrove swamp. This area receives sediment from the eastern slopes of the mountainous interior, particularly from Mount St. Catherine, which forms the western flank of the drainage basin for the Meadow Beach locality. Sediments drained from these mountains consist of kaolinitic clays from weathered interior soils, alluvial silt, and reworked volcanic deposits. The site also receives sands from tropical storms, which often impact the east coast. Additional vegetation in the immediate coring location was limited and marine detritus in the core vicinity indicated that tidal or storm surges occurred in the area. These surges would have introduced large amounts of seawater into the local environment, effectively creating a toxic saline environment for many plants. The coring location is approximately 125 m from the modern coastline, where beach strands of *Coccoloba uvifera* (sea grape) and other small shrubs, rare grasses, and *Ipomoea pescaprae* (beach morning glory) are found. The beach was also convenient for rinsing coring equipment and ourselves of mangrove swamp muck (fig. 6.2). Meadow Beach was selected for coring because augur testing indicated the presence of buried, reduced, organic-rich sediments of considerable depth. The core setting, in close proximity

Figure 6.2. Cleaning ourselves and coring equipment of mangrove muck fronting the Meadow Beach, Grenada coring location.

to the Saladoid and post-Saladoid Pearls, La Filette, and Simon Beach sites, made this an ideal location to potentially link Ceramic Age human activities to the environmental record.

The Meadow Beach core consisted of 490 cm of stratigraphically contiguous sediments. Three well-defined zones are readily apparent in the pollen record and three radiocarbon dates help frame the associated environmental history (tab. 6.2). The upper portion of the core comprised silty clay to a depth of 55 cm with pieces of undecomposed wood and charcoal (tab. 6.3). This cap deposit was underlain by reddish black peat extending to 165 cm, forming an abrupt boundary with a silty clay layer extending to 303 cm. A radiocarbon date of ca. 1060 B.C. was obtained from peat at 215–217 cm. Peat extended from 303 to 382 cm and a second radiocarbon date of ca. 3055 B.C. was recovered from peat at 330–332 cm. A layer of very cohesive, silty clay extended from 385 to 443 cm. From 455 to 488 cm silt loam and loam dominated, with increasing sand content. The bottom layer of the core was gleyed, fine to medium sand containing shells and peat. A radiocarbon date of ca. 4110 B.C. was recovered from the peat at the base of the core. Tables 6.3–6.6 provide sediment descriptions, laboratory particle size results, loss-on-ignition results, and sedimentation rates for the core.

Table 6.2. Radiocarbon Dates from the Grenada Cores.

Core Location	Lab Sample Number	Core Number/Sample Depth	^{14}C Age (BP)[a]	$^{13}C/^{12}C$ Ratio	2-Sigma Calibrated Date Range[b]	Median Cal Date
Meadow Beach	AA84798	MB08-1, 215–217 cm, Peat	2880±40	−27.0	1210–930 BC/ 2880–3160 BP	1060 BC/3010 BP
Meadow Beach	AA84799	MB08-1, 330–332 cm, Peat	4420±40	−30.4	3330–2920 BC/ 4870–5280 BP	3055 BC/5005 BP
Meadow Beach	AA82678	MB08-1, 492 cm, PW[c]	5270±50	−31.1	4230–3980 BC/ 5930–6180 BP	4110 BC/6060 BP
Lake Antoine	Beta-377885	Antoine 12-VII-08-3, 146 cm, PP[d]	1290±30	−23.2	AD 670–770/ 1180–1290 BP	AD 715/1240 BP
Lake Antoine	AA91729	Antoine 12-VII-08-3, 311–313 cm, LS[e]	2030±40	−34.2	160 BC–AD 60/ 1890–2110 BP	35 BC/1985 BP
Lake Antoine	AA91728	Antoine 12-VII-08-6, 611–613 cm, LS	4860±45	−29.2	3760–3530 BC/ 5480–5710 BP	3655 BC/5605 BP
Lake Antoine	Beta-377883	Antoine 12-VII-08-7, 700 cm, PP	7340±40	−28.4	6350–6075 BC/ 8300–8025 BP	6185 BC/8135 BP
Lake Antoine	AA91730	Antoine 12-VII-08-7, 736–738 cm, LS	8050±50	−28.6	7170–6780 BC/ 8730–9090 BP	6980 BC/8930 BP

a. 1-sigma range.
b. Dates were calibrated using the IntCal13 method of CALIB ver. 7.0 (Reimer et al. 2013).
c. Preserved wood.
d. Preserved plant matter.
e. Lake sediment.

Table 6.3. Sediment Descriptions of the Meadow Beach, Grenada Core (Core MB08-1).

Depth (cm)	Organics	Color	Texture	Notes
				Peat and sand at surface
5–13	Sapric	10YR 3/2	Silty	
13–30	Sapric	10YR 3/1-10YR 4/1	Clayey-silt	
30–35	Sapric	2.5Y 4/1	Clayey silt	Intact wood in matrix of sediment
35–40	Sapric	Alternating bands of 2.5Y 4/2 and 2.5Y 3/1	Clayey silt	
40–55	Hemic	5Y 2.5/2	Silty clay	Some wood; abundant black flecks
55–60	Sapric	2.5Y 2.5/1		Peat
60–70	Sapric	10YR 2/2	Silty	Peat
70–74				Undecomposed wood
74–95	Sapric	5YR 2.5/1		Reddish black peat
95–100	Hemic	5YR 2.5/1		Reddish black peat (bottom of Tube 1)
100–105				Slop; (top of Tube 2)
105–130	Sapric	10YR 2/1		Abundant black flecks
130–165	Sapric	5Y 2.5/1	Silty	Abrupt boundary @ 165
165–180	Sapric	2.5Y 3/2; 10YR 2/1 at base	Silty clay	(bottom of Tube 2)
180–200				Slop; (top of Tube 3)
200–209	Sapric	10YR 2/1	Silt	
209–215		2.5Y 3/2	Silty clay	
215–220	Sapric	2.5Y 3/1	Silty clay	
220–244	Sapric	5Y 2.5/1		peat
244–250	Sapric	2.5Y 3/2	Clayey silt	
250–266	Sapric	10YR 3/1	Clayey silt	
266–280	Sapric	10YR 2/2		Peat (bottom of Tube 3)
280–290				Slop; (top of Tube 4)
290–303	Sapric	2.5Y 3/1	Silty clay	
303–310	Hemic	2.5Y 2.5/1 (some 2.5Y 4/2)		peat
310–325	Sapric	5Y 2.5/1		Peat
325–343	Sparic	5Y 2.5/1		Peat (bottom of Tube 4)
343–365				Slop; (top of Tube 5)
365–382	Sapric	10YR 2/2	Silty	Peat
385–443	Sapric	10YR 2/2 - 10YR 2/1	Clayey silt (stiff clay)	(bottom of Tube 5)

(continued)

Table 6.3. *(continued)*

Depth (cm)	Organics	Color	Texture	Notes
443–455				Slop (Top of Tube 6)
455–470	Sapric	10YR 3/1	Silty (small amount grit)	
470–488		Gley1 2.5/10Y	Sandy silt (grit increases with depth)	
488–493		Gley1 2.5/5GY	Sand (fine – medium)	Shell layer with sapric peat; (bottom of Tube 6)

Table 6.4. Particle Size Percentages from the Meadow Beach, Grenada Core.

Depth (cm)	Sand	Silt	Clay	Depth (cm)	Sand	Silt	Clay
5–15	1	8	91	225–235	8	58	34
15–25	1	10	89	235–245	12	56	32
30–35	1	24	75	245–255	16	48	36
35–40	4	11	85	255–265	18	41	41
40–50	6	45	49	265–280	23	41	36
50–60	11	38	51	290–300	7	49	44
60–70	7	33	60	300–310	6	47	47
60–70	9	33	58	310–320	7	61	32
70–80	9	51	40	320–330	4	50	46
80–90	1	52	47	330–340	6	47	47
90–100	7	59	34	365–375	8	48	44
105–115	19	4	77	375–385	2	51	47
115–125	10	52	38	385–395	7	53	40
125–130	31	40	29	395–405	7	41	52
130–140	43	35	22	405–415	6	38	56
140–150	22	49	29	415–425	5	34	61
150–160	14	52	34	425–435	9	45	46
160–165	7	15	78	435–445	10	43	47
165–175	8	38	54	455–465	21	47	32
175–180	1	33	66	465–475	22	50	28
200–209	4	49	47	475–485	30	43	27
209–215	5	29	66	485–493	50	27	23
215–225	8	51	41				

Table 6.5. Loss-on-Ignition Results from the Meadow Beach, Grenada Core Sediments.

Depth (cm)	% Organic Carbon	% Carbonate	Depth (cm)	% Organic Carbon	% Carbonate
5–15	20.21	6.13	225–235	27.44	11.59
15–25	15.35	6.43	235–245	27.96	11.59
30–35	20.57	10.82	245–255	20.75	8.31
35–40	18.48	10.57	255–265	16.76	5.78
40–50	30.19	10.55	265–280	22.24	11.17
50–60	44.72	9.15	290–300	20.80	6.95
60–70	36.82	17.44	300–310	27.76	9.19
60–70	40.01	16.64	310–320	36.03	16.77
70–80	52.96	12.81	320–330	34.28	14.16
80–90	62.44	9.48	330–340	22.20	13.32
90–100	58.19	9.95	365–375	24.61	13.15
105–115	46.11	13.57	365–375	24.79	10.90
105–115	49.96	8.76	375–385	30.99	15.67
115–125	39.49	12.05	385–395	30.17	10.12
125–130	39.09	9.73	395–405	24.47	11.87
130–140	18.91	5.24	405–415	20.78	9.92
140–150	21.02	8.79	415–425	25.43	11.83
150–160	25.79	8.64	425–435	26.10	10.13
160–165	41.88	12.16	435–445	36.13	11.43
165–175	18.65	10.04	435–445	27.20	10.93
175–180	22.22	10.97	455–465	22.87	8.61
200–209	43.96	12.19	465–475	21.47	11.46
209–215	11.97	6.83	475–485	18.64	7.93
215–225	19.43	8.97	485–493	11.92	8.21
215–225	17.89	7.93			

Table 6.6. Sedimentation Rates for the Grenada Cores.

Core, ^{14}C sample depths	^{14}C Date Ranges (Median Cal Dates, BP)	Sedimentation Rate (cm/yr)
MB08-1, 0–216 cm	0–3010	.0717
MB08-1, 216–331 cm	3010–5010	.0382
MB08-1, 331–492 cm	5010–6060	.1533
LA 12-VII-08, 0–146 cm	0–1240	.1177
LA 12-VII-08, 146–312 cm	1240–1980	.2243
LA 12-VII-08, 312–612 cm	1980–5600	.0828
LA 12-VII-08, 612–700 cm	5600–8140	.0346
LA 12-VII-08, 700–737 cm	8140–8930	.0468

Pollen was found throughout the sequence and forty-four samples were examined (fig. 6.3). The basal zone (493–330 cm) was characterized by high grass, palm type H, Solanaceae, Arecaceae, Moraceae, Myrtaceae, Sapotaceae, *Spondias*, and *Zanthoxylum*. As a group, these taxa favor a freshwater swamp forest–type environment and their presence reflects a former marshy wetland. Other swamp-forest elements noted in this Early to Mid Holocene context include Anacardiaceae, Apocynaceae, *Coccoloba*, and Rubiaceae. The presence of grasses might suggest the swamp forest was surrounded by savanna-type vegetation; Asteraceae pollen, a type common in grasslands is also elevated during this zone. Although a number of ethnobotanically useful taxa were represented, sedimentation rate was high and pollen and charcoal concentrations were low, suggesting that these data may record a differentially preserved or deposited assemblage (tab. 6.6). Mangrove pollen is present in lower percentages in comparison to upper zones, suggesting that mangroves were in the area, but removed from the local environment. Palm type H, an unidentified form not comparable to any Caribbean palms examined, is common in these basal samples, suggesting it was locally abundant on the landscape. In the absence of a clear charcoal signal and with low pollen concentrations we concluded that this lowest zone of the core dates to prehuman occupations of Grenada.

Sustained and elevated charcoal concentration values consistent with anthropogenic burning activities are bracketed by the dates ca. 3055–1060 B.C. (330–215 cm). Sedimentation rate for this approximate two-thousand-year range is quite low (tab. 6.6), and this is among the wettest periods in Caribbean climate history. It is unlikely that the associated high charcoal concentrations were the result of widespread natural fires (Burney, Pigott Burney, and MacPhee 1994; Siegel et al.

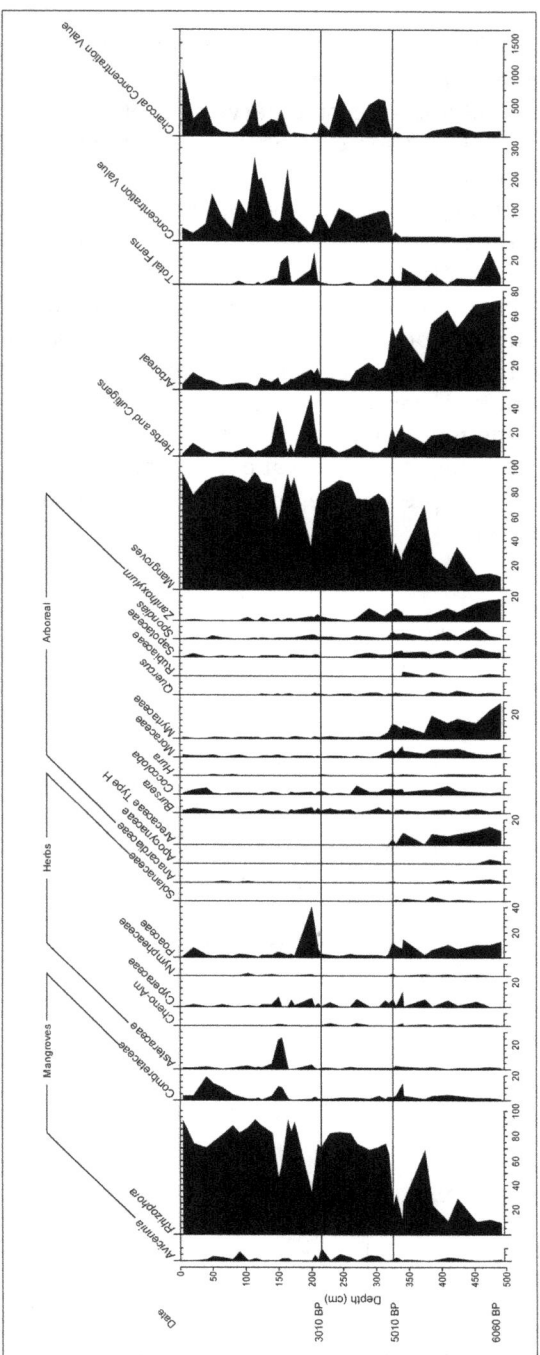

Figure 6.3. Meadow Beach, Grenada, core pollen-percentage diagram. Pollen and charcoal concentrations are expressed as grains and fragments, respectively, per cm³ of sediment.

2015; Siegel et al. 2005). Arecaceae phytolith concentrations declined significantly above 300 cm, shortly after the onset of large-scale burning, which may be either a secondary byproduct of landscape modifications or intentional and intensive harvesting of palms by newly arrived human colonists, or some combination of both factors (figs. 6.4a, 6.4b). Restructuring of the local plant community is apparent by ca. 3055 B.C. Clearing of local forests is apparent with reductions in arboreal taxa including Anacardiaceae, *Hura,* Moraceae, Myrtaceae, and Rubiaceae, although it is also possible that rising sea levels with a corresponding increase in water levels or salinization may account for the removal of these types. Both Asteraceae and Poaceae types are reduced in this section, again suggesting a significant local environmental perturbation. Red mangrove pollen became dominant, reflecting sea levels reaching modern levels. The 1,700- to 2,400-year period of human-induced burning and landscape modifications documented in this core most likely represent the impacts of the first colonizers to Grenada (tabs. 6.7, 6.8).

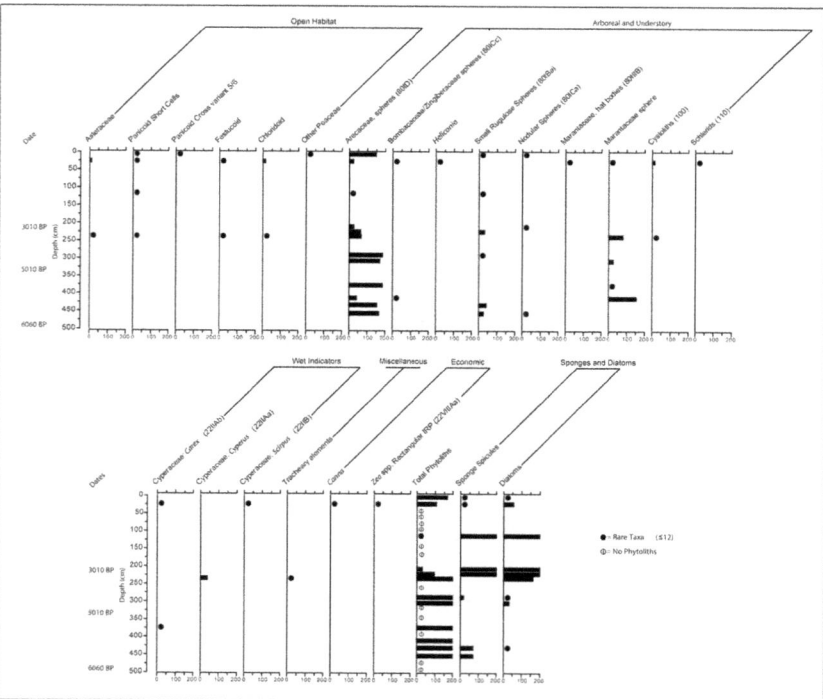

Figure 6.4a. Meadow Beach, Grenada, core phytolith diagram: resolved.

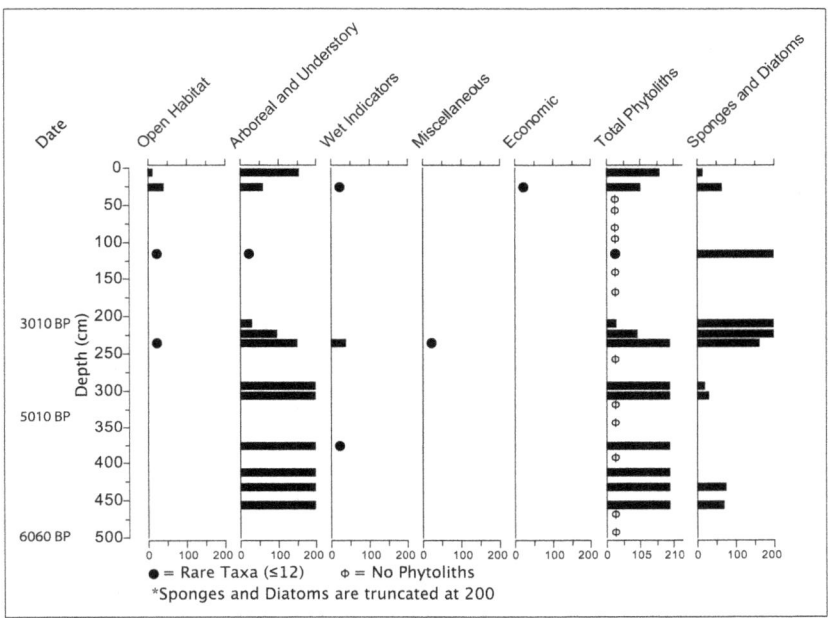

Figure 6.4b. Meadow Beach, Grenada, core phytolith diagram: composite.

Beginning with Pollen Zone 2 there was a total loss of palm type H from the record. Its disappearance coinciding with the arrival of humans suggests overharvesting, resulting in the removal of palms from the local plant community. Elsewhere in the neotropics forest clearance has been associated with selectively sparing of economically useful plant taxa (Jones 1994; Neff et al. 2006).

The uppermost zone (215–0 cm) dates from ca. 1060 B.C. to modern times. Red and to a lesser extent white mangrove pollen percentages are high, documenting the formation of the modern environment (fig. 6.3). Two periods of increased sustained deposition of particulate charcoal reflect (1) European activity (60 cm) and (2) probable Saladoid landscape modifications (160 cm). All documented sites on Grenada date to these periods, including the nearby Pearls, High Bluff, and Savanne Suazey sites.

Lake Antoine (Core 12-VII-08)

Lake Antoine is a water-filled volcanic caldera a few kilometers north of Meadow Beach. The Lake Antoine basin comprises tuff, scoria, and ash deposits. Previous unpublished studies of sediments from Lake

Table 6.7. Ethnobotanical Associations and Disturbance Indicators Represented in the Grenada Cores.[a]

Taxon	Ethnobotanical Association or Disturbance Indicator	Core MB08-1	Lake Antoine
MANGROVE			
Avicennia	Black mangrove. Throat pains, incontinence.	X[b]	
Combretaceae	White mangrove. Slows bleeding.	X	
Rhizophora	Red mangrove. Diarrhea, fever, malaria, excellent fuel wood.	X	X
HERBS/CULTIGENS			
Asteraceae	Aster or Composite family. Herbs and shrubs. Many are invasive weed species of cleared open areas.	X	X
Cheno-Ams	Chenopod and amaranth families. Favor disturbed or open habitats. Young greens and mature seeds are edible. Includes seablite, saltwort, chenopod, amaranth.	X[b]	X[b]
Croton	Some produce a latex used for medicinal purposes.		X[b]
Cyperaceae, *Cladium*	Sedge family. Grasslike herbaceous plants, many are weeds that invade cleared open areas.	X	X
Heliconia	Lobster claw, wild plantain, false bird-of-paradise. Frequent invasive taxon of edges of human clearings.	X[b]	
Marantaceae	Maranta family, starchy edible rhizomes. Includes West Indian arrowroot.	X	
Montrichardia	Yautia-madera. Edible fruits and seeds, medicinal, fish bait.		X[b]
Poaceae	Grass family. Often associated with areas frequently fired. Edible starchy grains.	X	X
Solanaceae	Nightshade family. Berries of some are edible. Includes *Capsicum* (pepper).	X	X[b]
Zea mays, *Zea* spp.	Maize. Edible grain.	X[b]	X[b]
ARBOREAL			
Anacardiaceae, *Spondias* sp.	Cashew family. Edible fruit, hogplum.	X[b]	X

(continued)

Table 6.7. *(continued)*

Taxon	Ethnobotanical Association or Disturbance Indicator	Core MB08-1	Lake Antoine
Apocynaceae	Dogbane family. Golden trumpet vine. Fibers used for cordage. Some produce edible flowers.	X[b]	
Arecaceae	Palm family. Edible fruit, thatching, cordage, needles, posts.	X	X
Bursera	Gumbo limbo. Resin has medicinal properties, leaves used for tea.	X	X
Cecropia	Pumpwood. Fast-growing colonizing trees common to disturbed forest habitats and clearings.		X
Celtis	Hackberry, edible fruit.		X
Coccoloba	Sea grape. Edible fruit, medicinal.	X	
Moraceae, *Ficus*, *Brosimum*	Mulberry family. Edible fruit, breadnut, medicinal. Often colonize open cleared areas.	X	X
Myrtaceae, *Eugenia*, *Psidium*	Myrtle family. Edible fruit, medicinal. Frequently found in windbreak and secondary forest growth. Includes guava, Eugenia, allspice.	X	X[b]
Rubiaceae	Madder family. Caribbean princewood. Bark has medicinal properties, quinine.	X	
Sapotaceae, *Chrysophyllum*	Sapote family. Edible fruit, medicinal, latex in some species. Includes edible fruits of chicle, sapote, lucuma.	X	X

a. See Table 5.5 for the sources of information.
b. Trace amounts.

Table 6.8. Plant Taxa Identified in the Grenada Cores with No Documented Ethnobotanical or Anthropogenic Correlates other than Perhaps Fuel Wood, Especially Arboreal Taxa.

Taxon	Common Name	Core MB08-1	Lake Antoine
HERBS/CULTIGENS			
Nymphaeacea	Water lily	X	X
ARBOREAL			
Hura	Sand box	X	
Quercus	Oak	X	
Zanthoxylum	Prickly ash	X	X
FERNS			
Unknown ferns		X	X

Antoine were limited (McAndrews and Ramcharan 2008) but did demonstrate the potential for significant paleoenvironmental data. We collected two sediment cores from the approximate deepest section of the lake. The lake is fringed by aquatic vegetation, most notably *Montrichardia*, a semiarboreal member of the Araceae (skunk cabbage family), and sedges, including *Eleocharis* and *Cladium*. Flat areas immediately surrounding the lake are under cultivation for bananas, breadfruit, melons, and other crops. Hilly vegetation farther from the lake was largely forested.

Lake sediments were collected by Jason Curtis following methods described in chapter 4, this volume. The water level of Lake Antoine was a few meters above sea level, and water depth at the coring location was approximately 8 m. The analyzed core was 8.4 m long. Basal sediments comprised palynologically sterile coarse sands. These sediments most likely were deposited prior to the formation of the modern lake. The organic record collected in the core represents a thorough archive of environmental history over the past ca. nine thousand years. The lake may not have begun to develop until sea levels rose to the point where the freshwater table was elevated.

Four pollen zones were recognized in this sequence, based on frequency changes of significant taxa (fig. 6.5). The basal zone (850–725 cm) was dominated by Moraceae Type F, a pollen type similar to *Ficus* spp. *Ficus* grains are poorly dispersed and rarely found in most sediments. These grains occur exclusively inside fig fruit and would be expected only through decomposition of figs. Many aquatic animals consume figs, including fish, reptiles, and amphibians; fruit passing through their digestive tracts would liberate the pollen grains, allowing entry into the lake sediments. However, positive identification of these grains is problematic and other members of the Moraceae family could be the source. Along with the possible *Ficus* grains, the basal zone is marked by elevated percentages of Myrtaceae (myrtle family), very slightly elevated red mangroves, *Croton*, Solanaceae, *Celtis*, and *Zanthoxylum* pollen grains. Collectively, these taxa suggest a composite picture of swamp-forest types along with some drier savanna-type vegetation. The absence of organic material in the lowest portion of the basal zone precluded a radiocarbon date, but organic sediment from 737 cm produced a date of ca. 6980 B.C. At that depth total phosphorus was quite high (1,000 mg/kg); Moraceae pollen dominated; and Arecaceae (palm family with edible fruit), herbs, and cultigens were relatively abundant. Palm pollen is normally scarce in most sequences because the trees are largely insect pollinated, pollen is produced in low numbers, and it is poorly dispersed. However, palm pollen was

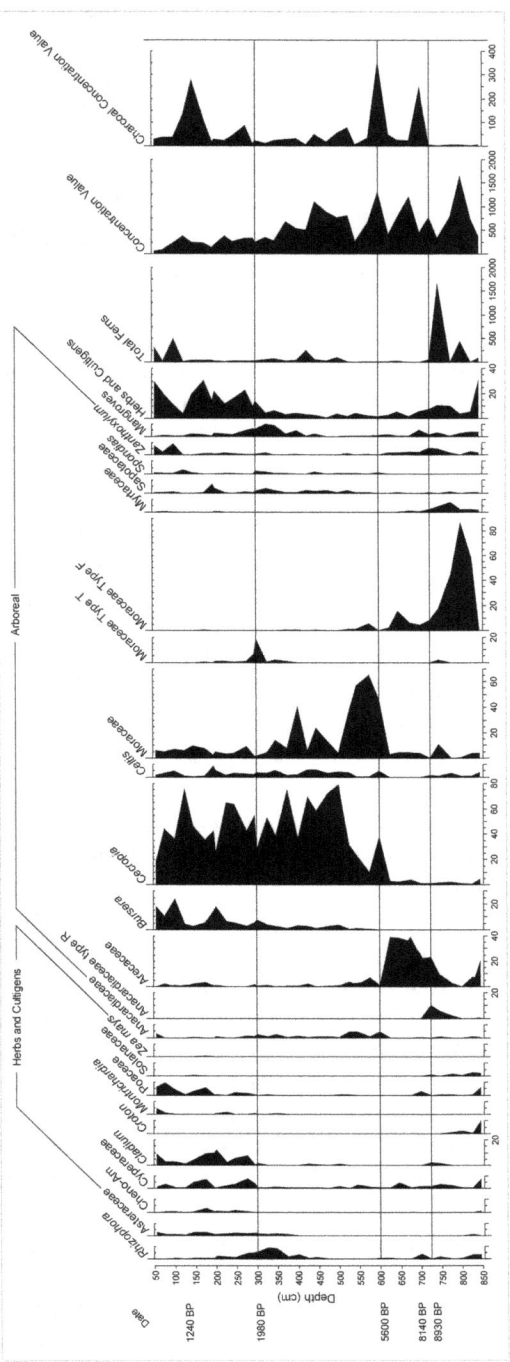

Figure 6.5. Lake Antoine, Grenada, core pollen-percentage diagram. Pollen and charcoal concentrations are expressed as grains and fragments, respectively, per cm³ of sediment.

abundant in the lower and upper samples of the basal zone, suggesting that palms were likely to have been common components of the forest in the caldera surrounding Lake Antoine at this time.

Pollen Zone 2 (725–600 cm) is marked by significant changes in local vegetation. Palm pollen, particularly Arecaceae types G and H became common during this time, while Moraceae Type F was less prevalent. These palms may be the dominant forms in the local forest, although efforts to identify them to the genus level were not possible. The sudden cessation of the accumulation of these grains at the end of this zone mirrors the pattern in the Meadow Beach core, likely the result of the removal of these plants from the local ecosystem. The decline in palm pollen and phytoliths, co-occurring with other proxies of human activities suggests that palms were overharvested with the arrival of first human colonists to Grenada (figs. 6.6a, 6.6b; tab. 6.7).

Two large spikes of particulate charcoal in this zone suggest that the forest in the caldera area, and likely beyond, was subjected to large-scale burning. The first major burn (700 cm) apparently had no major effect on the local palm population. The associated date (ca. 6185 B.C.) dates to a period of very dry conditions in the Holocene (ca. 10,000–7200 cal yr B.P.) (Banner et al. 1996; Curtis 1997; Curtis, Brenner, and Hodell 2001; Curtis and Hodell 1993; Hodell et al. 1991; Leyden 1985). We regard the early Lake Antoine assemblages to be linked to natural disturbances associated with dry conditions in the Early to Mid Holocene. Paleoclimate records indicate a period of dry conditions between approximately 10,000 and 7200 cal yr B.P. (Curtis, Brenner, and Hodell 2001). The spike in charcoal at this time is most likely a product of natural fires from the great amount of combustible fuel that would have been littering the landscape.

The fire event at 600 cm (ca. 3655 B.C.), however, coincided with the demise of palm types G and H. Significant changes following the 600 cm burn likely represent an effort by local people to modify and eventually manage the landscape in the vicinity of the caldera. Steady deposition of particulate carbon in the lake basin above 600 cm represents continuous landscape management through the Mid and Late Holocene. To further investigate anthropogenic impacts, total phosphate analyses were conducted on the lake sediments. Total phosphate concentrations increased at the beginning of Pollen Zone 2 and dropped by the end of the zone, a pattern possibly linked to the charcoal inputs (fig. 6.7).

At 600 cm there was a restructuring in the local floral community. Palm types G and H disappeared and Moraceae (probable *Brosimum alicastrum*) and *Cecropia* pollen became abundant. *Cecropia* (trumpet tree) is an early gap-colonizing tree in disturbed environments. In-

Grenada • 149

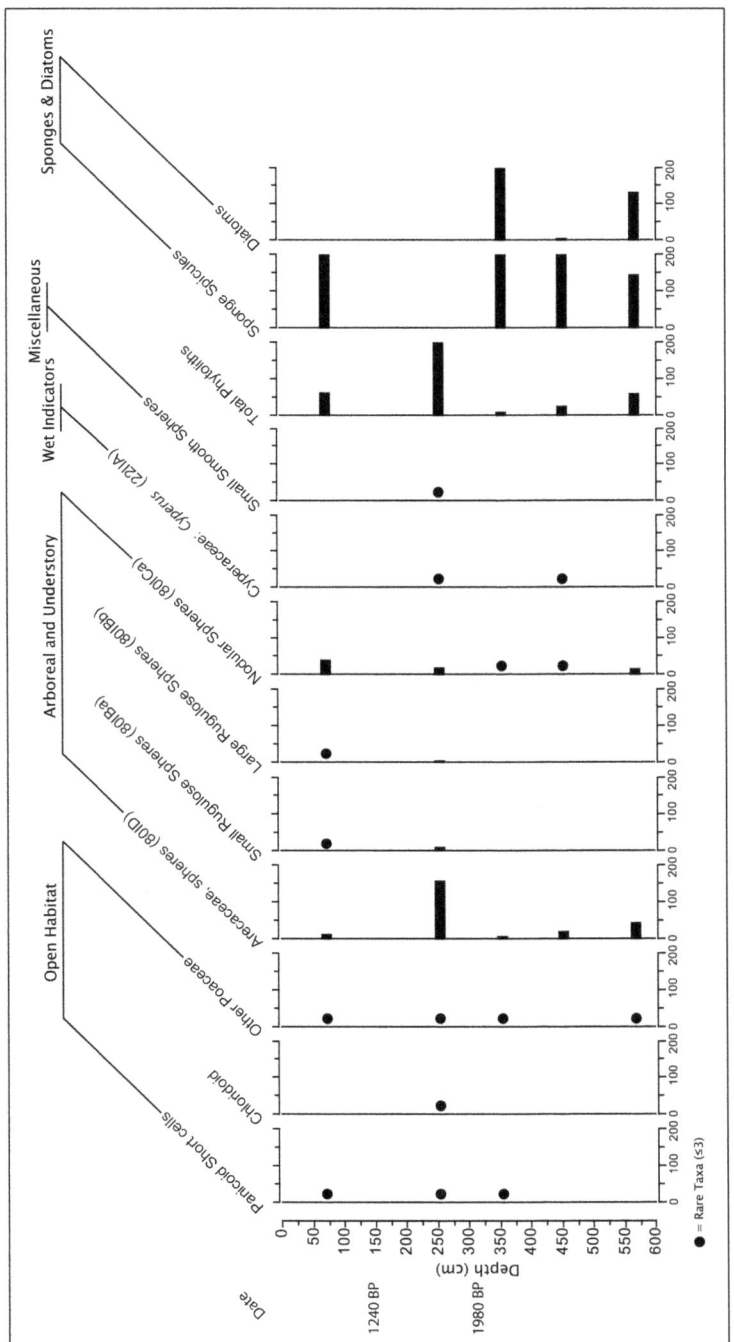

Figure 6.6a. Lake Antoine, Grenada, core phytolith diagram: resolved.

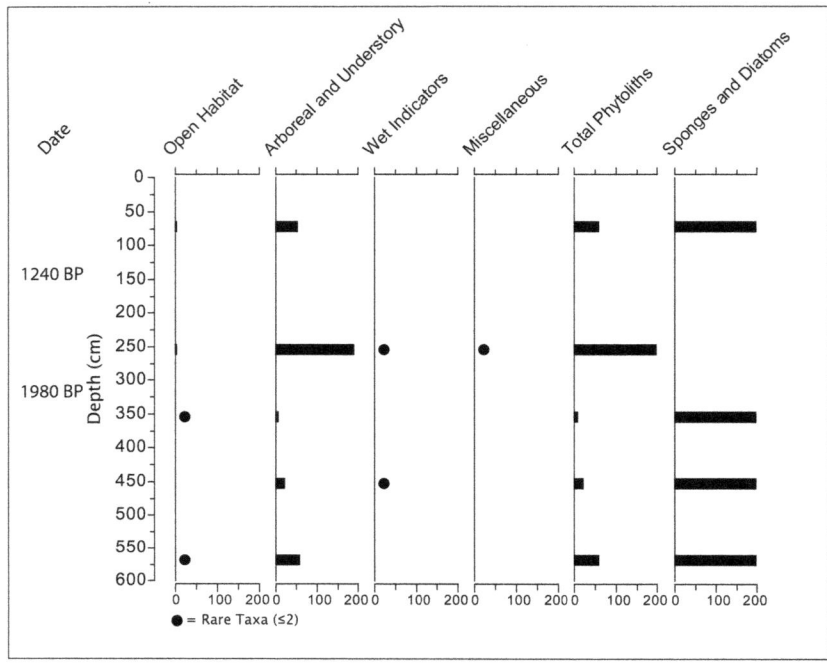

Figure 6.6b. Lake Antoine, Grenada, core phytolith diagram: composite.

creases in Sapotaceae, Anacardiaceae, and *Spondias* also occurred at this time. These are underrepresented trees and the removal of undesirable taxa would result in the apparent increase in these rarely seen pollen types. The floral community at this time was a product of human landscape management. *Brosimum*, Sapotaceae, some members of the Anacardiaceae family, *Celtis*, and *Spondias* all produce edible fruit. This managed garden forest was a hospitable place with a greater relative abundance of economically important native plants. Radiocarbon dates bracket this zone of Archaic human occupation in the caldera between ca. 3655 and 35 B.C. Depending on when Saladoid people settled the Pearls community, the ca. 35 B.C. date may be contemporaneous with those later colonists.

The uppermost zone (above 300 cm) dates to the Early and Late Ceramic Age as it is currently understood. Continued landscape management is reflected by sustained burning, total phosphate values, and increases in disturbance taxa (Asteraceae, Cyperaceae, Poaceae, Cheno-Ams). Sedge and *Cladium* (sawgrass) pollen increased as well, a product of increased siltation probably related to ongoing clearing

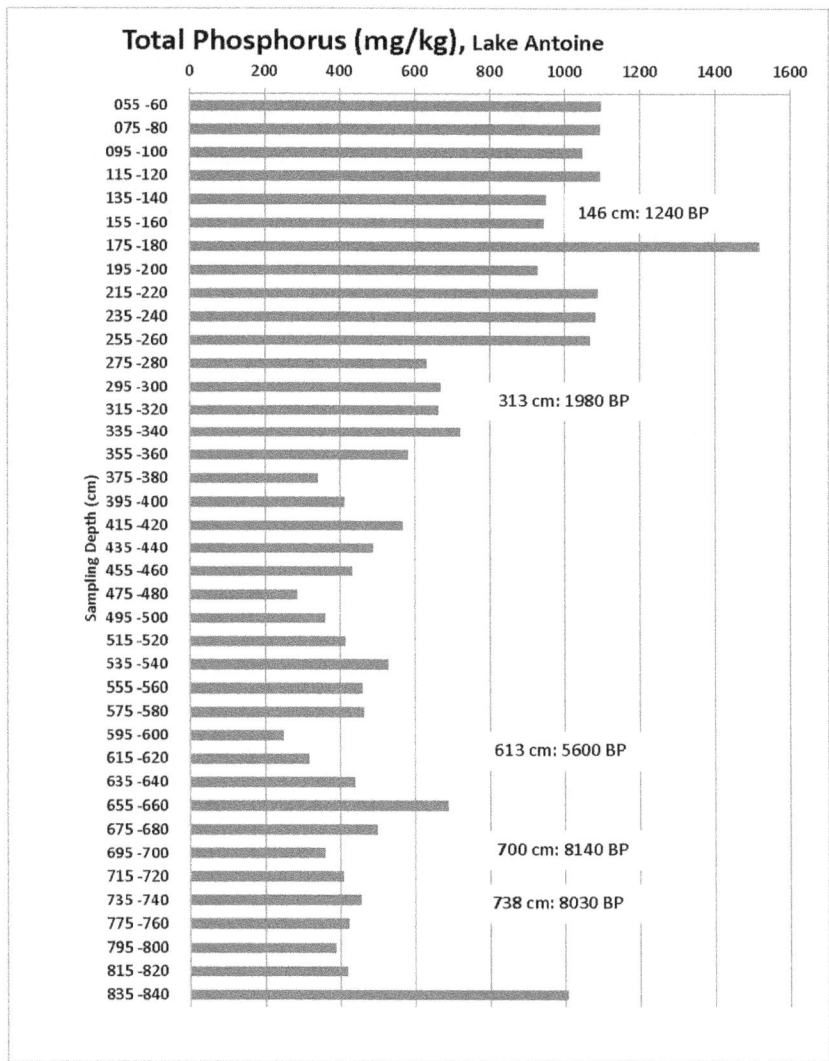

Figure 6.7. Total phosphorous values in the Lake Antoine core sediments.

activities by Saladoid and post-Saladoid groups in the region. A single *Zea mays* pollen grain was documented at 175 cm, indicating this plant was being cultivated near the lake edge. Interpolating between the radiocarbon dates straddling the 175-cm context dates to ca. A.D. 580, well into the Ceramic Age as it is generally understood in the Caribbean. Swamp-forest taxa continued to dominate the arboreal elements, with *Bursera* (Gumbo limbo) becoming common. *Bursera* is an important swamp-forest element and would be expected as a natural part of the local forest. Today, *Bursera* trees are common elements in the forest surrounding Lake Antoine. *Zanthoxylum* is another noneconomic swamp-forest tree whose pollen increased in the upper zone. *Montrichardia* pollen concentrations were slightly elevated in this zone. This arboreal member of the Araceae family is a conspicuous member of the modern local plant community, with expansive stands of the trees fringing the lake. The absence of *Montrichardia* pollen in deeper sediments of the core may be due to differential preservation. Most members of the Araceae family produce fragile pollen grains that are difficult to identify unless well preserved. Sediments from the uppermost 50 cm were not lost during collection but were poorly consolidated, typical of tropical lakes.

Discussion

Two sediment cores collected from northeastern Grenada documented paleoecology and anthropogenic landscapes, including the earliest evidence of human activity on the island. Dated sequences of pollen, phytoliths, charcoal particulates, and sediment chemistry span the transitions from prehuman occupations through earliest colonization events and into later prehistory.

The Meadow Beach core reflects a sequence starting with a swamp-forest environment, ca. 4000–3000 B.C. Human activity is not indicated during this time, though good evidence of human intrusion into the area defines the overlying zone, ca. 3000–1000 B.C. High frequencies of particulate charcoal, coupled with significant perturbation of local vegetation marks the activities of the earliest or near-earliest human colonists to the island. Among the impacts of these early colonizers is the decline of Arecaceae (palm) type H, an unknown form that was formerly common in the area. Whether this palm was decimated by climate change (unlikely, given the available climate record for the circum-Caribbean region), overharvested by humans (most likely scenario), or otherwise affected by the possible removal of seed-dispersing rodents (unlikely given the absence of zooarchaeological evidence) remains to be demonstrated. With the appearance of first colonizers (ca. 3000 B.C.), local habitats were permanently and dramatically altered. After ca. 1060 B.C., the uppermost zone in Meadow Beach records additional habitat changes likely to have been driven in part by human activities. Periods of sustained burning may coincide with the arrival of Saladoid settlers from the Orinoco Valley.

The sequence from Lake Antoine is approximately consistent with the one from Meadow Beach, although older by nearly three thousand years. This core represents an 8.4-m record of past conditions in the lake basin. Four zones were identified and dated, reflecting a period of high Moraceae (cf. *Ficus*) pollen near the base, followed by a zone dominated by palm pollen. As in the Meadow Beach core, there is a sudden and dramatic reduction in palm type H pollen coupled with a significant sustained period of burning reflected in the charcoal record. Palm type H never appears again in the sediment record, suggesting it was nearly removed from the environment at that time. This event was dated to ca. 3655 B.C., about 200–750 years before the same observation in the Meadow Beach core (based on 2-sigma calibrated date ranges). Above this zone, microfossils reflect a shifting managed landscape within the lake basin to one more favorable for human habitation, with increases in economically useful plants, including *Celtis,* Moraceae (*Brosimum*-type), Sapotaceae, and *Spondias* and continuous sustained burning. In the uppermost zone, straddling Saladoid and post-Saladoid occupations of Grenada, additional landscape modifications are marked by increases in open-habitat and disturbance indicators. A maize pollen grain at 175 cm suggests the presence of corn after ca. 35 B.C. and prior to ca. A.D. 715 (A.D. 580, interpolated).

Systematic archaeological and paleoenvironmental investigations on Grenada are limited (R. P. Bullen 1964, 1965, 1970; McAndrews 1996; McAndrews and Ramcharan 2008). No Archaic sites have been identified. Microfossils and organic material collected from the Meadow Beach and Lake Antoine cores reveal anthropogenic landscapes dating to ca. 3655–3055 B.C., thereby pushing back initial human colonization of the island approximately three thousand years prior to what the available archaeological data indicate.

Initial forest clearing is associated with the permanent loss of an unknown species of palm (Arecaceae) documented in both cores. Grenada served as a strategic stepping-stone during this earliest colonization pulse into the Lesser Antilles. Native plant communities on Grenada and Trinidad were similar based on coring results from both islands. First colonists on Grenada walked into landscapes sufficiently familiar and people quickly modified them to create enduring places of home. However, the biogeographic differences in landmass scale between the small island of Grenada and Trinidad/South America would have represented a major readjustment in exploitation strategies. Survival strategies followed for millennia on the mainland may have been deleterious to the small-island ecosystems of the Lesser Antilles. We argued elsewhere that the landscape learning curve was not steep for the first pioneering groups entering the islands (Siegel et al. 2015). We still partially agree with that assessment based on the similarities in the plant taxa between the islands and the mainland. However, we would now modify our earlier conclusion in terms of exploitation strategies of the first colonists to the first island occupied in the Lesser Antilles (Grenada). After nearly extirpating palms on Grenada through overharvesting, we argue that as early colonizers moved into other islands they learned that mainland approaches to procurement strategies needed to be modified for the small-island worlds of the Lesser Antilles, as will be seen in some of the other islands discussed in this book that contain approximately contemporaneous indicators of anthropogenic landscapes.

Traditional views of Archaic lifeways and adaptations in the Caribbean are based on notions of small groups of hunters, foragers, fishers, collectors, and gatherers. Implicit in this perspective is the expectation that these small transitory groups followed homogeneous survival strategies and trod lightly on the landscapes, resulting in little to no discernible environmental impacts. Our coring results from Grenada reveal people modifying and actively managing landscapes early in the Archaic period. Data from the Lake Antoine core indicate forest management by selective culling of some tree taxa to facilitate or encourage the growth of other economically useful tree taxa. This phenomenon has been documented elsewhere in core sediments from Belize (Jones 1994) and Puerto Rico (Burney, Pigott Burney, and MacPhee 1994; Siegel et al. 2005) also dating to the Archaic. With carefully designed systematic archaeological surveys in the northeastern region of Grenada, we expect Archaic sites will be identified and linked to those earliest colonists responsible for the anthropogenic landscapes documented in our cores.

7

Curaçao

*Nicholas P. Dunning, John G. Jones, Neil A. Duncan,
Deborah M. Pearsall, and Peter E. Siegel*

Background

Curaçao is one of a chain of islands formed along a now largely inactive subduction zone that marks the southern margin of the Caribbean tectonic plate. While volcanic activity helped create the island, more recently its emergence above sea level has been associated with tectonic uplift. The south coast of Curaçao is essentially a ria coast—that is, an area where former stream valleys have been partially drowned by sea-level rise in the Holocene and are now brackish water embayments, including San Juan Bay and Spaanse Water (fig. 1.1). These valleys/bays are incised into the basement rock of the island, which consists of ancient, weathered diabase and basalt: Curaçao Lava Formation (Beets and MacGillavry 1977). Subsequent to a period of surface exposure and weathering, these igneous rock structures were submerged or partially submerged under shallow seas and covered by layers of clastic sediments (Knip and Curaçao Midden Formations) and by coraliferous limestone (Seroe Domai Formation). Subsequent orographic uplift has led to the erosion and removal of limestone over wide areas, but sections are preserved in remnant highlands: Curaçao's famous table mountains. Curaçao's northeast coast has been struck several times by powerful tsunamis over the past 10,000 years (Scheffers 2004). However, no tsunami impacts have been identified on the south coast and associated inlets.

Curaçao has a land area of 444 km². It lies 72 km off the coast of Venezuela and is intervisible with the mainland (fig. 7.1). The 1,000-m-deep Bonaire Trench separates the island from the mainland. Cool, nutrient-rich water upwelling from the trench contributes to rich fishing grounds along the island's coasts.

Curaçao possesses a semiarid climate, receiving between 500 and 600 mm of rainfall on an average annual basis. Precipitation is highly sea-

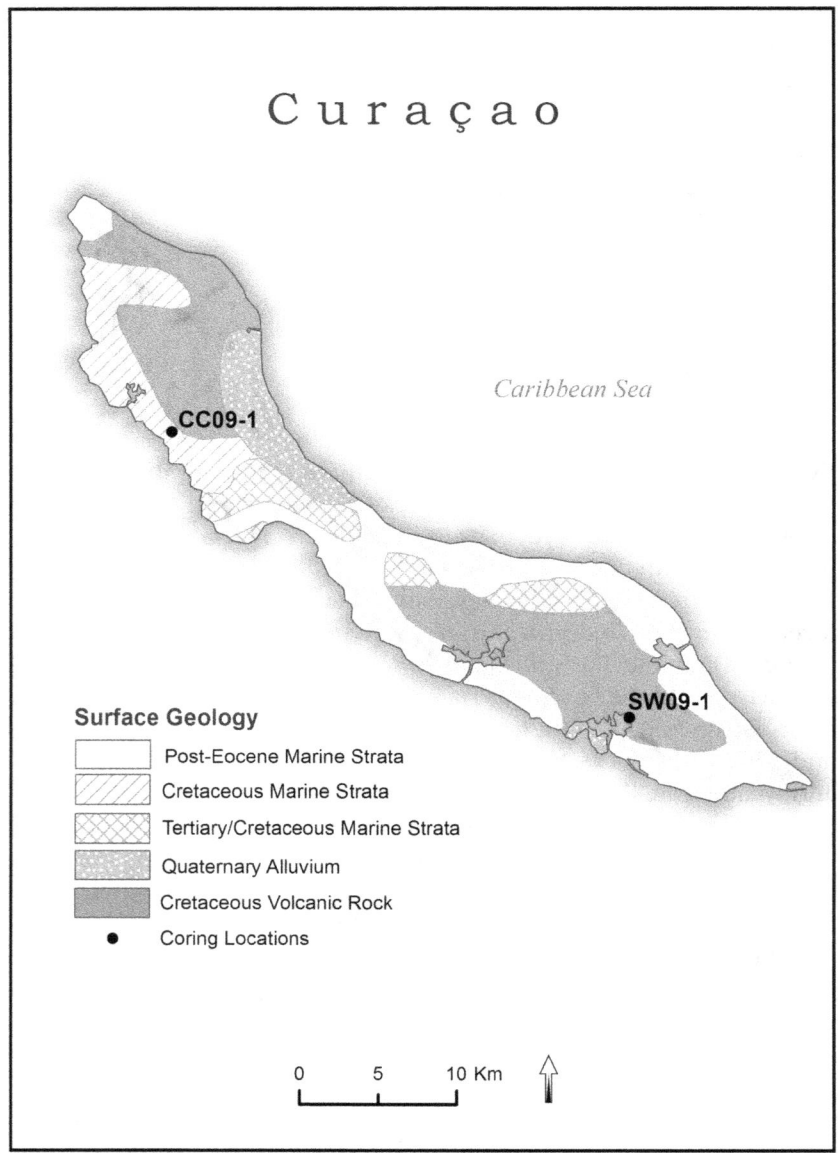

Figure 7.1. Map of Curaçao showing the surface geology and coring locations.

sonal, with most rainfall occurring during an October–December wet season. Although Curaçao is situated outside the hurricane belt, tropical storms occasionally strike the island and can produce devastating floods (Scheffers et al. 2009). Data from throughout the Caribbean Basin including the nearby coast of Venezuela indicate that regional climate has been episodically unstable over the past several thousand years, including persistent dry periods associated with shifts in the annual migration of the ITCZ (e.g., Haug et al. 2001). By analogy with nearby areas in Venezuela there are indications that the climate of Curaçao was wetter during the Mid Holocene and began drying into present-day trends about three thousand years ago.

Curaçao's semiarid climate has led to the development of xeric scrubland and very dry acacia-dominated forest. This vegetation is nearly identical to that found on adjacent areas of the South American coast in Venezuela. At present, the distribution of dry arboreal forest is highly limited, though early historical sources and archaeobotanical samples from excavations at Santa Barbara indicate that the forest was likely more widespread in precolonial times (Newsom and Wing 2004: 63–67). Archaeobotanical collections were made as part of excavations at Santa Barbara, a Ceramic Age site northeast of Spaanse Water. No seeds of food plants were recovered, but carbonized wood was abundant. Most prevalent were buttonwood (*Conocarpus erectus*), lignum-vitae or pokhout (*Guaiacum* sp.), caper tree (*Capparis* sp.), strong bark or watakeli (*Bourreria succulenta*), and trumpet tree (*Tabebuia* sp.) or calabash (*Cresentia* sp.). Ethnohistoric sources from the nearby mainland indicate that Caquetio Indians cultivated maize, manioc, and sweet potatoes, but also consumed wild cactus fruits and cocuy leaves (*Agave cocui*) (Hernandez de Alba 1963, cited in Haviser 1987). The Caquetio also resided on Curaçao at the time of European contact.

The distribution of soils on Curaçao reflects the island's semiarid climate, variation in parent materials, and the relative stability (slope and age) of the land surfaces (De Vries 2000). On low-slope, stable surfaces Aridisols predominate and are notable in the landscape by well-developed caliche within their B horizons. On sloping land underlain by igneous or metamorphic rock, shallow Inceptisols have formed, typically with gravelly, sandy C and Bw horizons. On the generally steeply sloping limestone hills shallow Entisols predominate, though small tracts of thin Mollisols (Rendolls) also occur. Valley fills with alluvial deposits have chiefly given rise to Inceptisols. Most of these alluvial soils are deep, well-drained, and base rich and have formed the island's principal agricultural resource in precolonial, colonial, and modern times. Although rainfall is not abundant on Curaçao, much of it arrives in the form of strong tropical downbursts and can potentially generate significant soil erosion on exposed land surfaces.

Archaeological data indicate that humans first arrived on Curaçao between four thousand and five thousand years ago. Evidence for these early occupations comes from several larger sites suggestive of possible permanent residence (including burials) and more numerous smaller sites thought to represent hunting and gathering camps (Haviser 1987, 2001a). All sites are characterized by abundant molluscan shell middens and are concentrated in near-coastal locations. Agricultural implements are lacking. There appears to be a period of widespread abandonment between Archaic and Ceramic Age settlement on the island, though this chronology is uncertain.

Ceramic Age sites are larger, more abundant, and were occupied by ca. A.D. 800. Most sites are concentrated in the vicinity of the ria inlets along the southern portion of the island (Haviser 1987). These locations allowed inhabitants to exploit both valley alluvial soils for farming and coastal marine resources. Additional information integrating the archaeological history of the ABC islands is presented in chapter 3 this volume.

Spanish explorers occupied Curaçao in 1499. Most of the indigenous population was quickly enslaved; many were shipped elsewhere or died from Old World diseases. The Spanish introduced a new land economy based on salt production, ranching, and plantation agriculture, including the Lanaha or Curaçao Orange. Coastal colonial plantations often walled off sections of inlets to create *saliñas*, or salt pans, to produce evaporative sea salt. In 1634 Curaçao came under the rule of the Dutch who were initially interested in salt production for their expanding fishing economy in the early seventeenth century (Goslinga 1971: 135–136). While salt production proved to be disappointing, the plantation and ranching land economy continued and expanded, and Curaçao became an important transshipment point in the African slave trade. When the Dutch took possession of Curaçao, they rounded up most of the island's Hispanic and remaining indigenous population and transported them to coastal Venezuela (Goslinga 1971: 268–269). In the past hundred years the island's economy has shifted predominantly to tourism and the refining of Venezuelan petroleum.

Environmental Coring on Curaçao

San Juan Bay (Core CC09-1)

San Juan Bay lies along the southwest coast of Curaçao. The bay takes the form of a narrow ria or drowned valley with shallow water behind a prominent beach bar at its southern (seaward) end, patches of red mangrove in places, and a complex estuary at the northern end (fig. 7.2). Archaeologically the bay is known for an oceanside cliff rock shelter with ancient pictographs of unknown age and a prominent Ceramic Age site

Figure 7.2. San Juan Bay, Curaçao. The San Juan Bay takes the form of a narrow ria or drowned valley.

lying about 2 km inland along the course of a prominent intermittent stream (Haviser 1987). Haviser noted that the alluvial soils along the stream near the site provided land suitable for maize cultivation, with larger areas of adjacent gently sloping terrain well suited to manioc.

Soils in the watershed contributing mineral sediment to San Juan Bay consist of shallow, sandy Inceptisols formed on igneous and clastic parent materials. The bay catchment also includes lesser areas of limestone hills on which have formed skeletal Entisols (on steep slopes) and deeper Aridisols with well-developed caliche (on stable surfaces) (De Vries 2000). Many land surfaces show evidence of historical and modern degradation in the form of soil truncation and gully development. Sedimentation in the bay has been altered in colonial times by wall construction, chiefly to create *saliñas*.

The entire catchment of San Juan Bay lies on land belonging to the San Juan plantation, a ranching-centered colonial operation, now a privately owned estate, but with nature conservation status. A network of moderate- to high-gradient intermittent streams contributes seasonal surface flow into the north end of the bay. Although annual rainfall in the area is only between 500 and 600 mm, its arrival in the form of intense tropical downbursts likely generated significant quantities of soil loss on exposed surfaces, particularly on steeper slopes (De Vries 2000). The semiarid climate naturally produces a relatively open vegetative cover and considerable areas of exposed soil. In the colonial era, ranching would have further exposed soil surfaces and likely generated larger amounts of erosion. In precolonial times, anthropogenic fires and land clearance for cultivation also may have contributed to soil loss.

Sediments within the CC09-1 core suggest that considerable quantities of inorganic sediment have been transported through the San Juan drainage network and deposited into the bay. During the colonial era the north end of the bay was partially walled off to create salt ponds. Our core was taken about 15 m beyond the seaward side of the last colonial *saliña* wall, in a wide swath of marshy land dominated by black mangrove. A section of the wall has recently been breached, contributing a gravel wash in the upper core strata. Behind (landward of) the *saliña* walls, sedimentation appears to have been heavier than in the coring location proper. Nevertheless, substantial quantities of terrestrial sediment accumulated at the coring location. Observations made along the tributary stream network indicate that considerable quantities of terrestrial sediment have also accumulated along the lower reaches of the valleys and have not yet been flushed into the bay. Increasing clast sizes and decreasing charcoal quantities are indicative of accelerating sedimentation rates over time.

The core reached a total depth of 311 cm, although stratigraphy may be compromised in a few areas due to hole collapse. Obvious zones of hole slop were discarded, but a few strata may still be problematic. Upper layers with significant quantities of gravel were particularly prone to slumping. However, overall stratigraphic integrity of the core is reasonably good.

The core is dominated by numerous layers of sands, silts, and clays, with five bands rich in shells (tab. 7.1). Sand is the dominant clast size in the majority of strata, reflective of the sandy texture of many of the soils within the catchment. Silts or clays dominate a number of strata, reflecting periods of lower-energy stream flow entering the north end of the bay or periods of ponding. Ponding may have been induced by vegetative stabilization or, during European settlement, by the construction of *saliña* walls, which slowed the velocity of runoff entering the bay and prevented sand from reaching the coring location except after heavy storms. An increase in overall sand deposition above 24 cm may be attributed to the filling of the outermost *saliña* with sediment, allowing larger clasts to more easily overtop the wall. Gravel lenses at 18–19 and 2–8 cm were likely created by the breakdown of portions of the outer wall. Sodium levels within the core gradually increased within the core

Table 7.1. Sediment Descriptions of the San Juan, Curaçao Core (Core CC09-1).

Depth (cm)	Color	OM % (LOI)	total P (ppm)	Na (ppm)	Ca (ppm)	Sand %	Silt %	Clay %	Notes
0–2	Very dark gray (5Y 3/1)	15.8	430	7592	4125	21	74	5	Sandy organic silt
2–8	Olive brown (2.5Y 4/3)	4.5							Silt and angular gravel (wall fragments?)
8–9	Very dark gray (2.5Y 3/1)	14.0	470	8364	4480	5	16	79	Organic clay
9–18	Dark olive gray (5Y 2.5/1)	6.1	610	7930	4607	80	3	17	Clayey fine sand; mangrove roots
18–19									Angular gravel in matrix of dark silt
19–20	Dark olive brown (2.5Y 3/3)	7.9	760	8002	4590	74	10	16	Clayey fine sand
20–21	Dark brown (10YR 3/3)	8.1	400	7876	5388	77	8	15	Clayey coarse sand
21–24	Dark olive brown (2.5Y 3/3)	10.2	470	8069	5145	61	35	4	Clayey fine sand
24–26	Black (5Y 2.5/1)	10.8	510	10788	5632	4	9	87	Organic clay
26–46	Dark olive gray (5Y 3/2)	5.0	500	12307	6491	3	11	86	Weakly banded clay
46–56									Top of Tube 2: Hole slop
56–76	Olive gray (5Y 4/2)	5.1	600	15375	4901	3	21	76	Silty clay
76–89	Dark olive gray (5Y 3/2)	4.0	580	14898	4824	4	11	85	Clay

(continued)

Table 7.1. (continued)

Depth (cm)	Color	OM % (LOI)	total P (ppm)	Na (ppm)	Ca (ppm)	Sand %	Silt %	Clay %	Notes
89–102	Black (Gley N 2.5/N)	11.8	510	14233	5240	7	24	69	Silty organic clay
102–105	Very dark gray (Gley N 3/N)	10.2	440	14460	4997	71	23	6	Silty organic sand
105–124	Black (Gley N 2.5/N)	12.3	400	13721	5109	6	21	73	Silty organic clay
124–126	Black (Gley N 2.5/N)	11.5	430	14025	7212	9	19	72	Silty organic clay with many small shells
126–134	Black (10Y 2.5/1)	10.4	480	12145	5389	21	9	70	Top of Tube 3: sandy organic clay
134–157	Dark olive gray (5Y 3/2)	5.1	530	13652	4768	6	71	23	Silt
157–173	Green black (10GY 2.5/1)	8.8	500	13427	5166	5	73	22	Clayey organic silt
173–178	Dark gray green (Gley 10Y 3/1)	6.9	470	13029	5382	18	76	6	Sandy organic silt
178–186	Black (Gley N 2.5/N)	9.7	410	12642	7948	17	79	4	Organic silt with many small shells (1)
186–196	Black (Gley N 2.5/N)	8.2	360	12016	6390	5	20	75	Silty organic clay; less shells
196–213	Black (Gley N 2.5/N)	8.7	380	11049	7435	24	74	2	Sandy organic silt with many shells (2)
213–214									Top of Tube 4; Hole slop
214–223	Black (5Y 2.5/2)	8.0	420	13013	5229	3	15	82	Laminated silty organic clay
223–225	Greenish black (10Y 2.5/1)	9.1	390	12814	5160	4	84	12	Organic silt

(continued)

Table 7.1. (continued)

Depth (cm)	Color	OM % (LOI)	total P (ppm)	Na (ppm)	Ca (ppm)	Sand %	Silt %	Clay %	Notes
225–226	Black (5Y 2.5/2)	9.2	410	13156	5471	5	15	80	Silty organic clay
226–238	Greenish black (10Y 2.5/1)	8.5	400	13339	6227	4	85	11	Organic silt
238–250	Black (Gley N 2.5/N)	9.7	330	12320	8018	67	25	8	Sandy organic silt with many shells
250–254	Black (Gley N 2.5/N)	10.2	310	12801	5444	3	18	79	Organic silty clay
254–259	Black (Gley N 2.5/N)	9.5	340	12002	7847	12	20	68	Organic silty clay with shells (3)
259–280	Black (Gley N 2.5/N)	10.7	320	10870	5025	11	85	4	Organic silt
280–291	Greenish black (Gley10Y2.5/1)	9.8	420	9765	6104	81	17	2	Organic silty sand with shells (4)
291–297	Greenish black (Gley10Y2.5/1)	10.5	310	10634	5943	3	90	7	Organic silt
297–301	Greenish black (Gley10Y2.5/1)	10.0	260	10198	7540	83	15	2	Organic silty sand with shells (5)
301–305	Black (Gley N 2.5/N)	10.6	240	10412	5351	5	89	6	Organic silt
305–306	Greenish black (Gley10Y2.5/1)	9.8	250	10035	7628	88	8	4	Organic fine sand with shells (6)
306–309	Black (Gley N 2.5/N)	9.9	230	10381	4969	6	82	12	Organic silt; Cal. date range: 1069 ± 27 BP [896–1020 AD]
309–311	Black (Gley N 2.5/N)	11.1	220	10101	4878	78	11	11	Organic medium sand

Notes:
Shells identified by Denis Nieweg: 1) *Crassostrea rhizophorae* (juv.), *Brachidontes exustus* (adult), *Tagelus* sp. (juv.), Barnacle sp. (adult), *Corbula caribea* (adult), *Chione cancellata* (juv.), *Anomalocardia brasiliana* (juv.), 2) *Melongena melongena* (juv.), *Tagelus* sp. (juv.), *Corbula caribea* (adult), *Chione cancellata* (juv.), *Spengleria rostrata* (juv.), *Macoma* sp. (juv.),
3) *Tagelus* sp. (adult), *Batillaria minima* (juv.), 4) *Batillaria minima* (adult), *Cerithium* sp. (juv.), *Brachidontes exustus* (adult), 5) *Brachidontes exustus* (adult), 6) *Tagelus* sp. (adult), *Chione cancellata* (juv. and adult)

from about 10,000 ppm at 311 cm to a peak of more than 15,000 ppm at 56–76 cm. This rise in sodium probably reflects greater amounts of ponding within the north end of the bay, especially that induced by colonial-era wall construction. Above 56 cm sodium levels declined markedly, probably due to sedimentation of the outer *saliña*, which allowed more freshwater runoff to reach the coring location. Organic matter within the core ranged from a high of 15.8 percent near the surface to a low of 4.0 percent at 76–89 cm. Overall, the amount of organic matter within the core was about 8.1 percent, with the remaining sediment largely consisting of clastic terrestrial material.

Shells from strata between 180 and 310 cm were identified by Denis Nieweg (Leiden University). All identifiable taxa are characteristic of sandy or muddy intertidal mangrove habitats (tab. 7.1). The notable decline in shells above 180 cm may be a product of accelerating sedimentation and habitat destruction.

Organic matter near the base at 308–309 cm produced a date of ca. A.D. 975 (tab. 7.2). This date falls within the Early Ceramic Age (Dabajuroid) on Curaçao, contemporaneous with the San Juan archaeological site lying upstream from the coring location (Haviser 1987). The lower strata within the core clearly contain information relating to the precolonial environment of San Juan Bay. A date of ca. A.D. 1305 was obtained from charcoal at a depth of 245 cm (Late Ceramic Age).

In total, thirty-two samples from Core CC09-1 were processed and counted for pollen. Preservation was good, but low pollen concentrations coupled with high concentrations of charcoal made pollen counting difficult. At least seventy plant taxa were identified, and concentration values ranged from 3,040 to 44,793 fossil grains/ml of sediment. Slightly lower concentration values in parts of the core probably reflect faster sedimentation rates.

The basal zone (308–240 cm) was dominated by sedges and grasses, with some woodland elements including *Celtis, Machaerium,* and other arboreal types (fig. 7.3). Both pollen and charcoal concentration values were high in this section, indicating low sedimentation rates. High charcoal counts are consistent with human settlement and clearing, although weedy pollen types often associated with agricultural clearing, including Asteraceae, *Borreria,* and Cheno-Ams, are all reduced in this zone (tab. 7.3, 7.4). Cyperaceae and Poaceae include invasive species associated with cleared, open, and frequently fired areas. High pollen concentrations of these taxa were present in the basal zone. Agricultural activities in the area are indicated by the presence of a single *Zea mays* grain in the basal sample from 305 cm. This zone probably reflects the late prehistoric period.

Table 7.2. Radiocarbon Dates from the Curaçao Cores.

Core Location	Lab Sample Number	Core Number/Sample Depth	^{14}C Age (BP)[a]	^{13}C/^{12}C Ratio	2-Sigma Calibrated Date Range[b]	Median Cal Date
Spanish Waters	AA92659	SW09-1, 95cm, OS[c]	1790±40	-25.2	AD 130–340/1620–1820 BP	AD 235/1715 BP
Spanish Waters	AA90821	SW09-1, 157–158cm, PW[d]	3970±45	-25.0	2620–2310 BC/4260–4570 BP	2490 BC/4440 BP
Spanish Waters	AA84144	SW09-1, 223cm, PW	4850±40	-25.4	3710–3530 BC/5480–5660 BP	3645 BC/5595 BP
San Juan	AA92660	CC09-1, 245cm, OS	680±35	-14.3	AD 1270–1390/560–680 BP	AD 1305/650 BP
San Juan	AA84145	CC09-1, 308–309 cm, OS	1070±30	-17.5	AD 900–1020/930–1050 BP	AD 975/975 BP

a. 1-sigma range.
b. Dates were calibrated using the IntCal13 method of CALIB ver. 7.0 (Reimer et al. 2013).
c. Organic sediment.
d. Preserved wood.

166 • Chapter 7

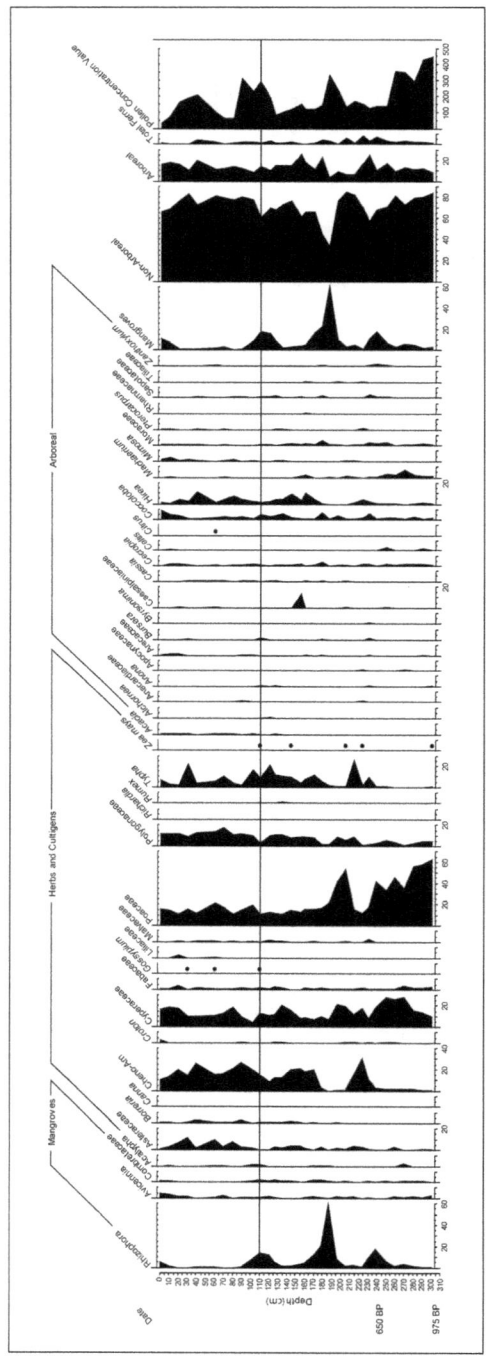

Figure 7.3. San Juan Bay, Curaçao, core pollen-percentage diagram. Pollen and charcoal concentrations are expressed as grains and fragments, respectively, per cm³ of sediment.

Table 7.3. Ethnobotanical Associations and Disturbance Indicators Represented in the Curaçao Cores.[a]

Taxon	Ethnobotanical Association or Disturbance Indicator	Core SW09-1	Core CC09-1
MANGROVE			
Avicennia	Black mangrove. Throat pains, incontinence.	X[b]	X[b]
Combretaceae	White mangrove. Slows bleeding.	X[b]	X[b]
Rhizophora	Red mangrove. Diarrhea, fever, malaria, excellent fuel wood.	X	X
HERBS/CULTIGENS			
Asteraceae	Aster or Composite family. Herbs and shrubs. Many are invasive weed species of cleared open areas.	X[b]	X
Borreria	Weedy herb in Madder family. Alkaloid and iridoid extracts have medicinal properties.		X
Cactaceae	Cactus. Some produce edible fruits.	X[b]	
Cheno-Ams	Chenopod and amaranth families. Favor disturbed or open habitats. Young greens and mature seeds are edible. Includes seablite, saltwort, chenopod, amaranth.	X[b]	X
Croton	Some produce a latex used for medicinal purposes.	X[b]	X[b]
Cyperaceae, *Cladium*	Sedge family. Grasslike herbaceous plants, many are weeds that invade cleared open areas.	X[b]	X
Fabaceae, *Desmodium*	Wild herbaceous legumes. Includes cohoba, edible beans. Species include plants with medicinal uses and for producing narcotic snuff, edible fruit, and fish poison.	X[b]	X
Gossypium	Cotton. Fibers used for textiles and cordage.		X[b]
Liliaceae	Lily. Bulbs of some are edible.		X[b]
Bombacaceae/ Malvaceae	Mallow family. Some have medicinal properties, others fruits and leaves are edible. Cotton (*Gossypium*) is in this family.	X[b]	X
Marantaceae, Maranta, Calathea		X[b]	
Poaceae	Grass family. Often associated with areas frequently fired. Edible starchy grains.	X	X
Polygonaceae, *Polygonum*	Knotweed. Some species have edible leaves.	X[b]	X

(continued)

Table 7.3. *(continued)*

Taxon	Ethnobotanical Association or Disturbance Indicator	Core SW09-1	Core CC09-1
Typha	Cattail. Colonizing plants to newly cleared wetlands. Edible rhizomes.	X	X
Zea mays, Zea spp.	Maize. Edible grain.		X[b]
ARBOREAL			
Acacia	Young spines used to relieve gum and tooth pain.		X
Alchornea	Many species have medicinal properties.	X[b]	X[b]
Anacardiaceae, *Anacardium*, *Spondias* sp.	Cashew family. Edible fruit, hogplum.	X	X[b]
Anona	In the pawpaw family. Edible fruits.		X[b]
Apocynaceae	Dogbane family. Golden trumpet vine. Fibers used for cordage. Some produce edible flowers.		X[b]
Arecaceae	Palm family. Edible fruit, thatching, cordage, needles, posts.	X	X[b]
Cecropia	Pumpwood. Fast-growing colonizing trees common to disturbed forest habitats and clearings.	X	X
Celtis	Hackberry, edible fruit.		X[b]
Citrus	Edible fruit.		X[b]
Coccoloba	Sea grape. Edible fruit, medicinal.	X	X
Hirea	Liana. Used for cordage.	X[b]	X
Moraceae, *Ficus*, *Brosimum*	Mulberry family. Edible fruit, breadnut, medicinal. Often colonize open cleared areas.	X	X[b]
Sapindaceae	Soapberry family. Fruits and seeds of some are edible, others poisonous.	X[b]	
Sapotaceae, *Chrysophyllum*, *Sideroxylon*	Sapote family. Edible fruit, medicinal, latex in some species. Includes edible fruits of chicle, sapote, lucuma.	X[b]	X[b]
Sebastiana	Flowers, leaves edible of some species.	X[b]	

a. See Table 5.5 for the sources of information.
b. Trace amounts.

The middle zone from 240 to 110 cm reflects a time of probable agricultural intensification. Maize pollen was present in four samples and increases in the weedy taxa Asteraceae, *Borreria,* Cheno-Ams, Malvaceae, Polygonaceae, and *Rumex* were documented. Decreases in pollen and charcoal concentrations reflect a faster sedimentation rate, consistent

Table 7.4. Plant Taxa Identified in the Curaçao Cores with No Documented Ethnobotanical or Anthropogenic Correlates Other than Perhaps Fuel Wood, Especially Arboreal Taxa.

Taxon	Common Name	Core SW09-1	Core CC09-1
HERBS/CULTIGENS			
Acalypha	Copperleaf, flowering shrub	X	
Polygonaceae, *Gymnopodium*	Common sorrel	X[a]	
ARBOREAL			
Machaerium	Escambrón, spiny climbing shrub or small tree. Form thickets in mangrove swamps.	X[a]	X
Pterocarpus	Swamp bloodwood tree. Grows in swamp forests, mainly on landward side of mangrove.	X	X
Quercus	Oak		
Trema	Elm trees. Small evergreens growing in open forests or clearings.	X	
Zanthoxylum	Prickly ash	X	X
FERNS			
Unknown ferns		X	X

a. Trace amounts.

with increased sediment runoff due to deforestation (tab. 7.5). *Rhizophora* (red mangrove) pollen appears in cyclic fashion throughout the zone, with higher concentrations when agricultural activity was reduced. *Rhizophora* may indicate periods when the local environment became too saline for crop production. The transition between the middle and upper zones may be coincident with initial European colonization of Curaçao.

The upper zone from 110 to 0 cm is marked by a near-complete reduction in mangroves; disturbance indicators of sedges and grasses remain high. Maize pollen is lacking and is replaced with *Gossypium* (cotton) pollen. A single *Citrus* (orange, lemon) pollen grain indicates that these sediments were deposited during colonial or later times, as this genus is Old World in origin. The low concentrations of both pollen and charcoal again reflect a faster sedimentation rate.

Phytoliths were well represented in all of the tested samples from Core CC09-1, with six producing 200-counts (figs. 7.4a, 7.4b). Phytolith influx was not uniform during the thousand years of deposition represented: low influx occurred around 150 cm and at the top of the core. Sponge spicules and diatoms were not common in the core.

Table 7.5. Sedimentation Rates for the Curaçao Cores.

Core/^{14}C sample depths	^{14}C Date Ranges (Median Cal Dates, BP)	Sedimentation Rate (cm/yr)
SW09-1, 0–95 cm	0–1715	.0553
SW09-1, 95–157 cm	1715–4440	.0227
SW09-1, 157–223 cm	4440–5595	.0571
CC09-1, 0–245 cm	0–650	.3769
CC09-1, 245–308 cm	650–975	.1928

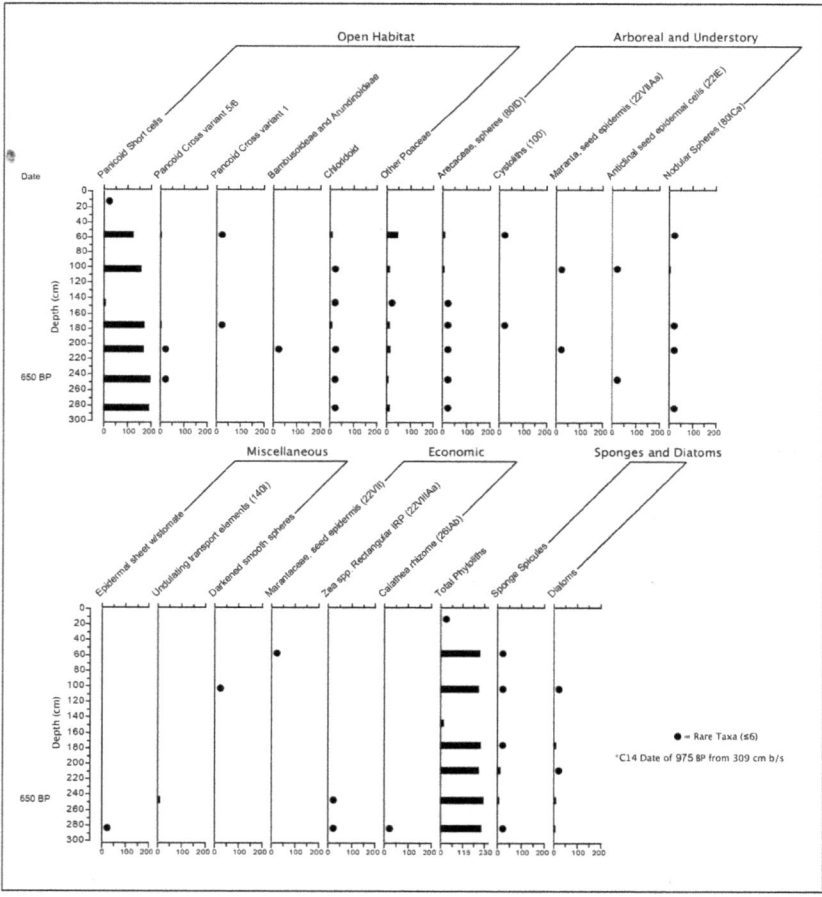

Figure 7.4a. San Juan Bay, Curaçao, core phytolith diagram: resolved.

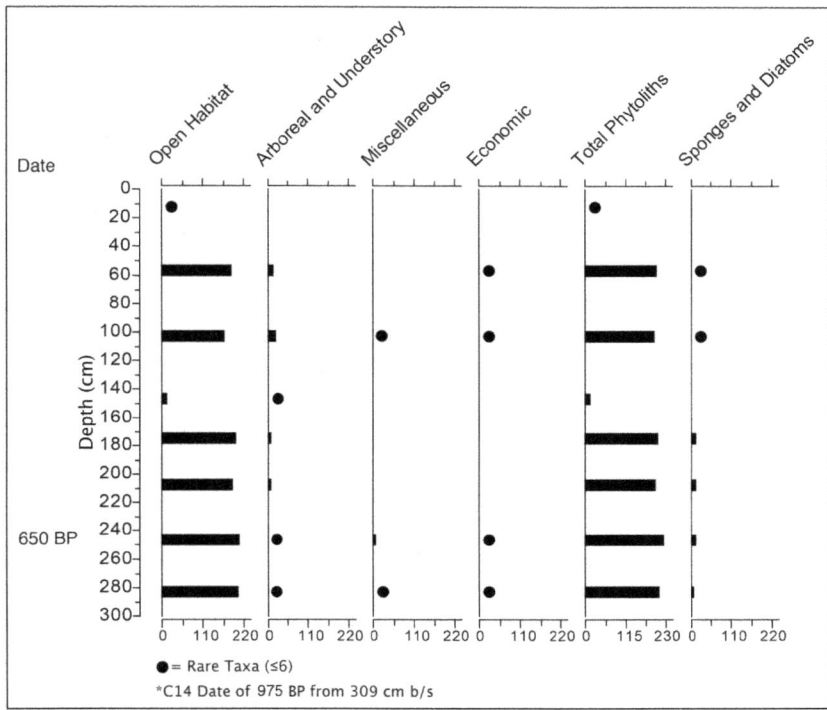

Figure 7.4b. San Juan Bay, Curaçao, core phytolith diagram: composite.

The overall pattern of phytolith occurrence is for open habitat indicators, interrupted by an interval of low influx in the middle of the core. Panicoid grasses dominated all productive samples and two Variant 1 crosses were recovered at 55–60 cm and 173–178 cm. While they were too small to be definitively identified as maize, maize pollen was identified in strata above and below the Variant 1 crosses and two maize cob phytoliths were recovered in the two lowest samples. Marantaceae phytoliths occurred in five samples, including the oldest analyzed, evidence that arrowroot and/or leren may have been cultivated. Four *Maranta* seed phytoliths in levels 102–105 cm and 205–210 cm further indicate arrowroot, and *Calathea* is represented by a rhizome phytolith in the deepest sample. Phytolith results suggest cultivation of arrowroot, leren, and maize in the context of an open environment with palms.

Spaanse Water (Core SW09-1)

Spaanse Water is a large, many-fingered bay situated on the southeastern coast of Curaçao (fig. 7.1). Archaeologically the bay is known for the

172 • *Chapter 7*

large resource-extraction site, Spaanse Water, situated on a peninsula within the bay just south of our coring location in the northeastern part of the bay. Spaanse Water was initially thought to be an exclusively Archaic Age site (Haviser 1987). However, excavations have since revealed a more complex history with pulses of utilization centered on several periods: 2550–2150 B.C. (Early Archaic), 1250 B.C.–A.D. 35 (Late Archaic and transitional to Ceramic Age), and A.D. 1345–1670 (Late Ceramic Age) (Hoogland and Hofman 2011). The large Ceramic Age Santa Barbara site is located 1 km inland of the coring location. This site lies along a prominent, complex intermittent stream or *rooi*. The catchment basin for the stream system has a fairly low gradient, seasonally contributing freshwater and sediment into the embayment. The basin contains significant areas of alluvial soils suitable for manioc and maize cultivation, forming an important resource for the occupants of Santa Barbara (Haviser 1987). A natural spring is located near the shoreline of the bay, creating a further amenity for settlement.

Soils in the watershed contributing mineral sediment to Spaanse Water are chiefly shallow, sandy Inceptisols formed on igneous and clastic sedimentary parent materials. However, the Spaanse Water catchment is also flanked by one large limestone hill on which have formed skeletal Entisols (on steep slopes) and deeper Aridisols with well-developed caliche (on stable surfaces) (De Vries 2000). Vegetation is xerophytic dry forest and scrub with a preponderance of cacti. Many land surfaces show evidence of historical and modern degradation in the form of surface truncation and gully development. Sedimentation in the bay has been altered since colonial times by wall construction.

In the Dutch colonial era, the eastern shore was part of the ranching-centered Santa Barbara plantation. The small embayment where we cored is partially surrounded by a limestone and mortar colonial wall. The core was taken from the end of what appeared to be a colonial stone pier connected to the wall and projecting into the bay. The presence of the wall on the landward side of the embayment is likely to have reduced the amount of colonial-era sediment entering the bay. The wall continues to shield this section of the bay from sedimentation, including that generated by development of the Santa Barbara plantation into an upscale condo-golf-marina complex in 2009. There is some black mangrove fringing the coast of the embayment. Red mangrove is well established on a barrier island about 30 m offshore from the coring site.

The core reached a depth of 230 cm, bottoming out in highly gleyed silty clay (tab. 7.6). Organic matter near the base of the core at 223 cm produced a date of ca. 3645 B.C. (tab. 7.2), around the time humans likely first arrived on Curaçao (Haviser 1987, 2001b). The lowest levels of the core (below 208 cm) reflect an estuarine environment dominated by terrestrial sediment deposition. Steadily rising sea levels are reflected in the sediments between 208 and 180 cm, most notably in the rise of sodium levels peaking between 180 and 190 cm (tab. 7.6). Above 180 cm sediments in the core reflect more stable sea-level conditions and the establishment of a brackish slack-water depositional environment, consistent with the fibric red mangrove-derived peat in several strata. Shells found within strata between 100 and 144 cm (identified by Denis Nieweg) all are found in intertidal mangrove habitats (tab. 7.6). Marls are found at depths of 54–55, 86–92, and 131–137 cm. The marl layers are likely autochthonous biogenic sediments forming either within algal mats or via pelletization during episodes of Ca supersaturation within stagnant, near-shore backwater contexts.

Human landscape disturbance is most evident in the core between 36 and 54 cm represented by pulses of sandy and silty sediments and steadily rising phosphate levels. These levels are most likely associated with colonial-era land clearance and land use. Human inputs are also probably associated with increased phosphate levels between 86 and 100 cm, possibly reflecting the establishment of the Ceramic Age site of Santa Barbara inland and upstream from the coring site. A lower increase in P levels and increased silt inputs between 137 and 157 cm may reflect human landscape disturbance associated with the nearby Archaic site of Spaanse Water. Three radiocarbon dates were obtained from the core (tab. 7.2).

In total, nineteen samples were processed and counted for pollen from the core (fig. 7.5). Pollen preservation was excellent and at least sixty-three taxa were identified. Concentration values ranged from 7,766 to 74,878 fossil grains/ml of sediment.

Four pollen zones were defined (fig. 7.5). These zones were empirically obvious; however, they have also been identified through a constrained sum of squares analysis. The basal zone, 220–180 cm, represents a swamp-forest environment, dominated by pollen from *Coccoloba* (sea grape), *Bursera* (Gumbo limbo), and Combretaceae (white mangroves). Swamp forests are regions where plant roots might be seasonally submerged, and are usually located immediately behind and somewhat higher than the mangrove zones. White mangroves are abundant in this zone, and in fact, may often be a dominant type. Other associated taxa included *Zanthoxylum* (prickly ash), *Sebastiana*-type (white poisonwood), *Gymnopodium,* and Anacardiaceae (cashew family). *Typha* (cattail), somewhat removed from the depositional area, is less represented in the pollen record. Charcoal concentrations were reduced, suggesting minimal human activity in the area.

Table 7.6. Sediment Descriptions of the Spaanse Water, Curaçao Core (Core SW09-1).

Depth (cm)	Color	%OM (LOI)	Total P (ppm)	Na (ppm)	Ca (ppm)	Sand %	Silt %	Clay %	Notes
0–24	Greenish black (Gley 10Y 2.5/1)	46.2	650	41352	17210	29	30	41	Sapric muck
24–36	Dark green gray (10Y 4/1)	47.5	480	38456	16784				Hemic muck
36–36.5	Dark olive brown (2.5Y 3/3)	38.7							Fibric peat and coarse sand
36.5–45	Olive (5Y 5/3)	29.3	210	40188	18111	43	11	46	Sandy organic clay; some mangrove roots
45–54	Light olive gray (5Y 6/2)	19.1	140	39139	16935	45	35	20	Sandy silt with some fibric layers and roots
54–55	Dark olive brown (2.5Y 3/3)			30645	45412	62	9	29	Sandy marl
55–72	Very dark brown (10YR 2/2)	52.6	120	37867	15715	39	21	40	Fibric and hemic peat
72–80									Top of Tube 2; hole slop
80–86	Greenish black (Gley 10Y 2.5/1)	53.7							Sapric OM; might be hole slop
86–92	Light olive gray (5Y 6/2)	4.1	220	26971	42586	44	16	40	Marl; mangrove roots
92–100	Light olive gray/black	9.2	200	31482	23160	50	12	38	Churned marl and hemic OM; storm mixing or bioturbation
100–124	Very dark brown (10YR 2/2)	55.7	130	35330	19276	61	17	22	Hemic and fibric peat; shell fragments (1)
124–131	Pale olive (5Y 6/3)	15.2	<100	34746	18549	74	14	12	Organic sand

(continued)

Table 7.6. (continued)

Depth (cm)	Color	%OM (LOI)	Total P (ppm)	Na (ppm)	Ca (ppm)	Sand %	Silt %	Clay %	Notes
131–137	Very pale brown (10YR 7/3)	1.2	120	29196	72468	36	34	30	Sandy marl; cemented lenses; 1 shell (2)
137–139									Finely laminated peat and gleyed silt
139–144	Grayish green (Gley 5G 5/2)	22.0	100	34621	30136	11	55	34	Silt; large shell fragment (3)
144–157	Greenish gray (Gley 10Y 5/1)	14.0	130	33924	22860	14	25	61	Silty clay
157–158									Wood
158–165	Dark brown (10YR 3/2)	60.1							Top of Tube 3; Sandy saprist; may be hole slop
165–180	Very dark brown (10YR 2/2)	48.4							Hemic peat
180–190	Very dark brown/pale olive	29.3	110	62128	84592	71	19	10	Laminated peat and organic sand
190–201	Pale olive (5Y 6/3)	13.7	<100	58299	41934	69	17	14	Organic sand
201–208	Very pale brown (10YR 7/3)	8.0	110	41647	33075	68	12	20	Sandy marl
208–217	Greenish gray (Gley 10Y 5/1)	9.8	240	35444	24189	13	44	43	Clayey silt
217–219	Very dark brown (10YR 2/2)	58.1							Fibric peat
219–230	Greenish gray (Gley 10Y 5/1)	10.7	220	37912	18641	26	35	39	Silty clay; charcoal

Notes:
Shells identified by Denis Nieweg:
1. *Brachidontes exustus* ("Scorched Mussel"); mangrove habitat.
2. Juvenile of the Tellinidae family.
3. *Melampus coffens*; mangrove habitat.

176 • Chapter 7

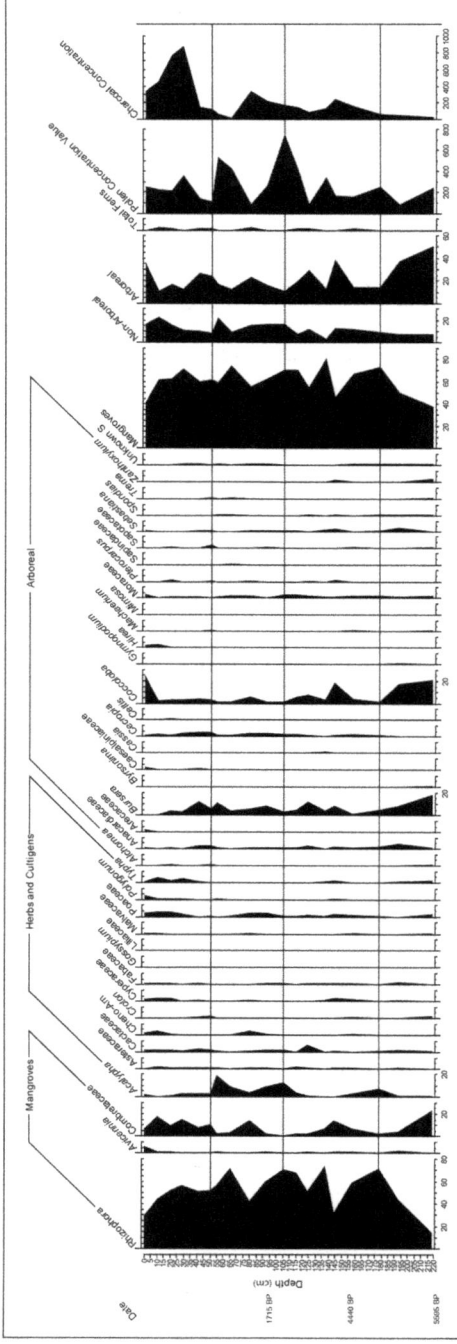

Figure 7.5. Spaanse Water, Curaçao, core pollen-percentage diagram. Pollen and charcoal concentrations are expressed as grains and fragments, respectively, per cm³ of sediment.

The next zone, 180–110 cm, is characterized by a notable increase in red mangrove pollen. This increase may be a product of sea-level rise or coastal subsidence, either of which could lead to slight salinization of the area, making the environment more favorable for salt-tolerant red mangroves. Swamp-forest types were reduced and *Cecropia* (trumpet) pollen and particulate charcoal concentrations increased. *Cecropia* is a fast-growing colonizer, favoring forest gaps or cleared areas where it grows quickly before becoming overwhelmed by more aggressive trees. Elevated values of *Cecropia* and charcoal concentrations reflect human activities in the area.

The third zone, 110–50 cm, was marked by increases in *Acalypha* (three-seeded mercury) and other weedy taxa, including Cheno-Ams and Poaceae (grass family). These groups favor disturbed, open, or otherwise well-drained areas, and may reflect either local site abandonment or, alternatively, an expansion of cleared areas. Charcoal concentrations remained elevated through much of the zone, indicating sustained land management in the area. At 75 cm there were significant declines in charcoal particulates and grass and Cheno-Am pollen concentrations, suggesting local abandonment sometime after ca. A.D. 235.

The uppermost zone, 50–0 cm, showed major increases in particulate charcoal, Combretaceae, and disturbance taxa including Cheno-Ams, Cyperaceae, Poaceae, *Typha*, and *Cecropia*. This zone represents recent human activities in the area, including clearing, agriculture, and possibly construction. Agriculture is represented directly by the occurrence of a single *Gossypium* (cotton) pollen grain at 20 cm.

Two samples from the core produced a near 200-count for phytoliths (figs. 7.5a, 7.5b). One was from the uppermost level and the other from 144 to 155 cm. The core midsection, 130–190 cm, otherwise lacked phytolith influx. At 144–155 cm palm phytoliths dominated the phytolith assemblage, with a significant contribution from Marantaceae (nodular spheres). This contribution may have come from cultivated arrowroot or leren. Marantaceae phytoliths were first documented at 188–193 cm. The interpretation of cultivation is supported by the pollen data. Pollen from *Cercopia,* an early colonizer in deforested areas, and elevated charcoal values identified in this section of the core may reflect forest clearing for cultivation.

At the top of the core panicoid grass phytoliths dominated the assemblage, with minor contributions from palm and Marantaceae, including a tentatively identified seed body. An open habitat with scattered trees is indicated, which is consistent with the pollen data. No Variant 1 crosses or other maize indicators were present; other panicoid grasses contributed to the observed assemblage.

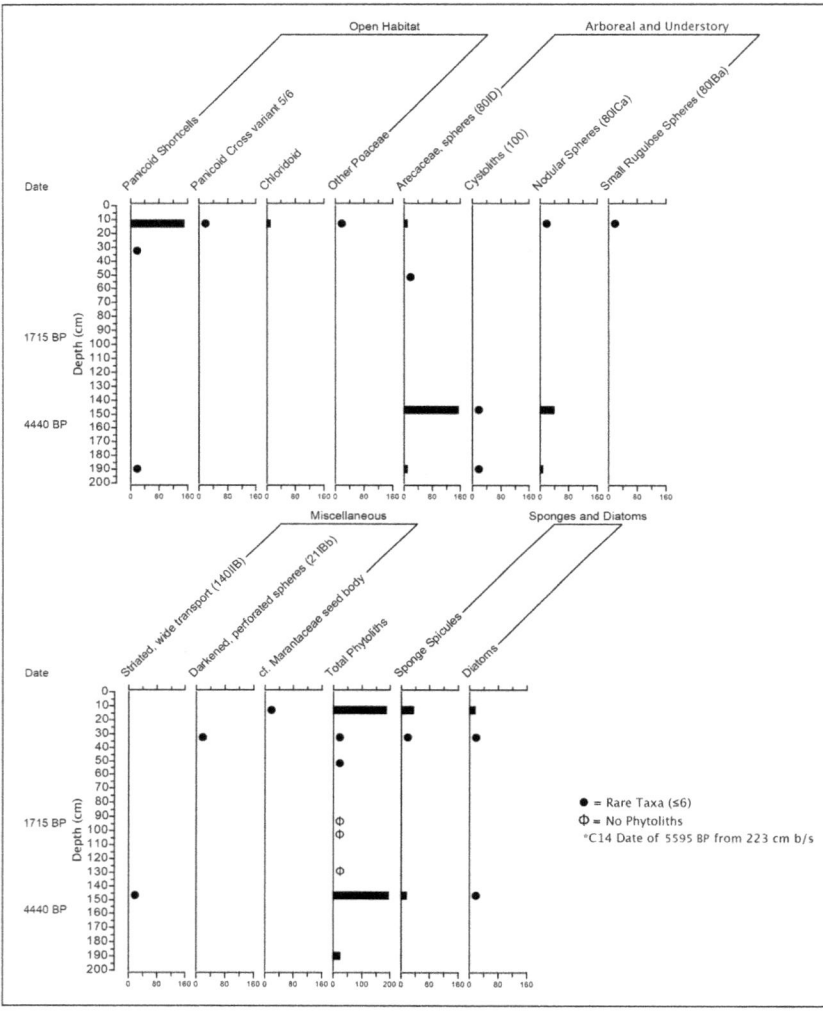

Figure 7.6a. Spaanse Water, Curaçao, core phytolith diagram: resolved.

Discussion

Core SW09-1 reached a total depth of 230 cm, with a near-basal date of ca. 3645 B.C. In contrast, Core CC09-1 was 311 cm deep and dated to ca. A.D. 975. The discrepancy in age versus depth between the two cores reflects variation in drainage-basin geometries, resulting in markedly different sedimentation rates (tab. 7.5). The San Juan Bay drainage is dominated by steeply sloping terrain and a high-gradient stream,

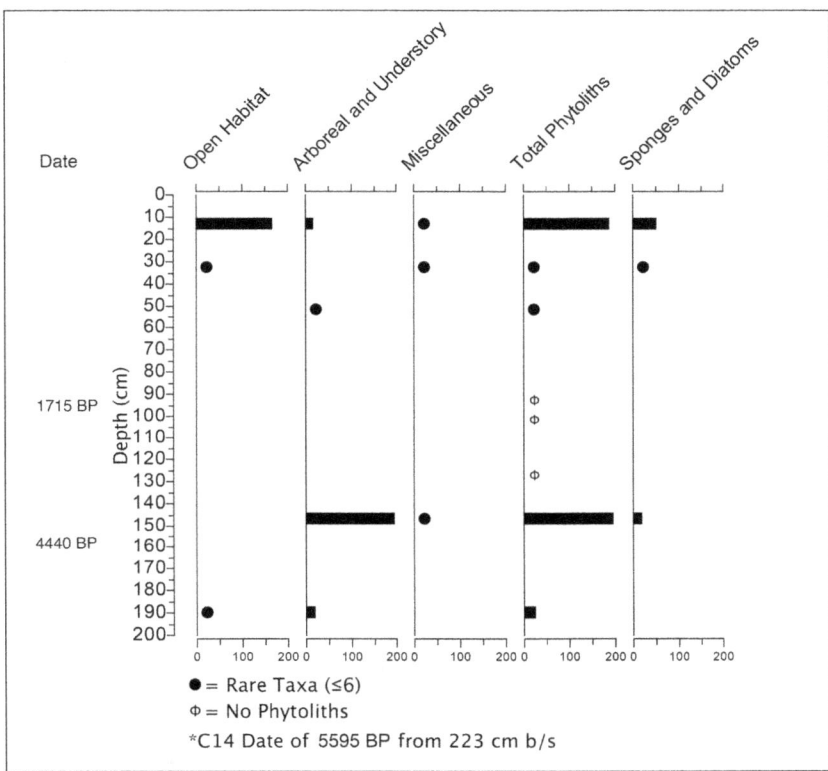

Figure 7.6b. Spaanse Water, Curaçao, core phytolith diagram: composite.

whereas the Spaanse Water/Santa Barbara drainage is characterized by gently rolling terrain feeding into a low-gradient intermittent stream. Soil erosion rates were high in the San Juan drainage basin both in precolonial and colonial times as reflected in the formation of a broad estuary at the north end of the bay and alluvial deposits along stream banks above the estuary. In contrast, sediment accumulation at the northeast end of Spaanse Water remained slow (also reflected by episodes of biogenic marl formation) with only moderate acceleration in colonial times. Colonial wall constructions clearly affected sediment deposition in both coring locations. The wall system at San Juan Bay was overwhelmed by inflowing sediments with a series of *saliñas* filling in over time.

Pollen preservation and productivity was good in both cores. Phytolith preservation and productivity was good in the CC09-1 core and variable in the SW09-1 core. The lowermost portions of SW09-1 predate by two hundred to eight hundred years the oldest-known documented human occupations on Curaçao and represent a landscape dominated by swamp forest, likely in an estuarine setting. Between ca. 5600 and 3500 cal yr B.P., gradually rising sea levels in the western Atlantic (Toscano and Macintyre 2003) slowly induced changes within Spaanse Water. At the northeast end of the inlet, sediment aggradation and ponding resulted in biogenic marl deposition and offshore sediment bars colonized with red mangrove. Around 3500 cal yr B.P., the first signs of human landscape disturbances were indicated by increases in silty sediment with elevated phosphate levels, increased levels of charcoal, *Cecropia* (trumpet) pollen, and Marantaceae (nodular spheres). These disturbance indicators likely are associated with the establishment of the nearby Archaic site of Spaanse Water. Although the subsistence economy of this site was clearly oriented toward the extraction of marine protein, it may be that some form of early horticulture was also practiced. *Cecropia* pollen and increased charcoal indicate nearby forest clearance, perhaps for the cultivation of arrowroot or leren as indicated by the Marantaceae (nodular spheres). Although this evidence for early horticulture is inconclusive, it contributes to a growing body of information suggestive of more widespread plant domestication or perhaps plant encouragement in the West Indies during the Archaic (Newsom and Wing 2004). Examination of Archaic grinding tool surfaces for starch grains could prove illuminating as it has elsewhere in the Caribbean (e.g., Pagán-Jiménez et al. 2005; Pagán-Jiménez et al. 2015). After roughly 3500 cal yr B.P., the near-shore environment appears to have been geomorphically stable, probably reflecting the persistence of a mangrove colonized baymouth bar. Terrestrial sediment deposition is periodically interrupted by episodes of biogenic marl formation typical of such lagoons. The Archaic Age disturbance indicators eventually declined, perhaps reflecting a period of abandonment of the Spaanse Water site. Sometime after 1800 cal yr B.P. (perhaps several hundred years later), there is a marked acceleration in land disturbance, likely associated with the establishment of the Ceramic Age site of Santa Barbara upstream of the coring location as well as reutilization of Spaanse Water. Disturbance indicators included increased phosphates, elevated charcoal levels, and pollen from *Acalypha* (three-seeded mercury) and other weedy taxa including Cheno-Ams and Poaceae (grass), all reflective of disturbed or otherwise opened area. This land clearance was likely associated with expanding agricultural land. The uppermost section of the core exhibits both phytolith and pollen evidence for widespread land clearance as would be expected in the colonial and modern eras.

Ceramic Age and colonial land use are more abundantly represented in the CC09-1 core. Sedimentation rates appear to have been relatively low near the base of the core reflecting the period around 1000 B.P., though abundant charcoal and one grain of maize pollen indicate nearby horticulture. Later precolonial sediments reflect accelerating land clearance, increased soil erosion, and cultivation of arrowroot, leren, and maize amidst an abundance of cleared land. The colonial era is marked by increased indications of land clearance, the disappearance of maize, and the introduction of cotton. A single grain of citrus pollen from the colonial era potentially indicates the introduction of Laraha, or bitter orange, the peel of which is used to flavor Curaçao's eponymous liquor.

8

Barbados

*Nicholas P. Dunning, John G. Jones,
Deborah M. Pearsall, and Peter E. Siegel*

> The island was so grown with wood that there could be found no champions, or savannas, for men to dwell in.
> Richard Ligon 1657, quoted in Watts 1966: 21

Background

Barbados is the most isolated of the Antillean islands, lying some 145 km east of St. Vincent and 210 km north-northeast of Tobago (fig. 1.1). This isolation initially limited the diversity of flora and fauna and shaped the processes of environmental change on the island between its first settlement around four thousand years ago and the colonial era. We review pertinent aspects of island physical geography, archaeology, and history followed by a discussion of the core results.

Barbados is located in an emergent portion of the Lesser Antilles forearc, an ill-defined, largely submarine ridge lying east of and parallel to the Lesser Antilles volcanic island arc along the subduction zone marking the boundary between the Caribbean and South American tectonic plates (Muhs 2001). The island is 440 km^2 in area (fig. 8.1). An underlying core of Tertiary clastic sedimentary rock is aerially exposed only in the northeast section of the island (the Scotland District). The remaining 85 percent of exposed rocks on the island consists of Quaternary limestones that originated as coral reefs. Episodic tectonic uplift has elevated these reefs in a step-like manner, manifest in a series of topographic terraces visible on the landscape. The highest terraces date to approximately 700,000 years ago and the lowest to about 80,000 years ago (Broeker et al. 1968; Fairbanks 1989; Muhs 2001). The island reaches a maximum elevation of 340 m at Hillaby Peak. Limestone dissolution processes have created a variety of karst landforms including sinkholes (dolines) and caves, particularly on the upper, older terraces, though some sinkholes have also developed on the lower ones (Day 1983).

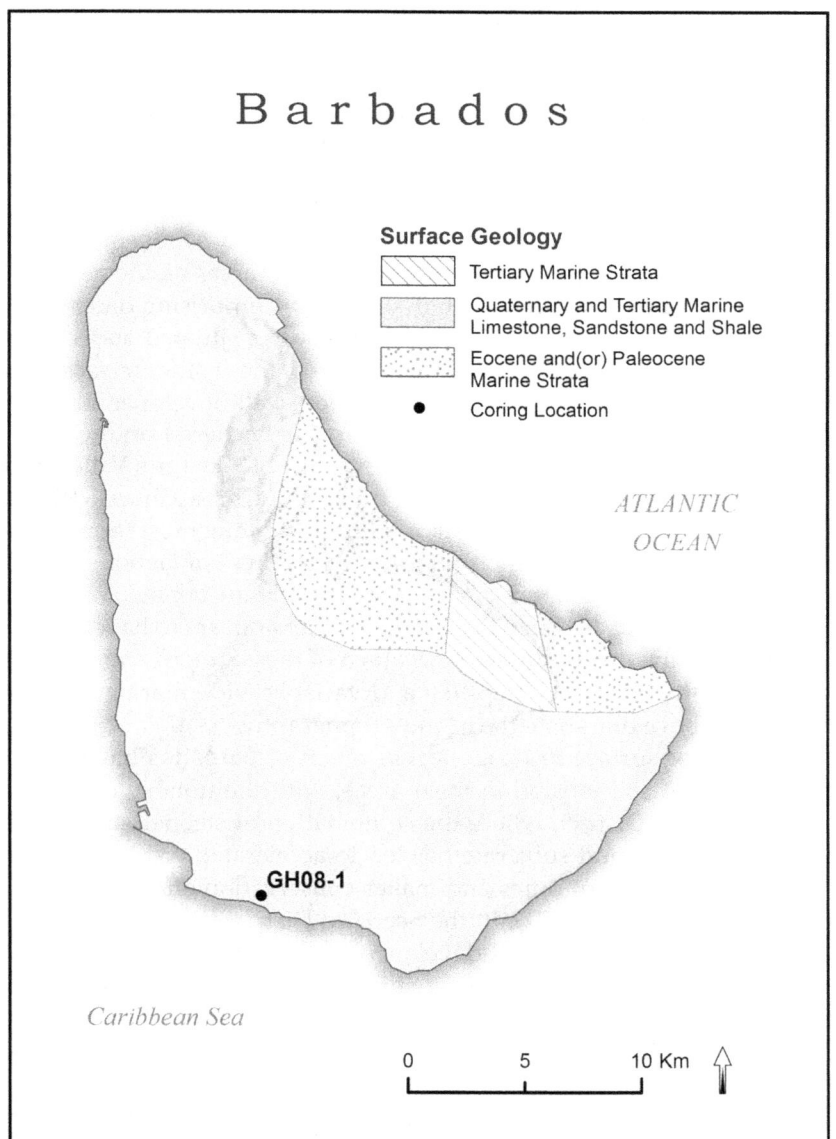

Figure 8.1. Map of Barbados showing the surface geology and coring location.

Drainage on the marine reefs is chiefly internal because of high limestone porosity and the presence of sinkholes; westward-flowing stream systems are not well developed. Within the Scotland District, deep fluvial dissection has taken place and steeply graded streams cascade eastward into the ocean.

Nine physiographic areas and several subareas have been outlined for Barbados (Ahmad 2011; Vernon and Carroll 1966). Most distinctive is the Scotland District that occupies much of the northeastern portion of the islands, where older clastic sedimentary strata are exposed. These relatively soft materials have been deeply eroded into a series of steep eastward-flowing drainages. Immediately to the south of the Scotland District is the Below the Cliff area where a few remnants of limestone terraces remain but steep slopes have accelerated mass movements and created long scree slopes. Surrounding these two areas on the west and south is the Above the Second High Cliff area, comprising older limestone terraces with well-developed karst features situated above a locally prominent escarpment. West and south of these older terraces lies the Below the Second High Cliff area with less well-developed karst on four semicontinuous low terraces. This area is bordered on the south by a set of structural depressions known as the St. George's Valley and St. Philip Plain and an adjacent rise called the Christ Church Ridge. The rise appears to be the product of uplift postdating most terrace formation, which resulted in the sporadic development of lagoons within the depressions. Another ancient lagoon is evident behind fossilized beach ridges on the St. Lucy Plain, an area that appears to have experienced relatively little uplift. Around much of the southern and western sections of the island the step-like and variably wide marine terraces discussed above dominate the island's topography.

The lack of surface drainage across much of Barbados has limited the severity of soil erosion in most areas, with the notable exception of the Scotland District, where the combination of steeper slopes and less-cohesive soil and substrate has led to accelerated erosion in both historical and modern times and makes conservation efforts challenging (Carson and Tam 1977). In the Scotland District, and in areas with steeper slopes and more-well-developed surface drainage, particularly in parts of western Barbados, severe historical soil erosion is evident in the form of truncated slope soils, alluvial fans, and valley fills. Soil erosion and declining fertility were problems that plagued colonial plantation agriculture on Barbados (Sheridan 1974; Watts 1987).

The climate on Barbados is tropical and maritime, with humid to subhumid precipitation ranging across the island. Island-wide rainfall averages about 1,500 mm, but varies with elevation, from slightly more than 2,000 mm at the highest elevation to less than 1,300 mm along most of the south coast. Rainfall is strongly seasonal, with about 75 percent arriving during the June to December wet season when trade winds are also pervasive under the influence of the ITCZ. Wet-season (June through December) temperatures typically range from 23° C to 30° C, while dry-season (January through May) temperatures range from 18° C to 29° C. Barbados lies south of most Atlantic hurricane tracks and strikes are rare, although historically the island was impacted by especially devastating storms in 1675, 1731, and 1780 (Mulcahy 2006). Storm deposits on the island have not been carefully studied. Tsunami deposits of unknown age have been identified on the west coast of Barbados (Scheffers and Kelletat 2006).

Data from around the Caribbean Basin indicate that regional climate has been episodically unstable over the past several thousand years, including persistent dry periods associated with shifts in the annual migration of the ITCZ (Haug et al. 2001; Hodell et al. 1991). Recent data from Anse à la Gourde, Guadeloupe, indicate climatic drying during several periods (200 B.C.–A.D. 400, A.D. 800–1000, A.D. 1300–1600) separated by intervals of wet conditions (Beets et al. 2006).

Edaphic patterns on Barbados are most closely linked to geologic parent materials (Ahmad 2011). Variations in underlying sedimentary rock structures and slope have created a relatively complex soilscape in the Scotland District. These soils are typically immature (Inceptisols) due to geomorphic instability and high erosion rates that limit the time available for pedogenic development. On the limestone marine terraces that cover most of the island, soil variation is conditioned by the relative age of the terraces and the corresponding degree of weathering of constituent clay minerals. Soils formed on older, higher-elevation terraces have been placed in the Barbadian Red Brown and Yellow Brown Associations (Ultisols) with well-developed argillic horizons featuring kaolinitic clays (Ahmad 2011; Muhs 2001; Vernon and Carroll 1966). Soils formed on younger, lower-elevation terraces belong to the Barbadian Gray Brown Association and Black Association (Vertisols and Mollisols) with less-well-developed argillic horizons comprising smectite clays.

Soils on the reef terraces were previously interpreted as residual—that is, developed from residual, noncarbonate impurities within underlying limestone (Vernon and Carroll 1966). More-recent research demonstrated that the majority of the mineral fraction of Barbadian terrace soils is derived from windblown volcanic ash from St. Vincent, trans-Atlantic Saharan silt (or dust), and possibly silt from the lower Mississippi River Valley (Muhs et al. 2007; Muhs et al. 1987).

The Below the First High Cliff and Christ Church Ridge physiographic districts are mantled primarily in soils of the Black Association: relatively shallow Mollisols and deeper Vertisols (Ahmad 2011; Muhs 2001; Vernon and Carroll 1966). These soils form a catena sequence, clearly visible in several construction-site exposures within 1 km of the Graeme Hall Nature Sanctuary (fig. 8.2). On areas with low slope, where clay sediment has accumulated and stability has provided time for a greater degree of pedogenesis, argilloturbation (shrinking, swelling, and vertical heaving) is well established in the deep smectite clay, and Vertisols are well developed (tab. 8.1). On bordering side slopes, geomorphic instability has prevented the accumulation of deeper clays, and dark Mollisols with underlying cambic or argillic horizons as well as shallower Mollisols with no B horizon (Rendolls) are most prevalent (tab. 8.2).

The middle marine terraces are mainly mantled with soils in the Black and Gray Brown Associations, again chiefly Mollisols and Vertisols (Ahmad 2011; Muhs 2001; Vernon and Carroll 1966). These soils are characterized by high cation exchange capacity and base saturation yielding high innate fertility, an important factor for early colonial period plantation agriculture (Watts 1987). Presumably, these soils were attractive to pre-European horticultural or farming groups as well. Some soils found on the uppermost terraces are less fertile; those of the Scotland District have limitations for agriculture, including lower fertility and high susceptibility to erosion.

Figure 8.2. View to the southwest from atop the first (lowest) marine terrace toward Graeme Hall wetland and the ocean beyond. Soils on the terrace and the coastal plain below are deep clay Mollisols and Vertisols that have been used for intensive sugarcane production.

Table 8.1. Description of Low Slope Soils in the Graeme Hall, Barbados Watershed.

Depth (cm)	Color	OM % (LOI)	Total P (ppm)	Na (ppm)	Ca (ppm)	Sand %	Silt %	Clay %	Notes
0–30	Black (7.5YR 2.5/1)	3.3	6	290	21560	9	5	86	A horizon; cracking to 30 cm depth
30–70	(10YR 4/1)	2.0	5	369	20421	7	3	90	ACss horizon; slickensides
70–110+	(10YR 5/2)	1.4	5	538	19663	11	6	83	Css horizon; slickensides

Table 8.2. Description of Bordering Side Slope Soils that are Geomorphically Unstable in the Graeme Hall, Barbados Watershed.

Depth (cm)	Color	OM % (LOI)	Total P (ppm)	Na (ppm)	Ca (ppm)	Sand%	Silt%	Clay%	Notes
0–15	Black (5YR 2.5/1)	4.6	15	183	19424	19	7	74	A1 horizon
15–40	Very dark gray (5YR 3/1)	4.0	14	191	19169	17	6	77	A2 horizon
40–50	(5YR 3/2)	3.9	16	265	21845	21	7	72	AC horizon; ±30% limestone gravel
50–65	(5Y 4/2)	1.0	12	364	23360	24	8	68	C horizon: ±50% limestone gravel
65+									Cr horizon: soft coral limestone

Previous research on native vegetation on Barbados comes principally from two sources: (1) early colonial accounts of island plants and (2) studies of remnant areas of largely pre-European vegetation. David Watts (1966) synthesized early European accounts of Barbados and its vegetative cover. European colonization of Barbados began in 1627.

Watts (1966) credited two early reports as particularly valuable for their description of island vegetation within three decades of British colonization: those of Sir Henry Colt (1631) and Richard Lignon (1657) (Colt and Lignon cited in Watts 1966: 166–168). By 1665 much of the Barbadian landscape had been stripped of its pre-European vegetation, though enough patches remained through the end of the seventeenth century to allow for the compilation of fourteen partial catalogues of native collected plants (Watts 1966). By 1750 timber was being imported from Tobago and St. Lucia to construct or repair sugar mills, because Barbados was then almost devoid of forest.

Early European visitors reported that most of Barbados was covered in dense tropical forest. The height, structure, and composition of the forest varied with rainfall distribution, edaphic factors, relative exposure to trade winds and tropical storms, and proximity to windblown salt along the coasts. Colt (1631) and Lignon (1657) (both cited in Watts 1966) noted that the first British settlers could find no open spaces (such as savannas) in which to place their settlements and immediately began clearing forested areas.

Historical sources combined with botanical studies of remnant native forest patches allow for a reconstruction of the late pre-Contact Barbadian landscape. The forest contained a two-story canopy structure. Prominent members of the relatively open upper canopy were deciduous species, 30–40 m in height, including *Cedrela mexicana, Ceiba pentandra, Hymenaea courbaril, Mastichidendron sloaneanum,* and *Citharexylum spinosa,* as well as the towering emergent palm *Roystonea oleracea.* Two evergreen species, *Sapium hippomane* and *Hernandia sonora,* were also likely prominent in the upper canopy. A dense lower canopy, about 20–25 m, was characterized by a complex mix of species including *Spondias mombin, Fagara* spp., *Cordia* spp., *Bursera simaruba, Chlorophoria tinctoria, Inga laurina, Dipholis salicifolia, Sapindus saponaria, Coccoloba pubescens,* and *Pimenta racemosa.* A varied understory consisted of shrubs and smaller trees, most notably *Aiphanes erosa.* This forest structure characterized the wetter and more sheltered parts of Barbados. Elsewhere, arboreal growth was retarded by pronounced seasonal moisture deficits and wind and salt exposure leading to stunted and beveled forest variants.

Smaller areas of xerophytic vegetation were also reported, including a coastal vegetation association associated with low, rocky, and sandy littoral areas. Prominent species included *Hippomane mancinella, Coccoloba uvifera, Tabebuia pallida, Caesalpinia bonduc,* and, in the driest areas, *Cephalocereus barbadensis* and *Agave barbadensis.*

Currently there is only one remaining mangrove wetland on Barbados, located in Graeme Hall. Mangroves were widely distributed in the seventeenth century (Watts 1966: 34). However, poorly developed natural surface drainage on Barbados likely limited the extent of mangroves due to the spatially constricted nature of estuarine areas. The largest area of mangroves seems to have been in the embayment that is now the harbor for Bridgetown. Based on the Graeme Hall wetland and historical accounts, *Rhizophora mangle* and *Laguncularia racemosa* predominated, with the sporadic presence of *Avicennia* spp. and *Conocarpus erectus* (Watts 1966: 37).

More than sixty pre-Columbian sites are documented for Barbados (Drewett 2000: 167–170, 2006: fig. 3). Prior to 1989, it was believed that no Archaic occupations were present on the island (Boomert 1987: 13–14; Drewett 1989a: 82). The Barbados Archaeological Survey, established in 1984 under the direction of the late Peter L. Drewett, greatly expanded our understanding of the prehistory of the island, including documentation of Archaic occupations (Drewett 1986, 1987, 1988, 1989a, 1989b, 1991, 1993, 1996/1997, 2000, 2002, 2006; Hackenberger 1988; Hinds, Jardine, and Watson 2000). Heywoods, located on the west-northwest coast, produced between two hundred and three hundred shell tools, probably of Archaic origin (Drewett 2000: 29). One of the tools made from *Strombus gigas* (Queen conch) was radiocarbon dated to 3980±100 B.P. (I-16840, 2320–1750 cal yr B.C., 2 sigma) (Drewett 2006: 212). More recently, Fitzpatrick (2011) obtained two additional dates of shell artifacts from Heywoods: 4230±50 B.P. (cal 2530–2220 B.C., 2 sigma) and 4360±40 B.P. (cal 3280–2940 B.C., 2 sigma). Another location along the south coast produced possible Archaic artifacts (Drewett 2000: fig. 72).

Five to eight early Ceramic Age Saladoid sites are documented for the island (Drewett 2000, 2006). Two radiocarbon dates from the Goddard site place Saladoid occupation on Barbados potentially as early as 400 B.C. (Drewett 2006: 212; 1950±150 B.P., cal 400 B.C.–A.D. 450 2 sigma [Beta-20723, charcoal]; 2253±55, cal 400 B.C.–A.D. 170, 2 sigma [Beta-19969, charcoal]). The timing and route(s) of Saladoid entry into the West Indies have been debated for decades (Keegan 1995, 2009; Rainey 1940; Rouse 1958, 1986, 1992; Siegel 1991a, 1991b). A traditional model posited island hopping from south to north (Rouse 1986, 1992). There has been some discussion that the Saladoids may not have settled Trinidad and the southern Lesser Antilles before the northern Lesser Antilles and Puerto Rico (Fitzpatrick 2006; Keegan 2009). Arie Boomert (2000: 129, 2009: 66) observed that Cedrosan Saladoid settlers occupied

Trinidad by approximately 300–400 B.C., although, as Keegan (2009) emphasized, older ^{14}C dates in Saladoid contexts are available from the northern Lesser Antilles and Puerto Rico (see also Siegel 1991b: tab. 1). However, if the lower ends of the calibrated date ranges of the Goddard ^{14}C dates accurately reflect Early Saladoid occupations on Barbados, then there is support for the island-hopping model proposed by Rouse (1986, 1992). Additional dating of Saladoid sites combined with paleoecological investigations on Barbados and other islands in the Lesser Antilles are needed to resolve this issue.

The Saladoid site of Hillcrest in the Scotland District includes ceramic sherds in colluvial deposits along the margins of gullies, a juxtaposition that led Drewett (1989a: 83) to posit that early agriculture generated substantial soil erosion in this vulnerable region. Drewett also suggested that a lack of hard stone on the island led its Saladoid inhabitants to craft tools from marine shell.

The post-Saladoid occupations of Barbados resulted in a dramatic increase in site frequency and presumably population, beginning around A.D. 600 and again by ca. A.D. 1000 (Drewett 2006: 206–209, fig. 5). Based on site sizes and distribution, population by A.D. 1100 is thought to have numbered "in the thousands" (Drewett 1989a: 93). It is unclear to what degree population dropped after A.D. 1100. It was commonly believed that the island was abandoned prior to the arrival of Europeans because two accounts written in 1518 and 1536 described the island as deserted (Drewett 1989a: 93, 2006: 210–211; Schomburgk 1971/1848). However, other documents reported that indigenous people were forcibly removed for slave labor in the early sixteenth century (Sauer 1966: 193–195; Watts 1987: 109). Sir William Courteen reported landing on "the unoccupied island of Barbados" in 1624 (Sheridan 1973: 81). British colonization of Barbados began in 1627 and 1628 (Sheridan 1973: 81–84). A handful of radiocarbon dates from late prehistoric or protohistoric deposits suggest that Barbados may still have been occupied by Amerindians at Contact. A Suazoid midden in the Port St Charles site (west-northwest coast) produced two suggestive dates: 1120±80 B.P. (I-16189, cal A.D. 1110–1420, 2 sigma) and 910±80 B.P. (I-16188, cal A.D. 1300–1570, 2 sigma), both from shell (*Strombus gigas*). Samples from Silver Sands, a Suazoid site located along the south coast, were dated to 990±80 B.P. (I-16218, cal A.D. 1260–1490, 2 sigma [*Strombus gigas*]), 650±100 B.P. (I-16215, cal A.D. 1160–1450, 2 sigma [human bone]), and 1000±150 B.P. (I-16268, cal A.D. 650–1300, 2 sigma [human bone]) (Drewett 2006: 209–212). Drewett (1989a: 93–94) suggested that late prehistoric population increases, dwindling supplies of freshwater, environmental degradation, and overfarming of marginal soils may have conspired to reduce population levels on Barbados prior to arrival of Europeans. To date, no intact archaeological deposits have been documented with both early colonial and Native American artifacts (Drewett 2006: 211) suggesting no overlap in settlement histories.

Throughout Barbados prehistory, people seemingly favored coastal settings, with very little evidence for interior habitations. However, this pattern may be a product of differential site destruction: "It is likely that especially in central Barbados numerous sites have been destroyed or at least disturbed due to ploughing for sugar cane cultivation, which has been going on now for some 350 years" (Boomert 1987: 11–12). Two Saladoid, three Troumassoid, and three Suazoid sites have been documented in the general vicinity of the Graeme Hall wetland (discussed below).

Archaeological deposits in several Barbadian sites produced a narrow range of terrestrial animal remains consumed from Archaic through post-Saladoid times, including rice rats, dogs, unknown species of snakes, and pigeons (Newsom and Wing 2004: 90–94). This dearth of terrestrial animals likely also influenced the choice of coastal locations, including mangroves, where marine protein sources were available. Marine resources are more extensively represented in the Barbadian zooarchaeological assemblages. Archaebotanical recovery of carbonized seeds and other nonwood remains from the Ceramic Age deposits in the Heywoods site indicate the use of several native forest species including *Spondias* sp., *Annona* sp., *Acromonia aculeate*, *Hymenaca courbaril*, and *Cresentia* sp. (Newsom and Wing 2004: tab. 6.4).

Europeans formally occupied Barbados in 1627 with British colonization. From the standpoint of the initial British colonists Barbados offered several environmental advantages: timber, fertile soil, and isolation. The island's position relative to the other Lesser Antilles left it safely outside patrolled Spanish shipping routes, but near enough to provide a convenient base of operations against Spanish interests.

The initial focus of British agricultural colonization was on smallholder tobacco and indigo cultivation, but the initial influx of colonists included a few aristocrats who were issued large land grants by the British crown. The goal of the British colonists was to produce commercial crops for export, which resulted in rapid and extensive removal of forest cover (Watts 1987: 154–155). A few tree species were sometimes selectively logged either for on-island construction (e.g., *Cedrela mexicana*) or for export to England (e.g., the dyewood *Chloraphora tinctoria* and the hardwood *Guajacum officinale*). However, most large trees were killed by bark ringing and left in place to dry as smaller trees and shrubs were cut around them and dried until the entire mass was burned and replaced by crops.

Sugarcane was first introduced in 1645 during a global tobacco glut when prices for tobacco were extremely low (Sheridan 1974: 128–140). While initial experiments resulted in poor quality molasses, better refining methods were soon put into use. The persistent trade winds were harnessed for milling and the sugar economy rose to prominence. Between 1645 and 1667 large sugar plantations replaced most of the smallholdings. Many small-hold farmers emigrated to other British Caribbean possessions, and the importation of enslaved Africans increased to meet the labor needs of the plantations. Initially confined to the island's coastal margins and St. George's Valley, land clearance and plantation agriculture spread inland to higher elevations through the end of the seventeenth century, until almost all arable land was under cultivation.

Although the soils of Barbados were noted for their high innate fertility during the first decades of the colonial era, by 1661 official records indicated a growing concern for declining soil fertility, erosion, weed invasions, and decreasing sugar yields (Watts 1987: 222). Several innovations helped to remediate these problems: (1) cross-channel dams, (2) extension of the cropping season, (3) specialized dung farms, and (4) cane holing. Cross-channel dams effectively arrested gully development and soil loss, especially where it was degrading sloping land along the edges of the island's natural reef terraces. Extension of the cropping season increased yields by allowing cane to grow for longer periods of time, but did not address the underlying decline in soil productivity.

Dung farms were created to produce large quantities of manure, which was otherwise in short supply on Barbados. Animals were raised in limited spaces and manure was collected and composted on site for sale to plantations. Sugar producers who could afford regular application of manure benefited from increased crop yields (Sheridan 1974: 140–141). The cane-hole method of planting also increased yields. This system employed a grid pattern of small furrows and low ridges, with spot-applications of manure in the furrows. The furrows and ridges also stabilized exposed soils by slowing surface flow and diminishing erosion (Watts 1987: 224).

Barbados was preeminent in West Indian sugar production until about 1710, when the expansion of plantations on larger islands saw the gradual decline of the island's importance. This decline apparently led many plantations to eventually abandon their labor-intensive conservation practices in the eighteenth century, resulting in the return of soil erosion problems, declining fertility, declining crop yields, and further diminishment of the Barbadian sugar industry (Watts 1987: 435).

Environmental Coring on Barbados

Graeme Hall Wetland (Core GH08-1)

To document environmental history on Barbados we extracted a core from the Graeme Hall mangrove wetland located along the south coast (fig. 8.1). Core sediments reflect the transition from an open embayment to a closed wetland spanning the past 1,400 years. Precolonial anthropogenic signals were muted compared to the early colonial era. Mangrove wetlands were once present in multiple coastal locations on Barbados and were important resource zones for prehistoric occupants, evidenced by the locations of archaeological sites in proximity to former wetlands. Several of these wetlands were located along the island's south coast, including one backing the Saladoid Chancery Lane site; this wetland was largely destroyed in the twentieth century. We investigated the location for a possible core but found conditions to be unfavorable for microfossil preservation; recent cut-and-fill episodes have effectively buried the residual wetlands.

The Graeme Hall wetland is the last surviving mangrove community on Barbados. It is embedded within the 81.1 acre Graeme Hall Nature Sanctuary, which was established in 1994 with the initial purchase of 34.25 acres of wetlands (Wallace and Pryor 2010). Historical records indicate that modern impacts on the wetland began in the early 1700s when a road was built along the sandbar, separating the wetland from the ocean and further restricting tidal exchanges. By the later eighteenth century, the wetlands were part of the Graeme Hall sugar plantation, which subsequently drained some wetland areas to expand sugar land and pasture. In the late 1900s a lake was dredged out of a section of remaining mangrove to create a shooting pond for wildfowl hunters. Despite these predations, portions of an intact mangrove ecosystem remain, including dense thickets of red (*Rhizophera mangle*) and white (*Avicennia racemosa*) mangroves. Most of the intact mangroves exist in the western portion of the wetland. Relict drainage canals and relatively recent freshwater wetlands occupy the eastern portion. Our sediment core (GH08-1) was retrieved from a shallow water context amidst mature red mangrove in the western part of the wetland.

The lowermost limestone reef terrace on the south side of Barbados contains a number of solution/collapse dolines; the Graeme Hall wetland occupies one such depression of approximately 35 ha in area. This cavity in the bedrock appears to have been open to the ocean during part of the Holocene. More recently, it has been closed off by the development of a sandy baymouth bar, now consolidated by modern road and residential construction. Similar Holocene beach and dune deposits are noticeable in embayments along the southern and western coasts of Barbados.

There are no surface streams flowing into the Graeme Hall wetland. However, sheet wash and a disorganized system of rills appear to bring in some surface flow, principally from sloping agricultural land on the northeast and east sides of the wetland. Groundwater flow likely brings freshwater recharge from the north. Terrain immediately surrounding the wetland is generally flat, but rises abruptly about 100–200 m to the northeast leading up to the second limestone terrace. Slopes along this rise vary from about 5 to 20 percent. The total surface catchment for the Graeme Hall wetland is likely less than 1 km^2. Sloping land north and east of the wetland is mantled by sandy clay dark Rendolls formed on weathering limestone; these soils are about 20 to 65 cm deep (e.g., fig. 8.2, tab. 8.1). Adjacent flatter areas are characterized by well-developed heavy clay Vertisols formed on marl; these soils are about 100 to 120 cm deep (e.g., tab. 8.2). Soils observed in the area surrounding the wetland show little evidence of pronounced erosion and likely have not contributed large quantities of mineral sediment to the wetland, though some sedimentation is evident in an increase in silicate minerals in the uppermost levels of a core taken from the wetland (Ramcharan 2005).

Eugene Ramcharan of the University of the West Indies extracted a 225-cm core from the Graeme Hall wetland in 2003 (Ramcharan 2005). The core bottomed out in biogenic sand, including small mollusk shells radiocarbon dated to 1409±40 B.P. (cal A.D. 855–1055, 2 sigma). A second radiocarbon date was derived from peat between 104 and 114 cm: 833±75 B.P. (cal A.D. 1040–1280, 2 sigma). The core showed a reduction in carbonates and increase in organic matter at around 190 cm; this was interpreted as the closure of the embayment and the establishment of the brackish water, mangrove-dominated ecosystem. Three pollen zones were identified in Ramcharan's core: Zone 1 (1300−700 B.P.) comprising "*Rhizophora* associated with *Bursera*, *Coccoloba* and other coastal plants"; Zone 2 (700–400 B.P.) associated with increased species diversity but continued dominance of *Rhizophora*; and Zone 3 (400 B.P. to present) marked by the increased presence of Cyperaceae, possibly associated with local land clearance (Ramcharan 2005: 149).

We collected a 283-cm core in shallow water amidst red mangrove. Gaps in the record were created by hole slop, where collapse of wet sediments into the hole between drives created admixture, necessitating the discard of compromised material (tab. 8.3). Three radiocarbon dates were obtained for the core (tab. 8.4). Since the core obtained by Ramcharan reached a similar depth and shows very similar composition, the basal date of the GH08-1 core is assumed to be roughly similar in age: 1410±40 B.P.

Table 8.3. Sediment Descriptions of the Graeme Hall, Barbados Core (GH08-1 Core).

Depth (cm)	Color	OM (LOI)	Total P (ppm)	Na (ppm)	Ca (ppm)	Sand %	Silt %	Clay %	Notes
0–15	Very dark brown (10YR 2/2)	48.3	183	5190	7825	9	8	83	Oozy fibric peat
15–41	Black (10YR 2/1)	58.5	235	4483	7146				Hemic peat
41–47	Black (10YR 2/1)	61.4	116	4240	7230				Firm hemic peat; Pomacaea shell Fragments
47–66	Very dark brown (10YR 2/2)	45.0	68	4476	6901	9	10	81	Hemic peat
66–84	Dark reddish brown (5YR 2.5/2)	64.7	61	4539	6359				Fibric peat (Mangrove); 85 cm: 270±35 BP
									???
96–101									Hole collapse
101–128	Black (5YR 5/1)	60.9	50	5064	3636				Hemic peat; 110 cm: 970±40 BP
128–172.5	Black (5YR 5/1)	63.3	45	5458	1922				Fibric peat 170–172 cm: 1120±60 BP
172.5–175	Light gray (2.5Y 7/1)	1.3	34	3329	27643	78	9	13	Sand is largely biogenic
175–177	Gray (2.5Y 5/1)					6	15	79	
177–184	Dark gray (2.5Y 5/1)	16.9	33	2087	30861	84	8	8	Sand is largely biogenic
									???
210–223	Dark gray (2.5Y 5/1)	4.8	36	1615	33296	80	9	11	Sand is largely biogenic

(continued)

Table 8.3. *(continued)*

Depth (cm)	Color	OM (LOI)	Total P (ppm)	Na (ppm)	Ca (ppm)	Sand %	Silt %	Clay %	Notes
223–230	Dark gray (2.5Y 5/1)	3.6	33	1692	31085	85	11	4	Sand is largely biogenic
230–247	Dark gray (2.5Y 5/1)	3.7	28	1539	32784	81	16	3	
247–251	Grayish brown (2.5Y 5/2)	3.0	17	6327	46419				Calcareous, biogenic marl
251–283	Dark gray (2.5Y 5/1)	4.2	19	11484	33838	79	17	4	Sand is largely biogenic

Table 8.4. Radiocarbon Dates from the Graeme Hall, Barbados Core.

Lab Sample No.	Sample Depth	^{14}C Age (BP)[a]	$^{13}C/^{12}C$ Ratio	2-Sigma Calibrated Date Range[b]	Median Cal Date
AA92658	85 cm, Peat	270±35	-25.6	AD 1490–1950/1–460 BP[c]	AD 1620/330 BP
Beta-268169	110 cm, Peat	970±40	-25.3	AD 1000–1160/790–950 BP	AD 1090/865 BP
AA82682	170–172 cm, Peat	1120±60	-24.9	AD 770–1020/930–1180 BP	AD 910/1040 BP
BGS2395[d]	225 cm, shell	1410±40	?	AD 850–1050/900–1100 BP	AD 970/990 BP

a. 1-sigma range.
b. CALIB ver. 7.0 was used to calibrate the dates (Reimer et al. 2013). Dates from organic samples were calibrated using the IntCal13 method. The shell date was calibrated using the Marine13 method, -27 for delta R, and 14 for delta R uncertainty. We used the delta R and uncertainty values calculated by Bright (2011: Appendix 2) for the same section of the Caribbean.
c. Suspect date range due to impingement on the end of the calibration data set.
d. Date from Ramcharan (2005) core.

The sediments in the GH08-1 core record a transition from more-open embayment to closed wetland. This transition became most pronounced at 172.5 cm. Organic sediments from 170 to 172 cm produced a date of ca. A.D. 910. Above 172.5 cm the core consisted largely of organic sediments (45–64.7% organic matter). Most of the remaining sediment in this zone consisted of carbonate precipitates, with silicate sediments never accounting for more than 10 percent of the sediment by weight. Sodium levels became relatively stable above 172.5 cm, ranging from 4,240 to 5,458 ppm, probably reflecting closure of the embayment by sandy deposits. This closure may be the result of offshore-to-onshore sediment surges associated with a major hurricane or a tsunami. Tsunami-generated boulder ridge deposits on the east coast of Barbados produced radiocarbon dates of 1550±70 B.P. and 1360±60 B.P. (Scheffers and Kelletat 2006). After closure, flow of marine water through the sand barrier appeared to continue, thus maintaining brackish conditions within the wetland, though this flow was compromised recently by historical and modern construction on the sandbar. Calcium levels steadily increased during this period (1922 to 7825 ppm), probably reflecting enhanced accumulation of Ca precipitation within the closed system. Phosphate levels gradually increased from 45 ppm in the lower part of the zone to 235 ppm between 15 and 41 cm, likely indicative of increased runoff associated with agriculture during the historical era. The decline in P level to 183 ppm between 0 and 15 cm may reflect the creation of a vegetative buffer around the wetland with the creation of the Graeme Hall Nature Sanctuary.

Core sediments between 172.5 and 283 cm reflect a more dynamic near-shore environment. Most strata within this zone consisted primarily of churned, coarse, biogenic sands (principally broken coral and shells). Ramcharan (2005) reported that identifiable shell fragments within these sands consisted of eleven mollusk species from rocky shore/sublittoral, soft bottom, and brackish-water habitats. The lack of stratification or zonation within the sands and shells suggests that these deposits were most likely brought into or redeposited within the then-open embayment by storm surges. Two zones of still-water deposits were identified in the sediments. At 247–251 cm there was a zone of calcareous, biogenic marl. The marl layer was likely an autochthonous biogenic deposit forming either within algal mats or via pelletization during episodes of Ca supersaturation within a stagnant backwater context. At 175–179 cm there was a stratum of clayey sediment likely laid down during a period of still water within a lagoonal environment. Sodium levels dropped abruptly from 11,484 ppm at 251–283 cm to 1,539 ppm at 230–247 cm, probably indicating partial closure of the embayment by sandy deposits during this time. This closure may be the result of the final stage of Late Holocene sea-level rise.

Three pollen zones were identified in the core (fig. 8.3). The basal zone (280–240 cm) is associated with biogenic sand and organic matter traces. Pollen preservation was good, although concentration values were low, making counting difficult. The assemblages were dominated by red mangrove grains, with an appreciable quantity of Arecaceae (Type H) pollen. Sedge and grass pollen are also slightly elevated. This section probably represents lagoon deposits behind a mangrove bar. The identification of the palm pollen is unknown but may represent *Geonoma*. Historical accounts record the presence of a palmetto (presumably a palm) as a mangrove understory plant. Based on morphological features of the palm grains this may be the same taxon represented in the Grenada cores. Proxies for human activities were not present in this zone.

Zone 2 (240–115 cm) represents a similar environment to the basal section, although there is a reduction (and total elimination) in palm pollen and increases in red mangrove pollen and charcoal concentrations. The concomitant decline in palm and increase in charcoal is similar to the pattern identified in the Grenada cores and may reflect forest modifications and overexploitation of palms by humans. This anthropogenic signature corresponds to Ramcharan's (2005) shell date of ca. A.D. 990 from 225 cm in his Graeme Hall core (tab. 8.4).

The uppermost section (115–0 cm) reflects a more freshwater system, with appreciably more sedge and grass pollen, along with an increased amount of *Acrostichum* fern spores. Although these ferns tolerate some salinity, they prefer a brackish setting and likely chart a shift to a less saline environment. Sustained charcoal, Poaceae, and Cyperaceae concentrations increased significantly and the sedimentation rate was elevated during this zone, indicative of active landscape modification and management practices (tab. 8.5). The zone dates from ca. A.D. 1100 to recent times. At 30 cm a single *Zea mays* pollen grain was identified, probably representing early historical agriculture.

Eight samples were processed and examined for phytoliths. All were completely devoid of preserved phytoliths.

Discussion

Barbados is more distant from its nearest neighbor than any other island in the West Indies. The prehuman diversity of vegetation was nevertheless comparable to other islands of the Lesser Antilles. Prior to the systematic investigations by Peter Drewett, it was believed that Archaic

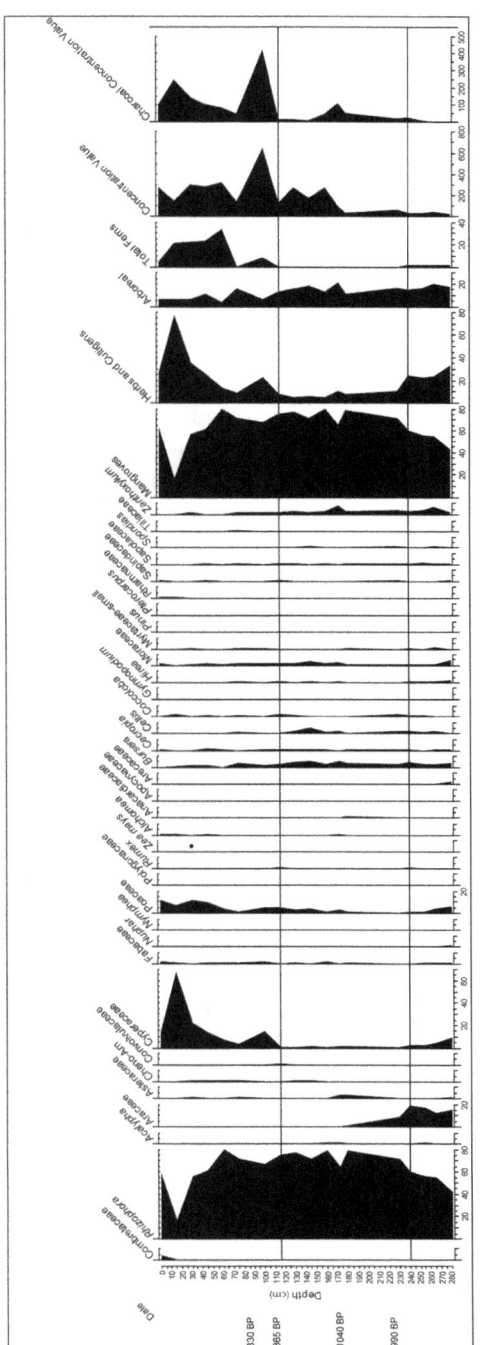

Figure 8.3. Graeme Hall, Barbados, core pollen-percentage diagram. Pollen and charcoal concentrations are expressed as grains and fragments, respectively, per cm³ of sediment.

Table 8.5. Sedimentation Rates for the Graeme Hall, Barbados Core.

¹⁴C sample depths	¹⁴C Date Ranges (Median Cal BP Dates)	Sedimentation Rate (cm/yr)
0–85 cm	0–330	.2575
85–110 cm	330–865	.0467
110–171 cm	865–1040	.3485

occupations did not exist on Barbados. Drewett clearly demonstrated that Archaic people had settled the island at least as early as ca. 3150 B.C. (Drewett 2000, 2006; also Fitzpatrick 2011).

The Graeme Hall wetland core did not penetrate Early or Mid Holocene sediments; our record of environmental history for Barbados relates to late Ceramic Age through early colonial occupations. Increasing levels of charcoal and disturbance indicators associated with cleared, open spaces in the core above 240 cm reflect an anthropogenic landscape well before ca. A.D. 800 (fig. 8.3, tabs. 8.6, 8.7). A significant spike in charcoal and attendant disturbance indicators at 170 cm, dated to ca. A.D. 870, reflects intensified management practices most likely by late Ceramic Age Troumassoid peoples and correlates with pre-European population growth on the island documented in the archaeological record (Drewett 2006: fig. 5). Declining charcoal concentration values between 140 and 115 cm may be due to abandonment of the local area, although by ca. A.D. 1090 (110 cm) reoccupation is reflected by dramatic increases in sustained charcoal concentrations and other disturbance indicators. This reoccupation is consistent with the pre-European demographic zenith for the island if site frequency is treated as a proxy for population size. The high disturbance-indicator values were sustained well into the European colonial period, suggesting that there was not a late pre-Columbian abandonment of Barbados, contrary to some of the early European accounts (Sheridan 1973; Watts 1987).

Table 8.6. Ethnobotanical Associations and Disturbance Indicators Represented in the Graeme Hall, Barbados Core.[a]

Taxon	Ethnobotanical Association or Disturbance Indicator	Core GH08-1
MANGROVE		
Combretaceae	White mangrove. Slows bleeding.	X[b]
Rhizophora	Red mangrove. Diarrhea, fever, malaria, excellent fuel wood.	X
HERBS/CULTIGENS		
Araceae	Arum family. Some species produce edible fruits. Others are toxic.	X
Asteraceae	Aster or Composite family. Herbs and shrubs. Many are invasive weed species of cleared open areas.	X[b]
Cheno-Ams	Chenopod and amaranth families. Favor disturbed or open habitats. Young greens and mature seeds are edible. Includes seablite, saltwort, chenopod, amaranth.	X[b]

(continued)

Table 8.6. *(continued)*

Taxon	Ethnobotanical Association or Disturbance Indicator	Core GH08-1
Convolvulaceae	Morning glory family. Includes species with edible tubers and leaves (sweet potatoes). Some with psychotropic and medicinal properties.	X[b]
Cyperaceae, *Cladium*	Sedge family. Grasslike herbaceous plants, many are weeds that invade cleared open areas.	X
Fabaceae	Wild herbaceous legumes. Includes cohoba, edible beans. Species include plants with medicinal uses and for producing narcotic snuff, edible fruit, and fish poison.	X[b]
Poaceae	Grass family. Often associated with areas frequently fired. Edible starchy grains.	X
Polygonaceae, *Polygonum, Rumex*	Knotweed. Some species cooked and eaten.	X[b]
Zea mays	Maize. Edible grain.	X[b]
ARBOREAL		
Alchornea	Many species have medicinal properties.	X[b]
Anacardiaceae, *Anacardium, Spondias* sp.	Cashew family. Edible fruit, hogplum.	X[b]
Arecaceae	Palm family. Edible fruit, thatching, cordage, needles, posts.	X[b]
Bursera	Gumbo limbo. Resin has medicinal properties, leaves used for tea.	X
Cecropia	Pumpwood. Fast-growing colonizing trees common to disturbed forest habitats and clearings.	X[b]
Celtis	Hackberry, edible fruit.	X
Coccoloba	Sea grape. Edible fruit, medicinal.	X[b]
Hirea	Liana. Used for rope.	X[b]
Moraceae, *Ficus, Brosimum*	Mulberry family. Edible fruit, breadnut, medicinal. Often colonize open cleared areas.	X
Myrtaceae, *Eugenia, Psidium*	Myrtle family. Edible fruit, medicinal. Frequently found in windbreak and secondary forest growth. Includes guava, Eugenia, allspice.	X[b]
Rhamnaceae	Buckthorn family. Edible berries.	X[b]
Sapindaceae	Soapberry family. Fruits and seeds of some are edible, others poisonous.	X[b]
Sapotaceae, *Chrysophyllum, Sideroxylon*	Sapote family. Edible fruit, medicinal, latex in some species. Includes edible fruits of chicle, sapote, lucuma.	X[b]

a. See Table 5.5 for the sources of information.
b. Trace amounts.

202 • Chapter 8

Table 8.7. Plant Taxa Identified in the Graeme Hall, Barbados Core with No Documented Ethnobotanical or Anthropogenic Correlates Other than Perhaps Fuel Wood, Especially Arboreal Taxa.

Taxon	Common Name	Core GH08-1
HERBS/CULTIGENS		
Acalypha	Copperleaf, flowering shrub	X[a]
ARBOREAL		
Pterocarpus	Swamp bloodwood tree. Grows in swamp forests, mainly on landward side of mangrove.	X[a]
Zanthoxylum	Prickly ash	X
FERNS		
Unknown ferns		X

a. Trace amounts.

The location of Barbados was not favorable for Spanish colonization because it lay well outside the shipping routes established in the sixteenth century and maintained thereafter. However, Spanish slave raiding in the early sixteenth century may have eliminated the indigenous Barbadian population (Sauer 1966: 193–195). When British colonists arrived in 1627, they reported the island to be deserted of humans and mantled in dense tropical forest.

To clear land for cultivation much of this forest was simply cut, allowed to dry, and burned. In 1631 Sir Henry Colt observed, "All the earth is black with cinders" (cited in Watts 1987: 166). Major forest clearance associated with the establishment of sugarcane plantations in the seventeenth century is reflected by significant increases in charcoal concentrations and disturbance-indicator pollen taxa (Cyperaceae, Poaceae) dating to ca. A.D. 1620 (fig. 8.3, tab. 8.4). Increased inputs of inorganic sediments after this level also reflect the effects of forest clearance. Although nearby lands were cultivated as part of the Graeme Hall sugar plantation, inorganic sediment inputs were not exceedingly great, reflecting the generally muted topography and lack of fluvial influx, thereby contributing to the preservation of portions of the mangrove wetland around the coring location. Elevated phosphate levels in the core during the historical period reflect the introduction of manuring practices and, later, the use of chemical fertilizers and, finally, runoff from increasingly urbanized landscapes. Other studies indicate that changes in water salinity and pulses of untreated effluents threaten the integrity and health of the Graeme Hall wetland as surrounding lands have become urbanized and water quality has been compromised (Wallace and Pryor 2010).

9

MARTINIQUE

Neil A. Duncan, Nicholas P. Dunning, John G. Jones, Deborah M. Pearsall, and Peter E. Siegel

Background

Martinique is situated midway along the chain of the Lesser Antilles and is part of the active volcanic island arc associated with the subduction zone created by the convergence of the Atlantic and Caribbean tectonic plates (Maury et al. 1990). Archaeologically, the island is well known for its Ceramic Age sites. It is considerably less well known for Archaic sites and, as will be discussed later, the perception of a paucity of Archaic sites may be strongly shaped by taphonomic factors, especially active volcanic activity during the Holocene.

Martinique is one of the Caribbean islands with well-documented volcanic activity during the Holocene, including in recent times (fig. 9.1). The active center of volcanism has shifted northward through time to its current center at Mount Pelée. Andesitic cones in the central portion of the island (Pitons du Carbet and Morne Jacob) were last active ca. 5.5 million to 1 million years ago, and the deeply dissected cones of the southern volcanic uplands were last active ca. 14 million to 6.5 million years ago (Adélaïde-Merlande and Hervieu 1996). The eruptive history of Mount Pelée may have played a role in the early human settlement of Martinique, most notably in the occupation of Saladoid communities on the northeast coast of the island (Allaire 1989). Mount Pelée seems to have an approximate 250-year eruptive cycle, with a notable change around A.D. 1000 from an earlier pattern of Plinian-type eruptions (upper cone destruction and huge ash clouds) to Pelean-type eruptions (down-flowing pyroclastic flows named for the devastating eruption of Mount Pelée in 1902) (Westercamp and Traineau 1983).

Precipitation on Martinique is strongly conditioned by elevation and orographic forcing, generating more than 2,500 mm annually in the central mountains, whereas near-desert conditions are found around Pointe des Salines at the low-lying extreme southeast end of the island.

204 • Chapter 9

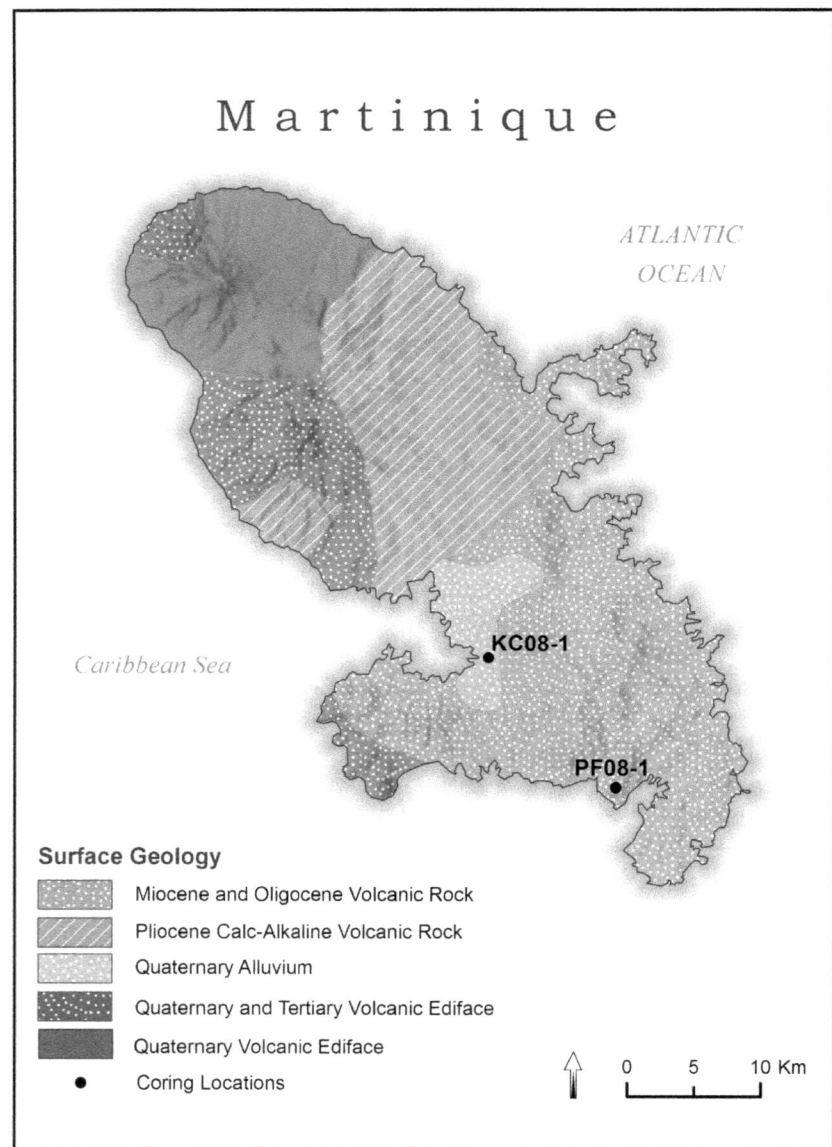

Figure 9.1. Map of Martinique showing the surface geology and coring locations.

The older volcanic cones in the south and central parts of the island have been deeply dissected by sustained tropical weathering and fluvial erosion. Drainage is essentially radial with streams flowing outward toward all coasts; the configuration of the ancient cones, however, concentrates the greatest amount of runoff into the large Baie de Fort-de-France on the west side of the island. The active Mount Pelée on the north side of the island exhibits only moderate fluvial dissection.

Soils on the island range from young Andisols formed in recent ash deposits in the north, Oxisols and Ultisols on deeply weathered saprolite in the central and southern hills, Aridisols and Vertisols in the desert southeast, to tracts of Histosols in the coastal wetlands. Many areas of sloping land show considerable evidence of soil cover degradation, most likely the effects of long-term sugar cultivation. Vegetation ranges from tropical moist forest in the central highlands to xerophytic scrub in the southeast. Mangrove ecosystems are prominent in coastal embayments, most notably around the Baie de Fort-de-France.

There is sparse archaeological evidence for Archaic occupations in the Lesser Antilles. Two possible Archaic (or at least aceramic) sites are documented for Martinique: Boutbois and Le Godinot (Allaire and Mattioni 1983). Both sites are located in upland settings overlooking the Rivière du Carbet approximately 2.5 km from the Caribbean Sea. The Rivière du Carbet flows west, emptying into the Caribbean along the west-northwest coast of Martinique.

In contrast to the Archaic, there are many Ceramic Age occupations documented for Martinique (Bérard 2004; Bright 2011). The archaeological map of the island shows fifty-six sites with occupations dating to 200/100 B.C. to A.D. 400 (Early Saladoid), eighty-four with occupations dating to A.D. 400–600/800 (Late Saladoid), fifty-five with occupations dating to A.D. 600/800–1200 (early Ostionoid), and sixty-three with occupations dating to A.D. 1200–1500 (late Ostionoid/protohistoric) (Bright 2011: fig. 3.5). The majority of sites are located along the coast or in near-coastal settings, except for a handful of sites identified in the southern tropical highlands. Most of the Ceramic Age sites contain deposits dating to two or more major cultural periods.

The earliest mention of European interest in Martinique dates to 1512 when the king of Spain authorized the enslavement of Native Americans living on the islands between Dominica and Tobago, inclusive (Watts 1987: 109). There does not appear to have been sustained European occupation of Martinique until after 1639 when the French began using the island as a place for their ship crews to rest after making trans-Atlantic journeys to the West Indies (Watts 1987: 171). During the 1650s approximately 10,000 white colonists left Barbados for other islands in the Antilles, Surinam, and North America (Chandler 1946; Watts 1987: 217). Some of these colonists settled on Martinique. The first sugar estates were established around 1670, when Dutch settlers from Brazil were allowed to occupy the island (Watts 1987: 297). By the 1690s much of the Martinique lowland forests had been removed for cane plantations, resulting in soil deterioration and erosion (Watts 1987: 395). The Martinique sugar industry intensified during the eighteenth and nineteenth centuries causing yet more environmental degradation. By the mid to late nineteenth century, fourteen central sugar-processing mills were established and Martinique was ranked fourth highest in sugar production across the Caribbean in censuses from 1835 to 1869 (Watts 1987: tab. 10.10, fig. 10.6).

Environmental Coring on Martinique

Baie de Fort-de-France (Core KC08-1)

Core KC08-1 was collected from an enormous mangrove swamp fringing the central-west coast of Martinique, backing the entire Baie de Fort-de-France. The bay receives runoff from several sizable perennial rivers that drain high, dissected peaks to the north and northeast, including the Pitons du Carbet and Morne Jacob, an area covering some 120 km^2. The Gros Ilet site is located on Pointe Vatable along the southwestern edge of the swamp (Bérard 2004).

The KC08-1 core was extracted from a large area of red mangrove toward the southeast end of Baie de Génipa, an embayment within the larger Baie de Fort-de-France. Mangroves extend along much of the eastern side of the bay, but at present are most extensive in the southeast. The southeastern corner of the bay from where the core was collected receives runoff mostly from areas more immediately to the east (ca. 30 km^2) and south (ca. 21 km^2) and it was in these areas of highly weathered and deeply dissected older volcanic uplands that soil reconnaissance was conducted. Immediately to the south of the coring site is a series of low hills, the lower flanks of which are currently used for sugarcane cultivation. Soils on the lower slopes appear to be well-developed Oxisols. The upper slopes of the hills are mantled chiefly with Oxic Inceptisols formed on saprolitic igneous rock. These more steeply sloping soils are often truncated, with A horizons lost to erosion, most probably during colonial-era or modern cultivation. East of the coring location is an extensive area of poorly drained flatland with

Histosols, much of which has been brought into cultivation through the use of a network of drainage ditches and canals.

Modern urbanization continues to spread across this area, generating considerable amounts of eroded sediments, which ultimately are channeled into the bay—a process that has been transforming the landscape for years. These same areas were previously under sugar cultivation, evidenced by ruins of abandoned mills. Upland soils consist of Oxisols and Inceptisols, many of which are truncated. Complex alluvial soils were observed along several small, steeply graded streams, including two large alluvial fans located at the mouths of the streams where they aggrade abruptly onto flatter terrain. A road cut through one fan exhibited an Ab horizon (buried surface soil) at a depth of 140 cm; the age of this buried soil is uncertain, but may well be historical.

The 676-cm KC08-1 core produced a basal ^{14}C date of ca. 3790 B.C. (tab. 9.1). Composition of the entire core is strongly organic, with much of its length consisting of 45–70 percent organic matter by dry weight (tab. 9.2). The mineral fraction of the core increased notably in the upper 2 m of the core, especially near the surface, reflecting changing land cover/use patterns in the watershed. Rising sea level is indicated by elevated sediment salinity values and aggradation between 600 and 450 cm, followed by a period of stabilization, then slightly more seawater incursion above 200 cm. The seawater incursion is possibly a product of instability in the mangrove ecosystem.

A prominent volcanic ash deposit was identified at 218–228 cm; organic sediment from 229 to 230 cm dated to ca. A.D. 335 (1550–1700 cal B.P., 2 sigma) (tab. 9.1), correlating the eruption with archaeological Horizon II on Martinique (Mid to Late Saladoid). The ash deposit most likely corresponds to the significant Plinian P2 eruption at Mount Pelée dated to 1670±40 B.P. (Allaire 1989; Westercamp and Traineau 1983).

Pollen preservation in the core was excellent; twenty-four samples were processed. Only twenty samples were countable because the basal sediments comprised almost exclusively organic material, with little silt or clay, thus pollen concentration values were very low (fig. 9.2). Pollen counts extended to around 625 cm. Despite good pollen preservation, concentration values were low, suggesting that fluctuations in pollen frequencies were due more to variations in sedimentation rates (tab. 9.6) than to factors of oxidation.

Five pollen zones were identified. The basal zone (625–575 cm) dating after ca. 3790 B.C. produced no proxies for anthropogenic inputs (tab. 9.3). This zone is dominated by *Cladium* (sawgrass), other sedges, *Byrsonima*, Moraceae, and *Zanthoxylum*. Red mangrove pollen was

Table 9.1. Radiocarbon Dates from the Martinique Cores.

Core Location	Lab Sample Number	Core Number/Sample Depth	^{14}C Age (BP)[a]	^{13}C/^{12}C Ratio	2-Sigma Calibrated Date Range[b]	Median Cal Date
Baie de Fort-de-France	AA92562	KC08-1, 229–230cm, OS[c]	1710±30	-27.7	AD 250–400/1550–1700 BP	AD 335/1615 BP
Baie de Fort-de-France	Beta-341060	KC08-1, 575cm, PP[d]	4420±30	-25.4	3320–2920 BC/4870–5270 BP	3050 BC/5000 BP
Baie de Fort-de-France	AA82676	KC08-1, 674–676cm, OS	5000±50	-27.3	3950–3670 BC/5620–5890 BP	3790 BC/5740 BP
Pointe Figuier	AA92561	PF08-1, 128cm, PW[e]	330±35	-27.8	AD 1480–1640/310–480 BP	AD 1560/390 BP
Pointe Figuier	AA82677	PF08-1, 222–223cm, OS	2600±50	-29.1	900–540 BC/2490–2840 BP	780 BC/2740 BP

a. 1-sigma range.
b. Dates were calibrated using the IntCal13 method of CALIB ver. 7.0 (Reimer et al. 2013).
c. Organic sediment.
d. Preserved plant matter.
e. Preserved wood.

Table 9.2. Sediment Descriptions of the Baie de Fort-de-France, Martinique Core (Core KC08-1).

Depth (cm)	Color	OM (LOI)	P ppm	Ca ppm	Na ppm	Sand%	Silt %	Clay%	Notes
0–19	Black (5Y 2.5/1)	30.2							Sapric peat
19–34	Very dark gray (2.5Y 3/1)	32.9	3020	62600	32667	7	70	23	Gytja
34–45	Very dark gray (10YR 3/1)	28.7							Hemic peat
45–100	Very dark gray (2.5Y 3/1)	34.8	2140	27380	39469	8	69	23	Silty peat; some fibric OM and roots
109–200	Black (5Y 2.5/1)	45.4				7	64	29	Hemic peat with some fibric material
200–217	Very dark brown (7.5YR 2.5/2)	41.0							Hemic peat with some fibric material
217–226	Greenish black (Gley10Y 2.5/1)	15.3	2750	16340	20311	70	22	8	Organic sand
226–228	Gray (10YR 6/1)	9.0				61	18	21	Volcanic ash
228–246	Black (10YR 2/1)	40.5				3	67	30	Hemic peat; some mangrove roots
246–263	Black (2.5Y 2.5/1)	38.6	320	10480	42628	8	71	21	Silty hemic peat
263–290	Black (5Y 2.5/1)	46.3				13	60	27	Hemic to fibric peat
290–300	Black (Gley 2.5/N)	48.2							Hemic peat
300–303									Slop? Or gytja
302–310									Wood
305–336	Black (7.5YR 2.5/1)	49.8							Sapric peat
336–351	Very dark brown (7.5YR 2.5/2)	53.9	130	8020	60097	13	65	22	Hemic silty peat

(continued)

Table 9.2. *(continued)*

Depth (cm)	Color	OM (LOI)	P ppm	Ca ppm	Na ppm	Sand%	Silt %	Clay%	Notes
351–363	Very dark brown (7.5YR 2.5/2)	54.7							Sapric peat
363–394	Black (5Y 2.5/1)	56.0							Hemic peat; roots
394–400	Very dark brown (7.5YR 2.5/2)	44.3	410	8650	5872	7	24	69	Organic clay; charcoal
400–404	Very dark brown (7.5YR 2.5/2)								Organic clay; charcoal
404–414	Black (10YR 2/1)	52.6							Silty hemic peat
414–443	Black (Gley 2.5/N)	53.9							Silty hemic peat; charcoal
443–489	Black (10YR 2/1)	55.5	110	10100	68015	11	59	30	Hemic to fibric peat
489–500	Black (2.5Y 2.5/1)	58.2							Fibric peat and wood
500–533	Black (Gley 2.5/N)								Hemic to fibric peat
533–590	Black (Gley 2.5/N)	60.8	<100	9630	62737	4	71	25	Silty hemic peat
590–600	Black (5Y 2.5/1)								Fibric peat and wood
600–611.5	Black (5Y 2.5/1)	63.1							Fibric peat and wood; some silt
611.5–612.5	Very dark gray (5Y 3/1)								Sand lens
612.5–623	Black (2.5Y 2.5/1)	65.8							Fibric peat and wood; some silt
623–634	Black (2.5Y 2.5/1)	62.7							Increasing silt
634–655	Black (2.5Y 2.5/1)	61.0	<100	5425	64101	10	72	18	Silty hemic to fibric peat
655–656									Charcoal lens
656–676	Black (10YR 2/1)	71.7							Fibric mangrove peat; some charcoal

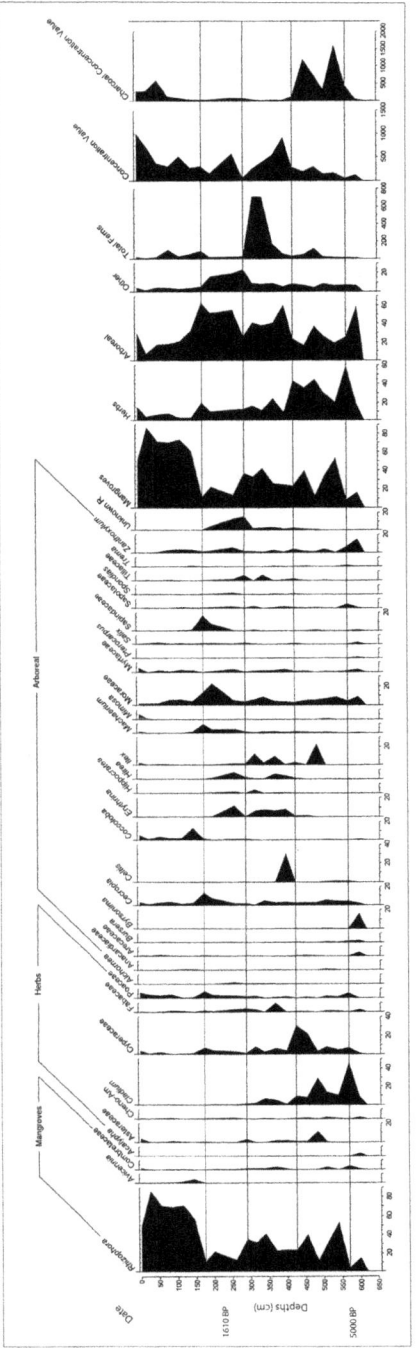

Figure 9.2. Baie de Fort-de-France, Martinique, core pollen-percentage diagram. Pollen and charcoal concentrations are expressed as grains and fragments, respectively, per cm³ of sediment.

present but was sparse compared to later quantities. This record reflects a swamp forest in a slightly brackish environment. Mangroves are present nearby, but probably not at the coring location.

The next zone (575–425 cm) represents a similar environment with elevated amounts of mangroves and fewer arboreal elements. *Cladium* and other sedges remain common. Charcoal values began to increase in the upper portion of the basal zone by 600 cm, as did Poaceae and Cyperaceae, colonizing taxa associated with open, cleared spaces. One pollen sample revealed a spike in Sapotaceae, an edible fruit–bearing tree. Preserved plant matter from 575 cm was dated to ca. 3050 B.C. Increases in Asteraceae and Cyperaceae pollen were documented by approximately 500 cm. These herbaceous families include weedy invaders of cleared, open areas. The pollen and charcoal assemblage from this zone represents a modified, if not actively managed, landscape (tab. 9.4). Strong signals of human activity from ca. 575 to 425 cm occurred

Table 9.3. Plant Taxa Identified in the Martinique Cores with No Documented Ethnobotanical or Anthropogenic Correlates Other than Perhaps Fuel Wood, Especially Arboreal Taxa.

Taxon	Common Name	Core KC08-1	Core PF08-1
HERBS/CULTIGENS			
Acalypha	Copperleaf, flowering shrub	X	
Polygonaceae, *Gymnopodium*	Common sorrel		X
ARBOREAL			
Erythrina	Leguminosae family, cockspur, cockscomb coraltree	X	X
Hura	Sand box	X	
Ilex	Holly	X	X
Machaerium	Escambrón, spiny climbing shrub or small tree. Form thickets in mangrove swamps.	X	X
Pterocarpus	Swamp bloodwood tree. Grows in swamp forests, mainly on landward side of mangrove.	X	X
Trema	Elm trees. Small evergreens growing in open forests or clearings.	X	
Zanthoxylum	Prickly ash	X	X
FERNS			
Unknown ferns		X	X

during the mesic conditions of the Mid Holocene. Halfway through this zone, at around 500 cm, there were changes in vegetation, including increases in fern spores, Asteraceae, *Ilex* pollen, and Unknown R pollen that probably reflect disturbances in the area.

Following the earliest evidence of human intervention in the area, charcoal concentration values declined to negligible levels, suggesting that human activities in the local area were minimal, although indicators of clearings remained elevated (*Cladium,* Cyperaceae, *Cecropia*). Increases were documented in some savanna types, including *Erythrina, Celtis,* and Tiliaceae. These changes in the local plant community defined the beginning of Zone 3 (425–290 cm).

Concentration values are higher in this zone, suggesting that sedimentation rates were lower (tab. 9.6). All indicators in this zone suggest that areas in the vicinity of the coring location were abandoned. Interpolating between the calibrated midpoint radiocarbon dates bracketing the 425-cm context resulted in an estimated abandonment date of ca. 1580 B.C. Later in this zone, fern spores increased dramatically. Charcoal concentration values remained low, suggesting human activity near the coring location was minimal. Nevertheless, there is good archaeological evidence for settlements on the island by ca. 450 B.C. (Bright 2011).

Zone 4 (290–180 cm) was marked by increases in swamp-forest pollen types. Red mangroves were reduced, while *Hirea, Machaerium* (rosewood), Moraceae, Sapindaceae, *Zanthoxylum,* and Unknown R became common. Ferns were reduced and charcoal concentrations remained low. The overall pollen and charcoal assemblage in Zone 4 indicates a continuation of no human habitation or landscape-management activities in the coring vicinity.

The uppermost zone (180–0 cm) revealed significant increases in red mangrove pollen. Most arboreal elements were reduced, although *Coccoloba* (sea grape) increased. At around 50 cm charcoal increased sharply, reflecting historical activities in the coring area.

Phytolith preservation in the core was excellent, although deposition was inconsistent. No phytoliths were recovered from the basal deposits (675–490 cm). Phytolith deposition varied for the rest of the sequence, with the highest influxes in the middle of the core (490–390 cm) and upper 50 cm (figs. 9.3a, 9.3b). Three highly productive phytolith samples from 490 to 390 cm are similar in composition: an abundance of woody plants such as small rugulose spheres overwhelmingly dominated the counts, with few Arecaceae spinulose spheres and Marantaceae large rugulose and nodular spheres, rare sclerids, and sedge phytoliths. The phytoliths in this section of the core present a strong arboreal signature rather than a palm-dominated swamp forest (i.e., mangrove indicated),

Table 9.4. Ethnobotanical Associations and Disturbance Indicators Represented in the Martinique Cores.[a]

Taxon	Ethnobotanical Association or Disturbance Indicator	Core KC08-1	Core PF08-1
MANGROVE			
Avicennia	Black mangrove. Throat pains, incontinence.	X	X[b]
Combretaceae	White mangrove. Slows bleeding.	X	X[b]
Rhizophora	Red mangrove. Diarrhea, fever, malaria, excellent fuel wood.	X	X
HERBS/CULTIGENS			
Asteraceae	Aster or Composite family. Herbs and shrubs. Many are invasive weed species of cleared open areas.	X	X
Borreria	Weedy herb in Madder family. Alkaloid and iridoid extracts have medicinal properties.		X[b]
Canna	Canna. Rhizomes rich in starch, seeds are edible.		X
Cheno-Ams	Chenopod and amaranth families. Favor disturbed or open habitats. Young greens and mature seeds are edible. Includes seablite, saltwort, chenopod, amaranth.	X[b]	X
Convolvulaceae	Morning glory family. Includes species with edible tubers and leaves (sweet potatoes). Some with psychotropic and medicinal properties.		X[b]
Croton	Some produce a latex used for medicinal purposes.		X
Cyperaceae, *Cladium*	Sedge family. Grasslike herbaceous plants, many are weeds that invade cleared open areas.	X	X
Euphorbiaceae	Spruge family. A number of species produce a latex high in isoprene polymers that when processed can be made into rubber. Cassava (*Manihot esculenta*) is a member of the family.		X[b]
Fabaceae, *Desmodium*	Wild herbaceous legumes. Includes cohoba, edible beans. Species include plants with medicinal uses and for producing narcotic snuff, edible fruit, and fish poison.	X	X
Malvaceae/Tiliaceae	Mallow family. Some have medicinal properties, others fruits and leaves are edible. Cotton (*Gossypium*) is in this family.	X	

(continued)

Table 9.4. *(continued)*

Taxon	Ethnobotanical Association or Disturbance Indicator	Core KC08-1	Core PF08-1
Poaceae	Grass family. Often associated with areas frequently fired. Edible starchy grains.	X	X
ARBOREAL			
Acacia	Young spines used to relieve gum and tooth pain.		X[b]
Alchornea	Many species have medicinal properties.	X[b]	
Anacardiaceae, *Spondias* sp.	Cashew family. Edible fruit, hogplum.	X[b]	X[b]
Apocynaceae	Dogbane family. Golden trumpet vine. Fibers used for cordage. Some produce edible flowers.		X
Arecaceae	Palm family. Edible fruit, thatching, cordage, needles, posts.	X	X
Byrsonima	Edible fruit, nance.	X	X
Bursera	Gumbo limbo. Resin has medicinal properties, leaves used for tea.	X	X[b]
Cecropia	Pumpwood. Fast-growing colonizing trees common to disturbed forest habitats and clearings.	X	X
Celtis	Hackberry, edible fruit.	X	X[b]
Coccoloba	Sea grape. Edible fruit, medicinal.	X	X[b]
Guazuma	West Indian elm, pigeon wood. Seeds of some have medicinal properties and others are edible.		X
Hippocratea	Medicine vine, medicinal, anti-inflammatory.	X	X[b]
Hirea	Liana. Used for rope.	X	
Moraceae, *Ficus*, *Brosimum*	Mulberry family. Edible fruit, breadnut, medicinal. Often colonize open cleared areas.	X	X
Myrtaceae, *Eugenia*, *Psidium*	Myrtle family. Edible fruit, medicinal. Frequently found in windbreak and secondary forest growth. Includes guava, Eugenia, allspice.	X	X
Sapindaceae	Soapberry family. Fruits and seeds of some are edible, others poisonous.	X	X
Sapotaceae, *Chrysophyllum*	Sapote family. Edible fruit, medicinal, latex in some species. Includes edible fruits of chicle, sapote, lucuma.	X[b]	X
Verbenaceae	Verbena family. Some with aromatic and medicinal properties.		X[b]

a. See Table 5.5 for the sources of information.
b. Trace amounts.

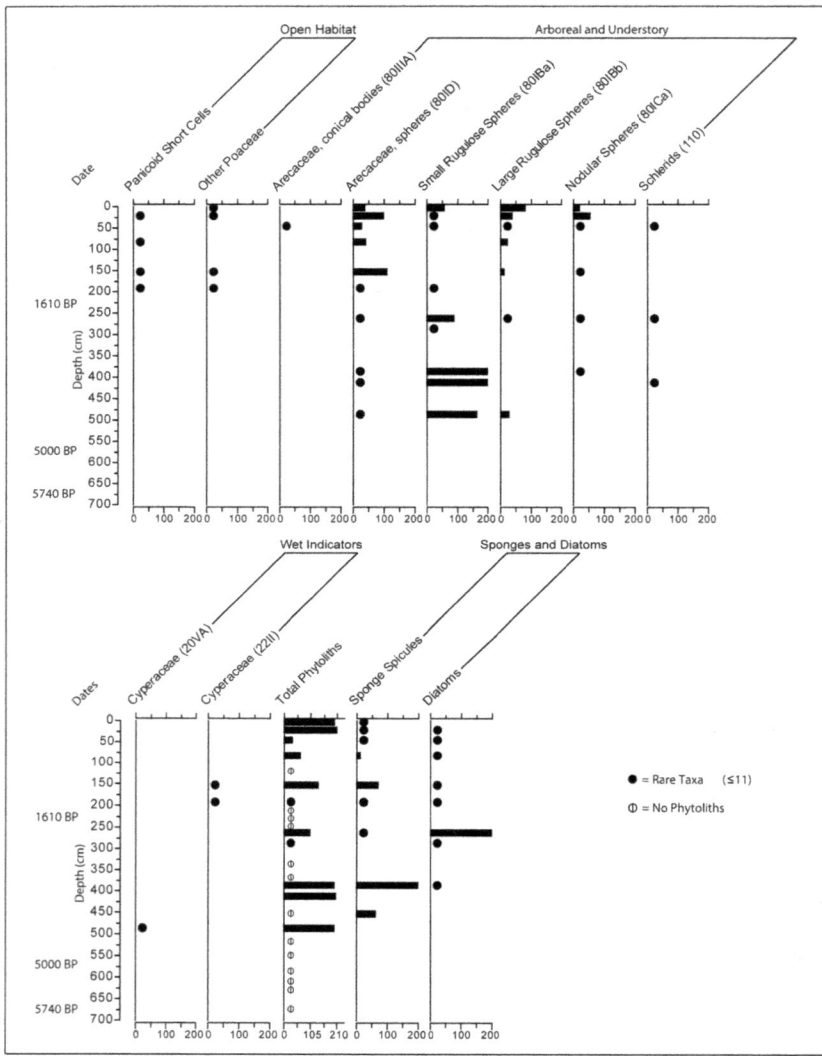

Figure 9.3a. Baie de Fort-de-France, Martinique, core phytolith diagram: resolved.

with a minor influx of freshwater indicators. By 195–190 cm, panicoid grass and other Poaceae phytoliths entered the record. Arecaceae phytoliths were highly represented in the upper section of the core, while woody plant phytoliths (small rugulose spheres) declined. Phytolith patterning in the upper 2 m of the core is consistent with an increase in palm forest.

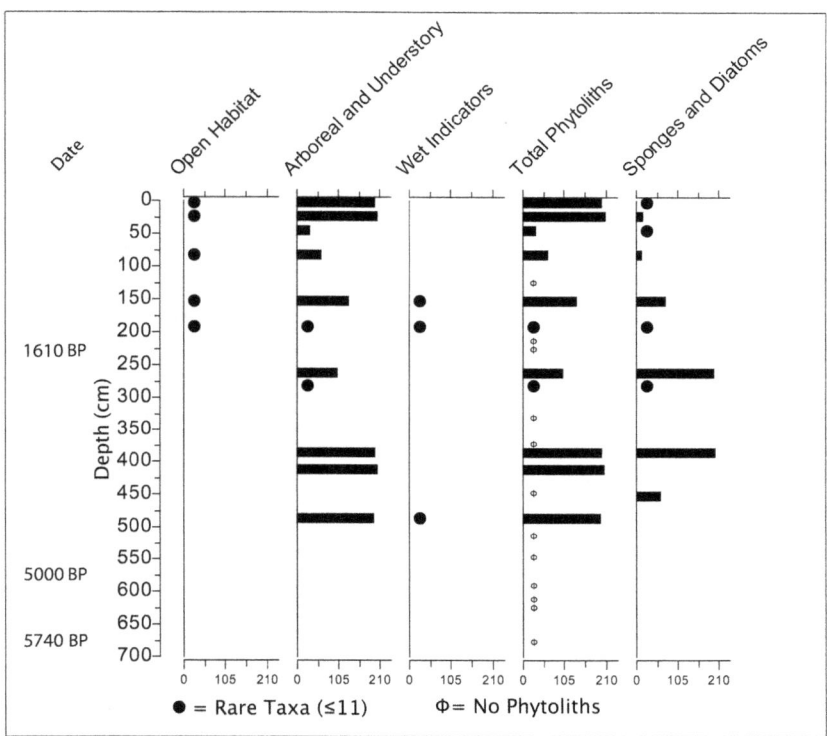

Figure 9.3b. Baie de Fort-de-France, Martinique, core phytolith diagram: composite.

Pointe Figuier (Core PF08-1)

We collected a core from the Pointe Figuier wetland (PF08-1), along a low-grade stream embayment on the south-central coast within the deeply dissected ancient southern volcanic uplands (fig. 9.1). Anse Figuier, lying just to the east of Pointe Figuier, fronts this embayment and contains a Mid to Late Saladoid period site (ca. A.D. 600–700) documented by Benoît Bérard (2004).

Pointe Figuier is part of a large, steep-sided headland separating the Baie du Trou au Diablo and Baie du Marin. The small valley behind (north of) Anse Figuier is drained by a sluggish seasonal stream that meanders through accumulated sediment on the flat valley floor. The north–south axis of this valley is about 2 km in length and the valley has an average east–west width of about 700 m, producing a watershed catchment area of approximately 1.4 km². The sides of the valley are very steep, with grades approximating 70–80 percent in some areas, but more typically 30–50 percent. These slopes aggrade abruptly onto the valley floor. Numerous landslide scars of varying ages are visible on the hill slopes.

Soils on the valley floor are chiefly alluvial Inceptisols with pockets of Histosols. Soils on the slopes are mainly shallow, unstable Entisols. Hillside Entisols have a dominantly clayey texture, though coarse sand is found in the subsoil. This clay dominance is reflected in the clayey nature of the mineral component of the majority of strata in the sediment core. However, the lower strata are sandy, reflecting earlier more-pronounced marine influences.

The core reached a total depth of 233 cm. Within the core deposits were numerous prehistoric ceramic fragments, probably associated with the Anse Figuier site (Bérard 2004: fig. 57). Two radiocarbon dates were obtained: ca. 780 B.C. (222–223 cm) and ca. A.D. 1560 (128 cm) (tab. 9.1). Coarse sand in the lower part of the core comprised chiefly pulverized coral and marine shells (tab. 9.5). Prior to ca. 780 B.C., the coring location was either closer to the shoreline or more open to the ocean, and possibly was a tidal flat before aggradation. Proximity to the shoreline is reflected in elevated Na levels in the lower strata. A stratigraphic break at 162 cm likely reflects a scouring event and truncation of sedimentation. The composition of sediments, including terrestrial gravels and other large clasts above the unconformity suggests that the scouring event was fluvial in nature. The most likely scenario is a major storm and consequent flooding. The position of Anse Figuier in a small embayment on the south coast of Martinique could have made it particularly vulnerable to hurricanes. Storms may have also reconfigured coastal bars and beaches, isolating the coring location from the coast as reflected in decreasing Na levels in the sediments. P levels show two prominent spikes: the earliest occurred at 113–127 cm, and was probably linked to colonial-era activities. Another spike was associated with the uppermost strata, and was most likely related to modern pasturing in the area. A less prominent spike occurred between 200 and 224 cm and may represent Late Archaic or Early Saladoid activities.

Twelve pollen samples were processed from the Pointe Figuier core, and preservation was excellent. Three zones were identified in the pollen record (fig. 9.4). The basal zone (233–165 cm) dates to the period after ca. 780 B.C. and is dominated by red mangrove pollen, although savanna- and forest-favoring taxa are also common. These grains could have been carried into the coring location through fluvial action, but indicate that forests and savannas may have been present in the vicinity in the past. Sustained quantities of charcoal are noted in most of the samples, indicating that human activities likely took place in the area in the past.

Table 9.5. Sediment Descriptions of the Pointe Figuier, Martinique Core (Core PF08-1).

Depth (cm)	Color	OM (LOI)	Total P (ppm)	Na (ppm)	Sand%	Silt%	Clay%	Notes
0–20	Very dark grayish brown (2.5Y 3/2)	13.9	1620	7325	8	11	81	Organic clay; ±10% gravel Oxidation mottles
20–26	Dark greenish gray (10Y 4/1); Greenish gray (5GY 5/1)	15.6	1530	6713	12	9	79	Highly mottled; includes ±10% small shell fragments
26–53	Dark gray (Gley 4/N)	14.6	370	6548	20	6	74	Sand fraction is fine
53–100	Very dark greenish gray (10Y 3/1)	18.7	550	6672	8	15	77	Organic clay; sand fraction is coarse
100–113								Hole slop
113–127	Very dark gray (5Y 3/1)	20.1	590	6909	5	30	65	Organic silty clay
127–162	Very dark gray (5Y 3/1)	22.3	270	7480	19	9	72	±5 gravel; much of the clay is aggregated into larger clasts
162–188	Very dark gray (Gley 3/N)	26.8	110	9831	27	48	25	Hemic peat; charcoal flecks
188–190	Very dark brown							Fibric peat
190–200								Wood
200–211	Black (Gley 2.5/N)	59.5	180	9944				Fibric peat
211–224	Black (5Y 2.5/1)	44.1	170	10745	44	26	30	Fibric peat
224–230	Dark gray (Gley 4/N)	10.2	<100	14383	80	8	18	Coarse sand composed of tiny shell fragments and coral sand
230–233	Black (5Y 2.5/1)	5.8			71	9	20	

220 • Chapter 9

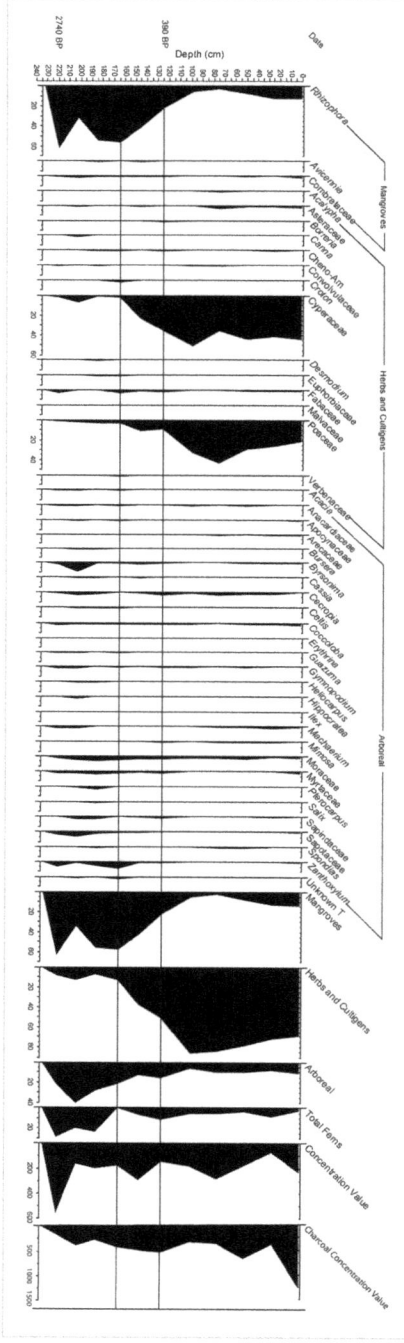

Figure 9.4. Pointe Figuier, Martinique, core pollen-percentage diagram. Pollen and charcoal concentrations are expressed as grains and fragments, respectively, per cm³ of sediment.

Zone 2 (165–125 cm) was characterized by a reduction in red mangrove pollen and increases in grass and sedge pollen. Forest taxa also declined and charcoal concentrations remained high. The uppermost zone (125–0 cm) was similar to Zone 2, with slight increases in Asteraceae (disturbance) grains. Charcoal concentrations remained high and increased in the uppermost sample.

Eight samples were processed for phytoliths from Pointe Figuier. Six were productive for phytoliths, although deposition was inconsistent (figs. 9.5a, 9.5b). The two lower samples (200–225 cm, 231–234 cm) did not produce phytoliths, most likely due to an abundance of mangroves in the area, as evidenced in the pollen record (fig. 9.4). Above 200 cm, phytoliths included arboreal and understory indicators reflecting Arecaceae, woody plants (small rugulose spheres, sclerids), and Marantaceae (large rugulose spheres, nodular spheres), but none dominated the assemblage.

Open indicators, including panicoid grasses, were also represented. Sedge occurred in three of the samples (120 cm and above). This pattern suggests that mixed arboreal vegetation (rather than palm-dominated swamp forest) grew near the coring locality and that the setting was somewhat open. There is also a consistent Marantaceae signature in this core. *Heliconia* sp., a robust understory/edge herb, occurred in one sample (75–80 cm).

Discussion

Human activity is indicated quite early in the KC08-1 core in the form of significant amounts of charcoal and disturbance indicators from pollen taxa associated with open, cleared spaces. Phytoliths were absent below 490 cm; influx between 490 and 390 cm was associated with slight increases in herbaceous and arboreal pollen types, however, suggesting freshwater input from forested habitat. Phosphate values from 400 to 394 cm were indicative of human activities.

In the upper portion of the KC08-1 core (above the ash lens at 227 cm) pollen and phytoliths indicate significant changes in the local environment. Phytoliths suggest a more open environment with greater contributions of palms, grasses, and herbaceous Marantaceae. *Maranta arundinacea, Calathea latifolia,* and *Calathea lutea* have been collected on Martinique; these could be sources of the Marantaceae phytoliths recovered in both of the Martinique cores. At the very top of the KC08-1 core, Marantaceae, woody plants, and palms occurred in roughly equal quantities, with some grass phytoliths. There is a consistent Marantaceae

222 • Chapter 9

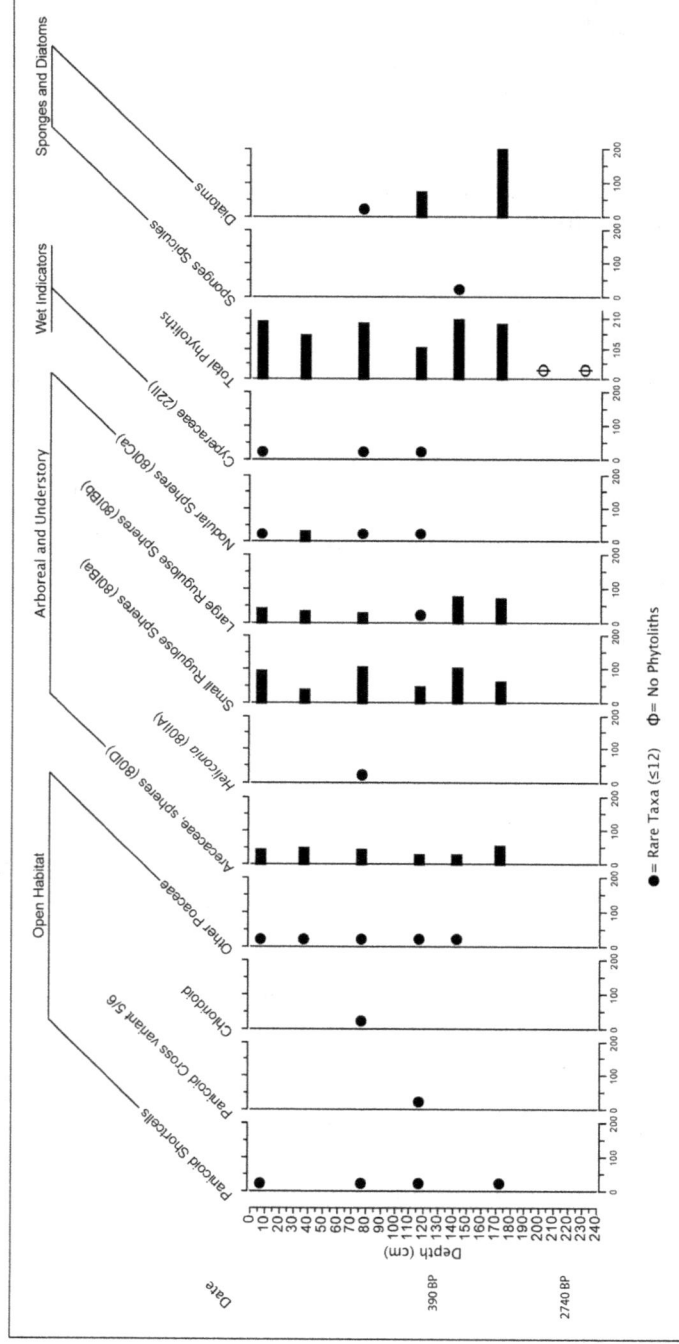

Figure 9.5a. Pointe Figuier, Martinique, core phytolith diagram: resolved.

Martinique • 223

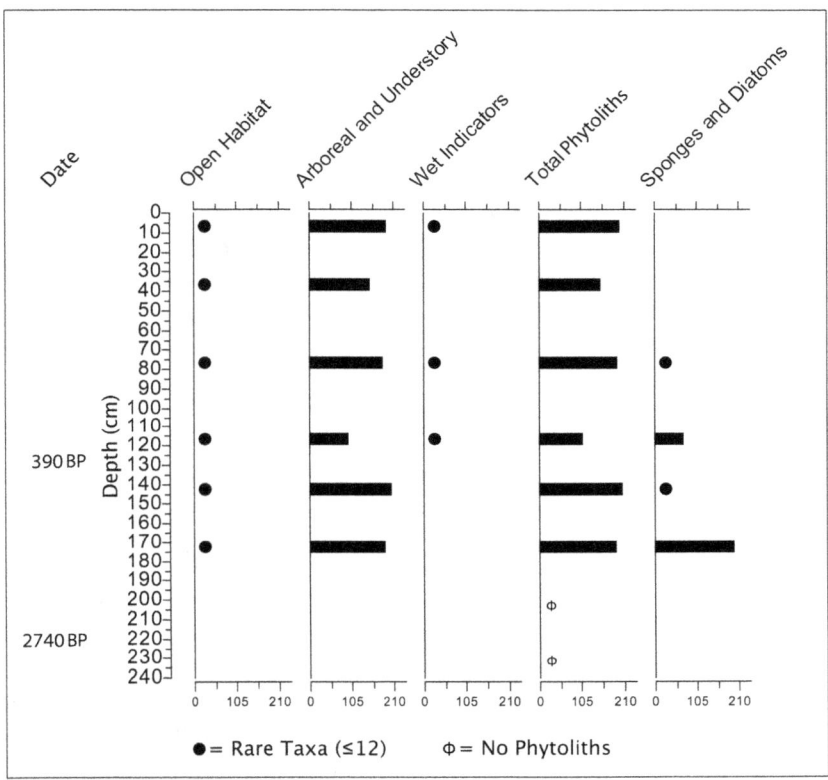

Figure 9.5b. Pointe Figuier, Martinique, core phytolith diagram: composite.

Table 9.6. Sedimentation Rates for the Martinique Cores.

Core, ^{14}C sample depths	[14]C Date Ranges (Median Cal Dates, BP)	Sedimentation Rate (cm/yr)
Baie de Fort-de-France, 0–230 cm	0–1610	.1428
Baie de Fort-de-France, 230–575 cm	1610–5000	.1017
Baie de Fort-de-France, 575–675 cm	5000–5740	.1351
Pointe Figuier, 0–128 cm	0–390	.3282
Pointe Figuier, 128–222 cm	390–2740	.0404

signature that strengthened in the upper meter of the core. Mangrove pollen began to dominate the pollen assemblage by 190 cm, associated with a sharp reduction of arboreal pollen types. This apparent discrepancy between pollen and phytolith indicators may be explained by influx of phytoliths from arboreal and understory plants from more-distant upstream locations, whereas mangroves dominated the immediate coring locality. The change in upstream phytolith influx from forest-dominated indicators to more-open habitat with greater palm presence may be associated with Plinian eruptions of Mount Pelée. Following heavy ash fall, open habitat indicators should be expected; the pollen record is less telling, however, showing a reduction in arboreal types and a dramatic resurgence of mangrove pollen above 175 cm.

It is unclear from which volcanic source the ash lens is derived. Previous volcanological investigations on Martinique suggest that the maximum dispersal of ejecta from Mount Pelée eruptions was in the area of present-day Fort-de-France, approximately 7 km north of the KC08-1 coring location (Allaire 1989: fig. 6; Westercamp and Traineau 1983). The ca. A.D. 335 date associated with the ash lens overlaps with the second Plinian (A.D. 280±60) and *nuées ardentes* Marne Ponce (A.D. 220±80) eruptions reported by Westercamp and Traineau (1983; see also Allaire 1989: fig. 5). If our ash lens is associated with either of those eruptions, then the geographic extent of the ash fall will need to be somewhat revised. There are no documented archaeological sites in the vicinity of the coring location that are contemporaneous with the ash lens, although there are quite a few sites farther north closer to Mount Pelée that range in age from 200 B.C. to A.D. 400 (Bright 2011: fig. 3.5).

Signals of human activity are quite strong in the Pointe Figuier core. One nearby archaeological site, Anse Figuier, a Mid to Late Saladoid site (ca. A.D. 600–700), is known (Bérard 2004). Buried ceramics were also noted within the core sediments, indicating a buried archaeological site in this location. Charcoal concentrations were elevated throughout the core, suggesting human activity through the sequence from ca. 780 B.C. The absence of phytoliths in the lower portion of the core (below 175 cm) is associated with high mangrove pollen counts, suggesting low phytolith influx from freshwater sources. The coring location was likely open to the ocean still at this point. Beginning in Pollen Zone 2, there was a marked decline in mangroves beginning at 165 cm, reflected by an influx of freshwater (lower Na levels in the sediments). Phytoliths also appeared in this zone around 170 cm and represent palm, arboreal, and herbaceous taxa. A disjunction in the sediments around 162 cm appears to be associated with a major storm event. Above 165 cm, mangroves declined, while pollen from sedges, grasses, and herbaceous plants became more dominant beginning just before 120 cm. At this point, a significant reduction was documented in phytolith counts associated with an upward spike in phosphates at 113–127 cm. Major landscape modifications revealed by these changes in the pollen and phytolith assemblages are linked to large-scale historic period agriculture on the island dated to after ca. A.D. 1560.

Once Europeans arrived to the West Indies with their views of globalization, market economies, and appropriate ways to benefit from these new lands and the occupants of them, they embarked on profit-driven strategies of landscape modification. In particular the English, French, and Dutch converted many of the previously forested islands of the Lesser Antilles into landscapes of single species of plants: tobacco (*Nicotiana rustica* or *N. tabacum*), indigo (*Indigofera suffruticosa*), and especially sugarcane (*Saccharum officinarum*) (Sheridan 1973; Watts 1966, 1987). On many of the islands, the sugar industry consumed ever-increasing amounts of forest to clear land for cultivation, mills, and housing, and to provide fuel wood for the mills and refineries.

Early colonial planters were under the misconception "that all West Indian soils exposed from beneath species-rich tropical rain-forest … would be fertile, and would stay that way, for the whole landscape *looked* rich in resources" especially compared to the lands of their home countries (Watts 1987: 396, emphasis in original). Of course, within about a century of intensive plantation agriculture many of these tropical landscapes were described as "barren, rocky gullies, runaway land [eroded], waste land, and all the rest much worn out and not so fertile as it was … [and] now lies waste[d]" (Anonymous 1710, cited in Watts 1987: 397).

The 94 cm of basal sediments in the Pointe Figuier core accumulated over approximately 2,300 years, from ca. 780 B.C. to ca. A.D. 1560 (tabs. 9.1, 9.6). The upper 128 cm of sedimentation occurred largely after the arrival of Europeans. The plantation system on Martinique was established in the 1670s. By 1736 there were 447 sugar plantations documented, and nearly the entire lowlands of the island were cleared for cultivation (Watts 1987: 299–300, fig. 7.4). Over the past four hundred years (14% of the time span since 780 B.C.), 58 percent of the sediments in the Figuier core resulted from colluvial erosional deposits (tab. 9.6).

 10

Marie-Galante

*John G. Jones, Nicholas P. Dunning,
Deborah M. Pearsall, and Peter E. Siegel*

Background

Marie-Galante is a remarkably circular island of about 158 km² lying some 27 km southeast of the larger island of Guadeloupe, a French overseas department (figs. 1.1, 10.1). The island's circular and relatively flat appearance has given it the nickname *la grande galette* (the big pancake). Until the recent finding of an Archaic burial in Grotte du Morne Rita (Fouéré et al. 2015), archaeological investigations to date have indicated that human occupations on Marie-Galante did not begin until Early Saladoid times. Along with the Archaic burial, paleoenvironmental data reported here suggest that occupation began much earlier.

Marie-Galante is situated along the forearc of the Lesser Antilles subduction zone, a mainly submarine ridge of uplifted seafloor. The island comprises uplifted Pliocene to Holocene Age coral limestone reef structures of generally very low relief. Karst features, including sinkholes and caves, are evident in many places on the island. Normal faulting has produced locally dramatic topographic breaks on the north half of the island. A prominent 500- to 800-m wide graben, known locally as *le bar*, runs from the west to east coast from Anse du Vieux Fort to Anse Piton. The horst upland on the south side of the graben is clearly defined by a 90- to 110-m escarpment. Short, very steep drainages have begun to dissect the escarpment. A sluggish, spring-fed, low-grade surface stream, the Rivière du Vieux Fort, drains the western half of the graben. The horst upland on the north side of the graben slopes upward to the north at an average slope of 5 to 10 percent. This sloping terrain has been dissected by several dendritic surface stream systems.

Marie-Galante's climate reflects its tropical maritime location and lack of significant elevation. There is little variation in either daily or annual temperature with monthly average minimum-maximum ranges from 22.5° C to 27.8° C in February and from 25.5° C to 30.5° C in

Marie-Galante • 227

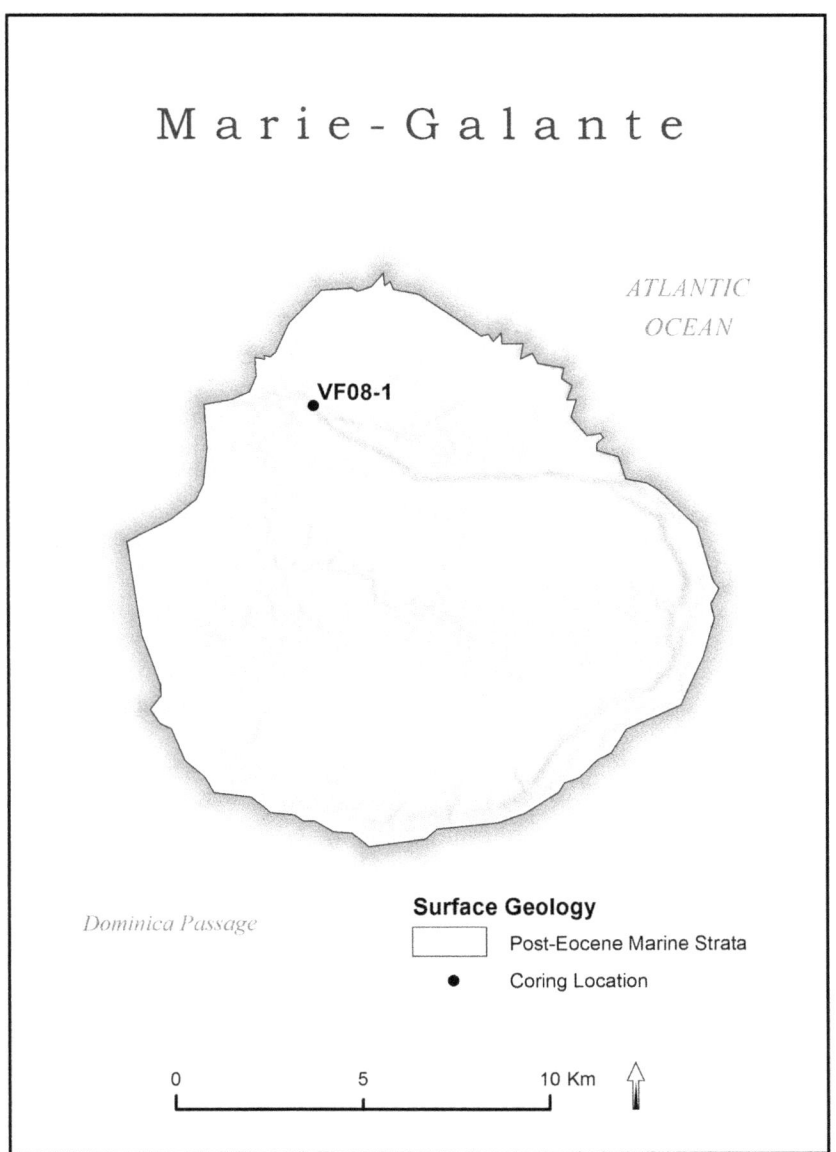

Figure 10.1. Map of Marie-Galante showing the surface geology and coring location.

August/September. Rainfall on Marie-Galante averages about 900 mm annually, but with significant interannual variation and significant seasonality; most precipitation occurs from July through December. Hurricanes impact the area on average once every four to five years (Zahibo et al. 2007).

Soils within the *le bar* graben comprise mainly wetland Histosols (organic mucks and peats), and soils on the horst uplands range from skeletal Entisols on steep slopes to Lithic Rendolls (Rendzinas) on moderate slopes, to Vertisols on flatter surfaces. All soils are predominantly clayey in texture, though the Entisols and Rendolls have a significant sand (chiefly weathered limestone grit) component in their C-horizons. The clay is predominantly smectite and is likely derived chiefly from volcanic ash deposited from eruptions on neighboring islands. The soils have a high base-saturation status due to elevated levels of calcium. Phosphorus is notably low.

Today the flora of Marie-Galante includes both pantropical native species and introduced species from the continental Americas, Europe, and Asia (Casile 2010). The VF08-1 core was collected in a former lagoon within *le bar*, which is now a waterlogged sedge meadow lying behind a white mangrove forest. Formerly, this waterway was open to the sea, but it has silted in over time. Modern vegetation in the coring area is dominated by sedges (*Cyperus, Eleocharis, Cladium*), white mangroves (*Conocarpus, Laguncularia*), and various grasses (*Phragmites, Paspalum*); at slightly higher elevations sugarcane is being cultivated. The steep hills framing the graben are dominated by semideciduous tropical vegetation. Trees identified in the area include *Pimienta* (bay rum), *Inga, Ficus,* Sapotaceae, and *Coccoloba.*

In total, fifty-nine pre-Columbian sites are registered for Marie-Galante (Direction Regionale des Affaires Culturelles [DRAC] 2008; Stouvenot and Gineste 2002: 11). The sites date to the Saladoid and Troumassoid periods, although a possible Archaic presence has been documented on the main island of Guadeloupe (Clerc 1976; de Waal 2006: 71). Most of the sites on Marie-Galante are coastal, three are inland (more than 2 km from the coast), and nine are intermediate between the coast and interior (about 0.5 to 2 km from the shore). Folle Anse and Talisseronde are two of the more notable Early Ceramic Age sites on Marie-Galante (Hofman et al. 2004). Folle Anse, Grotte du Morne Rita, Pavillon, and Talisseronde contain late Cedrosan Saladoid deposits (de Waal 2006). Two post-Saladoid sites (Vieux Fort 2, Anse Bambou Sud) occur within 0.5 km of the coring location and a third (Pointe du Cimetière) is found approximately 3 km away (DRAC 2008).

Christopher Columbus stopped on Marie-Galante during his second voyage in 1493; the island is named for one of his vessels. The first European settlement was established in 1648, a colony of about fifty French settlers, all of whom died within five years from disease or starvation, or at the hands of indigenous people. A peace treaty was signed in 1660 between the French and the Caribs allowing for the establishment of a permanent European settlement. With the exception of a British occupation between 1759 and 1763, Marie-Galante has remained under French control. Indigo and tobacco were initially important colonial crops on the island, although sugarcane eventually dominated the agricultural system. Marie-Galante was largely deforested during the seventeenth and eighteenth centuries as the sugar industry expanded. In the eighteenth century the island was famous for its numerous windmills and boasted more than a hundred small sugar mills. Sugarcane remains the most important crop on Marie-Galante, though processing is now centralized in one mill and several rum distilleries.

Environmental Coring on Marie-Galante

Vieux Fort (Core VF09-1)

The nearly 7-m core was collected from a sedge wetland along Rivière du Vieux Fort a little more than 1 km east of the island's west coast at a current elevation of less than 1 m above mean sea level (figs. 4.1c, 10.1). Based on evidence in the core, the western portion of the graben aggraded significantly during the Holocene, though much of the sediment is organic. It is likely that deeper coring would reveal multiple episodes of Pleistocene aggradation and degradation.

From 657 to 464 cm the core comprised hemic and fibric histic material derived largely from red mangroves (*Rhizophora*). A basal peat sample dated to ca. 4580 B.C. (tab. 10.1). At that time, mean sea level was approximately 2 m lower than today and was slowly rising. High Na and S levels and good organic matter preservation in the basal sediments reflect a stable, brackish, but moderately high saline mangrove-forest habitat (tab. 10.2).

The estuary where these sediments were deposited was closer to the ocean shore at the time, and the predominance of red mangrove indicates that the system would have been brackish to full marine. Sedimentation rates in the core ranged from low to moderate throughout (tab. 10.3). Pollen from disturbance-indicating vegetation was sparse and particulate charcoal was almost wholly lacking in all samples from

Table 10.1. Sediment Descriptions for the Vieux Forte, Marie-Galante Core (Core VF08-1).

Depth (cm)	Color	OM (LOI)	P ppm	Ca ppm	Na ppm	Sand%	Silt%	Clay%	Notes
0–5	Greenish black (Gley 10Y 2.5/1)	29.8							Fibric peat
5–31	Dark green gray (Gley 10Y 3/1)	25.9	1300	167600	6434	86	7	7	Sapric peat; many roots; charcoal smears
31–51	Black (2.5Y 2.5/1)	32.1	1140	99100	6825	59	17	24	Hemic peat
51–65	Black (5Y 2.5/1)	39.9				55	19	26	Hemic peat
65–76	Black (Gley N 2.5/N)	46.3				49	22	29	
76–115	Black (2.5Y 2.5/1)	52.7	620	94000	8960	38	32	30	Hemic peat with some fibric material
115–142	Black (Gley N 2.5/N)	61.8	590	101400	11511	41	28	31	Hemic peat
142–143	Very dark gray (10YR 3/1)								Clayey ash
143–157	Black (Gley N 2.5/N)	64.2				37	23	40	Hemic peat
157–161	Light brownish gray (10YR 6/2)	13.7	530	201600	22762	62	7	31	Sticky marl
161–172	Dark green gray (Gley 10Y 3/1)	22.6	340	106000	19666	10	12	78	Peaty clay
172–206	Black (Gley N 2.5/N)	58.0				41	31	28	Sapric peat
206–214	Black and light gray	27.8							Bands of strata above and below
214–232	Light gray (10YR 7/2)	18.1	470	225300	21381	70	8	22	Sticky marl with root casts
232–257	Very dark gray (10YR 3/1)	44.4							Weakly banded hemic peat

(continued)

Table 10.1. (continued)

Depth (cm)	Color	OM (LOI)	P ppm	Ca ppm	Na ppm	Sand%	Silt%	Clay%	Notes
257–261	Greenish black (Gley 10Y 2.5/1)	29.4				11	20	69	Clayey sapric peat
261–263	Very pale brown (10YR 7/4)	11.0							Sticky marl
263–280	Black (Gley N 2.5/N)	73.5	310	97300	18433	36	23	41	Hemic peat
280–282	Greenish gray (Gley 10Y 5/1)					26	14	60	Clayey ash
282–390	Black (Gley N 2.5/N)	81.0	220	91700	20084	44	35	21	Hemic peat with some fibric material
390–394.5	Black (Gley N 2.5/N)	51.6				10	14	76	Sapric peaty clay
394.5–396	Black (2.5Y 2.5/1)								Sapric peaty clay
396–397.5	Dark brown (7.5YR 3/3)								Sapric peaty clay with fine shell fragments
397.5–401.5	Light reddish brown (5YR 6/4)	4.0							Gritty marl; red mottles
401.5–402.5	Pink (5YR 7/3)	1.1							Shells in marly matrix
402.5–404	Dark red brown (2.5YR 3/4)	18.7							Weakly banded marl and peat
404–412	Pink (7.5YR 7/3)	16.1	260	215700	21828	68	9	23	Sticky marl
412–414	Brown (7.5YR 4/3)								Sticky marl
414–415	Brown (7.5YR 4/3)								Marl with charcoal and many shells
415–425	Very dark brown (10YR 2/2)	66.3							Weakly banded hemic peat
425–440	Grayish brown (10YR 5/2)	14.0				7	8	85	Clay

(continued)

Table 10.1. (continued)

Depth (cm)	Color	OM (LOI)	P ppm	Ca ppm	Na ppm	Sand%	Silt%	Clay%	Notes
440–464	Dark grayish brown (10YR 4/2)	9.8	180	64300	19375	37	12	51	Sandy clay with many marine shells
464–657	Dark reddish brown (2.5YR 2.5/3)	80.2	520	82600	18469	79	9	12	Hemic and fibric peat and roots (Red Mangrove)

Notes:
Shells identified by Denis Nieweg:
396–398 cm:
Within this sample two mollusc and one ostracod (Crustacea) species were recognised.
The molluscs consisted of :
-*Neritina virginea* (L. 1758), Neritidae. Two individuals and one dorsal fragment.
-*Hydrobia sp.*, Hydrobiidae. Two individuals of which one complete. Due to the fact that literature about these small molluscs is scarce, the specimen could not be analysed to species level.
The ostracod remains (>10) were likely to be one species namely: *Strandesia cf. sphaeroidea* Broodbakker 1983.

414–415 cm:
Only the mollusc *Neritina virginea* was present consisting of four specimens, which were very eroded and decalcified.
Two species of ostracods were recognised within this sample, namely: *Strandesia cf. sphaeroidea* (>15) and another not identified (two notched valve) (>10).
From the location Rivière Vieux Fort, Marie-Galante other ostracods are known such as *Perissocytheridea sp.*, *Chlamydotheca unispinosa*, *Cypris subglobosa*, *Tanycypris meridian*, and *Strandesia trispinosa galantis*. These species are probably not the ostracod species recognised from this sample. This due to the fact, that the genera from these species have other characteristics.

440–464 cm:
From this sample four mollusc species were recognised as:
Bivalves:
-*Chione cancellata* (L. 1767), Veneridae. One left valve.
-*Crassostrea rhizophorae* (Guilding 1828), Ostreidae. Three upper valves, two lower valves and additional fragments (not compatible, NISP [Number of Identified Specimens]=5).
-*Brachidontes exustus* (L. 1758), Mytilidae. Two fragments.
And the gastropod: *Nassarius antillarum* (d'Orbigny 1842), Nassaridae. Two juveniles and one adult.
-Cirripedia (Crustacea), barnacle fragment. Heavily eroded.

Table 10.2. Radiocarbon Dates from the Vieux Fort, Marie-Galante Core (Core VF08-1).

Lab Sample Number	Sample Depth	^{14}C Age (BP)[a]	^{13}C/^{12}C Ratio	2-Sigma Calibrated Date Range[b]	Median Cal Date
Beta-379163	60–65 cm, PP[c]	230±30	-25.3	AD 1530–1950/ 1–420 BP	AD 1690/ 260 BP
Beta-383083	60–65 cm, OS[d], alkali insoluble	660±30	-27.2	AD 1280–1390/ 560–670 BP	AD 1340/ 610 BP
Beta-378827	60–65 cm, OS	630±30	-27.0	AD 1290–1400/ 550–660 BP	AD 1350/ 600 BP
AA84800	205–207 cm, Peat	1980±35	-26.3	50 BC–AD 120/ 1830–2000 BP	AD 20/ 1930 BP
AA84883	255–257 cm, OS	2960±30	-31.2	1290–1050 BC/ 3000–3210 BP	1170 BC/ 3120 BP
AA84884	414.5 cm, CW[e]	4380±60	-26.7	3330–2890 BC/ 4840–5280 BP	3020 BC/ 4970 BP
AA82675	655–657 cm, Peat	5730±70	-27.4	4730–4370 BC/ 6320–6710 BP	4580 BC/ 6530 BP

a. 1-sigma range.
b. Dates were calibrated using the IntCal13 method of CALIB ver. 7.0 (Reimer et al. 2013).
c. Preserved plant matter.
d. Organic sediment.
e. Carbonized wood.

Table 10.3. Sedimentation Rates for the Vieux Fort, Marie-Galante Core (Core VF08-1).

^{14}C sample depths	^{14}C Date Ranges (Median Cal Dates, BP)	Sedimentation Rate (cm/yr)
0–63 cm	0–600	.1050
63–206 cm	600–1930	.1075
206–256 cm	1930–3120	.0420
256–414.5 cm	3120–4960	.0861
414.5–656 cm	4960–6530	.1538

this basal zone, representing a nonanthropogenic landscape (fig. 10.2). Also represented in this basal zone, forest composition of the nearby hills above the coring location was dominated by semideciduous elements, including Moraceae (mostly *Brosimum alicastrum*), *Byrsonima*, *Bursera*, *Coccoloba*, *Cecropia*, and *Machaerium*. The slightly elevated percentages of *Byrsonima* pollen (nance) hint at slightly drier conditions because these trees were probably local and favor savanna-like settings.

With rising sea levels the red mangrove environment was destabilized, reflected by sandy, shell-rich deposits beginning at 464 cm. Superadjacent sediments indicate a nearer-to-shore lagoonal environment with frequent bands of biogenic marls and increased salinity. A high concentration of mollusk shells between 464 and 440 cm is indicative of the die-off of species present in formerly stable mangroves (tab. 10.2). The marl layers are a product of autochthonous biogenic sediments forming either within algal mats or via pelletization during episodes of Ca supersaturation within stagnant backwater contexts. Clay strata were deposited during still-water episodes. Periods of marl and clay precipitation were interrupted by development of organic strata, reflecting resurgence of mangrove forest in the area. Concentrations of *Neritina* shells with evidence of in situ predation at 396–398 cm also indicate a period of brackish mangrove habitat stabilization (also indicated by ostracods sharing this habitat) (tab. 10.2).

Sustained increases in particulate charcoal concentrations were documented by 400 cm (fig. 10.2). This period of elevated charcoal concentrations was bracketed by the dates of ca. 3020 and 1170 B.C., which is associated with the Mid Holocene period of wet conditions in the Caribbean. Pollen concentration values for invasive weedy and economically useful taxa increased at this time. Disturbance-indicator taxa included Asteraceae, Poaceae, Cyperaceae, and *Cecropia* (tabs. 10.4, 10.5). With the clearing of local forests, plants of economic value were selectively spared and encouraged, resulting in higher pollen concentrations of what were previously scarce types. Economically useful plant taxa included Arecaceae (palm family) and Sapotaceae (Sapote family). It is not clear what accounts for the replacement of the *Rhizophora* (red) by the Combretaceae (white) mangrove communities, although evidence of rising sea level by 464 cm may be linked to the reduction in red mangrove at about 410 cm. Myrtaceae pollen concentrations also declined markedly at this time. Major increases in charcoal concentration values beginning at 400 cm may or may not be related to the shift in mangrove communities. Red mangrove has been documented to be a superior fuel wood (Morton 1965), although its diminished presence in the Marie-Galante pollen record predates by an unknown number of years the

Marie-Galante • 235

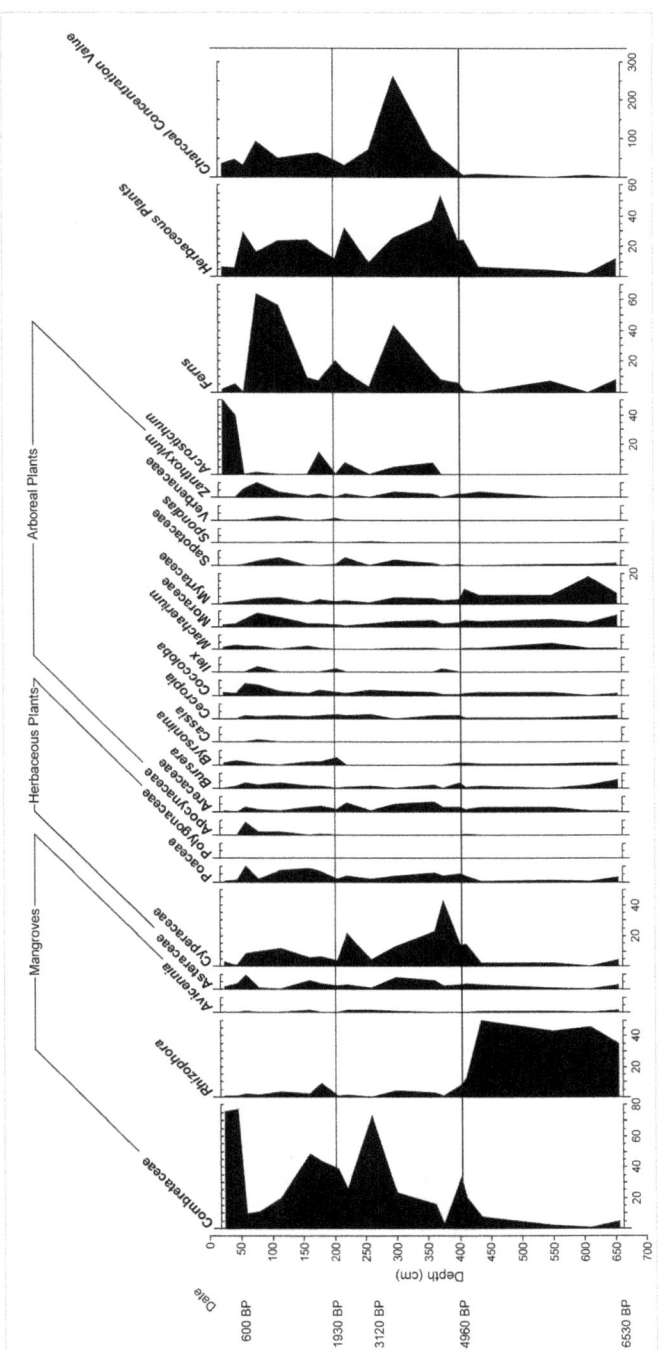

Figure 10.2. Vieux Fort, Marie-Galante, core pollen-percentage diagram. Pollen and charcoal concentrations are expressed as grains and fragments, respectively, per cm³ of sediment.

Table 10.4. Ethnobotanical Associations and Disturbance Indicators Represented in the Marie-Galante Core.[a]

Taxon	Ethnobotanical Association or Disturbance Indicator	Core VF08-1
MANGROVE		
Avicennia	Black mangrove. Throat pains, incontinence.	X[b]
Combretaceae	White mangrove. Slows bleeding.	X
Rhizophora	Red mangrove. Diarrhea, fever, malaria, excellent fuel wood.	X
HERBS/CULTIGENS		
Asteraceae	Aster or Composite family. Herbs and shrubs. Many are invasive weed species of cleared open areas.	X
Cyperaceae	Sedge family. Grasslike herbaceous plants, many are weeds that invade cleared open areas.	X
Poaceae	Grass family. Often associated with areas frequently fired. Edible starchy grains.	X
ARBOREAL		
Anacardiaceae, *Spondias* sp.	Cashew family. Edible fruit, hogplum.	X[b]
Apocynaceae	Dogbane family. Golden trumpet vine. Fibers used for cordage. Some produce edible flowers.	X
Arecaceae	Palm family. Edible fruit, thatching, cordage, needles, posts.	X
Byrsonima	Edible fruit, nance.	X
Bursera	Gumbo limbo. Resin has medicinal properties, leaves used for tea.	X
Cecropia	Pumpwood. Fast-growing colonizing trees common to disturbed forest habitats and clearings.	X
Coccoloba	Sea grape. Edible fruit, medicinal.	X
Moraceae	Mulberry family. Edible fruit, breadnut, medicinal. Often colonize open cleared areas.	X
Myrtaceae	Myrtle family. Edible fruit, medicinal. Frequently found in windbreak and secondary forest growth. Includes guava, Eugenia, allspice.	X
Sapotaceae	Sapote family. Edible fruit, medicinal, latex in some species. Includes edible fruits of chicle, sapote, lucuma.	X
Verbenaceae	Verbena family. Some with aromatic and medicinal properties.	X

a. See Table 5.5 for sources of information.
b. Trace amounts.

Table 10.5. Plant Taxa Identified in the Marie-Galante Core Samples with No Documented Ethnobotanical or Anthropogenic Correlates Other than Perhaps Fuel Wood, Especially Arboreal Taxa.

Taxon	Common Name	Core VF08-1
ARBOREAL		
Ilex	Holly	X
Machaerium	Escambrón, spiny climbing shrub or small tree. Form thickets in mangrove swamps.	X
Zanthoxylum	Prickly ash	X
FERNS		
Unknown ferns		X

significant increase in probable anthropogenic fires. Combined, the charcoal and pollen data reflect a human-modified if not actively managed landscape by ca. 3000 B.C., considerably earlier than archaeological evidence for human occupations on Marie-Galante, except for the recently excavated Archaic burial in Morne Rita (Fouéré et al. 2015).

Volcanic ash was documented at 280–282 cm and 142–143 cm, probably attributable to activity of La Soufrière volcano on nearby Guadeloupe. At least twelve eruptions are recorded for La Soufrière between 3,000 and 1,500 years ago (Komorowski et al. 2005). Above 157 cm, marl layers no longer formed and mineral sediment input became more pronounced (although the sediment remained histic), indicating aggradation of the graben after sea levels further stabilized about two thousand years ago and the shoreline was farther removed from the coring location. Increased levels of P and K in the upper 50 cm of the core reflect contributions of modern fertilizers and increases in mineral sediment associated with agricultural land clearance (tab. 10.2). The uppermost pollen zone was poorly defined, marked by subtle shifts in flora. Changes in forest composition during this time included slight increases in pollen from Apocynaceae, *Bursera*, *Coccoloba*, *Machaerium*, Moraceae, Sapotaceae, and *Zanthoxylum*. These taxa are all important members of the modern local forests. The spike in charcoal along with an increase in grass pollen in the uppermost 20 cm marked the onset of sugarcane production in the immediate area.

Eighteen samples were processed for phytoliths but only one from 265 to 270 cm produced four phytoliths: Asteraceae (2), palm, and *Heliconia*.

Discussion

Marie-Galante is an exclusively limestone island believed to have been first occupied by humans in the Ceramic Age (Saladoid). Our 657-cm core from the northwestern part of the island produced a basal date of ca. 4580 B.C. The landscape at that time was characterized by red mangrove with no evidence of a human presence. The lower sediments of the core formed in an evolving environment close to the ocean. The red mangrove thicket was gradually replaced by a less saline environment as local sea-level rise led to aggradation within the low-gradient Rivière du Vieux Fort fluvial system and increasingly distanced the coring location from the ocean. Around the time of this transformation, human settlers first occupied Marie-Galante, evidenced by significant increases in charcoal and pollen from disturbance-indicator and economically useful taxa. These elevated charcoal values and associated disturbance indicators dated to ca. 3000 B.C. during the mesic conditions of the Holocene. Human activities on Marie-Galante continued uninterrupted through the remainder of pre-Columbian history and accelerated in the past few hundred years as colonial indigo and sugar plantation economies radically altered the island's landscape.

The landscapes created and managed by the early Archaic colonists to the island were eventually occupied by the Early Ceramic Age Neolithic settlers to Marie-Galante. The apparently larger and archaeologically more visible Ceramic Age occupants came to an island with already-managed landscapes, onto which they grafted their distinctively lowland South American lifestyles.

11

ANTIGUA

John G. Jones, Nicholas P. Dunning, Deborah M. Pearsall, Neil A. Duncan, and Peter E. Siegel

Background

Antigua is purported to have 365 beaches, one for every day of the year, as the Antigua and Barbuda Department of Tourism puts it. Whether this count is accurate really depends on how one counts, and what one counts, as a beach. Like almost all the small islands of the West Indies, Antigua has no natural lakes. Fortunately, there are several areas along its coast with extant mangrove wetlands that contain accumulating terrestrial sediment and preserved paleoenviromental proxies such as pollen and phytoliths. Several wetlands were sampled during the course of our investigations, with two yielding significant results. Several of Antigua's many beaches did prove useful for rinsing coring equipment and ourselves of mangrove swamp muck.

Antigua is located about two thirds of the way north along the chain of the Lesser Antilles and is part of an older volcanic island arc marking the junction of the Caribbean and South American tectonic plates that developed some 40 million years ago; volcanoes on the island have been inactive for about the past 29 million years. The southwestern third of the island comprises highly eroded, deeply dissected remnants of ancient volcanic cones, including Boggy Peak, the highest point on the island at 402 m. The northeastern third consists of a more recent limestone shelf created during episodes of submergence. The central plain of the island is underlain by both igneous and sedimentary formations and is notable as a pronounced graben (structural trough) running across the island, within which Quaternary Age sediments have accumulated (fig. 11.1).

The eastern shoreline of Antigua is a classic ria coast consisting of roughly parallel deep embayments separated by steep ridges. This coast formed as the result of deep fluvial dissection of the landscape during the various lower sea-level stands of the Pleistocene and the

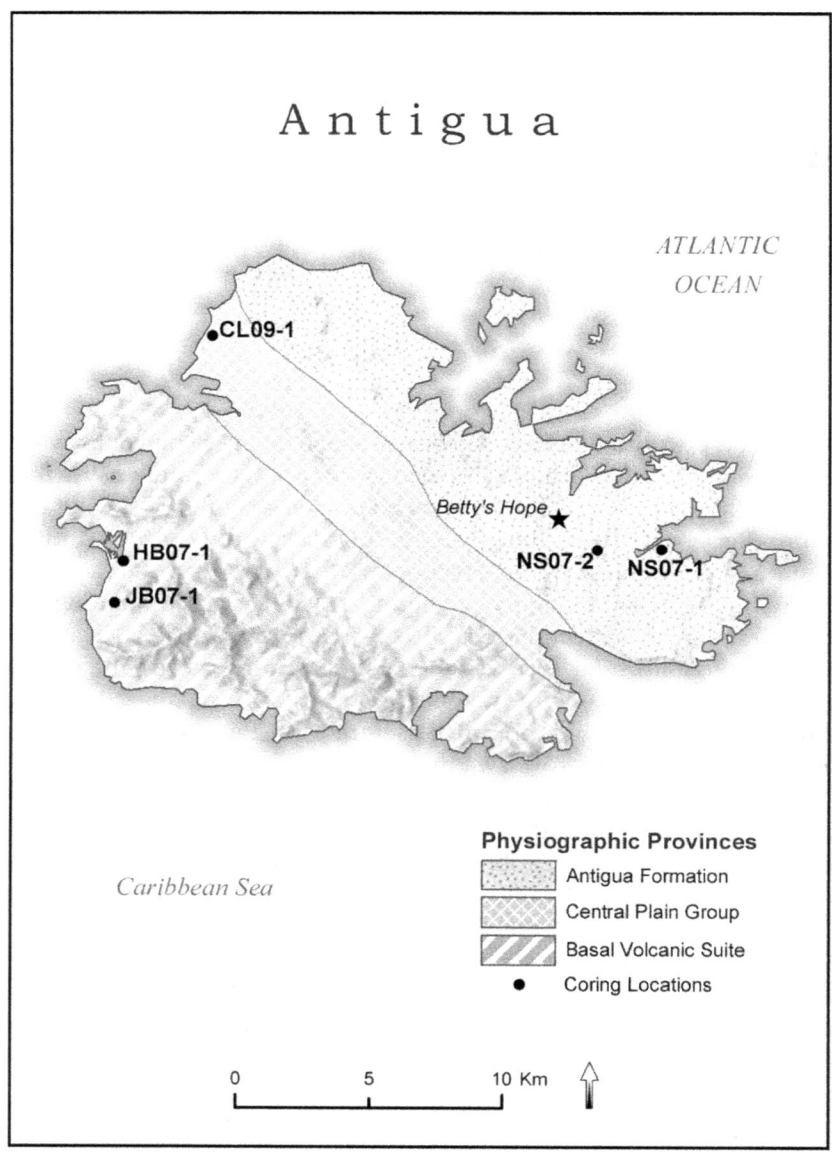

Figure 11.1. Map of Antigua showing the surface geology and coring locations.

partial drowning of these deep valleys following Holocene sea-level increases. Nonsuch Bay lies in the largest of these valleys.

The climate of Antigua is tropical maritime with little variation in either daily or annual temperature. Monthly average minimums range from 22.4°C in February to 25.4°C in August, and monthly average maximums range from 27.9°C in February to 30.5°C in September. Rainfall averages about 1,050 mm annually, but since 1960 annual highs and lows of 1,708 mm and 667 mm have been recorded in the capital city of St. John's. Historically, droughts have been a frequent problem for Antigua's farmers. Following orographic patterns, rainfall totals are lowest in the north and east (typically around 1,050 mm) and highest in the hilly southwest where annual rainfall reaches about 1,400 mm. Rainfall is strongly seasonal with a pronounced December—May dry season. Antigua is struck by a hurricane approximately every twelve years.

Very little of Antigua's pre-European vegetative cover still exists. From early European accounts, the island was largely mantled in forest and scrubland in the early seventeenth century, with the height and complexity of vegetative cover linked to rainfall distributions (Loveless 1960). Based on historical accounts and a few remnant patches of relatively undisturbed forest, the wet volcanic uplands appear to have been mantled in tropical seasonal forest with *Cedrela mexicana, Ceiba occidentalis, Ficus citrifolia, Hymenaea courbaril, Inga laurina,* and *Pisonia subcortata* among the dominant trees. At lower elevations and more northerly latitudes, the forest cover became progressively lower in height and more deciduous, interdigitating with scrubland or thickets dominated by *Acacia, Bursera,* and *Pisonia* spp. Areas with little rainfall and very shallow soil cover possessed more-open, more-xerophytic cover. Coastal zones along sheltered bays and inlets contained areas of swamp-forest and mangrove ecosystems.

For the size of the island, Antigua has an extraordinary number of pre-Columbian sites (Archaic and Ceramic Age), in addition to numerous above- and below-ground remains of colonial occupations. Many documented Archaic sites are located along the coast, many of them backed by mangroves (Davis 1974, 1982, 2000: 101, fig. 23). Pregill et al. (1988) recovered faunal remains of twelve extinct species of animals dating to Archaic occupations of the island, suggesting that people were responsible for the animals' demise. Jolly Beach is one of the most prominent and well-known Archaic sites in the Caribbean and is located next to two salt ponds along the west-southwest coast (Davis 2000). Another Archaic and two Ceramic Age coastal sites are within

2 km to the north and south of Jolly Beach (Davis 2000: fig. 23). Nonsuch Bay is located along the east-southeast coast, approximately 22 km nearly due east of Jolly Beach. This bay, and Ayres Creek that flows into it, were the loci of considerable prehistoric activity, judging from the density of documented archaeological sites (Davis 2000: fig. 23; Stokes 1991: 74–87, 96–109, figs. 4 and 5).

In addition to evidence for fairly intensive human occupation on Antigua during Archaic times, a significant source of chert is located on Long Island, a small island immediately north of the Antigua mainland (Knippenberg 2007). This chert source was exploited during the Archaic and Ceramic Ages. At least during the Ceramic Age, Long Island flint was dispersed in far-flung exchange networks from Martinique in the south through the northern Lesser Antilles, Virgin Islands, and Puerto Rico (Knippenberg 2007).

Colonial activities were a significant factor in restructuring the landscape ecology of Antigua. Spanish, French, and English colonists visited Antigua in the late sixteenth and early seventeenth centuries, although the first documented settlement was not until 1632, when Edward Warner arrived from St. Kitts where his father had settled in 1628. In these early years of occupation "tobacco was listed as Antigua's chief crop, whilst sugar was the only other worthy of mention" (Multer, Weiss, and Nicholson 1986: 4-9). Sugar supplanted tobacco by 1672, though indigo, cotton, and ginger were also cultivated commercially; the first major sugar plantation was in operation at Betty's Hope plantation by 1674, established by Christopher Codrington, who had experience in running a plantation from his previous home on Barbados (Fox 2007; Goodwin 1994; Multer, Weiss, and Nicholson 1986: 4–10). Over the next century sugar dramatically transformed the physical and cultural landscapes of many of the islands in the Lesser Antilles (Meniketti 2015; Richardson 2004; Sheridan 1973; Watts 1987):

> There is little question that the economy of Antigua underwent a remarkable transformation during the first three quarters of the eighteenth century. This was the period when the large sugar plantation became the dominant unit of production; when the race to acquire land, slaves, and sugar works sometimes made for conditions approaching a Hobbesian state of nature. The white population increased from approximately 2,300 in 1678 to 5,200 in 1724. From this peak it then declined to 2,590 in 1774, as the process of consolidating small farms and plantations into sugar estates gained momentum. The slave population, on the other hand, experienced an almost continuous growth; it was reported in scattered census returns at 570 in 1672, 2,172 in 1678, 12,943 in 1708, 27,892 in 1745, and 37,808 in 1774. (Sheridan 1973: 194)

The sugar industry consumed ever-increasing amounts of forest to clear land for cultivation, mills and housing, and to provide fuel wood for the mills and refineries: "Extensive timber felling took place from the 1730s in Antigua ... in order to pave the way for the creation of new sugar estates. In Antigua, by 1750, virtually every district was under cane, there being no forest left on the island, a situation which was maintained at least until the 1790s, when Sir William Young reiterated that the 'country is open, with very few trees or shrubs ... [and] cultivation covers every acre (Young 1801)" (Watts 1987: 434–435). A 1747 map of Antigua shows a thriving and intensive sugarcane industry on the island. By 1775 the island had been stripped of approximately 97 percent of its native vegetative cover (Technical Advisory Committee 2006; Watts 1987).

By the middle of the nineteenth century, sugar markets across much of the Antilles were collapsing, resulting in the abandonment of plantations, including many on Antigua (Armstrong 2001; Fox 2007). By the early twentieth century, over 70 percent of Antigua's former sugar lands lay idle or were being used for other kinds of production, most typically as low-quality pasture. Pasturing and feral stock (notably goats) led to overgrazing and further soil erosion in many areas. The last of Antigua's sugar operations closed in the mid 1970s, but damage to the island's soilscape has endured. A full 90 percent of the soils on Antigua are considered degraded, suffering either from erosion or nutrient depletion resulting from centuries of deforestation, cultivation, and overgrazing (Technical Advisory Committee 2006). Our landscape surveys within the Ayres Creek and Jolly Beach watersheds confirmed this assessment. Almost all soils observed on sloping land were significantly truncated—that is, the A-horizons (topsoil) and often portions of the subsoil had been lost to erosion. At the bases of slopes, buried soil surfaces were sometimes visible where aggradation had accumulated eroded sediments atop older soils. A good example of these processes is illustrated in figure 11.2, a pair of topographically related soils observed on a hillslope in Brooks Township. The 2Ab horizon in the lower soil likely represents the pre-European soil surface, which was buried by colonial-era sediments (C horizon) washing down onto this location from upslope erosion; a modern soil has begun to develop on the lower slope since stabilization (probably resulting from nineteenth-century reforestation). On the upper slope, colonial-era erosion removed all but the lowest part (2C horizon) of the pre-European soil; a thin modern soil has begun to develop on the truncated upper slope.

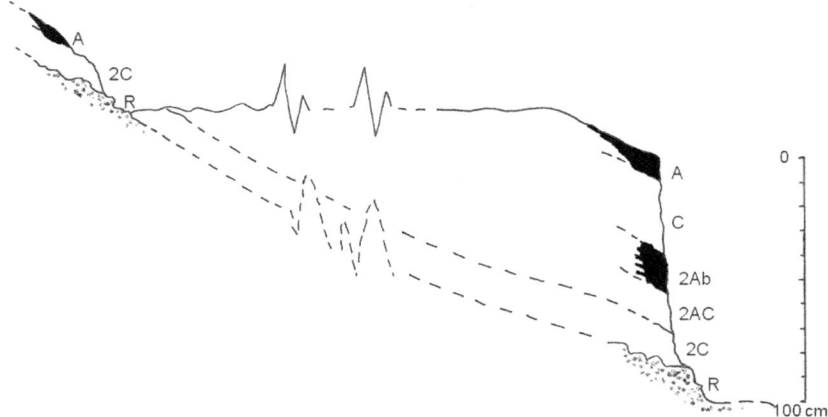

A: Dark grayish brown (10YR4/2) sandy loam; large crumbs; ± 10% gravel.
C: Light yellowish brown (10YR6/4) loamy sand; small crumbs; ± 20% gravel.
2Ab: Very dark grayish brown (10YR3/2) loam; subangular blocks; ± 5% gravel.
2AC: Yellowish brown (10YR5/4) sandy loam; subangular blocks.
2C: Yellow (10YR7/6) sapolitic andesite.
R: Andesite.

Figure 11.2. Cross-section of two soil profiles exposed on a hillslope in the Ayres Creek watershed (Brooks Township, Antigua). The lower profile reveals a mature soil surface (2Ab horizon) buried beneath colluvium (C horizon) generated by colonial-era erosion, atop which a modern soil is developing. The upper profile revealed the severe truncation of the early soil as the result of erosion, leaving behind only some of the original 2C horizon, out of which a modern soil is developing.

Environmental Coring on Antigua

A number of potential coring locations were examined in the coastal periphery of the island. The Nonsuch Bay (Ayres Creek, also known as Collins Creek) area along the east coast was selected because of the likelihood of recovering stratified terrigenous sediments. The core was extracted from an embayed estuary of Ayres Creek. The estuary has formed where the low-grade stream enters Nonsuch Bay and has been dumping large quantities of sediment. The coring location is about 1 km inland from the current marine shoreline and less than 1 m in elevation.

Ayres Creek originates in the volcanic highlands in the southwest, but its 33.5 km^2 watershed lies chiefly in the central plain and limestone shelf. Flow within the watershed is largely seasonally intermittent with many lengths drying to stagnant pools in the winter/spring dry season. The drainage system was largely unchecked until the late 1960s when two earthen dams were constructed on middle sections of the creek, creating the Potsworks and Collins reservoirs, significantly reducing sediment loads in the lower portions of the drainage (both reservoirs are now choked with sediment).

Soils within the watershed fall into three broad groups. The limestone shelf area in the lower portions of the watershed is mantled with skeletal calcareous Entisols on the steepest lands and dark, shallow Rendolls (perhaps the most fertile soils on the island) on flatter ground. Within the central plain or graben, deep, reddish Ultisols have developed on more-acidic sediments, whereas dark, cracking Vertisols have formed on calcareous sediments. The volcanic uplands are mantled by a complex suite of shallow Entisols, Inceptisols, and Ultisols developing out of weathered andesite and other igneous materials.

One sediment core (NS07-1) was initially collected in a red mangrove marsh near the mouth of Nonsuch Bay (fig. 11.1). This short core (1.24 m) appeared to be very young, representing poorly consolidated organic remains overlying decomposed bedrock material, with the organic material likely deposited since the most recent hurricane or major storm event. The Nonsuch Bay area, however, contains substantial numbers of documented Archaic and Ceramic Age sites. In this area sedimentary deposits offered the potential to provide a long and detailed record of past human–environment relations, thus we decided to investigate areas farther up the drainage basin. Approximately 800 m inland from our initial coring location, we identified a mangrove swamp that appeared to contain a substantial sediment record. Precore augering of the sediments revealed a long and potentially complex sediment history in the area; the sediments appeared to be primarily reduced organic-rich clays, silts, and peats. Aceramic archaeological surface deposits were documented in the vicinity of the locality. The decision was made to collect a second core in this new location: Core NS07-2.

The setting of the NS07-2 coring location consisted of standing pools of brackish water, and was dominated by red mangrove (*Rhizophora mangle*) and black mangrove (*Avicennia germinans*) trees, with white mangrove (*Laguncularia* sp.) and buttonwood (*Conocarpus erectus*) occurring on drier islands rising no more than 2 m above the swamps. Other taxa noted on these drier areas included the ubiquitous introduced *Acacia,* as well as *Leucaena, Prosopis, Sideroxylon, Eugenia, Hura,* and *Canella,* as well as assorted grasses, sedges, and herbs. Mongooses and crabs and recent human activity extensively disturbed the drier sandy ridges, but the wetlands proper appeared to contain primary stratified deposits. In total, 456 cm of sediments were collected in Core

NS07-2, although organic-rich sediments continued to greater depths. These deeper sediments could not be collected with our coring apparatus because of the stiffness of the clays and limitations of the equipment. After radiocarbon dating we were surprised to learn that the nearly 5 m of sediment has almost all been deposited in the past five hundred years.

Another core (JB07-1) was collected on the western side of the island near the Jolly Beach archaeological site (fig. 11.1). This location for a core was selected because the sediments contained organic-rich clays with good potential for preserved pollen. Furthermore, because the environment in this part of the island is volcanic and, thus, silica-rich, the likelihood was high for the recovery of well-preserved fossil phytoliths. Mineral sediments in the core are derived from a small (approximately 0.5 km^2), steep watershed largely mantled with shallow, stony, well-drained Mollisols and Inceptisols that formed on weathered volcanic bedrock. Soil profiles observed in nearby construction cuts revealed signs of truncation, both modern and historical.

The immediate setting of the Jolly Beach core was characterized by backwater lagoon, fringed by red, black, and white mangroves, with a groundcover of grasses, *Ipomoea*, small shrubby plants in the Apocynaceae family, and *Acacia* trees. Much of the area is currently being filled as a dump for construction material and was largely disturbed by modern human activity, but was likely to have been an open lagoon in the past. The specific location selected for coring appeared to have been minimally disturbed by recent human activity. The Jolly Beach archaeological site was located about 125 m north of the coring location. A basal date on the Jolly Beach core yielded an age of ca. 1570 B.C., making this core a prime candidate for analysis despite its relatively short length.

A 1.34-m core was collected from Crosby Lagoon in the extreme northwestern part of the island (Core CL09-1). Given the relatively recent basal-sample date of ca. A.D. 1305 and the short length of the core, we decided to forgo any further analysis of it (tab. 11.1). Another short core was collected from Hermitage Bay, approximately 1 km north of the Jolly Beach location and it was deemed to be unproductive (HB07-1).

In total, twenty-four pollen samples were processed from Nonsuch Bay and twelve from Jolly Beach; well-preserved pollen was present in all samples. Concentration values ranged from 2,562 to 40,413 fossil grains/ml of sediment at Nonsuch Bay and 1,896 to 55,742 grains/ml at Jolly Beach. Although concentration values were often fairly low, the generally excellent preservation of the pollen grains indicates rapid sedimentation rates rather than poor or differential preservation. All samples from the two cores produced 200-plus grain counts.

Table 11.1. Radiocarbon Dates from the Antigua Cores.

Core Location	Lab Sample Number	Core Number/Sample Depth	¹⁴C Age (BP)[a]	¹³C/¹²C Ratio	2-Sigma Calibrated Date Range[b]	Median Cal Date
Jolly Beach	AA82473	JB07-1, 115 cm, OS[c]	1470±35	-25.5	AD 540–650/1300–1410 BP	AD 595/1360 BP
Jolly Beach	AA82474	JB07-1, 235 cm, OS	3290±60	-28.0	1730–1440 BC/3390–3680 BP	1570 BC/3520 BP
Crosby Lagoon	AA86581	CL09-1, 132–133 cm, OS	680±35	-24.4	AD 1270–1390/560–680 BP	AD 1305/650 BP
Nonsuch Bay	AA77644	NS07-2, 221 cm, PW[d]	110±30	-28.2	AD 1680–1940/10–270 BP[f]	AD 1835/115 BP
Nonsuch Bay	AA82476	NS07-2, 349 cm, CW[e]	190±40	-25.2	AD 1650–1950/1–310 BP[f]	AD 1770/180 BP
Nonsuch Bay	AA82475	NS07-2, 398 cm, OS	250±35	-26.3	AD 1520–1950/1–430 BP[f]	AD 1655/295 BP
Nonsuch Bay	AA77643	NS07-2, 445 cm, OS	580±35	-26.5	AD 1300–1420/530–650 BP	AD 1350/600 BP

a. 1-sigma range.
b. Dates were calibrated using the IntCal13 method of CALIB ver. 7.0 (Reimer et al. 2013).
c. Organic sediment.
d. Preserved wood.
e. Carbonized wood.
f. Suspect date range due to impingement on the end of the calibration data set.

At least sixty-four pollen taxa were identified in the Nonsuch Bay (NS07-2) core, in addition to seven or more unknown or otherwise unidentified types and several different ferns. Approximately sixty pollen taxa were documented in the Jolly Beach samples, along with five or more indeterminate or unknown types (tab. 11.2). Eight samples from Jolly Beach were processed for phytoliths but none was recovered. Poor phytolith preservation may be due to the relatively high pH of the calcareous sediments, or to the high clay and peat content (phytoliths being silt-size particles).

Nonsuch Bay (Core NS07-2)

Sediments in the Nonsuch Bay core relate primarily to the land-use history during the colonial era (tab. 11.3). Organic matter ranged from a high of 48.1 percent (387–409 cm) to a low of 4.2 percent (19–27 cm). Banding between inorganic and organic-rich sediments appears to be the result of alternating periods of landscape instability (inorganic dominated deposition) and relative stability (organic peats and clays). Inorganic clays typically exhibited little to no stratification except where interbanded with sandy lenses indicative of fluvial deposition. Fine banding (laminae) was often present within the organic-rich clays, indicative of more-gradual deposition. Lack of stratification within the inorganic clays is indicative of rapid pulses of deposition, most likely attributable to heavy rain events, such as tropical storms, during periods when the watershed was largely deforested. The stratum of coarse sand and small marine shell fragments at 387–382 cm represents a storm-surge event, likely associated with a hurricane or tsunami (tab. 11.3).

Table 11.2. Pollen Taxa Identified in the Nonsuch Bay and Jolly Beach, Antigua Cores.

Taxon	Common Name	Taxon	Common Name
Avicennia	Black Mangrove	*Acacia*	Acacia
Combretaceae	White Mangrove	*Alchornea*	*Alchornea*
Rhizophora	Red Mangrove	Anacardiaceae	Cashew Family
Acalypha	Three-Seeded Mercury	Apocynaceae	Dogbane Family
Agave	Century Plant	Arecaceae	Palm Family
Alismataceae	Pickerelweed Family	Bombacaceae	Bombax Family
Alternanthera	Joseph's Coat	*Bursera*	Gumbo limbo
Araceae	Arum Family	*Byrsonima*	Nance
Asteraceae	Aster Family	Caesalpiniaceae	Fabaceae Subfamily
Borreria	Buttonweed	*Cassia*	Cassia

(continued)

Table 11.2. *(continued)*

Taxon	Common Name	Taxon	Common Name
Cactaceae	Cactus Family	*Casuarina*	Australian Pine
Canna	Canna	*Cecropia*	Trumpet
Cheno-Am	Goosefoot, Pigweed	*Ceiba*	Ceiba
Convolvulaceae	Morning Glory Family	*Celtis*	Hackberry
Croton	Croton	*Coccoloba*	Sea Grape
Cucurbitaceae	Squash Family	*Guazuma*	Bay Cedar
Cyperaceae	Sedge Family	*Gymnopodium*	Canelita
Desmodium	Tick Seed	*Haematoxylon*	Logwood
Euphorbiaceae	Spurge Family	*Hampea*	Tree Cotton
Fabaceae	Bean or Legume Family	*Hirea*	Barbados Cherry-Type
Geraniaceae	Cranesbill Family	*Hura*	Sandbox
Hamelia	Redhead	*Leucaena*	Lead Tree
Hypericaceae	St John's Wort Family	Loranthaceae	Mistletoe Family
Lamiaceae	Mint Family	*Machaerium*	Rosewood
Liliaceae	Lily Family	*Maytenus*	Maytenus
Malvaceae	Mallow Family	Meliaceae	Mahogany Family
Nymphea	Water Lily	Moraceae	Mulberry Family
Onagraceae	Evening Primrose Family	*Myrica*	Wax Myrtle
Opuntia	Prickly Pear	Myrtaceae	Myrtle Family
Poaceae	Grass Family	*Pinus*	Pine
Polemoniaceae	Phlox Family	*Piper*	Pepper
Polygonaceae	Knotweed Family	*Pterocarpus*	
Polygonum	Knotweed	*Quercus*	Oak
Rosaceae	Rose Family	Rhamnaceae	Buckthorn Family
Rumex	Dock	Rubiaceae	Madder Family
Solanaceae	Nightshade Family	Rutaceae	Rue Family
Typha	Cattail	Sapindaceae	Soapberry Family
Utricularia	Bladderwort	Sapotaceae	Sapodilla Family
Verbenaceae	Vervain Family	*Sebastiana*	Poisonwood
Zea mays	Maize	*Spondias*	Hogplum
		Symplocos	Sweetleaf
		Tiliaceae	Basswood Family
		Trema	Trema
		Zanthoxylum	Prickly Ash
		Indeterminate	poor preservation

Table 11.3. Sediment Descriptions of the Nonsuch Bay, Antigua Core (Core NS07-2).

Depth (cm)	Color	OM (LOI)	Total P (ppm)	Sand (%)	Silt (%)	Clay (%)	Notes
0–3	Black						Fibric OM (mangrove)
3–19	Greenish black (Gley 10Y 2.5/1)	6.9	422	3	27	70	Some fibric OM
19–27	Greenish gray (Gley 10Y 5/1)	4.2	397	2	19	79	Clay
27–52	Dark green gray (Gley 10Y 4/1)	10.4	433	4	36	60	Hemic clay
52–66	Dark green gray (Gley 10Y 3/1)	8.8	336	2	32	66	Hemic clay
66–77	Dark green gray (Gley 10Y 3/1)	13.2	291	1	24	75	Hemic clay
77–100	Greenish gray (Gley 10Y 5/1)	16.4	280	2	34	64	Hemic clay; one small snail; some fibric bands
100–113							Hole slop
113–117	Greenish gray (Gley 10Y 5/1)		246				Hemic clay
117–122	Greenish gray (Gley 10Y 6/1)	11.8	279	7	33	60	Hemic clay; small snails
122–124	Very dark gray (10YR 3/1)	35.3					Thinly bands of peat
124–133	Dark green gray (Gley 10Y 4/1)	12.5	254	4	27	69	Hemic clay
133–171	Greenish gray (Gley 10Y 5/1)	17.0	187	3	34	63	Hemic clay with thin fibric bands
171–181							Hole slop
182–186	Dark green gray (Gley 10Y 4/1)	4.5	243	4	16	80	Numerous small snail shells
186–193	Dark green gray (Gley 10Y 4/1)	11.7	220	8	21	71	Hemic clay
193–222	Greenish gray (Gley 10Y 5/1)	5.8	235	3	27	70	Sapric clay; wood at 220
222–226	Greenish gray (Gley 10Y 5/1)	5.1	272	9	30	61	Sapric clay
226–231	Greenish gray (Gley 10Y 6/1)	4.6	283	3	28	69	Sapric clay

(continued)

Table 11.3. (continued)

Depth (cm)	Color	OM (LOI)	Total P (ppm)	Sand (%)	Silt (%)	Clay (%)	Notes
231–249	Greenish gray (Gley 10Y 5/1)	6.9	254	0	33	67	Sapric clay with darker bands
249–261	Greenish gray (Gley 10Y 5/1)						Same as above; more dark bands
261–262	Very dark gray (Gley N 3/N)						Sapric clay
262–274	Dark gray (5Y 4/2)	6.6	173	1	15	84	Clay
274–281							Hole slop
281–295	Dark green gray (Gley 10Y 4/1)		201	2	26	72	Sapric clay
295–299	Dark green gray (Gley 10GY 4/1)	5.2	186	1	18	81	Clay
299–308	Greenish gray (Gley 10Y 5/1)	6.3	144	4	27	69	Sapric clay
308–312	Dark green gray (Gley 10GY 4/1)	4.6		10	13	77	Banded clay; ash /sand lens at 311
312–326	Greenish gray (Gley 10Y 5/1)	6.7	138	3	24	73	Sapric clay; a few lighter bands
326–330	Greenish gray (Gley 10Y 6/1)	5.4		4	25	71	Sapric clay
330–331	Greenish gray (Gley 5GY 5/1)		113				Sapric clay
331–333	Greenish gray and dark greenish gray						Tightly banded sapric clay; thin ash lens at top
333–335	Greenish gray (Gley 5GY 5/1)	4.9	77	2	18	80	Clay
335–340	Greenish gray (Gley 10Y 5/1)	6.6	118	1	27	72	Sapric clay
340–348	Dark green gray (Gley 10Y 4/1)	7.0	125	2	29	69	Sapric clay
348–351	Greenish gray (Gley 5GY 6/1)			38	9	52	Irregular band of volcanic ash
351–358	Greenish gray (Gley 5GY 5/1)	4.4	89	3	30	77	Clay
358–360	Greenish gray (Gley 10Y 5/1)		101	2	33	75	Clay

(continued)

Table 11.3. (continued)

Depth (cm)	Color	OM (LOI)	Total P (ppm)	Sand (%)	Silt (%)	Clay (%)	Notes
360–362	Greenish gray (Gley 10GY 5/1)			33	8	59	Irregular band of fine volcanic ash
362–367	Greenish gray (Gley 10Y 5/1)	5.0	128	7	25	68	Sapric clay
367–371				44	30	26	Fibric band atop coarse sand with micro snail shells
371–374							Hole slop
374–382	Greenish gray (Gley 10Y 5/1)	8.8	140	6	27	77	Sapric clay; Irregular bands
382–387	Greenish gray (Gley 10Y 6/1)	6.1	135	46	11	43	Coarse sand and micro shells
387–409	Greenish black (Gley 10Y 2.5/1)	48.1	142				Banded hemic peats
409–456	Dark green gray (Gley 10Y 3/1)	7.0	164	3	26	71	Sapric clay with thin peat bands

Notes:
Shells identified by Denis Nieweg:
117–122 cm: One bivalve and three gastropod species are present within this level.
The bivalve specimen is a very small fragment of a mytilid (mussel), Mytilidae, but not recognisable on a genus or species level.
The gastropods are:
-*Neritina virginea* (L. 1758), Neritidae, one adult specimen.
-*Bulimulus guadalupensis* (Bruguiere 1789), Bulimulidae, one complete juvenile and one fragment belonging to different specimens. This species is a land mollusc
-Planorbidae fragment (not to be recognised on a genus or species level). This is a freshwater mollusc
382–387 cm: Only one species is present within this sample:
-*Perna perna* (L. 1758), Mytilidae, juvenile, one left and one right valves belonging together, NISP=1.

The highest Na levels were documented in the deepest strata (456–362 cm). During the time that these sediments were deposited, the marine shoreline was likely considerably closer to the coring location than it is today. The probable storm-surge deposit of sand and broken shells at 387–382 cm supports this supposition. As sediment began to rapidly fill the embayment at the mouth of Ayres Creek during the colonial era, the marine shoreline shifted eastward—reflected by lower Na levels in the sediment and no further storm-surge deposits. Shells deposited at 122–117 cm are from species preferring either freshwater or brackish-water habitats, indicating that aggradation within the estuary had proceeded to the point that the coring location had become effectively isolated from the ocean.

Phosphate levels show notable increases at 250 cm and 60 cm. The 60-cm spike relates to modern inputs, most likely from fertilizers. The nineteenth-century Manure Act (prompted by declining sugar yields) may account for the spike at 250 cm. Below 250 cm P levels declined in association with pulses of inorganic clay sediments (tab. 11.3).

Bands of volcanic ash were documented in several strata of the core. Relatively thick ash bands at 351–348 cm and 362–360 cm may be linked to the 1797–1798 eruptions of La Soufrière on Guadeloupe (Adélaïde-Merlande and Hervieu 1996; Komorowski et al. 2005). Eruptions on other more-distant islands during the appropriate period are not likely to have dropped these quantities of ash on Antigua (Hincks et al. 2005; Robertson 2005; Simpson 2005; Smith 2005). The only comparably explosive eruptions on Guadeloupe occurred in 1976–1977 and reportedly dropped some ash on Antigua. The layer of clay between the ash lenses at 351–348 cm and 362–360 cm produced large amounts of microscopic volcanic glass. The biggest blasts of the 1797–1798 eruptions occurred in September 1797 and April 1798 and heavy ash fall was reported on Antigua. The clay and glass layer likely resulted from in-washing of weathered ash being flushed out of the Ayres Creek watershed between the September 1797 and April 1798 blasts. The radiocarbon date of ca. A.D. 1770 at 349 cm is consistent with this dating of the ash. However, the range of the radiocarbon date "is suspect due to impingement on the end of the calibration data set" (Reimer et al. 2013). La Soufrière also erupted less explosively in 1836–1837 but still produced significant ash clouds, which could account for the ash lenses identified at 331 cm or 311 cm.

Three pollen zones were identified in the Nonsuch Bay core (fig. 11.3). The lowest zone (456–370 cm), bracketed by the dates of ca. A.D. 1350 and A.D. 1655, straddles the late pre-Columbian/early colonial eras. The three date ranges from the historic era are suspect "due to impinge-

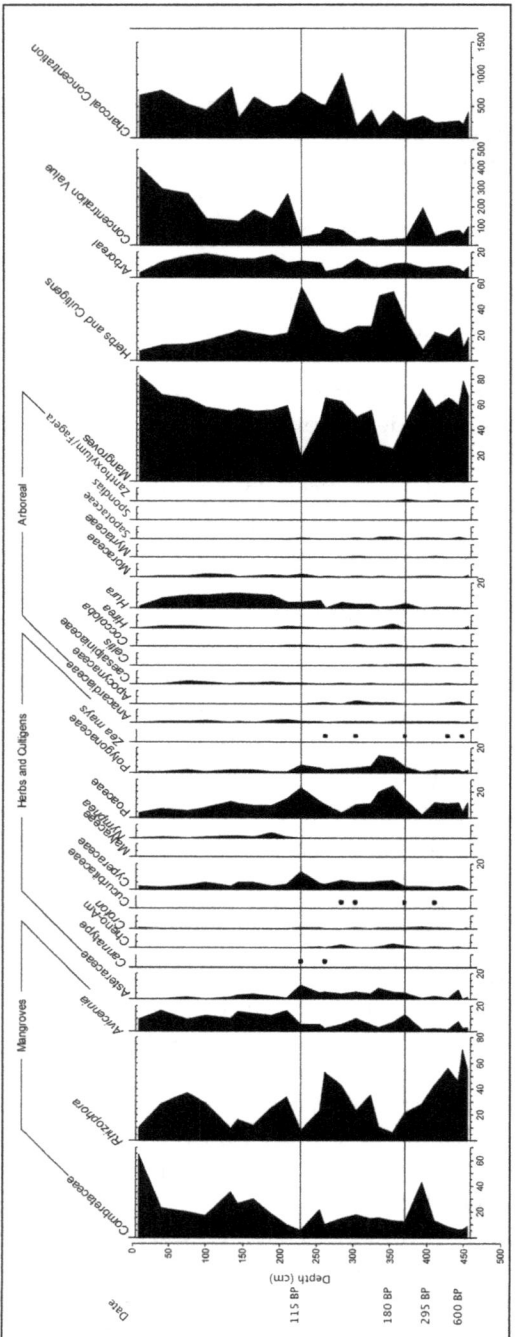

Figure 11.3. Nonsuch Bay, Antigua, core pollen-percentage diagram. Pollen and charcoal concentrations are expressed as grains and fragments, respectively, per cm³ of sediment.

ment on the end of the calibration data set" (Reimer et al. 2013). That said, they are correctly ordered stratigraphically from oldest to most recent (tab. 11.1). The historic-era sediments likely represent erosional material introduced into the Ayres Creek (Nonsuch Bay) basin from aggressive agricultural practices. These materials and associated organic components are likely to date somewhat older than the age of their introduction into the basin. Sediments from this zone largely comprised sapric and fibric peaty clays, although a band of irregularly laminated sapric clays occurred from 382 to 374 cm. Pollen concentrations were relatively high in this zone, suggesting a somewhat slower sedimentation rate (tab. 11.4). The pollen assemblage overall was dominated by red and white mangroves, with notable percentages of disturbance flora including Asteraceae, Poaceae, and Polygonaceae. Forest types were reduced and cultigens were well represented by *Zea mays* throughout the zone and Cucurbitaceae (cf. *Cucurbita*) by 410 cm.

A clear division between the pre-Columbian/early colonial periods is not visible in the pollen record (fig. 11.3). The presence of maize and possibly squash pollen indicates that these plants were being cultivated in the immediate site area because both taxa produce large and heavy pollen grains that rarely travel far from their source. Overall, this zone presents a picture of a mangrove environment, with human settlement and agriculture occurring nearby.

The middle zone (370–231 cm) reflects major landscape modifications directly linked to colonial agricultural pursuits, largely sugarcane cultivation. The Betty's Hope plantation, established in 1651 and located in the uplands of the Ayres Creek drainage basin, was one of the largest, longest continuous-running, and most-productive sugar plantations in the British West Indies (Fox 2014; Goodwin 1994). The sedimentation rate documented in the Nonsuch Bay core following the establishment of Betty's Hope plantation spiked by more than 460 percent to 1.9692

Table 11.4. Sedimentation Rates for the Antigua Cores.

Core/^{14}C sample depths	^{14}C Date Ranges (Median Cal BP Dates)	Sedimentation Rate (cm/yr)
JB07-1, 0–115 cm	0–1360	.0845
JB07-1, 115–235 cm	1360–3520	.0555
CL09-1, 0–132 cm	0–650	.2030
NS07-2, 0–221 cm	0–115	1.9217
NS07-2, 221–349 cm	115–180	1.9692
NS07-2, 349–398 cm	180–295	.4260
NS07-2, 398–445 cm	295–600	.1540

cm/yr, compared to 0.4260 cm/yr prior to extensive British deforestation (tab. 11.4). Sediments from this middle section comprise clays and sapric clays, with several bands of volcanic ash. As discussed, the large volcanic ash lenses likely relate to the eruptions of 1797–1798 of La Soufrière on Guadeloupe, while the smaller lenses may be related to eruptions of La Soufrière in 1836–1837. If these correlations are correct, the core radiocarbon dates are somewhat older than the actual ages of the sediments as would be expected under conditions of rapid upstream erosion and sedimentation.

While mangrove pollen concentrations remain high throughout much of this zone, there are notable increases in disturbance taxa including Asteraceae, Cheno-Ams, Polygonaceae, and Poaceae, all types likely associated with agricultural clearing (tabs. 11.5, 11.6). Cyperaceae pollen also increased; these plants favor open wet areas. The Poaceae

Table 11.5. Ethnobotanical Associations and Disturbance Indicators Represented in the Antigua Cores.[a]

Taxon	Ethnobotanical Association or Disturbance Indicator	Core JB07-1	Core NS07-2
MANGROVE			
Avicennia	Black mangrove. Throat pains, incontinence.	X	
Combretaceae	White mangrove. Slows bleeding.	X	X
Rhizophora	Red mangrove. Diarrhea, fever, malaria, excellent fuel wood.	X	X
HERBS/CULTIGENS			
Agave	Sap, stalk, flowers, and leaves are edible.	X[b]	
Asteraceae	Aster or Composite family. Herbs and shrubs. Many are invasive weed species of cleared open areas.	X	X
Canna	Canna. Rhizomes rich in starch, seeds are edible.	X[b]	X[b]
Cheno-Ams	Chenopod and amaranth families. Favor disturbed or open habitats. Young greens and mature seeds are edible. Includes seablite, saltwort, chenopod, amaranth.	X	X
Croton	Some produce a latex used for medicinal purposes.		X[b]
Cucurbitaceae	Gourd family. Edible fruits and some used as vessels.		X[b]
Cyperaceae, *Cladium*	Sedge family. Grasslike herbaceous plants, many are weeds that invade cleared open areas.	X	X
Fabaceae, *Desmodium*	Wild herbaceous legumes. Includes cohoba, edible beans. Species include plants with medicinal uses and for producing narcotic snuff, edible fruit, and fish poison.	X	

(continued)

Table 11.5. *(continued)*

Taxon	Ethnobotanical Association or Disturbance Indicator	Core JB07-1	Core NS07-2
Malvaceae	Mallow family. Some have medicinal properties, others fruits and leaves are edible. Cotton (*Gossypium*) is in this family.	X[b]	
Nymphaea	Water lilies. Leaves, flower buds, and seeds are edible.		X
Poaceae	Grass family. Often associated with areas frequently fired. Edible starchy grains.	X	X
Polygonaceae, *Rumex*	Docks and sorrels. Edible leaves.	X	X
Zea mays	Maize. Edible grain.		X[b]
ARBOREAL			
Acacia	Young spines used to relieve gum and tooth pain.	X[b]	
Alchornea	Many species have medicinal properties.	X	
Anacardiaceae, *Spondias* sp.	Cashew family. Edible fruit, hogplum.	X	X
Apocynaceae	Dogbane family. Golden trumpet vine. Fibers used for cordage. Some produce edible flowers.	X[b]	X
Arecaceae	Palm family. Edible fruit, thatching, cordage, needles, posts.	X[b]	X
Byrsonima	Edible fruit, nance.	X[b]	
Bursera	Gumbo limbo. Resin has medicinal properties, leaves used for tea	X	
Caesalpiniaceae	Anthraquinone glycosides from the seeds and leaves used as a laxative and anti-inflammatory agent.	X[b]	X
Celtis	Hackberry, edible fruit	X	X[b]
Chrysobalanaceae	Coco-Plum family. Edible fruits.		X[b]
Coccoloba	Sea grape. Edible fruit, medicinal.	X	X
Guazuma	West Indian elm, pigeon wood. Seeds of some have medicinal properties and others are edible.	X[b]	
Hirea	Liana. Used for rope.	X[b]	X
Moraceae	Mulberry family. Edible fruit, breadnut, medicinal. Often colonize open cleared areas.	X	X
Myrtaceae, *Eugenia, Psidium*	Myrtle family. Edible fruit, medicinal. Frequently found in windbreak and secondary forest growth. Includes guava, Eugenia, allspice.	X	X[b]
Sapindaceae	Soapberry family. Fruits and seeds of some are edible, others poisonous.	X[b]	
Sapotaceae, *Chrysophyllum*	Sapote family. Edible fruit, medicinal, latex in some species. Includes edible fruits of chicle, sapote, lucuma.	X[b]	X

a. See Table 5.5 for the sources of information.
b. Trace amounts.

Table 11.6. Plant Taxa Identified in the Antigua Cores with No Documented Ethnobotanical or Anthropogenic Correlates Other than Perhaps Fuel Wood, Especially Arboreal Taxa.

Taxon	Common Name	Core JB07-1	Core NS07-2
HERBS/CULTIGENS			
Acalypha	Copperleaf, flowering shrub	X[a]	
Polygonaceae, *Gymnopodium*	Common sorrel	X[a]	X
ARBOREAL			
Hura	Sand box	X[a]	X
Maytenus	Caribbean Mayten, staff vine	X	
Trema	Elm trees. Small evergreens growing in open forests or clearings.	X	
Zanthoxylum	Prickly ash	X	X[a]
FERNS			
Unknown ferns		X	

a. Trace amounts.

grains, although unidentifiable below the family level, are consistent in size and surface texture and may represent the same species, possibly sugarcane (*Saccharum officinarum*). Pollen from *Zea mays*, Cucurbitaceae, and *Canna* (achira) persisted through this zone, indicating that subsistence farming was still taking place in the local area. Pollen concentration values overall were reduced in this middle zone and relate to the rapid sedimentation compared to the basal zone.

The uppermost pollen zone (231–0 cm) dates to the late colonial/recent period. Stratigraphic breaks were not noted and the sediments may reflect continuous, rapid deposition until modern times. Assemblages continued to be dominated by red and white mangroves, although black mangroves became more common during this period. Black mangroves thrive in hyper-saline areas, and increases in this diagnostic pollen might reflect the proximity of low-lying areas where brackish to saline water accumulated, or increased capillary rise and deposition of salt as vegetation was removed along the flanks of the wetland. Stands of black mangroves currently dominate the area. Cultigens were lacking and disturbance vegetation much reduced, although charcoal concentrations remained high throughout, reflecting input from a regional, rather than a local, area. Increases in pollen from *Hura*, Moraceae, Anacardiaceae, and Caesalpiniaceae were documented in the upper zone. These taxa represent common arboreal elements suggesting that in part some forested areas were becoming reestablished, consistent with a reduction in cane farming in the Ayres Creek drainage.

A single set of phytolith samples was processed given the late date of the Nonsuch Bay core. Two samples in the middle of the core (150–155 cm, 255–261 cm) returned a 200-count, with low phytolith influx above and below, and no phytolith deposition at the base of the core (445–450 cm).

The productive sample at 255–261 cm was dominated by arboreal and understory indicators, overwhelmingly palm (figs. 11.4a, 11.4b). Palms are nearly completely absent from the pollen assemblage; thus,

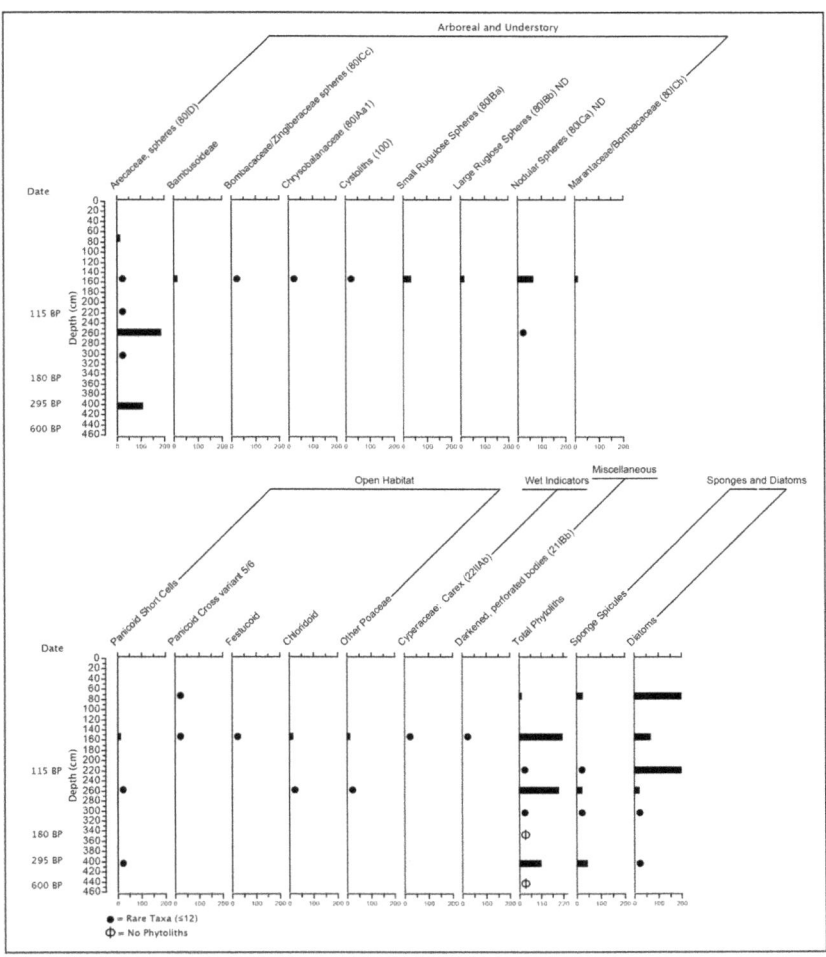

Figure 11.4a. Nonsuch Bay, Antigua, core phytolith diagram: resolved.

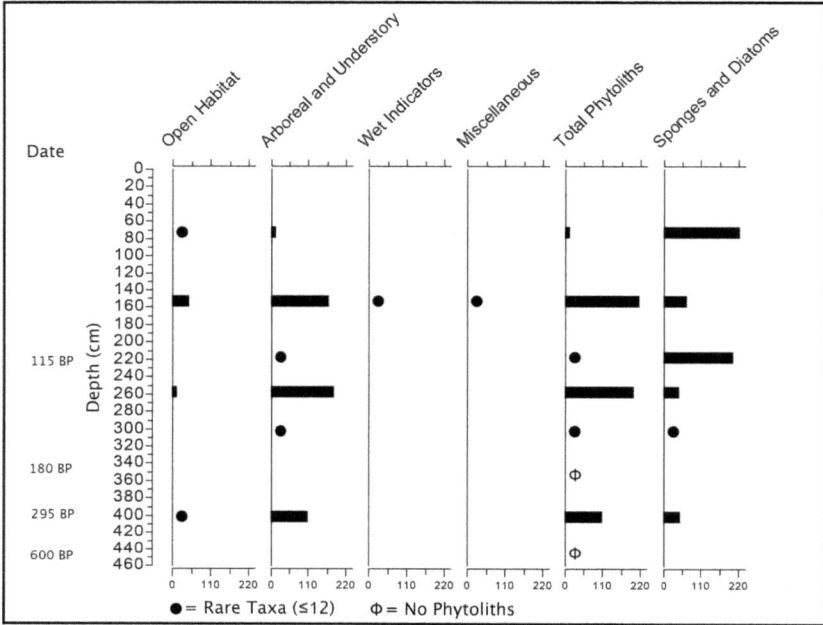

Figure 11.4b. Nonsuch Bay, Antigua, core phytolith diagram: composite.

the prevalence of palm phytoliths highlights the mutually complementary nature of tandem pollen and phytolith studies. This sample represents what is likely to be late-eighteenth- or early-nineteenth-century deposits, reflecting intensive sugarcane production. The abundance of palms coupled with the dearth of other phytolith types is consistent with large-scale clearing in the area, but with local mangrove forests filtering out regional phytolith influx.

The phytolith sample at 150–155 cm was also predominantly arboreal and understory, but with a much more diverse combination of types represented—palms, bamboo, Chrysobalanaceae, small rugulose (woody dicots), and Marantaceae and Marantaceae/Bombacaceae forms. There are also more grasses in this zone, reflecting local disturbances. The pollen assemblage records less-intensive agriculture in what may have been a seriously depleted environment. Increases in phytoliths reflecting woody and shrubby vegetation may be consistent with the pollen record. Changes occurred in the area that involved palm and Marantaceae. *Maranta arundinacea* (arrowroot) is documented on the islands. The appearance of palm phytoliths and Marantaceae (255–261 cm) may indicate the local cultivation of these ethnobotanically useful plants, along with *Canna,* Cucurbitaceae, and maize, as reflected in the pollen record.

The Nonsuch Bay pollen, phytolith, and sedimentary records provide a direct view into early historical activities on Antigua. With basal sediments dating to the period just prior to European contact, the entire sequence represents a record of early and later colonial landscape modifications. The point of European contact with the island, if even present in this sequence, is not clearly identifiable from the pollen record. With maize pollen occurring in many samples, including a sample 7 cm above the base of the core dating to ca. A.D. 1350, the presence of maize in a pre-European context cannot be assumed. In the basal and middle zones, agricultural efforts near the coring locality were taking place represented by the occurrence of maize, squash, and achira (*Canna*) pollen. More regional evidence of agriculture is also represented in the core, particularly in the middle zone where grass pollen and associated weedy vegetation (Asteraceae, Cheno-Am, Cyperaceae, Polygonaceae) increased significantly. Increases in grass pollen probably reflect the production of sugarcane; many of those grains may represent sugarcane, although this taxon is not positively identifiable from its pollen. The generally consistent sizes of the grass grains in the core midsection suggest a narrow range of similar source taxa. This zone dates from the early-eighteenth to early-nineteenth century, the zenith of sugar cultivation on Antigua. Low pollen concentrations suggest rapid sedimentation during this period, consistent with the massive erosion documented in the sequence beginning by approximately A.D. 1650. Phytoliths from the middle zone are derived from two additional possible cultigens not present in the pollen record: palms and Marantaceae.

Geoarchaeological research in the upper reaches of the Ayres Creek watershed has documented landscape impacts from the Betty's Hope plantation activities (Wells, Pratt, and Fox 2015). Our coring data from Nonsuch Bay (mouth of the watershed) complement results from Wells et al.'s project (fig. 11.5) (see also Wells et al. 2018). From the base of our core (445 cm) to 398 cm, the sedimentation rate was relatively low to moderate, spanning the late prehistoric to early colonial era for the eastern Caribbean. Organic sediment from 398 cm produced a date of ca. A.D. 1655, coinciding with the establishment of the Betty's Hope plantation. Between the dates of ca. A.D. 1655 and 1770, the sedimentation rate increased by more than 400 percent. From 1770 to the present, sedimentation increased to nearly 2.0 cm a year, the fastest rate documented in the current project.

The uppermost zone of Nonsuch Bay reflects reduced efforts at sugarcane farming; in fact all evidence of cultivation in the area is lacking in this section of the core. The reduction in plant cultivation at this time, after around 1839, may be due in large part to the loss of Antigua's soils as noted in Zone 2, and is consistent with a documented reduction in sugarcane cultivation on the island (Armstrong 2001; Fox 2007). Higher pollen concentrations in this upper zone would suggest reduced sedimentation rates; the upper 115 cm of deposition since ca. A.D. 1835, however, indicates otherwise. Sugarcane production was active in Betty's Hope plantation until the late twentieth century, thus accounting for continued erosion in the watershed in recent times, again possibly because there was simply less soil to erode into the rivers and catchments (Weaver 1988). Increases in *Hura*, Caesalpiniaceae, and Anacardiaceae pollen indicate some reestablishment of forest in the vicinity or upstream of Nonsuch Bay. Phytoliths from this section likely also reflect reforestation in a disturbed environment.

Jolly Beach (Core JB07-1)

Sediments collected in the Jolly Beach core represented a continuous sequence (tab. 11.7). Sediments from 208 to 262 cm are largely compact marine clays interrupted by a few thin bands of organic matter and darker silts. These sediments were likely deposited in a lagoon that was readily open to the ocean much of the time, with the few organic bands probably representing brief periods of closure. Shells found within these lower strata are typical shallow-water marine species (tab. 11.7).

Sediments deposited between 122 and 208 cm indicate increasing terrestrial inputs entering the lagoon, possibly associ-

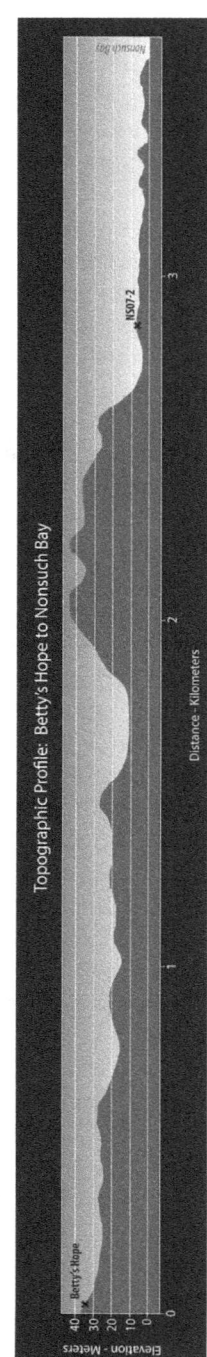

Figure 11.5. Cross-section of the terrain between Betty's Hope plantation and Nonsuch Bay. Although vertical relief is not extreme, the clear-cutting of surface vegetation for the plantation resulted in massive erosional deposits accumulating in the bay.

Table 11.7. Sediment Descriptions of the Jolly Beach, Antigua Core (Core JB07-1).

Depth (cm)	Color	OM (LOI)	Total P (ppm)	Sand%	Silt%	Clay%	Notes
0–47	Greenish gray (Gley 10Y 5/1)	7.0	416	30	19	51	Many small shell fragments
47–63	Dark green gray (Gley 10Y 4/1)	8.8	338	22	25	53	Few large shell pieces; many small shell fragments
63–82	Black (5Y 2.5/1)	34.5	299	44	38	18	Peaty; many small shell fragments decreasing with depth
82–100	Black (10Y 2.5/1)	42.5	185	39	37	24	Peaty; shells absent
106–122	Black (10Y 2.5/1)						Continuation of stratum above
122–130	Gray (5Y 5/1)	10.9	145	48	42	10	Some mangrove roots
130–147	Greenish gray (Gley 10Y 5/1)	11.8	122	42	43	15	Large clam at 135–139 cm
147–150	Dark gray (5Y 4/1)	33.2	111				Peaty with super abundant shell fragments
150–184	Gray (5Y 5/1)	6.1	130	8	49	43	A few small shell fragments
184–186	Dark green gray (Gley 10Y 4/1)	3.2	69	5	21	74	
198–208	Dark gray (5Y 4/1)	6.4	46	28	38	34	Numerous small shell fragments
208–226	Dark green gray (Gley 10Y 4/1)	2.3	47	8	24	68	Massive clay with thin shell and dark silt lenses
226–262	Greenish gray (Gley 10Y 6/1)	2.1	38	6	24	70	Massive clay with shell fragment lenses at 228 and 230 cm, peat lens at 235 cm, silty lens at 240 cm, charcoal flecks at 251–257 cm.

(*continued*)

Table 11.7. *(continued)*

Notes:
Shells identified by Denis Nieweg:
0–47 cm:
Two gastropod species and two bivalve species are present.
Gastropods:
- *Melampus coffeus* (L. 1758), Melampidae, top fragment, adult.
- *Diodora listeri* (d'Orbigny 1842), Fissurellidae, Very eroded juvenile.
Bivalves:
- *Arca imbricata* (Bruguiere 1789), Arcidae, very eroded fragment from a left valve.
- *Codakia* sp., Lucinidae, very eroded, very juvenile specimen, right valve.

47–63 cm:
Very eroded shell fragments primarily belonging to one bivalve:
- *Codakia orbicularis* (L.1758), Lucinidae, five fragments and one hinge (right valve), (NISP=1)
And two eroded (right valve) fragments of:
- *Brachidontes exustus* (L.1758), Mytilidae, NISP=2

63–82 cm:
Also this sample consists of very eroded shell (bivalve) fragments probably belonging to
- *Codakia orbicularis* (L.1758), Lucinidae, 15 fragments and one very juvenile left valve, NISP=1
Two very eroded gastropod fragments are present, one belonging to:
- *Turbo castanea* (Gmelin, 1791), Turbinidae, operculum.
And the other belonging to:
- *Astraea caelata* (Gmelin, 1791), Turbinidae, only a top fragment.

135–139 cm:
Within this sample two bivalve species were recognised:
- *Phacoides pectinatus* (Gmelin, 1791), Lucinidae, three fragments probably belonging to the same specimen (NISP=1).
- *Chione cancellata* (L.1767), Veneridae, two right valves, NISP=2.
Two small bivalve fragments were not recognisable.

147–150 cm:
Five species of gastropods and two bivalve species are present within this sample.
- *Cerithium lutosum* Menke 1828, Cerithiidae, six adult specimens.
- *Bulla striata* Bruguiere 1792, Bullidae, one eroded specimen.
- *Neritina virginea* (L. 1758), Neritidae, one adult specimen and one fragment, NISP=2.
- *Modulus modulus* (L.1758), Modulidae, one adult specimen.
- cf. *Engoniophos unicinctus* (Say, 1825), Buccinidae, very juvenile specimen.
The two bivalve species are:
- *Codakia orbicularis* (L.1758), Lucinidae, one very eroded fragment.
- *Tellina* sp., Tellinidae, three very juvenile valves, two left and one right valve, NISP=3

150–184 cm:
One bivalve and three gastropod species are present within this sample.
- cf. *Tellina martinicensis* Orbigny 1842, Tellinidae, juvenile left valve. Bivalve.
Gastropods:
- *Bulla striata* Bruguiere 1792, Bullidae, two juvenile specimens.
- *Cerithium lutosum* Menke 1828, Cerithiidae, one adult specimen.
- *Astraea caelata* (Gmelin, 1791), Turbinidae, one juvenile fragment.

228–230 cm:
Two gastropod species and two bivalve species are present.
Gastropods:
- *Cerithium lutosum* Menke 1828, Cerithiidae, three adult specimens.
- *Bulla striata* Bruguiere 1792, Bullidae, two juvenile specimens.
Bivalves:
- cf. *Tellina martinicensis* Orbigny 1842, Tellinidae, two very juvenile specimens, NISP=2.
- *Chione cancellata* (L.1767), Veneridae, one very eroded specimen.
Furthermore a few fragments of calcified algae were found.

ated with land clearance within the watershed. Variable, but increasing, phosphate levels also reflect local human presence. Most notably, peak phosphates between 150 and 184 cm may be linked to the occupations of the nearby Jolly Beach site. Bands of shells within these strata are consistent with a shallow lagoon, likely with abundant seagrass.

Above 122 cm sediments became markedly more organic and root casts below this zone indicate the probable establishment of a red mangrove ecosystem. The bay mouth bar enclosing the lagoon was probably well developed by this point. This ecosystem appears to have stabilized over time with mollusk populations adapting to the new habitat. However, instability was later introduced in the form of increased in-washing terrestrial mineral sediments, although mollusk populations indicate the ecosystem likely remained fairly healthy until near the time of its destruction. Increasingly higher phosphate levels throughout this zone reflect more human activities in the local area.

Four pollen zones were apparent in the Jolly Beach core samples, identified by a stratigraphically constrained sum of squares analysis (fig. 11.6). The basal zone occurred from 234 to 185 cm, and dates to the period sometime after ca. 1570 B.C. Sediments in this zone largely comprised blue-gray clay with occasional bands of fragmented shells and brown-colored silts. Here we see evidence for a red and white mangrove lagoon system represented by relatively high percentages of mangrove pollens (*Rhizophora* and Combretaceae), and the area was likely to have been fringed by a nearby swamp forest, indicated by high percentages of *Coccoloba* (sea grape) pollen. A number of species of *Coccoloba* are known from the Caribbean, and many are edible. These plants generally favor swamp forests, where their roots remain wet throughout much of the year, although some species, such as *Coccoloba uvifera*, are frequently found near beaches or dunes. Pollen percentages from another swamp-forest or upland forest taxon, *Bursera* (Gumbo limbo) were also slightly elevated in this basal zone. Charcoal concentrations were low in this zone but increased with time.

The middle zone from the Jolly Beach core (185–80 cm) consisted of banded blue-gray clay, fragmented shell and silty lenses, although sediments above 122 cm almost entirely comprised organic-rich peat. An increase in red mangrove pollen was documented, probably reflecting a new or more-substantial connection to the nearby sea. White mangrove pollen decreased slightly and increasing *Celtis* (hackberry) pollen suggests there may have been some drying in the area, although a reduction in forest cover could also account for that finding. An increase in particulate carbon, most notably around 170 cm, is probably associated with human activities in the nearby Jolly Beach site. Interpolating between

266 • Chapter 11

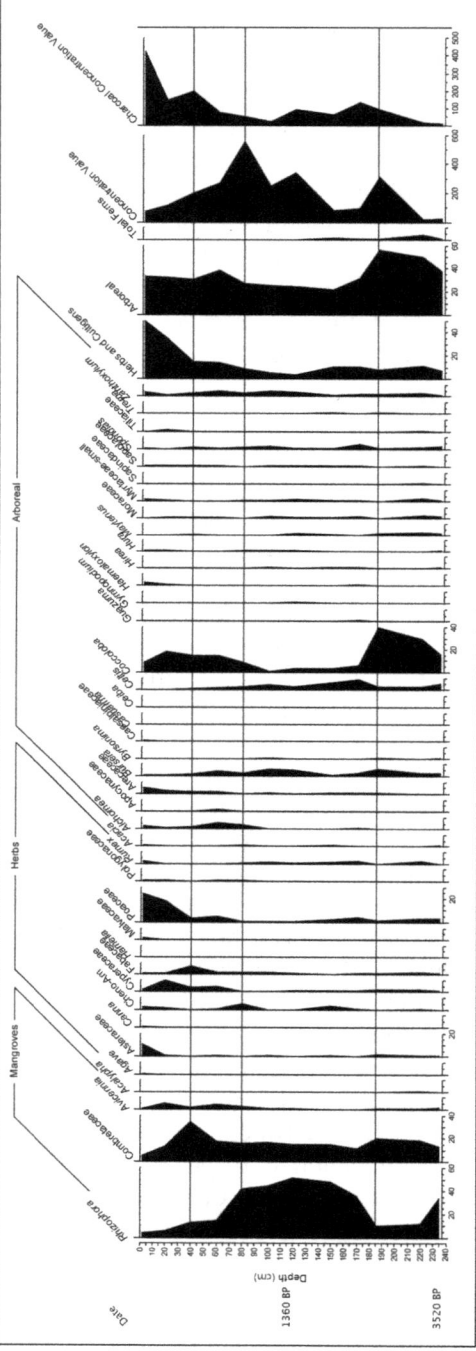

Figure 11.6. Jolly Beach, Antigua, core pollen-percentage diagram. Pollen and charcoal concentrations are expressed as grains and fragments, respectively, per cm³ of sediment.

the two Jolly Beach median calibrated radiocarbon dates places the 170-cm charcoal peak at ca. 400 B.C., around the Archaic/Saladoid interface in this portion of the Caribbean.

The third zone (80–40 cm), although undated, reflects late prehistoric or early historic occupations. Sediments below 63 cm comprised peats, while those from the upper portion of the zone consist of shells and grayish clays. Decreases were documented in red mangrove pollen along with slight increases in white and black mangrove pollen in this zone. Cyperaceae, Poaceae, and charcoal concentrations also increased, indicating local disturbance. *Alchornea* (Euphorbiaceae) pollen increased at this time, reflecting a shift in the local floral community. Arecaceae (palm) pollen increased above 60 cm, extending through the uppermost zone. Nonnative coconut palms (*Cocos nucifera*) are common in the Jolly Beach area today, and may be reflected by the palm pollen in the upper zone of the core.

The uppermost zone (above 40 cm) shows major increases in disturbance indicators (Asteraceae, Poaceae, Arecaceae) associated with recent human activities in the locality. The presence of a single pollen grain from the introduced *Casuarina* (Australian pine) in the uppermost sample was noted. These trees are common in the Jolly Beach area today. A single *Agave* (century plant) grain was also identified in the uppermost sample, again reflecting modern horticultural efforts in the area.

Although not as detailed as the Nonsuch Bay core, the sediment core from Jolly Beach (JB07-1) recorded a longer history, with a basal date of ca. 1570 B.C. Based on limited dating of the Jolly Beach archaeological site, Davis (2000: 97) "suggest[ed] occupation sometime during the period between about 1400 and 2100 B.C." If Davis's assessment of the site's occupational range is correct, our basal core date is linked to the more-recent end of the Archaic occupation. Our core represents the oldest paleoecological record for Antigua.

Four zones were represented in the Jolly Beach core pollen sequence. The basal zone reflects what is probably a swamp-forest environment surrounding a red, black, and white mangrove system. This type of environment would have been a favored occupation area, being ecotonal; the forest and mangrove zones, coupled with the nearby sea, would have afforded multiple opportunities for food procurement.

The next zone reflects a reduction in swamp forest–type pollen, but shows that the area became more open around this time. Increases in red mangroves, along with slight increases in Cheno-Ams, Poaceae, and *Celtis* pollen coupled with a reduction in white mangrove and *Coccoloba* pollen, suggest that an environmental shift had taken place.

This may represent a newly opened channel to the sea, allowing greater amounts of saline water to enter the area. *Celtis* and disturbance taxa suggest the area was now more open, allowing weeds to flourish. At this time increases in particulate charcoal (170 cm core depth) may reflect an increase in human-caused burning in the area. By interpolation, the elevated charcoal concentration at 170 cm dates to ca. 400 B.C. This interpolated date may mark the arrival of the first Saladoid colonists to Antigua. Rouse reported two dates from the base of a Saladoid midden in the Indian Creek site (Ayres Creek drainage): both 2785±80 B.P. (1190–800 cal B.C., 2 sigma) (Rouse and Morse 1999: tab. 1). Rouse rejected the date as too early for Saladoid, but if it accurately represents the Saladoid date-of-entry to Antigua (and other nearby islands?), then our 400 B.C. core date may be associated with an already-established Saladoid presence on the island.

Sediments from the uppermost two zones in the Jolly Beach core likely represent late prehistoric/historic occupations. Increases in grass and sedge pollen along with those of *Alchornea* and palm probably reflect historical disturbances. Palm pollen, although unidentified to the genus level, is consistent with pollen produced by *Cocos nucifera* (coconut palm, an introduced economic and ornamental type common in the Jolly Beach area today). The presence of the introduced *Casuarina* (Australian pine) and *Agave* (century plant) also reflect modern efforts at landscaping. Significant increases in charcoal, mostly above 60 cm, are also indicative of historic or recent clearing in the area.

Crosby Lagoon (Core CL09-1)

Given the core's young age, no pollen samples were analyzed. Three samples were tested for phytoliths and only the uppermost sample contained phytoliths: predominantly palm spheres, with a few grass phytoliths and nodular spheres. Arrowroot is documented on Barbuda, and was potentially a source of the nodular spheres.

Discussion

Long sediment records were recovered from Jolly Beach and Nonsuch Bay. An additional core from Crosby Lagoon in the northwestern part of the island was collected but was relatively short and too recent. Coring locations were selected for their proximity to documented prehistoric archaeological sites and it was anticipated that the environmental records would relate to local activities of the settlement occupants.

The sediment core from Jolly Beach recorded environmental conditions over the past 3,520 years. Microfossils and sediments reflected an ecotonal environment, favorable for human settlement. Particulate charcoal distributions indicate episodes of human-caused burning during prehistoric and historic occupations. Phytoliths were lacking in this sequence.

The Nonsuch Bay core provided a record of landscape modifications from the protohistoric through colonial and recent periods on Antigua. The pollen and phytolith records documented shifts in the local environment and increases in agricultural activities, particularly in the eighteenth century. The sequence of radiocarbon dates through the 445-cm core revealed massive sediment runoff linked to the plantation activities in Betty's Hope plantation. In this core we have direct geoarchaeological evidence of the phenomenon described by Douglas Armstrong (2013a) as "an emerging landscape of power and enslavement." Economically useful plants represented in the pollen record include maize, squash, *Canna* (Achira), and, in the phytolith record, possibly palms and Marantaceae. Sugarcane, the primary historic-period crop on Antigua was not unequivocally documented in the microfossil record but its cultivation clearly was behind massive transformations in the regional landscape. Deforestation in this portion of the island during the seventeenth and eighteenth centuries resulted in large-scale loss of soil. To address Early to Mid Holocene landscapes, future coring in the Nonsuch Bay area will require longer cores using different coring apparatus that can penetrate thick historic-period erosional deposits.

12

Barbuda

*John G. Jones, Nicholas P. Dunning, Neil A. Duncan,
Deborah M. Pearsall, and Peter E. Siegel*

Background

Barbuda is located approximately 40 km north of Antigua (fig. 1.1). Geopolitically, Antigua and Barbuda form a two-island nation; given the distance between them and their geologically distinct histories, however, will treat them separately (McCann and Sykes 1984). Barbuda is located along the forearc of the Lesser Antilles subduction zone, a mainly submarine ridge of uplifted seafloor. The island comprises Pliocene to Holocene Age coral limestone of generally very low relief. It is approximately 170 km² in extent, the southern half comprising The Highlands formation, a limestone shelf with a maximum elevation of 31 m. Much of the northern and western portions of Barbuda consist of an inland lagoon system (fig. 12.1). In some areas the lagoon is separated from the surrounding ocean by narrow sandbars only a few meters in width. Eolian and coastal geomorphic processes have repeatedly reshaped the large lagoonal part of the island throughout the Holocene. Extensive tracts of mostly vegetated sand dunes define the area along the southeastern side of the lagoon (Hill 1966).

Barbuda's climate reflects its tropical maritime location and lack of significant elevation. There is little variation in either daily or annual temperatures with monthly average minimums ranging from 22.4º C in February to 25.4º C in August, and monthly maximum averages ranging from 27.9º C in February to 30.5º C in September. Rainfall on Barbuda averages 889 mm annually, but with significant interannual and seasonal variations much of the rainfall is from July through December. On average, the island is impacted by a hurricane once every twelve years.

Soils on Barbuda range from skeletal Entisols on unstable, typically sandy surfaces, to deeper, clayey Rendolls on areas of topographically sheltered hard limestone and marl in the highlands (Hill 1966). Eolian

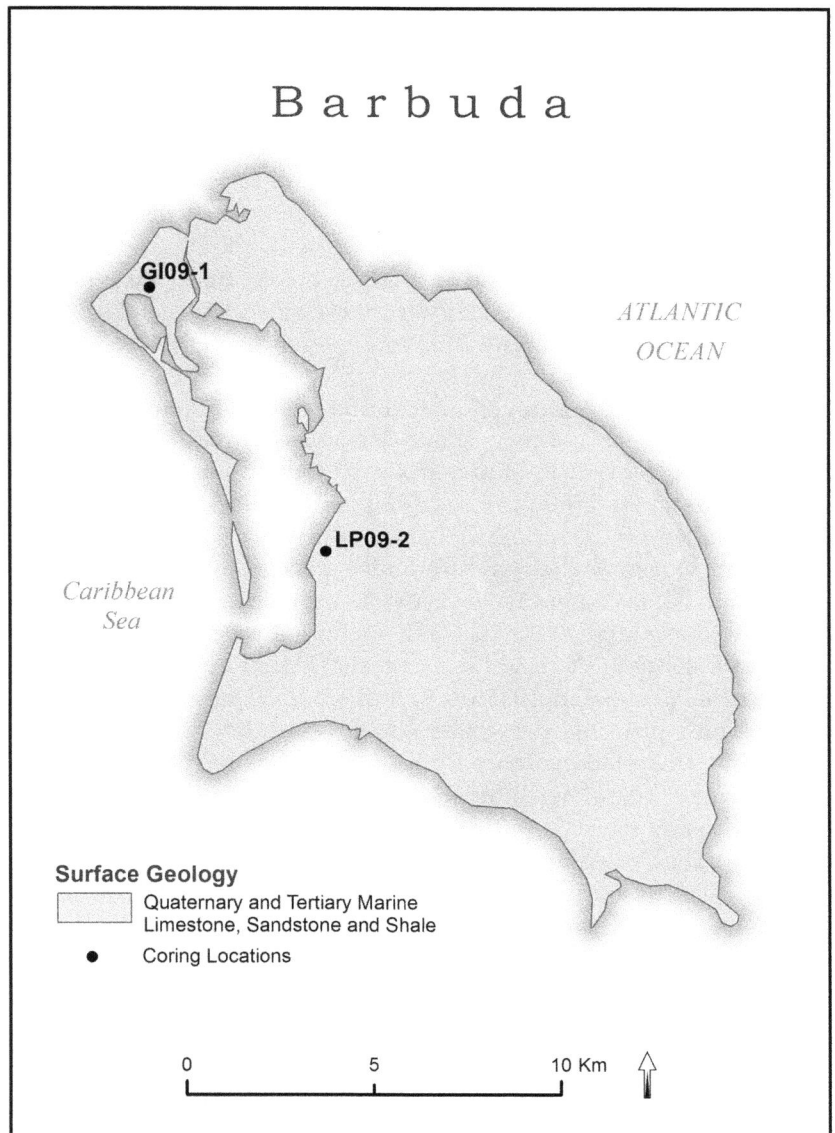

Figure 12.1. Map of Barbuda showing the surface geology and coring locations.

silt from Africa (or Saharan dust) constitutes a sizeable fraction of the inorganic component of soils on Barbuda just as it does on other limestone islands in the Caribbean, such as Barbados (Muhs et al. 2007). This windblown sediment was probably deposited in the Barbuda lagoon both directly and as in-washing fluvial material. However, the low physical relief of the island produces low fluvial sedimentation rates. Organic-based Histosols are found within some mangrove areas.

European interest in Barbuda dates to 1493 when Columbus made landfall during his second voyage to the New World. Colonization in earnest took place in the late seventeenth century with the establishment of the town of Codrington. The introduction of livestock (goats, hogs, and guinea fowl) had a profound effect on the island's vegetation. Beard (1949) characterized Barbuda as belonging to the evergreen bushland formation, while Harris (1965) classified the island's vegetation as evergreen woodland. While few references to the island's specific native vegetation exist, our survey revealed that the major woody taxa currently found on much of Barbuda were dominated by indigenous *Haematoxylum* (logwood) and introduced *Acacia*. The island is fringed by several species of mangrove, particularly in the Codrington lagoon area, where are found red (*Rhizophora*), black (*Avicennia*), and white (*Conocarpus, Laguncularia*) mangroves.

In total, sixteen Archaic and Ceramic Age sites are known for Barbuda (Look 2011; Watters 1980a, 2001). In his transect survey of the island, David Watters (1980a: 333–341) identified seven pre-Columbian sites: one Saladoid (Site BA3 [Sufferers site], Mill Reef complex), three Mamora Bay post-Saladoid (Sites BA1, BA5, BA7), and three small generic ceramic probable post-Saladoid sites. In a later survey, Watters (2001: 103) presented evidence for a series of Archaic occupations situated along a 3-km-long lithified paleoshoreline "trending SSE from the southeast corner of the Codrington Lagoon to the south coast of Barbuda." The Early Saladoid Seaview site (Site BA16), located along the northeast coast of Barbuda was identified by Look (2011). Watters, Donahue, and Stuckenrath (1992) published a number of dates from sites spanning the Archaic and Ceramic Ages, which we calibrated using CALIB 7.0 (tab. 12.1). Early colonial occupations are documented on the island, represented by approximately ten historic sites, including a plantation complex, fields, and structures of various kinds (Watters 1980a: 351–356; Watters 1980b, 1997, 2003; Watters and Miller 2000; Watters and Nicholson 1982).

With the assistance of archaeologist Reg Murphy and staff from the Codrington Lagoon National Park, we surveyed much of the island for suitable coring locations. Two locations were identified: Low Pond on the northern border of the town of Codrington and Grassy Island in Codrington Lagoon National Park. Inland lagoons were also investigated in the southern half of the island, but these were deemed to have too little sediment to provide useful information.

Table 12.1. Barbuda Dates Reported by Watters et al. (1992).

Location	Lab Sample Number	Material	¹⁴C Age (BP)	2-sigma Calibrated Date Range[a]	Cal Median Date
River Site	PITT-0717	*Strombus*	3650±35	1740–1520 BC	1640 BC
River Site	PITT-0731	*Strombus*	3830±25	1950–1750 BC	1860 BC
Indiantown Trail Site	Beta-18492	Charcoal	910±220	AD 680–1420	AD 1090
Indiantown Trail Site	PITT-0594	*Cittarium pica*	445±30	AD 1720–1949	AD 1870
Indiantown Trail Site	PITT-0595	*Strombus gigas*	1070±45	AD 1220–1400	AD 1300
Strombus line, Location 1[b]	SI-6695	*Strombus*	3340±70	1450–1070 BC	1280 BC
Strombus line, Location 1	PITT-0590	*Strombus*	3560±45	1640–1410 BC	1530 BC
Strombus line, Location 1	PITT-0718	*Strombus*	2100±35	AD 130–350	AD 240
Strombus line, Location 2	SI-6879	*Strombus*	5480±100	4200–3700 BC	3940 BC
Strombus line, Location 2	PITT-0592	*Strombus*	2900±50	880–580 BC	760 BC
Strombus line, Location 2	PITT-0719	*Strombus*	1755±80	AD 440–760	AD 620
Strombus line, Location 3	SI-6696	*Strombus*	4090±90	2460–1980 BC	2220 BC
Strombus line, Location 3	PITT-0591	*Strombus*	2830±80	800–420 BC	650 BC
Strombus line, Location 3	PITT-0720	*Strombus*	1930±70	AD 270–600	AD 440
Strombus line, Location 4	SI-6880	*Strombus*	3150±60	1200–870 BC	1020 BC
Strombus line, Location 4	PITT-0593	*Strombus*	2650±50	610–260 BC	420 BC
Strombus line, Location 4	PITT-0721	*Strombus*	3350±60	1430–1120 BC	1290 BC
South coast, Location 5	PITT-0589	*Strombus* artifact	1080±60	AD 1180–1400	AD 1290

a. CALIB ver 7.0 was used to calibrate the dates and compute the cal median values (Reimer et al. 2013). Dates from charcoal were calibrated using the IntCal13 method. Shell dates were calibrated using the Marine13 method: -27 for delta R and 14 for delta R uncertainty. We used the R and uncertainty values calculated elsewhere for the same section of the Caribbean (Bright 2011).
b. These locations along the *Strombus* line and south coast are plotted on the map presented by Watters et al. (1992: Figure 11).

Environmental Coring on Barbuda

Low Pond (Core LP09-2)

The core at Low Pond was collected near the northern edge of the town of Codrington. Vegetation in the immediate area consisted of red (*Rhizophora*), black (*Avicennia*), and white mangroves (Combretaceae), with occasional saltwort (*Salicornia*) and grasses on elevated areas. The area was used for fishing and launching boats, thus we selected a location removed from heavily trafficked areas. In total, 149 cm of stratigraphically continuous sediments were collected. Basal sediments consisted of gravelly marls with shells. Organic sediment from 148 cm dated to ca. 535 B.C. (tab. 12.2). Low Pond itself, not sampled for this study, is an eighteenth-century well feature constructed on behalf of Lord Codrington for the purpose of watering livestock. Accordingly, we expected historic-period disturbances in the core collected about 100 m west of this feature. No prehistoric sites are documented in the immediate vicinity of the coring location vicinity.

Sixteen samples were analyzed for pollen, of which thirteen provided 200-plus grain counts. Pollen concentration values ranged from 3,516 to 50,168 fossil grains/ml of sediment. Many of the concentration values were fairly low, but since pollen preservation was generally excellent, the lower values probably signal fluctuations in sedimentation rates rather than periods of desiccation or sediment oxidation. Overall, sediments comprised various clays and organic-rich gyttjas. Three basal samples from 130 to 149 cm comprised organic clays; pollen grains were present in the organic-rich sediments, but were exceedingly rare and counts could not be achieved. Concentration values from these three basal samples were too low to provide reliable counts (Bryant and Hall 1993; Hall 1981). In total, forty-six taxa were identified in the pollen assemblage (tab. 12.3). In addition, two unknown types were noted.

Table 12.2. Radiocarbon Dates from the Barbuda Cores.

Core Location	Lab Sample Number	Core Number/ Sample Depth	^{14}C Age (BP)[a]	^{13}C/^{12}C Ratio	2-Sigma Calibrated Date Range[b]	Median Cal Date
Low Pond	AA86579	LP09-2, 148–149cm, OS[c]	2430±45	−24.3	750–400 BC/ 2350–2700 BP	535 BC/ 2485 BP
Grassy Island	AA86580	GI09-1, 169–170cm, Peat	2820±40	−20.4	1110–850 BC/ 2800–3060 BP	975 BC/ 2925 BP

a. 1–sigma range.
b. Dates were calibrated using the IntCal13 method of CALIB ver. 7.0 (Reimer et al. 2013).
c. Organic sediment.

Table 12.3. Pollen Taxa Identified in the Barbuda Cores.

Taxon	Common Name	Taxon	Common Name
Avicennia	Black Mangrove	*Bursera*	Gumbo limbo
Combretaceae	White Mangrove	*Byrsonima*	Nance
Rhizophora	Red Mangrove	*Cassia*	Cassia
Asteraceae	Aster Family	*Cecropia*	Trumpet
Borreria	Buttonweed	*Celtis*	Hackberry
Cactaceae	Cactus Family	*Citrus*	Orange, Grapefruit
Cheno-Am	Goosefoot, Pigweed	*Coccoloba*	Sea Grape
Croton	Croton	*Guazuma*	Bay Cedar
Cyperaceae	Sedge Family	*Gymnopodium*	Canelita
Cladium	Sawgrass	*Haematoxylon*	Logwood
Euphorbiaceae	Spurge Family	*Hippomane*	Manchineel
Fabaceae	Bean or Legume Family	*Hirea*	Barbados Cherry Type
Geraniaceae	Cranesbill Family	*Hura*	Sandbox
Liliaceae	Lily Family	*Machaerium*	Rosewood
Poaceae	Grass Family	Moraceae	Mulberry Family
Polygonaceae	Knotweed Family	Myrtaceae	Myrtle Family
Polygonum	Knotweed	*Pinus*	Pine
Solanaceae	Nightshade Family	*Pterocarpus*	
Verbenaceae	Vervain Family	*Quercus*	Oak
Acacia	Acacia	Sapotaceae	Sapodilla Family
Alchornea	*Alchornea*	*Sebastiana*	Poisonwood
Anacardiaceae	Cashew Family	*Trema*	Trema
Apocynaceae	Dogbane Family	*Zanthoxylum*	Prickly Ash
Arecaceae	Palm Family	Indeterminate	poor preservation

Four samples were tested for phytoliths from the core; none contained phytoliths, although the uppermost did have some sponge spicules.

Above 125 cm the core contained abundant well-preserved fossil pollen, and three zones are apparent (fig. 12.2). The lowest zone occurred from 125 to 75 cm, and postdates ca. 535 B.C. Samples were dominated by white and red mangrove pollen characteristic of an environment similar to today's. Other taxa were also well represented at the time, including *Cladium* (sawgrass), *Alchornea,* and Moraceae (mulberry family, probably largely *Trophis* and possibly *Ficus*). Fern spores were higher during this period as well; nearly all of them were from *Acrostichum,*

276 • Chapter 12

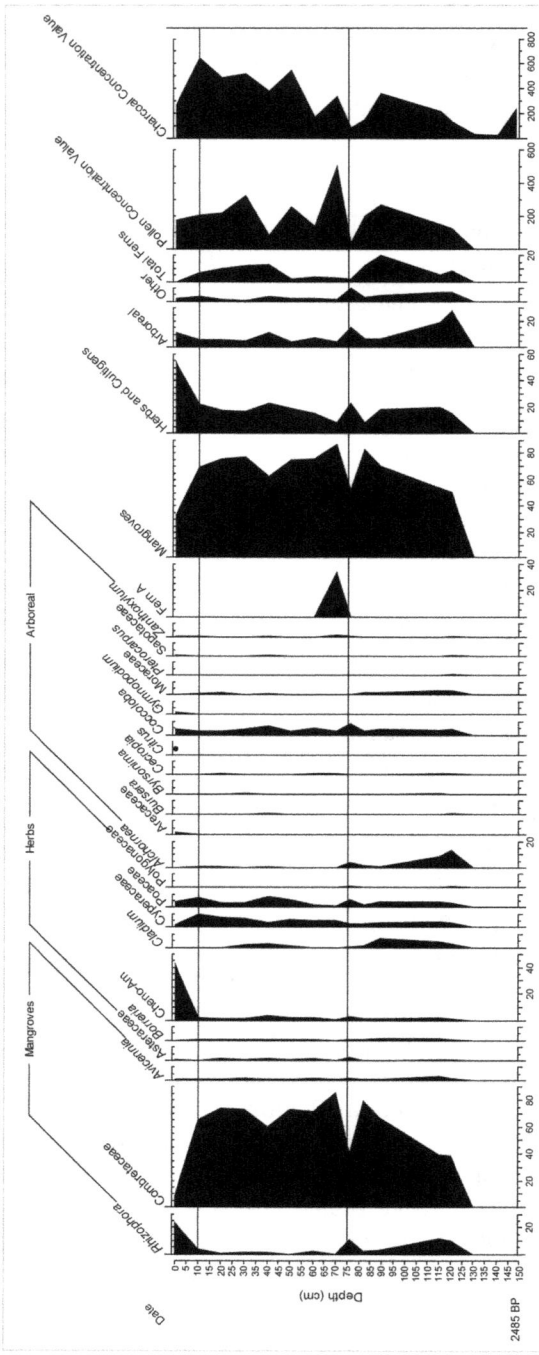

Figure 12.2. Low Pond, Barbuda, core pollen-percentage diagram. Pollen and charcoal concentrations are expressed as grains and fragments, respectively, per cm^3 of sediment.

a salt-tolerant fern species. Elevated values of this taxon along with salt-tolerant *Cladium* and increased percentages of red mangroves suggest higher salinity levels in the lagoon at the time. Particulate charcoal concentration values were elevated and sustained indicating human activities.

Between 75 and 10 cm, shifts were documented in the frequencies of some taxa. *Rhizophora, Cladium, Alchornea,* and Moraceae pollen counts were reduced, while sedge and Combretaceae pollen increased slightly. These changes likely reflect changes in lagoon salinity. Possibly, the lagoon was sealed off from the ocean at this time, although other factors could account for the increase in less-salt-tolerant species. There is a dramatic spike in fern type-A spores, a type largely comprising ferns in the Polypodiaceae family. These ferns would not be expected in a marine environment, and also probably signal a reduction in local salinity. This zone likely extends into the historical period, but there is no clear pollen evidence for the prehistoric–historic transition in the Low Pond core.

The uppermost zone (10–0 cm) shows a distinctive increase in Cheno-Am pollen; these grains could represent disturbance types (*Chenopodium* [goosefoot] or Amaranthaceae [pigweed]), but more likely indicate the prevalence of saltwort (*Salicornia*) in the area. This taxon was noted in the coring vicinity today. Red mangrove increased notably while white mangrove decreased. Both taxa are also abundant in the area today. Cultigens were noted by the occurrence of a few grains of introduced palm (probably *Cocos nucifera,* coconut) and by the occurrence of a single grain of *Citrus* (orange, lemon, or grapefruit).

Particulate charcoal concentration values were relatively high at the core base (fig. 12.2). The ca. 535 B.C. date from that context was associated with a charcoal peak that probably reflects human activities on the island, although pollen values were too low and phytoliths nonexistent to provide additional lines of evidence.

Grassy Island (Core GI09-1)

The Grassy Island core was collected from Codrington Lagoon National Park, adjacent to a shell marl island and ridge. The coring location is currently adjacent to the lagoon estuary and the deposits will likely be eroded in the future. The depositional environment of Grassy Island was a closed organic-accumulating lagoon surrounded by mangroves. Vegetation in the area included red, black, and white mangroves; saltwort; grasses (Poaceae); Cyperaceae; unidentified trees; and columnar cactus (cf. *Pilosocereus*) on the higher ridges. In total, 185 cm of continuous sediments were collected. A peat sample from 170 cm produced a date of ca. 975 B.C. Most of the core comprised fibric peat and bands of calcareous marls. Basal sediments consisted of gravelly marl with shells. A band of volcanic ash was noted at 122–123 cm.

Twelve samples were examined for pollen. Except for the basal sample, pollen preservation was excellent and concentration values ranged from 14,293 to 126,674 fossil grains/ml of sediment. In total, twenty-seven identifiable and four unknown pollen taxa were documented. Four samples were tested for phytoliths and recovery was found to be very low. No phytoliths were identified below 145 cm. Other samples contained palm spheres, a sedge phytolith, and single spheres from the Bombacaceae and Zingiberaceae families.

Two pollen zones were documented in the core (fig. 12.3). From 185 to 170 cm, sediments consisted of gravelly marl, shells, and some organic material. Pollen and phytoliths were absent. All samples above 167 cm produced well-preserved pollen. Between 167 and 125 cm, high levels of red mangrove and appreciable quantities of grass pollen were documented. Combretaceae and *Borreria* pollen were also somewhat elevated in this zone, though Cheno-Am pollen, a major component in the uppermost section of the core was significantly reduced. This zone reflects an environment with a stronger marine influence than today. Since this core was collected from the same lagoon as Low Pond, we may be seeing the same signal where the estuary was more open to the sea at an earlier time, but closed at some unspecified time. A relatively higher amount of salt in the system likely suppressed many plants in the Grassy Island area, but allowed mangroves to flourish. These findings are consistent with observations by David Watters and colleagues regarding the timing of the prograded Palmetto Point south of Codrington Lagoon (Watters 2001; Watters, Donahue, and Stuckenrath 1992; also Brasier and Donahue 1985).

The uppermost zone from 125 cm and above reflects a different environment. Red mangrove pollen was reduced, while *Avicennia* (black mangrove) pollen increased significantly. Cheno-Ams (almost certainly saltwort [*Salicornia*]), *Alchornea*, and *Coccoloba* also increased. Cheno-Am grains noted in this section all appear identical and probably reflect the presence of a single species of plant. The Grassy Island coring location may have increased in salinity levels at this time, thereby resulting in a setting not conducive to red mangrove vegetation. Black mangrove and saltwort are halophytic, thriving in hyper-saline environments, and the closing of the estuary to periodic flushing of fresh or saltwater may have created an environment favorable for these plants. In the

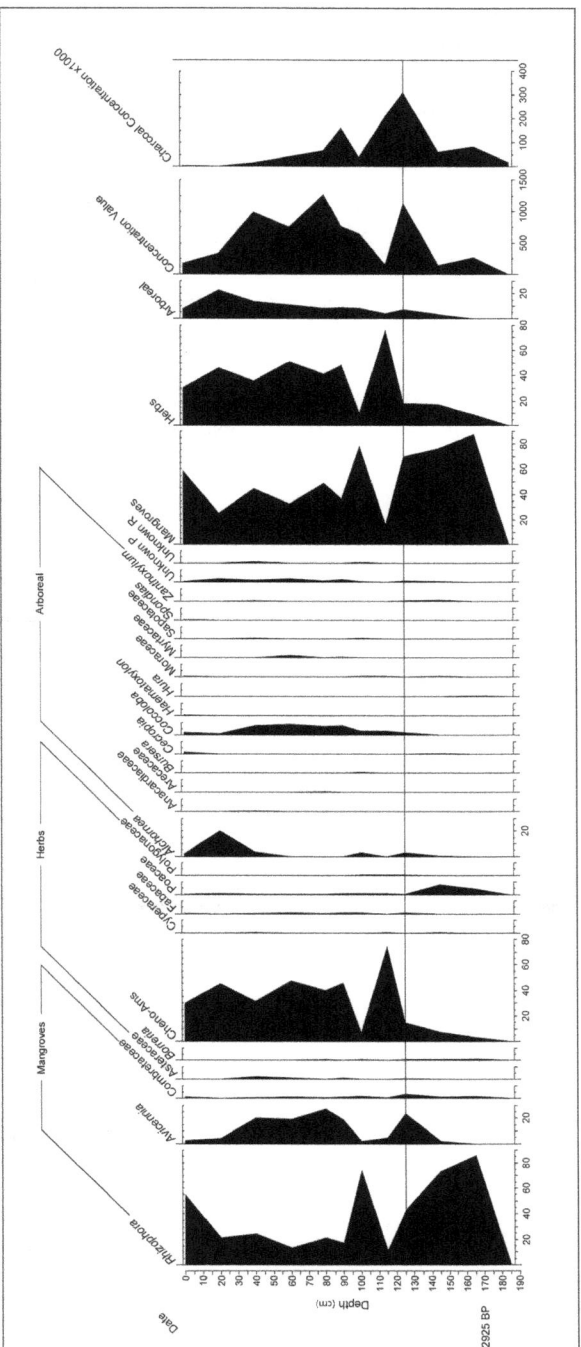

Figure 12.3. Grassy Island, Barbuda, core pollen-percentage diagram. Pollen and charcoal concentrations are expressed as grains and fragments, respectively, per cm³ of sediment.

absence of freshwater input or periodic marine-water flushing, the evaporation of salty water in the area might have created an environment where these taxa could thrive at the expense of other taxa. *Alchornea* and *Coccoloba* were likely found on the slightly higher ridges on the islands still present in the coring area. Particulate charcoal was relatively low throughout the Grassy Island core, but reached a peak at around the time of transition between the lower and upper zones, around 125 cm; there was also a small peak at 90 cm. These peaks may reflect human activity elsewhere on Barbuda. There was a gradual increase in arboreal pollen in the upper zone, probably reflecting the maturation of local forests.

Three sediment samples from the upper zone produced only a few phytoliths, with counts too low for meaningful interpretations. The phytolith types were from taxa poorly represented in the pollen record, including palms and a single phytolith each of Bombacaceae/Zingiberaceae and sedge (fig. 12.4).

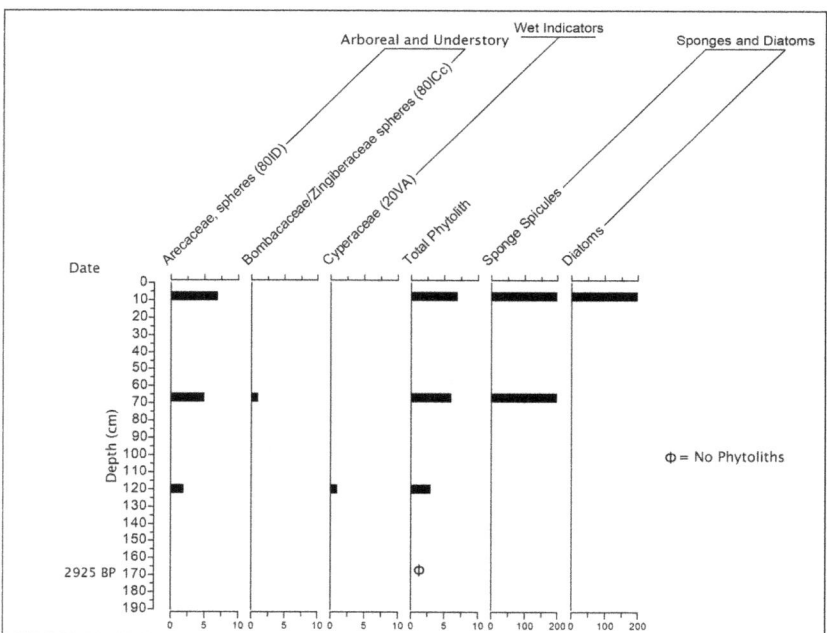

Figure 12.4. Grassy Island, Barbuda, core phytolith diagram: resolved. Given the low phytolith counts only the resolved diagram is presented.

Discussion

The Barbuda sediment cores document a significant environmental event occurring sometime after approximately three thousand years ago. Observed shifts in pollen spectra likely reflect the same event across Codrington Lagoon. The event is associated with changes in relative degrees of salinity within the lagoon: a decrease in Low Pond and an increase in Grassy Island. Such shifts in salinity are not unexpected given the geomorphically dynamic nature of Codrington Lagoon. Today, the lagoon is separated from the ocean only by narrow sandbars in places; the locations of openings to the ocean undoubtedly changed repeatedly during the Holocene. Hurricanes and tsunamis are the most likely agents for rapid redistribution of sediments, reconfiguration of the lagoon, and overall coastal transformations, especially on low-lying islands like Barbuda (Engel 2012; Engel et al. 2010).

The environmental record in the Low Pond core revealed a moderate amount of charcoal deposition, reflecting nearby human activities. After ca. 580 B.C., saline levels increased in the local area with greater occurrence of salt-tolerant species, including red mangrove and sawgrass (*Cladium*). Later, the relative importance of these taxa decreased, along with a near total removal of *Alchornea* from the record. White mangrove pollen (taxa favoring fresh- rather than saltwater environments) became somewhat more common, again reflecting a change in local water salinity.

An inverse pattern was documented in the Grassy Island core, where basal sediments deposited after ca. 975 B.C. represented an environment dominated by red mangroves, with grasses occurring on drier ridges. At 125 cm, an event occurred whereby grasses and red mangrove decreased significantly, while hyper-saline-loving taxa *Avicennia* and Cheno-Am (probably *Salicornia*) became abundant. A 1-cm-thick volcanic ash lens was recorded at 122–123 cm, but its relationship to the environmental shift is not known. Given its approximate age and spatial proximity the most likely source of the ash is a series of pyroclastic eruptions at Liamuiga volcano on St. Kitts between 1,800 and 2,000 years ago (Robertson 2005). Ash deposition was not identified in the Low Pond core, though the distribution patterns of settling eolian sediments such as volcanic ash can exhibit great variability even over short distances. The past environment of Grassy Island was an open wetland where organic-rich sediments accumulated and ash from a remote volcano was preserved. This environment deprived of freshwater or even marine-water flushing lead to a hyper-saline setting where black mangrove and saltwort plants flourished. The upper zone showed changes in upland vegetation. Whereas the lower zone of the Grassy Island sequence revealed relatively high percentages of grass pollen, the upper zone produced significant quantities of *Coccoloba* (sea grape) and *Alchornea* pollen. Fluctuations in particulate charcoal at 125 and 90 cm indicate human activities in the area.

Despite the challenges of working on what appears to be a young island with little apparent sediment accumulation, two cores in excess of 2,400 years old were collected. Pollen preservation was excellent in both sequences, although concentration values were exceedingly low in the basal sediments from the cores. A significant event occurred in both cores, where it appears that dramatic shifts in local salinity levels resulted in changing composition of local vegetation. We believe that this event is related to the progradation of Palmetto Point and associated silting of portions of Codrington Lagoon in the Mid to Late Holocene, resulting in the restriction of water flow to and from the lagoon (Brasier and Donahue 1985; Watters, Donahue, and Stuckenrath 1992). Both cores reveal the presence of humans, although evidence is lacking for intensive landscape modifications and encouragement of economically useful plant taxa (tabs. 12.4, 12.5). The pollen and charcoal data are consistent with the assessment by Watters (2001) for small encampments of coastally oriented shellfish gatherers during the Mid to Late Holocene Archaic period.

Table 12.4. Ethnobotanical Associations and Disturbance Indicators Represented in the Barbuda Cores.[a]

Taxon	Ethnobotanical Association or Disturbance Indicator	Core GI09-1	Core LP09-2
MANGROVE			
Avicennia	Black mangrove. Throat pains, incontinence.	X	X
Combretaceae	White mangrove. Slows bleeding.	X[b]	X
Rhizophora	Red mangrove. Diarrhea, fever, malaria, excellent fuel wood.	X	X
HERBS/CULTIGENS			
Asteraceae	Aster or Composite family. Herbs and shrubs. Many are invasive weed species of cleared open areas.	X[b]	X
Borreria	Weedy herb in Madder family. Alkaloid and iridoid extracts have medicinal properties.	X[b]	X

(continued)

Table 12.4. *(continued)*

Taxon	Ethnobotanical Association or Disturbance Indicator	Core GI09-1	Core LP09-2
Cheno-Ams	Chenopod and amaranth families. Favor disturbed or open habitats. Young greens and mature seeds are edible. Includes seablite, saltwort, chenopod, amaranth.	X	X
Cyperaceae, *Cladium*	Sedge family. Grasslike herbaceous plants, many are weeds that invade cleared open areas.		X
Fabaceae	Wild herbaceous legumes. Includes cohoba, edible beans. Species include plants with medicinal uses and for producing narcotic snuff, edible fruit, and fish poison.	X	
Poaceae	Grass family. Often associated with areas frequently fired. Edible starchy grains.	X	X
Polygonaceae	Docks and sorrels. Edible leaves.	X[b]	X[b]
ARBOREAL			
Alchornea	Many species have medicinal properties.	X	X
Arecaceae	Palm family. Edible fruit, thatching, cordage, needles, posts.	X[b]	X[b]
Byrsonima	Edible fruit, nance.		X[b]
Bursera	Gumbo limbo. Resin has medicinal properties, leaves used for tea.		X[b]
Cecropia	Pumpwood. Fast-growing colonizing trees common to disturbed forest habitats and clearings.	X[b]	X[b]
Citrus	Edible fruit.		X[b]
Coccoloba	Sea grape. Edible fruit, medicinal.	X	X
Moraceae	Mulberry family. Edible fruit, breadnut, medicinal. Often colonize open cleared areas.		X
Myrtaceae	Myrtle family. Edible fruit, medicinal. Frequently found in windbreak and secondary forest growth. Includes guava, Eugenia, allspice.	X[b]	
Sapotaceae	Sapote family. Edible fruit, medicinal, latex in some species. Includes edible fruits of chicle, sapote, lucuma.	X[b]	X[b]

a. See Table 5.5 for the sources of information.
b. Trace amounts.

Table 12.5. Plant Taxa Identified in the Barbuda Cores with No Documented Ethnobotanical or Anthropogenic Correlates Other than Perhaps Fuel Wood, Especially Arboreal Taxa.

Taxon	Common Name	Core GI09-1	Core LP09-1
HERBS/CULTIGENS			
Polygonaceae, *Gymnopodium*	Common sorrel	X[a]	X[a]
ARBOREAL			
Hura	Sand box	X[a]	
Maytenus	Caribbean Mayten, staff vine	X	
Pterocarpus	Swamp bloodwood tree. Grows in swamp forests, mainly on landward side of mangrove.		X[a]
Zanthoxylum	Prickly ash	X[a]	
FERNS			
Unknown ferns			X

a. Trace amounts.

13

St. Croix

*Deborah M. Pearsall, Nicholas P. Dunning,
John G. Jones, Neil A. Duncan, and Peter E. Siegel*

Background

St. Croix is one of the more isolated West Indian islands, lying some 70 km south of the other Virgin Islands, its closest neighbors (fig. 1.1). This relative isolation may have contributed to its apparent late settlement, although this observation may also be a product of sampling bias. Its relative proximity to Puerto Rico may also have led to a late Taíno occupation.

Geologically, St. Croix is distinct from the northern Virgin Islands and Puerto Rico. Located in the Anegada Passage, along the tectonic boundary between the Greater and Lesser Antilles, St. Croix was subjected to different sedimentary, convergence, and sediment-folding processes than the northern Virgins and Puerto Rico (Lewis et al. 1990: 118–120; Maury et al. 1990: 147). In terms of Holdridge's classification of life zones, St. Croix consists mostly of a subtropical dry forest (83%), followed by subtropical moist forest (17%) (Ewel and Whitmore 1973: tab. 2). The island has a landmass of about 215 km².

St. Croix, like Cuba, Hispaniola, and Puerto Rico, formed along a deformed convergent plate boundary. The boundary along this section of the North American–Caribbean boundary was once convergent and subductive, generating both uplift and volcanism (Nagle and Hubbard 1989). This juncture has since become a transform boundary with strong tectonic extension forces resulting in the separation and folding of bedrock formations. Lithology includes older igneous rocks, clastic sedimentary formations formed in near-shore contexts, limestone laid down in a central graben during high sea-level stands, and Quaternary coastal deposits.

St. Croix has two areas of elevated terrain: higher, steeper mountains in the west and a broader, longer, and lower range in the east (fig. 13.1). Both upland areas are deeply dissected by numerous steep, narrow valleys most typically draining toward the south. The southern

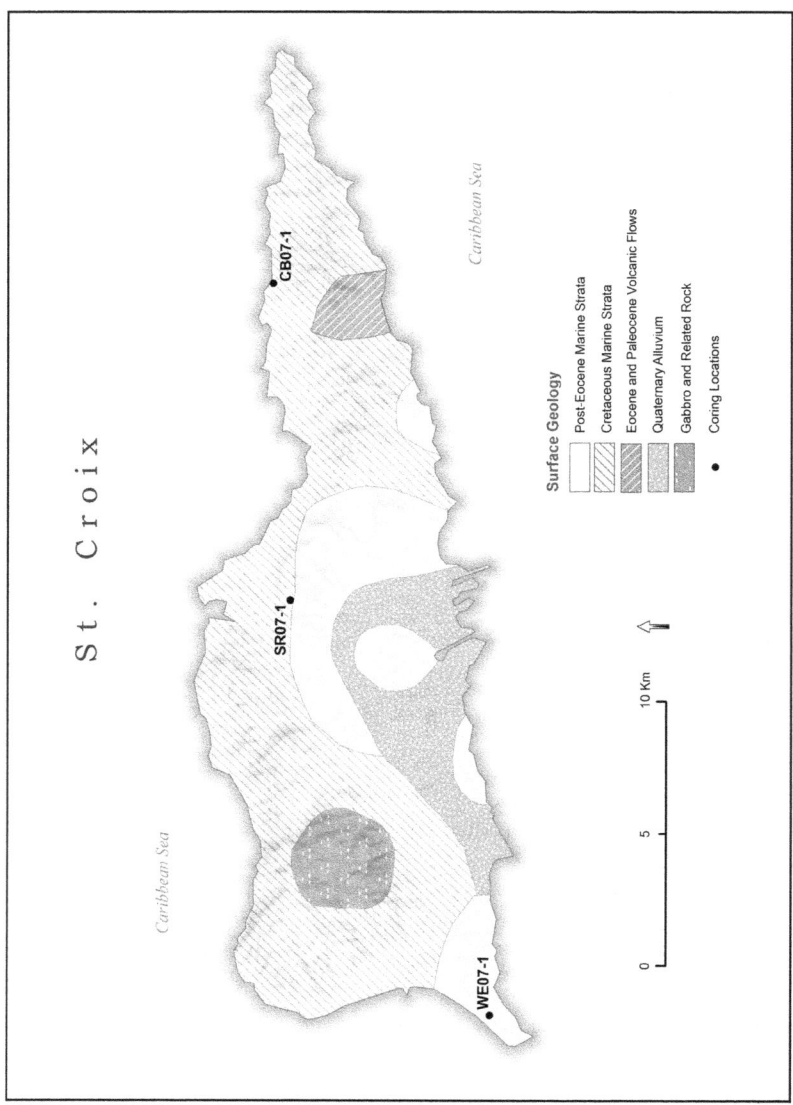

Figure 13.1. Map of St. Croix showing the surface geology and coring locations.

flanks of the mountain systems include a series of marine terraces created by both uplift and long-term sea-level fluctuations. Alluvial fans and aprons have formed where valleys disgorge onto the terraces and broad coastal plain. Coastal currents have reshaped sediments into numerous baymouth bars and spits along the coast of the island.

The distribution of soils across St. Croix reflects variation in topography and parent material. Generally shallow Mollisols predominate on stable upland surfaces, whereas very shallow Inceptisols are found on more–steeply sloping terrain. Argillic Mollisols and Vertisols have developed on stable lowland surfaces, most notably in the central graben between the eastern and western highlands. Sandy Entisols and mucky Histosols are found along the coasts.

Rainfall on St. Croix is governed by elevation because orographic forcing generates the majority of precipitation. Average annual rainfall totals range from a low of about 500 mm near the eastern end of the island to about 1,300 mm on the slopes of Mount Eagle (elevation 355 m) in the western mountains. Rainfall is normally heaviest from June through November.

Small areas of the coast were home to mangrove ecosystems, principally where baymouth bars and sand spits created sheltered basins of brackish water. Other coastal locations typically bore scrubby, xerophytic vegetation with *Hippomane mancinella, Coccoloba uvifera,* and various palm species locally dominant in some areas. Upland areas across eastern St. Croix are dominated by woody thicket or bush vegetation. Several species of *Croton* are dominant, interspersed with a wide variety of other taxa including *Lantana, Wedelia, Melochia,* and wild cotton (*Gossypium*). Higher tropical deciduous forest occurs in areas of greater rainfall in the western uplands and valleys with *Ceiba pentandra, Spondias mombin, Hura crepitans,* and *Bursera simarumba* as notable members.

There are no documented Archaic archaeological sites on St. Croix, although Hardy (2009: 101) noted that an aceramic archaeological deposit was identified in the vicinity of Salt River (north-central coast). In terms of the St. Croix prehistoric chronology, nine sites date to the Prosperity period (Early Saladoid), thirty-seven to Coral Bay-Longford (Late Saladoid), forty-nine to Magens Bay-Salt River I (early Ostionoid), thirty-two to Magens Bay-Salt River II (middle Ostionoid), and nineteen to Magens Bay-Salt River III (late Ostionoid/protohistoric/Contact) (Hardy 2009: 105–106; Morse 1989, 1995, 2004; Vescelius 1952, 1980).

Archaeological investigations in Coakley Bay identified two sites with Coral Bay–Longford/Magens Bay–Salt River I deposits in the vicinity of our Coakley Bay coring location (Soltec International 2007). In addition, the mid-eighteenth-century Coakley Bay plantation is located within the watershed.

Archaeobotanical data are reported from one Ceramic Age site on St. Croix: Aklis (Saladoid/Ostionoid) (Newsom and Pearsall 2003). Only charred wood was recovered. Two Archaic sites with archaeobotanical remains are reported from St. Thomas and St. John, Virgin Islands: Beach Access, St. John; and Krum Bay, St. Thomas (Newsom and Pearsall 2003; Pearsall 1989). Krum Bay provides the most detailed macroremains record for the Archaic Age in the Caribbean. Edible fruit-bearing trees identified among the plant remains from seed or fruit fragments include West Indian cherry (*Malpighia* sp.), wild fig (*Ficus* sp.), sapodilla (*Manilkara* sp.), and mastic-bully (*Sideroxylon* sp.). Sapotaceae seed fragments (*Manilkara* and *Sideroxylon*) occurred in about half of the samples analyzed at Krum Bay. Herbaceous plants include *Trianthema*, cactus family (Cactaceae), bean family (Fabaceae), and purslane (*Portulaca*). No seeds or nonwood remains were recovered from the Beach Access site.

Two Ceramic Age sites on St. Thomas and St. John have published archaeobotanical records: Trunk Bay, St. John (Ostionoid); and Tutu, St. Thomas (Saladoid/Ostionoid) (Newsom and Pearsall 2003). The fruit trees guava (*Psidium guajava*), mastic (*Sideroxylon* sp.), and cockspur (*Celtis* sp.) are represented at Trunk Bay.

The Tutu village site provides a detailed macroremains record for plant foods from the Cedrosan Saladoid and Chican Ostionoid occupations of St. Thomas (Pearsall 2002). From the earlier period were identified Sapotaceae seed coat fragments and wild fig (*Ficus*) and seeds from the herbaceous plants grass (Poaceae), wild bean (Fabaceae), and purslane (*Portulaca*). Cotton (*Gossypium*) seeds were also present, as were fragments of dense cotyledon tissue, porous endosperm tissue, and root/tuber tissue. In addition to these plants, but excepting purslane, the record of the later period also included two maize kernel fragments, *doncella* (*Brysonima* sp.), an edible fruit in the Malpighiaceae family, Cheno-Am, passion fruit (*Passiflora*), and guava (*Psidium*). The two periods differed markedly in the quantity of charred wood and food remains recovered, with five to six times the material recovered from Chican Ostionoid samples than from Cedrosan Saladoid. The better-preserved record from the later period documents a mixed subsistence system that included maize, roots and tubers, tree fruits, and a variety of wild annuals favoring disturbed habitats.

Phytoliths add arrowroot (Marantaceae), palm (Arecaceae), squash (*Cucurbita* sp.), and Chrysobalanaceae, a family that includes the edible fruit–bearing tree *Chrysobalanus icaco* to the record of plants used during the early and later occupations of Tutu (Piperno 2002). A study of microfossils from dental calculus was conducted by Mickleburgh and Pagán-Jiménez (2012) on three individuals from Tutu: one from the early period, one probably from the early period, and one from the late period. The early individuals produced starch from canna (cf. Cannaceae), bean (Fabaceae), sweet potato (cf. *Ipomoea batatas*), cocoyam (cf. *Xanthosoma*), and maize (cf. *Zea mays*). Starch from the single late individual resembled bean (cf. Fabaceae) and maize (cf. *Zea mays*).

The microfossil (phytolith and starch) evidence from Tutu provides insight into the kinds of root or tuber foods consumed by the occupants: arrowroot family, canna family, sweet potato, and cocoyam. The list of utilized tree fruits is expanded to include palm and Chrysobalanaceae. Maize is corroborated in the Late Ceramic Age, and identified for the first time in the early period (two cf. *Zea mays* grains from the confirmed early individual).

In comparison to the other Virgin Islands, St. Croix has more level surface area, which has been extensively used for sugarcane cultivation (Eggers 1879). More than 16,000 acres were under sugar cultivation in 1889; seventy-two plantations were in operation at the turn of the twentieth century. Other estate-raised crops included bananas, pineapple, cocoa, coffee, mango, citrus, and coconuts (Millspaugh 1902). The *Croton* vegetation formation—a dry, shrubby formation that dominates on the eastern and southern parts of the island—also occurs more generally in areas in which soil has been exhausted from cane cultivation (Eggers 1879). Small-scale horticulture on St. Croix and the Virgin Islands has included cultivation of yam (*Dioscorea alata, D. altissima*), sweet potato (*Ipomoea batatas*), okra (*Abelmoschus esculentus*), tanier (*Xanthosoma sagittaefolium*), pigeon pea (*Cajanus cajan*), tomato (*Solanum lycopersicum,* syn. *Lycopersicon esculentum*), and peppers (*Capsicum*), as well as various squashes and melons (Cucurbitaceae) (Eggers 1879). As is the case more widely in the Virgin Islands, pastures planted in introduced guinea grass (*Panicum maximum*) occur, and most of the commonly occurring tropical fruit trees (e.g., tamarind, mango, papaya, avocado, tree gourd, guava, sapote, soursop) have been naturalized (Eggers 1879; Millspaugh 1902).

Environmental Coring on St. Croix

Cores were extracted from three wetlands across the island (fig. 13.1). Core WE07-1 was collected from the West End Saltpond near the southwestern point of the island. The large, intensively occupied Saladoid Aklis site is located in this area (Hayward and Cinquino 2002; Morse 1989, 1995, 2004; Vescelius 1952). This is an area characterized by a complex history of shoreline sediment movement and deposition. Unfortunately, sediments within the saltpond were dominated by thick marine sands with only thinner bands of histic material, a poor environment for conservation of plant microfossils. Core SR07-1 was collected from a black mangrove swamp in the estuary of the Salt River near the north-central coast of the island. The Salt River has a complex drainage basin of about 12 km², much of it moderately to steeply sloping terrain. While extracting the core it became apparent that the estuary included a heavy burden of silty sediment likely derived from historic-period erosion. We were unable to penetrate this mantle of recent sediment. A more productive coring site was identified at Coakley Bay, located along the northeast coast of the island.

Coakley Bay (Core CB07-1)

The CB07-1 core was extracted from the east end of a small lagoon situated behind a baymouth bar along the north coast of St. Croix (fig. 13.1). Until recently, the end of the lagoon was an area of mixed mangrove forest, most of which has been removed for modern residential development. Several very small intermittent streams feed into the lagoon, draining a total area of about 1.5 km², much of it moderately to steeply sloping terrain. This hilly landscape is mantled by soils of the Cramer, Glynn, and Southgate Series: shallow, stony, well-drained Mollisols and Inceptisols formed on weathered volcanic bedrock (Natural Resource Conservation Service 2000). Soils in the wetland itself belong to the Sandy Point Series: Histic Tropic Fluvaquents–poorly developed, hydromophic soils formed in alluvial sediment and organic muck. All of the soils examined on the slopes above the wetland show signs of moderate to severe truncation, with many missing A-horizons completely and with erosion proceeding into the C-horizon. Most of these lands were part of the former Coakley Bay plantation, which produced sugar in the area beginning in the mid eighteenth century (Law Engineering and Environmental Services 2002). Much of the erosion and consequent sedimentation in the Coakley Bay wetland is likely attributable to that period. Some of the surrounding area is currently being converted from pasture and open land to upscale residential land use, which is generating a new wave of erosion and sedimentation.

A 274-cm core was extracted from the eastern end of the Coakley Bay Lagoon (tab. 13.1). The core bottomed out in dark green–gray gleyed clay. Fibric organic material at a depth of 249 cm produced a radiocarbon date of ca. 1820 B.C. (tab. 13.2). A wood sample from 67 cm was dated to ca. A.D. 665, indicating that much of the core has considerable antiquity. Heavy clay sediments between 2 and 50 cm reflect colonial-era land clearance and erosion accumulating mineral sediment relatively rapidly in an area of red mangrove (evidenced by root casts). Organic-matter levels were appreciably higher between 82 and 130 cm, representing a relatively stable red mangrove-dominated lagoon. Much of the core between 130 and 250 cm consisted of weakly stratified sandy

Table 13.1. Sediment Descriptions of the Coakley Bay, St. Croix Core (CB07-1).

Depth (cm)	Color	OM (LOI)	Total P (ppm)	Sand%	Silt%	Clay%	Notes
0–2	Black						Organic muck
2–16	Very dark gray (5Y 3/1)	6.9		5	38	57	±20% red-orange mottles
16–30	Dark green gray (Gley 10Y 3/1)	8.6		4	36	60	
30–50	Olive gray (5Y 5/2)	7.7		7	40	53	Irregular, dark organic zone (root cast/crab burrow?)
50–53	Very dark gray brown (10YR 3/2)						
53–70	Dark green gray (Gley 10Y 4/1)	8.4		11	33	56	Charcoal flecks; wood piece at 67 cm
70–82	Dark green gray (Gley 10Y 3/1)	9.7		13	30	57	Root casts with lighter clay
82–91	Greenish black (Gley 10Y 2.5/1)	28.5		21	33	46	Root casts with lighter clay
91–130	Black (Gley N 2.5/N	33.2		30	32	38	Weakly laminated
130–132							Hole slop
132–147	Black (Gley N 2.5/N						Continuation of 91–130; weakly laminated
147–148							Lens of coarse sand
148–153	Greenish black (Gley 10Y 2.5/1)	15.0		32	28	40	
153–160	Dark green gray (Gley 10Y 4/1)	6.9		39	31	30	Abundant small marine shells
160–167	Greenish black (Gley 10Y 2.5/1)	7.6		42	31	27	

(continued)

Table 13.1. (continued)

Depth (cm)	Color	OM (LOI)	Total P (ppm)	Sand%	Silt%	Clay%	Notes
167–182	Dark green gray (Gley 10Y 3/1)	6.5		39	29	32	A few small marine shells
182–195	Greenish black (Gley 10Y 2.5/1)	8.0		44	33	23	Superabundant small marine shells
195–216							Hole slop
216–243	Dark green gray (Gley 10GY 4/1)						Possible hole slop; almost liquid
243–250	Greenish black (Gley 10Y 2.5/1)	7.9		45	35	20	Probable continuation of 182–195 cm
250–274	Dark green gray (Gley 10BG 4/1)	2.7		10	22	68	Massive clay

Table 13.2. Radiocarbon Dates from the Coakley Bay, St. Croix Core (CB07-1).

Lab Sample No.	Sample Depth, Material	^{14}C Age (BP)[a]	^{13}C/^{12}C Ratio	2-Sigma Calibrated Date Range (BP)[b]	Median Cal Date
AA82471	67 cm, PW[c]	1350±35	-26.9	AD 630–770/1180–1320 BP	AD 665/1285 BP
AA99901	140 cm, OS[d]	2320±30	-9.4	430–240 BC/2180–2380 BP	390 BC/2340 BP
Beta-376843	228 cm, OS	2900±30	-15.8	1210–1000 BC/2950–3160 BP	1085 BC/3035 BP
AA77642	249 cm, OS	3500±40	-18.8	1935–1700 BC/3650–3880 BP	1820 BC/3770 BP

a. 1-sigma range.
b. Dates were calibrated using the IntCal13 method of CALIB ver. 7.0 (Reimer et al. 2013).
c. Preserved wood.
d. Organic sediment.

or clayey mineral sediments, with some banded organic matter indicative of a moderately stable depositional environment.

Two zones within the core produced abundant mollusk shells: 153–160 cm and 182–195 cm (tab. 13.1). Shells were analyzed by Denis Nieweg of Leiden University. All species in both levels are suggestive of a shallow marine environment with sandy or muddy bottom. It is likely that the barrier beach was breached during these periods, allowing more open access to the ocean than currently exists. The shells appear to have been deposited in situ and not washed in by storms. However, storm events may have been responsible for breaching the barrier beach. The stratum of coarse sand at 147–148 cm may represent a storm surge event and the probable closing of the lagoon by the building of the barrier beach. Marine shells are absent above this level.

Particulate charcoal is abundant in much of the core, suggesting a long sequence of human activity and land clearance in the area (tab. 13.3). At least two Late Saladoid/Early Ostionod sites are known from the vicinity of the Coakley Bay lagoon, dating to "approximately A.D. 400 to 700" (Soltec International 2007: 35).

Twelve samples were processed for pollen. Pollen was noted, although the grains were present in low concentrations due to an abundance of organic detritus and particulate charcoal. Further analysis of pollen was not undertaken. As noted, particulate charcoal was very abundant in the core, but was especially noteworthy beginning at 229–230 cm and continuing through 74–75 cm (tab. 13.3).

Table 13.3. Coakley Bay, St. Croix Core Charcoal Counts.

Depth (cm)	Charcoal Concentration (fragments/cm^3)
34–35	119,776
55–56	854,050
74–75	1,693,170
94–95	4,966,632
114–115	3,750,058
134–135	4,490,036
159–160	3,045,914
174–175	4,364,616
194–195	1,952,561
229–230	2,559,708
254–255	149,539
273–274	58,719

Phytoliths were recovered from eighteen of the twenty-four samples processed, although quantities were rarely high. Phytolith influx was poor to lacking below 164 cm, fairly abundant between 164 and 60 cm, and low above 60 cm.

Unlike other cores studied for the project, samples from Coakley Bay often contained more open-habitat indicators than arboreal and understory phytoliths. This is true of all the samples with higher phytolith counts between 165–60 cm, with the exception of the sample at 91–85 cm. Samples with more open-habitat indicators had relatively abundant panicoid grass phytoliths, with fewer quantities of other grass types (figs. 13.2a, 13.2b). Arboreal and understory plants are not absent in this section of core; small numbers of phytoliths from palms, Chrysobalanaceae, woody plants (small rugulose, cystoliths, sclerids), and Marantaceae were identified.

The sample from 91 to 85 cm differed from other samples in this core midsection with somewhat higher numbers of nodular and large rugulose spheres, Marantaceae indicators, and lower counts of grass phytoliths. Arboreal and understory indicators were much the same as other samples in this part of the core.

The overall assemblage of phytoliths from the midsection of the Coakley Bay core suggests an open habitat with some arboreal ele-

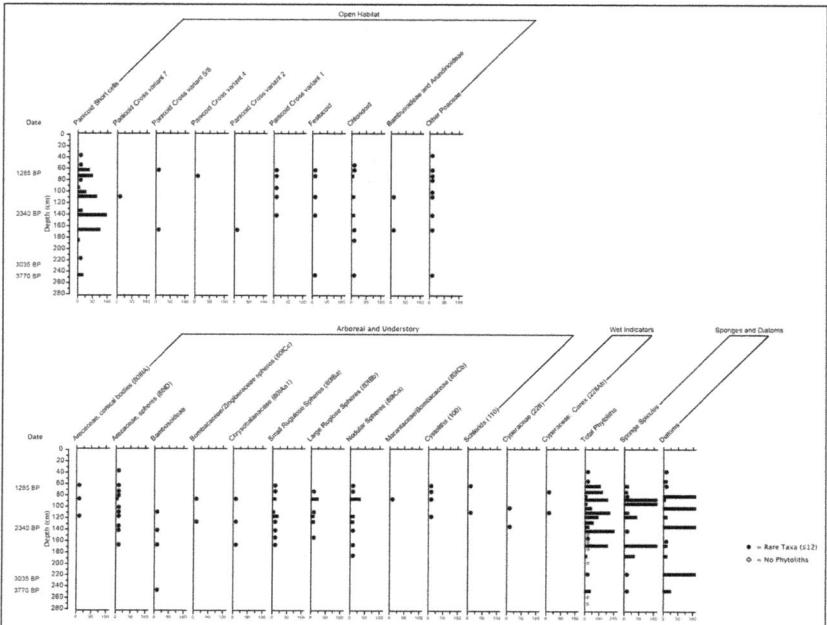

Figure 13.2a. Coakley Bay, St. Croix, core phytolith diagram: resolved.

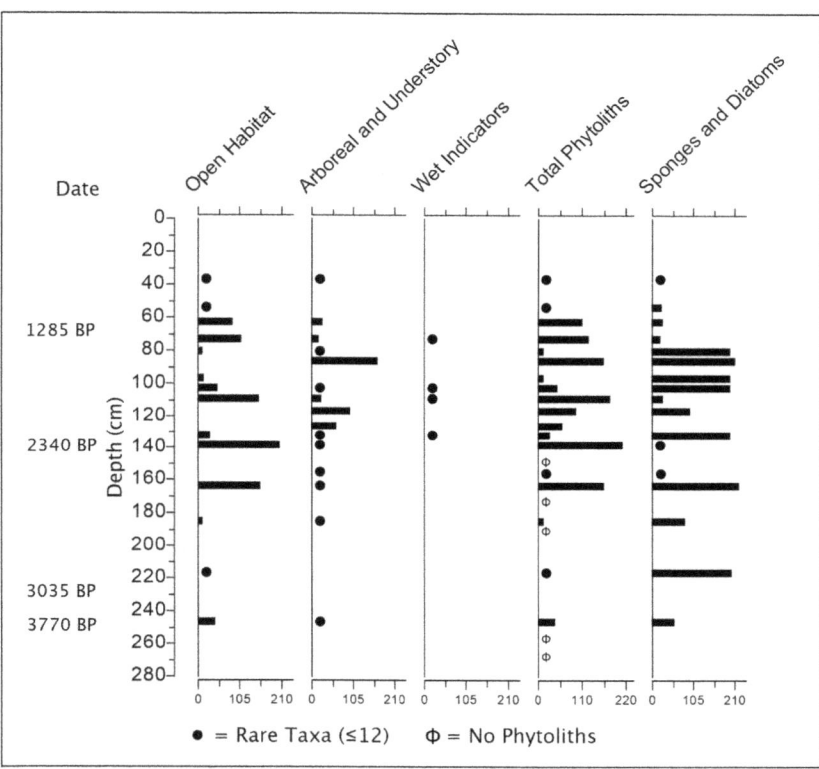

Figure 13.2b. Coakley Bay, St. Croix, core phytolith diagram: composite.

ments. Marantaceae are represented throughout the midsection, indicating the presence of arrowroot and/or leren (or wild Marantaceae). Nine Variant 1 cross-phytoliths were present in five levels, all from the core midsection. While none of the crosses was large enough to identify definitively as maize (Pearsall 2015), the presence of so many Variant 1 crosses in combination with the absence of Variant 5/6 crosses, which are produced more commonly in wild panicoid grasses, is suggestive of maize. The identification of sedge phytoliths indicates freshwater habitat near the coring locality.

Discussion

Heavy clay sediments above 50 cm are interpreted as likely colonial land clearance. Phytolith deposition was very sparse in this section of core so no additional insights into land use were possible. Sediments indicated a stable to moderately stable depositional environment throughout the core (tab. 13.4). More regular phytolith influx was represented in the deposit from 164 to 60 cm. The phytolith assemblage from this section of core reflects an open habitat with some arboreal elements.

Until the 1980s the Coakley Bay area included multiple inflowing streams and mangroves. Current vegetation is dry and open and the phytolith assemblage indicates this pattern was consistent in the past. Particulate charcoal concentrations are high in much of the core, suggesting a long history of land clearance that may have resulted in or contributed to the vegetation pattern seen today. Variant 1 crosses appear earliest in the sequence at 140 cm. Organic sediment from that context produced a date of ca. 390 B.C. (tab. 13.2). If these cross-shaped phytoliths were produced by maize, this date is earlier than the cf. *Zea mays* starch recovered from dental calculus of an individual from the early period at the Tutu site (Cedrosan Saladoid, A.D. 65–950) but falls squarely within the Prosperity complex of the Cedrosan Saladoid subseries for Virgin Islands chronology. Prosperity is comparable to Hacienda Grande on Puerto Rico.

The overall open-habitat pattern of phytoliths, the abundant charcoal, and the presence of Variant 1 cross-phytoliths are consistent with (but not definitive of) maize cultivation in the Coakley Bay watershed by ca. 390 B.C. Economically useful taxa in the phytolith record include Chrysobalanaceae and palm (both arboreal elements) and Marantaceae. This combination of arboreal resources, annuals, and root/tuber resources has parallels at earlier and later sites on St. Thomas and more widely in the Caribbean. The open look of the Coakley Bay phytolith record begins around 160 cm. Therefore, anthropogenic landscapes in the area may extend to at least about ca. 510 B.C. (interpolated) or possibly earlier, to ca. 1085 B.C. (229–230 cm), the lowest depth with exceedingly high particulate charcoal concentrations.

Table 13.4. Coakley Bay, St. Croix Core Sedimentation Rates.

^{14}C sample depths	^{14}C Date Ranges (Median Cal BP Dates)	Sedimentation Rate (cm/yr)
0–67 cm	0–1285	.0521
67–140 cm	1285–2340	.0691
140–228 cm	2340–3035	.1266
228–249 cm	3035–3770	.0285

PART III

SYNTHESIS AND FUTURE DIRECTIONS IN ISLAND HISTORICAL ECOLOGY

14

ASSESSING COLONIZATION, LANDSCAPE LEARNING, AND SOCIONATURAL CHANGES IN THE CARIBBEAN

Peter E. Siegel, Deborah M. Pearsall, Nicholas P. Dunning, John G. Jones, Pat Farrell, Neil A. Duncan, and Jason H. Curtis

Our investigation of island historical ecology was framed by intertwined questions concerning colonization processes, identification of anthropogenic landscapes, introductions of new plant species to native landscapes, and socioenvironmental landscapes as dynamic systems all in the context of the archipelago setting of the southern and eastern Caribbean. We have sought to address the full range of environmental variability and human occupational history across the study region. In this chapter we synthesize and integrate the data presented in the previous island chapters.

Colonization of the Caribbean

The Caribbean archipelago may be thought of as a superhighway, with plants, animals, and people constantly moving from continents to islands, from islands to other islands, and from islands to continents. Prior to human colonization, approximately eight thousand years ago, fish, birds, insects, spiders, amphibians, mammals, trees, weeds, and bushes dispersed at various rates and intervals (Woods 1989; Woods and Sergile 2001). Once humans arrived on the islands, natural landscapes were transformed into modified and managed places reflecting survival strategies of these newest interlopers. Modifications to landscapes were sometimes gradual and other times dramatic depending on a range of interrelated factors, including group composition and size, mobility patterns, social and political organization, subsistence strategies, and supply–demand considerations. Teasing out these factors is challenging and will be most successful when integrating multiple lines of evidence, including archaeological excavations, paleoenvironmental reconstructions, and ethnohistoric observations.

In the history of Caribbean archaeology, numerous models and explanations have been proposed to account for the initial and ensuing occupations of the islands (Siegel 2013). Ideas have ranged from migrations of large communities of mission-directed people to small parties of scouts investigating new places to live or resources to exploit. Siegel (2010: 303–305) suggested that there may have been some combination of scouting followed by larger groups of colonizers. Researchers now agree that colonization events and processes and adjustments to or modifications of landscapes varied through time and space and with shifting survival strategies (Boomert 2013; Hofman et al. 2007).

As discussed in previous chapters, the earliest solid archaeological evidence for human occupations in the West Indies comes from the Oropuche Lagoon along the west coast of Trinidad (Boomert 2000; Harris 1973). Based on assemblage compositions and locations, a handful of sites in the lagoon reflect a broad-spectrum foraging, collecting, fishing, and hunting subsistence adaptation dating to approximately 6000 cal yr B.C. (Boomert 2000: 55–69). Assemblages consist of bone projectile points, peccary teeth fashioned into fishhooks, ground stone pestles and manos, faceted edge grinders, and stone anvils. Results of zooarchaeological investigations of the St. John midden conducted by Elizabeth Wing are consistent with a broad-spectrum subsistence adaptation (Boomert 2000: tab. 2; Wing 1977; Wing and Reitz 1982). Boomert (2000: 68–74) linked this Early Banwari Trace complex to the Alaka and El Conchero complexes located in coastal swamp, marsh, or riverine settings of northwestern Guyana and the Paria Peninsula of eastern Venezuela, respectively. More widely, Boomert (2000: 74) related these early complexes to other Early to Mid Holocene sites in Ecuador, Colombia, and Panama as discussed by Piperno and Pearsall (1998: 185–190) and Ranere (1992). The southern Caribbean ABC islands contain Archaic sites linked to occupations along the north-central coast of Venezuela.

It is unclear to what extent Archaic colonists to the Caribbean occupied islands between Tobago and Antigua. Richard Callaghan (2010) investigated the apparent paucity of Archaic sites documented south of the Guadeloupe Passage and offered suggestions to account for this situation. He examined oceanographic conditions as a constraint on Archaic voyaging, volcanic activity limiting human occupations, and volcanism as a constraint on finding buried sites. After simulating ocean currents, wind directions, and mean wind forces, Callaghan discounted "oceanographic conditions or technological deficiencies" of Archaic people as factors to explain the apparent lack of sites south of the Guadeloupe Passage (Callaghan 2010: 137). He found no convincing correlations between volcanism and lack of human settlements, especially when considering "settlement on these islands by later peoples" (Callaghan 2010: 141). Likewise, he argued that volcanic deposits are not uniformly deep across affected areas, except perhaps on St. Vincent, therefore it is unlikely that the absence of Archaic sites is a result of sampling bias from volcanism. Concerning volcanic activity and site visibility, Douglas Armstrong observed years ago, "The presence of Archaic middens at some depth beneath the surface forces a reevaluation of assumptions regarding the distribution of Archaic sites, or any sites occupied prior to volcanic activity. It cannot be assumed that because the sites do not show on the surface, that they are non-existent" (Armstrong 1980: 157). Despite these caveats, Callaghan concluded that Archaic settlement of the islands between Tobago and Antigua may not have occurred.

Additional factors should be considered regarding the apparent sparseness of Archaic sites on many of the islands. First, lacking systematic surveys, poor representation of Archaic sites may be the product of sampling bias and issues of visibility. We know from other tropical regions that Archaic sites are often underrepresented compared to later, more-visible Ceramic Age occupations. Yet paleoecological records reveal the presence of active Archaic occupations in those same regions (e.g., Burney 1997a; Neff et al. 2006). Second, massive erosion resulting from colonial plantation practices has buried former surfaces under meters of colluvial deposits on many islands, thus sealing archaeological sites within difficult-to-access contexts. Third, the role of sea-level changes should be considered in the drowning of former shoreline or near-shoreline terrestrial landscapes that potentially contain Archaic sites. This process no doubt will be exacerbated as global warming continues. Postglacial relative sea level predictions based on glacial isostatic adjustment modeling in the Caribbean reveals relative sea level values of approximately −2 m MSL (4000 cal B.P.), −4 m MSL (5000 cal B.P.), −8 m MSL (7000 cal B.P.), and −13 m MSL (8000 cal B.P.) (Toscano, Peltier, and Drummond 2011). Depending on seafloor topography and cal B.P. age there is the potential for submerged Archaic landscapes (and thus sites) associated with the islands. This would require examining bathymetric maps and sea-level curves in connection with specific islands and conducting underwater surveys, the last of which is a daunting enterprise. Again, Armstrong discussed this issue in regard to the apparent absence of Archaic sites: "A relatively lower sea level would have made areas which are now inundated available as habitation [or extraction] areas" (Armstrong 1980: 157). More recently, Cooper and Boothroyd (2011: 399) documented dramatic shoreline changes around Cuba during the Holocene with "implications for ... the loss of paleo-coastal pre-Columbian coastal sites." They emphasized "that relative sea level change in the past ... has not been constant and uniform but rather dynamic and *locally contingent*" (Cooper and Boothroyd 2011: 402, emphasis added).

To date, Archaic occupations have been documented in three sites between Tobago and Antigua: Heywoods on Barbados (Drewett 2006), and Boutbois and Le Godinot on Martinique, discussed below (Allaire and Mattioni 1983). One of the shell artifacts from Heywoods produced a radiocarbon date of 3980±100 B.P. (Drewett 2006, 2007). Bright (2011: Appendix 2: 10) calibrated the date, taking into consideration the marine-reservoir effect, resulting in 2365–1761 B.C. (2 sigma). Fitzpatrick (2011) obtained two additional dates of shell artifacts from Heywoods: 4230±50 B.P. (cal 2350–2220 B.C., 2 sigma), and 4360±40 B.P. (cal 3280–2940 B.C., 2 sigma).

John Cherry and colleagues reported on tantalizing evidence for an Archaic presence on Montserrat. Chipped-stone artifacts including "blade-cores, blades, backed blades and blade-flakes ... [reminiscent of] the earliest Archaic sites in the Greater Antilles" were surface collected from the Upper Blake's site in the north-central portion of the island (Cherry, Ryzewski, Leppard, and Bocancea 2012: 1). Hopefully in the future similar assemblages will be found in excavated contexts with associated organic material for radiocarbon dating.

By approximately 500 B.C. and certainly by the time of Christ and shortly after, the archaeological record of the Lesser Antilles/southern Caribbean islands suggests a dramatic infilling of the region compared to earlier times. This better-known and more intensively studied era is broadly referred to as the Early Ceramic Age. Again, the observation of greater site frequency after 500 B.C. in part may be artifacts of sampling bias, sea-level changes, relative visibility of distinct site types, and depositional or sedimentary histories. The extent to which Ceramic Age occupations represent distinctively different groups of people from the earlier Archaic occupants is currently the center of considerable debate (Rodríguez Ramos, Pagán-Jiménez, and Hofman 2013). Based on settlement organization and artifact assemblages, some investigators have strongly argued for an Amazonian origin for these later arrivals to the Lesser Antilles (Boomert 2000; Roe 1989; Rouse 1992; Siegel 2010). As in the case of the Archaic, timing and mode of colonization have been the source of disagreement. Fitzpatrick suggested that the earliest Ceramic Age colonists bypassed much of the Antilles when moving in from the south (Fitzpatrick 2013; Fitzpatrick, Kappers, and Giovas 2010). Based on their review of existing radiocarbon dates, Fitzpatrick, Kappers, and Giovas (2010: 166) concluded that the initial Saladoid colonists from South America "jumped directly from the northern coast of South America to Puerto Rico and the northern Lesser Antilles and then worked their way southward through the Leeward and Windward islands." This idea is similar to old views of monolithic mission-directed groups of people systematically working their way en masse through groups of islands.

European exploration and colonization of the West Indies commenced in 1492; as a process it continued and ramified over the next five centuries. From an ecological perspective, this history of colonial activities resulted in some of the most dramatic landscape modifications documented over the entire span of human occupations in the archipelago. As global supply and demand flows evolved, the New World was increasingly recognized as a crucially important player in rapidly expanding post-Renaissance markets (Anderson-Córdova, Barnes, and Siegel 2004). It is in this context of world systems and core-periphery relations at international scales that the Caribbean became an intensely contested region by European powers (e.g., Carr 1984). The Spanish, English, French, and Dutch variously battled and negotiated with each other for access to land, resources, and people resulting, eventually, in a remarkable blend or mosaic of traditions, including European, African, Asian, and Native American (Farnsworth 2001; Wilson 1993). The cultural mosaic was the outcome of brutal exploitation of Africans and Native Americans by Europeans in their consuming quests for and control over gold, sugar, and labor.

As European powers jostled for space, the Caribbean was gradually divided into broad regions associated with specific nations: Spain, France, Holland, and England. Gold was the mineral that fueled Spanish colonization of the Caribbean, so they concentrated their efforts on the Greater Antilles (Ewen 2001: 8). The French and British were more interested in sugarcane production and competed with each other in the Lesser Antilles and Trinidad for plantation land (Delpuech 2001; Watters 2001; Watts 1987). The Dutch specialized in marketing and exchange pursuits, although they did maintain large plantations on Sint Maarten and St. Eustatius (Haviser 2001b: 64–66).

Data from our project inform on the full span of human history in the Caribbean, from the first tentative steps on the islands through the arrival and eventual domination of the landscapes and indigenous people by the Europeans. In some areas, our data complement archaeological, paleoecological, and historical findings from the Lesser Antilles, and in others amplify understanding of colonization history as both event and process. We will highlight relevant project results that provide more-nuanced insights into pre-Columbian colonization and the aftermath of post-Columbian occupations. In particular, our data from Trinidad, Grenada, Marie-Galante (Guadeloupe), Martinique, and St. Croix provide a basis for revisiting initial colonization models of the Caribbean.

Human-induced Landscape Modifications Shortly after Initial Colonization of the Islands

In his review of Caribbean landscapes and fire history, geographer Bonham Richardson observed, "The Caribbean's insular and fragmented physical environments have been severely modified and degraded by human occupation for several millennia; such modification—often by fire—has been particularly notable in the five centuries since European intrusion" (Richardson 2004: 5). Richardson's account was based on archival research, literature reviews, and oral histories; his focus was primarily on the British West Indies between the mid to late nineteenth to early twentieth century. In our project, we extended this perspective of landscape modification to the earliest human occupations of the islands—not only British—using primary data buried in the sediments.

When investigating human interactions and engagements with and impacts to landscapes it is essential to disentangle natural from cultural disturbances documented in paleorecords. To this end, paleoenvironmental/climatic reconstructions for the region under study must be considered. Specifically, evaporation/precipitation ratios over time represent one line of evidence to be viewed, along with dated sequences of microfossils, sediment chemistries, and landscape histories. These reconstructions provide an interpretive framework within which disturbance indicators may be evaluated.

The longest most-detailed sequence of Caribbean climate history during the Holocene comes from the investigations of ^{18}O-isotope values of ostracods buried in the lakebed sediments from Lake Miragoâne, Haiti. This work was conducted by David Hodell and his team (Brenner and Binford 1988; Curtis and Hodell 1993; Curtis, Brenner, and Hodell 2001; Higuera-Gundy 1991; Higuera-Gundy et al. 1999; Hodell et al. 1991). The chronological resolution for the Miragoâne sediments analyzed by Jason Curtis was 16.8 years per sample. Within a seventeen-year span there may be unusual dry or wet episodes that are not possible to detect. Mangini et al. (2007) analyzed ^{18}O-isotope values of a ca. 7,000-year-old stalagmite collected from a cave on Barbados. Although Mangini et al. (2007: 1332) generally documented "increased rainfall intensity between 6.7 and 3 ka B.P. in agreement with records from Lake Miragoâne" they observed that "high oxygen isotope values in stalagmite [lower precipitation] ... are synchronous with periods of lower stable isotope values recorded in Lake Miragoâne [higher precipitation]." They indicated that "stalagmites ... record only summer precipitation, whereas $\delta^{18}O$ in ostracods record the whole year average water budget ... [and that analysis of many ostracods] average out any seasonal noise" (Mangini et al. 2007: 1337). The degree of resolution may be finer in the stalagmite data, thus allowing for assessments in seasonal variability that cannot be tracked in ostracod records. It has also been suggested that "shifts in the mean latitude of the Atlantic Intertropical Convergence Zone" (Haug et al. 2001: 1304) through time affect "the distribution and timing of rainfall around the equatorial region" (Mangini et al. 2007: 1332). Based on analysis of the Cariaco Basin sediment record and comparing their data to other tropical Atlantic locations, Haug et al. (2001) found broad regional congruence in climate reconstructions ranging from West Africa to northern South America and the circum-Caribbean region (Curtis, Brenner, and Hodell 2001; Goni et al. 2009; Haug et al. 2001; Hodell et al. 2005).

Climate history documented for the circum-Caribbean region provides the context for interpreting the microfossil, sediment, and landscape records obtained in the current project. Tables 14.1 and 14.2 present summaries of the economically useful plant taxa and disturbance indicators identified in the sediment cores collected during the project. The core taken in the vicinity of the Cedros archaeological site in southwestern Trinidad produced evidence of human occupations in the area prior to the documented Saladoid occupations of the site (Boomert 2000; Boomert, Faber-Morse, and Rouse 2013; Rouse 1953; Rouse and Allaire 1978). A charcoal sample from a Saladoid context in the Cedros site yielded a date of 2140±70 B.P. (cal 380–0 B.C., 2 sigma) (Boomert 2000: 518; Rouse and Allaire 1978: tab. 13.4). A *Maranta* phytolith (arrowroot) was recovered from a depth in our core predating 4730±40 B.P. (cal 3640–3380 B.C., 2 sigma), straddling the Late Banwari and Poonah Road Archaic complexes as defined by Boomert (2000: fig. 7; Boomert, Faber-Morse, and Rouse 2013: fig. 31) and, as discussed by Pearsall and Duncan in chapter 5 (this volume), may represent an early introduction of this economically useful plant from mainland South America.

A core taken from Oropuche Lagoon near the St. John site produced a date of 4790±40 B.P. (cal 3650–3380 B.C., 2 sigma) associated with a suite of economically useful plants, including *Canna,* Poaceae, *Anacardium,* Moraceae, Myrtaceae, and Sapotaceae, although very little in the way of clear disturbance indicators were present at that time.

Table 14.1. Summary of Ethnobotanically Useful Plant Taxa Identified in Project Core Sections Dating to the Archaic and Ceramic Ages.

Island	Context	Taxa Associated with Archaic Age	Taxa Associated with Ceramic Age
Trinidad	Cedros site Core CE07-1	Arecaceae (phytoliths), *Maranta* (seed phytolith), Bombacaceae/Zingiberaceae (trace phytoliths), Poaceae (trace phytoliths) Chrysobalanceae (trace phytoliths)	Arecaceae (phytoliths), *Maranta/Calathea* (phytoliths), Bombacaceae/Zingiberaceae (phytoliths), Poaceae (trace phytoliths) Chrysobalanceae (trace phytoliths)
	St. John site Core SJ07-2	*Avicennia* (trace pollen), Combretaceae (pollen), *Rhizophora* (pollen), Cheno-Ams (trace pollen), Poaceae (pollen), *Anacardium* (pollen), Arecaceae (pollen), Caesalpiniaceae (pollen), *Guazuma* (trace pollen), Moraceae (pollen), Myrtaceae (pollen), Sapotaceae (pollen)	*Avicennia* (pollen), Combretaceae (pollen), *Rhizophora* (pollen), Poaceae (pollen, major increase), *Typha* (trace pollen), *Zea mays* (trace pollen), *Anacardium* (pollen), Arecaceae (pollen, major increase; phytoliths), *Brysonima* (trace pollen), Caesalpiniaceae (trace pollen), *Coccoloba* (minor pollen), Moraceae (pollen), Myrtaceae (trace pollen), Sapindaceae (trace pollen), *Spondias* (trace pollen), *Symphonia* (pollen)
	Nariva Swamp Core NV08-1	*Avicennia* (pollen), Combretaceae (trace pollen), *Rhizophora* (pollen), Fabaceae (pollen), Marantaceae (trace phytoliths), *Nymphaea*, Poaceae (pollen), *Alchornea*, Anacardiaceae (pollen), Arecaceae (phytoliths), Chrysobalanceae (trace phytoliths), *Coccoloba* (pollen), *Eugenia* (trace pollen), Moraceae (pollen), *Psidium* (trace pollen), Rhamnaceae (trace pollen), Sapindaceae (trace pollen), Sapotaceae (pollen)	
	Nariva Swamp Core NV08-3	Combretaceae (trace pollen), *Rhizophora* (pollen), *Borreria* (trace pollen), Fabaceae (trace pollen), Poaceae (trace pollen, trace phytoliths), *Polygonum* (trace pollen), *Acacia* (trace pollen), Anacardiaceae (trace pollen), Apocynaceae (trace pollen), Arecaceae (pollen), *Byrsonima* (pollen), *Cassia* (trace pollen), *Coccoloba* (trace pollen), *Hippocratea* (trace pollen), *Hirea* (trace pollen), Moraceae (pollen), Sapindaceae (minor pollen), Sapotaceae (trace pollen), *Sebastiana* (trace pollen), *Spondias* (pollen)	Combretaceae (trace pollen), *Rhizophora* (pollen), Cheno-Ams (trace pollen), Fabaceae (trace pollen), Poaceae (pollen), Arecaceae (trace pollen, phytoliths), *Byrsonima* (pollen), *Cassia* (trace pollen), *Hirea* (trace pollen), Moraceae (pollen), *Polygonum* (pollen), Sapindaceae (pollen), Sapotaceae (trace pollen), *Symphonia* (pollen)

(continued)

Table 14.1. (continued)

Island	Context	Taxa Associated with Archaic Age	Taxa Associated with Ceramic Age
	Nariva Swamp Core NV08-4	Combretaceae (trace pollen), *Rhizophora* (pollen), Poaceae (trace pollen, trace phytoliths), *Typha* (trace pollen), *Alchornea* (trace pollen), Anacardiaceae (minor pollen), Apocynaceae (trace pollen), Arecaceae (phytoliths, pollen), *Byrsonima* (pollen), Caesalpiniaceae (trace pollen), *Celtis* (trace pollen), *Coccoloba* (trace pollen), Moraceae (minor pollen), Myrtaceae (pollen), Sapindaceae (pollen), Sapotaceae (pollen), *Spondias* (pollen), *Symphonia* (pollen), Marantaceae: *Maranta* (trace phytoliths), *Maranta/Calathea* (trace phytoliths)	Combretaceae (trace pollen), *Rhizophora* (pollen), Marantaceae/*Maranta* (trace phytoliths), Onagraceae (trace pollen), Poaceae (pollen, trace phytoliths), Polygonaceae (trace pollen), *Alchornea* (trace pollen), Anacardiaceae (trace pollen), Apocynaceae (trace pollen), Arecaceae (phytoliths, pollen), *Byrsonima* (pollen), Caesalpiniaceae (trace pollen), *Cassia* (trace pollen), *Celtis* (trace pollen), *Coccoloba* (trace pollen), Ebenaceae (trace phytoliths), *Hippocratea* (trace pollen), Moraceae (trace pollen), Myrtaceae (pollen), Sapindaceae (pollen), Sapotaceae (pollen), *Spondias* (pollen), *Symphonia* (pollen)
Grenada	Meadow Beach wetland Core MB08-1	*Avicennia* (trace pollen), Combretaceae (trace pollen), *Rhizophora* (pollen), Cheno-ams (pollen), Poaceae (pollen), Solanaceae (trace pollen), Anacardiaceae (trace pollen), Apocynaceae (trace pollen), Arecaceae (phytoliths, pollen), *Bursera* (pollen), *Coccoloba* (pollen), Moraceae (pollen), Marantaceae (phytoliths), Myrtaceae (pollen), Rubiaceae (pollen), Sapotaceae (pollen), *Spondias* (pollen)	*Avicennia* (trace pollen), Combretaceae (trace pollen), *Rhizophora* (pollen), Poaceae (pollen), *Zea* spp. (trace phytoliths), Arecaceae (phytoliths), *Bursera* (pollen), *Coccoloba* (pollen), Moraceae (trace pollen), Myrtaceae (trace pollen), Sapotaceae (trace pollen), *Spondias* (pollen)
	Lake Antoine core	*Rhizophora* (pollen), *Croton* (trace pollen), Anacardiaceae (pollen), Arecaceae (trace phytoliths, pollen), *Bursera* (pollen), *Celtis* (pollen), Moraceae (pollen), Myrtaceae (trace pollen), Sapotaceae (pollen), *Spondias* (trace pollen)	*Rhizophora* (pollen), Cheno-ams (trace pollen), *Montrichardia* (trace pollen), Poaceae (pollen), Solanaceae (trace pollen), *Zea mays* (pollen grain, 175 cm), Anacardiaceae (trace pollen), Arecaceae (trace pollen, phytoliths), *Bursera* (pollen), *Celtis* (pollen), Moraceae (pollen), Sapotaceae (pollen), *Spondias* (pollen)

(continued)

308 • Chapter 14

Table 14.1. (continued)

Island	Context	Taxa Associated with Archaic Age	Taxa Associated with Ceramic Age
Curaçao	Spaanse Water Core SW09-1	*Avicennia* (trace pollen), Combretaceae (trace pollen), *Rhizophora* (pollen), Cactaceae (trace pollen), *Croton* (trace pollen), *Polygonum* (trace pollen), *Typha* (trace pollen), Fabaceae (trace pollen), Malvaceae (trace pollen), Poaceae (pollen), Anacardiaceae (pollen), Arecaceae (phytoliths), *Coccoloba* (pollen), Moraceae (pollen), Sapotaceae (trace pollen), *Sebastiana* (trace pollen)	*Avicennia* (trace pollen), Combretaceae (trace pollen), *Rhizophora* (pollen), Fabaceae (trace pollen), Cactaceae (trace pollen), Cheno-ams (trace pollen), *Croton* (trace pollen), *Polygonum* (trace pollen), Malvaceae (trace pollen), Poaceae (pollen), *Typha* (trace pollen), *Alchornea* (trace pollen), Anacardiaceae (pollen), *Hirea* (trace pollen), Sapindacaea (trace pollen), *Coccoloba* (pollen), Moraceae (pollen), Sapotaceae (trace pollen), *Sebastiana* (trace pollen)
	San Juan Bay Core CC09-1		*Avicennia* (trace pollen), Combretaceae (trace pollen), *Rhizophora* (pollen), Fabaceae (trace pollen), *Borreira* (pollen), Cheno-ams (pollen), *Croton* (trace pollen), Fabaceae (pollen), Liliaceae (trace pollen), Polygonaceae (pollen), *Gossypium* (3 pollen grains), Malvaceae (trace pollen), Poaceae (pollen), *Zea mays* (5 pollen grains), *Zea* spp. (2 phytoliths), *Acacia* (trace pollen), Anacardiaceae (trace pollen), *Anona* (trace pollen), Apocynaceae (trace pollen), Arecaceae (trace phytoliths, trace pollen), *Celtis* (trace pollen), *Citrus* (1 pollen grain), *Coccoloba* (pollen), *Hirea* (pollen), Marantaceae (1 phytolith), *Maranta* (2 phytoliths), *Calathea* (1 phytolith), Moraceae (trace pollen), Sapotaceae (trace pollen)
Barbados	Graeme Hall Core GH08-1		Combretaceae (trace pollen), *Rhizophora* (pollen), Araceae (pollen), Arecaceae (trace pollen), Cheno-ams (trace pollen), Convolvulaceae (trace pollen), Fabaceae (trace pollen), Poaceae (pollen), *Zea mays* (1 pollen grain), *Alchornea* (trace pollen), Anacardiaceae (trace pollen), *Bursera* (pollen), *Celtis* (pollen), *Coccoloba* (trace pollen), *Hirea* (trace pollen), *(continued)*

Island	Context	Taxa Associated with Archaic Age	Taxa Associated with Ceramic Age
Antigua	Jolly Beach Site Core JB07-1	*Avicennia* (trace pollen), Combretaceae (pollen), *Rhizophora* (pollen), Cheno-ams (trace pollen), *Rumex* (pollen), Fabaceae (pollen), *Bursera* (pollen), Caesalpiniaceae (trace pollen), *Celtis* (pollen), Poaceae (pollen), Arecaceae (trace pollen), *Brysonima* (trace pollen), *Coccoloba* (pollen), *Guazuma* (trace pollen), Moraceae (pollen), Myrtaceae (pollen), Sapindaceae (trace pollen), Sapotaceae (trace pollen), *Spondias* (pollen)	Moraceae (pollen), Myrtaceae (trace pollen), Rhamnaceae (trace pollen), *Rumex* (trace pollen), Sapindacaea (trace pollen), Sapotaceae (trace pollen)
	Nonsuch Bay Core NS07-2[a]		*Avicennia* (pollen), Combretaceae (pollen), *Rhizophora* (pollen), Agave (trace pollen), *Canna* (trace pollen), Cheno-ams (pollen), Fabaceae (pollen), Malvaceae (trace pollen), *Rumex* (pollen), Poaceae (pollen), *Acacia* (trace pollen), *Alchornea* (pollen), Apocynaceae (pollen), Arecaceae (minor pollen), *Bursera* (pollen), Caesalpiniaceae (trace pollen), *Celtis* (pollen), *Coccoloba* (pollen), *Hirea* (trace pollen), Moraceae (pollen), Myrtaceae (pollen), Sapotaceae (minor pollen), *Spondias* (pollen)
			Avicennia (pollen), Combretaceae (pollen), *Rhizophora* (pollen), Agave (trace pollen), *Canna* (trace pollen), Cheno-ams (trace pollen), *Croton* (pollen), Cucurbitaceae (4 pollen grains), *Nymphaea* (pollen), Poaceae[b] (pollen), Polygonaceae (pollen), *Zea mays*[b] (5 pollen grains), *Coccoloba* (trace pollen), Anacardiaceae[b] (trace pollen), Apocynaceae (pollen), Arecaceae (phytoliths), Caesalpiniaceae (pollen), *Celtis* (trace pollen), *Hirea* (pollen), Moraceae (pollen), Myrtaceae (trace pollen), Sapotaceae[b] (trace pollen)
Barbuda	Low Pond Core LP09-2		*Avicennia* (pollen), Combretaceae (pollen), *Rhizophora* (pollen), *Borreria* (pollen), Cheno-ams (pollen), Poaceae (pollen), Polygonaceae (trace pollen), *Byrsonima* (trace pollen), *Bursera* (trace pollen), *Citrus* (trace pollen), *Alchornea* (pollen), Arecaceae (trace pollen), *Coccoloba* (pollen), Moraceae (pollen), Sapotaceae (trace pollen)

(continued)

310 • Chapter 14

Table 14.1. (continued)

Island	Context	Taxa Associated with Archaic Age	Taxa Associated with Ceramic Age
	Grassy Island Core GI09-1	Combretaceae (trace pollen), *Rhizophora* (pollen), *Borreria* (trace pollen), Cheno-ams (trace pollen), Poaceae (trace pollen),	*Avicennia* (pollen), Combretaceae (trace pollen), *Rhizophora* (pollen), *Borreria* (trace pollen), Cheno-ams (pollen), Fabaceae (trace pollen), Poaceae (pollen), Polygonaceae (trace pollen), *Alchornea* (pollen), Arecaceae (trace pollen, phytoliths), *Coccoloba* (pollen), Myrtaceae (trace pollen), Sapotaceae (trace pollen)
Martinique	Baie de Fort-de-France Core KC08-1	Combretaceae (trace pollen), *Rhizophora* (pollen), Cheno-ams (trace pollen), Fabaceae (trace pollen), Poaceae (pollen), Anacardiaceae (trace pollen), Arecaceae (pollen, core base; trace phytoliths), *Byrsonima* (pollen, core base), *Bursera* (trace pollen), *Celtis* (pollen, core mid-section), *Hirea* (pollen), Moraceae (pollen), Myrtaceae (pollen), Sapotaceae (trace pollen),	*Avicennia* (trace pollen), Combretaceae (trace pollen), *Rhizophora* (pollen), Fabaceae (pollen), Poaceae (pollen, trace phytoliths), Tiliaceae (pollen), *Alchornea* (trace pollen), Anacardiaceae (pollen), Arecaceae (phytoliths), *Coccoloba* (pollen), *Hippocratea* (trace pollen), *Hirea* (pollen), Moraceae (pollen), Myrtaceae (pollen), Sapindaceae (pollen), Sapotaceae (trace pollen), *Spondias* (trace pollen)
Martinique	Pointe Figuier Core PF08-1		*Avicennia* (trace pollen), Combretaceae (trace pollen), *Rhizophora* (pollen), *Borreria* (trace pollen), *Canna* (trace pollen), Cheno-ams (trace pollen), Convulaceae (trace pollen), *Croton* (trace pollen), Euphorbiaceae (trace pollen), *Desmodium* (trace pollen), Fabaceae (pollen), Poaceae (phytoliths, pollen), *Acacia* (trace pollen), *Spondias* (trace pollen), Anacardiaceae (trace pollen), Apocyanaceae (trace pollen), Arecaceae (trace pollen, phytoliths), *Bursera* (trace pollen), *Byrsonima* (pollen), *Celtis* (trace pollen), *Coccoloba* (trace pollen), *Guazuma* (trace pollen), *Hippocratea* (trace pollen), Moraceae (pollen), Myrtaceae (pollen), Sapindaceae (pollen), Sapotaceae (pollen), Verbenaceae (trace pollen)

(continued)

Table 14.1. (continued)

Island	Context	Taxa Associated with Archaic Age	Taxa Associated with Ceramic Age
Marie-Galante	Vieux Fort Core VF08-1	*Avicennia* (trace pollen), Combretaceae (pollen), *Rhizophora* (pollen), Poaceae (pollen), Arecaceae (pollen), *Bursera* (pollen), *Byrsonima* (trace pollen), *Coccoloba* (pollen), Moraceae (pollen), Myrtaceae (pollen), Sapotaceae (pollen), *Spondias* (trace pollen)	*Avicennia* (trace pollen), Combretaceae (pollen), *Rhizophora* (trace pollen), Poaceae (pollen), Apocynaceae (pollen), Arecaceae (pollen), *Bursera* (pollen), *Byrsonima* (pollen), *Coccoloba* (pollen), Moraceae (pollen), Myrtaceae (pollen), Sapotaceae (pollen), *Spondias* (trace pollen), Verbenaceae (pollen)
St. Croix	Coakley Bay Core CB07-1		Arecaceae (phytoliths)

a. This nearly 5-m-long core dates almost entirely to the historic era. An organic sample from the base of the core was dated to cal 530–650 BP (2 sigma). Microfossils at that depth represent a pre-Columbian landscape. Sediments above that depth are a result of land-use history following European colonization of the island. Unless otherwise noted, results reported for this core post-date European contact.

b. Pre- and post-Columbian context.

312 • Chapter 14

Table 14.2. Summary of Disturbance Indicators Identified in Project Core Sections Dating to the Archaic and Ceramic Ages.

Island	Context	Taxa Associated with Archaic Age	Taxa Associated with Ceramic Age
Trinidad	Cedros site Core CE07-1	Poaceae (trace phytoliths)	Poaceae (trace phytoliths)
	St. John site Core SJ07-2	Cheno-ams (trace pollen), *Cecropia* (pollen), Moraceae (pollen), Myrtaceae (pollen)	*Typha* (trace pollen), Asteraceae (pollen), Cyperaceae (pollen), Poaceae (pollen), *Cecropia* (pollen), Moraceae (pollen), Myrtaceae (trace pollen), charcoal (pollen slides), open-habitat indicators (phytoliths), elevated phosphates (sediments)
	Nariva Swamp Core NV08-1	Asteraceae (trace pollen, trace phytoliths), Cyperaceae (trace pollen, trace phytoliths), Poaceae (pollen), *Typha* (pollen), *Cecropia* (pollen), Moraceae (pollen), charcoal (base of core, pollen slides), open-habitat indicators (phytoliths), sustained elevated charcoal by cal 5900 BP.	
	Nariva Swamp Core NV08-3	Asteraceae (pollen), Cyperaceae (trace pollen), Poaceae (trace pollen, trace phytoliths), *Typha* (pollen), *Cecropia* (pollen), Moraceae (pollen)	Cheno-ams (trace pollen), Cyperaceae (pollen), Poaceae (pollen, trace phytoliths), *Cecropia* (pollen), Moraceae (pollen), charcoal (pollen slides)
	Nariva Swamp Core NV08-4	Asteraceae (pollen, trace phytoliths), Poaceae (trace pollen, trace phytoliths), *Typha* (trace pollen), *Cecropia* (trace pollen), Moraceae (trace pollen), Myrtaceae (pollen), charcoal (pollen slides)	Asteraceae (pollen, trace phytoliths), Cyperaceae (pollen), Poaceae (pollen, trace phytoliths), *Cecropia* (trace pollen), Moraceae (trace pollen), Myrtaceae (pollen), charcoal (pollen slides), open-habitat indicators (phytoliths)
Grenada	Meadow Beach wetland Core MB08-1	Asteraceae (trace pollen), Cheno-ams (trace pollen), Cyperaceae (pollen), Poaceae (pollen, core base), Moraceae (pollen), Myrtaceae (pollen), charcoal (pollen slides, core mid-section)	Asteraceae (pollen), Cyperaceae (pollen), Poaceae (pollen), *Heliconia* (trace phytoliths), Moraceae (trace pollen), Myrtaceae (trace pollen), charcoal (pollen slides)

(continued)

Table 14.2. *(continued)*

Island	Context	Taxa Associated with Archaic Age	Taxa Associated with Ceramic Age
	Lake Antoine core	*Cecropia* (pollen, core midsection), Moraceae (pollen), Myrtaceae (trace pollen), relatively high phosphorous values (sediments, two mid-sections of core)	Asteraceae (pollen), Cheno-ams (trace pollen), Cyperaceae (pollen), Poaceae (pollen), *Cecropia*, charcoal (pollen slides), Moraceae (pollen), high phosphorous values (sediments)
Curaçao	Spaanse Water Core SW09-1	Asteraceae (trace pollen), Cyperaceae (trace pollen), Poaceae (pollen), *Typha* (trace pollen), *Cecropia* (pollen, core mid-section), Moraceae (pollen), charcoal (pollen slides)	Asteraceae (trace pollen), Cyperaceae (trace pollen), Poaceae (pollen), *Typha* (trace pollen), *Acalypha* (pollen), Cheno-Ams (trace pollen), Poaceae (pollen), Moraceae (pollen), charcoal (pollen slides)
	San Juan Bay Core CC09-1		Asteraceae (pollen), Cheno-ams (pollen), Cyperaceae (pollen), Poaceae (pollen), *Typha* (pollen), *Cecropia* (pollen), Moraceae (trace pollen), charcoal (pollen slides), open-habitat indicators (phytoliths)
Barbados	Graeme Hall Core GH08-1		Asteraceae (trace pollen), Cheno-ams (trace pollen), Poaceae (pollen), Cyperaceae (pollen), *Cecropia* (trace pollen), Moraceae (pollen), Myrtaceae (trace pollen), charcoal (pollen slides)
Antigua	Jolly Beach Site Core JB07-1	Asteraceae (pollen), Cheno-ams (trace pollen), Cyperaceae (pollen), Poaceae (pollen), Moraceae (pollen), Myrtaceae (pollen), charcoal (pollen slides, upper portion of zone)	Cheno-Ams (pollen), Cyperaceae (pollen), Poaceae (pollen), Moraceae (pollen), Myrtaceae (pollen), charcoal (pollen slides)
	Nonsuch Bay Core NS07-2[a]		Asteraceae (pollen), Cheno-Ams (pollen), Cyperaceae (pollen), Poaceae[b] (pollen), Moraceae (pollen), charcoal (pollen slides), open-habitat indicators (phytoliths)
Barbuda	Low Pond Core LP09-2	Cheno-Ams (trace pollen), Poaceae (trace pollen),	Asteraceae (pollen), Cheno-Ams (pollen), *Cladium* (pollen), Cyperaceae (pollen), Poaceae (pollen), *Cecropia* (trace pollen), Moraceae (pollen), charcoal (pollen slides)

(continued)

314 • Chapter 14

Table 14.2. (continued)

Island	Context	Taxa Associated with Archaic Age	Taxa Associated with Ceramic Age
	Grassy Island GI09-1		Asteraceae (trace pollen), Cheno-Ams (pollen), Poaceae (pollen), *Cecropia* (trace pollen), Myrtaceae (trace pollen), charcoal (pollen slides)
Martinique	Baie de Fort-de-France Core KC08-1	Asteraceae (pollen, zone midsection), Cheno-Ams (trace pollen), *Cladium* (pollen), Cyperaceae (pollen, trace phytoliths), Poaceae (pollen), *Cecropia* (pollen), Moraceae (pollen), Myrtaceae (pollen), charcoal (pollen slides, zone mid-section)	Cyperaceae (pollen, phytoliths), Poaceae (pollen, trace phytoliths), *Cecropia* (pollen), Moraceae (pollen), Myrtaceae (pollen), charcoal (pollen slides, reduced but sustained)
	Pointe Figuier Core PF08-1	Charcoal (pollen slides)	Asteraceae (pollen), Cheno-Ams (trace pollen), Cyperaceae (pollen), Poaceae (pollen, trace phytoliths), *Cecropia* (pollen), Moraceae (pollen), Myrtaceae (pollen), charcoal (pollen slides), open-habitat indicators (phytoliths)
Marie-Galante	Vieux Fort Core VF08-1	Asteraceae (pollen), Cyperaceae (pollen), Poaceae (pollen), *Cecropia* (pollen), Moraceae (pollen), Myrtaceae (pollen), charcoal (pollen slides, upper portion of zone)	Asteraceae (pollen), Cyperaceae (pollen), Poaceae (pollen), *Cecropia* (pollen), Moraceae (pollen), Myrtaceae (pollen), charcoal (pollen slides)
St. Croix	Coakley Bay Core CB07-1	Open-habitat indicators (phytoliths), charcoal (pollen slides, particularly high from 230–150 cm)	Open-habitat indicators (phytoliths), charcoal (pollen slides, particularly high from 150–174 cm)

a. This nearly 5-m-long core dates almost entirely to the historic era. An organic sample from the base of the core was dated to 530–650 cal BP (2 sigma). Microfossils at that depth represent a pre-Columbian landscape. Sediments above that depth are a result of land-use history following European colonization of the island. Unless otherwise noted, results reported for this core post-date European contact.

b. Pre- and post-Columbian context.

Cores collected from Nariva Swamp along the east coast of Trinidad produced a longer record of environmental history than did the Cedros or Oropuche cores. A near-basal context in the Nariva 1 core was dated to 6160±70 B.P. (cal 5300–4940 B.C., 2 sigma) and there is evidence for the presence of people in the area at that time or earlier documented in the pollen profile. Associated with this early date are pollen and phytoliths from a number of economically useful plant taxa, including Fabaceae, Poaceae, Anacardiaceae, Arecaceae, *Coccoloba*, Moraceae, Sapindaceae, and Sapotaceae as well as disturbance indicators of *Typha* and *Cecropia*. The top of this zone dates to 5900±30 B.P. (cal 4840–4710 B.C., 2 sigma), at which point a dramatic and sustained increase in the concentration of charcoal particulates occurred, also indicative of human intervention in the area.

The Nariva 4 core taken from the edge of a sandy island in the swamp produced a date of 5910±50 B.P. (cal 4930–4620 B.C., 2 sigma) at 685 cm, near the base. The presence of sustained relatively high charcoal concentration at this time is evidence of human activity in the area, especially during the wettest era documented in Caribbean climate history over the past 10,500 years (Curtis, Brenner, and Hodell 2001: 41–46; Higuera-Gundy et al. 1999; Hodell et al. 1991: 791–792, fig. 2; also Haug et al. 2001) (fig. 14.1).

In studying long sequences of paleoenvironmental records in other low-latitude regions of the world, researchers have documented oscillations in the incidence of fires in the absence of human occupations (Behling 1995; Burney 1996a, 1996b, 1997b; Haberle and Ledru 2001). It is important to relate fire periodicity to other environmental variables, including precipitation patterns (arid vs. mesic conditions), potential sources of fire ignition (volcanic activity, amount of leaf litter), and vegetation cover in the area (moist forest [e.g., Moraceae, *Cecropia*], dry forest [e.g., dry-adapted palms like *Pseudophoenix vinifera* and dry-forest trees like *Ampelocera, Guazuma*, Myrtaceae, and Fabacae]) (Behling 1995; Burney 1996b: 52; Higuera-Gundy et al. 1999).

Following the early presence of people in the vicinity of the Nariva 4 core (ca. cal 6,700 years ago), the area appears to have been abandoned until approximately 3,500–4,000 years ago. At that time, economically useful plants along with disturbance indicators are represented in the pollen taxa. At this time, too, charcoal-particle concentration values are moderately and continuously elevated.

In his review of Archaic occupations in southeastern and eastern Trinidad, Boomert observed that the shell-midden sites of Ortoire and Cocal 1 are situated within 600 m of each other on a sandbar between Nariva Swamp and the ocean (Boomert 2000: 84–87; Boomert, Faber-Morse, and Rouse 2013: 16–18; De Booy 1917; Rouse 1953). Two charcoal

316 • Chapter 14

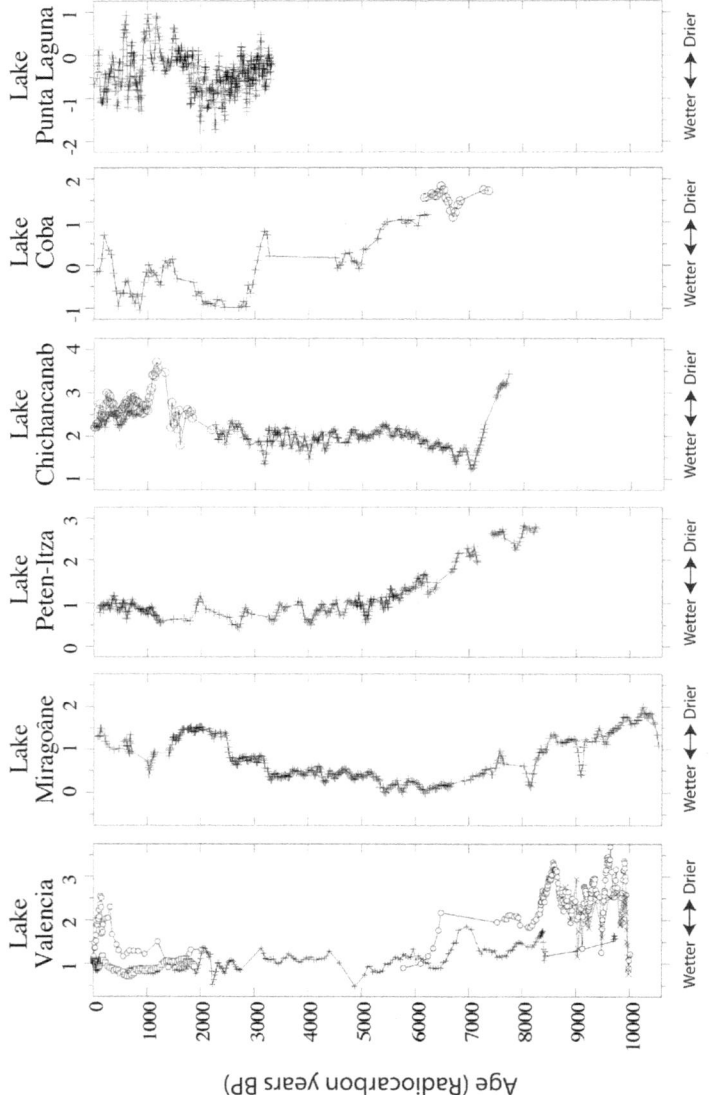

Figure 14.1. Paleoclimatic reconstructions for the circum-Caribbean region based on oxygen isotopic measurement of carbonate shell material (from Curtis, Brenner, and Hodell 2001). Data graphed in permil (‰) units versus VPDB (Vienna Pee Dee Belemnite), which is the international reference standard for oxygen and carbon isotopes used in paleoclimate studies.

samples from Ortoire produced dates of 2760±130 B.P. (cal 1370–550 B.C., 2 sigma) and 2750±130 B.P. (cal 1310–540 B.C., 2 sigma). Based on similarities in assemblage composition, Boomert suggested that the North Manzanilla 2, Chip Chip Hill, and Kernahan Trace shell middens, all associated with Nariva Swamp, were contemporaneous with Ortoire and Cocal 1; he assigned the sites to an Ortoire complex dating from about 1200 to 500 B.C. (Boomert 2000: 84–87, fig. 7). Based on coring results from the current project, it is now clear that people were in the area approximately 3,500 years prior to the Ortoire period. To what extent people occupying the Nariva Swamp around 5900 B.P. were related to or had interactions with Late Banwari people on the west coast will remain unknown until archaeological sites of these early occupations are identified.

On Grenada, our core in the Meadow Beach mangrove, a few kilometers north of the early Ceramic Age Pearls site, provided evidence for earlier human occupations than the evidence currently available archaeologically for this island (Benz 2010). Heretofore, no Archaic sites have been documented on Grenada. As Hofman and Hoogland observed in chapter 3 (this volume), a variety of factors may have conspired to obscure the presence of Archaic sites. Material collected from the base of the core (492 cm) produced a date of 5270±50 B.P. (cal 4230–3980 B.C., 2 sigma), which is associated with a swamp-forest environment, and at that time there is no indication of human inputs. Sustained elevated charcoal concentration values within the core are bracketed by dates of 4420±40 B.P. (cal 3330–2920 B.C., 2 sigma) and 2880±40 B.P. (cal 1210–930 B.C., 2 sigma). Again, this is during a period documented to be among the wettest in Caribbean climate history so it is unlikely that these high charcoal concentrations are the result of large-scale natural fires. In addition, pollen from disturbance indicators is present by ca. cal 3300 B.C.: Cyperaceae, Poaceae, and herbs and cultigens. If this approximate 1,700- to 2,400-year period of human-induced burning and landscape modification represents initial colonization of Grenada, then expectations should be built into future systematic archaeological surveys for the potential of identifying Archaic sites.

A core 8.4 m in depth was collected from the sediments of Lake Antoine, Grenada. Lake sediment from 737 cm produced a date of 8050±50 B.P. (cal 7170–6780 B.C., 2 sigma). At that depth there is no clear evidence of human inputs. However, the total phosphorus value at 835–840 cm was extraordinarily high. At 700 cm there is a dramatic spike in charcoal, although the pollen spectra do not indicate human disturbance factors or encouragement of economically useful taxa. It is conceivable that there was a short dry interval within the long era of mesic conditions (fig. 14.1) that is not visible within the oxygen isotope sequence. In that case we may be documenting a natural fire event at 700 cm. Preserved plant matter collected from 700 cm was dated to 7340±40 B.P. (cal 6350–6070 B.C., 2 sigma).

By 600 cm, or shortly below, there is a major increase in charcoal inputs followed by sustained and elevated concentration values. Lake sediment from 611 cm dated to 4860±45 B.P. (cal 3760–3530 B.C., 2 sigma) placing that fire event in the Mid to Early-Late Holocene. Associated with this sudden onset and sustained presence of fire were elevated values of pollen concentrations from disturbance indicators and economically useful taxa. The Meadow Beach and Lake Antoine data are consistent regarding the arrival of humans to Grenada no later than ca. cal 3700–3000 B.C.

Curaçao has a fairly well-documented Archaic presence (Haviser 1987, 1989, 2001a; Hofman and Hoogland, this volume; Hoogland and Hofman 2015). The Archaic Rooi Rincón site located near the north-central coast produced a series of radiocarbon dates, the oldest of which is 4490±60 B.P. (cal 3360–2940 B.C., 2 sigma) (Haviser 1987: tab. 1). Recent work at the Seru Boca Rockshelter and Spaanse Water sites reveal a complex occupational history spanning the Archaic and Ceramic Ages, with activities centered around intermittent "shell collecting and processing" (Hoogland and Hofman 2011: 635; Hoogland and Hofman 2015). Our core taken in the vicinity of the Spaanse Water site produced a near-basal sample date of 4850±40 B.P. (cal 3710–3530 B.C., 2 sigma). Associated pollen and phytoliths reflect a swamp-forest environment, dominated by white mangroves. Reduced charcoal particulates, too, suggest no human activity in the region at that time, perhaps reinforcing the Rooi Rincón date as the earliest evidence of human occupations on Curaçao (Haviser 1987; see also Hoogland and Hofman 2011).

A nearly 7-m-long core extracted from a wetland along Rivière du Vieux Fort on Marie-Galante (Guadeloupe) produced a long record of environmental history (Casile 2010). A basal-sediment sample was dated to 5730±70 B.P. (cal 4730–4370 B.C., 2 sigma). At that time, the environment was characterized by a mangrove forest habitat with no evidence of human activity. By the core midsection a dramatic and sustained increase in particulate charcoal was documented, along with the presence of pollen from economically useful plant species. The initial period of elevated charcoal concentration was bracketed by the dates 4380±60 B.P. (cal 3330–2890 B.C., 2 sigma) and 2960±30 B.P. (cal 1290–1050 B.C.). This date range is associated with the Mid Holocene period of increased wet conditions in the Caribbean (Curtis, Brenner, and Hodell 2001). Currently there is only sketchy archaeological evidence for an Archaic presence on Marie-Galante. Three documented post-Saladoid sites are located within 3 km of the coring location. Our coring evidence clearly indicates human activities in the area dating to the Middle to Late Archaic period.

We obtained a nearly 7-m core from the Baie de Fort-de-France of Martinique. The basal section of the core (676 cm) dating to 5000±50 B.P. (cal 3950–3670 B.C., 2 sigma) yielded no evidence of human activity in the area. From 575 to 425 cm a continuous and elevated density of charcoal was documented, along with a range of economically useful and disturbance-indicator taxa, reflecting human occupations in the area. Preserved plant material collected from 575 cm produced a radiocarbon date of 4420±30 B.P. (cal 3310–2920 B.C., 2 sigma), indicating human activities on Martinique at least by that time. The strong signal of human activity from 575 to 425 cm occurred during the mesic conditions of the Mid Holocene (Archaic Age) (Curtis, Brenner, and Hodell 2001: 44). A core taken from a wetland in Pointe Figuier, along the south coast of Martinique, displayed nearly continuous elevated charcoal concentration values from ca. cal 800 B.C. through historic occupations revealing again the presence of humans during the Archaic and later.

Two possible Archaic sites (Boutbois, Le Godinot) were identified in northern Martinique (Allaire and Mattioni 1983; Hofman and Hoogland, this volume). Benoît Bérard (2002, 2006a, 2006b) reexamined these sites and concluded that they may or may not be of Archaic Age; they may be special-purpose aceramic sites dating to the Ceramic Age. In addition, he reported a radiocarbon date from charcoal collected in the Boutbois site of 1600±90 B.P. (cal A.D. 250–630, 2 sigma), clearly postdating the Archaic Age (Bérard 2006a: 9).

Antigua has among the best-documented and most extensive set of Archaic sites known in the Caribbean (Davis 1974, 1982, 1993, 2000; Olsen 1976; Stokes 1991: 68–87; van Gijn 1993). Undated sites without pottery may be aceramic components of Ceramic Age settlement systems (Lundberg 1985; Stokes 1991). The Jolly Beach site on Antigua is among the oldest documented on the island and in the Leeward Islands generally (Armstrong 1980; Davis 2000). Davis (2000: 24) reported a charcoal date from the site of 3775±90 B.P. (cal 2470–1970 B.C., 2 sigma). Our core from Jolly Beach bottomed out in greenish-gray gley with dense fragments of shell at 262 cm. Organic sediment from 235 cm produced a date of 3290±60 B.P. (cal 1730–1440 B.C., 2 sigma). Although not as old as the date from the archaeological context, it is close. Our core date is associated with an edge environment characterized by a swamp forest adjacent to a red, black, and white mangrove system. A low yet sustained level of charcoal particulates and *Celtis* and other disturbance taxa are linked to the activities represented by the human occupants of the nearby habitation.

On St. Croix we obtained a nearly 3-m core from Coakley Bay along the northeast coast. A near-basal sample from 249 cm produced a date of 3500±40 B.P. (cal 1935–1700 B.C., 2 sigma). Starting at 229 cm, charcoal concentrations were extraordinarily high and were sustained until 75 cm. Based on interpolation between available radiocarbon dates, the

229-cm depth dates to approximately cal 1480 B.C. Hardy (2009: 101) hinted at the presence of an Archaic deposit ("an aceramic component") near Salt River. Our findings provide support for Hardy's suggestion of Archaic occupations on St. Croix.

Summary

Table 14.3 presents radiocarbon dates from the southern and eastern Caribbean falling within the range of Archaic occupations in the Caribbean and that are associated with archaeological deposits or sediments containing good evidence of human activities. Contrary to recent suggestions for a minimal to nonexistent presence of Archaic occupations in the islands south of the Guadeloupe Passage (Callaghan 2010), it is clear that groups of people were well established at that time. If Archaic inhabitants followed a strong coastal adaptation and sea level is 2–4 m higher today than four thousand to five thousand years ago it is likely that many of those old sites are now inundated.

Human-induced Landscape Modifications Well after Initial Colonization of the Islands

In the previous section, we concluded that much of the Lesser Antillean archipelago was inhabited earlier than previously thought. The intensity of occupations remains unknown, although evidence from the current project indicates a sustained presence of Archaic inhabitants from about 5000 B.C. We will now address human-induced landscape modifications over the ensuing centuries, beginning approximately 1000 B.C. In contrast to the first scouting parties and settlers to the islands, later colonists came to places that were already imprinted with signatures of human activities. This less-than-profound observation is important to keep in mind when considering the kinds of landscapes new colonists confronted and continued to modify or create.

Until recently, it was generally accepted that the earliest Neolithic groups entered the West Indies from greater Amazonia around 500 B.C. (Lathrap 1970; Rouse 1992; Siegel 1991a, 2010). Along with this acceptance was the notion that the earlier Archaic occupants conveniently disappeared or were absorbed by the purportedly larger and better-organized farmers from South America. A number of recent investigations indicate that what really happened was not so simple (Keegan 2006; Rodríguez Ramos 2005, 2010; Rodríguez Ramos et al. 2008; Rodríguez Ramos, Pagán-Jiménez, and Hofman 2013; Siegel et al. 2005).

Table 14.3. Early Radiometric Dates from the Eastern and Southern Caribbean Associated with Archaeological Deposits or Sediments with Evidence of Human Activities.

Island/Location/Material[a]	Lab Sample/ Date (BP)	2σ Cal Age Range[b]	Cal Median Date	Method of Dating	Source
Trinidad/Banwari Trace site/Ch	IVIC-888/7180±80	8170–7850 BP/ 6220–5900 BC	8000 BP/ 6050 BC	Conventional ^{14}C	Boomert 2000
Trinidad/St. John site/Sh	UGAMS-12305/6980±30	7560–7430 BP/ 5610–5480 BC	7500 BP/ 5550 BC	AMS ^{14}C	Pagán-Jiménez et al. 2015
Trinidad/St. John site/Ch	UGAMS-12303/6890±30	7790–7670 BP/ 5840–5720 BC	7720 BP/ 5770 BC	AMS ^{14}C	Pagán-Jiménez et al. 2015
Trinidad/St. John site/Sh	UGAMS-12304/6870±25	7470–7330 BP/ 5525–5380 BC	7410 BP/ 5460 BC	AMS ^{14}C	Pagán-Jiménez et al. 2015
Trinidad/Banwari Trace site/Ch	IVIC-889/6780±70	7780–7510 BP/ 5830–5560 BC	7630 BP/ 5680 BC	Conventional ^{14}C	Boomert 2000
Trinidad/St. John site/Sh	UGAMS-12306/6710±25	7340–7180 BP/ 5390–5230 BC	7270 BP/ 5320 BC	AMS ^{14}C	Pagán-Jiménez et al. 2015
Trinidad/St. John site/Sh	ARC-1153/6870±50	7500–7300 BP/ 5560–5350 BC	7410 BP/ 5460 BC	Conventional ^{14}C	Boomert 2000
Trinidad/Banwari Trace site/Ch	IVIC-891/6190±100	7310–6800 BP/ 5360–4850 BC	7080 BP/ 5130 BC	Conventional ^{14}C	Boomert 2000
Trinidad/St. John site/Sh	UGAMS-12307/6190±25	6750–6570 BP/ 4800–4620 BC	6660 BP/ 4710 BC	AMS ^{14}C	Pagán-Jiménez et al. 2015
Trinidad/Banwari Trace site/Ch	IVIC-887/6170±90	7270–6800 BP/ 5320–4850 BC	7070 BP/ 5120 BC	Conventional ^{14}C	Boomert 2000
Trinidad/Nariva Swamp/PW	AA-82681/6160±70	7250–6890 BP/ 5300–4940 BC	7060 BP/ 5110 BC	AMS ^{14}C	Current project

(continued)

322 • Chapter 14

Table 14.3. (continued)

Island/Location/Material[a]	Lab Sample/ Date (BP)	2σ Cal Age Range[b]	Cal Median Date	Method of Dating	Source
Trinidad/Banwari Trace site/Ch	IVIC-890/6100±90	7240–6740 BP/ 5290–4800 BC	6980 BP/ 5030 BC	Conventional ¹⁴C	Boomert 2000
Trinidad/St. John site/Sh	UGAMS-12308/6050±25	6600–6410 BP/ 4650–4460 BC	6500 BP/ 4550 BC	AMS ¹⁴C	Pagán-Jiménez et al. 2015
Trinidad/Nariva Swamp/PW	AA-82680/5910±50	6880–6570 BP/ 4930–4690 BC	6730 BP/ 4780 BC	AMS ¹⁴C	Current project
Trinidad/Nariva Swamp/PW	Beta-343380/5900±30	6790–6660 BP/ 4840–4710 BC	6720 BP/ 4770 BC	AMS ¹⁴C	Current project
Trinidad/Banwari Trace site/Ch	IVIC-783/5650±100	6670–6280 BP/ 4720–4330 BC	6450 BP/ 4500 BC	Conventional ¹⁴C	Boomert 2000
Barbuda/*Strombus* line/Sh	SI-6879/5480±100	6150–5650 BP/ 4200–3700 BC	5890 BP/ 3940 BC	Conventional ¹⁴C	Watters et al. 1992
Trinidad/St. John site/Sh	UGAMS-13634/5080±30	5570–5380 BP/ 3390–3380 BC	5480 BP/ 3530 BC	AMS ¹⁴C	Pagán-Jiménez et al. 2015
Grenada/Lake Antoine/LS	AA-91728/4860±45	5710–5470 BP/ 3760–3530 BC	5600 BP/ 3650 BC	AMS ¹⁴C	Current project
Trinidad/Cedros swamp/OS	AA-77444/4730±40	5580–5330 BP/ 3635–3380 BC	5480 BP/ 3530 BC	AMS ¹⁴C	Current project
Tobago/Milford 1 site/Sh	GrN-14965/4880±45	5380–5030 BP/ 3440–3090 BC	5220 BC/ 3280 BC	Conventional ¹⁴C	Boomert 2000
St. Martin/Etang Rouge 3 site/Sh	KIA-28815/4830±40	5290–5020 BP/ 3340–3070 BC	5160 BP/ 3210 BC	AMS ¹⁴C	Bonnissent 2008
Curaçao/Rooi Rincon site/Ch	IVIC-247/4490±60	5310–4890 BP/ 3360–2940 BC	5150 BP/ 3195 BC	Conventional ¹⁴C	Haviser 1987

(continued)

Table 14.3. (continued)

Island/Location/Material[a]	Lab Sample/ Date (BP)	2σ Cal Age Range[b]	Cal Median Date	Method of Dating	Source
Antigua/Birgits site/Sh	UM-4005/4810±45	5280–4980 BP/ 3330–3030 BC	5140 BP/ 3190 BC	Conventional ^{14}C	de Mille 2011; Nodine 1990
St. Martin/Etang Rouge 3 site/Sh	KIA-28108/4770±40	5255–4930 BP/ 3300–2980 BC	5080 BP/ 3130 BC	AMS ^{14}C	Bonnissent 2008
Grenada/Meadow Beach/Pe	AA-84799/4420±40	5280–4870 BP/ 3330–2920 BC	5010 BP/ 3060 BC	AMS ^{14}C	Current project
Martinique/Baie de Fort-de-France/ PPM	Beta-341060/4420±30	5270–4870 BP/ 3320–2920 BC	5000 BP/ 3050 BC	AMS ^{14}C	Current project
Marie-Galante/Vieux Fort/CW	AA-84884/4380±60	5280–4840 BP/ 3330–2890 BC	4960 BP/ 3020 BC	AMS ^{14}C	Current project
Antigua/ Twenty Hill site/Sh	Beta-31931/4660±90	5240–4700 BP/ 3290–2760 BC	4940 BP/ 2990 BC	Conventional ^{14}C	de Mille 2011; Nodine 1990
Curaçao/Seru Boca site/Sh	GrN-32015/4570±35	4925–4695 BP/ 2980–2745 BC	4820 BP/ 2870 BC	Conventional ^{14}C	Hoogland and Hofman 2015
St. Martin/Etang Rouge 1 site/Sh	KIA-28116/4505±35	4830–4605 BP/ 2880–2660 BC	4740 BP/ 2790 BC	AMS ^{14}C	Bonnissent 2008
Curaçao/Rooi Rincon site/Ch	IVIC-246/4160±80	4860–4450 BP/ 2910–2500 BC	4690 BP/ 2740 BC	Conventional ^{14}C	Haviser 1987
Curaçao/Rooi Rincon site/Ch	IVIC-234/4110±70	4830–4440 BP/ 2880–2490 BC	4640 BP/ 2690 BC	Conventional ^{14}C	Haviser 1987
Curaçao/Spanish Water/Sh	GrN-32018/4455±20	4790–4570 BP/ 2840–2620 BC	4685 BP/ 2730 BC	Conventional ^{14}C	Hoogland and Hofman 2015
Curaçao/Spanish Water/Sh	GrN-31917/4435±15	4775–4550 BP/ 2830–2600 BC	4650 BP/ 2700 BC	Conventional ^{14}C	Hoogland and Hofman 2015

(continued)

Table 14.3. (continued)

Island/Location/Material[a]	Lab Sample/ Date (BP)	2σ Cal Age Range[b]	Cal Median Date	Method of Dating	Source
Curaçao/Spanish Water/Sh	GrN-31915/4415±20	4770–4515 BP/ 2780–2560 BC	4615 BP/ 2665 BC	Conventional ^{14}C	Hoogland and Hofman 2015
Curaçao/Spanish Water/Sh	GrN-31916/4400±20	4760–4495 BP/ 2770–2540 BC	4590 BP/ 2640 BC	Conventional ^{14}C	Hoogland and Hofman 2015
Curaçao/Rooi Rincon site/Ch	IVIC-242/4070±70	4820–4420 BP/ 2870–2470 BC	4580 BP/ 2640 BC	Conventional ^{14}C	Haviser 1987
Barbados/Heywoods site/Sh	Beta-297522/4360±40	4690–4410 BP/ 2740–2460 BC	4540 BP/ 2585 BC	Conventional ^{14}C	Fitzpatrick 2011
Curaçao/Rooi Rincon site/Ch	IVIC-240/3990±50	4780–4290 BP/ 2830–2340 BC	4470 BP/ 2520 BC	Conventional ^{14}C	Haviser 1987
Tobago/Milford 1 site/Sh	GrN-14963/4320±45	4630–4340 BP/ 2690–2400 BC	4480 BP/ 2530 BC	Conventional ^{14}C	Boomert 2000
St. Martin/Etang Rouge 1 site/Sh	KIA-28115/4275±30	4525–4310 BP/ 2580–2360 BC	4430 BP/ 2480 BC	AMS ^{14}C	Bonnissent 2008
Barbados/Heywoods site/Sh	Beta-297521/4230±50	4510–4280 BP/ 2570–2260 BC	4360 BP/ 2410 BC	Conventional ^{14}C	Fitzpatrick 2011
St. Martin/Sandy Ground 2 site/Sh	Erl-9066/4200±50	4470–4150 BP/ 2500–2200 BC	4320 BP/ 2370 BC	AMS ^{14}C	Bonnissent 2008
Barbuda/*Strombus* line/Sh	SI-6696/4090±90	4410–3910 BP/ 2465–1960 BC	4180 BP/ 2230 BC	Conventional ^{14}C	Watters et al. 1992
St. Martin/Etang Rouge 1 site/Ch	KIA-28121/3830±25	4400–4105 BP/ 2450–2150 BC	4225 BP/ 2270 BC	AMS ^{14}C	Bonnissent 2008
Antigua/Jolly Beach site/Ch	Unreported/3780±90	4420–3920 BP/ 2470–1970 BC	4160 BP/ 2210 BC	Conventional ^{14}C	Davis 2000

(continued)

Table 14.3. (continued)

Island/Location/Material[a]	Lab Sample/ Date (BP)	2σ Cal Age Range[b]	Cal Median Date	Method of Dating	Source
Barbados/Heywoods site/Sh	I-16840/3980±100	4320–3740 BP/ 2370–1790 BC	4020 BP/ 2070 BC	Conventional ^{14}C	Bright 2011; Drewett 2006
Tobago/Milford 1 site/Sh	GrN-14964/4020±70	4290–3860 BP/ 2340–1910 BC	4070 BP/ 2120 BC	Conventional ^{14}C	Boomert 2000
St. Martin/Etang Rouge 1 site/Ch	KIA-28123/3685±30	4140–3925 BP/ 2190–1975 BC	4030 BP/ 2080 BC	AMS ^{14}C	Bonnissent 2008
St. Martin/Etang Rouge 1 site/Ch	KIA-28119/3660±25	4085–3900 BP/ 2130–1950 BC	3985 BP/ 2030 BC	AMS ^{14}C	Bonnissent 2008
St. Martin/Etang Rouge 1 site/Ch	KIA-28124/3600±30	3980–3840 BP/ 2030–1890 BC	3905 BP/ 1960 BC	AMS ^{14}C	Bonnissent 2008
Trinidad/Nariva Swamp/PW	AA-85864/3580±45	3980–3720 BP/ 2110–1770 BC	3880 BP/ 1930 BC	AMS ^{14}C	Current project
Curaçao/St. Michielsberg site/Sh	GrN-9994/3820±70	4000–3600 BP/ 2050–1650 BC	3800 BP/ 1850 BC	Conventional ^{14}C	Haviser 1987
Curaçao/St. Michielsberg site/Sh	AAINA-102/3820±65	3980–3610 BP/ 2030–1660 BC	3800 BP/ 1850 BC	Conventional ^{14}C	Haviser 1987
Barbuda/River site/Sh	PITT-0731/3830±25	3915–3705 BP/ 1960–1755 BC	3820 BP/ 1870 BC	Conventional ^{14}C	Watters et al. 1992
Antigua/North Crabb's Bay site/Sh	Beta-164057/3800±70	3970–3580 BP/ 2020–1635 BC	3780 BP/ 1830 BC	Conventional ^{14}C	de Mille 2011
St. Martin/Trou David 1 site/Ch	ErI-9074/3515±45	3905–3645 BP/ 1950–1700 BC	3785 BP/ 1830 BC	AMS ^{14}C	Bonnissent 2008
Curaçao/St. Michielsberg site/Sh	AAINA-103/3790±50	3910–3620 BP/ 1960–1670 BC	3760 BP/ 1810 BC	Conventional ^{14}C	Haviser 1987

(continued)

Table 14.3. (continued)

Island/Location/Material[a]	Lab Sample/ Date (BP)	2σ Cal Age Range[b]	Cal Median Date	Method of Dating	Source
St. Martin/Etang Rouge 1 site/Sh	KIA-28114/3800±30	3880–3670 BP/ 1930–1720 BC	3775 BP/ 1830 BC	AMS ^{14}C	Bonnissent 2008
St. Martin/Etang Rouge 1 site/Ch	Beta-190805/3490±40	3865–3645 BP/ 1920–1690 BC	3765 BP/ 1810 BC	AMS ^{14}C	Bonnissent 2008
St. Martin/Etang Rouge 1 site/Sh	KIA-28112/3775±30	3845–3635 BP/ 1900–1690 BC	3750 BP/ 1800 BC	AMS ^{14}C	Bonnissent 2008
St. Martin/Norman Estate 1 site/Sh	GrN-20159/3780±40	3875–3625 BP/ 1925–1680 BC	3755 BP/ 1800 BC	?	Henocq and Petit 1995
St. Martin/Salines d'Orient site/Sh	Erl-9071/3750±50	3860–3570 BP/ 1910–1620 BC	3720 BP/ 1770 BC	AMS ^{14}C	Bonnissent 2008
St. Martin/Etang Rouge 1 site/Ch	KIA-28126/3445±25	3825–3635 BP/ 1880–1690 BC	3700 BP/ 1750 BC	AMS ^{14}C	Bonnissent 2008
St. Martin/Norman Estate 1 site/Sh	GrN-20157/3730±30	3810–3590 BP/ 1860–1640 BC	3690 BP/ 1740 BC	?	Henocq and Petit 1995
St. Martin/Etang Rouge 1 site/Ch	KIA-28127/3430±35	3825–3590 BP/ 1880–1640 BC	3685 BP/ 1730 BC	AMS ^{14}C	Bonnissent 2008
Antigua/Jolly Beach site/Sh	Beta-31930/3630±80	3780–3370 BP/ 1830–1420 BC	3570 BP/ 1620 BC	Conventional ^{14}C	de Mille 2011; Nodine 1990 Bonnissent 2008
St. Martin/Etang Rouge 1 site/Ch	KIA-28120/3365±25	3690–3560 BP/ 1740–1610 BC	3610 BP/ 1660 BC	AMS ^{14}C	Watters et al. 1992
Barbuda/River site/Sh	PITT-0717/3650±35	3695–3470 BP/ 1740–1520 BC	3590 BP/ 1640 BC	Conventional ^{14}C	Bonnissent 2008
St. Martin/Salines d'Orient site/Sh	Erl-9072/3610±50	3680–3400 BP/ 1730–1450 BC	3540 BP/ 1590 BC	AMS ^{14}C	Henocq and Petit 1995

(continued)

Table 14.3. (continued)

Island/Location/Material[a]	Lab Sample/ Date (BP)	2σ Cal Age Range[b]	Cal Median Date	Method of Dating	Source
St. Martin/Norman Estate 1 site/Sh	Beta-41782/3580±90	3760–3300 BP/ 1810–1350 BC	3510 BP/ 1560 BC	Conventional ^{14}C	Crock et al. 1995
Anguilla/Whitehead's Bluff site/Sh	Pitt-1263/3605±45	3665–3405 BP/ 1710–1460 BC	3530 BP/ 1580 BC	Conventional ^{14}C	
Antigua/Jolly Beach site/OS	AA-82474/3290±60	3640–3380 BP/ 1730–1440 BC	3520 BP/ 1570 BC	AMS ^{14}C	Current project
St. Martin/Norman Estate 1 site/Sh	GrN-20158/3590±50	3640–3380 BP/ 1700–1430 BC	3520 BP/ 1570 BC	?	Henocq and Petit 1995
Saba/Plum Piece site/LC	GrN-27562/3430±30	3585–3410 BP/ 1640–1460 BC	3510 BP/ 1560 BC	Conventional ^{14}C	Hofman and Hoogland 2003 Watters et al. 1992
Barbuda/*Strombus* line/Sh	PITT-0590/3560±45	3600–3365 BP/ 1650–1410 BC	3480 BP/ 1530 BC	Conventional ^{14}C	de Mille 2011
Antigua/North Crabb's Bay site/Sh	Beta-164058/3540±70	3640–3290 BP/ 1690–1340 BC	3460 BP/ 1510 BC	Conventional ^{14}C	
St. Martin/Etang Rouge 1 site/Ch	KIA-28125/3235±25	3555–3385 BP/ 1610–1440 BC	3450 BP/ 1500 BC	AMS ^{14}C	Bonnissent 2008
St. Martin/Trou David 1 site/Sh	ErI-9073/3510±50	3570–3310 BP/ 1620–1360 BC	3430 BP/ 1480 BC	AMS ^{14}C	Bonnissent 2008
Antigua/Deep Bay site/Sh	UM-4003/3450±100	3590–3080 BP/ 1650–1140 BC	3350 BP/ 1400 BC	Conventional ^{14}C	de Mille 2011; Nodine 1990 Hofman and Hoogland 2003
Saba/Plum Piece site/LC	GrN-27564/3320±30	3460–3325 BP/ 1510–1330 BC	3390 BP/ 1440 BC	Conventional ^{14}C	Crock et al. 1995
Anguilla/Whitehead's Bluff site/Sh	Beta-60775/3410±60	3450–3140 BP/ 1510–1200 BC	3310 BP/ 1360 BC	Conventional ^{14}C	

(continued)

Table 14.3. (continued)

Island/Location/Material[a]	Lab Sample/ Date (BP)	2σ Cal Age Range[b]	Cal Median Date	Method of Dating	Source
Antigua/Hand Point site/Sh	UM-4002/3390±120	3600–3000 BP/ 1600–1000 BC	3300 BP/ 1300 BC	Conventional ^{14}C	de Mille 2011; Nodine 1990 Bonnissent 2008
St. Martin/Pointe du Bluff/Sh	Erl-9064/3460±50	3500–3220 BP/ 1550–1270 BC	3370 BP/ 1420 BC	AMS ^{14}C	Hofman and Hoogland 2003
Saba/Plum Piece site/LC	GrN-27563/3300±30	3445–3260 BP/ 1500–1310 BC	3370 BP/ 1420 BC	Conventional ^{14}C	Bonnissent 2008
St. Martin/Baie Longue 2 site/Ch	Beta-187937/3140±40	3450–3245 BP/ 1500–1300 BC	3365 BP/ 1410 BC	AMS ^{14}C	Crock et al. 1995
Anguilla/Whitehead's Bluff site/Sh	Beta-63158/3380±90	3490–3010 BP/ 1540–1060 BC	3270 BP/ 1320 BC	Conventional ^{14}C	Watters et al. 1992
Barbuda/*Strombus* line/Sh	SI-6695/3340±70	3400–3020 BP/ 1450–1070 BC	3230 BP/ 1275 BC	Conventional ^{14}C	Bonnissent 2008
St. Martin/Baie Longue 2 site/Sh	Beta-187936/3450±40	3460–3235 BP/ 1510–1280 BC	3360 BP/ 1410 BC	Conventional ^{14}C	Bonnissent 2008
Antigua/North Crabb's Bay site/Sh	Beta-164056/3430±50	3460–3190 BP/ 1510–1240 BC	3330 BP/ 1380 BC	Conventional ^{14}C	de Mille 2011
St. Martin/Etang Rouge 1 site/Ch	KIA-28117/3095±25	3370–3235 BP/ 1420–1290 BC	3300 BP/ 1350 BC	AMS ^{14}C	Bonnissent 2008
St. Martin/Etang Rouge 1 site/Sh	KIA-28111/3380±40	3380–3220 BP/ 1430–1210 BC	3275 BP/ 1330 BC	AMS ^{14}C	Bonnissent 2008
Barbuda/*Strombus* line/Sh	PITT-0721/3350±60	3390–3060 BP/ 1440–1110 BC	3240 BP/ 1290 BC	Conventional ^{14}C	Watters et al. 1992
St. Martin/Sandy Ground 1 site/Sh	Erl-9065/3340±50	3360–3080 BP/ 1410–1120 BC	3230 BP/ 1280 BC	AMS ^{14}C	Bonnissent 2008

(continued)

Table 14.3. (continued)

Island/Location/Material[a]	Lab Sample/ Date (BP)	2σ Cal Age Range[b]	Cal Median Date	Method of Dating	Source
St. Martin/Etang Rouge 1 site/Sh	KIA-28113/3320±30	3325–3095 BP/ 1375–1150 BC	3205 BP/ 1255 BC	AMS ^{14}C	Bonnissent 2008
St. Martin/Etang Rouge 1 site/Ch	KIA-28118/2950±50	3320–2960 BP/ 1370–1010 BC	3110 BP/ 1160 BC	AMS ^{14}C	Bonnissent 2008
Anguilla/Whitehead's Bluff site/Sh	Beta-21865/3240±80	3320–2880 BP/ 1370–920 BC	3090 BP/ 1140 BC	Conventional ^{14}C	Crock et al. 1995
St. Martin/Norman Estate 2 site/Sh	Beta-224793/3240±60	3290–2910 BP/ 1340–960 BC	3090 BP/ 1140 BC	Conventional ^{14}C	Bonnissent 2008
Marie-Galante/Vieux Fort/OS	AA-84883/2960±30	3210–3010 BP/ 1260–1055 BC	3120 BP/ 1170 BC	AMS ^{14}C	Current project
Curaçao/Spanish Water/Sh	GrN-31918/3195±20	3135–2940 BP/ 1190–990 BC	3030 BP/ 1080 BC	Conventional ^{14}C	Hoogland and Hofman 2015 de Mille 2011; Nodine 1990
Antigua/Parham Road site/Sh	UM-4004/3140±100	3220–2740 BP/ 1270–790 BC	2970 BP/ 1020 BC	Conventional ^{14}C	
Trinidad/Ortoire site/Ch	Y-260-2/2760±130	3240–2490 BP/ 1400–500 BC	2890 BP/ 900 BC	Conventional ^{14}C	Boomert 2000
St. Croix/Coakley Bay/OS	Beta-376843/2900±30	3160–2950 BP/ 1130–1000 BC	3030 BP/ 1080 B	AMS ^{14}C	Current project
St. Martin/Etang Rouge 1 site/Sh	KIA-28110/3185±30	3140–2905 BP/ 1190–960 BC	3020 BP/ 1070 BC	AMS ^{14}C	Bonnissent 2008
Grenada/Meadow Beach/Pe	AA-84798/2880±40	3160–2880 BP/ 1210–930 BC	3010 BP/ 1060 BC	AMS ^{14}C	Current project
Barbuda/*Strombus* line/Sh	SI-6880/3150±60	3150–2810 BP/ 1200–860 BC	2970 BP/ 1020 BC	Conventional ^{14}C	Watters et al. 1992

(continued)

Table 14.3. (continued)

Island/Location/Material[a]	Lab Sample/ Date (BP)	2σ Cal Age Range[b]	Cal Median Date	Method of Dating	Source
St. Martin/Etang Rouge 1 site/Sh	KIA-28109/3105±30	3020–2800 BP/ 1070–850 BC	2910 BP/ 960 BC	AMS ^{14}C	Bonnissent 2008
St. Martin/Norman Estate 2 site/Ch	Beta-224792/2610±40	2840–2540 BP/ 890–590 BC	2750 BP/ 800 BC	Conventional ^{14}C	Bonnissent 2008
Antigua/Twenty Hill site/Sh	UM-4000/2940±90	2960–2650 BP/ 1010–520 BC	2740 BP/ 790 BC	Conventional ^{14}C	de Mille 2011; Nodine 1990 Watters et al. 1992
Barbuda/*Strombus* line/Sh	PITT-0592/2900±50	2820–2530 BP/ 880–580 BC	2710 BP/ 760 BC	Conventional ^{14}C	Bonnissent 2008
St. Martin/Baie Orientale 1 site/Sh	Beta-146427/2850±60	2700–2440 BP/ 820–490 BC	2640 BP/ 690 BC	Conventional ^{14}C	Gérard 1994
Guadeloupe/Pointe des Pies site/Sh	Ly-6423/2830±50	2740–2550 BP/ 790–500 BC	2620 BP/ 670 BC	Conventional ^{14}C	Watters et al. 1992
Barbuda/*Strombus* line/Sh	PITT-0591/2830±80	2760–2360 BP/ 810–410 BC	2600 BP/ 650 BC	Conventional ^{14}C	Bonnissent 2008
St. Martin/Baie Orientale 1 site/Ch	Beta-145372/2420±40	2700–2350 BP/ 750–400 BC	2460 BP/ 510 BC	AMS ^{14}C	de Mille 2011; Nodine 1990
Antigua/Cloverleaf W site/Sh	Beta-23547/2680±80	2690–2210 BP/ 740–260 BC	2430 BP/ 480 BC	Conventional ^{14}C	Hoogland and Hofman 2015 Watters et al. 1992
Curaçao/Spanish Water/Sh	GrN-31921/2680±20	2490–2320 BP/ 540–370 BC	2400 BP/ 450 BC	Conventional ^{14}C	Hoogland and Hofman 2015
Barbuda/*Strombus* line/Sh	PITT-0593/2650±50	2600–2250 BP/ 650–300 BC	2380 BP/ 430 BC	Conventional ^{14}C	Hoogland and Hofman 2015
Curaçao/Spanish Water/Sh	GrN-31922/2625±20	2430–2285 BP/ 480–335 BC	2335 BP/ 385 BC	Conventional ^{14}C	Gérard 1994

(continued)

Table 14.3. (continued)

Island/Location/Material[a]	Lab Sample/ Date (BP)	2σ Cal Age Range[b]	Cal Median Date	Method of Dating	Source
Guadeloupe/Pointes des Mangles site/Sh	Beta-239750/2620±20	2420–2300BP/ 475–330 BC	2330 BP/ 380 BC	Conventional ¹⁴C	
St. Martin/Baie Orientale 1 site/Ch	Beta-146425/2270±40	2350–2155 BP/ 400–210 BC	2250 BP/ 300 BC	AMS ¹⁴C	Bonnissent 2008
Curaçao/Spanish Water/Sh	GrN-31923/2450±15	2255–2040 BP/ 305–90 BC	2130 BP/ 180 BC	Conventional ¹⁴C	Hoogland and Hofman 2015 de Mille 2011; Nodine 1990
Antigua/Five Islands site/Sh	UM-4001/2390±50	2220–1900 BP/ 270 BC–AD 50	2050 BP/ 100 BC	Conventional ¹⁴C	Bonnissent 2008
St. Martin/Trou David 2 site/Hu	Erl-8235/2070±50	2280–1900 BP/ 330 BC–AD 50	2040 BP/ 90 BC	AMS ¹⁴C	Bonnissent 2008
St. Martin/Baie Orientale 1 site/Ch	Beta-146424/2020±40	2110–1885 BP/ 160 BC–AD 70	1970 BP/ 20 BC	AMS ¹⁴C	

a. Ch: charcoal, Sh: shell, OS: organic sediment, PW: preserved wood, LS: lake sediment, CW: carbonized wood, Pe: Peat, PPM: preserved plant matter, Hu: human bone, LC: land crab.

b. CALIB ver. 7.0 was used to calibrate the dates and compute the cal median values (Reimer et al. 2013). Dates from charcoal and organic samples were calibrated using the IntCal13 calibration dataset. Shell dates were calibrated using the Marine13 calibration dataset: -27 for ΔR and 14 for ΔR uncertainty. Dates from land crab remains were calibrated using the Mixed Marine/Northern Hemisphere calibration dataset: 50% marine, -27 for ΔR, and 14 for ΔR uncertainty. We used the ΔR and uncertainty values calculated elsewhere for the same section of the Caribbean (Bright 2011).

It has been suggested that the earliest Saladoid colonists did not follow the stepping-stone route up the Lesser Antilles proposed long ago by Rouse, but instead jumped directly from Venezuela to the northern Lesser Antilles or the Greater Antilles (Callaghan 2001; Fitzpatrick 2013; Fitzpatrick, Kappers, and Giovas 2010). Probably the best support for this argument comes from Rouse's (1976; Rouse and Morse 1999) excavation of the Indian Creek site on Antigua. Charcoal samples collected from the two deepest levels in one of the Saladoid middens produced two identical dates of 2785±80 B.P. (cal 1190–800 B.C., 2 sigma). At the time of his excavation in the 1970s, Rouse rejected the validity of those dates "because they were 800 years earlier than any other Ceramic Age dates in the West Indies" (Rouse and Morse 1999: 45). If the dates in fact reflect an initial Caribbean crossing by Early Saladoid explorers into the islands then perhaps later Saladoid occupations (post-ca. 900 B.C.) elsewhere on Antigua and to the west and south of the island represent continued colonization from an Antiguan founding group. Alternatively, or in addition, there may have been an early ca. 900 B.C. jump from Venezuela to Antigua and subsequent colonizing episodes following the stepping-stone route up the chain of the Lesser Antilles. We suspect that some combination of long-distance scouting, followed by founding communities, more exploration, and local expansion and settlement, in addition to island hopping from South America, occurred during the Neolithic colonization of the Caribbean. Throwing out the stepping-stone model for a long-distance leap is simply replacing one monolithic heavy-arrow idea for another.

There is growing support for some amount of interaction between the resident Archaic populations and the Saladoid colonists (Siegel et al. 2005). Some archaeologists believe there is sufficient evidence for marked similarities between Archaic and post-Saladoid ceramic-vessel technology and morphology to argue for an Archaic source for the late and protohistoric Taíno societies (Keegan 2006; Rodríguez Ramos et al. 2008).

Earlier (see chaps. 6, 9, 10; Siegel et al. 2015) we demonstrated the presence of Archaic people on a number of islands in the absence of documented archaeological sites, and discussed factors of preservational bias and visibility that need to be considered when drawing conclusions about landscape occupational histories. We will continue that line of investigation in the context of later colonization events and in situ developments.

Project Contributions to Understanding Later Pre-Columbian and Early European Socionatural Landscapes

Signals of human activity were recorded in a number of contexts dating to the later Archaic, Ceramic Age, and early historic era. The core taken near the Archaic site of St. John in Oropuche Lagoon, Trinidad, produced a date of 820±30 B.P. (cal A.D. 1165–1265, 2 sigma). Microfossils associated with this context reveal a time of active landscape management and clearing. Saladoid settlers were well established on Trinidad no later than A.D. 0; data from our core suggest that by the twelfth century A.D. landscape impacts were quite extensive. The Bontour type site and four known Saladoid sites are located within approximately 10 km of the coring location (Boomert 2000: fig. 16; Boomert, Faber-Morse, and Rouse 2013: fig. 3). The occupants of these and other undocumented nearby settlements may have produced the signal recorded in the core.

Phytolith data from the Cedros core, dating to 2490±40 B.P. (cal 790–420 B.C., 2 sigma), are associated with open-habitat indicators suggesting a more arid environment than prior to this era. This finding is consistent with a period of transition from moist to drier conditions seen in the available climate data (Curtis, Brenner, and Hodell 2001; Higuera-Gundy et al. 1999; Hodell et al. 1991) (fig. 14.1). In addition, the phytolith record at this time reveals an environment with increased availability of economically useful plants, including edible fruits. Shortly after this time, based on current dating, the Cedros archaeological site was occupied by the earliest known Ceramic Age settlers to Trinidad (Boomert, Faber-Morse, and Rouse 2013; Rouse and Allaire 1978). We would not be surprised if more-extensive excavations and dating in the Cedros site produced older Saladoid dates consistent with our 2490 B.P. date. These first settlers of the Cedros community may have been drawn to the location precisely for the drier conditions, newly available resources, and a more-open forested setting than during the previous mesic period. Drier conditions in tropical-forest environments have been documented to be "favourable to the niche expansions of crop plants through the cutting and burning of vegetation" (Piperno 1989: 549).

Evidence for Late Archaic/Early Ceramic Age landscape modifications in Nariva Swamp is variable. Core NV08-3 taken near the center of the swamp produced clear signals of human activity by 2480±30 B.P. (cal 770–420 B.C., 2 sigma), with elevated and sustained levels of charcoal and *Cecropia* and somewhat elevated levels of Poaceae pollen and phytolith traces of open-habitat indicators. In addition, the previous pollen assemblage of brackish-water-adapted plants like red mangrove was reduced and replaced by freshwater-loving sedges, reflecting environmental changes conducive for human settlement. The mid to upper section of the NV08-4 core, associated with the Ceramic Age, displays a cluster of elevated concentrations in economically useful plant taxa, charcoal particulates, and disturbance/open-habitat indicators all pointing to an increasingly managed landscape.

On Grenada the Meadow Beach core reveals continued human activities by cal 1210–930 B.C. (2 sigma), prior to currently accepted dates for a Saladoid presence in this section of the West Indies. Among other economically useful plants identified in the Ceramic Age portion of the Lake Antoine core *Zea mays* was present after cal 160 B.C.–A.D. 60, possibly contemporaneous with the Saladoid occupation of the Pearls site. It is notable that peaks in the lake-core total phosphate values are directly preceded by elevated charcoal-particulate concentrations. Farrell argued that there is a lag between human-induced fires and the introduction of phosphorus into the lake sediments (chap. 5, this volume).

On Curaçao coring along Spaanse Water Bay in the vicinity of known Archaic and Ceramic Age sites documented pulses of human activity from approximately cal 2490 B.C., cal A.D. 235, and by interpolation during the early colonial era. Given the nature of Archaic shell deposits dotting the island, Hoogland and Hofman (2011: 637) suggested that Curaçao "was frequented ... by groups from other islands or the South American mainland." Our coring data support this interpretation of limited human engagement on the island during the earliest periods of occupation. However, by post ca. cal 2490 B.C., pollen, phytolith, charcoal, and phosphorus data reveal distinct episodes of sustained and more-intrusive human activities. Our second core on Curaçao taken near the Ceramic Age site of San Juan produced data relevant for the San Juan occupations and other nearby Ceramic Age activities. *Zea mays* pollen associated with a 2-sigma cal date of A.D. 900–1020 indicates some amount of cultivation by the Mid Ceramic Age in this portion of the island, although, as seen in the Spaanse Water core, human use and management of the landscape appears to have been less than intensive.

Our core in the one remaining mangrove on Barbados produced evidence of human-induced landscape modification dating to cal A.D. 720–1020 (2 sigma). This date is quite a bit later than archaeologically documented Archaic and Early Ceramic Age occupations on the island. A sustained and elevated presence of charcoal microparticulates combined with the reduction and elimination of palm pollen at this time suggests intentional burning of the forest.

One of our cores on Martinique was extracted from the large mangrove swamp ringing the Baie de Fort-de-France along the west coast. As discussed in chap. 9 (this volume) this core produced good evidence of human activities deep in the Archaic, prior to any well-documented archaeological sites dating to that time. In contrast, the upper section of the core dating to ca. cal A.D. 335 and later revealed reduced presence of disturbance indicators, although economically useful taxa are still well represented. Disturbance indicators are present but less prominently than during the Archaic, especially charcoal microparticulate concentrations. Perhaps economically useful plants introduced or selected by earlier Archaic people continued to thrive naturally when this part of Martinique was less intensively occupied by later Ceramic Age groups. Ceramic Age archaeological sites are well represented on the island, although not as many are documented around the Baie de Fort-de-France as elsewhere (Bérard 2004: fig. 57; Bright 2011: fig. 3.5). Four pottery scatters dating to ca. A.D. 400–800 have been identified along the edge of the bay within a few kilometers of the coring location (Bright 2011: fig. 3.5). Our core results may reflect a reduced local presence and intensity of activities during the Ceramic Age compared to the previous Archaic Age. It would be useful to obtain more information about the nature of the occupations represented by the four known pottery-scatter sites. Bright (2011: 78) distinguished between what he called settlement sites versus pottery scatters.

The core from Pointe Figuier along the south coast of Martinique revealed nearly continuous human activities in the area dating from ca. cal 800 B.C. through historic times. The nearby Anse Figuier site was occupied during the Late Saladoid/Early Troumassoid era (ca. A.D. 400–1000) (Bérard 2004; Bright 2011: Appendix 1: 115). Two radiocarbon dates were obtained from conch shells collected from the site: 1775±40 B.P. (ARL-1147, cal A.D. 490–685, 2 sigma), and 1485±40 B.P. (ARL-1148, cal A.D. 780–995, 2 sigma) (Bérard, personal communication 2013). Both dates were calibrated for the marine-reservoir effect using the Marine13 calibration data set of Calib7.02 (Delta R = –27±7) (Reimer et al. 2013). Compared to the Baie de Fort-de-France area, the density of known archaeological sites along the south coast is quite high (Bérard 2004; Bright 2011: Appendix 1: 111). Again, as emphasized in other chapters, our assessments of site distributions are based on very little in the way of systematic surveys, and Martinique is no different. Therefore, discussions of relative site frequency should be treated as testable hypotheses rather than as empirically confirmed patterns. From about 800 B.C. to the midsection of the Figuier core dating to the protohistoric/Contact period (cal A.D. 1480–1640, 2 sigma) there appears to be relatively constant sedimentation rate and uniform influx of charcoal particulates resulting from human activities. The cal A.D. 1480–1640 date is from 128 cm, a little more than halfway down the core. From ca. cal med 780 B.C. to cal med A.D. 1560 there is about 94 cm of sedimentation, with the remaining sediments accumulating after the arrival of Europeans. The plantation system on Martinique was established in the 1670s and massive deforestation occurred shortly after. By 1736 nearly the entire lowlands of the island were under plantation agriculture, the results of which are apparent in the Pointe Figuier core. Over approximately the past four hundred years, 58 percent of the sediments accumulated in the ca. 2,800-year core.

On Marie-Galante the Vieux Fort core displays continued human activities during the Late Archaic and Early Ceramic Ages. The 2960±30 B.P. date (from 256 cm depth) is associated with the onset of drying conditions documented in Caribbean climate records (Curtis, Brenner, and Hodell 2001). Interestingly, the concentration values of charcoal particulates in the Vieux Fort core declined beginning with this date. The values are still elevated and continuous through the Ceramic Age and into the European-colonial era, but at considerably reduced levels compared to the earlier Archaic discussed previously. The earliest settlers to the island during the Early to Mid Archaic engaged in a considerable amount of landscape modification activities. They unwittingly set the stage for later colonists who apparently continued a program of landscape maintenance beginning by 1980±35 B.P. (cal 50 B.C.–A.D. 120; 206 cm depth), which coincides with the approximate arrival time of the initial Saladoid colonizers.

Jolly Beach on Antigua is one of the major Archaic sites documented in the Caribbean (Davis 2000); as discussed above our core collected from the area revealed human activities contemporaneous with the early occupations of the site. Microbotanical remains collected from approximately the core midsection and dated to 1470±35 B.P. (cal A.D. 540–650, 2 sigma) indicate continued human activities, although no archaeological evidence for a Late Saladoid presence was observed in the Jolly Beach site. There is one known Ceramic Age site located about 1.5 km to the southwest of Jolly Beach (Davis 2000: fig. 23); activities of those occupants may be represented in our core midsection.

The other interesting Antiguan core was collected from wetlands fringing Nonsuch Bay, where Ayres Creek empties into the bay. Numerous Archaic and Ceramic Age sites are known for this area (Stokes 1991). Indian Creek, one of the premier Saladoid sites known in the Caribbean, is located within the Ayres Creek watershed (Rouse and Morse 1999). A nearly 5-m long core was obtained; based on its great depth and the presence of several ash bands we were confident that a long record of environmental history was represented. Siegel was convinced that organic sediment from 445 cm would return a radiocarbon date from the Early to Mid Holocene. It was with much surprise that the near-basal sample produced a date of 580±35 B.P. (cal A.D. 1300–1420), clearly before Columbus but barely so. Three subsequent samples submitted for dates from selected depths in the column were successively more recent, all within the European colonial era. We see in this core dramatic direct evidence for what Armstrong (2013a, 2013b: 530–533) called "an emerging landscape of power and enslavement" in the sixteenth- and seventeenth-century Caribbean plantation economy. Massive deforestation resulted in soil loss and colluvial deposition, discussed by Watts (1987) in his masterful overview of the Caribbean during the early colonial era (see also Wells et al. 2018). Our results in Nonsuch Bay have implications for future paleoecological investigations in similar conditions. Cores in the range of 10–15 m may need to be extracted in order to penetrate Early to Mid Holocene sediments, thus requiring equipment capable of achieving these depths.

As on Antigua, Archaic and Ceramic Age occupations have been documented on Barbuda. The two cores collected from Barbuda were relatively short (150 cm and 185 cm) with ambiguous evidence for clear human-induced landscape modifications. Charcoal particulate concentrations followed by other disturbance-indicator pollen taxa (Cheno-Ams, Poaceae) are most suggestive of vegetation clearing during Late Archaic/Early Saladoid times.

The core from Coakley Bay on St. Croix continued to display elevated charcoal concentration values during the Saladoid and post-Saladoid periods. In addition to other disturbance indicators in the phytolith assemblage, probable maize phytoliths were recovered from a context dated to cal 430–240 B.C. (2 sigma). This date associates the presence of maize with the Early Saladoid Prosperity complex on St. Croix.

There is increasingly more evidence from microbotanical data in the Caribbean for the introduction of maize during the Archaic (Fortuna 1981: 86–89; Newsom 2009; Newsom and Pearsall 2003; Pagán-Jiménez 2013; Sanoja 1989; Siegel et al. 2005: 111–112). However, based on the sparse and spotty occurrence of maize macro- and microremains, the aggressive measures archaeologists have been taking over the past twenty-five years to retrieve subsistence data, and the growing conditions required for abundant yields, Newsom (2010: 124) argued that maize never obtained the status of a staple crop in the Caribbean, unlike elsewhere in the Americas (but see Pagán-Jimenez 2013: 401–403).

Our findings from St. Croix and elsewhere in this project where maize pollen or phytoliths were identified support Newsom's assessment.

Caribbean Socionatural Landscapes across Space and Time

The perspective of historical ecology provides a framework for investigating culture and nature in a synergistic context rather than as a form of dualistic opposition. By recognizing the adjectival aspect of history in regard to ecology, we explicitly embrace the temporal dimension in the synergy between human behavior and the physical environment (Winterhalder 1994: 18–21). In our project of Caribbean historical ecology, we use the word "socionatural" as an adjective to modify the word "landscapes," thus emphasizing the inextricably intertwined domains of human action and physical environment.

The field of historical ecology got its start with and theoretical foundations based mostly on investigations of continental zones and contiguous landmasses (Balée 1998a; Balée and Erickson 2006a; Crumley 1994a; McIntosh et al. 2000; Russell 1997). That may simply be a product of historical accident and there are now quite a few applications of historical ecology in island settings (Fitzpatrick and Keegan 2007; Kirch and Hunt 1997; McGovern 1994). As Balée and Erickson (2006b: 1) observed, "Wherever humans have trodden, the natural environment is somehow different, sometimes in barely perceptible ways, sometimes in dramatic ways." In our Caribbean case study, we can certainly attest to anthropogenic landscapes at times when and places where archaeologists traditionally have assumed people were not present.

In many cases, the effects of human actions may be more apparent or dramatic on island ecosystems than elsewhere because of their circumscribed relatively isolated geographies (Kirch 1997c: 2–3). In terms of island historical ecology, the Pacific has been the center of the most extensive and detailed studies (e.g., Athens et al. 2002; Kirch 1996, 2010b; Kirch and Hunt 1997; McCoy and Hartshorn 2007; Rolett 1998; Vitousek et al. 2003; Vitousek et al. 2004). In the Caribbean, we have a few decades worth of subsistence, settlement pattern, and environmental studies; some of the more recent of these have been conducted more or less within the framework of a historical-ecological approach without explicitly saying so (e.g., Newsom and Wing 2004). Fitzpatrick and Keegan (2007) presented a useful overview on the applicability of historical ecology in Caribbean archaeology. They made an important observation: "One of the main issues for an historical ecology of the Caribbean is deciphering the impact of the islands' earliest human inhabitants. ... Research shows that the cumulative effects of ongoing cultural development in conjunction with land clearing activities using fire, for example, can be devastating" (Fitzpatrick and Keegan 2007: 34). As documented in our study, fire seems to have been the tool of choice in modifying and managing landscapes from the earliest human through European colonial occupations.

In her review of Caribbean paleoethnobotany, Lee Newsom (2008: 181) observed that the "challenge ... is to build on the archaeobotanical database ... [and] to provide a clearer spatial and temporal framework of understanding, on a regional, subregional, and island-by-island basis." Our goals in this project have been to address Caribbean historical ecology at the "regional, subregional, and island-by-island" scales and to confront the interrelated challenges of identifying traces of human activities on landscapes, understanding island colonization, and gaining insight into landscape management or modification through time. To achieve these goals, we implemented a consistent and systematic approach to collecting and sampling core sediments from wetlands with good potential to yield reliable data relevant for our interests in past human actions. Specific islands were selected between Venezuela and Puerto Rico, which as a group encompasses the full range of environmental and topographic variability across the Lesser Antilles and southern Caribbean.

Table 14.4 displays the single oldest radiocarbon dates from each of the islands presented in table 14.3. At 2 sigmas, every date overlaps with each of the two adjacent dates. However, there is a general geographic progression from south to north in the distribution of the oldest dates on each island. Clearly, Trinidad was the earliest occupied island with the dates from the Banwari Trace and St. John sites, and Nariva Swamp. If the remaining dates reflect general colonization rates of the islands, then there is a significant temporal gap between Trinidad and Grenada. Geologically and culturally Trinidad and northern South America are connected (Bellizzia and Dengo 1990; Boomert 2000, 2013). Indeed, Boomert (2013: 142) suggested, "Bands of ... hunters/foragers ... frequented Trinidad perhaps as early as about 8000 cal B.C., prior to the island's separation from the mainland" following sea-level increases.

It is unlikely to be a coincidence that there is a temporal gap of about 2,500–3,000 years between the earliest evidence of human activities on Trinidad and Grenada and that the shortest straight-line distance between the two islands is about 140 km, considerably longer than interisland distances among any of the Windward Islands except for Barbados (Bright 2011: 24–26). In their visual-sight analysis of the same islands, Torres and Rodríguez Ramos (2008: 22) suggested, "Trinidad and Grenada are joined by intersecting visibility ranges, thus posing a

340 • Chapter 14

Table 14.4. Earliest Single Radiometric Dates Per Island from the Eastern and Southern Caribbean Associated with Archaeological Deposits or Sediments with Evidence of Human Activities.

Island/Location/Material[a]	Lab Sample/ Date (BP)	2σ Cal Age Range[b]	Cal Median Date	Method of Dating	Source
Trinidad/Banwari Trace site/Ch	IVIC-888/7180±80	8170–7850 BP/ 6220–5900 BC	8000 BP/ 6050 BC	Conventional ^{14}C	Boomert 2000
Barbuda/*Strombus* line/Sh	SI-6879/5480±100	6150–5650 BP/ 4200–3700 BC	5890 BP/ 3940 BC	Conventional ^{14}C	Watters et al. 1992
Grenada/Lake Antoine/LS	AA-91728/4860±45	5710–5470 BP/ 3760–3530 BC	5600 BP/ 3650 BC	AMS ^{14}C	Current project
Tobago/Milford 1 site/Sh	GrN-14965/4880±45	5380–5030 BP/ 3440–3090 BC	5220 BC/ 3280 BC	Conventional ^{14}C	Boomert 2000
St. Martin/Etang Rouge 3 site/Sh	KIA-28815/4830±40	5290–5020 BP/ 3340–3070 BC	5160 BP/ 3210 BC	AMS ^{14}C	Bonnissent 2003, 2008
Curaçao/Rooi Rincon site/Ch	IVIC-247/4490±60	5310–4890 BP/ 3360–2940 BC	5150 BP/ 3195 BC	Conventional ^{14}C	Haviser 1987
Antigua/Birgits site/Sh	UM-4005/4810±45	5280–4980 BP/ 3330–3030 BC	5140 BP/ 3190 BC	Conventional ^{14}C	de Mille 2011; Nodine 1990
Martinique/Baie de Fort-de-France/PPM	Beta-341060/4420±30	5270–4870 BP/ 3320–2920 BC	5000 BP/ 3050 BC	AMS ^{14}C	Current project
Marie-Galante/Vieux Fort/CW	AA-84884/4380±60	5280–4840 BP/ 3330–2890 BC	4960 BP/ 3020 BC	AMS ^{14}C	Current project
Barbados/Heywoods site/Sh	Beta-297522/4360±40	4690–4410 BP/ 2740–2460 BC	4540 BP/ 2585 BC	Conventional ^{14}C	Fitzpatrick 2011

(continued)

Table 14.4. (continued)

Island/Location/Material[a]	Lab Sample/ Date (BP)	2σ Cal Age Range[b]	Cal Median Date	Method of Dating	Source
Anguilla/Whitehead's Bluff site/Sh	Pitt-1263/3605±45	3665–3405 BP/ 1710–1460 BC	3530 BP/ 1580 BC	Conventional ^{14}C	Crock et al. 1995
Saba/Plum Piece site/LC	GrN-27562/3430±30	3585–3410 BP/ 1640–1460 BC	3510 BP/ 1560 BC	Conventional ^{14}C	Hofman and Hoogland 2003
St. Croix/Coakley Bay/OS	Beta-376843/2900±30	3160–2950 BP/ 1130–1000 BC	3030 BP/ 1080 BC	AMS ^{14}C	Current project
Guadeloupe/Pointe des Pies site/Sh	Ly-6423/2830±50	2740–2550 BP/ 790–500 BC	2620 BP/ 670 BC	Conventional ^{14}C	Gérard 1994

a. Ch: charcoal, Sh: shell, OS: organic sediment, PW: preserved wood, LS: lake sediment, CW: carbonized wood, Pe: Peat, PPM: preserved plant matter, Hu: human bone, LC: land crab.

b. CALIB ver. 7.0 was used to calibrate the dates and compute the cal median values (Reimer et al. 2013). Dates from charcoal and organic samples were calibrated using the IntCal13 calibration dataset. Shell dates were calibrated using the Marine13 calibration dataset: -27 for ΔR and 14 for ΔR uncertainty. Dates from land crab remains were calibrated using the Mixed Marine/Northern Hemisphere calibration dataset: 50% marine, -27 for ΔR, and 14 for ΔR uncertainty. We used the ΔR and uncertainty values calculated elsewhere for the same section of the Caribbean (Bright 2011).

scenario in which the two landmasses are actually within sight of each other." However, that scenario contradicts their map of the visibility ranges for this portion of the Caribbean (Torres and Rodríguez Ramos 2008: fig. 1.7). Using the visibility areas depicted by Torres and Rodríguez Ramos, at best a canoe would need to travel approximately 54 km from Trinidad before entering Grenada's visibility range. Without the ability of traveling back to ca. cal 3700 B.C. Trinidad, it is impossible to ascertain with any certainty what the push or pull factors were that prompted the first individuals to venture into the waters beyond their range of interisland visibility and make it to Grenada.

By approximately cal 3600 B.C., Grenada and then a couple of hundred years later many if not all of the remaining islands in the Lesser Antilles up to and including Antigua were being investigated, if not settled by people. Given the high percentages of disturbance indicators in many of the core samples dating to the Archaic, we would suggest that more than brief forays or scouting investigations were taking place. Another option to consider is that some landscapes were being prepared for later use and then people moved on, and that the paucity of Archaic archaeological sites in some cases could be linked to that dynamic. However, a single human-generated conflagration followed by departure of the people without returning would be difficult if not impossible to distinguish from a natural fire because of the spike in microfossil indicators of disturbance without follow-up sustained elevated percentages of those microfossils.

Data from the current project reveal blended strategies of scouting, initial colonization, population infilling, abandonment, and relocations as a continuous process throughout the full range of human history in the Caribbean. As such, we have documented survival strategies seamlessly shifting between modalities of opportunistic foraging, collecting, farming, and hunting. Underlying, or perhaps driving the direction of survival strategies, were the decidedly human and interrelated historical factors of politics, religion, ideology, sociology, demography, and needs of sustenance. All human actions are based on human needs and agendas. From the actions of the first canoe-load of aimless wanderers or directed voyagers (we will never know) to those of larger groups of later settlers to the explicit nation-building efforts of European colonists, the record of human behavior is encoded in the sediments of Caribbean landscapes. The challenge for us has been to painstakingly and judiciously sample the record, maintain the integrity of the sample, and learn how to decipher the clues left from eight millennia of human actions across a diverse range of ecological settings all in the context of natural environmental change during the Holocene.

Island Historical Ecology and Socionatural Landscapes

In her comments on colonization processes and adaptations, Carole Mandryk observed, "People do not travel across a landscape, they interact with it" (Mandryk 2003: xiii). Or, as Balée emphasized, "The landscape is a place of interaction with a temporal dimension that is as historical and cultural as it is evolutionary [and that] ... past events have been inscribed, sometimes subtly, on the land" (Balée 2006: 77). Traditionally, for archaeologists "past events have been inscribed ... on the land" in the form of the archaeological record. However, we are increasingly finding that relying exclusively on the archaeological record may result in a myopic or distorted view when accounting for past events, especially when they are "inscribed subtly on the land."

In many respects, the theoretical foundations of historical ecology are congruent with those of landscape ecology in the biological sciences (Pickett and Cadenasso 1995; Pickett and White 1985; Turner 2005). Just as historical ecologists reacted to the ahistorical aspects of cultural ecology (Balée 2006; Crumley 1994b), so too did landscape ecologists react to the equilibrium models of systems ecology (Turner 2005: 331–335). In their discussion of spatial heterogeneity in ecological systems, Pickett and Cadenasso observed, "[Systems] ecology sought or assumed spatial homogeneity for convenience or simplicity ... and heterogeneity was taken as a necessary evil or an unwanted complication. In contrast, landscape ecology regards spatial heterogeneity as a central causal factor in ecological systems, and it considers spatial dynamics and ecology's founding concern with the *temporal dynamics of systems* to be of equal importance" (Pickett and Cadenasso 1995: 331, emphasis added).

Historical and landscape ecologists take the long view and investigate multiple interrelated factors, resulting in dynamic landscapes. In landscape ecology, a disturbance is defined as "any relatively discrete event in time that disrupts ecosystem, community, or population structure and changes resources, substrate availability, or the physical environment" (White and Pickett 1985: 7). With some modification, this is the sense in which we have been using the term in our investigation of island historical ecology. As archaeologists, ethnobiologists, geographers, and climatologists we are also concerned specifically in distinguishing between natural and human-caused disturbances. For example, fire as a disturbance factor may occur as a relatively discrete event or as an interval of time ranging from decades to hundreds of years. The discrete firing event may be the result of nature, such as a lightning strike. The elevated and continuous presence of fire may be the result of landscape management. Each of these two scenarios will produce alternative signatures in the paleoecological record: (1) discrete fire event equals spike in charcoal concentration value with little to no sustained presence, or (2) longer phase of fire presence equals elevated and sustained charcoal concentration values. However, it is important to consider the context of documented disturbances, including climate conditions (wet vs. dry) and relative percentages of ethnobotanically useful taxa.

In a number of cores we documented disturbance indicators and attendant economically useful plant taxa early in the Archaic followed by the absence or considerably diminished presence of disturbance indicators but continued presence of economically useful taxa. Landscape ecologist Monica Turner remarked, "All landscapes have a history [and] … disturbances can also leave legacies that persist for decades to centuries" (Turner 2005: 321). And, as historical ecologist Balée observed, "Intermediate disturbance may have lasting legacies, of the *longue durée* sort, in terms of redefining vegetation patterns" (Balée 2006: 78).

From the *longue durée* perspective, people in the Caribbean have been interacting with their landscapes for at least eight thousand years, sometimes in ways that leave only subtle traces of actions and in other ways that leave dramatic traces. Over this span we see variable trajectories of landscape engagements, ranging from early relatively intense activities followed by abandonment, to continuous occupations throughout pre-Columbian history to places occupied late in the historical sequence.

To identify these trajectories, our research was explicitly interdisciplinary, engaging the expertise and perspectives of archaeologists, geographers, soil scientists, ethnobotanists and paleoecologists, and climate scientists. In doing so, we are attempting to further our understanding of interrelated domains of island survival, including colonization patterns, modifications of and adjustments to varying landscapes, and the continuum between environmental degradation and sustainability. The successes of these kinds of studies hinge on carefully considered, systematic, and fine-grained data-collecting protocols; close collaboration among disciplinary specialists; and willingness to consider alternative perspectives as research progresses. It is crucial to continue systematic historical-ecological investigations in the Caribbean, especially to fill out topographic and geographic variability, not only in the Lesser Antilles and southern Caribbean but also in the large islands of the Greater Antilles. As the effects of modern climate change, economic development, and globalization continue, it is essential that these kinds of studies be conducted in a timely manner. Otherwise, the settings that contain preserved residues of ancient to not-so-ancient to recent human–land interactions will be gone before we know about them.

15

INSIGHTS FROM THE OUTSIDE

Some Wider Perspectives and Future Directions
in Caribbean Island Historical Ecology

John F. Cherry

In his preface, the editor introduces this chapter as by "a senior scholar" who "brings the perspective of an outsider and insider to the issues and findings" reported in the book. As regards the first characterization, I have no choice but to plead guilty as charged. On the second, though, it may be helpful to frame what follows by providing some context. I was born on a large island (Great Britain), and have had a career-long interest in comparative global island archaeology, with fieldwork experience in settings as varied as the barrier islands of the Gulf of Mexico, the Outer Hebrides, the Orkney Islands, and, especially, for much of the past four decades, in Greece, on several of the Cycladic islands and on Crete. But having followed Caribbean archaeology for many years from afar, I now find myself actually there — on Montserrat in the Lesser Antilles, where, with Dr. Krysta Ryzewski, I codirect a multiperiod survey and excavation project that has now completed numerous periods of fieldwork (Cherry, Ryzewski, Leppard, and Bocancea 2012; Cherry, Ryzewski, Leppard 2013; Opitz et al. 2015; Ryzewski and Cherry 2015). This makes me a reasonably knowledgeable outsider, but also a relatively newly arrived insider. In other ways, though, I am decidedly an outsider. While I have certainly put my back into helping drill pollen cores in both Greece and Italy, I profess no expertise whatsoever in most of the specializations on display in the research described in this book: palynology, palaeoethnobotany, phytolith analysis, malacology, geomorphology, soil science, palaeovolcanology, even what our French colleagues refer to as *anthracologie* (the study of charcoal). My comments, then, are based on no first-hand knowledge of these archaeologically related scientific disciplines. But, if truth be told, that is doubtless true of the majority of the archaeologists who will benefit from this book.

Unfamiliar and highly technical terminology is certainly an issue that readers must face. Hands up, all those who know the difference between Andisols, Oxisols, Ultisols, Aridisols, Vertisols, Entisols, Histosols, and Rendolls (quite aside from identifying them in the field). Are we clear about what the hemic versus sapric classification means, as applied to clays, peats, and even muck (not to be confused with hole slop)? What, precisely, do panicoid shortcells, or chloridoids, or small rugulose spheres tell the phytolith analyst? As one scans across the top of the pollen diagrams, many of the taxa or plant families will likely mean little to the nonspecialist from Europe or North America: in the neotropics, so many plants are strange and new, unfamiliar even when Linnaean taxonomy is glossed with English common names. Of course, the use of precise, technical language, meaningful to professionals in that field, is a sine qua non in scientific reporting. In my own work on lithics, for example, I feel no compunction to explain terms such as a tranchet blow, a *pièce esquillée,* or a right ventral invasive pressure retouch: experts will know what I mean. More important are the interpretative inferences about past human behavior that ultimately rest on such observations in the data. In the case of the present research, the crucial element is the extent to which the patterns emerging from each of several quite different types of data and their analysis agree—or at least broadly converge—on plausible, solidly grounded pictures of changing socionatural landscapes across the eastern Caribbean. That is why the data integration and discussion sections at the end of each of the individual island case studies are the most rewarding and intriguing for the nonspecialist archaeological reader.

Great Opportunities in the Caribbean Islands!

Although this sounds like advertising copy from a realtor or tourist agent, it is actually a section heading in David Burney's influential 1997 article in *Human Ecology:* "Tropical Islands as Paleoecological Laboratories: Gauging the Consequences of Human Arrival" (Burney 1997a). His paper surveyed the role of human versus background-level disturbances in tropical island ecosystems, focusing especially on "the earliest stratigraphic proxy evidence for initial human impacts (including increased charcoal particle influx to sediments, first appearance of exotic pollen, increase in ruderal pollen, and paleolimnological evidence for cultural eutrophication of lake waters)" (Burney 1997a: 437). The article concluded that in general the available data confirm, but sometimes predate, the earliest conventional archaeological evidence for human activity. The case studies surveyed came from his own and others' work on Madagascar and the Hawai'ian islands, but there was at that time little he could say about the Caribbean, despite the great promise he felt the area held for work of this type. The only studies he could cite were a core from Lake Miragoâne, Haiti, that provided the general outlines of Holocene climate change, as inferred from oxygen-isotope studies of ostracods (Hodell et al. 1991) and a sediment core from Laguna Tortuguero on the northern coast of Puerto Rico, in which an abrupt and sustained increase in charcoal values ca. 5300 B.P., suggested that the date of the first human occupation of the island might have been underestimated by as much as two millennia (Burney, Pigott Burney, and MacPhee 1994). But, Burney also noted, "Palynological studies addressing the ecological changes before and after human arrival are unfortunately not available" (Burney 1997a: 446).

What a difference nearly two decades can make! There has been a growing swell of ecologically based studies, mainly in the Greater Antilles, that have tackled issues such as changing shorelines, past climates, "palaeotempestology," the dates of the introduction of exotic and economically valuable plant species, human–plant dynamics in general, human palaeodiet as indicated by stable isotope analysis, and a range of problems to which zooarchaeology, bioarchaeology, starch analysis, stable carbon and nitrogen analysis, global human ecodynamics, and several other approaches besides are making notable contributions (see Keegan, Hofman, and Rodriguéz Ramos 2013). One can readily monitor the growth of interest in, and the impact of, such approaches from the growing numbers of papers on these themes delivered at the biennial congresses of the International Association of Caribbean Archaeologists over the past couple of decades (Siegel 2013). Fitzpatrick and Keegan (2007) offer an invaluable, and still relatively up-to-date, synthetic overview of how archaeological, palaeoecological, historical, and modern biological data can be combined as the basis for a historical ecology approach to the effects of humans on Caribbean island ecosystems.

But now we have the fruits of the collaborative research reported in the preceding chapters of this volume—an enterprise whose ambitious scope takes historical ecology in the eastern Caribbean to a new level. Let's take stock. It has involved programs of palaeoenvironmental coring on no fewer than nine islands in the southern and eastern Caribbean, from Trinidad and Curaçao in the south to St. Croix in the north. In all, a total of twenty-four cores were drilled. The periods they span are anchored by almost fifty ^{14}C dates. Two hundred and ninety samples were examined for plant phytoliths. And so on. In addition, we should not forget the complex and time-consuming logistics of such an operation: scouting for locations likely to yield productive sediments;

seeking permissions; acquiring and transporting bulky equipment to the core sites (sometimes mucky spots); the tedious tasks of splitting the core, minutely describing the color and identifying the composition of its sediments, band-by-band, and extracting samples for ^{14}C dating and for submission to a varied group of expert analysts; and, of course, the countless hours spent with the microscope sorting, identifying, and counting pollen grains, phytoliths, molluscs, particulate charcoal, and so on. With so many samples from so many cores on so many islands, this must have been an exercise in herding cats, and I salute the participants in this research endeavor for bringing it all to a coherent conclusion.

Conference organizers and editors often enlist an outsider discussant for comments on the (hoped for) importance of the research presented. What I have just written, I trust, already indicates the unprecedented scope and significance of this research program; its impact will become apparent as the details are digested and commented on by others. In what follows, I offer some thoughts, from the perspective of a nonexpert outsider–insider (in the sense noted at the outset), on just a few themes, albeit very big ones: fire; volcanoes, risk, and environmental disaster; colonization patterns; extinctions and introductions; and future directions.

Fire

Without question, fire has been a crucial element in the creation of socionatural landscapes throughout the Caribbean archipelago, from the very beginning. A ground-base in the interpretation of the various cores reported in this volume is the moment at which the presence of particulate charcoal first spikes, or begins to appear at sustained, significantly elevated levels. In most cases, this has been read as a reliable signature of first human presence on the island in question. That may very well be so, but let's take a step back and consider some wider context.

Fire is dangerous and hard to control: I wrote this on the day in 2013 that nineteen experienced firefighters died together battling a huge forest fire in Arizona. But it has many benefits for humans, including heat, light, the enlargement of the day, a measure of protection from predators, the varied uses of pyrotechnology to create new materials, the modification of landscapes and their plant and animal communities, and, most importantly, the ability to transform foods through cooking in ways that provide higher caloric returns and lower energetic costs of digestion—a development that has been regarded as critical to evolutionary success by writers from Charles Darwin to Richard Wrangham (2010). Humans are the only living species to control fire. So detecting fire use in the archaeological and palaeoanthropological record is an important and fascinating problem.

But distinguishing anthropogenic from natural fires is extremely tricky (Alperson-Afil 2012). To be sure, our knowledge of the prehistory of fire has advanced enormously in recent decades, as is clear from comparing earlier studies such as Catherine Perlès's book *Préhistoire du feu* (1977) with recent evaluations. The overall picture is relatively clear. There are no contexts from the Pliocene (> 2.5 million years ago [Ma]) that preserve evidence for anthropogenic fire; by contrast, fire-use is ubiquitous at sites associated with *Homo sapiens*. In between, things are less clear. In Europe, habitual fire-use is well documented in the Middle Pleistocene after ca. 0.3–0.4 Ma (Roebroeks and Villa 2011), although it is hard to conceive of how the hominins present there from ca. 1.2 Ma could have survived without the use of fire in cold European habitats, even if we currently have no solid evidence for it. In the Early Pleistocene, anthropogenic fire seems to be well documented at Gesher Benot Ya'aqov in Israel at ca. 0.8 Ma (Alperson-Afil and Goren-Inbar 2010; Goren-Inbar et al. 2004) and perhaps at Wonderwerk Cave in South Africa at ca. 1.0 Ma (Berna et al. 2012). Earlier claims—for example at Chesowanja and Koobi Fora (Kenya) and Swartkrans (South Africa), all between 1.4 and 1.6 Ma—are mired in controversy, however.

Clearly, the first humans to arrive in the Caribbean archipelago had knowledge of using and controlling fire. But what we don't know is how, why, and to what extent they used fire beyond the immediate needs of cooking, heat, and light within domestic settlements. The global evidence just mentioned all relates to excavated archaeological sites, while that reported in this volume comes from coring out in the landscape—sometimes, to be sure, in the vicinity of known archaeological sites, in the hope that activities there would reveal themselves in the various signatures of the cores. Among these cores, those on Trinidad, Grenada, Curaçao, Marie-Galante, Martinique, Antigua, and St. Croix have all revealed up-ticks in the rate of influx of particulate charcoal associated with ^{14}C dates that, in Caribbean archaeological terms, are Archaic. If the wider landscape is revealing fire-use signatures at this early stage, then we must ask ourselves what kinds of activities this reflects. Earlier understandings of the Caribbean Archaic portrayed its inhabitants as living in small, mobile bands, without ceramics or agriculture, and a stone and shell technology. But mounting evidence (mainly, but not only, from the Greater Antilles) now suggests that fisher-forager Archaic populations sometimes produced pottery, intensively exploited different suites of locally available foods (moving seasonally to utilize certain resource concentrations), managed a range of subsistence plants, apparently even introducing some species not indigenous to the Caribbean (sapodilla, yellow sapote, and wild avocado), and—to judge from the evidence of fossil birds and other animal remains—contributed to the degradation of island ecologies well before the arrival of Saladoid peoples (Fitzpatrick and Keegan 2007: 34; Pagán-Jiménez 2013; Rodríguez Ramos, Pagán-Jiménez, and Hofman 2013). How would fire-induced modifications of the landscape fit into such a picture, and how could we know that they were deliberate?

I am pessimistic about quick and easy answers to such questions in the Caribbean, because it has proved so difficult to answer them in other regions. Australia provides a telling example. More than forty years ago, Rhys Jones (1969; cf. Bliege Bird et al. 2008) proposed his "firestick farming" hypothesis, which suggests that indigenous Australians regularly used fire to burn vegetation in order to facilitate hunting and to change the composition of plant and animal communities in an area. Expectable effects would be to turn dry rainforest into savanna, and increase populations of grass-eating species such as kangaroos, while at the same time perhaps playing some role in the extinction of the Australian megafauna. Not so fast, claims a recent paper (Mooney et al. 2011) that provides sedimentary charcoal records from 223 locations in Australasia dating back 70,000 years, and that asserts that the arrival of the first inhabitants ca. 50 ± 10 ka did not result in a distinct change in fire regimes across the continent, concluding that fire in Australasia predominantly reflects climate. (Not surprisingly, fire activity accelerated dramatically with the arrival of European colonists after 1788.) These questions have been playing out in particularly interesting ways with respect to the evidence from Tasmania (e.g., Bowman and Brown 1986; Horton 1982) and New South Wales (Black and Mooney 2006). Another salutary comparative study is that of Haberle and Ledru (2001), which uses microscopic charcoal from sediments at ten sites in Indonesia and Papua New Guinea and five in Panama, Brazil, and Ecuador to reconstruct very long-term fire histories. It concludes that fire is promoted during periods of rapid climate change and high climate variability, irrespective of whether humans are present. This type of comparison of charcoal records from regions with utterly different human histories "provides one of the most reliable means available of decoupling climate influences from human influences in the fossil record" (Haberle and Ledru 2001: 99).

The fire-signatures in the various cores reported in this volume may indeed provide solid and unexpected proxy evidence for the presence of humans on certain eastern Caribbean islands well before the horizons attested from the earliest known archaeological sites. But, if so, for what purposes were landscapes being modified by anthropogenic fires? Given the biotically depauperate condition of the Caribbean as a whole in terms of mammalian and other fauna, it is hard to imagine a fire regime aimed expressly at modifying these resources. Equally, considering the modestly sized, and probably also mobile or seasonal, Archaic populations of the Lesser Antilles, is it reasonable to envision wide-scale forest clearance for horticultural purposes? As the fascinating discussion here of the Grenada data suggests, anthropogenic forest modification was probably more subtle and complex, and it is certainly difficult to disentangle the interplay of multiple factors. For example, the permanent disappearance of pollen of the unidentified palms type G and H in the mid-third millennium B.C., coincident with evidence of major burning, could implicate clearance by fire, but it could also be a result of overexploitation by humans, or even overharvesting of the rodents that likely served as the palms' main propagation vector. Or again, it could be that salinization resulting from rising sea levels played a role. Likewise, an apparent increase in pollen from various fruit-bearing trees at just this time might be a function of the removal (perhaps by fire) of undesirable taxa, but could equally well reflect deliberate planting or even cultivation. We just don't know. There are many unresolved issues here requiring further study, and conclusions based on current data should be treated with some caution.

These sorts of quandaries have been playing out in the Pacific somewhat earlier than in the history of scholarship in the Caribbean. For example, Kirch and Ellison (1994) proposed human settlement, based on evidence from sediment cores, on Mangaia in East Polynesia much earlier than anything visible archaeologically, but there still exist no sites or acceptable ^{14}C dates prior to about A.D. 1000 or so. Similar kinds of claims have been made for Palau and the Marianas (e.g., Athens, Dega, and Ward 2008), yet this tantalizing evidence is some one thousand or two thousand years prior to the earliest known archaeological sites. Hunter-Anderson (2009) has argued that these same data can be reinterpreted as a natural outcome of geoclimatic conditions. Such arguments from another island theater should be taken on board as a cautionary tale as we consider these new data from the Caribbean.

At the other end of the chronological spectrum comes the clear-felling of the neotropical forest, on an unimaginable scale and almost everywhere, as the European plantation system took hold from the early seventeenth century. Of course, humans have dramatically modified the landscapes they have inhabited and exploited all over the world, but the speed with which the entire Caribbean was utterly transformed by fire is staggering. It is hard to think of parallels for it, except for the ongoing devastation of the Amazon through uncontrolled and generally illegal logging and grazing. On Montserrat, for example, sugar cultivation and the importation of the first enslaved Africans began in the 1650s. Yet already by 1673, when the famous Blathwayt Atlas map of Montserrat was compiled (a drawing of all sides of the island as seen from various points out at sea), it is apparent that fire-cleared cane fields had supplanted the native vegetation virtually to the top of every hill (Pulsipher 1986). The traces of this environmental disaster, not surprisingly, are clear to see in the cores drilled for this project—although one hardly needs to go to the time and expense of coring to confirm the date and severity of a process that is already known in abundant detail from a very wide variety of historical documentation. What is much less well studied and understood are the long-term impacts of the implantation of an entirely novel form of socionatural landscape: not just the deleterious consequences of farming an industrial monocrop and introducing species such as the cane toad and mongoose, but the extent of local extinctions of plants and animals, and the subtler effects of the creation of ecological patchiness on the numbers and viability of those that have survived.

Fire has played a critical role in the social, as well as ecological, history of the Lesser Antilles, as Bonham Richardson set out in his wonderful book *Igniting the Caribbean's Past* (2004): arson in the cane fields as acts of protest; the terror induced by the night-time *cannes brulées* processions before Lent in Trinidad and the Windwards; dreadful conflagrations, such as that which consumed much of Port of Spain in 1895. In an act of vivid historical imagination, Richardson reminds us that the scramble for new cane land involved the felling, chopping, and ring-barking of trees year-round, and—even if burning occurred mainly in the drier months—the smoke from charred logs and smoldering stumps likely resulted in lingering hazy conditions throughout the year. Thus, as he writes (Richardson 2004: 28), "Among the first sensations that some African slaves had of the Caribbean region, as they stumbled from the holds of slave vessels, were sights of smoky skies and smells from local clearing fires, initial sensual impressions that were in many ways accurate precursors of what the inferno of Caribbean slavery would be like."

Volcanoes, Risk, and Environmental Disaster

To read the *Volcanic Hazard Atlas of the Lesser Antilles* (Lindsay et al. 2005) is a sobering experience. The arcuate linear arrangement of the islands of the Lesser Antilles of course marks the outer edge of the

Caribbean Plate, where subduction of the oceanic crust of the South American Plate is taking place. All of them are the product of this plate tectonism, although only the western string of islands comprised volcanic rocks. It is a geologically tortured zone. In the Volcanic Caribbees there are twenty-one live volcanoes (i.e., active or recently active volcanoes that pose a threat and require monitoring) on eleven different islands—Grenada, St. Vincent, St. Lucia, Martinique, Dominica (which has nine), Guadeloupe, Montserrat, Nevis, St. Kitts, St. Eustatius, and Saba, with two additional underwater volcanoes (Kick 'Em Jenny and Île de Caille) north of Grenada.

We know a good deal about the eruptive histories of these volcanoes. Two are currently very active (Soufrière Hills on Montserrat, and Kick 'Em Jenny), while others have erupted violently in modern times, including the Soufrière of St. Vincent (1718, 1812, 1902, 1979) and Mount Pelée on Martinique (May 8, 1902), the worst volcanic disaster of the twentieth century. In fact, at least thirty-four eruptions have occurred since European settlement in the Lesser Antilles, twenty-one of them since 1900 (Lindsay et al. 2005: xiv). The current volcanic disaster on Montserrat comes as no real surprise, given geological evidence indicating that the Soufrière Hills volcano has been intermittently active throughout the past four thousand years, including during the Saladoid and early historic periods (Roobol and Smith 1998). The same is true on several other islands: from Basse-Terre on Guadeloupe there are eighty-eight ^{14}C dates on Quaternary pyroclastic deposits ranging from ca. 40,000 to 280 years ago; St. Kitts has provided fourteen ^{14}C dates for volcanic rocks dating from 4270±140 B.P. to 1620±50 B.P.; recent eruptive history at the Soufrière volcano on St. Vincent is charted by eighty-two ^{14}C dates reaching from the radiocarbon present back to 5140±55 B.P. (Lindsay et al. 2005: 79–80, 207, 249–250).

In short, there is abundant evidence of frequent volcanic activity spanning the entire period of human occupation of these islands. Geological and archaeological investigations have from time to time discovered evidence of the inevitable intersection of human settlement and volcanism. On Saba, for example, a pit dug in The Bottom found a dense andesite surge deposit containing accretionary lapilli, ^{14}C-dated to 280±80 B.P. This was below laharic mudflow deposits containing European ceramics, and above two Amerindian occupation levels, the more recent dated to 525±66 B.P. (Roobol and Smith 2004). In a separate location not far away, several conch tools (possibly from a burial) were found inserted in a young pyroclastic deposit, one of them with a radiocarbon date of 3155±65 B.P. (Roobol and Smith 1980: 168–169). On St. Kitts these same scholars (1980: 170–171) and Armstrong (1980) were able to correlate a well-dated sequence of eruptions of Mount Misery with the sequence at the Sugar Factory Pier site, with Archaic middens dated to 2,175±60 and 4,100±60 B.P. lying beneath a soil developed in the top of a tephra layer dated to 1750±90 B.P. and containing Saladoid material. The past five thousand years of volcanic activity at Mount Pelée on Martinique are now well studied (Westercamp and Traineau 1983), and the significance of tephra layers found in the stratigraphy of the Cedrosan Saladoid sites of Vivé and Fond Brûlé on the island has been explored in detail by Allaire (1989) and others.

Against this backdrop, it is hardly surprising that some of the cores drilled for this project encountered lenses or other indications of volcanic ash. The majority of the mineral fraction of Barbadian terrace soils, we are told, is derived from windblown volcanic ash from St. Vincent. On Martinique a prominent volcanic ash lens, with an uncalibrated ^{14}C date of 1730±30 B.P. just above it, is interpreted as corresponding to the significant Plinian eruption at Mount Pelée dated to A.D. 280±60. In another core (KC08-1), pollen and phytoliths both indicate significant changes in the local environment, immediately above an ash lens dated to 1710±30 B.P., and possibly associated with the same event (although it is unclear from which volcanic source this ash lens is derived). On Marie-Galante predominantly smectite clays probably derive from ash deposited from neighboring islands, and prominent ash layers in the cores are most likely attributable to eruptions of La Soufrière on Guadeloupe, which was hyperactive between ca. 3000 and 1500 B.P. The Antiguan cores have relatively thick ash bands, most plausibly associated with the 1797–1798 eruptions of the same volcano, supported by a nearly overlapping ^{14}C date of 190±40 B.P. (1721–1797 A.D.); significant ash clouds from the 1836–1837 eruption may also be marked in these cores. Finally, an ash lens in the Barbuda core may, with some uncertainty, be sourced to the pyroclastic eruptions of the Liamuiga volcano on St. Kitts between 1800 and 2000 B.P. In several cases, these correlations are approximate: the distribution patterns of settling aeolian sediments, such as ash, are extremely variable over short distances, and may also display time-lags.

Two inferences are clear from these data. One is that the impact of eruptive events is not limited to a single island. Indeed, in the current crisis on Montserrat, complaints are common from the neighboring islands of Antigua, Nevis, and Guadeloupe (and even as far afield as St. Croix) about the inconvenience of ash blowing in from Montserrat. The list of phenomena associated with Lesser Antillean volcanism is a terrifying litany: ashfalls, ballistic projectiles, debris avalanches, earthquakes and seismic tremors, laharic mudflows, lateral blasts, unstable lava dome formations, lava flows, lightning strikes (probably a major cause of natural fires), pyroclastic flows and surges, tsunamis, and deadly hot volcanic gases (Lindsay et al. 2005: xvii–xviii). Most of these have relatively local impacts around the eruptive source, but aerial ashfalls can have far wider effects—not only on entire landscapes for many kilometers around a volcano, but also reaching neighboring islands. They can collapse buildings, destroy vegetation, create serious respiratory problems for humans and livestock, and cause other problems that may persist long after the eruption itself has ended. A second conclusion, obviously, is that these terrifying types of events happened regularly, on multiple islands, throughout the recent history of human settlement in the Lesser Antilles. We should not underestimate the physical devastation of the landscape and the potentially devastating impacts on the humans who occupied it, but we should also consider the psychological repercussions of such tremendous forces, ones that early islanders doubtless perceived as supernatural (Blong 1987).

There are great opportunities for further work here, and it is surprising that relatively little has been done. While the Holocene and later Pleistocene eruptive histories of many of the Lesser Antillean volcanoes are now reasonably well known, there exists far less information about the scale and extent of individual events. These produce volcanic products (tephra, pumice, aeolian deposits, etc.) with distinctive, identifiable, geochemical signatures; with care, these can be anchored via radiocarbon dating in stratigraphic sequences, wherever these may be available (in natural exposures, excavation trenches, or drilling cores, including deep-sea). With sufficient samples, it is possible to produce isopach maps that chart the distribution over the landscape and the varying depths of volcanic debris produced by specific, dated eruptions. A good example is Westercamp and Traineau's (1983) mapping of the second and third Plinian eruptions of Mount Pelée on Martinique. The former, in the opinion of Allaire (1989: 154), was of a magnitude sufficient to have caused the entire northern half of the island to have become uninhabitable and abandoned, as indicated by a cultural hiatus after ca. A.D. 350.

This type of tephrochronological research, and more generally the collaboration of archaeologists and volcanologists, has paid huge dividends in a number of other parts of the world. Space does not allow me to provide even brief summaries, but I would draw attention especially to the following as models. In Central America, Payson Sheets (1983, 2006) explored the Cerén site in El Salvador, deeply encased in volcanic ash ca. A.D. 600, and later (Sheets and McKee 1994) worked at Arenal in Costa Rica, using a variety of remote sensing technologies to explore an entirely ash-buried archaeological landscape in a jungle environment. Recent work in the volcanic landscapes of Iceland has been notably productive, especially in relating detailed tephrochronological mapping to the Norse settlement of the island, environmental change, glacier fluctuations, erosion, deforestation, farmstead abandonment, and so on (Dugmore et al. 2000; Dugmore et al. 2007). On the other side of the globe, Robin Torrence and colleagues have made notable progress in exploring the contributions of volcanism to landscape histories in the Willaumez Peninsula on New Britain in Papua New Guinea, showing how fine-grained stratigraphic analysis and dating over the past several thousand years can assist in understanding how human groups have developed strategies to cope with the demands of repeated refuging and recolonization (Parr et al. 2009; Torrence, Neall, and Boyd 2009; Torrence et al. 2000). The mother of all such studies, of course, is the Bronze Age eruption of Santorini in the Aegean, where decades of research have produced a finely detailed ashfall isopach map of the eruption and detailed stratigraphic correlations of this event in excavated stratigraphic sequences throughout the eastern Mediterranean. As yet, however, there has been no decisive agreement among scholars on the absolute date of the eruption, which is a lynchpin for the tie between Egyptian absolute chronologies and those of the eastern Mediterranean and the Aegean (Warburton 2009). Several recent books have explored such issues at a general scale (e.g., Balmuth et al. 2005; Bawden and Reycraft 2000; Cooper and Sheets 2012; Grattan and Torrence 2007; Sheets and Grayson 1979; Torrence and Grattan 2002). Caribbean archaeologists would do well to pay closer attention to such work elsewhere.

Here is one final thought, about the perception of volcanic risk. I happened to be engaged in fieldwork on Montserrat, amid heavy ashfalls, only days before the catastrophic event of February 11, 2010, in which the Soufrière Hills lava dome collapsed, producing dramatic pyroclastic flows that prograded the shoreline on the east of the island by ca. 0.5 km and dealt the final death-blow to the important Early Ceramic site of Trants (Cherry, Ryzewski, and Leppard 2012: fig. 3). This led me to wonder how prehistoric populations on the island had prepared for or responded to such threats, and whether there might exist some signature of volcanic risk awareness in the archaeological record. I now think that is unlikely. A fascinating recent paper (Lalubie 2011) examined Père Breton's famous 1665 *Dictionnaire caraïbe-français* for those lexical items used to describe the environment, and the hazards it poses. Breton listed many Kalinago words having to do with finely graded perceptions of natural risk: different types and strengths of storms, hurricanes, floods, sea-swells, earthquakes, landslides, and so on—but nothing specifically about volcanic activity. This makes sense. Direct hits by hurricanes or severe tropical storms are not predictable, but everyone in the Caribbean, past and present, knows they can be expected quite frequently. One can take steps to mitigate risk, for example by choice of settlement location, or, as Samson's (2010) research in the Dominican Republic has suggested, by developing distinctive types of domestic architecture that constitute a logical response in terms of resilience to such threats. Volcanic disasters, on the other hand, are much less frequent, largely unpredictable, and generally occur at intervals that exceed the limits of intergenerational memory. That volcanic dome on the skyline may be rumbling, venting sulphurous steam, and making the ground shake, but such warning signals have in general, throughout human history, not sufficed to deter settlement in the very path of extreme danger. The victims of Vesuvius, buried at Pompeii and Herculaneum, are testimony to that.

Colonization Patterns

The results of this program of environmental coring provide many fascinating insights on a wide range of issues that are important for a better understanding of human occupational history across the southern Caribbean and Lesser Antilles: colonization processes, the development of anthropogenic landscapes, the introduction and extinction of plant species, the impacts of fire and volcanism, and so on. These have been ably synthesized in chapter 14. One outcome, however, deserves repeated emphasis. This is the clear evidence—from increased and sustained influxes of particulate charcoal, greater representation of economically useful plant taxa (tab. 14.1), indications of environmental disturbance seen in the pollen and phytolith counts (tab. 14.2), elevated phosphate values in sediments, etc.—of human modifications to the landscapes of several islands, associated with clearly Archaic ^{14}C dates (tabs. 14.3, 14.4). In some cases (Trinidad, Antigua; see chap. 3, this volume), this represents welcome proxy confirmation of what we knew already from well-dated deposits at archaeological sites. In others, however, these environmental data index a human presence earlier—sometimes substantially earlier—than the periods of the first known archaeological sites. In fact, eight of the twenty earliest dates associated with either archaeological deposits or sediments in the southern Caribbean and Lesser Antilles now come from the work of this project.

Is this important result a surprise? It should certainly force a rethink of the dates, extent, and patterns of earliest island colonization in this region. Finding and understanding the Archaic period in the eastern Caribbean has been a decades-long struggle, but perhaps the battle is beginning to be won. In fact, the list of islands in the northern Lesser Antilles with Archaic sites has become quite long: aside from the unusual situation on Antigua (with Jolly Beach and more than forty other locations), it includes Anguilla (Whitehead's Bluff), Barbuda (the River site), Guadeloupe (Pointe des Pies), Montserrat (Upper Blake's), Nevis (Hichman's Shell Heap, Nisbett), Saba (Plum Piece), St. Eustatius (Corre Corre Bay), St. Kitts (Sugar Factory Pier, and perhaps Ballast Bay and Great Salt Pond), St. Martin (Norman Estate, Etang Rouge, Baie Orientale), and St. Thomas (Krum Bay). Even so, it is notable that few islands have more than one known site, and furthermore that a number of these sites date to what Hofman and Hoogland (in chap. 3, this volume) term the Late Archaic, after 800 B.C., thus partially overlapping with ^{14}C dates from some Early Ceramic sites. Meanwhile, in the southern Lesser Antilles, Archaic sites are far rarer: Heywoods on Barbados is now firmly dated at 3980±100 B.P. (Drewett 2006), but claimed examples on Martinique and Tobago are less certain.

This picture provides too few data points to allow firm conclusions about colonization paths. Did Archaic settlers originating in South America skip quickly over the more southerly islands, before establishing more regular settlements on islands farther north (Callaghan 2010)? Did Archaic peoples who were already firmly established in the Greater Antilles spread south, in a movement that petered out in the Windwards? Or are such questions moot, because the data are so skewed and incomplete?

The obstacles in the path of locating Archaic sites have often been noted. Recall that the traces of anthropogenic landscape modifications of Archaic Age recovered by environmental coring are generally 2 or 3 m deep and, by extension, archaeological sites may be equally deeply buried. In some cases volcanic debris, ashfall, or sediments may be the cause (which is why more-precise isopach maps are urgently needed). More often, the culprit is likely to be the thick erosional deposits created by the massive clear-felling of neotropical jungle for the sugar plantations of the colonial era. Changes in postglacial relative sea level are also a likely factor, with the potential for large-scale coastal inundation and salinization as a result of the rise of mean levels from −4 m at 5000 cal B.P. and −8 m at 7000 cal B.P. This may certainly have resulted in the loss of palaeocoastal pre-Columbian sites, although—given the present state of knowledge—it can be only a guess that Archaic settlement patterns were as strongly focused on the coast as they seem to have been in Saladoid and later times; Hofman and Hoogland's notion (chap. 3, this volume) of yearly mobility cycles in pursuit of resources in different locations implies settlements, or at least activity areas, that are *not* on the shore—as seems to be borne out by Plum Piece and Upper Blake's, both of which are well inland and at considerable elevation. I return briefly below to what could be done in the face of such site-finding challenges.

What strikes an outsider such as myself is the fact that, even after a century of field investigations, the pattern, process, and strategy of Caribbean island colonization are hotly debated topics still actively under investigation, and very far from resolution. This applies not only to the Archaic, but also equally to the first major expansion of pottery-making horticulturalists in the Early Ceramic period from the mid-first millennium B.C. It is agreed that they migrated from the Orinoco region of South America, but a seemingly logical stepping-stone progression northward through the Lesser Antilles (as has often been proposed) is in fact undermined by the fact that sites with early ^{14}C dates occur in the north, in the Leeward Islands and Puerto Rico, rather than south of the Guadeloupe Passage. A variant proposal ("the southward route hypothesis" [Fitzpatrick 2013]), suggesting that the Caribbean islands were settled in the north first, by a more direct route from South America, with subsequent southward migration and settlement through the islands, is attractive, but as yet is far from being widely accepted (as already discussed in chap. 14, this volume).

These continuing uncertainties stand in contrast to the situation in most other island archipelagoes, both small (e.g., the Kuril, Ryuku, or Californian Channel Islands) and large (the Pacific and Mediterranean). In the Pacific, there has been an explosion over the past thirty years of new archaeological, linguistic, and bioanthropological data that have largely resolved previously obdurate questions about when and how people entered the Pacific and eventually managed to discover and settle on virtually all of its thousands of islands (see, most recently, Kirch 2010a). This is not to say that all problems are solved and no matters are still in dispute. But this part of the world enjoys the unique advantage of affording data on the biology (via population genetics and molecular biology) and languages (via comparative linguistics, now enhanced by cladistic procedures) of the descendants of the original colonizing populations, which provide cross-checks against the archaeological evidence, now available in vastly greater quantity over an area encompassing millions of square miles. The possibilities for similar work in the Caribbean are inevitably far more limited, especially where premodern languages are concerned. And while there is newly developing research on mitochondrial haplogroup lineages as a means of exploring modern population relationships that may reflect historic and prehistoric patterns in the peopling of the islands (e.g., Vilar et al. 2013), it is controversial and has quickly become politicized.

One has to admire the rather grand certainties of the Pacific colonization story, as we now know it (cf. Leppard, chap. 2): the crossing of Wallacea into the super-continent of Sahul (New Guinea–Australia–Tasmania) in the later Pleistocene, as documented by more than 150 sites, the earliest at Huon in northern New Guinea some 60–40 ky B.P.; expansion into Near Oceania on the large islands of New Britain and New Ireland in the Bismarck Archipelago by ca. 35 ky B.P. and the northern Solomons by ca. 28 ky B.P.; and thirty subsequent millennia in which high degrees of linguistic and biological diversity evolved, followed by an Austronesian incursion from island Southeast Asia around 4000–3500 B.P., setting up the Lapita expansion into the southwestern archipelagoes of Remote Oceania between ca. 3200 and 2900 B.P.; and then, after the settlement of Micronesia, the final push into Eastern Polynesia, including the remotest corners of the Polynesian triangle (Hawai'i no earlier than A.D. 800, Rapa Nui ca. A.D. 800–1000, and New Zealand around A.D. 1250–1300). Considering the need to transport domestic animals and crop plants, as well as the formidable gaps of open ocean to be crossed in outrigger canoes, this is among the greatest achievements of human exploration, one that makes the Caribbean experience (whatever its details may turn out to be) seem puny by comparison.

In the Mediterranean—a far smaller, inland sea whose islands were, almost by definition, settled from adjacent mainlands or along short, insular stepping-stone routes—the general picture is clear, to some extent conforms to biogeographical predictions, and has not changed very much between the earliest attempts to bring order to the data (Cherry 1981, 1984, 1990) and current syntheses (Phoca-Cosmetatou 2011). Although ^{14}C dates remain scarcer than they should be, it is clear that most islands were settled by farming communities in the Neolithic or Early Bronze Age. Within some regions, such as the Cycladic islands, colonization paths can be reconstructed with some precision (Broodbank 2000). After years of searching (somewhat akin to the missing Archaic of the Caribbean, see more below), solid evidence is now coming to light for a maritime Mesolithic or even Late Epipalaeolithic on Cyprus, Crete, and several Aegean islands, reaching back in some cases as early as the eleventh millennium cal B.C. (Knapp 2013: 48–74). The data for earlier visitation or settlement on Mediterranean islands are sparse and often disputed; some modern islands with Middle Palaeolithic finds were reachable dry-shod at times of lowered sea-level, or across trivial water gaps. One has to agree with Broodbank's assessment (2006) that there exists only very limited evidence at present for any kind of maritime activity in the Mediterranean before the end of the Pleistocene (although he was writing before the recent controversial announcement of the discovery of crude quartz tools of Lower Palaeolithic types in the Plakias area of southern Crete: Strasser et al. 2010). The possible colonization of Mediterranean islands by premodern hominins is, in fact, a problem on which historical ecology might help shed light: for instance, studies of the impact of apex predators on island ecologies following colonization could be of use in modeling the palaeoenvironmental signatures of hominin arrivals on islands (Leppard 2014a).

Extinctions and Introductions

This brings me to a final area of Caribbean–Mediterranean contrast worth noting. One cannot help but be impressed by the sheer range of plants and trees picked up in the palynological and phytolith evidence from this project's cores, including especially the ruderal and economically useful species that help point to anthropogenic landscape impacts at different stages of Caribbean island settlement. In these environments, it seems, such evidence preserves well. Such finds, alongside those from previous and ongoing palaeoecological projects elsewhere in the Caribbean, serve as a vital complement to the already superbly rich store of palaeoethnobotanical information provided by plant macrofossils from excavated archaeological sites (for a comprehensive listing, see Newsom and Wing 2004: tabs. 7.7–7.8). This must be accounted one of the great triumphs of Caribbean archaeology. While chronological resolution is generally rather coarse (Archaic–Early Ceramic–Late Ceramic–colonial), we have an immensely detailed regional picture of which plants and trees were exploited and which were extirpated (at least locally, although human agency is often difficult to demonstrate) at different stages of the past. It also includes evidence for those species that have been introduced into local island ecologies through human intervention: aside from the three species noted earlier as Archaic arrivals, they are found in Ceramic Age sites, and include manioc, maize, annatto, Panama tree, papaya, tobacco, Cojoba, pepper, peanut, and (probably) sweet potato (Fitzpatrick and Keegan 2007: tab. 1).

The islands of the Mediterranean fare poorly in comparison, and the evidence is much sparser. In part, this may be because they have always seemed peripheral to the big story, namely, the process of plant domestication in Southwest Asia and the mechanisms of northwestward spread throughout Europe. New species were certainly brought to the islands by the first agricultural colonists, but the story of domestication had already taken place, far away. Routine flotation for macrobotanical remains, in any case, is largely a development of the past generation. Coring for pollen and other palaeoenvironmental evidence has been quite rare; a colleague who works in the West Mediterranean islands could not point me in the direction of any such work. This is not so much because of lack of interest or expertise, but because finding suitable locations is very difficult in these semiarid environments, has taken years to develop, and faces severe challenges of preservation. Even on so large and environmentally diverse an island as Crete, the number of cores can be counted on the fingers of both hands and, while some of them have been successful in charting Holocene environmental changes and human impacts (e.g., Bottema and Sarpaki 2003), others have been a disappointment, because they were largely devoid of pollen for important segments of the sequence (e.g., Bottema 1980). The more-promising environments for this type of research are, in fact, not the islands, but rather the littoral fringes of the surrounding Mediterranean mainlands, especially areas such as southern France (Leveau et al. 1999: 9–24).

But if we focus on animals rather than plants, this archipelagic comparison operates in the other direction. In the Mediterranean, once again, the macrolevel picture of the domestication and spread of animals from Southwest Asia into Mediterranean Europe is now quite well understood, anchored by a huge number of ^{14}C dates and, increasingly, by genetically based studies (Colledge et al. 2013). On the islands, however, the introduction of these fauna directly or indirectly impacted a wide range of endemic Pleistocene fauna—many of them gigantized or nanized, and all of them now extinct—and these have been intensively studied in cave and rockshelter contexts throughout the insular Mediterranean by palaeontologists and archaeologists (e.g., for Crete [Reese 1996]). Thus a significant research area, as in a number of other parts of the world, concerns the possible role of human colonizers of island environments in the extinction of these fauna, whether pygmy hippopotami on Cyprus (Simmons 1999) or *Myotragus* in the Balearics (Alcover 2008). On some islands the picture is a dramatic one: the endemic mammalian fauna of Corsica, for example, has been *entirely* wiped out and replaced by anthropogenically introduced species over the past several thousand years (Vigne 1988; cf. Cherry 1990: 194–197).

In the Caribbean, the picture is quite different. We should acknowledge immediately the excellent research on shells, fish, and terrestrial invertebrates that has taken place at a multitude of sites throughout the islands. Newsom and Wing (2004: 194–200) provide an invaluable summary of the data, especially at sites with long sequences, emphasizing the significant decline over time (especially in the post-Saladoid periods) in the sizes of reef fishes, a shift in the estimated biomass of reef versus pelagic fishes, the decline in quantities and size of land crabs, and so on (cf. also Carlson and Keegan 2004). But so far as mammalian fauna are concerned, the picture is less well researched. Endemic species were few and small-bodied; definite introductions, all in the Ceramic Age, seem confined to dog, opossum, agouti, guinea pig, shrew, and *hutía,* but other native species (such as the cony *Geocapromys* and other large rodents) may also have been kept in captivity and moved from island to island. All these species have known origins, with limited (mainly South American), native ranges, and in this sense constitute translocated exotic species whose movements could provide an excellent proxy record for the dispersal, movements, and interactions of human populations (Giovas et al. 2011), but research in this vein is still in its infancy. Even more surprising is how little we yet know about the endemic Pleistocene fauna of the Caribbean, and humans' impact on it. Of course, the native fauna were far less varied than those in the Mediterranean, and those small-bodied taxa that were introduced (at least prior to European intervention) may have had minimal effects on endemic island biotas, because they were effectively managed in captivity. Still, we have very little information, except for a few studies (Steadman et al. 2005; Steadman, Pregill, and Olson 1984; Turvey et al. 2007), about animal extinctions in the prehistoric Caribbean, and humans' possible role, directly or indirectly, in them. Clear examples, such as the intermingling of cultural remains and the fossils of now-extinct Late Holocene vertebrates, as found at the Burma Quarry close to the end of the airport runway on Antigua (Pregill et al. 1988), are vanishingly rare.

What this rather crude comparison between the Caribbean and the Mediterranean suggests, I think, is that much depends on the types of evidence that have survived for our examination, but equally on research traditions and the questions on which archaeologists have chosen to focus their efforts.

Future Directions

The editor asked me for thoughts on future directions, which, not being a historical ecologist, I am hesitant to do. Nonetheless, the richness and novelty of the results from the current research endeavor lead to the obvious suggestion: Keep up the good work! (Or, as the team itself puts it in chap. 14, this volume, "It is crucial to continue systematic historical-ecological investigations in the Caribbean.") It would be difficult to replicate the sheer scope of the work reported in this volume, but that is probably not necessary to do: it has laid an admirable foundation for future research that might most profitably now focus in greater detail on individual islands (perhaps in additional kinds of local topographic settings, where other types of sediment accumulation processes might yield different sorts of data), and of course, also, in order to increase coverage and geographic variability, on islands for which little or no palaeoenvironmental record yet exists.

The focus of this book has been on the southern Caribbean and Lesser Antilles, naturally enough, since that was the location of the fieldwork reported here. The next step is to widen the framework and integrate these new data more fully with results from comparable past and ongoing work in the Greater Antilles, where there exist studies of considerable sophistication. Selecting just a few examples at random, I would point to recent work on environment-culture correlations in Puerto Rico (Siegel et al. 2005), on the past four thousand years of fire and forest history in the Dominican Republic (Kennedy, Horn, and Orvis 2006), on sea-level change and pre-Columbian landscapes in Cuba (Cooper and Boothroyd 2011), and ongoing palaeoecological and geoarchaeological investigations in the Río Grande de Manatí region of the central-north coast of Puerto Rico (Rivera-Collazo 2011). Certainly, there is a continued need for multidisciplinary engagement of the kind that has made the research reported in this book so successful, but we also need engagement with other research groups pursuing similar goals within the wider region in order to build toward ever-more-comprehensive syntheses. For example, active research is ongoing on Barbuda (recently expanded to Antigua), under the auspices of the Barbuda Historical Ecology Project, the Islands of Change Project, and the Global Human Ecodynamics Alliance, exploring long-term environmental and climate history, human settlement, and ecosystem response.

There is definitely some urgency about pursuing such studies. Rising sea levels as a consequence of climate change, together with fast-accelerating economic development, are likely to make many types of locations with real promise for palaeoenvironmental research increasingly hard to find. This has been my own experience on Montserrat. We had hoped to locate places suitable for coring, but with more than half the island volcanically damaged and inaccessible for the foreseeable future, with steep coastal cliffs almost everywhere (and, thus, a lack of lagoon or back-swamp environments), and no pools, lakes, or wetlands in the interior, the sole candidate we could identify was a small area of mangrove swamp in a brackish inlet known as Piper's Pond, in the northwest of the island. But before we could organize coring there, the Pond was bulldozed and in-filled, as part of landscaping for the development of the Carr's Bay/Little Bay area, the intended new capital town of the island. That opportunity has now been lost for good.

As primarily a Mediterranean archaeologist, I do have recommendations concerning future landscape search strategies. A key question set up by this book is the following: We have unequivocal evidence, from palaeoenvironmental coring, for the presence and impact of human populations on several islands well before their earliest currently known archaeological sites. So where are these earlier (Archaic) sites? We will find them only by survey—including in that term not only pedestrian reconnaissance, but also the close inspection of road cuts, erosion gullies, and other such locations where deeply buried sites might express themselves. But, in general, I am not impressed by the ways in which survey has been conducted in the Caribbean, at least compared to how it has developed in a number of other parts of the world. There have been, it is true, some systematic random transect surveys (e.g., Armstrong 1980 on St. Kitts; Watters 1980a on Montserrat), but most claims to have surveyed an island usually turn out to refer to very low-intensity, judgmental inspection. Certainly, those of us who have conducted Caribbean surveys know the very real difficulties: steep slopes, deeply eroded ghauts, prickly and even dangerous vegetation, dense neotropical forest (including regrowth over former clear-felled sugar plantations). Yet despite such obstacles, thorough survey—informed by geomorphology and historical ecology—remains the only way to gain data about the earliest settlement of the Lesser Antilles.

What does "thorough" imply? It means taking survey seriously, devoting significant time and resources to it, and not treating it as merely a casual warm-up for the main bout (i.e., excavation). After all, cultural landscapes comprise not only stratified settlement sites, but also many other anthropogenic features—boundary walls, quarry sites, field clearance cairns, rock art, bread ovens, and a myriad of other elements, including off-site artifact scatters. The latter are especially important, not only in providing a fuller understanding of how people have interacted with their wider environments in the past, but also by mapping where artifacts are or are not to be found, in helping assess the dates of currently exposed land surfaces, and thus what portions of earlier landscapes may now be obscured as a result of depositional or erosional processes.

In the Mediterranean, hundreds of systematic, high-intensity surveys have now been conducted, many of them in island environments (Cherry 2003). In a very impressive recent instance, one project completed the inspection of every square meter of the modern surface of an Aegean island, albeit it a fairly small one (Antikythera, 21 km^2 [Bevan and Connolly 2013]). It would be fair to say that, as a proportion of overall archaeological time and effort, intensive, survey-based regional research on Mediterranean islands is now an order of magnitude greater than it was two or three decades ago (Alcock and Cherry 2004). It is strange that these changes in archaeological practice have seemingly had so little impact in the Caribbean; I do not think that is entirely because it does not offer the relatively light ground vegetative cover found in other parts of the world that have been especially conducive to survey.

This is not to say that more-extensive, more-judgmental survey strategies (i.e., single-person surveys, or essentially so) do not continue to play an important role. Indeed, this, in addition to intensive survey, may be key to making progress on the missing Archaic problem. Thirty-five years ago in his work on St. Kitts, Douglas Armstrong (1980) adopted a purposive, problem-oriented approach to locating Archaic sites on the island. Considering what was then known about the Archaic in the Caribbean, and considering factors that impede our ability to find sites, he developed a model setting out criteria for expected site location; this model was then tested, with some success, using first a general island-wide random survey (demonstrating that recent volcanic activity does inhibit Archaic site discovery), followed by targeted intensive transects on the lower peninsula of St. Kitts (which is largely free of volcanic impacts). Comparable strategies have proven very effective in recent years in the Aegean for making progress on a rather similar missing Mesolithic problem, both on the mainland and in the islands, including Crete. Again, the model was developed from the locations and environmental contexts of the few known Mesolithic sites in Greece; took account of the loss of coastal plains in the Early Holocene due to marine transgression; and assumed a strong preference for coastal locations with caves and rockshelters, freshwater, and access to extensive wetlands offering the widest range of plant, animal, and other resources (Runnels et al. 2005; Strasser et al. 2010). This style of work surely provides useful pointers for what could now be attempted more systematically in the Caribbean.

Historical ecology has at its very heart the goal of identifying and understanding environmental changes in past anthropogenic landscapes: that is what is intended by the word "socionatural" of this book's subtitle. Its authors have amply demonstrated how critical interdisciplinary collaboration is for making progress. As part of this necessary mix of data and disciplines, historical ecology in the Caribbean could, in my view, benefit enormously from the wider availability of higher-grade, spatially controlled, geomorphologically informed, regional archaeological data on past landscape use.

References

Aceituno, Francisco J., Nicolás Loaiza, Miguel Eduardo Delgado-Burbano, and Gustavo Barrientos. 2013. "The Initial Human Settlement of Northwest South America during the Pleistocene/Holocene Transition: Synthesis and Perspectives." *Quaternary International* 301: 23–33.

Adélaïde-Merlande, Jacques, and Jean-Paul Hervieu. 1996. *Les volcans dans l'histoire des Antilles*. Paris: Karthala.

Ahmad, Nazeer. 2011. *Soils of the Caribbean*. Kingston, Jamaica: Ian Randle.

Alcock, Susan E., and John F. Cherry. 2004. "Introduction." In *Side-by-Side Survey: Comparative Regional Studies in the Mediterranean World*, edited by Susan E. Alcock and John F. Cherry, 1–9. Oxford: Oxbow Books.

Alcover, Josep Antoni. 2008. "The First Mallorcans: Prehistoric Colonization in the Western Mediterranean." *Journal of World Prehistory* 21: 19–84.

Allaire, Louis. 1977. "Later Prehistory in Martinique and the Island Caribs: Problems in Ethnic Identification." Ph.D. dissertation. New Haven, CT: Yale University.

———. 1989. "Volcanic Chronology and the Early Saladoid Occupation of Martinique." In Siegel, *Early Ceramic Population Lifeways*, 147–169.

———. 1990. "Prehistoric Taino Interaction with the Lesser Antilles." Paper presented at the 55th Annual Meeting of the Society for American Archaeology. Las Vegas, NV, April 18–22, 1990.

———. 1991. "Understanding Suazey." *Proceedings of the International Congress for Caribbean Archaeology* 13(2): 715–728.

———. 1997. "Anse Trabaud: rapport 1997." In *Le néolithique de la Martinique dans son contexte antillais*, edited by J. P. Giraud. Martinique: Projet Collectif de Recherche.

———. 2013. "Ethnohistory of the Caribs." In Keegan, Hofman, and Rodríguez Ramos, *Oxford Handbook of Caribbean Archaeology*, 97–108.

Allaire, Louis, and Mario Mattioni. 1983. "Boutbois et Le Godinot: deux gisements acéramiques de la Martinique." *Proceedings of the International Congress for the Study of the Pre-Columbian Cultures of the Lesser Antilles* 9: 27–38.

Allen, Jim. 1997. "The Impact of Pleistocene Hunters and Gatherers on the Ecosystems of Australia and Melanesia: In Tune with Nature?" In Kirch and Hunt, *Historical Ecology in the Pacific Islands*, 22–38.

Alperson-Afil, Nira. 2012. "Archaeology of Fire: Methodological Aspects of Reconstructing Fire History of Prehistoric Archaeological Sites." *Earth-Science Reviews* 113(3–4): 111–119.

Alperson-Afil, Nira, and N. Goren-Inbar. 2010. *The Acheulian Site of Gesher Benot Ya'aqov, Vol. 2: Ancient Flames and Controlled Use of Fire*. London: Springer.

Anderson, Atholl. 1997. "Prehistoric Polynesian Impact on the New Zealand Environment: Te Whenua Hou." In Kirch and Hunt, *Historical Ecology in the Pacific Islands*, 271–283.

Anderson, Atholl. 2003. "Entering Uncharted Waters: Models of Initial Colonization in Polynesia." In Rockman and Steele, *Colonization of Unfamiliar Landscapes*, 169–189.
Anderson, Atholl, James H. Barrett, and Katherine V. Boyle, eds. 2010. *The Global Origins and Development of Seafaring*. Cambridge, UK: McDonald Institute for Archaeological Research, Cambridge University.
Anderson, Atholl, John Chappell, Michael Gagan, and Richard Grove. 2006. "Prehistoric Maritime Migration in the Pacific Islands: An Hypothesis of ENSO Forcing." *The Holocene* 16: 1–6.
Anderson, Atholl, and Geoffrey Clark. 1999. "The Age of Lapita Settlement in Fiji." *Archaeology in Oceania* 34: 31–39.
Anderson-Córdova, Karen F., Mark R. Barnes, and Peter E. Siegel. 2004. "Interaction between the Caribbean and Eastern North America in the Colonial Period." In *An Annales Approach to Contact-Era Archaeology*, edited by Michael Klein. *Journal of Middle Atlantic Archaeology* 20: 29–34.
Andersson, Bengt Lennart. 1977. "The Genus *Ischnosiphon* (Marantaceae)." *Opera Botanica* 43: 1–114.
Anctzak, A., and M. Anctzak. 2006. *Los ídolos de las islas prometidas: Arqueología prehispanicá del Archipélago de los Roques*. Caracas, Venezuela: Editoral Equinoccio.
Anctzak, Maria Magdalena, and Andrzej Anctzak 2015. "Late Pre-Colonial and Early Colonial Archaeology of the Las Aves Archipelagos, Venezuela." *Contributions in New World Archaeology* 8: 7–44.
Anthony, David W. 1990. "Migration in Archeology: The Baby and the Bathwater." *American Anthropologist* 92: 895–914.
———. 1997. "Prehistoric Migration as Social Process." In Chapman and Hamerow, *Migrations and Invasions in Archaeological Explanation*, 21–32.
Arculus, Richard. 1976. "Geology and Geochemistry of the Alkali Basalt-Andesite Association of Grenada, Lesser Antilles Island Arc." *Geological Society of America Bulletin* 87: 612–624.
Armstrong, Douglas V. 1980. "Shellfish Gatherers of St. Kitts: A Study of Archaic Subsistence and Settlement Patterns." *Proceedings of the International Congress for the Study of the Pre-Columbian Cultures of the Lesser Antilles* 8: 152–167.
———. 2001. "A Venue for Autonomy: Archaeology of a Changing Cultural Landscape, the East End Community, St. John, Virgin Islands." In Farnsworth, *Island Lives*, 142–164.
———. 2013a. "Archaeology of an Emerging Landscape of Power and Enslavement in Early 17th-century Barbados." Paper presented at the New York Academy of Science's Anthropology Section and the Wenner-Gren Foundation, New York, 28 January.
———. 2013b. "New Directions in Caribbean Historical Archaeology." In Keegan, Hofman, and Rodríguez Ramos, *Oxford Handbook of Caribbean Archaeology*, 525–541.
Athens, J. Stephen. 1997. "Hawaiian Native Lowland Vegetation in Prehistory." In Kirch and Hunt, *Historical Ecology in the Pacific Islands*, 248–270.
Athens, J. Stephen, Michael F. Dega, and Jerome V. Ward. 2008. "Austronesian Colonization of the Mariana Islands: The Palaeoenvironmental Evidence." *Bulletin of the Indo-Pacific Pacific Association* 24: 21–30.
Athens, J. Stephen, H. David Tuggle, Jerome V. Ward, and David J. Welch. 2002.

"Avifaunal Extinctions, Vegetation Change, and Polynesian Impacts in Prehistoric Hawai'i." *Archaeology in Oceania* 37: 57–78.

Athens, J. Stephen, Timothy M. Rieth, and Thomas S. Dye. 2014. "A Paleoenvironmental and Archaeological Model-Based Age Estimate for the Colonization of Hawai'i." *American Antiquity* 79: 144–155.

Ayes Suárez, Carlos M. 1988. *Evaluación arqueológica tipo fase 2 Angostura, Florida Afuera, Barceloneta, Puerto Rico*. AYES: Investigaciones Arqueológicas e Historicas, Manatí, Puerto Rico. Submitted to Custodio, Roe & Asociados, Hato Rey, Puerto Rico. Copies available from the Instituto de Cultura Puertorriqueña, San Juan.

Baldacchino, Godfrey. 2008. "Studying Islands: On Whose Terms? Some Epistemological and Methodological Challenges to the Pursuit of Island Studies." *Island Studies Journal* 3(1): 37–56.

Balée, William, ed. 1998a. *Advances in Historical Ecology*. New York: Columbia University Press.

———. 1998b. "Historical Ecology: Premises and Postulates." In Balée, *Advances in Historical Ecology*, 13–29.

———. 2006. "The Research Program of Historical Ecology." *Annual Review of Anthropology* 35: 75–98.

———. 2013. *Cultural Forests of the Amazon: A Historical Ecology of People and their Landscapes*. Tuscaloosa: University of Alabama Press.

Balée, William, and Clark L. Erickson, eds. 2006a. *Time and Complexity in Historical Ecology: Studies in the Neotropical Lowlands*. New York: Columbia University Press.

———. 2006b. "Time, Complexity, and Historical Ecology." In Balée and Erickson, *Time and Complexity*, 1–17.

Balmuth, Miriam S., David K. Chester, and Patricia A. Johnston, eds. 2005. *Cultural Responses to the Volcanic Landscape: The Mediterranean and Beyond*. Boston: Archaeological Institute of America.

Bandaranayake, W. M. 1998. "Traditional and Medicinal Uses of Mangroves." *Mangroves and Salt Marshes* 2: 133–148.

Banner, Jay L., MaryLynn Musgrove, Yemane Asmerom, R. Lawrence Edwards, and John A. Hoff. 1996. "High-Resolution Temporal Record of Holocene Ground-Water Chemistry: Tracing Links between Climate and Hydrology." *Geology* 24: 1049–1053.

Barkeley, Fred A. 1934. "The Statistical Theory of Pollen Analysis." *Ecology* 47: 439–447.

Barker, David. 1998. "The North-East Trades and Temperature Inversions: Notes for the Classroom." *Caribbean Geography* 9(1): 58–65.

Barnett, William K. 2000. "Cardial Pottery and the Agricultural Transition in Mediterranean Europe." In Price, *Europe's First Farmers*, 93–116.

Barr, K. K. 1981. "Geological Outline." In Cooper and Bacon, *Natural Resources of Trinidad and Tobago*, 2–12.

Bartone, Robert N., and Aaad H. Versteeg. 1997. "The Tanki Flip Features and Structures." In Versteeg and Rostain, *Archaeology of Aruba*, 23–126.

Bawden, Garth, and Richard Martin Reycraft, eds. 2000. *Environmental Disaster and the Archaeology of Human Response*. Anthropological Papers 7. Albuquerque: Maxwell Museum of Anthropology, University of New Mexico.

Beard, J. S. 1944. "Climax Vegetation in Tropical America." *Ecology* 25(2): 127–158.
———. 1946. *Natural Vegetation of Trinidad.* Oxford Forestry Memoirs 20. Oxford: Clarendon Press.
———. 1949. *The Natural Vegetation of the Windward and Leeward Islands.* Oxford Forestry Memoirs 21. Oxford: Clarendon Press.
Beets, C. J., and H. J. MacGillavry. 1977. "Outline of the Cretaceous and Early Tertiary History of Curaçao, Bonaire, and Aruba." Guide to the Field Excursions on Curaçao, Bonaire, and Aruba. *GUA Papers of Geology Series* 1(10): 1–6.
Beets, C. J., S. R. Troelstra, P. M. Grootes, M.-J. Nadeau, K. van der Borg, A. F. M. de Jong, C. L. Hofman, and M. L. P. Hoogland. 2006. "Climate and Pre-Columbian Settlements at Anse à la Gourde, Guadeloupe, Northeastern Caribbean." *Geoarchaeology: An International Journal* 21(3): 271–280.
Behling, Hermann. 1995. "A High Resolution Holocene Pollen Record from Lago do Pires, SE Brazil: Vegetation, Climate and Fire History." *Journal of Paleolimnology* 14: 253–268.
Belfer-Cohen, Anna, and Nigel Goring-Morris. 2009. "For the First Time." *Current Anthropology* 50(5): 669–672.
Bellizzia, Alirio, and Gabriel Dengo. 1990. "The Caribbean Mountain System, Northern South America; A Summary." In Dengo and Chase, *Caribbean Region*, Vol. H, 167–175.
Bellwood, Peter. 2001. "Early Agriculturalist Population Diasporas? Farming, Languages, and Genes." *Annual Review of Anthropology* 30: 181–207.
Bennett, John W. 1976. *The Ecological Transition: Cultural Anthropology and Human Adaptation.* New York: Pergamon Press.
Benz, Emily Jane. 2010. "A Paleoenvironmental Reconstruction from the Island of Grenada, Caribbean Environments during the Time of Human Occupation." M. A. thesis. Pullman, WA: Washington State University.
Bérard, Benoît. 2002. "De l'occupation précéramique de la Martinique." In *Archéologie précolombienne et coloniale des Caraïbes*, edited by A. Delpuech, J.-P. Giraud, and A. Hesse, 55–66. Actes du congrès national des sociétés historiques et scientifiques 123. Paris: CTHS.
———. 2004. *Les premières occupations agricoles de l'arc antillais, migration et insularité: le cas de l'occupation saladoïde ancienne de la Martinique.* BAR International Series 1299. Oxford: British Archaeological Reports.
———. 2006a. "Le Carbet: Boutbois." *Bilan Scientifique de la Région Martinique* 2004: 9–11.
———. 2006b. "Le Carbet: Godinot." *Bilan Scientifique de la Région Martinique* 2004: 12–13.
———. 2013. "The Saladoid." In Keegan, Hofman, and Rodríguez Ramos, *Oxford Handbook of Caribbean Archaeology,* 184–197.
Berman, Mary Jane, and Deborah M. Pearsall. 2000. "Plants, People, and Culture in the Prehistoric Central Bahamas: A View from the Three Dog Site, An Early Lucayan Settlement on San Salvador Island, Bahamas." *Latin American Antiquity* 11: 219–239.
Berman, Mary Jane, and Deborah M. Pearsall. 2008. "At the Crossroads: Starch

Grain and Phytolith Analyses in Lucayan Prehistory." *Latin American Antiquity* 19: 181–203.
Berna, Francesco, Paul Goldberg, Liora Kolska Horwitz, James Brink, Sharon Holt, Marion Bamford, and Michael Chazan. 2012. "Microstratigraphic Evidence of In Situ Fire in the Acheulian Strata of Wonderwerk Cave, Northern Cape Province, South Africa." *Proceedings of the National Academy of Sciences of the United States of America* 109(20): E1215–E1220.
Berridge, C. E. 1981. "Climate." In Cooper and Bacon, *Natural Resources of Trinidad and Tobago*, 2–12.
Bertran, Pascal, Dominique Bonnissent, Daniel Imbert, Pierre Lozouet, Nathalie Serrand, and Christian Stouvenot. 2004. "Paléoclimat des Petites Antilles depuis 4000 ans BP: l'enregistrement de la lagune de Grand-Case à Saint-Martin." *C.R. Geoscience* 336: 1501–1510.
Bevan, Andrew, and James Conolly. 2013. *Mediterranean Islands, Fragile Communities and Persistent Landscapes: Antikythera in Long-term Perspective*. Cambridge, UK: Cambridge University Press.
Black, Manu P., and Scott D. Mooney. 2006. "Holocene Fire History from the Greater Blue Mountains World Heritage Area, New South Wales, Australia: The Climate, Humans and Fire Nexus." *Regional Environmental Change* 6: 41–51.
Blancaneaux, A. F. 2009. "Contribution à l'étude de la disparition de la culture saladoïde aux petites antilles. Corrélation préhistorique posible entre climat et culture." Ph.D. dissertation. Paris: Université des Antilles et de la Guyane and Université Paris I, Panteón Sorbonne.
Bliege Bird, R., D. W. Bird, B. F. Codding, C. H. Parker, and J. H. Jones. 2008. "The 'Fire Stick Farming' Hypothesis: Australian Aboriginal Foraging Strategies, Biodiversity, and Anthropogenic Fire Mosaics." *Proceedings of the National Academy of Sciences of the United States of America* 105(39): 14796–14801.
Blong, R. J. 1987. *Volcanic Hazards: A Sourcebook of the Effects of Eruptions*. New York: Academic Press.
Bonnissent, Dominque 2003. "St. Martin, Etang Rouge-lot 401." *Bilan Scientifique, Direction Regionale des Affaires Culturelles de la Guadeloupe* 2003: 39–43.
———. 2008. "Archéologie précolombienne de l'île de Saint-Martin, Petites Antilles (3300 B.C.–1600 A.D.)." Ph.D. dissertation. Marseille: Université Aix-Marseille I.
———. 2013 *Les gisements précolombiens de la baie orientale: campements du Mésoindien et du Néoindien sur l'île de Saint-Martin, Petites Antilles*. Paris: Éditions de la maison des sciences de l'homme.
Bonnissent, D., P. Bertran, A. Chancerel, and Th. Romon. 2001. "Le gisement précéramique de la Baie Orientale à Saint-Martin (Petites Antilless), résultats préliminaires." *Proceedings of the International Congress for Caribbean Archaeology* 19(1): 78–88.
Boomert, Arie. 1983. "The Saladoid Occupation of Wonotobo Falls, Western Surinam." *Proceedings of the International Congress for the Study of the Pre-Columbian Cultures of the Lesser Antilles* 9: 97–120.
———. 1985. "The Guayabitoid and Mayoid Series: Amerindian Culture History in Trinidad during the Late Prehistoric and Protohistoric Times." *Pro-

ceedings of the International Congress for the Study of the Pre-Columbian Cultures of the Lesser Antilles 10: 93–148.

———. 1986. "The Cayo Complex of St. Vincent: Ethnohistorical and Archaeological Aspects of the Island-Carib Problem." *Antropológica* 66: 3–68.

———. 1987. "Notes on Barbados Prehistory." *Journal of Barbados Museum and Historical Society* 38: 8–43.

———. 2000. *Trinidad, Tobago and the Lower Orinoco Interaction Sphere: An Archaeological/Ethnohistorical Study.* Alkmaar, The Netherlands: Cairi.

———. 2001. "Saladoid Sociopolitical Organization." *Proceedings of the International Congress for Caribbean Archaeology* 18: 55–77.

———. 2006. "Between the Mainland and the Islands: The Amerindian Cultural Geography of Trinidad." *Antropologando* 5(15): 149–179.

———. 2007. "Plymouth: A Late-Prehistoric Ceramic Complex of Tobago." *Leiden Journal of Pottery Studies* 23: 121–158.

———. 2009. "Between the Mainland and the Islands: The Amerindian Cultural Geography of Trinidad." *Bulletin of the Peabody Museum of Natural History* 50: 63–73.

———. 2011. "From Cayo to Kalinago." In Hofman and van Duijvenbode, *Communities in Contact,* 291–306.

———. 2013. "Gateway to the Mainland: Trinidad and Tobago." In Keegan, Hofman, and Rodríguez Ramos, *Oxford Handbook of Caribbean Archaeology,* 141–154.

Boomert, Arie, and Alistair J. Bright. 2007. "Island Archaeology: In Search of a New Horizon." *Island Studies Journal* 2(1): 3–26.

Boomert, Arie, Birgit Faber-Morse, and Irving Rouse. 2013. *The 1946 and 1953 Yale University Excavations in Trinidad.* Yale University Publications in Anthropology 92. New Haven, CT: Department of Anthropology, Yale University.

Boomert, Arie, and Léonid Kameneff. 2005. "Preliminary Report on Archaeological Investigations at Great Courland Bay, Tobago." *Proceedings of the International Congress for Caribbean Archaeology* 20(2): 457–468.

Bottema, Sytze. 1980. "Pollen Analytical Investigations on Crete." *Review of Palaeobotany and Palynology* 31: 193–217.

Bottema, Sytze, and Anaya Sarpaki. 2003. "Environmental Change in Crete: A 9000-Year Record of Holocene Vegetation History and the Effect of the Santorini Eruption." *The Holocene* 13(5): 733–749.

Bouyoucos, George J. 1936. "Directions for Making Mechanical Analysis of Soils by the Hydrometer Method." *Soil Science* 42(3): 27–40.

Bowman, D. M. J. S., and M. J. Brown. 1986. "Bushfires in Tasmania: A Botanical Approach to Anthropological Questions." *Archaeology in Oceania* 21(3): 166–171.

Bradford, Margaret A. C. 2001. "Caribbean Perspectives on Settlement Patterns: The Windward Island Study." Ph.D. dissertation. Iowa City: University of Iowa.

Brasier, Martin, and Jack Donahue. 1985. "Barbuda—An Emerging Reef and Lagoon Complex on the Edge of the Lesser Antilles Island Arc." *Journal of the Geological Society* 142: 1101–1117.

Brenner, Mark. 1994. "Lakes Salpeten and Quexil, Peten, Guatemala, Central America." In *Global Geological Record of Lake Basins,* edited by E. Gierlowski-

Kordesch and K. Kelts, vol. 1, 377–380. Cambridge, UK: Cambridge University Press.
Brenner, Mark, and Michael W. Binford. 1988. "A Sedimentary Record of Human Disturbance from Lake Miragoâne, Haiti." *Journal of Paleolimnology* 1: 85–97.
Brenner, M., B. W. Leyden, J. H. Curtis, R. M. Medina González, B. H. Dahlin. 2000. "Un registro de 8000 anos del paleoclima del noroeste de Yucatan, Mexico." *Revista de la Universidad Autónoma de Yucatán* 213: 52–65.
Brereton, Bridget. 1981. *A History of Modern Trinidad 1783–1962*. Kingston: Heinemann.
Bright, Alistair J. 2011. *Blood is Thicker than Water: Amerindian Intra- and Interinsular Relationships and Social Organization in the Pre-Colonial Windward Islands.* Leiden, Netherlands: Sidestone Press.
Broeker, W. S., D. L. Thurber, J. Goddard, T. L. Ku, R. K. Matthews, and K. J. Mesolella. 1968. "Milankovitch Hypothesis Supported by Precise Dating of Coral Reefs and Deep Sea Sediments." *Science* 159: 297–300.
Broodbank, Cyprian. 1999. "The Insularity of Island Archaeologists: Comments on Rainbird's 'Islands Out of Time.'" *Journal of Mediterranean Archaeology* 12(2): 235–239.
———. 2000. *An Island Archaeology of the Early Cyclades*. Cambridge, UK: Cambridge University Press.
———. 2006. "The Origins and Early Development of Mediterranean Maritime Activity." *Journal of Mediterranean Archaeology* 19(2): 199–230.
———. 2010. "'Ships a-Sail from Over the Rim of the Sea': Voyaging, Sailing and the Making of Mediterranean Societies c. 3500–800 B.C." In Anderson, Barrett, and Boyle, *Global Origins and Development of Seafaring*, 249–264.
Broodbank, Cyprian, and Thomas F. Strasser. 1991. "Migrant Farmers and the Neolithic Colonization of Crete." *Antiquity* 65: 233–245.
Brown, Nicole A. 2000. *Environmental Advocacy in the Caribbean: The Case of the Nariva Swamp, Trinidad.* CANARI Technical Report 268. London: United Kingdom Department for International Development.
Bryant, Vaughn M. Jr., and Stephen A. Hall. 1993. "Archaeological Palynology in the United States: A Critique." *American Antiquity* 58: 277–286.
Buffett, Alice, and Donald C. Laycock. 1988. *Speak Norfolk Today: An Encyclopædia of the Norfolk Island Language.* Norfolk Island: Himi.
Bullen, K. E. 1965. *Theory of Seismology*. London: Cambridge University Press.
Bullen, Ripley P. 1964. *The Archaeology of Grenada, West Indies*. Social Sciences 11. Gainesville: Florida State Museum, University of Florida.
———. 1965. "Archaeological Chronology of Grenada." *American Antiquity* 31: 237–241.
———. 1970. "The Archaeology of Grenada, West Indies, and the Spread of Ceramic Peoples in the Antilles." *Proceedings of the International Congress of the Pre-Columbian Cultures of the Lesser Antilles* 3: 147–152.
Burney, David A. 1993. "Late Holocene Environmental Changes in Arid Southwestern Madagascar." *Quaternary Research* 40: 98–106.
———. 1996a. "Paleoecology of Humans and their Ancestors." In *East African Ecosystems and their Conservation*, edited by Tim R. McClanahan and Truman P. Young, 19–36. New York: Oxford University Press.

———. 1996b. "Climate Change and Fire Ecology as Factors in the Quaternary Biogeography of Madagascar." *Biogéographie de Madagascar* 1996: 49–58.

———. 1997a. "Tropical Islands as Paleoecological Laboratories: Gauging the Consequences of Human Arrival." *Human Ecology* 25(3): 437–457.

———. 1997b. "Theories and Facts Regarding Holocene Environmental Change Before and After Human Colonization." In *Natural Change and Human Impact in Madagascar,* edited by Steven M. Goodman, 75–89. Washington, DC: Smithsonian Institution Press.

Burney, David A., Lida Pigott Burney, and R. D. E. MacPhee. 1994. "Holocene Charcoal Stratigraphy from Laguna Tortuguero, Puerto Rico, and the Timing of Human Arrival on the Island." *Journal of Archaeological Science* 21: 273–281.

Burney, David A., R. V. DeCandido, Lida Pigott Burney, F. N. Kostel-Hughes, T. W. Stafford Jr., and Helen F. James. 1995. "A Holocene Record of Climate Change, Fire Ecology and Human Activity from Montane Flat Top Bog, Maui." *Journal of Paleolimnology* 13: 209–217.

Burnham, Robyn, and Alan Graham. 1999. "The History of Neotropical Vegetation: New Developments and Status." *Annals of the Association of the Missouri Botanical Garden* 86(2): 546–589.

Bush, M. B., D. R. Piperno, P. A. Colinvaux, L. Krissek, P. E. De Oliveira, M. C. Miller, and W. Rowe. 1992. "A 14,300 Year Paleoecological Profile of a Lowland Tropical Lake in Panama." *Ecological Monographs* 62: 251–276.

Butzer, Karl W. 1982. *Archaeology as Human Ecology: Method and Theory for a Contextual Approach.* Cambridge, UK: Cambridge University Press.

———. 1996. "Ecology in the Long View: Settlement, Agrosystem Strategies, and Ecological Performance." *Journal of Field Archaeology* 23: 141–150.

Caffrey, Maria A. 2011. "Holocene Climate and Environmental History of Laguna Saladilla, Dominican Republic." Ph.D. dissertation. Knoxville: University of Tennessee.

Caffrey, Maria A., and Sally P. Horn. 2015. "Long-term Fire Trends in Hispaniola and Puerto Rico from Sedimentary Charcoal: A Comparison of Three Records." *The Professional Geographer* 67: 229–241.

Callaghan, Richard T. 2001. "Ceramic Age Seafaring and Interaction Potential in the Antilles: A Computer Simulation." *Current Anthropology* 42: 308–313.

———. 2003. "Comments on the Mainland Origins of the Preceramic Cultures of the Greater Antilles." *Latin American Antiquity* 14: 323–338.

———. 2010. "Crossing the Guadeloupe Passage in the Archaic Age." In Fitzpatrick and Ross, *Island Shores, Distant Pasts,* 127–147.

Carlson, Lisbeth A., and William F. Keegan. 2004. "Resource Depletion in the Prehistoric Northern West Indies." In *Voyages of Discovery: The Archaeology of Islands,* edited by Scott M. Fitzpatrick, 85–107. Westport, CT: Praeger.

Carr, Raymond. 1984. *Puerto Rico: A Colonial Experiment.* New York: Vintage.

Carretero, M. E., J. L. López-Pérez, M. J. Abad, P. Bermejo, S. Tillet, A. Israel, and B. Noguera-P. 2008. "Preliminary Study of the Anti-Inflammatory Activity of Hexane Extract and Fractions from *Bursera simaruba* (Linneo) Sarg. (Burseraceae) Leaves." *Journal of Ethnopharmacology* 116(1): 11–15.

Carson, M. A., and S. W. Tam. 1977. "The Land Conservation Conundrum of Eastern Barbados." *Annals of the Association of American Geographers* 67: 185–203.

Case, J.E., T.L. Holcombe, and R.G. Martin. 1984. "Map of Geologic Provinces in the Caribbean Region." In *The Caribbean-South American Plate Boundary and Regional Tectonics*, edited by William E. Bonini, Robert B. Hargraves, and Reginald Shagam, pp. 1–30. Memoir 162. Boulder, Colorado: The Geological Society of America.

Casile, Claudette Antonia. 2010. "A Paleoenvironmental Investigation of the Island of Marie-Galante, FWI: The Human and Environmental Nexus in the Caribbean during Human Occupation." M. A. thesis. Pullman: Washington State University.

Chandler, Alfred D. 1946. "The Expansion of Barbados." *Journal of the Barbados Museum and Historical Society* 13: 106–136.

Chanlatte Baik, Luis A. 1981. "La Hueca y Sorcé (Vieques, Puerto Rico): primeras migraciones agroalfareras Antillanas: nuevo esquema para los procesos culturales de la arqueología Antillana." Santo Domingo: Privately printed.

———. 1983. "Sorcé-Vieques: climax cultural del Igneri y su participación en los procesos socioculturales Antillanos." *Proceedings of the International Congress for the Study of the Pre-Columbian Cultures of the Lesser Antilles* 9: 73–95.

———. 2013. "Huecoid Culture and the Antillean Agroalfarero Farmer-Potter Period." In Keegan, Hofman, and Rodríguez Ramos, *Oxford Handbook of Caribbean Archaeology*, 171–183.

Chanlatte Baik, Luis A., and Yvonne M. Narganes Storde. 1990. "La nueva arqueología de Puerto Rico: su proyección en las antillas." Santo Domingo: Privately printed.

Chapman, John, and Helena Hamerow, eds. 1997. *Migrations and Invasions in Archaeological Explanation*. BAR International Series 664. Oxford: British Archaeological Reports.

Chapman, Robert W. 1990. "Producing Inequalities: Regional Sequences in Later Prehistoric Southern Spain." *Journal of World Prehistory* 21: 195–260.

Chapman, V. J. 1976. *Mangrove Vegetation*. Vaduz: J. Cramer.

Chenery, E. M. 1952. *The Soils of Central Trinidad*. Port of Spain, Trinidad: Government Printing Office.

Cherry, John F. 1981. "Pattern and Process in the Earliest Colonization of the Mediterranean Islands." *Proceedings of the Prehistoric Society* 47: 41–68.

———. 1984. "The Initial Colonization of the West Mediterranean Islands in the Light of Island Biogeography and Paleogeography." In *The Deyà Conference of Prehistory: Early Settlement in the Western Mediterranean Islands and the Peripheral Areas*, edited by W. Waldren, R. Chapman, J. Lewthwaite, and R.-C. Kennard, 7–28. BAR International Series 229. Oxford, UK: British Archaeological Reports.

———. 1990. "The First Colonization of the Mediterranean Islands: A Review of Recent Research." *Journal of Mediterranean Archaeology* 3: 145–221.

———. 2003. "Archaeology Beyond the Site: Regional Survey and its Future." In Papadopoulos and Levanthal, *Theory and Practice in Mediterranean Archaeology*, 137–160.

Cherry, John F., Krysta Ryzewski, and Thomas P. Leppard. 2012. "Multi-period Landscape Survey and Site Risk Assessment on Montserrat, West Indies." *Journal of Island and Coastal Archaeology* 7: 282–302.

Cherry, John F., Krysta Ryzewski, Thomas P. Leppard, and Emanuela Bocancea. 2012. "The Earliest Phase of Settlement in the Eastern Caribbean: New Evidence from Montserrat." *Antiquity* 86(333): Project Gallery.

———. 2013. "Diachronic, Multi-scalar Landscape Archaeology on Montserrat: Opportunities and Challenges." Paper Presented at the 25th Congress of the International Association of Caribbean Archaeologists, San Juan, Puerto Rico, 15–20 July.

CIMAS. 2008. Electronic document. Retrieved 1 August 2012 from http://oceancurrents.rsmas.miami.edu/atlantic/Guiana.html. Miami, FL: The Cooperative Institute for Marine and Atmospheric Studies, University of Miami.

Claiborne, Robert. 1970. *Climate, Man, and History*. New York: W. W. Norton.

Clark, Geoffrey, Foss Leach, and Sue O'Connor, eds. 2008. *Islands of Inquiry: Colonisation, Seafaring and the Archaeology of Maritime Landscapes*. Terra Australis 29. Canberra: Australian National University Press.

Cleland, Charles E. 1976. "The Focal-Diffuse Model: An Evolutionary Perspective on the Prehistoric Cultural Adaptations of the Eastern United States." *Midcontinental Journal of Archaeology* 1: 59–76.

Clerc, Edgar. 1976. "Possibilité d'un peuplement précéramique en Guadeloupe." *Proceedings of the International Congress for the Study of the Pre-Columbian Cultures of the Lesser Antilles* 6: 44–45.

Cody, Anne. 1991a. "From the Site of Pearls, Grenada: Exotic Lithics and Radiocarbon Dates." *Proceedings of the International Congress for Caribbean Archaeology* 13: 589–604.

———. 1991b. "Distribution of Exotic Stone Artifacts through the Lesser Antilles: Their Implications for Prehistoric Interaction and Exchange." *Proceedings of the International Congress for Caribbean Archaeology* 14: 204–226.

Colinvaux, Paul. 1987. "Amazon Diversity in Light of the Paleoecological Record." *Quaternary Science Reviews* 6:93–114.

———. 1993. "Pleistocene Biogeography and Diversity in Tropical Forests of South America." In *Biological Relationships between Africa and South America*, edited by P. Goldblatt, pp. 473–499. New Haven: Yale University Press.

———. 2007. *Amazon Expeditions: My Quest for the Ice-age Equator*. New Haven: Yale University Press.

Colledge, Sue, James Conolly, Keith Dobney, Katie Manning, and Stephen Shennan, eds. 2013. *Origins and Spread of Domestic Animals in Southwest Asia and Europe*. UCL Institute of Archaeology Publication 59. Altamira, CA: Left Coast Press.

Colten, Craig E. 1998. "Historical Geography and Environmental History." *Geographical Review* 88(2): iii–iv.

Cooper, Jago. 2010. "Modelling Mobility and Exchange in Precolumbian Cuba: GIS Led Approaches to Identifying Pathways and Reconstructing Journeys from the Archaeological Record." *Journal of Caribbean Archaeology, Special Publication* 3: 122–137.

———. 2013. "The Climatic Context for Pre-Columbian Archaeology in the Caribbean." In Keegan, Hofman, and Rodríguez Ramos, *Oxford Handbook of Caribbean Archaeology*, 47–58.

Cooper, Jago, and Richard Boothroyd. 2011. "Living Islands of the Caribbean: A

View of Relative Sea Level Change from the Water's Edge." In Hofman and van Duijvenbode, *Communities in Contact*, 393–405.

Cooper, Jago, and Payson Sheets, eds. 2012. *Surviving Sudden Environmental Change: Answers from Archaeology*. Boulder: University of Colorado Press.

Cooper, St. G. C., and P. R. Bacon, eds. 1981. *The Natural Resources of Trinidad and Tobago*. London: Edward Arnold.

Coppa, Alfredo, Andrea Cucina, Menno L. P. Hoogland, Michaela Lucci, Fernando Luna Calderón, Raphaël G. A. M. Panhuysen, Glenis Tavarez María, Roberto Valcárcel Rojas, and Rita Vargiu. 2008. "New Evidence of Two Different Migratory Waves in the Circum-Caribbean Area during the Pre-Columbian Period from the Analysis of Dental Morphological Traits." In Hofman, Hoogland, and van Gijn, *Crossing the Borders*, 195–213.

Crock, John G. 2000. "Interisland Interaction and Development of Chiefdoms in the Eastern Caribbean." Ph.D. dissertation. Pittsburgh, PA: University of Pittsburgh.

Crock John G., and Nanny Carder. 2011. "Diet and Rank in a Caribbean Maritime Society." *Latin American Antiquity* 22: 573–594.

Crock, John G., James B. Petersen, and Nicholas Douglas. 1995. "Preceramic Anguilla: A View from the Whitehead's Bluff Site." *Proceedings of the International Congress for Caribbean Archaeology* 15: 283–292.

Crumley, Carole, L., ed. 1994a. *Historical Ecology: Cultural Knowledge and Changing Landscapes*." Sante Fe, NM: School of American Research Press.

———. 1994b. "Historical Ecology: A Mutlidimensional Ecological Orientation." In Crumley, *Historical Ecology*, 1–6.

Cruxent, J. M., and Irving Rouse. 1961. *Arqueología chonológica de Venezuela*. Social Science Monographs No. 6. Washington, DC: Pan American Union.

Curet, L. Antonio. 2005. *Caribbean Paleodemography: Population, Culture History, and Sociopolitical Processes in Ancient Puerto Rico*. Tuscaloosa: University of Alabama Press.

Curet, L. Antonio, and Mark W. Hauser, eds. 2011. *Islands at the Crossroads: Migration, Seafaring, and Interaction in the Caribbean*. Tuscaloosa: University of Alabama Press.

Curtis, Jason H. 1997. "Climatic Variation in the Circum-Caribbean during the Holocene." Ph.D. dissertation. Gainesville: University of Florida.

Curtis, Jason H., Mark Brenner, and David A. Hodell. 2001. "Climate Change in the Circum-Caribbean (Late Pleistocene to Present) and Implications for Regional Biogeography." In Woods and Sergile, *Biogeography of the West Indies*, 2nd ed., 35–54.

Curtis, Jason H., and David A. Hodell. 1993. "An Isotopic and Trace Element Study of Ostracods from Lake Miragôane, Haiti: A 10,500 Year Record of Paleosalinity and Paleotemperature Changes in the Caribbean." Climate Change in Continental Isotopic Records. *American Geophysical Monograph* 78: 135–152.

Curtis, Jason H., David A. Hodell, and Mark Brenner. 1996. "Climate Variability on the Yucatan Peninsula (Mexico) during the Past 3500 Years, and Implications for Maya Cultural Evolution." *Quaternary Research* 46: 37–47. Davis, Dave D. 1974. "Some Notes Concerning the Archaic Occupation of Antigua." *Proceedings of the International Congress for the Study of Pre-Columbian Cultures of the Lesser Antilles* 5: 65–71.

———. 1982. "Archaic Settlement and Resource Exploitation in the Lesser Antilles: Preliminary Information from Antigua." *Caribbean Journal of Science* 17(1–4): 107–121.

———. 1993. "Archaic Blade Production on Antigua, West Indies." *American Antiquity* 58: 688–697.

———. 2000. *Jolly Beach and the Preceramic Occupation of Antigua, West Indies.* Yale University Publications in Anthropology 84. New Haven, CT: Department of Anthropology, Yale University.

Davis, Dave, and Kevin Oldfield. 2003. "Archaeological Reconnaissance of Anegada, British Virgin Islands." *Journal of Caribbean Archaeology* 4: 1–11.

Dawson, Helen. 2011. "Island Colonization: Settling the Neolithic Question." In Phoca-Cosmetatou, *First Mediterranean Islanders*, 31–54.

Day, Michael J. 1983. "Doline Morphology and Development in Barbados." *Annals of the Association of American Geographers* 73: 206–219.

Day, Michael J., and M. Sean Chenworth. 2004. "The Karstlands of Trinidad and Tobago, their Land Use and Conservation." *Geographical Journal* 170(3): 256–266.

De Booy, Theodore. 1917. "Certain Archaeological Investigations in Trinidad, British West Indies." *American Anthropologist* 19: 471–486.

de Mille, Christy. 2011. "New Evidence and Understanding of the Antiguan Preceramic." *Proceedings of the International Congress for Caribbean Archaeology* 23: 428–446.

De Vries, A. J. 2000. "The Semi-Arid Environment of Curaçao: A Geochemical Soil Survey." *Netherlands Journal of Geosciences* 79: 479–494.

de Waal, Maaike S. 2006. "Pre-Columbian Social Organisation and Interaction Interpreted through the Study of Settlement Patterns: An Archaeological Case-Study of the Pointe des Châteaux, La Désirade and les îlles de la Petite Terre Micro-Region, Guadeloupe, F. W. I." Ph.D. dissertation. Leiden, Netherlands: Leiden University.

Dean, Walter E. Jr. 1974. "Determination of Carbonate and Organic Matter in Calcareous Sediments and Sedimentary Rocks by Loss on Ignition: Comparison with Other Methods." *Journal of Sedimentary Petrology* 44: 242–248.

DeBoer, Warren R. 1975. "The Archaeological Evidence for Manioc Cultivation: A Cautionary Note." *American Antiquity* 40: 419–432.

Deevey, E. S., M. Brenner, and M. W. Binford. 1983. "Paleolimnology of the Peten Lake District, Guatemala, III. Late Pleistocene and Gambian Environments of the Maya Area." *Hydrobiologia* 103: 211–216.

deFrance, Susan D. 2013. "Zooarchaeology in the Caribbean: Current Research and Future Prospects." In Keegan, Hofman, and Rodríguez Ramos, *Oxford Handbook of Caribbean Archaeology*, 378–390.

deFrance, Susan D., William F. Keegan, and Lee A. Newsom. 1996. "The Archaeobotanical, Bone Isotope, and Zooarchaeological Records from Caribbean Sites in Comparative Perspective." In *Case Studies in Environmental Archaeology*, edited by Elizabeth J. Reitz, Lee A. Newsom, and Sylvia J. Scudder, 289–304. New York: Plenum Press.

deFrance, Susan D., and Lee A. Newsom. 2005. "The Status of Paleoethnobiological Research on Puerto Rico and Adjacent Islands." In Siegel, *Ancient Borinquen,* 122–184.

Delpuech, André. 2001. "Historical Archaeology in the French West Indies: Recent Research in Guadeloupe." In Farnsworth, *Island Lives,* 21–59.

———. 2004. "Espaces naturels et territories amérindiens dans la Caraïbe orientale." In Delpuech and Hofman, *Late Ceramic Age Societies in the Eastern Caribbean,* 3–16.

Delpuech, Andre, and Corinne L. Hofman, eds. 2004. *Late Ceramic Age Societies in the Eastern Caribbean.* BAR International Series 1273. Oxford: British Archaeological Reports

Delpuech, André, Corinne L. Hofman, and Menno L. P. Hoogland. 2001. "Excavations at the Site of Anse à la Gourde, Guadeloupe. Organisation, History, Environmental Setting." *Proceedings of the International Congress for Caribbean Archaeology* 18: 156–161.

Demetrius, L., V. M. Gundlach, and G. Ochs. 2004. "Complexity and Demographic Stability in Population Models." *Theoretical Population Biology* 65: 211–225.

Dengo, Gabriel, and J. E. Chase, eds. 1990. *The Caribbean Region. The Geology of North America,* Vol. H. Boulder, CO: Geological Society of America.

Descantes, Christophe, Robert J. Speakman, Michael D. Glascock, and Matthew T. Boulanger, eds. 2008. *An Exploratory Study into the Chemical Characterization of Caribbean Ceramics.* Special Publication No. 2. *Journal of Caribbean Archaeology.*

Diamond, Jared. 2005. *Collapse: How Societies Choose to Fail or Succeed.* New York: Penguin.

Dijkhoff, R. A. C. F. 1997. "Tanki Flip/Henriquez: An Early Urumaco Site in Aruba." M.A. thesis. Leiden, Netherlands: Leiden University.

Dijkhoff, R. A. C. F., and M. S. Linville. 2004. *The Archaeology of Aruba: The Marine Shell Heritage.* Publications of the Archaeological Museum of Aruba 10. Aruba: Archaeological Museum.

Direction Regionale des Affaires Culturelles (DRAC). 2008. "Archaeological Site Files." Basse-Terre, Guadeloupe: Service Regional de l'Archeologie, Ministere de la Culture.

Donovan, Stephen K. 1994. "Trinidad." In *Caribbean Geology: An Introduction,* edited by Stephen K. Donovan and Trevor A. Jackson, 209–228. Kingston, Jamaica: University of the West Indies Association.

Dorst, Marc. 2008. "The Pre-Columbian SAN-1 Site, Manzanilla, Trinidad, Preliminary Research Report, Fieldwork October 2007." St. Augustine, Trinidad and Tobago: National Archaeological Committee of Trinidad and Tobago.

Drewett, Peter L. 1986. "A Survey of Prehistoric Barbados." *Caribbean Conservation News* 4(5): 16–18.

———. 1987. "Archaeological Survey of Barbados. 1st Interim Report." *Journal of the Barbados Museum and Historical Society* 38: 44–80.

———. 1988. "Archaeological Survey of Baarbados. 2nd Interim Report." *Journal of the Barbados Museum and Historical Society* 38: 196–204.

———. 1989a. "Prehistoric Ceramic Population Lifeways and Adaptive Strategies on Barbados, Lesser Antilles." In Siegel, *Early Ceramic Population Lifeways*, 79–118.

———. 1989b. "Archaeological Survey of Baarbados. 3rd Interim Report." *Journal of the Barbados Museum and Historical Society* 38: 338–352.

———. 1991. *Prehistoric Barbados*. London: Archetype.

———. 1993. "Excavations at Heywoods, Barbados, and the Economic Basis of the Suazoid Period in the Lesser Antilles." *Proceedings of the Prehistoric Society* 59: 113–137.

———. 1996/1997. "Excavations at the Prehistoric Sites at Silver Sands, Little Welches and Heywoods, 1995: A Preliminary Report." *Journal of the Barbados Museum and Historical Society* 43: 59–68.

———. 2000. *Prehistoric Settlements in the Caribbean: Fieldwork in Barbados, Tortola and the Cayman Islands*. St. Michael, Barbados: Archetype and Barbados Museum and Historical Society.

———. 2002. *Amerindian Stories: An Archaeology of Early Barbados*. St. Michael, Barbados: Barbados Museum and Historical Society.

———. 2004. "Post-Saladoid Society on Barbados." In Delpuech and Hofman, *Late Ceramic Age Societies in the Eastern Caribbean*, 215–230.

———. 2006. "Dating the Prehistoric Settlement of Barbados." *Journal of the Barbados Museum and Historical Society* 52: 202–214.

———. 2007. *Above Sweet Waters: Cultural and Natural Change at Port St. Charles, Barbados, c. 1750 B.C.–A.D. 1850*. London: Archetype.

Dubelaar, Cornelius N. 1995. *The Petroglyphs of the Lesser Antilles, the Virgin Islands and Trinidad*. Amsterdam: Foundation for Scientific Research in the Caribbean Region.

Dugmore, Andrew J., Mike J. Church, Kerry-Anne Mairs, Thomas H. McGovern, Sophia Perdikaris, and Orri Vésteinsson. 2007. "Abandoned Farms, Volcanic Impacts, and Woodland Management: Revisiting Þjórsárdalur, the 'Pompeii of Iceland.'" *Arctic Anthropology* 44: 1–11.

Dugmore, Andrew J., Anthony J. Newton, Gudrún Larsen, and Gordon T. Cook. 2000. "Tephrochronology, Environmental Change and the Norse Settlement of Iceland." *Environmental Archaeology* 5: 21–34.

Efstratiou, Nikos, Paolo Biagi, Panagiotis Karkanas, and Elisabetta Starnini. 2013. "A Late Palaeolithic Site at Ouriakos (Limnos, Greece) in the North-Eastern Aegean." *Antiquity* 87(335): Project Gallery.

Eggers, Baron H. F. A. 1879. *The Flora of St. Croix and the Virgin Islands*. Bulletin of the United States National Museum 13. Washington DC: Government Printing Office.

Ellison, Joanna C., and David R. Stoddart. 1991. "Mangrove Ecosystem Collapse during Predicted Sea-Level Rise: Holocene Analogues and Implications." *Journal of Coastal Research* 7(1): 151–165.

Engel, Max, Helmut Brückner, Sascha Fürstenberg, Peter Frenzel, Anna Maria Konopczak, Anja Scheffers, Dieter Kelletat, Simon Matthias May, Frank Schäbitz, and Gerhard Dau. 2012. "A Prehistoric Tsunami Induced Long-Lasting Ecosystem Changes on a Semi-Arid Tropical Island—The Case of Boka Bartol (Bonaire, Leeward Antilles)." *Naturwissenschaften* 14:

51–67. Erdtman, G. 1960. "The Acetolysis Method: A Revised Description." *Svensk Botanisk Tidskrift* 54: 561–564.
Evans, J. D., J. R. Cann, A. C. Renfrew, I. W. Cornwall, and A. C. Western. 1964. "Excavations in the Neolithic Settlement of Knossos, 1957–60. Part 1." *Annual of the British School at Athens* 59: 132–240.
Ewel, J. J., and J. L. Whitmore.1973. *The Ecological Life Zones of Puerto Rico and the U.S. Virgin Islands.* Forest Service Research Paper ITF-18. Río Piedras, Puerto Rico: Institute of Tropical Forestry, U.S. Forest Service.
Ewen, Charles R. 2001. "Historical Archaeology in the Colonial Spanish Caribbean." In Farnsworth, *Island Lives*, 3–20.
Eyre, L. Alan. 1998. "The Tropical Rainforests of the Eastern Caribbean: Present Status and Conservation." *Caribbean Geography* 9(2): 101–120.
Fairbanks, Richard G. 1989. "A 17,000 Year Glacio-Eustatic Sea Level Record: Influences of Glacial Melting Rates in the Younger Dryas Event and Deep-Ocean Circulation." *Nature* 342: 637–642.
Farnsworth, Paul, ed. 2001. *Island Lives: Historical Archaeologies of the Caribbean.* Tuscaloosa: University of Alabama Press.
Fiedel, Stuart J., and David W. Anthony. 2003. "Deerslayers, Pathfinders, and Icemen: Origins of the European Neolithic as Seen from the Frontier." In Rockman and Steele, *Colonization of Unfamiliar Landscapes*, 144–168.
Fitzhugh, Ben, and Terry L. Hunt. 1997. "Introduction: Islands as Laboratories: Archaeological Research in Comparative Perspective." *Human Ecology* 25(3): 379–383.
Fitzpatrick, Scott M. 2006. "A Critical Approach to ^{14}C Dating in the Caribbean: Using Chronometric Hygiene to Evaluate Chronological Control and Prehistoric Settlement." *Latin American Antiquity* 17: 389–418.
———. 2011. Verification of an Archaic Age Occupation on Barbados, Southern Lesser Antilles. *Radiocarbon* 53(4): 595–604.
———. 2012. "On the Shoals of Giants: Natural Catastrophes and the Overall Destruction of the Caribbean's Archaeological Record." *Journal of Coastal Conservation* 16: 173–186.
———. 2013. "The Southward Route Hypothesis." In Keegan, Hofman, and Rodríguez Ramos, *Oxford Handbook of Caribbean Archaeology*, 198–204.
Fitzpatrick, Scott M., and Richard Callaghan. 2009. "Examining Dispersal Mechanisms for the Translocation of Chicken (*Gallus gallus*) from Polynesia to South America." *Journal of Archaeological Science* 36(2): 214–223.
Fitzpatrick, Scott M., Michiel Kappers, Quetta Kaye, Christina M. Giovas, Michelle J. LeFebvre, Mary Hill Harris, Scott Burnett, Jennifer A. Pavia, Kathleen Marsaglia, and James Feathers. 2009. "Precolumbian Settlements on Carriacou, West Indies." *Journal of Field Archaeology* 34(3): 247–266.
Fitzpatrick, Scott M., Michiel Kappers, and Christina M. Giovas. 2010. "The Southward Route Hypothesis: Examining Carriacou's Chronological Position in Antillean Prehistory." In Fitzpatrick and Ross, *Island Shores, Distant Pasts*, 163–176.
Fitzpatrick, Scott M., and William F. Keegan. 2007. "Human Impacts and Adaptations in the Caribbean Islands: An Historical Ecology Approach." *Earth and Environmental Science Transactions of the Royal Society of Edinburgh* 98: 29–45.

Fitzpatrick, Scott M., and Ann H. Ross, eds. 2010. *Island Shores, Distant Pasts: Archaeological and Biological Approaches to the Pre-Columbian Settlement of the Caribbean*. Gainesville: University Press of Florida.

Fix, Alan G. 1999. *Migration and Colonization in Human Microevolution*. Cambridge Studies in Biological and Evolutionary Anthropology 24. Cambridge, UK: Cambridge University Press.

Forenbaher, Stasŏ, and Timothy Kaiser. 2011. "Palagruža and the Spread of Farming in the Adriatic." In Phoca-Cosmetatou, *First Mediterranean Islanders*, 99–113.

Fortuna, Luis. 1981. "Informe palinológico." In *Estudio de cuatro nuevos sitios paleoarcaicos de la isla de Santo Domingo*, edited by Elpidio Ortega and José Guerrero, 83–89. Serie Investigaciones Antropológicas 17. Santo Domingo: Museo del Hombre Dominicano.

Fouéré, P., S. Bailon, D. Bonnissent, A. Chancerel, P. Courtaud, M. F. Deguilloux, S. Grouard, A. Lenoble, P. Mora, J. Monney, K. Pinçon, A. Queffelec, and C. Stouvenout. 2015. "La grotte de Morne Rita, Capesterre de Marie-Galante (Guadeloupe): nouvelles données." Paper presented at the 26th Congress of the International Association for Caribbean Archaeology, Sint Maarten, 19–25 July.

Fox, Georgia. 2007. "Continuing Investigations of English Settlement in the Caribbean: A Multifaceted Approach." *Proceedings of the International Congress for Caribbean Archaeology* 21(1): 163–169.

———. 2014. "Archaeological Investigations at Betty's Hope Plantation, Antigua: Some Preliminary Thoughts on Theory." In *Bitasion archaeologie des habitations—plantations des Petites Antilles*, edited by Kenneth G. Kelly and Benoît Bérard, 33-41. Leiden, Netherlands: Sidestone Press.

Gamble, Clive. 1996. *Timewalkers: The Prehistory of Global Colonization*. Cambridge, MA: Harvard University Press.

Garcia-Casco, Antonio, Sebastiaan Knippenberg, Reniel Rodríguez Ramos, George E. Harlow, Corinne Hofman, José Carlos Pomo, and Idael F. Blanco-Quintero. 2013. "Pre-Columbian Jadeitite Artifacts from the Golden Rock Site, St. Eustatius, Lesser Antilles, with Special Reference to Jadeitite Artifacts from Elliot's, Antigua: Implications for Potential Source Regions and Long-Distance Exchange Networks in the Greater Caribbean." *Journal of Archaeological Science* 408: 3153–3169.

Geophysics Study Committee. 1990. *Sea-Level Change*. Washington, DC: National Academy Press.

Gérard, R. 1994. "Premier indice d'une occupation précéramique en Guadeloupe continentale." *Journal de la Société des Américanistes* 80: 241–242.

Giovas, Christine M., Michelle J. LeFebvre, and Scott M. Fitzpatrick. 2011. "New Records for Prehistoric Introduction of Neotropical Mammals to the West Indies: Evidence from Carriacou, Lesser Antilles." *Journal of Biogeography* 39(3): 476–487.

Gischler, Eberhard 2006. "Comment on 'Corrected Western Atlantic Sea-level Curve for the Last 11,000 Years based on Calibrated ^{14}C Dates from *Acropora Palmate* Framework and Intertidal Mangrove Peat' by Toscano and Macintyre." *Coral Reefs* 22: 257–270 (2003), and their response in *Coral Reefs* 24: 187–190 (2005)." *Coral Reefs* 25: 273–279.

Goni, M. A., H. Aceves, B. Benitez-Nelson, E. Tappa, R. Thunell, D. E. Black, F. Muller-Karger, Y. Astor, and R. Varela. 2009. "Oceanographic and Climatologic Controls on the Compositions and Fluxes of Biogenic Materials in the Water Column and Sediments of the Caricao Basin over the Late Holocene." *Deep-Sea Research I* 56: 614–640.

Goodwin, Conrad M. 1994. "Betty's Hope Windmill: An Unexpected Problem." *Historical Archaeology* 28(1): 99–110.

Goren-Inbar, Naama, Nira Alperson, Mordechai E. Kislev, Orit Simchoni, Yoel Melamed, Adi Ben-Nun, and Ella Werker. 2004. "Evidence of Hominin Control of Fire at Gesher Benot Ya'aqov, Israel." *Science* 304(5671): 725–727.

Goslinga, Cornelis Ch. 1971. *The Dutch in the Caribbean and on the Wild Coast 1580–1680*. Gainesville: University Press of Florida.

Goudie, Andrew. 2000. *The Human Impact on the Natural Environment*. Fifth edition. Cambridge: MIT Press.

Graham, Alan. 1995. "Diversification of Gulf/Caribbean Mangrove Communities through Cenozoic Time." *Biotropica* 27: 20–27.

Grattan, John, and Robin Torrence, eds. 2007. *Living Under the Shadow: The Cultural Impacts of Volcanic Eruptions*. Walnut Creek, CA: Left Coast Press.

Greenfield, Haskel J. 2010. "The Secondary Products Revolution: The Past, the Present, and the Future." *World Archaeology* 42(1): 29–54.

Grimm, Eric C. 1988. "Data Analysis and Display." In *Vegetation History*, edited by B. Huntley and T. Webb III, 43–76. Dordrecht: Kluwer.

Grouard, Sandrine. 1997. "Tanki Flip Faunal Remains." In Versteeg and Rostain, *Archaeology of Aruba*, 257–264.

———. 2001. "Subsistance, systèmes techniques et gestion territoriale en mileu insulaire antillais précolombien. Exploitation des vertébrés et des crustacées aux époques Saladoïdes et Troumassoïdes de Guadeloupe (400 av. J.C. à 1500 ap. J.C.)." Ph.D. dissertation. Paris: Université de Paris X-Nanterre.

Grouard, Sandrine, Sophia Perdikaris, and Karyne Debue. 2013. "Dog Burials Associated with Human Burials in the West Indies during the Early Pre-Columbian Ceramic Age (500 B.C.–600 A.D.)." *Anthropozoologica* 48(2): 447–465.

Guilaine, Jean, and Claire Manen. 2007. "From Mesolithic to Neolithic in the Western Mediterranean." *Proceedings of the British Academy* 144: 21–51.

Guilderson, Thomas P., Richard G. Fairbanks, and James L. Rubenstone. 1994. "Tropical Temperature Variations since 20,000 Years Ago: Modulating Interhemispheric Climate Change." *Science* 263(5147): 663–665.

Gunn, Joel D. 1994. "Global Climate and Regional Biocultural Diversity." In Crumley, *Historical Ecology*, 67–97.

Haberle, Simon G., and Marie-Pierre Ledru. 2001. "Correlations among Charcoal Records of Fires from the Past 16,000 Years in Indonesia, Papua New Guinea, and Central and South America." *Quaternary Research* 55: 97–104.

Hackenberger, Steven. 1988. "An Abstract of Archaeological Investigations by the Barbados Museum 1986." *Journal of the Barbados Museum and Historical Society* 38(2): 155–162.

Hall, Stephen A. 1981. Deteriorated Pollen Grains and the Interpretation of Quaternary Pollen Diagrams. *Review of Paleobotany and Palynology* 32: 193–206.

Hanski, Ilkka. 2010. "The Theories of Island Biogeography and Metapopulation Dynamics: Science Marches Forward, but the Legacy of Good Ideas Lasts for

a Long Time." In Losos and Ricklefs, *Theory of Island Biogeography Revisited,* 186–213.
Hardy, F. 1981. "Soils." In Cooper and Bacon, *Natural Resources of Trinidad and Tobago,* 23–42.
Hardy, Meredith D. 2009. "The St. Croix Archaeology Project and the Vescelius Collection: A Reexamination." *Bulletin of the Peabody Museum of Natural History* 50(1): 99–118.
Harris, David R. 1965. *Plants, Animals, and Man in the Outer Leeward Islands, West Indies: An Ecological Study of Antigua, Barbuda, and Anguilla.* Berkeley: University of California Press.
Harris, David R., and Gordon C. Hillman, eds. 1989. *Foraging and Farming: The Evolution of Plant Exploitation.* London: Unwin Hyman.
Harris, Peter O'Brien. 1972a. "Notes on Trinidad Archaeology." Pointe-à-Pierre: Trinidad and Tobgao Historical Society.
———. 1972b. "The Early Trinidadian." *Art and Culture (San Fernando)* 1972: 23–30.
———. 1973. "Preliminary Report on Banwari Trace, a Preceramic Site in Trinidad." *Proceedings of the International Congress for the Study of the Pre-Columbian Cultures of the Lesser Antilles* 4: 115–125.
———. 1978. "A Revised Chronological Framework for Ceramic Trinidad and Tobago." *Proceedings of the International Congress for the Study of the Pre-Columbian Cultures of the Lesser Antilles* 7: 47–63.
———. 1991. "A Paleo-Indian Stemmed Point from Trinidad, West Indies." *Proceedings of the International Congress for Caribbean Archaeology* 14: 73–93.
Haug, Gerald H., Konrad A. Hughen, Daniel M. Sigman, Larry C. Peterson, and Ursula Röhl. 2001. "Southward Migration of the Intertropical Convergence Zone through the Holocene." *Science* 293(5533): 1304–1308.
Haug, Gerald H., Detlef Gunther, Larry C. Peterson, Daniel M. Sigman, Konrad A. Hughen, and Beat Aeschlimann. 2003. "Climate and the Collapse of Maya Civilization." *Science* 299: 1731–1735.
Haviser, Jay B. Jr. 1987. "Amerindian Cultural Geography of Curaçao." Ph.D. dissertation. Leiden, Netherlands: Leiden University.
———. 1989. "A Comparison of Amerindian Insular Adaptive Strategies on Curaçao." In Siegel, *Early Ceramic Population Lifeways,* 3–28.
———. 1991a. *The First Bonaireans.* Reports of the Archaeological-Anthropological Institute of the Netherlands Antilles 10. Curaçao: Archaeological-Anthropological Institute of the Netherlands Antilles.
———. 1991b. "Development of an Interaction Sphere in the Northern Lesser Antilles." *New West Indian Guide* 65(3/4): 129–151.
———. 1997. "Settlement Strategies in the Early Ceramic Age." In Wilson, *Indigenous People of the Caribbean,* 57–69.
———. 2001a."New Data for the Archaic Age on Curaçao." *Proceedings of the International Congress for Caribbean Archaeology* 19(1): 110–121.
———. 2001b. "Historical Archaeology in the Netherlands Antilles and Aruba." In Farnsworth, *Island Lives,* 60–81.
Hawai'i Biocomplexity Project Team. 2010. "The Hawai'i Biocomplexity Project in Retrospect." In Kirch, *Roots of Conflict,* 163–171.

Hayward, Michele H., and Michael A. Cinquino, eds. 2002. *Archaeological Investigations at the Aklis Site, Sandy Point National Wildlife Refuge, St. Croix, U.S. Virgin Islands.* SEAC Technical Reports No. 10. Tallahassee, FL: Southeast Archaeological Center.

Henocq, Christophe, and François Petit. 1995. "Présentation de six gisements archéologiques de St Martin et de leur environnement." *Proceedings of the International Congress of Caribbean Archaeology* 16(1): 300–315.

Higham, T. F. G., and L. Johnson. 1997. "The Prehistoric Chronology of Raoul Island, the Kermadec Group." *Archaeology in Oceania* 32(3): 207–213.

Higuera-Gundy, Antonia. 1991. "Antillean Vegetational History and Paleoclimate Reconstructed from the Paleolimnological Record of Lake Miragone, Haiti." Ph.D. dissertation. Gainesville: University of Florida.

Higuera-Gundy Antonia, Mark Brenner, David A. Hodell, Jason H. Curtis, Barbara W. Leyden, and Michael W. Binford. 1999. "A 10,300 ^{14}C Yr Record of Climate and Vegetation Change from Haiti." *Quaternary Research* 52: 15–170.

Higuera, Philip E., Linda B. Brubaker, Patricia M. Anderson, Feng Sheng Hu, and Thomas A. Brown. 2009. "Vegetation Mediated the Impacts of Postglacial Climate Change on Fire Fegimes in the South-Central Brooks Range, Alaska." *Ecological Monographs* 79: 201–219.

Higuera, P. E., D. C. Gavin, P. J. Bartlein, and D. J. Hallett. 2010. "Peak Detection in Sediment-Charcoal Record: Impacts of Alternative Data Analysis Methods on Fire-History Interpretations." *International Journal of Wildland Fire* 19: 996–1014.

Hill, I. D. 1966. "Soil and Land Use Surveys, No. 19A and 19B: Antigua and Barbuda." St. Augustine, Trinidad and Tobago: Regional Research Center, University of the West Indies.

Hincks, Thea, Steve Sparks, Peter Dunkley, and Paul Cole. 2005. "Montserrat." In Lindsay et al., *Volcanic Hazard Atlas*, 148–167.

Hinds, Ronald, Bruce Jardine, and Karl Watson. 2000. "A Preliminary Report on a Saladoid Site at Spring Garden, Barbados." *Journal of the Barbados Museum and Historical Society* 46: 77–92.

Hodell, David A., Mark Brenner, Jason H. Curtis, Roger Medina-González, Enrique Ildefonso-Chan Can, Alma Albornaz-Pat, and Thomas P. Guilderson. 2005. "Climate Change on the Yucatan Peninsula during the Little Ice Age." *Quaternary Research* 63: 109–121.

Hodell, David A., Jason H. Curtis, Glenn A. Jones, Antonia Higuera-Gundy, Mark Brenner, Michael W. Binford, and Kathleen T. Dorsey. 1991. "Reconstruction of Caribbean Climate Change Over the Past 10,500 Years." *Nature* 352: 790–793.

Hofman, Corinne L. 1993. "In Search of the Native Population of Pre-Columbian Saba (400–1450 A.D.), Part One: Pottery Styles and their Interpretations." Ph.D. dissertation. Leiden, Netherlands: Leiden University.

———. 1995a. "Three Late Prehistoric Sites in the Periphery of Guadeloupe: Grande Anse, Les Saintes and Morne Cybele 1 and 2, La Desirade." Paper presented at the 16th International Congress for Caribbean Archaeology, Guadeloupe.

———. 1995b. "Inferring Inter-Insular Relationships from Ceramic Style: A View from the Leeward Islands." *Proceedings of the International Congress for Caribbean Archaeology* 15: 233–241.

———. 1999. "The Pottery." In Hofman and Hoogland, *Archaeological Investigations on St. Martin,* 149–188.

———. 2013. "The Post-Saladoid in the Lesser Antilles (A.D. 600/800–1492)." In Keegan, Hofman, and Rodríguez Ramos, *Oxford Handbook of Caribbean Archaeology,* 205–220.

Hofman, Corinne L., Arie Boomert, Alistair J. Bright, Menno L. P. Hoogland, Sebastiaan Knippenberg, and Alice V. M. Samson. 2011. "Ties with the 'Homelands': Archipelagic Interaction and the Enduring Role of the Continental American Mainland in the Precolumbian Lesser Antilles." In Curet and Hauser, *Islands at the Crossroads,* 73–85.

Hofman, Corinne L., and Eric Milton Branford. 2011. "Lavoutte Revisited, Preliminary Results of the 2009 Rescue Excavations at Cas-en-Bas, St. Lucia." *Proceedings of the International Congress for Caribbean Archaeology* 23: 690–700.

Hofman, Corinne L., Alistair J. Bright, Arie Boomert, and Sebastiaan Knippenberg. 2007. "Island Rhythms: The Web of Social Relationships and Interaction Networks in the Lesser Antillean Archipelago between 400 B.C. and A.D. 1492." *Latin American Antiquity* 18: 243–268.

Hofman, Corinne L., Alistair J. Bright, and Menno L. P. Hoogland. 2006. "Archipelagic Resource Mobility. Shedding light on the 3000 Years Old Tropical Forest Campsite at Plum Piece, Saba (Northern Lesser Antilles)." *Journal of Island and Coastal Archaeology* 1(2): 145–164.

Hofman, Corinne L., Alistair J. Bright, and Reniel Rodríguez Ramos. 2010. "Crossing the Caribbean Sea: Towards a Holistic View of Pre-Colonial Mobility and Exchange." *Journal of Caribbean Archaeology* 10: 1–18.

Hofman, Corinne L., André Delpuech, Menno L. P. Hoogland, and Maaike S. de Waal. 2004. "Late Ceramic Age Survey of the Northeastern Islands of the Guadeloupean Archipelago: Grande-Terre, La Desirade and Petite-Terre." In Delpuech and Hofman, *Late Ceramic Age Societies in the Eastern Caribbean,* 159–182.

Hofman, Corinne L., and Menno L. P. Hoogland, eds. 1999. *Archaeological Investigations on St. Martin (Lesser Antilles): The Sites of Norman Estate, Anse des Pères and Hope Estate with a Contribution to the "La Hueca Problem."* Archaeological Studies Leiden University 4. Leiden, Netherlands: Faculty of Archaeology, Leiden University.

———. 2001. "Spatial Organization at a Troumassoid Settlement, The Case of Anse à la Gourde, Guadeloupe." *Proceedings of the International Congress for Caribbean Archaeology* 19: 124–131.

———. 2003. "Plum Piece: Evidence for Archaic Seasonal Occupation on Saba, Northern Lesser Antilles around 3300 B.P." *Journal of Caribbean Archaeology* 4: 12–27.

———. 2004. "Social Dynamics and Change in the Northern Lesser Antilles." In Delpuech and Hofman, *Late Ceramic Age Societies in the Eastern Caribbean,* 47–58.

———. 2011. "Unravelling the Multi-Scale Networks of Mobility and Exchange in the Circum-Caribbean." In Hofman and van Duijvenbode, *Communities in Contact*, 15–44.

———. 2012. "Caribbean Encounters: Rescue Excavations at the Early Colonial Island Carib Site of Argyle, St. Vincent." *Analecta Praehistoria Leidensia* 43/44: 63–76.

———. 2015. "Beautiful Tropical Islands in the Caribbean Sea. Human Responses to Floods and Droughts and the Indigenous Archaeological Heritage of the Caribbean." In *Water and Heritage: Material, Conceptual and Spiritual Connections*, edited by Willem J. H. Willems and Henk P. J. van Schaik, 99–119. Leiden, Netherlands: Sidestone Press.

Hofman, Corinne L., Menno L. P. Hoogland, and B. Roux. 2015. "Reconstruire le táboüi, le manna et les pratiques funéraires au village caraïbe d'Argyle, Saint-Vincent." In *À la recherche du Caraïbe perdu: Les populations amérindiennes des Petites Antilles de l'époque précolombienne à la période coloniale*, edited by B. Grunberg, 41–50. Paris: L'Harmattan.

Hofman, Corinne L., Menno L. P. Hoogland, and Annelou L. van Gijn, eds. 2008. *Crossing the Borders: New Methods and Techniques in the Study of Archaeological Materials from the Caribbean*. Tuscaloosa: University of Alabama Press.

Hofman, Corinne L., Menno L. P. Hoogland, Darlene A. Weston, Jason E. Laffoon, Hayley L. Mickleburgh, and Mike H. Field. 2012. "Rescuing the Dead: Settlement and Mortuary Data from Rescue Excavations at the Pre-Colonial Site of Lavoutte, Saint Lucia." *Journal of Field Archaeology* 37: 209–225.

Hofman, Corinne L., and Loe F. H. C. Jacobs. 2000/2001. "The Dynamics of Technology, Function and Style: A Study of Early Ceramic Age Pottery from the Caribbean." *Newsletter of the Department of Pottery Technology* 18/19: 7–44.

———. 2004. "Different or Alike? A Technological Comparison between Late Prehistoric Ceramics and Modern Day Folk Pottery from St. Lucia, W.I." *Leiden Journal of Pottery Studies* 20: 23–52.

Hofman, Corinne L., Angus A. A. Mol, Menno L. P. Hoogland, and Roberto Valcárcel Rojas. 2014. "Stage of Encounters: Migration, Mobility and Interaction in the Pre-Colonial and Early Colonial Caribbean." *World Archaeology* 46: 590–609.

Hofman, Corinne L., and Anne van Duijvenbode, eds. 2011. *Communities in Contact: Essays in Archaeology, Ethnohistory & Ethnography of the Amerindian Circum-Caribbean*. Leiden, Netherlands: Sidestone Press.

Holliday, Vance T., and William G. Gartner. 2007. "Methods of Soil P Analysis in Archaeology." *Journal of Archaeological Science* 34: 301–333.

Holmes, J. A., F. A. Street-Perrott, M. Ivanovich, and R. A. Perrott.1995. "A Late Quaternary Paleolimnological Record from Jamaica based on Trace-element Chemistry of Ostracod Shells." *Chemical Geology* 124: 143–160.

Hoogland, Menno L. P. 1996. "In Search of the Native Population of Pre-Columbian Saba. Part Two: Natural and Social Environment." Ph.D. dissertation. Leiden, Netherlands: Leiden University.

———. 2011. "Archaeological Investigations at Spanish Water, Curaçao." *Proceedings of the International Congress for Caribbean Archaeology* 23: 631–639.

———. 2013. "From Corpse Taphonomy to Mortuary Behavior in the Caribbean: A Case Study from the Lesser Antilles." In Keegan, Hofman, and Rodríguez Ramos, *Oxford Handbook of Caribbean Archaeology*, 452–469.

Hoogland, Menno L. P. and Corinne L. Hofman. 2015. "Archaeological Assessment in Compliance with the Valetta Treaty: Spanish Water, Curacao." In *Managing Our Past into the Future: Archaeological Heritage Management in the Dutch Caribbean*, edited by Corinne L. Hofman and Jay B. Haviser, 183–194. Leiden, Netherlands: Sidestone Press.

Hoogland, Menno L. P., Corinne L. Hofman, Henry Hooghiemstra, and Mike H. Field. 2015. "Under the Mangrove: Coastal Dynamics and Deeply Buried Deposits at the Site of Anse Trabaud, Martinique." Paper presented at the 26th Congress of the International Association for Caribbean Archaeology, Sint Maarten, 19–25 July.

Horton, D. R. 1982. "The Burning Question: Aborigines, Fire, and Australian Ecosystems." *Mankind* 13: 237–251.

Hunt, Terry L., and Carl P. Lipo. 2006. "Late Colonization of Easter Island." *Science* 311(5767): 1603–1606.

Hunter-Anderson, Rosalind L. 2009. "Savanna Anthropogenesis in the Mariana Islands, Micronesia: Re-interpreting the Palaeoenvironmental Data." *Archaeology in Oceania* 44: 125–141.

Im Thurn, Everard F. 1883. *Among the Indians of Guiana being Sketches Chiefly Anthropologic from the Interior of British Guiana*. London: Kegan Paul, Trench.

Instituto Nacional Indigenista. 2009. "Biblioteca digital de la medicina tradicional Mexicana." Universidad Nacional Autónoma de México, Mexico City. Retrieved 13 May 2015 from http://www.medicinatradicionalmexicana.unam.mx/index.php.

Iriarte, José, and Eduardo Alonso Paz. 2009."Phytolith Analysis of Selected Native Plants and Modern Soils from Southeastern Uruguay and its Implications for Paleoenvironmental and Archeological Reconstruction." *Quaternary International* 193: 99–123.

Iriarte, José, Irene Holst, Oscar Marozzi, Claudia Listopad, Eduardo Alonso, Andrés Rinderknecht, and Juan Montaña. 2004. "Evidence for Cultivar Adoption and Emerging Complexity during the Mid-Holocene in the La Plata Basin." *Nature* 432: 614–617.

Irwin, Geoffrey. 1990. "Human Colonisation and Change in the Remote Pacific." *Current Anthropology* 31(1): 90–94.

———. 1999. "Commentary on Paul Rainbird, 'Islands out of Time: Towards a Critique of Island Archaeology.'" *Journal of Mediterranean Archaeology* 12(2): 252–254.

Isendoorn, J. Daan, Corinne L. Hofman, and Mathijs Booden. 2008. "Back to the Source: Provenance Areas of Clays and Temper Materials of Pre-Columbian Caribbean Ceramics." *Journal of Caribbean Archaeology Special Issue* 2: 15–24.

Islebe, Gerald A., Henry Hooghiemstra, Mark Brenner, Jason H. Curtis, and David A. Hodell. 1996. "A Holocene Vegetation History from Lowland Guatemala." *The Holocene* 6: 265–271.

Jermy A. C., and T. G. Walker. 1985. "Cytotaxonomic Studies of the Ferns of Trinidad." *Bulletin of the British Museum of Natural History, Botany* 13(2): 133–276.

Jones, John G. 1994. "Pollen Evidence for Early Settlement and Agriculture in Northern Belize." *Palynology* 18: 205–211.
Jones, John G., and Deborah M. Pearsall. 1999. "Pollen and Phytolith Evidence for Settlement, Agriculture and Paleoenvironment at the Maisabel Site, a Multicomponent Site in Puerto Rico." Paper presented at the 64th Annual Meeting of the Society for American Archaeology, Chicago.
Jones, Rhys. 1969. "Firestick Farming." *Australian Natural History* 16: 224–231.
Keegan, William F. 1985. "Dynamic Horticulturalists: Population Expansion in the Prehistoric Bahamas." Ph.D. dissertation. Los Angeles: University of California.
———. 1992. *The People Who Discovered Columbus: The Prehistory of the Bahamas.* Gainesville: University Press of Florida.
———. 1995. "Modeling Dispersal in the Prehistoric West Indies." *World Archaeology* 26: 400–420.
———. 1999. "Comment on Paul Rainbird 'Islands Out of Time: Towards a Critique of Island Archaeology.'" *Journal of Mediterranean Archaeology* 12(2): 255–258.
———. 2004. "Islands of Chaos." In Delpuech and Hofman, *Late Ceramic Age Societies in the Eastern Caribbean*, 33–44.
———. 2006. "Archaic Influences in the Origins and Development of Taíno Societies." *Caribbean Journal of Science* 42(1): 1–10.
———. 2009. "Central Plaza Burials in Saladoid Puerto Rico: An Alternative Perspective." *Latin American Antiquity* 20: 375–385.
———. 2010. "Demographic Imperatives for Island Colonists." In Anderson, Barrett, and Boyle, *Global Origins and Development of Seafaring*, 171–178.
Keegan, William F., and Jared M. Diamond. 1987. "Colonization of Islands by Humans: A Biogeographical Perspective." In *Advances in Archaeological Method and Theory*, edited by Michael B. Schiffer, vol. 10, 49–92. New York: Academic Press.
Keegan William F., and Corinne L. Hofman. 2017. *The Caribbean before Columbus*. New York: Oxford University Press.
Keegan, William F., Corinne L. Hofman, and Reniel Rodriguéz Ramos, eds. 2013. *The Oxford Handbook of Caribbean Archaeology*. New York: Oxford University Press.
Keegan, William F., and Reniel Rodríguez Ramos. 2004. "Sin rodeos." *El Caribe Arqueológico* 7: 9–13.
Kennedy, H. 2003. "Marantaceae." In *Manual de Plantas de Costa Rica*, edited by B. E. Hammel, M. H. Grayum, C. Herrera, and N. Zamora. *Monographs in Systematic Botany* 92: 629–665.
Kennedy, Lisa M., Sally P. Horn, and Keneth H. Orvis. 2006. "A 4000-year Record of Fire and Forest History from Valle de Bao, Cordillera Central, Dominican Republic." *Palaeogeography, Palaeoclimatology, Palaeoecology* 231: 279–290.
Kennett, Douglas, Atholl Anderson, and Bruce Winterhalder. 2006. "The Ideal Free Distribution, Food Production, and Colonization in Oceania." In *Behavioral Ecology and the Transition to Agriculture*, edited by Douglas Kennett and Bruce Winterhalder, 265–288. Berkeley: University of California Press.

Kenny, Julian S. 2008. *The Biological Diversity of Trinidad and Tobago: A Naturalist's Notes.* Port of Spain: Prospect Press.

Kidder, Tristram R. 2006. "Climate Change and the Archaic to Woodland Transition (3000–2500 Cal B.P.) in the Mississippi River Basin." *American Antiquity* 71: 195–231.

Kimura, Birgitta K., Michelle J. LeFebvre, Susan D. deFrance, Hilary I. Knodel, Michelle S. Turner, Natalie S. Fitzsimmons, Scott M. Fitzpatrick, and Connie J. Mulligan. 2016. "Origin of Pre-Columbian Guinea Pigs from Caribbean Archeological Sites Revealed through Genetic Analysis." *Journal of Archaeological Science Reports* 5: 442–452.

King, Russell. 2007. *The History of Human Migration.* London: New Holland.

Kirby, I. A. Earle. 1974. "The Cayo Pottery of St. Vincent—A Pre-Calivigny Series." *Proceedings of the International Congress for the Study of the Pre-Columbian Cultures of the Lesser Antilles* 5: 61–64.

Kirch, Patrick V. 1982. "The Impact of the Prehistoric Polynesians on the Hawaiian Ecosystem." *Pacific Science* 36: 1–4.

———. 1984. *The Evolution of the Polynesian Chiefdoms.* Cambridge: Cambridge University Press.

———. 1988. "Polynesia's Mystery Islands." *Archaeology* 41(3): 26–31.

———. 1990. "Specialization and Exchange in the Lapita Complex of Oceania (1600–500 B.C.)." *Asian Perspectives* 29: 117–133.

———. 1996. "Late Holocene Human-induced Modifications to a Central Polynesian Island Ecosystem." *Proceedings of the National Academy of Sciences of the United States of America* 93: 5296–5300.

———. 1997a. *The Lapita Peoples: Ancestors of the Oceanic World.* London: Blackwell.

———. 1997b. "Changing Landscapes and Sociopolitical Evolution in Mangaia, Central Polynesia." In Kirch and Hunt, *Historical Ecology in the Pacific Islands,* 147–165.

———. 1997c. "Introduction: The Environmental History of Oceanic Islands." In Kirch and Hunt, *Historical Ecology in the Pacific Islands,* 1–21.

———. 2000. *On the Road of the Winds: An Archaeological History of the Pacific Islands before European Contact.* Berkeley: University of California Press.

———. 2005. "Archaeology and Global Change: The Holocene Record." *Annual Review of Environmental Resources* 30: 409–440.

———. 2010a. "Peopling of the Pacific: A Holistic Anthropological Perspective." *Annual Review of Anthropology* 39: 131–148.

———, ed. 2010b. *Roots of Conflict: Soils, Agriculture, and Sociopolitical Complexity in Ancient Hawai'i.* Santa Fe: School for Advanced Research Press.

———. 2011. "When Did the Polynesians Settle Hawai'i? A Review of 150 Years of Scholarly Inquiry and a Tentative Answer." *Hawaiian Archaeology* 12: 3–26.

Kirch, Patrick V., Eric Conte, Warren Sharp, and Cordelia Nickelsen. 2010. "The Onemea Site (Taravai Island, Mangareva) and the Human Colonization of Southeastern Polynesia." *Archaeology in Oceania* 45: 66–79.

Kirch, Patrick V, and J. Ellison. 1994. "Palaeoenvironmental Evidence for Human Colonization of Remote Oceanic Islands." *Antiquity* 68 (259): 310–321.

Kirch, Patrick V., and Terry L. Hunt, eds. 1997. *Historical Ecology in the Pacific Islands: Prehistoric Environmental and Landscape Change.* New Haven, CT: Yale University Press.

Kirch, Patrick V., and J-L. Rallu, eds. 2007. *The Growth and Collapse of Pacific Island Societies: Archaeological and Demographic Perspectives.* Honolulu: University of Hawai'i Press.
Kjellmark, Eric. 1996. "Late Holocene Climate Change and Human Disturbance on Andros Island, Bahamas." *Journal of Paleolimnology* 15: 133–145.
Knapp, A. Bernard. 2010. "Cyprus's Earliest Prehistory: Seafarers, Foragers and Settlers." *Journal of World Prehistory* 23: 79–120.
———. 2013. *The Archeology of Cyprus: From Earliest Prehistory through the Bronze Age.* Cambridge, UK: Cambridge University Press.
Knappett, Carl, Tim Evans, and Ray Rivers. 2008. "Modelling Maritime Interaction in the Aegean Bronze Age." *Antiquity* 82: 1009–1024.
———. 2011. "The Theran Eruption and Minoan Palatial Collapse: New Interpretations Gained from Modelling the Maritime Network." *Antiquity* 85: 1008–1023.
Komorowski, Jean-Christophe, Georges Boudon, Michel Semet, Francois Beauduce, Christian Anténor-Habazac, Sara Bazin, and Gilbert Hammouya. 2005. "Guadeloupe." In Lindsay et al., *Volcanic Hazard Atlas,* 67–105.
Kraan, Claudia, Amy Victorina, Scott M. Fitzpatrick, Taylor Dodrill, Maggie Gebhardt, Paul Gerard, Haden Kingrey, Natasha Minugh, Martin Nelson-Harrington, and Mark Rempel. 2016. "New Archaeological Research on Curaçao," *Journal of Island and Coastal Archaeology* 12: 138–144
Krook, L. 1979. "Sediment Petrographical Studies in Northern Suriname." Ph.D. dissertation. Amsterdam, Netherlands: Amsterdam Vrije Universiteit.
Laffoon, Jason E., and Bart R. de Vos. 2011. "Diverse Origins, Similar Diets: An Integrated Isotopic Perspective from Anse à la Gourde, Guadeloupe." In Hofman and van Duijvenbode, *Communities in Contact,* 187–203.
Laffoon, Jason E., Menno L. P. Hoogland, Gareth R. Davies, and Corinne L. Hofman. 2016. "Human Dietary Assessment in the Pre-Colonial Lesser Antilles: New Stable Isotope Evidence from Lavoutte, Saint Lucia." *Journal of Archaeological Science Reports* 5: 168–180.
Laffoon, Jason E., Reniel Rodríguez Ramos, Luis A. Chanlatte Baik, Yvonne Narganes Storde, Miguel Rodríguez Lopez, Gareth R. Davies, and Corinne L. Hofman. 2014. "Long-Distance Exchange in the Precolonial Circum-Caribbean: A Multi-Isotope Study of Animal Tooth Pendants from Puerto Rico." *Journal of Anthropological Archaeology* 35: 220–233.
Lalubie, Guillaume. 2011. "La perception des aléas naturels aux Petites Antilles par les Amérindiens Kalinago." Paper Presented at the 24th Congress of the International Association of Caribbean Archaeologists, Martinique, 25–29 July.
Lane, Chad S., Sally P. Horn, and Matthew T. Kerr. 2014. "Beyond the Mayan lowlands: Impacts of the Terminal Classic Drought in the Caribbean Antilles." *Quaternary Science Reviews* 86: 89–98.
Lathrap, Donald W. 1970. *The Upper Amazon.* Ancient Peoples and Places 70. Southampton: Thames and Hudson.
Law Engineering and Environmental Services. 2002. *Archaeological Assessment of Existing Conditions for the Slave Worker Village, Coakley Bay Historic Plantation, St. Croix, U.S. Virgin Islands.* Submitted to T. K. Properties, St. Croix, U.S. Virgin Islands. Law Engineering and Environmental Services, Miami

Lakes, Florida. St. Thomas, Virgin Islands: Department of Planning & Natural Resources, VI State Historic Preservation Office.

Leppard, Thomas P. 2014a. "Modeling the Impacts of Mediterranean Island Colonization by Archaic Hominins: The Likelihood of an Insular Lower Palaeolithic." *Journal of Mediterranean Archaeology* 27(2): 231–254.

———. 2014b. "Similarity and Diversity in the Prehistoric Colonization of Islands and Coasts by Food-Producing Communities. *Journal of Island and Coastal Archaeology* 9(1): 1–15.

———. 2015. "Adaptive Responses to Demographic Fragility: Mitigating Stochastic Effects in Early Island Colonization." *Human Ecology* 43(5): 721–734.

Leveau, Philippe, Frédéric Trément, Kevin Walsh, and Graeme Barker, eds. 1999. *Environmental Reconstruction in Mediterranean Landscape Archaeology.* Oxford: Oxbow Books.

Lewis, John F., Grenville Draper, C. Bourdon, C. Bowin, P. Mattson, F. Maurrasse, F. Tagle, and G. Pardo. 1990. "Geology and Tectonic Evolution of the Northern Caribbean Margin." In Dengo and Chase, *Caribbean Region*, Vol. H, 77–140.

Lewthwaite, J. 1982. "Cardial Disorder: Ethnographic and Archaeological Comparisons for Problems in the Early Prehistory of the West Mediterranean." In *Le Néolithique Ancien Mediteranéen*, edited by R. Montjardin, 311–318. Sète: La Féderation Archaéologique de l'Hérault.

Leyden, Barbara W. 1985. "Late Quaternary Aridity and Holocene Moisture Fluctuations in the Lake Valencia Basin, Venezuela." *Ecology* 66: 1279–1295.

———. 1987. "Man and Climate in the Maya Lowlands." *Quaternary Research* 28: 407–414.

Liddle, R. A. 1946. *The Geology of Venezuela and Trinidad.* Ithaca: Paleontology Research Institute.

Lindsay, Jan M., Richard E. A. Robertson, John B. Shepherd, and Shahiba Ali, eds. 2005. *Volcanic Hazards Atlas of the Lesser Antilles.* Trinidad and Tobago: Seismic Research Unit, University of the West Indies.

Liogier, Henri Alaine, and Luis F. Martorell. 2000. *Flora of Puerto Rico and Adjacent Islands: A Systematic Synopsis*, 2nd ed. revised. San Juan: Editorial de la Universidad de Puerto Rico.

Lippi, Ronald D. 1988. "Paleotopography and Phosphate Analysis of a Buried Jungle Site in Ecuador." *Journal of Field Archaeology* 15: 85–97.

Little, Elbert L. Jr., and Frank H. Wadsworth. 1964. *Common Trees of Puerto Rico and the Virgin Islands.* Agriculture Handbook 249. Washington, DC: Forest Service, U.S. Department of Agriculture.

Little, Elbert L. Jr., Roy O. Woodbury, and Frank H. Wadsworth. 1974. *Trees of Puerto Rico and the Virgin Islands, Second Volume.* Agriculture Handbook 449. Washington, DC: Forest Service, U.S. Department of Agriculture.

Logan, Amanda. 2006. "The Application of Phytolith and Starch Grain Analysis to Understanding Formative Period Subsistence, Ritual, and Trade on the Taraco Peninsula, Highland Bolivia." M.A. thesis. Columbia: University of Missouri.

Look, Cory. 2011. "The Use of GIS in Better Understanding Prehistoric and Historic Use of Space and Resources in Barbuda, West Indies." *Proceedings of the International Congress of Caribbean Archaeology* 23: 402–410.

Losos, Jonathan B., and Robert E. Ricklefs, eds. 2010. *The Theory of Island Biogeography Revisited*. Princeton, NJ: Princeton University Press.
Loveless, A. R. 1960. "The Vegetation of Antigua, West Indies." *Journal of Ecology* 48: 495–527.
Lundberg, Emily R. 1985. "Interpreting the Cultural Associations of Aceramic Deposits in the Virgin Islands." *Journal of Field Archaeology* 12(2): 201–212.
———. 1989. "Preceramic Procurement Patterns at Krum Bay, Virgin Islands." Ph.D. dissertation. Urbana-Champaign: University of Illinois.
MacArthur, Robert H., and Edward O. Wilson. 1963. "An Equilibrium Theory of Insular Zoogeography." *Evolution* 17: 373–387.
———. 1967. *The Theory of Island Biogeography*. Princeton, NJ: Princeton University Press.
Malaizé, B., P. Bertran, P. Carbonel, D. Bonnissent, K. Charlier, D. Galop, D. Imbert, N. Serrand, Ch. Stouvenot, and C. Pujol. 2011. "Hurricanes and Climate in the Caribbean during the Past 3700 Years BP." *The Holocene* 21(6): 911–924.
Malone, Caroline. 2003. "The Italian Neolithic: A Synthesis of Research." *Journal of World Prehistory* 17(3): 235–312.
Mandryk, Carole. 2003. "Foreword." In Rockman and Steele, *Colonization of Unfamiliar Landscapes*, xiii–xv.
Mangini, A., P. Blumbach, P. Verdes, C. Spötl, D. Scholz, H. Machel, and S. Mahon. 2007. "Combined Records from a Stalagmite from Barbados and from Lake Sediments Reveal Variable Seasonality in the Caribbean between 6.7 and 3 ka BP." *Quaternary Science Reviews* 26: 1332–1343.
Manning, Patrick. 2005. *Migration in World History*. New York: Routledge.
Manning, Stuart W., Carole McCartney, Bernd Kromer, and Sarah T. Stewart. 2010. "The Earlier Neolithic in Cyprus: Recognition and Dating of a Pre-Pottery Neolithic A Occupation." *Antiquity* 84: 693–706.
Maria Conserva, Lucia, and Jesu Costa Ferreira Jr. 2012. "*Borreria* and *Spermacoce* Species (Rubiaceae): A Review of Their Ethnomedicinal Properties, Chemical Constituents, and Biological Activities." *Pharmacognosy Review* 6(11): 46–55.
Marks, Kathy. 2009. *Lost Paradise: From Mutiny on the Bounty to a Modern-Day Legacy of Sexual Mayhem, the Dark Secrets of Pitcairn Island Revealed*. London: Free Press.
Marquardt, William H., and Carole L. Crumley. 1987. "Theoretical Issues in the Analysis of Spatial Patterning." In *Regional Dynamics: Burgundian Landscapes in Historical Perspective*, edited by Carole L. Crumley and William H. Marquardt, 1–18. New York: Academic Press.
Mattioni, Mario, and Ripley P. Bullen. 1970. "A Chronological Chart for the Lesser Antilles: Sites Dated by Ceramic Typology." *Proceedings of the International Congress for the Study of the Pre-Columbian Cultures of the Lesser Antilles* 3: 1–4.
Maury, R. C., G. K. Westbrook, P. E. Baker, P. Bouysse, and D. Westercamp. 1990. "Geology of the Lesser Antilles." In Dengo and Chase, *Caribbean Region*, Vol. H, 141–166.
Mayle, Francis E., and Mitchell J. Power. 2008. "Impact of a Drier Early-Mid Holocene Climate Upon Amazonian Forests." *Philosophical Transactions of the Royal Society B* 363: 1829–1838.

McAndrews, J. H. 1996. "Pollen Analysis on Grenada, West Indies." *Abstract in Palynology* 20: 247.
McAndrews, J. H., and E. K. Ramcharan. 2008. "Holocene Pollen and Climate from Lake Antoine, Grenada." *Abstract in Palynology* 32: 264.
McCann, William R., and Lynn R. Sykes. 1984. "Subduction of Aseismic Ridges Beneath the Caribbean Plate: Implications for the Tectonics and Seismic Potential of the Northeastern Caribbean." *Journal of Geophysical Research* 89: 4493–4519.
McCoy, Mark D., and Anthony S. Hartshorn. 2007. "Wind Erosion and Intensive Prehistoric Agriculture: A Case Study from the Kalaupapa Field System, Hawai'i." *Geoarchaeology: An International Journal* 22: 511–532.
McGovern, Thomas H. 1994. "Management for Extinction in Norse Greenland." In Crumley, *Historical Ecology*, 127–154.
McIntosh, Roderick J., Joseph A. Tainter, and Susan Keech McIntosh, eds. 2000. *The Way the Wind Blows: Climate, History, and Human Action*. New York: Columbia University Press.
McKusick, Marshall B. 1960. "Distribution of Ceramic Styles in the Lesser Antilles, West Indies." Ph.D. dissertation. New Haven, CT: Yale University.
Meggers, Betty J. 1954. "Environmental Limitation on the Development of Culture." *American Anthropologist* 56: 801–824.
———. 1995. "Judging the Future by the Past: The Impact of Environmental Instability on Prehistoric Amazonian Populations." In *Indigenous Peoples and the Future of Amazonia: An Ecological Anthropology of an Endangered World*, edited by Leslie E. Sponsel, 15–43. Tuscon: University of Arizona Press.
Mehlich, A. 1984. "Mehlich-3 Soil Test Extractant: A Modification of Mehlich-2 Extractant." *Communications in Soil Science and Plant Analysis* 15(12): 1409–1416.
Meltzer, David J. 2003. "Lessons in Landscape Learning." In Rockman and Steele, *Colonization of Unfamiliar Landscapes*, 222–241.
Meniketti, Marco G. 2015. *Sugar Cane Capitalism and Environmental Transformation: An Archaeology of Colonial Nevis, West Indies*. Tuscaloosa: University of Alabama Press.
Mickleburgh, Hayley L., and Jaime R. Pagán-Jiménez. 2012. "New Insights into the Consumption of Maize and Other Food Plants in the Pre-Columbian Caribbean from Starch Grains Trapped in Human Dental Calculus." *Journal of Archaeological Science* 39: 2468–2478.
Milliken, W., B. Klitgård, and A. Baracat, eds. 2009 onwards. "Neotropikey— Interactive Key and Information Resources for Flowering Plants of the Neotropics." Retrieved 13 May 2015 from http://www.theplantlist.org/.
Millspaugh, Charles F. 1902. "Flora of the Island of St. Croix." Field Columbian Museum Publication 68. *Botanical Series* 1(7): 441–546.
Mol, Angus A. A. 2014. *The Connected Caribbean: A Socio-Material Network Approach to Patterns of Homogeneity and Diversity in the Pre-Colonial Period*. Leiden, Netherlands: Sidestone Press.
Mol, Angus A. A., and Jimmy L. J. A. Mans. 2013. "Old Boy Networks in the Indigenous Caribbean." In *Network Analysis in Archaeology: New Approaches to Regional Interaction*, edited by Carl Knappett, 307–335. Oxford, UK: Oxford University Press.

Montgomery, Homer, Emile A. Pessagno Jr., and Ivette M. Muñoz. 1992. "Jurassic (Tithonian) Radiolaria from La Désirade (Lesser Antilles): Preliminary Paleontological and Tectonic Implications." *Tectonics* 11(6): 1426–1432.

Mooney, S. D., S. P. Harrison, P. J. Bartlein, A.-L. Daniau, J. Stevenson, K. C. Brownlie, S. Buckman, M. Cupper, J. Luly, M. Black, E. Colhoun, D. D'Costa, J. Dodson, S. Haberle, G. S. Hope, P. Kershaw, C. Kenyon, M. McKenzie, and N. Williams. 2011. "Late Quaternary Fire Regimes of Australasia." *Quaternary Science Reviews* 30: 28–46.

Moran, Emilio F. 1993. *Through Amazonian Eyes: The Human Ecology of Amazonian Populations.* Iowa City: University of Iowa Press.

Moran, Emilio F., and Elinor Ostrom, eds. 2005. *Seeing the Forest and the Trees: Human-Environment Interactions in Forest Ecosystems.* Cambridge, MA: MIT Press.

Morse, Birgit Faber. 1989. "Saladoid Settlement Patterns on St. Croix." In Siegel, *Early Ceramic Population Lifeways,* 29–42.

———. 1995. "The Sequence of Occupations at the Salt River Site, St. Croix." *Proceedings of the International Congress for Caribbean Archaeology* 15: 471–484.

———. 2004. "At the Onset of Complexity: Late Ceramic Developments in St. Croix." In Delpuech and Hofman, *Late Ceramic Age Societies in the Eastern Caribbean,* 183–193.

Morton, Julia F. 1965. "Can the Red Mangrove Provide Food, Feed and Fertilizer?" *Economic Botany* 19: 113–123.

Moscoso, Francisco, Carlos M. Ayes Suárez, and Ovidio Dávila. 1999. *Arcaicos de Angostura: pasado remoto de Puerto Rico.* Vega Baja, Puerto Rico: Sociedad de Investigaciones Arqueológicas e Históricas Sebuco.

Muhs, Daniel R. 2001. "Evolution of Soils on Quaternary Reef Terraces, Barbados, West Indies." *Quaternary Research* 56: 66–78.

Muhs, Daniel R., James R. Budahn, Joseph M. Prospero, and Steven N. Carey. 2007. "Geochemical Evidence for African Dust Inputs to Soils of Western Atlantic Islands: Barbados, the Bahamas, and Florida." *Journal of Geophysical Research* 112: F02009, doi:10.1029/2005JF000445.

Muhs, Daniel R., Russell C. Criterden, John H. Rosholt, Charles A Bush, and Kathleen C. Stewart. 1987. "Genesis of Marine Terrace Soils, Barbados, West Indies: Evidence from Minerology and Geochemistry." *Earth Surface Processes and Landforms* 12: 605–618.

Mulcahy, Matthew. 2006. *Hurricanes and Society in the British Greater Caribbean, 1624–1783.* Baltimore: John Hopkins University Press.

Multer, H. G., M. P. Weiss, and D. V. Nicholson. 1986. *Antigua: Reefs, Rocks, and Highways of History.* Contribution No. 1. St. John's: Leeward Islands Science Associates.

Myrbo A., and H. E. Wright. 2008. "Limnological Research Center Core Facility, SOP Series." Livingstone-bolivia.pdf. Draft v.3.1, 10/13/08.

Nagle, Frederick, and Dennis K. Hubbard. 1989. "St. Croix Geology Since Whetten: An Introduction." In *Terrestrial and Marine Geology of St. Croix, U.S. Virgin Islands,* edited by Dennis K. Hubbard, 1–9. St. Croix: West Indies Laboratory.

Natural Resource Conservation Service. 2000. *Soil Survey of the United States Virgin Islands.* Washington, DC: U.S. Department of Agriculture.

Neff, Hector, Deborah M. Pearsall, John G. Jones, Bárbara Arroyo, Shawn K. Collins, and Dorothy E. Freídel. 2006. "Early Maya Adaptive Patterns: Mid-Late Holocene Paleoenvironmental Evidence from Pacific Guatemala." *Latin American Antiquity* 17: 287–315.

Newsom, Lee A. 1993. "Native West Indian Plant Use." Ph.D. dissertation. Gainesville: University of Florida.

———. 2008. "Caribbean Paleoethnobotany: Present Status and New Horizons (Understanding the Evolution of an Indigenous Ethnobotany)." In Hofman, Hoogland, and van Gijn, *Crossing the Borders*, 173–194.

———. 2010. "Caribbean Maize: First Farmers to Columbus." In *Histories of Maize in Mesoamerica: Multidisciplinary Approaches to the Prehistory, Linguistics, Biogeography, Domestication, and Evolution of Maize*, edited by John E. Staller, Robert H. Tykot, and Bruce F. Benz, 118–128. Walnut Creek, CA: Left Coast Press.

Newsom, Lee A., and Deborah M. Pearsall. 2003. "Trends in Caribbean Island Archaeobotany." In *People and Plants in Ancient Eastern North America*, edited by Paul E. Minnis, 347–412. Washington, DC: Smithsonian Institution Press.

Newsom, Lee A., and Elizabeth S. Wing. 2004. *On Land and Sea: Native American Uses of Biological Resources in the West Indies*. Tuscaloosa: University of Alabama Press.

Nodine, Bruce K. 1990. "Aceramic Interactions in the Lesser Antilles: Evidence from Antigua, West Indies." Paper presented at the 55th Annual Meeting of the Society for American Archaeology, Las Vegas, NV.

Nokkert, Mark, Alex J. Brokke, Sebastiaan Knippenberg, and Tom D. Hamburg. 1995. "An Archaic Occupation at Norman Estate, St. Martin." *Proceedings of the International Congress for Caribbean Archaeology* 16(1): 333–351.

Norwine, Jim. 1978. *Climate and Human Ecology*. Houston: D. Armstrong.

Nuñez Meléndez, Esteban. 1992. *Plantas medicinales de Puerto Rico: folklore y fundamentos científicos*. Río Piedras: Editorial de la Universidad de Puerto Rico.

Nunn, Patrick D., Tomo Ishimura, William R. Dickinson, Kazumichi Katayama, Frank Thomas, Roselyn Kumar, Sepeti Mataraba, Janet Davidson, and Trevor Worthy. 2007. "The Lapita Occupation at Naitabale, Moturiki Island, Central Fiji." *Asian Perspectives* 46(1): 96–132.

Nyberg, Johan, Antoon Kuijpers, Björn A. Malmgren, and Helmar Kunzendorf. 2001. "Late Holocene Changes in Precipitation and Hydrography Recorded in Marine Sediments from the Northeastern Caribbean Sea." *Quaternary Research* 56: 87–102.

Nyberg, J., A. Winter, B. Malmgren, and J. Christy. 2001. "Surface Temperatures in the Eastern Caribbean during the 7th Century AD Average up to 4 Deg C Cooler than Present." *Eos Transaction, American Geophysical Union* Abstract Number OS51B-0480.

Oliver, José R. 1989. "The Archaeological, Linguistic and Ethnohistorical Evidence for the Expansion of Arawakan into Northweestern Venezuela and Northeastern Colombia." Ph.D. dissertation. Urbana-Champaign: University of Illinois.

———. 1997. "Dabajuroid Archaeology, Settlements and House Structures: An

Overview from Mainland Western Venezuela." In Versteeg and Rostain, *Archaeology of Aruba*, 363–428.

———. 1999. "The La Hueca Problem in Puerto Rico and the Caribbean: Old Problems, New Perspectives, Possible Solution." In Hofman and Hoogland, *Archaeological Investigations on St. Martin*, 253–297.

Olsen, Fred. 1974. *On the Trail of the Arawaks*. Norman: University of Oklahoma Press.

———. 1976. "Preceramic Findings in Antigua." *Proceedings of the Puerto Rican Symposium in Archaeology* 1: 85–94.

Opitz, Rachel S., Krysta Ryzewski, John F. Cherry, and Brenna Moloney. 2015. "Using Airborne LiDAR Survey to Explore Historic-era Archaeological Landscapes of Montserrat in the Eastern Caribbean." *Journal of Field Archaeology* 40: 523–541.

Orliac, M. 1997. "Human Occupation and Environmental Modifications in the Papeno'o Valley, Tahiti." In Kirch and Hunt, *Historical Ecology in the Pacific Islands*, 200–229.

Pagán-Jimenez, Jaime R. 2011. "Early Phytocultural Processes in the Pre-Colonial Antilles: A Pan-Caribbean Survey for an Ongoing Starch Grain Research." In Hofman and van Duijvenbode, *Communities in Contact*, 87–117.

———. 2013. "Human-Plant Dynamics in the Precolonial Antilles: A Synthetic Update." In Keegan, Hofman, and Rodríguez Ramos, *Oxford Handbook of Caribbean Archaeology*, 391–406.

Pagán-Jiménez, Jaime R., Miguel A. Rodríguez López, Luis A. Chanlatte Baik, and Yvonne Narganes Storde. 2005. La temprana introducción y uso de algunos plantas domésticas, silvestres, y cultivos en Las Antillas precolombianas. *Diálogo Antropológico* 3: 7–33.

Pagán-Jiménez, Jaime R., Reniel Rodríguez Ramos, Basil A. Reid, Martijn van den Bel, and Corinne L. Hofman. 2015. "Early Dispersals of Maize and Other Food Plants into the Southern Caribbean and Northeastern South America." *Quaternary Science Reviews* 123: 231–246.

Papadopoulos, John K., and Richard M. Leventhal, eds. 2003. *Theory and Practice in Mediterranean Archaeology: Old World and New World Perspectives*. Cotsen Advanced Seminars 1. Los Angeles: Cotsen Institute of Archaeology, University of California.

Parkes, Annette. 1997. "Environmental Change and the Impact of Polynesian Colonization: Sedimentary Records from Central Polynesia." In Kirch and Hunt, *Historical Ecology in the Pacific Islands*, 166–199.

Parkinson, Randall W., Ron D. DeLaune, and John R. White. 1994. "Holocene Sea-Level Rise and the Fate of Mangrove Forests within the Wider Caribbean Region." *Journal of Coastal Research* 10: 1077–1086.

Parr, J. F., W. E. Boyd, V. Harriott, and R. Torrence. 2009. "Human Adaptive Responses to Catastrophic Landscape Disruptions during the Holocene at Numundo, PNG." *Geographical Research* 47(2): 155–174.

Patton, Mark A. 1996. *Islands in Time: Island Sociogeography and Mediterranean Prehistory*. London: Routledge.

Pearsall, Deborah M. 1989. "Plant Utilization at the Krum Bay Site, St. Thomas USVI." In "Preceramic Procurement Patterns at Krum Bay, Virgin Islands."

E. R. Lundberg, 290–361. Ph.D. dissertation. Urbana-Champaign: University of Illinois.

———. 1995. "'Doing' Paleoethnobotany in the Tropical Lowlands: Adaptation and Innovation in Methodology." In Stahl, *Archaeology in the Lowland American Tropics*, 113–129.

———. 1997. "Evolution of Agricultural Systems in the Caribbean." Paper presented at the 62nd Annual Meeting of the Society for American Archaeology, Nashville, Tennessee.

———. 2002. "Analysis of Charred Botanical Remains from the Tutu Site." In Righter, *Tutu Archaeological Village Site*, 109–134.

———. 2003. "Integrating Biological Data: Phytoliths and Starch Grains, Health and Diet, at Real Alto, Ecuador." In *Phytolith and Starch Research in the Australian-Pacific-Asian Regions: The State of the Art*, edited by D. M. Hart and L. A. Wallis, 187–200. Terra Australis Vol. 19. Canberra: Pandanus Books.

———. 2015. *Paleoethnobotany: A Handbook of Procedures*, 3rd ed. New York: Routledge.

Pearsall, Deborah M., Karol Chandler-Ezell, and Alex Chandler-Ezell. 2003. "Identifying Maize in Neotropical Sediments and Soils using Cob Phytoliths." *Journal of Archaeological Science* 30: 611–627.

Perlès, Catherine. 1977. *Préhistoire du feu*. Paris: Masson.

Peros, M.C. 2004. "A 7000 C-14 Year Record of Environmental Change from North Central Cuba: Implications for Regional Sea Level and Climate Change." *Eos Transaction, American Geophysical Union* 85(46), Fall Meeting Supplement, Abstract Number GC53A-11.

Perry, Linda. 2005. "Reassessing the Traditional Interpretation of "Manioc" Artifacts in the Orinoco Valley of Venezuela." *Latin American Antiquity* 16: 409–426.

Perry, Linda , Ruth Dickau, Sonia Zarrillo, Irene Holst, Deborah M. Pearsall, Dolores R. Piperno, Mary Jane Berman, Richard G. Cooke, Kurt Rademaker, Anthony R. Ranere, J. Scott Raymond, Daniel H. Sandweiss, Franz Scaramelli, Kay Tarble, and James A. Zeidler. 2007. "Starch Fossils and the Domestication and Dispersal of Chili Peppers (*Capsicum* spp. L.) in the Americas." *Science* 315: 986–988.

Petersen, James B., Corinne L. Hofman, and L. Antonio Curet. 2004. "Time and Culture: Chronology and Taxonomy in the Eastern Caribbean and the Guianas." In Delpuech and Hofman, *Late Ceramic Age Societies in the Eastern Caribbean*, 17–33.

Petitjean Roget, Henri. 2005. "Une collection archéologique des Petites Antilles entre au Musée Régional d'Histoire et d'Ethnographie de la Martinique." *La Revue des Musées de France. La Revue du Louvre* 2005: 37–46.

———. 2015. *Taíno et Kalina*. Basse-Terre, Guadeloupe: Association de l'Árchéologie de la Caraibe.

Phoca-Cosmetatou, Nellie, ed. 2011. *The First Mediterranean Islanders: Initial Occupation and Survival Strategies*. School of Archaeology Monograph 74. Oxford: School of Archaeology, University of Oxford.

Pickett, S. T. A., and M. L. Cadenasso. 1995. "Landscape Ecology: Spatial Heterogeneity in Ecological Systems." *Science* 269(5222): 331–334.

Pickett, S. T. A., and P. S. White. 1985. *The Ecology of Natural Disturbance and Patch Dynamics.* Orlando, FL: Academic Press.

Piperno, Dolores R. 1988. *Phytolith Analysis: An Archaeological and Geological Perspective.* San Diego, CA: Academic Press.

———. 1989. "Non-Affluent Foragers: Resource Availability, Seasonal Shortages, and the Emergence of Agriculture in Panamanian Tropical Forests." In Harris and Hillman, *Foraging and Farming,* 538–554.

———. 2002. "Phytolithic Remains from the Tutu Site." In Righter, *Tutu Archaeological Village Site,* 135–140.

———. 2006. *Phytoliths: A Comprehensive Guide for Archaeologists and Paleoecologists.* Lanham, Maryland: AltaMira Press.

Piperno, Dolores R., Mark B. Bush, and Paul A. Colinvaux. 1990. "Paleoenvironments and Human Settlements in Late-Glacial Panama." *Quaternary Research* 33: 108–116.

Piperno, Dolores R., and Deborah M. Pearsall. 1998. *The Origins of Agriculture in the Lowland Neotropics.* San Diego, CA: Academic Press.

Piperno, Dolores R., Anthony J. Ranere, Irene Holst, and Patricia Hansell. 2000. "Starch Grains Reveal Early Root Crop Horticulture in the Panamanian Tropical Forest." *Nature* 407: 894–897.

Pohl, Mary D., Kevin O. Pope, John G. Jones, John S. Jacob, Dolores R. Piperno, Susan D. deFrance, David L. Lentz, John A. Gifford, Marie E. Danforth, and J. Kathryn Josserand. 1996. "Early Agriculture in the Maya Lowlands." *Latin American Antiquity* 7: 355–372.

Pope, Kevin, Mary D. Pohl, John G. Jones, David L. Lentz, Christopher von Nagy, Francisco J. Vega, and Irvy R. Quitmyer. 2001. "Origin and Environmental Setting of Ancient Agriculture in the Lowlands of Mesoamerica." *Science* 292: 1370–1373.

Potter, Robert, David Barker, Dennis Conway, and Thomas Klak. 2004. *The Contemporary Caribbean.* New York: Pearson.

Pregill, Gregory K., David W. Steadman, Storrs L. Olson, and Frederick V. Grady. 1988. *Late Holocene Fossil Vertebrates from Burma Quarry, Antigua, Lesser Antilles.* Smithsonian Contributions to Zoology 463. Washington, DC: Smithsonian Institution Press.

Prentice, Carol S., John C. Weber, J. Christopher Crosby, and Daniel Ragona. 2010. "Prehistoric Earthquakes on the Caribbean-South American Plate Boundary, Central Range Fault, Trinidad." *Geology* 38(8): 675–678.

Price, T. Douglas, ed. *Europe's First Farmers.* Cambridge, UK: Cambridge University Press.

Pulsipher, Lydia M. 1986. *Seventeenth Century Montserrat: An Environmental Impact Statement.* Historical Geography Research Series 17. Norwich, UK: Geo Books.

Pyne, Stephen J. 1998. "Forged in Fire: History, Land, and Anthropogenic Fire." In Balée, *Advances in Historical Ecology,* 64–103.

Rainbird, Paul. 1999. "Islands Out of Time: Towards a Critique of Island Archaeology." *Journal of Mediterranean Archaeology* 12(2): 216–234.

———. 2007. *The Archaeology of Islands.* Cambridge, UK: Cambridge University Press. Rainey, Froelich G. 1940. *Porto Rican Archaeology.* Scientific Survey of

Porto Rico and the Virgin Islands, 18(1). New York: New York Academy of Sciences.

Ramcharan, Eugene K. 1980. "Flora History of the Nariva Swamp, Trinidad." Ph.D. dissertation. St. Augustine, Trinidad and Tobago: University of the West Indies.

———. 2004. "Mid-Late Holocene Sea Level Influence on Coastal Wetland Development in Trinidad." *Quaternary International* 120: 145–151.

———. 2005. "Late Holocene Ecological Development of the Graeme Hall Swamp, Barbados, West Indies." *Caribbean Journal of Science* 41: 147–150.

Ramcharan, Eugene K., and John McAndrews. 2006. "Holocene Development of Coastal Wetland at Maracas Bay, Trinidad, West Indies." *Journal of Coastal Research* 2(3): 581–586.

Ranere, Anthony J. 1992. "Implements of Change in the Holocene Environments of Panama." In *Archaeology and Environment in Latin America*, edited by Omar R. Ortíz-Troncoso and Thomas van der Hammen, 25–44. Amsterdam: Universiteit van Amsterdam.

Redman, Charles L. 1999. *Human Impact on Ancient Environments*. Tuscon: University of Arizona Press.

———. 2005. Resilience Theory in Archaeology. *American Anthropologist* 107: 70–77.

Reese, David, ed. 1996. *Pleistocene and Holocene Fauna of Crete and its First Settlers*. Monographs in World Archaeology 28. Madison, Wisconsin: Prehistory Press.

Reimer, Paula J., Edouard Bard, Alex Bayliss, J. Warren Beck, Paul G. Blackwell, Christopher Bronk Ramsey, Caitlin E. Buck, Hai Cheng, R. Lawrence Edwards, Michael Friedrich, Pieter M. Grootes, Thomas P. Guilderson, Haflidi Haflidason, Irka Hajdas, Christine Hatté, Timothy J. Heaton, Dirk L. Hoffmann, Alan G. Hogg, Konrad A. Hughen, K. Felix Kaiser, Bernd Kromer, Stuart W. Manning, Mu Niu, Ron W. Reimer, David A. Richards, E. Marian Scott, John R. Southon, Richard A. Staff, Christian S. M. Turney, and Johannes van der Plicht. 2013. "IntCal13 and Marine13 Radiocarbon Age Calibration Curves 0–50,000 Years Cal BP." *Radiocarbon* 55: 1869–1887.

Reitz, Elizabeth J. 1989. "Vertebrate Fauna from Krum Bay, St. Thomas, Virgin Islands." In "Preceramic Procurement Patterns at Krum Bay, Virgin Islands." Emily R. Lundberg, 274–289. Ph.D. dissertation. Urbana-Champaign: University of Illinois.

Richardson, Bonham C. 2004. *Igniting the Caribbean's Past: Fire in British West Indian History*. Chapel Hill: University of North Carolina Press.

Richardson, W. D. 1963. "Observations on the Vegetation and Ecology of the Aripo Savannas, Trinidad." *Journal of Ecology* 51(2): 295–313.

Righter, Elizabeth, ed. *The Tutu Archaeological Village Site: A Multidisciplinary Case Study in Human Adaptation*. London: Routledge.

Rival, Laura. 1998. "Domestication as a Historical and Symbolic Process: Wild Gardens and Cultivated Forests in the Ecuadorian Amazon." In Balée, *Advances in Historical Ecology*, 232–250.

Rivera-Collazo, Isabel C. 2011. "Palaeoecology and Human Occupation during the Mid-Holocene in Puerto Rico: The Case of Angostura." In Hofman and van Duijvenbode, *Communities in Contact*, 407–420.

Roberts, Patrick, Chris Hunt, Manuel Arroyo-Kalin, Damian Evans, and Nicole Boivin. 2017. "The Deep Human Prehistory of Global Tropical Forests and its Relevance for Modern Conservation." *Nature Plants* 3(Article 17093). DOI: 10.1038/nplants.2017.93.

Robertson, Richard. 2005. "St. Kitts." In Lindsay et al., *Volcanic Hazard Atlas*, 204–217.

Rockman, Marcy. 2003. "Knowledge and Learning in the Archaeology of Colonization." In Rockman and Steele, *Colonization of Unfamiliar Landscapes*, 3–24.

Rockman, Marcy, and James Steele, eds. 2003. *Colonization of Unfamiliar Landscapes: The Archaeology of Adaptation*. London: Routledge.

Rodríguez López, Miguel A. 1989. "The Zoned Incised Crosshatch ZIC Ware of Early Precolumbian Ceramic Age Sites in Puerto Rico and Vieques Island." In Siegel, *Early Ceramic Population Lifeways*, 637–671.

———. 1999. "Excavations at Maruca, a Preceramic Site in Southern Puerto Rico." *Proceedings of the Congress of the International Association for Caribbean Archaeology* 17: 166–180.

Rodríguez Ramos, Reniel. 2005. "The Crab-Shell Dichotomy Revisited: The Lithics Speak Out." In Siegel, *Ancient Borinquen*, 1–54.

———. 2007. "Puerto Rican Precolonial History Etched in Stone." Ph.D. dissertation. Gainesville: University of Florida.

———. 2010. *Rethinking Puerto Rican Precolonial History*. Tuscaloosa: University of Alabama Press.

Rodríguez Ramos, Reniel, Elvis Babilonia, L. Antonio Curet, and Jorge Ulloa. 2008. "The Pre-Arawak Pottery Horizon in the Antilles: A New Approximation." *Latin American Antiquity* 19(1): 47–63.

Rodríguez Ramos, Reniel, Jaime R. Pagán-Jiménez, and Corinne L. Hofman. 2013. "The Humanization of the Insular Caribbean." In Keegan, Hofman, and Rodríguez Ramos, *Oxford Handbook of Caribbean Archaeology*, 126–140.

Roe, Peter G. 1989. "A Grammatical Analysis of Cedrosan Saladoid Vessel Form Categories and Surface Decoration: Aesthetic and Technical Styles in Early Antillean Ceramics." In Siegel, *Early Ceramic Population Lifeways*, 267–382.

Roebroeks, Wil, and Paola Villa. 2011. "On the Earliest Evidence for the Habitual Use of Fire in Europe." *Proceedings of the National Academy of Sciences of the United States of America* 108(13): 5209–5214.

Rolett, Barry Vladimir. 1998. *Hanamiai: Prehistoric Colonization and Cultural Change in the Marquesas Islands (East Polynesia)*. Yale University Publications in Anthropology 81. New Haven, CT: Department of Anthropology, Yale University.

———. 2007. "Avoiding Collapse: Pre-European Sustainability on Pacific Islands." *Quaternary International* 184: 4–10.

Roobol, M. John, and Alan L. Smith. 1980. "Archaeological Implications of Some Radiocarbon Dating on Saba and St. Kitts." *Proceedings of the International Congress for the Study of the Pre-Columbian Cultures of the Lesser Antilles* 8: 168–176.

———. 1998. "Pyroclastic Stratigraphy of the Soufrière Hills Volcano, Montserrat: Implications for the Present Eruption." *Geophysical Research Letters* 25(18): 3393–3396.

———. 2004. *Volcanology of Saba and St. Eustatius, Northern Lesser Antilles.* Amsterdam: Koninklijke Nederlandse Akademie van Wetenschappen.

Roosevelt, Anna C. 1980. *Parmana: Prehistoric Maize and Manioc Subsistence along the Amazon and Orinoco.* New York: Academic Press.

———. 1989. "Resource Management in Amazonia before the Conquest: Beyond Ethnographic Projection." *Advances in Economic Botany* 7: 30–62.

———. 1991. *Moundbuilders of the Amazon: Geophysical Archaeology on Marajo Island, Brazil.* San Diego: Academic Press.

Roth, Walter E. 1924. *An Introductory Study of the Arts, Crafts, and Customs of the Guiana Indians.* 38th Annual Report of the Bureau of American Ethnology. Washington, DC: Smithsonial Institution.

Rouse, Irving. 1947. "Prehistory of Trinidad in Relation to Adjacent Areas." *Man* 47: 93–98.

———. 1953. "Indian Sites in Trinidad." In *On the Excavation of a Shell Mound at Palo Seco, Trinidad, B.W.I.* Appendix B. John A. Bullbrook, 99–111. Yale University Publications in Anthropology 50. New Haven, CT: Department of Anthropology, Yale University.

———. 1958. "The Inference of Migrations from Anthropological Evidence." In *Migrations in New World Culture History,* edited by Raymond Thompson, 63–68. Social Science Bulletin 27. Tuscon: University of Arizona.

———. 1976. "The Saladoid Sequence on Antigua and its Aftermath." *Proceedings of the International Congress for the Study of the Pre-Columbian Cultures of the Lesser Antilles* 6: 35–41.

———. 1986. *Migrations in Prehistory: Inferring Population Movement from Cultural Remains.* New Haven, CT: Yale University Press.

———. 1989. "Peopling and Repeopling of the West Indies." In Woods, *Biogeography of the West Indies,* 119–135.

———. 1992. *The Tainos: Rise and Decline of the People Who Greeted Columbus.* New Haven, CT: Yale University Press.

Rouse, Irving, and Ricardo E. Alegría. 1990. *Excavations at the Maria de la Cruz Cave and Hacienda Grande Village Site, Loiza, Puerto Rico.* Yale University Publications in Anthropology 80. New Haven, CT: Department of Anthropology, Yale University.

Rouse, Irving, and Louis Allaire. 1978. "Caribbean." In *Chronologies in New World Archaeology,* edited by R. E. Taylor and C. W. Meighan, 432–481. New York: Academic Press.

Rouse, Irving, Louis Allaire, and Arie Boomert. 1985. "Eastern Venezuela, the Guianas, and the West Indies." Chapter prepared for an unpublished volume, *Chronologies in New World Archaeology,* edited by Clement W. Meighan and R. E. Taylor, 2nd ed.

Rouse, Irving, and Birgit Faber Morse. 1999. *Excavations at the Indian Creek Site, Antigua, West Indies.* Yale University Publications in Anthropology 82. New Haven, CT: Department of Anthropology, Yale University.

Rull, Valentí. 2000. "Holocene Sea Level Rising in Venezuela: A Preliminary Curve." *Boletin de la Sociedad Venezolana de Geólogos* 25: 32–36.

Rull, Valentí, Teresa Vegas-Vilarrúbia, and Narcisana Espinoza de Pernía. 1999. "Palynological Record of an Early-Mid Holocene Mangrove in Eastern Venezuela. Implications for Sea-Level Rise and Disturbance History." *Journal of Coastal Research* 15(2): 496–504.

Runnels, Curtis, Eleni Panagopoulou, Priscilla Murray, Georgia Tsartsidou, Susan Allen, Kevin Mullen, and Evangelos Tourloukis. 2005. "A Mesolithic Landscape in Greece: Testing a Site-Location Model in the Argolid at Kandia." *Journal of Mediterranean Archaeology* 18: 259–285.

Russell, Emily W. B. 1997. *People and the Land through Time: Linking Ecology and History.* New Haven, CT: Yale University Press.

Ryzewski, Krysta, and John F. Cherry. 2015. "Struggles of a Sugar Society: Surveying Plantation-Era Montserrat, 1650–1850." *International Journal of Historical Archaeology* 19(2): 356–383.

Sampson, Adamantios, Malgorzata Kaczanowska, and Janus K. Kozłowski. 2010. *The Prehistory of the Island of Kythnos (Cyclades, Greece) and the Mesolithic Settlement at Maroulas.* Kraków: Polish Academy of Arts and Sciences.

Samson, Alice V. M. 2010. *Renewing the House: Trajectories of Social Life in the Yucayeque (Community) of El Cabo, Higüey, Dominican Republic, A.D. 800 to 1504.* Leiden, Netherlands: Sidestone Press.

Samson, A. V. M., C. A. Crawford, M. L. P. Hoogland, and C. L. Hofman. 2015. "Resilience in Pre-Columbian Caribbean House-Building: Dialogue between Archaeology and Humanitarian Shelter." *Human Ecology* 43: 323–337.

Sanoja, Mario. 1989. "From Foraging to Food Production in Northeastern Venezuela and the Caribbean." In Harris and Hillman, *Foraging and Farming*, 523–537.

Sauer, Carl O. 1966. *The Early Spanish Main.* Berkeley: University of California Press.

Scarry, C. Margaret, and Vincas P. Steponaitis. 1997. "Between Farmstead and Center: The Natural and Social Landscape of Moundville." In *People, Plants, and Landscapes: Studies in Paleoethnobotany*, edited by Kristen J. Gremillion, 107–122. Tuscaloosa: University of Alabama Press.

Scheffers, Anja. 2004. "Tsunami Imprints on the Leeward Netherlands Antilles (Aruba, Curaçao, Bonaire) and their Relation to Other Coastal Problems." *Quaternary International* 120(1): 163–172.

Scheffers, Sander R., Jay Haviser, Tony Browne, and Anja Scheffers. 2009. "Tsunamis, Hurricanes, the Demise of Coral Reefs and Shifts in Prehistoric Human Populations in the Caribbean." *Quaternary International* 195(1–2): 69–87.

Scheffers, Sander R., and D. Kelletat. 2006. "Recent Advances in Paleo-Tsunami Field Research in the Intra-Americas Sea (Barbados, St. Martin, and Anguilla)." In *Caribbean Tsunami Hazard: Proceedings of the NSF Caribbean Tsunami Workshop*, edited by A. Mercado-Irizarri and P. Liu, 178–202. Puerto Rico: World Scientific.

Schomburgk, Robert Hermann. 1971 [1848]. *The History of Barbados.* London: Frank Cass.

Sheets, Payson, ed. 1983. *Archeology and Volcanism in Central America: The Zapotitan Valley of El Salvador.* Austin: University of Texas Press.

———. 2006. *The Ceren Site: An Ancient Village in Central America Buried by Volcanic Ash.* Revised and expanded edition. Belmont, California: Wadsworth.

Sheets, Payson, and Donald K. Grayson, eds. 1979. *Volcanic Activity and Human Ecology*. New York: Academic Press.

Sheets, Payson, and Brian R. McKee, eds. 1994. *Archaeology, Volcanism and Remote Sensing in the Arenal Region, Costa Rica*. Austin: University of Texas Press.

Sheppard, Peter J. 2011. "Lapita Colonization across the Near/Remote Oceania Boundary." *Current Anthropology* 52(6): 799–840.

Sheridan, Richard B. 1973. *Sugar and Slavery: An Economic History of the British West Indies 1623–1775*. Baltimore: Johns Hopkins University Press.

Sherratt, Andrew. 1981. "Plough and Pastoralism: Aspects of the Secondary Products Revolution." In *Pattern of the Past: Studies in Honour of David Clarke*, edited by Ian Hodder, Glynn Isaac, and Norman Hammond, 261–305. Cambridge, UK: Cambridge University Press.

Siegel, Peter E., ed. 1989a. *Early Ceramic Population Lifeways and Adaptive Strategies in the Caribbean*. BAR International Series 506. Oxford: British Archaeological Reports.

———. 1989b. "Site Structure, Demography, and Social Complexity in the Early Ceramic Age of the Caribbean." In Siegel, *Early Ceramic Population Lifeways*, 193–245.

———. 1991a. "Migration Research in Saladoid Archaeology: A Review." *Florida Anthropologist* 44(1): 79–91.

———. 1991b. "On the Antilles as a Potential Corridor for Cultigens into Eastern North America." *Current Anthropology* 32: 332–334.

———. 1993. "Saladoid Survival Strategies: Evidence from Site Locations." *Proceedings of the International Congress for Caribbean Archaeology* 14: 315–337.

———. 1996. "Ideology and Culture Change in Prehistoric Puerto Rico: A View from the Community." *Journal of Field Archaeology* 23(3): 313–333.

———. 2010. "Continuity and Change in the Evolution of Religion and Political Organization on Pre-Columbian Puerto Rico." *Journal of Anthropological Archaeology* 29: 302–326.

———, ed. 2005. *Ancient Borinquen: Archaeology and Ethnohistory of Native Puerto Rico*. Tuscaloosa: University of Alabama Press.

———. 2013. "Caribbean Archaeology in Historical Perspective." In Keegan, Hofman, and Rodríguez Ramos, *Oxford Handbook of Caribbean Archaeology*, 21–46.

Siegel, Peter E., John G. Jones, Deborah M. Pearsall, Nicholas P. Dunning, Pat Farrell, Neil A. Duncan, Jason H. Curtis, and Sushant K. Singh. 2015. "Paleoenvironmental Evidence for First Human Colonization of the Eastern Caribbean." *Quaternary Science Reviews* 129: 275–295.

Siegel, Peter E., John G. Jones, Deborah M. Pearsall, and Daniel P. Wagner. 2001. "Culture and Environment in Prehistoric Puerto Rico." *Proceedings of the International Congress for Caribbean Archaeology* 18(2): 281–290.

Siegel, Peter E., John G. Jones, Deborah M. Pearsall, and Daniel P. Wagner. 2005. "Environmental and Cultural Correlates in the West Indies: A View from Puerto Rico." In Siegel, *Ancient Borinquen*, 88–121.

Simmons, Alan H. 1999. *Faunal Extinctions in an Island Society: Pygmy Hippopotamus Hunters of Cyprus*. Boston: Kluwer Academic/Plenum.

———. 2011. "Re-writing the Colonization of Cyprus: Tales of Hippo Hunters and Cow Herders." In Phoca-Cosmetatou, *First Mediterranean Islanders*, 55–76.

Simpson, Kirstie. 2005. "Nevis." In Lindsay et al., *Volcanic Hazard Atlas*, 169–178.
Sjöberg, Alf. 1976. "Phosphate Analysis of Anthropic Soils." *Journal of Field Archaeology* 3: 447–454.
Smith, Alan L., and M. John Roobol. 2005. "Saba." In Lindsay et al., *Volcanic Hazard Atlas*, 179–190.
Smith, Guy D., L. M. Arya, and J. Stark. 1975. "The Densipan, a Diagnostic Horizon of Densiaquults for Soil Taxonomy." *Soil Science Society of America Journal* 39: 369–370.
Snow, David. 1985. "Affinities and Recent Histories of the Avifauna of Trinidad and Tobago." Ornithological Monograph. *Neotropical Ornithology* 36: 238–246.
Soltec International. 2007. *Phase I Archaeological Survey, Parcels 2A, 3A and 4 and Additional Archaeological Testing for Pre-Columbian Cultural Resource, Estate Coakley Bay, St. Croix, U.S. Virgin Islands*. Submitted to Mr. Rick Willis, Mount Pleasant, South Carolina. Soltec International, Weston, Florida. St. Thomas, Virgin Islands: Department of Planning & Natural Resources, VI State Historic Preservation Office.
Soodyall, Himla, Almut Nebel, Bharti Morar, and Trefor Jenkins. 2003. "Genealogy and Genes: Tracing the Founding Fathers of Tristan da Cunha." *European Journal of Human Genetics* 11: 705–709.
Speed, R. C., and C. A. Keller. 1993. "Synopsis of the Geological Evolution of Barbados." *Journal of the Barbados Museum and Historical Society* 41: 113–139.
Stahl, Peter W., ed. 1995. *Archaeology in the Lowland American Tropics: Current Analytical Methods and Recent Applications*. Cambridge, UK: Cambridge University Press.
Steadman, David W. 1997. "Extinctions of Polynesian Birds: Reciprocal Impacts of Birds and People." In Kirch and Hunt, *Historical Ecology in the Pacific Islands*, 51–79.
Steadman, David W., Paul S. Martin, Ross D. E. MacPhee, A. J. T. Jull, H. Gregory McDonald, Charles A. Woods, Manuel Iturralde-Vinent, and Gregory W. L. Hodgins. 2005. "Asynchronous Extinction of Late Quaternary Sloths on Continents and Islands." *Proceedings of the National Academy of Sciences of the United States of America* 102: 11763–11768.
Steadman, David W., Gregory K. Pregill, and Storrs L. Olson. 1984. "Fossil Vertebrates from Antigua, Lesser Antilles: Evidence for Late Holocene Human-Caused Extinctions in the West Indies." *Proceedings of the National Academy of Sciences of the United States of America* 81: 4448–4451.
Stevens, Charles J. 1999. "Review of *Historical Ecology in the Pacific Islands: Prehistoric Environmental and Landscape Change*, edited by Patrick V. Kirch and Terry L. Hunt." *Journal of Political Ecology* 6: 1–7.
Stockmarr, Jens. 1971. "Tablets with Spores Used in Absolute Pollen Analysis." *Pollen et Spores* 13: 615–621.
Stokes, Anne Vaughn. 1991. "A Settlement Survey of Nonsuch Bay: Implications for Prehistoric Subsistence in the Caribbean." M.A. thesis. Gainesville: University of Florida.
Stouvenot, C., and F. Casagrande. 2015. "Recherche des occupations précolumbiennes dans les hauteurs de Capesterre-Belle-Eau (Guadeloupe): résultats préliminaires." Paper presented at the 26th Congress of the International Association for Caribbean Archaeology, Sint Maarten, 19–25 July.

Stouvenot, Christian, and Marie Christine Gineste. 2002. "Guadeloupe carte archéologigue." Service Regional de l'Archéologie, Direction Regionale des Affaires, Culturelles, Basse Terre, Guadeloupe. *Bilan Scientifique* 2001: 10–13.

Strasser, Thomas F., Eleni Panagopoulou, Curtis N. Runnels, Priscilla M. Murray, Nicholas Thompson, Panayiotis Karkanas, Floyd W. McCoy, and Karl W. Wegmann. 2010. "Stone Age Seafaring in the Mediterranean: Evidence from the Plakias Region for Lower Palaeolithic and Mesolithic Habitation of Crete." *Hesperia* 79: 145–190.

Strasser, Thomas F., Curtis Runnels, Karl Wegmann, Eleni Panagopoulou, Floyd McCoy, Chad Digregorio, Panagiotis Karkanas, and Nick Thompson. 2011. "Dating Palaeolithic Sites in Southwestern Crete, Greece." *Journal of Quaternary Science* 26(5): 553–560.

Street-Perrott, F. A., , P. E. Hales, R. A. Perrott, J. C. Fontes, V. R. Switsur, and A. Pearson. 1993. "Late Quaternary Palaeolimnology of a Tropical Marl Lake: Wallywash Great Pond, Jamaica." *Journal of Paleolimnology* 9: 3–22.

Sutty, Leslie. 1983. "Liaison Arawak-Caliviny-Carib between Grenada and St. Vincent, Lesser Antilles." *Proceedings of the International Congress for the Study of the Pre-Columbian Cultures of the Lesser Antilles* 9: 145–153.

Tarrus, Josep. 2008. "La Draga (Banyoles, Catalonia), an Early Neolithic Lakeside Village in Mediterranean Europe." *Catalan Historical Review* 1: 17–33.

Taverne, Yvon, and Aad H. Versteeg. 1992. "Golden Rock Shells." In Versteeg and Schinkel, *The Archaeology of St. Eustatius*, 84–92.

Taylor, Leslie. 1996 onwards. "Tropical Plant Database." Retrieved 13 May 2015 from http://www.rain-tree.com/plants.htm.

Technical Advisory Committee. 2006. "National Action Plan to Combat Desertification on Antigua and Barbuda." St. John's, Antigua and Barbuda: Environmental Division, Ministry of Public Works and Environment.

Ternan, J. L., A. G. Williams, and C. Francis. 1989. "Land Capability Classification in Grenada, West Indies." *Mountain Research and Development* 9(1): 71–82.

Terrell, John Edward. 1997. "The Postponed Agenda: Archaeology and Human Biogeography in the Twenty-First Century." *Human Ecology* 25(3): 419–436.

———. 1999. "Comment on Paul Rainbird, 'Islands out of Time: Towards a Critique of Island Archaeology.'" *Journal of Mediterranean Archaeology* 12(2): 240–245.

Terrell, John Edward, John P. Hart, Sibel Barut, Nicoletta Cellinese, Antonio Curet, Tim Denham, Chapurukha M. Kusimba, Kyle Latinis, Rahul Oka, Joel Palka, Mary E. D. Pohl, Kevin O. Pope, Patrick Ryan Williams, Helen Haines and John E. Staller. 2003. "Domesticated Landscapes: The Subsistence Ecology of Plant and Animal Domestication." *Journal of Archaeological Method and Theory* 10(4): 323–368.

Tickell, Crispin. 1977. *Climate Change and World Affairs*. Cambridge, MA: Center for International Affairs, Harvard University.

Torrence, Robin, and John Grattan, eds. 2002. *Natural Disasters and Cultural Change*. London: Routledge.

Torrence, Robin, Vince Neall, and W. E. Boyd. 2009. "Volcanism and Historical Ecology on the Willaumez Peninsula, Papua New Guinea." *Pacific Science* 63: 507–535.

Torrence Robin, Christine Pavlides, Peter Jackson, and John Webb. 2000. "Volcanic Disasters and Cultural Discontinuities in Holocene Time of West New

Britain, Papua New Guinea." In *The Archaeology of Geological Catastrophes*, edited by W. J. McGuire, D. R. Griffiths, P. L. Hancock, and I. S. Stewart, 225–244. Geological Society Special Publication No. 171. London: The Geological Society.

Torres, Joshua M. 2010. "Tibes and the Social Landscape: Integration, Interaction, and the Community." In Curet and Stringer, *Tibes*, 231–260.

Torres, Joshua M., and Reniel Rodríguez Ramos. 2008. "The Caribbean: A Continent Divided by Water." In *Archaeology and Geoinformatics: Case Studies from the Caribbean*, edited by Basil A. Reid, 13–29. Tuscaloosa: University of Alabama Press.

Toscano, M. A., and I. G. Macintyre. 2003. "Corrected Western Atlantic Sea-Level Curve for the Last 11,000 Years based on Calibrated ^{14}C Dates from *Acropora palmata* Framework and Intertidal Mangrove Peat." *Coral Reefs* 22: 257–270.

———. 2006. "Reply to Gischler, E, Comment on Toscano and Macintyre (2003): Corrected Western Atlantic Sea-Level Curve for the Last 11,000 Years based on Calibrated ^{14}C Dates from *Acropora palmata* Framework and Intertidal Mangrove Peat, *Coral Reefs* 22: 257–270 (2003), and their response in *Coral Reefs* 24: 187–190 (2005)." *Coral Reefs* 25: 281–286.

Toscano, Marguerite A., W. Richard Peltier, and Rosemarie Drummond. 2011. "ICE-5G and ICE-6G Models of Postglacial Relative Sea-Level History Applied to the Holocene Coral Reef Record of Northeastern St Croix, U.S.V.I.: Investigating the Influence of Rotational Feedback on GIA Processes at Tropical Latitudes." *Quaternary Science Reviews* 30: 3032–3042.

Turner, Monica G. 2005. "Landscape Ecology: What Is the State of the Science?" *Annual Review of Ecology, Evolution, and Systematics* 36: 319–344.

Turvey, S. T., J. R. Oliver, Y. M. Narganes Storde, and P. Rye. 2007. "Late Holocene Extinction of Puerto Rican Native Land Mammals." *Biology Letters* 3: 193–196.

Ulloa Hung, Jorge, and Roberto Valcárcel Rojas. 2002. *Cerámica temprana en el centro del oriente de Cuba*. Santo Domingo: View Graph Impresos.

U.S. Geological Survey (USGS). 2010. "Poster of the Seismicity of the Caribbean Plate and Vicinity." United States Geological Survey. Retrieved 20 September 2012 http://earthquake.usgs.gov/earthquakes/eqarchives/poster/regions/caribbean.php

Valentin, Frédérique, Hallie R. Buckley, Estelle Herrscher, Rebecca Kinaston, Stuart Bedford, Matthew Spriggs, Stuart Hawkins, and Ken Neal. 2010. "Lapita Subsistence Strategies and Food Consumption Patterns in the Community of Teouma (Efate,Vanuatu)." *Journal of Archaeological Science* 37: 1820–1829.

Van Andel, Tjeerd, and Peter Sachs. 1964. "Sedimentation in the Gulf of Paria during the Holocene Transgression: A Subsurface Reflection Study." *Journal of Marine Research* 22(1): 30–50.

van den Bel, Martijn, and Thomas Romon. 2010. "A Troumassoid Site at Trois Rivières, Guadeloupe FWI: Funerary Practices and House Patterns at La Pointe de Grande Anse." *Journal of Caribbean Archaeology* 9: 1–17.

van der Hammen, Thomas. 1974. "The Pleistocene Changes of Vegetation and Climate in Tropical South America." *Journal of Biogeography* 1: 3–26.

———. 1988. "South America." In *Vegetation History*, edited by B. Huntley and T. Webb III, 307–337. Dordrecht: Kluwer.

van der Klift, Heleen M. 1992. "Faunal Remains of Golden Rock." In Versteeg and Schinkel, *The Archaeology of St. Eustatius*, 74–84.
van der Leeuw, Sander, and Charles L. Redman. 2002. "Placing Archaeology at the Center of Socio-Natural Studies." *American Antiquity* 67: 597–605.
van Gijn, A. L. 1993. "Flint Exploitation on Long Island, Antigua, West Indies." *Analecta Praehistorica Leidensia* 26: 183–197.
Van Soest, Matthijs C. 2000. *Sediment Subduction and Crustal Contamination in the Lesser Antilles Island Arc: The Geochemical and Isotopic Imprints on Recent Lavas and Geothermal Fluids*. Publication 20000101. Amsterdam: Netherlands Research School of Sedimentary Geology.
Vaughan, Hague H., Edward S. Deevey, and Samuel E. Garrett-Jones. 1985. "Pollen Stratigraphy of Two Cores from the Peten Lake District." In *Prehistoric Lowland Maya Environment and Subsistence Economy*, edited by Mary D. Pohl, 73–89. Memoirs of the Peabody Museum of American Archaeology and Ethnology 77. Cambridge, MA: Harvard University.
Veloz Maggiolo, Marcio. 1976. *Medioambiente y adaptación humana en la prehistoria de Santo Domingo*. Vol. 1. Santo Domingo: Universidad Autonoma de Santo Domingo.
———. 1977. *Medioambiente y adaptacion humana en la prehistoria de Santo Domingo*. Vol. 2. Santo Domingo: Universidad Autonoma de Santo Domingo.
Vernon, K. C., and D. M. Carroll. 1966. *Soil and Land Use Surveys No. 18*. Barbados. St. Augustine, Trinidad: The Imperial College of Tropical Agriculture.
Versteeg, Aad H. 1997. "Conclusions." In Versteeg and Rostain, *Archaeology of Aruba*, 447–458.
Versteeg, Aad H., and Stéphen Rostain, eds. 1997. *The Archaeology of Aruba: the Tanki Flip Site*. Publications of the Archaeological Museum Aruba 8. Aruba and Amsterdam: Foundation for Scientific Research in the Caribbean Region.
Versteeg, Aad H., and Kees Schinkel, eds. 1992. *The Archaeology of St. Eustatius, the Golden Rock Site*. Publication of the St. Eustatius Historical Foundation 2. Amsterdam: Foundation for Scientific Research in the Caribbean Region.
Versteeg A. H., J. Tacoma, and P. van de Velde, eds. 1990. *Archaeological Investigations on Aruba: The Malmok Cemetery*. Publication of the Archaeological Museum of Aruba 2. Aruba and Amsterdam: Foundation for Scientific Research in the Caribbean Region.
Vescelius, Gary S. 1952. "The Cultural Chronology of St. Croix." B.A. thesis. New Haven, CT: Yale University.
———. 1980. "A Cultural Taxonomy for West Indian Archaeology." *Journal of the Virgin Islands Archaeological Society* 10: 36–39.
Vigne, Jean-Denis. 1988. *Les mammifères post-glaciaires de Corse: Etude zooarchéologique*. Gallia Préhistoire Supplément 26. Paris: Centre National de la Recherche Scientifique.
Vilar, Miguel G., Carlalynne Melendez, Akiva Sanders, Akshay Walia, Jill B. Gaieski, Amanda C. Owings, and Theodore Schurr. 2013. "Analysis of Genetic Diversity in Southeastern Puerto Rico and the Implications for the Prehistoric and Historic Peopling of the Island and the Greater Antilles." Paper presented at the 25th Congress of the International Association of Caribbean Archaeologists, San Juan, Puerto Rico, 15–20 July.
Vitousek, Peter, Oliver Chadwick, Pamela Matson, Steven Allison, Louis Derry, Lisa Kettley, Amy Luers, Esther Mecking, Valerie Monastra, and Stephen

Porder. 2003. "Erosion and the Rejuvenation of Weathering-derived Nutrient Supply in an Old Tropical Landscape." *Ecosystems* 6: 762–772.

Vitousek, P. M., T. N. Ladefoged, P. V. Kirch, A. S. Hartshorn, M. W. Graves, S. C. Hotchkiss, S. Tuljapurkar, and O. A. Chadwick. 2004. "Soils, Agriculture, and Society in Precontact Hawai'i." *Science* 304(5677): 1665–1669.

Wallace, Robert E., and Richard H. Pryor. 2010. *Mangrove Ecosystem Assessment, Graeme Hall Nature Sanctuary, Barbados*. Environmental Engineering Consultants, Tampa, FL. Submitted to Graeme Hall Nature Sanctuary, Christ Church, Barbados.

Warburton, David A., ed. 2009. *Time's Up! Dating the Minoan Eruption of Santorini: Acts of the Minoan Eruption Chronology Workshop, Sandbjerg, November 2007*. Santa Barbara, CA: Aarhus University Press.

Watters, David R. 1980a. "Transect Surveying and Prehistoric Site Locations on Barbuda and Montserrat, Leeward Islands, West Indies." Ph.D. dissertation. Pittsburgh, PA: University of Pittsburgh.

———. 1980b. "Observations on the Historic Sites and Archaeology of Barbuda." *Walter E. Roth Museum Journal of Archaeology and Anthropology* 3(2): 125–154.

———. 1997. "Historic Documentation and Archaeological Investigation of Codrington Castle, Barbuda, West Indies." *Annals of the Carnegie Museum* 66: 229–288.

———. 2001. "Historical Archaeology in the British Caribbean." In Farnsworth, *Island Lives*, 82–99.

———. 2003. "Deterioration of Historic Structures on Barbuda." *Proceedings of the International Congress of Caribbean Archaeology* 20: 751–758.

Watters, David R., Jack Donahue, and Robert Stuckenrath. 1992. "Paleoshorelines and the Prehistory of Barbuda, West Indies." In *Paleoshorelines and Prehistory: An Investigation of Method*, edited by Lucille Lewis Johnson and Melanie Stright, 15–52. Boca Raton, FL: CRC Press.

Watters, David R., and R. B. Miller. 2000. "Wood Identification in Historic Sites: Inferences for Colonial Trade and Modification of Vegetation on Barbuda." *Caribbean Journal of Science* 36(1–2): 19–30.

Watters, David R., and Desmond V. Nicholson. 1982. "Highland House, Barbuda: An 18th-Century Retreat." *Florida Anthropologist* 34(4): 223–242.

Watts, David. 1966. *Man's Influence on the Vegetation of Barbados: 1627 to 1800*. Occasional Papers in Geography 4. Willerby, UK: University of Hull Publications.

———. 1987. *The West Indies: Patterns of Development, Culture and Environmental Change since 1492*. Cambridge Studies in Historical Geography 8. Cambridge, UK: Cambridge University Press.

Weaver, David B. 1988. "The Evolution of a 'Plantation' Tourism Landscape on the Caribbean Island of Antigua." *Tijdschrift voor economische en sociale geografie* 79(5): 319–331.

Webb, Robert S., David H. Rind, Scott J. Lehman, Richard J. Healy, and Daniel Sigman. 1997. "Influence of Ocean Heat Transport on the Climate of the Last Glacial Maximum." *Nature* 385: 695–699.

Webster, Gary S. 1996. *A Prehistory of Sardinia 2300–500 B.C.* Sheffield, UK: Academic Press.

Weiss, Kenneth M., and Peter E. Smouse. 1976. "The Demographic Stability of Small Human Populations." *Journal of Human Evolution* 5: 59–73.

Wells, E. Christian, Suzanna M. Pratt, and Georgia L. Fox. 2015. "The Landscape Legacies of Sugar and Rum in Antigua, West Indies." Paper presented at the 26th Congress of the International Association for Caribbean Archaeology, Sint Maarten-Saint Martin, Netherlands Antilles, 19–25 July.

Wells, E. Christian, Suzanna M. Pratt, Georgia L. Fox, Peter E. Siegel, Nicholas P. Dunning, and A. Reginald Murphy. 2018. "Plantation Soilscapes: Initial and Cumulative Impacts of Colonial Agriculture in Antigua, West Indies." *Environmental Archaeology: The Journal of Human Palaeoecology* 23(1): 23–35, in press.

Weng, Chengyu, Mark B. Bush, and J. Stephen Athens. 2002. "Holocene Climate Change and Hydrarch Succession in Lowland Amazonian Ecuador." *Review of Palaeobotany and Palynology* 120: 73–90.

Westercamp, Denis, and H. Traineau. 1983. "The Past 5000 Years of Volcanic Activity at Mt. Pelée, Martinique (F.W.I.): Implications for Assessment of Volcanic Hazards." *Journal of Volcanological and Geothermal Research* 17: 159–185.

White, P. S., and S. T. A. Pickett. 1985. "Natural Disturbance and Patch Dynamics: An Introduction." In Pickett and White, *Ecology of Natural Disturbance and Patch Dynamics*, 3–13.

Whittaker, Robert J., and José María Fernández-Palacios. 2007. *Island Biogeography: Ecology, Evolution, and Conservation*. Oxford, UK: Oxford University Press.

Willey, Gordon R. 1971. *An Introduction to American Archaeology*, Vol. 2, *South America*. Englewood Cliffs, NJ: Prentice-Hall.

Williamson, Ian, and Michael D. Sabath. 1982. "Island Population, Land Area, and Climate: A Case Study of the Marshall Islands." *Human Ecology* 10(1): 71–84.

Wilmshurst, Janet M., Atholl J. Anderson, Thomas F. G. Higham, and Trevor H. Worthy. 2008. "Dating the Late Prehistoric Dispersal of Polynesians to New Zealand Using the Commensal Pacific Rat." *Proceedings of the National Academy of Sciences of the United States of America* 105(22): 7676–7680.

Wilmshurst, Janet M., Terry L. Hunt, Carl P. Lipo, and Atholl J. Anderson. 2011. "High-precision Radiocarbon Dating Shows Recent and Rapid Initial Human Colonization of East Polynesia." *Proceedings of the National Academy of Sciences of the United States of America* 108(5): 1815–1820.

Wilson, Samuel M. 1993. "The Cultural Mosaic of the Indigenous Caribbean." *Proceedings of the British Academy* 81: 37–66.

———, ed. 1997. *The Indigenous People of the Caribbean*. Gainesville: University Press of Florida

———. 2007. *The Archaeology of the Caribbean*. New York: Cambridge University Press.

Wilson, Samuel M., Harry B. Iceland, and Thomas R. Hester. 1998. "Preceramic Connections between Yucatan and the Caribbean." *Latin American Antiquity* 9: 342–352.

Wilson, Brent, Keith Miller, Anna-Lisa Thomas, Nicholas Cooke, and Reece Ramsingh. 2008. "Foraminifera in the Mangal at Caroni Swamp, Trinidad: Diversity, Population Structure and Relation to Sea Level." *Journal of Foraminiferal Research* 38: 127–136.

Wing, Elizabeth S. 1977. "Factors Influencing Exploitation of Marine Re-

sources." In *The Sea in Pre-Columbian World*, edited by Elizabeth P. Benson, 47–64. Washington, DC: Dumbarton Oaks Research Library Collection.
Wing, Elizabeth S. 2001. "Native American Use of Animals in the Caribbean." In Woods and Sergile, *Biogeography of the West Indies*, 2nd ed., 481–518.
Wing, Elizabeth S., and Elizabeth J. Reitz. 1982. "Prehistoric Fishing Economies of the Caribbean." *Journal of New World Archaeology* 5(2): 13–32.
Wing, Elizabeth S., Susan D. deFrance, and Laura Kozuch. 2002. "Faunal Remains from the Tutu Site." In Righter, *Tutu Archaeological Village Site*, 141–165.
Winterhalder, Bruce P. 1994. "Concepts in Historical Ecology: The View from Evolutionary Theory." In Crumley, *Historical Ecology*, 17–41.
Wong, Th. E. 1989. *Revision of the Stratigraphy of the Coastal Plain of Suriname*. Studiekring voor Suriname en de Nederlandse Antillen 125. Amsterdam: Uitgaven Natuurwetenschapelijke.
Woodroffe, C. D. 1981. "Mangrove swamp stratigraphy and Holocene transgression, Grand Cayman Island, West Indies." *Marine Geology* 41(3–4): 271–294.
Woodroffe, Colin D., and John Grindrod. 1991. "Mangrove Biogeography: The Role of Quaternary Environmental and Sea-Level Change." *Journal of Biogeography* 18(5): 479–492.
Woods, Charles A., ed. 1989. *Biogeography of the West Indies: Past, Present, and Future*. Gainesville, FL: Sandhill Crane Press.
Woods, Charles A., and Florence E. Sergile, eds. 2001. *Biogeography of the West Indies: Patterns and Perspectives*. 2nd ed. Boca Raton, FL: CRC Press.
Wrangham, Richard. 2010. *Catching Fire: How Cooking Made Us Human*. New York: Basic Books.
Wright, A. C. S. 1959. "A New Zealand Pedologist on the Caribbean." Wellington, New Zealand: New Zealand Soil Bureau.
Wright, H. E. Jr. 1967. "A Square-Rod Piston Sampler for Lake Sediments." *Journal of Sedimentary Petrology* 37: 975–976.
Young, William. 1801. "A Tour through the Several Islands of Barbadoes, St. Vincent, Antigua, Tobago, and Grenada, in the Years 1791 & 1792." In *An Historical Survey of the Island of Saint Domingo*, edited by B. Edwards, 245–328. London: privately printed.
Zahibo, Narcisse, Efim Pelinovsky, Tatiana Talipova, Alexander Rabinovich, Andrey Kurkin, and Irina Nikolkina. 2007. "Statistical Analysis of Cyclone Hazard for Guadeloupe, Lesser Antilles." *Atmospheric Research* 84: 13–29.
Zent, Stanford. 1998. "Independent Yet Interdependent "Isode": The Historical Ecology of Traditional Piaroa Settlement Pattern." In Balée, *Advances in Historical Ecology*, 251–286.
Zilhão, João. 2000. "From the Mesolithic to the Neolithic in the Iberian Peninsula." In Price, *Europe's First Farmers*, 144–182.
———. 2001. "Radiocarbon Evidence for Maritime Pioneer Colonization at the Origins of Farming in West Mediterranean Europe." *Proceedings of the National Academy of Sciences of the United States of America* 98(24): 14180–14185.

Glossary

Aggradation: Building up of a surface through deposition of sediment.
Alfisol: Forest soil with moderate fertility and subsoil clay accumulation.
Alluvial: Landforms or sediment formed by running water.
Andisol: Soil derived from weathering volcanic ash.
Anthropogenic landscape: Human-modified landscape.
Anticlinal structure: A landform or geological feature that is folded in a convex, upward orientation, like an arch, with the stratigraphically oldest rocks in the core.
Atlantic hurricane belt: Equitorial through subtropical zone of the North Atlantic that is prone to hurricane development annually between June and December.
Argillic horizon: Subsoil soil horizon with notable clay accumulation.
Aridisol: Soil characteristic of warm, arid regions with surface or subsurface accumulation of soluble minerals.
Base saturation: A measure of soil fertility referencing the number of basic cations (e.g., Ca^+, K^+) that occupy cation exchange sites in a soil relative to the total number of sites.
Caldera: A basin-shaped depression formed by a volcanic eruption and collapse.
Caliche: Subsoil horizon cemented by accumulating calcium carbonate.
Cambic horizon: Incipient form of a subsoil horizon characteristic of immature or weakly developed soil.
Catena sequence: Soils sharing a common parent material but varying according to relative topographic position.
Cation exchange: Chemical reaction whereby surface cations of a solid like a clay mineral are replaced by cations from the matrix solution (also base exchange).
Colluvial deposit: Loose sediment that collects at the base of a slope (also slope wash).
Colonization pulse: Small-scale excursions or exploratory forays by groups of people when investigating new areas to settle.
Coriolis effect: Earth's rotational force causing fluid bodies on the planet's surface to deflect to the right in the northern and to the left in the southern hemispheres.
Detrital fans: Fan-shaped sediment deposit with the apex pointing upstream.

Earth's rotational state: Refers to changes in earth's rotation caused by redistribution of ice and water as glaciers melt and sea-level rises.

El Niño Southern Oscillation (ENSO): Irregular cyclical wind and sea surface temperature variations over the tropical eastern Pacific, with effects over much of the tropical and subtropical regions of the world.

Entisol: Immature soil with no well-developed pedogenic horizons.

Eustatic sea level: Global sea level related to the volume of water contained in the ocean at a given time.

Gley: Characteristic of waterlogged soils with reduced iron compounds, blue-gray or green-gray colors, and sometimes rust-colored mottles.

Graben: A slender depression in a portion of the earth's crust, bordered by normal faults on the long sides; sometimes forming a valley between horsts.

Gyttja: Very loose or gel-like sediment derived chiefly from organic matter.

Halophytic: Adapted to growing in saline conditions.

Histic: Comprising partially decomposed organic matter.

Histosol: Soil formed principally from partially decomposed organic matter; characteristic of poorly drained areas where organic decomposition is arrested by anaerobic conditions.

Horst: Linear block of upland terrain in a region of normal faulting; ridge of higher ground adjacent to a graben.

Illuvial: Subsoil accumulation of particles (e.g., clay) or soluble minerals transported downward in the soil by percolating water.

Inceptisol: Immature soil with only incipient soil horizon formation.

Intertropical Convergence Zone (ITCZ): A band of unstable air encircling the earth along the equator generated by maximal solar heating and the generation of upwelling convection cells that draw in air parcels from the north and south (northeast and southeast trade winds).

Isobath: A line marking equal water depth elevations.

Isostatic response: Adjustment to the earth's lithosphere in response to changes in weight loads resulting from various earth processes, including sedimentation, erosion, glaciation, and deglaciation.

Karst: Landscape that forms from the chemical dissolution of carbonate bedrock such as limestone (calcium carbonate), dolomite (calcium magnesium carbonate), or gypsum (hydrous calcium sulfate), or some combination of these. Karst topography is characterized by dissolution features, including sinkholes, caves, and underground caverns and drainage networks.

Landscape learning: The process of becoming familiar with the biotic and abiotic components of new places during exploration and colonization.

Laterite: An oxic soil horizon, composed of oxides of iron and aluminum.
Llanos landscape: A large plain usually devoid of trees.
Marine terraces: A relatively flat or gently inclined surface created by wave erosion, but isolated above the level of current wave action by either tectonic uplift or a drop in sea level.
Marl: Clay or silt sediment rich in calcium carbonate; typically poorly consolidated.
Mesic climate: Characterized by moderate to high levels of precipitation.
Mollisol: Soil with a relatively thick, organic-rich (mollic) A horizon with high base saturation status.
Orographic uplift: Forced upslope flow of air, resulting in cooler air, higher relative humidity, and increased probability of cloud formation and precipitation.
Oxisol: Highly chemically weathered, generally infertile soil with a well-developed oxic (typically iron or aluminum oxide) horizon.
Pedogenesis: Soil formation.
Phytoliths: Microscopic inorganic silica bodies that form in the cell walls of plants.
Plinthite: A component of highly weathered mineral soils, consisting of aluminum and iron oxides, quartz, and kaolinite clay forming from prolonged leaching and oxidation in weathered tropical soils.
Pollen: Microscopic grains produced in the anther, or male portion, of flowering plants and dispersed for sexual reproduction.
Progradation: Seaward extension of a river delta or beach, caused by increased sediment deposition by drainages or shoreline processes.
Rendoll (Rendzina): Mollisol consisting of a mollic horizon directly overlying carbonate bedrock.
Ria coast: Coast consisting of alternating bays and headlands, typically formed by rapid sea-level rise in an area of deep fluvial dissection.
Saprolitic rock: Deeply chemically weathered rock typical of humid tropical environments.
Scree slope: Sloping accumulation of broken rock fragments.
Sediment sink: Topographic low point where sediments accumulate over time.
Smectite clay: A group of clays comprising phyllosilicate minerals and characterized by high shrink-swell capacity.
Socionatural landscape: The aggregate landforms and associated biota of a region that have been modified in any way by the presence of humans.
Structural trough: A landscape depression or valley created by normal faulting (graben) or crustal folding (syncline).

Subduction: The downward movement of a lithospheric plate along a zone of plate convergence.

Synclinal basin: Topographic low created by a trough within folded bedrock with stratigraphically youngest rocks at its core.

Tectonic uplift: Upward vertical displacement of a land mass resulting from tectonic plate convergence.

Terraces: See Marine terraces.

Terrigenous sediments: Sediments derived from the weathering and erosion of land surfaces.

Ultisol: Highly weathered, usually acidic, low fertility soils with subsoil accumulation of clay and often plinthite.

Vertisol: Soils with high clay content found in regions with highly seasonal rainfall and characterized by shrinking and cracking in the dry season and swelling in the wet season.

Xeric climate: Climate with summer minimal and winter maximal precipitation.

🌿 Contributors

William Balée is professor of anthropology at Tulane University. He previously held postdoctoral appointments at the New York Botanical Garden and the Museu Paraense Emilio Goeldi in Belém, Brazil. He took his Ph.D. in anthropology at Columbia University. Among his books are the monographs *Footprints of the Forest: Ka'apor Ethnobotany—A Historical Ecology of Plant Utilization by an Amazonian People* (Columbia University Press, 1994) and *Cultural Forests of the Amazon: A Historical Ecology of People and Their Landscapes* (University of Alabama Press, 2013); both won the Mary W. Klinger Book Award from the Society for Economic Botany. His specialties include research in the Amazon Basin on historical–ecological questions concerning Tupi-Guaranian indigenous societies and, most recently, applied historical ecology among forest peasants.

John F. Cherry is Joukowsky Family Professor of Archaeology and professor of classics at Brown University. His teaching, research interests, and publications reflect a background in classics, anthropology, and archaeology, as well as educational training on both sides of the Atlantic, and archaeological fieldwork experience in Great Britain, the United States, Yugoslav Macedonia, Italy, Armenia, and (especially) Greece and (currently) Montserrat in the Caribbean, where since 2010 he has codirected a diachronic program of survey and excavation entitled *Survey and Landscape Archaeology in Montserrat*. He has published 140 papers and chapters, and coauthored or coedited twelve books. He has been coeditor of the *Journal of Mediterranean Archaeology* for twenty-six years and is general series editor for *Joukowsky Institute Publications*.

Jason H. Curtis is senior associate in geochemistry in the Department of Geological Sciences at the University of Florida, Gainesville. He received his B.S. degree in geology from the University of Michigan, Ann Arbor, in 1989 and his M.S. and Ph.D. degrees in geological sciences from the University of Florida, Gainesville, in 1992 and 1997, respectively. He was post-doctoral research fellow at the Smithsonian Tropical Research Institute, Panama, 1997–1998. Since 1998 he has been at the University of Florida. His position is a state-funded, nontenure accruing faculty member responsible for management of the Light Stable Isotope Mass Spectrometry Lab.

Neil A. Duncan is assistant professor of anthropology at the University of Central Florida, Orlando. He is an archaeologist and paleoethnobotanist specializing in analyses of phytoliths, starch grains, and macrobotanical remains. His research focuses on paleoenvironmental reconstruction and the interrelationships of humans, plants, and landscapes in the past. He has extensive fieldwork experience and collaboration in multidisciplinary projects from Peru, Ecuador, Colombia, the Caribbean, and China.

Nicholas P. Dunning is professor of geography at the University of Cincinnati. He is a geoarchaeologist and cultural ecologist specializing in the neotropics, where he has carried out extensive fieldwork. He has published several books and more than 120 articles and book chapters. In his spare time he is an organic farmer.

Pat Farrell is associate professor of geography at the University of Minnesota, Duluth. Her research interest in soils include pedo-archaeological investigations in the Maya region of Mexico and Central America, the Great Lakes region of North America, and the Caribbean, and contributions to soil-art collaborations in the geohumanities.

John G. Jones is senior paleoethnobotanist at Archaeological Consulting Services, Ltd., in Tempe, Arizona. He received his B.A. degree in anthropology (1983) from Youngstown State University, and his M.A. and Ph.D. degrees in anthropology (1988, 1991) from Texas A&M University. He was a Smithsonian and Mellon post-doctoral fellow at the Smithsonian Tropical Research Institute in Panama from 1991 through 1995. Author of more than eighty articles, his research focuses largely on the origins of agriculture and settlement in the neotropics and he has directed more than forty-five coring projects throughout Central and South America, China, and Kenya.

Corinne L. Hofman is professor of Caribbean archaeology and dean of the faculty of archaeology, Leiden University in the Netherlands. She has conducted fieldwork in many of the Caribbean islands over the past thirty years. Her research and publications are highly multidisciplinary; major themes of interest center around mobility and exchange, colonial encounters, intercultural dynamics, settlement archaeology, artifact analyses, and provenance studies. Hofman's projects are designed to contribute to the historical awareness, preservation, and valorization of indigenous heritage. Hofman has obtained numerous research grants from the Netherlands Organisation for Scientific Research (NWO), the Humanities in the European Research Area (HERA), and the European Research Council (ERC), as well as prestigious prizes. In 2012 she obtained an ERC-Synergy grant for the project "Nexus 1492: New World Encounters in a Globalizing World." In 2013 she was awarded the KNAW Merian prize for Women in Science, and in 2014 she was awarded the Spinoza Prize, which is the highest Dutch award in science. Among her recent books are *The Oxford Handbook of Caribbean Archaeology* (coedited with W. F. Keegan and R. Rodríguez Ramos, Oxford University Press, 2013) and *The Caribbean before Columbus* (coedited with W. F. Keegan, Oxford University Press, 2017). She is coeditor (with M. E. R. G. N. Jansen) of the Brill series "The Early Americas."

Menno L. P. Hoogland is associate professor in the faculty of archaeology at Leiden University in the Netherlands and professor by special appointment at the University of Groningen. Hoogland previously studied cultural anthropology in Leiden with a focus on prehistory and physical anthropology, and wrote his Ph.D. thesis on settlement patterns of the Amerindian population of Saba, Netherlands Antilles. He is an expert in archaeothanatology and Caribbean archaeology. Hoogland's research focuses on the funerary practices of precolonial and early colonial Amerindian societies in the Caribbean and the application of taphonomical methods for the reconstruction of funerary behaviour. He was principal investigator of the NWO project *Houses for the Living and the Dead*. Currently he is a senior researcher in the ERC-Synergy project "Nexus 1492."

Thomas P. Leppard is Renfrew Fellow in Archaeology in the McDonald Institute for Archaeological Research at Cambridge University. His current research addresses the emergence of social complexity in environments that might be expected to discourage such emergence, particularly on islands in the Mediterranean, Caribbean, and Pacific. More generally, he is interested in and has published on the transition to hierarchical communities, the question of Pleistocene maritime dispersal, palaeodemography and ecodynamics, and colonization and its environmental effects.

Deborah M. Pearsall is Professor Emerita of Anthropology at the University of Missouri, Columbia. Retired from MU in 2013 after thirty-five years, Debby Pearsall holds a B.A. from the University of Michigan, Ann Arbor, and M.A. and Ph.D. from the University of Illinois, Urbana-Champaign; all are degrees in anthropology. Her interests within this discipline center on South American archaeology and paleoethnobotany—the study of people–plant interrelationships through the archaeological record. She has conducted paleoethnobotanical research in numerous locations in the Americas. Her research has two broad themes: the origins and spread of agriculture in the lowland neotropics, and methods and approaches in paleoethnobotany. She is the author of three books: *Paleoethnobotany. A Handbook of Procedures* (3rd ed., Routledge Press, 2015); *Plants and People in Ancient Ecuador: The Ethnobotany of the Jama River Valley* (Wadsworth, 2004); and Piperno and Pearsall, *The Origins of Agriculture in the Lowland Neotropics* (Academic Press, 1998), and was the general editor of Academic Press's 2008 *Encyclopedia of Archaeology*. She has published in numerous professional journals and edited books.

Peter E. Siegel is professor and chair of anthropology at Montclair State University, Montclair, New Jersey. He earned B.A. (anthropology) and B.S. (entomology and applied ecology) degrees from the University of Delaware, Newark, and his M.A. and Ph.D. (anthropology) degrees from the State University of New York, Binghamton. Siegel is a New World archaeologist with research interests in historical ecology, ethnoarchaeology, heritage management and preservation, spatial analysis, and cosmological and political organization. He has conducted projects throughout eastern North America, much of the West Indies, lowland South America, and eastern Bolivia.

🌿 Index

Acalypha, 91, 133, 169, 177, 180, 202, 212, 248, 258, 313
Acrostichum, 91, 198, 275
Adornos, 49, 53
agave, 157
Agouti, 35, 47, 49
Aklis site, St. Croix, 287, 289
Alchornea, 93, 134, 168, 201, 215, 248, 257, 267, 268, 275, 277, 278, 280, 281, 282, 283, 306, 307, 308, 309, 310
amethyst, 44
Anguilla, 10, 35, 41, 358
Anse à la Gourde site, Guadeloupe, 49, 50
Anse Bambou Sud site, Marie-Galante, 228
Anse Figuier site, Martinique, 217, 218, 224, 335
Anse Lavoutte site, Saint Lucia, 50
Anse Trabaud site, Martinique, 40, 50
Anthropogenic landscapes, 366, 412
    and microfossils, 11, 13
    and proxies for, 57
Antigua, 8, 10, 41, 300, 319, 332, 336, 342
    and geology and climate, 239–241
    and soils, 243–246
    and European colonization, 242–243
Antillean beaked whale, 55
Archaeological survey, 365–366
Archaic age, 300–303, 315–320, 349, 365–366
    and challenges to identify archaeologically, 13–14
    and horticulture, 13, 59
    and landscape management, 8, 12, 13, 59
    and migration, 4
Arenal site, Costa Rica, 355–356
Argyle site, St. Vincent, 53–54

armadillo, 49
Arrowroot, leren (Marantaceae, *Maranta* sp., *Calathea*), 100, 103, 125, 171, 177, 180, 181, 260, 268, 288, 289, 295, 305
Aster family (Asteraceae), 89, 109, 110, 112, 124, 140, 142, 150, 164, 168, 212, 213, 221, 234, 237, 255, 256, 261, 267
Australia, 350
Avicennia (Black mangrove), 92, 104, 133, 144, 167, 172, 214, 236, 245, 248, 256, 258, 275, 278, 282–283, 289

Baie Orientale site, St. Martin, 42–43
Banwari Trace site, Trinidad, 37, 38, 75, 83, 98, 103, 300, 305, 317, 339
Balearic Islands, 22, 24
Barbados, 8, 10, 37, 40, 49, 57, 59, 70, 302, 334, 339
    and geology and climate, 182–185, 304
    and soils, 185–187
    and European colonization, 186, 188, 191–192, 202
Barbuda, 8, 10, 41, 57, 69, 70, 337, 354, 358, 364
    and geology and climate, 270
    and soils, 270–272
    and European colonization, 272
Barrera-Mordan site, Dominican Republic, 41
Beach Access site, St. John, 287–288
Betty's Hope plantation site, Antigua, 242, 255, 261, 262, 269
Biche point, Trinidad, 37, 126, 128
Big Man society, 44
Bismarck archipelago, 30
Boca Urirama site, Aruba, 46
Bonaire, 35, 36, 37, 38, 39, 46, 51, 52
Bonaire Trench, 35, 155

Bontour site and complex, Trinidad, 51, 98, 99, 333
Borreria, 92, 164, 167, 168, 214, 248, 275, 278, 283, 306, 309, 310
Boutbois site, Martinique, 40, 205, 302, 319
Breton, Père, *Dictionnaire caraïbe-français*, 357
Byrsonima, 94, 112, 114, 119, 123, 133, 207, 215, 234, 236, 248, 257, 275, 283, 306, 307, 309, 310, 311

Caesalpiniaceae, 94, 133, 189, 248, 257, 258, 262, 306, 307, 309
Caliviny style pottery, 49, 132
Canashitu site, Aruba, 46
Canna (achira), 70, 71, 214, 249, 256, 258, 261, 269, 288, 289, 305, 309, 310
Capesterre Belle Eau site, Basse Terre, Guadeloupe, 41
Caraipé temper, 55
Cardial-impressed ware, 29–31
Carnelian, 44
Cashew family (Anacardiaceae, *Spondias*), 93, 108, 109, 123, 134, 140, 142, 144, 150, 153, 248, 249, 257, 258, 262
Casuarina (Australian pine), 249, 267, 268
Cattail (*Typha*), 93, 168, 173, 177, 249, 306, 307, 308, 312, 313, 315
Cayo Redondo site, Cuba, 41
Cedros site, Trinidad, 46, 83, 99, 104, 305, 315, 333
Cerén site El Salvador, 355
Cerro Iguanas shell midden, Tucacas area, Venezuela, 38
Chancery Lane site, Barbados, 193
Cheno-Ams, 92, 133, 144, 150, 164, 167, 168, 177, 180, 200, 214, 249, 256, 261, 267, 275, 277, 278, 281, 283, 288, 306, 307, 308, 309, 310, 312, 313, 314, 337
Chip Chip Hill site, Trinidad, 127, 128, 316
Chrysobalanaceae, 94, 100, 104, 124, 125, 306

Chrysophyllum, 95, 109, 145, 168
Chilean wine palm (*Jubaea*), 23
Cittarium pica, 47, 52
Cladium, 92, 133, 144, 146, 150, 167, 201, 207, 212, 213, 214, 228, 256, 275, 277, 281, 283, 313, 314
climate change
  see Holocene climate change
Coakley Bay plantation, St. Croix, 287, 290
Coastal Falcón, 53
Cocal 1 site, Trinidad, 127, 315–316
Cohoba, edible beans (Fabaceae), 92, 108, 133, 167, 201, 214, 248, 249, 256, 275, 283, 288, 306, 308, 309, 310, 315
Corre Corre site, St. Eustatius, 42
Cotton (*Gossypium*), 49, 93, 167, 169, 177, 214, 242, 249, 257, 287, 288, 308
Colonization, 299–301
  and diversity of island ecologies, 4
  and environmental legacy, 3, 11, 338, 343, 344
  and exploration, 3–6, 339–342
  as historical process, xviii
  and interaction, 3
  of islands, 1–22, 357–361
  and landscape degradation, 11
  and landscape learning, 5
  and lines of communication, 5
  versus migrations, 6, 300
  motivating circumstances of, 3, 342
  pulses of, 4–6
  and trafficking of things, 3
Commensal species, 23
Corsica, 362
Crete, 20, 21, 22, 345, 360, 361, 362
Croton, 133, 144, 146, 167, 214, 249, 256, 275, 287, 289, 307, 308, 309, 310
Cucurbita, 133, 249, 255, 256, 258, 261, 288, 289, 309
Cuba, 364
Cul-de-Sac Marin site, Guadeloupe, 40

cultural classification
  Arauquinoid series, 46, 48, 51
  Barrancoid series, 46, 47, 48
  Bontour complex, 51
  Cedros complex, 46
  Chicoid series, 53, 54
  Dabajuroid series, 46, 51, 52, 55
  El Heneal complex, 39
  Erin complex, 46
  Huecoid series, 43, 44, 45
  Mayoid series, 55
  Meillacoid series, 55
  Ocumaroid series, 46, 51
  Ostionoid series, 48
  Palo Seco complex, 46
  Saladoid series, 37, 43, 44, 50, 51
  Suazoid series, 48, 49, 55
  Troumassoid series, 47, 48, 49
  Valencioid series, 51
Cupey, 35
Curaçao, 8, 35, 36, 37, 38, 39, 46, 51, 52, 55
  geology and climate, 155–157
  soils, 157, 159–160
Cyprus, 16, 24, 25, 26, 360, 362

De Savaan site, Curaçao, 51
Dogbane family (Apocynaceae), 93, 134, 140, 145, 168, 215, 236, 237, 246, 248, 257, 275, 306, 307, 308, 309, 310, 311
demography, 15, 19, 26–29
Diorite, 44
Dominica, 53, 353
Dominican Republic, Hispaniola, 41, 43, 46, 357, 364
down-the-line exchange, 44

eco-niches, 5
El Niño Southern Oscillation (ENSO), 20, 413
environmental coring
  Cedros archaeological site, Trinidad, 99–104
  in the current project, 8, 57–63
  Maisabel site, Puerto Rico, 12
  methods of, 60–63
  Nariva Swamp, Trinidad, 104–128
  St. John archaeological site, Trinidad, 84–99
environmental degradation
  See Antigua (European colonization); *see* Barbados (European colonization); *see* Betty's Hope plantation site, Antigua; *see* Colonization (and landscape degradation); *see* European colonists (impacts to landscapes); *see* Martinique (European colonization)
extinctions of plants and animals on islands, 350, 352, 357, 361–363
Erythrina, 91, 212, 213
Escambrón (*Machaerium*), 91, 133, 164, 169, 212, 213, 234, 237, 249, 275
European colonists
  human-land relations, 4
  impacts to landscapes, 188, 191, 200, 205, 206, 225, 241–244, 255, 260–262, 269

Falkland Islands, 19
Fan palms (*Pritchardia*), 23
Fiji, 28
fire, 348–352
  benefits for humans, 349
  fire-stick farming hypothesis, 350
  at Gesher Benot Ya'aqov, Israel, 349
  prehistory of, 349
  at Wonderwerk Cave, South Africa, 349
Folle Anse site, Marie-Galante, 228
Fort Bay site, Saba, 42
Freshwater sponge spicules (*cauixí*), 51

Galapagos Islands, 22
Geonoma, 198
Ginger family (Zingiberaceae), 242, 278, 280, 306
Goddard site, Barbados, 189, 190
Golden Rock site, St. Eustatius, 47
Golden Rock *maloca* structure, 47
Goto Lake shell deposits, Aruba, 38, 39

Gourd family (Cucurbitaceae), 133, 249, 255, 256, 258, 261, 288, 289, 309
Grand Bay site, Carriacou, 50
Grass family (Poaceae), 68, 69, 71, 81, 82, 89, 92, 93, 97, 98, 100, 106, 108, 109, 110, 116, 123, 124, 128, 133, 134, 140, 144, 150, 164, 167, 169, 171, 177, 180, 198, 201, 202, 212, 215, 216, 221, 224, 228, 234, 236, 237, 245, 246, 249, 255, 256, 257, 260, 261, 267, 268, 274, 275, 277, 278, 281, 282, 283, 288, 294, 295, 305, 306, 307, 308, 309, 310, 311, 312, 313, 314, 315, 317, 333, 337
Greenstone, 44
Grenada, 8, 10, 35, 44, 45, 49, 53, 54, 55
  geology, 129–130
Gros Îlet site, Martinique, 206
Grotte du Morne Rita site, Marie-Galante, 226, 228, 237
Guadeloupe, 226, 228, 237, 300, 304, 318, 320, 353, 354, 358, 359
  La Soufrière volcano on, 237, 353, 354
Guaizas, 53
Gullies (*rooien*), 36, 38, 52, 172
Gumbo limbo (*Bursera*), 94, 133, 145, 152, 173, 188, 194, 201, 215, 234, 236, 237, 241, 248, 257, 265, 275, 283, 287, 307, 308, 309, 310, 311
Gymnopodium, 91, 133, 169, 173, 212, 249, 258, 275, 284

Hackberry (*Celtis*), 94, 100, 104, 133, 145, 146, 150, 153, 164, 168, 201, 213, 215, 249, 257, 265, 267, 268, 275, 288, 307, 308, 309, 310, 319
Hawai'i, 16, 19, 23, 26
Heliconia, 97, 144, 221, 237, 312
Heywoods site, Barbados, 40, 189, 191, 358
Hillcrest site, Barbados, 190
High Bluff site, Grenada, 143
Hirea, 94, 133, 168, 201, 213, 215, 249, 257, 275, 306, 308, 309, 310

historical ecology
  interpretive framework of, 7, 10–11, 343–344
  in islands, xvi, xviii–xx, 3–4, 299, 338–339, 343–344
Hitchman's site, Nevis, 42
Holocene climate history, 8, 36, 78–80, 157, 193, 304–305, 318, 319, 362
  and human-environment interactions, 8, 10, 13
  and sea-level rise, 37, 78, 155, 198, 241, 301–302, 366
  and Trinidad, 37, 77
Holly (*Ilex*), 91, 123, 133, 212, 213, 237
Hope Estate site, St. Martin, 43, 44
human-land relations
  and archaeological discernibility, 4
  and climate, 7–8, 59–60
  and colonization strategies, 3–4, 152–154
  distinguished from natural environmental perturbations, 11, 60, 304, 315, 343–344
  see European colonists
  history of research in, xv–xvii
  and landscape modification, 4, 23–24
  variability in, 13
hunter-fisher-foragers, 38
Hutia, 35

Iceland, 19, 356
Indian Creek site, Antigua, 268, 332, 336
Indios Curacaos, 55
Intermediate culture area, 37
Intertropical Convergence Zone (ITCZ), 32, 130, 157, 184, 185, 305, 413
Introductions of plants and animals on islands, 349–350, 361–363
Island biogeography, 19, 20, 22–23, 27–28
Island dwarfs, 24, 25, 33
Isopach maps, 355–356

Jadeite, 44, 47

Jolly Beach site, Antigua, 41, 241, 246, 265

Kalinago, 53, 54
Kelbey's Ridge site, Saba, 53, 54
Kerguelen, 19
Kermadec Islands, 26, 28
Kernahan Trace site, Trinidad, 127–128, 316–317
Kiritimati Island, 26, 28
Knip site, Curaçao, 51
Knossos site, Crete, 21
Knotweed (Polygonaceae, *Polygonum*), 91, 93, 116, 133, 167, 168, 169, 201, 212, 249, 255, 256, 257, 258, 261, 275, 283, 284, 306, 307, 308, 309, 310
Koriabo ceramics, 54
Krum Bay site, St. Thomas, 42, 287–288, 358
Kythnos, 27, 28

La Filette site, Grenada, 135
Lagun Site, Aruba, 38, 39
Lake Miragoâne, Haiti, 80, 304–305, 347
Landscape learning, xix, xx, 4, 154, 413
La Orchila group, 35, 38
Lapita, 21, 30, 360
La Poterie site, Grenada, 53, 54
Las Aves archipelago, 38
Leapfrog migration, 5
Le Godinot site, Martinique, 40, 205, 302, 319
Level site, Saba, 41
Long Island area (Flinty Bay), 41
Long Island flint, 41, 43
Lord Howe Island, 22
Los Aves site, Bonaire, 51
Los Roques archipelago, 35, 37, 38, 51

Macabou site, Martinique, 50
Maisabel site, Puerto Rico
paleoenvironmental research, 12
Maize (*Zea mays*), 36, 38, 49, 51, 52, 71, 84, 89, 93, 96, 97, 98, 99, 100, 116, 125, 134, 144, 151, 153, 157, 159, 164, 168, 169, 171, 172, 177, 181, 198, 201, 249, 255, 257, 258, 261, 269, 288, 289, 295, 296, 306, 307, 308, 309, 334, 337, 338, 361
Mallow family (*Bombacaceae/Malvaceae/Tiliaceae*), 69, 93, 133, 134, 167, 168, 213, 214, 248, 249, 257, 260, 278, 280, 306, 308, 309, 310
Malmok site, Aruba, 46
Malta, 24, 30, 31
Mammalian fauna, 351, 362, 363
managed landscapes, 6, 7, 8, 35, 108, 148, 150, 153, 154, 177, 198, 200, 212, 213, 237, 238, 299, 333, 334, 339, 343
Mangaia, East Polynesia, 351
Manná, 53
Manzanilla (SAN1) site, Trinidad, 51
Marantaceae, 69, 70, 71, 84, 92, 93, 96, 97, 100, 103, 104, 110, 116, 125, 144, 167, 171, 177, 180, 181, 213, 221, 260, 261, 268, 269, 288, 289, 294, 295, 296, 305, 306, 307
Marie-Galante (Guadeloupe), 10, 35, 42, 45, 226–238, 349, 354
Marine flint nodules, 41
Maroula site, Kynthos, 27
Martinique, 8, 10, 40, 45, 49, 302, 304, 318, 319, 335, 336, 358
  European colonization, 205–206, 225, 336
  geology and climate, 203–205
  Mt. Pelée volcano on, 203, 205, 224, 353, 354, 355
  soils, 205–207
Mastic-bully, 36
Mediterranean, xvii, xx, 15–33, 356, 359, 360, 361, 362, 363, 365, 366
Melongena melongena, 52
Melos, 27
Mesolithic period, 16, 24, 27, 28, 360, 366
Metates, 51
Microflakes, 8, 51
Micronesia, 26
Modified Livingstone rod-piston corer, 60–61

Montserrat, xx, 10, 41, 44, 45, 302, 345, 352, 353, 354, 356, 358, 364, 365
  Blathwayt Atlas map of, 352
  Soufrière Hills volcano on, 353, 356
Morne Cybèle site, La Désirade, 53, 54
Morne Rita cave, Marie-Galante, 42
Morne Souffleur site, La Désirade, 53
Mulberry family (Moraceae), 94, 106, 108, 114, 133, 140, 142, 145, 146, 148, 153, 168, 201, 207, 213, 215, 234, 236, 237, 249, 257, 258, 275, 277, 283, 305, 306, 307, 308, 309, 310, 311, 312, 313, 314, 315
Multiconvex vessel, 54
Mt. Pelée, Martinique, 203, 205, 207, 224, 353, 354, 355
Myrtle family (Myrtaceae), 95, 133, 140, 142, 145, 146, 201, 215, 234, 236, 249, 257, 275, 283, 305, 306, 307, 309, 310, 311, 312, 313, 314, 315
Mystery islands, 26, 28

Nariva Swamp, Trinidad, 104–128
Neolithic colonization of Europe, 4–5
Neolithicization, 22
New Zealand, 19, 21, 26, 28, 360
Nevis, 10, 42, 353, 354, 358
Nightshade family (Solanaceae), 133, 140, 144, 146, 249, 275, 307
Norfolk Island, 19
Nor'fuk language, 19
North Manzanilla 2 site, Trinidad, 127, 316

Orange, lemon (*Citrus*), 168, 169, 181, 275, 277, 283, 289, 308, 309
Oropuche Lagoon, Trinidad, 58, 78, 81, 82, 84, 85, 98, 300, 305, 315, 333
Ortoire site and complex, Trinidad, 126, 127, 128, 315, 316, 317

Pacific, xx, 15–33, 338, 351, 359, 360

Pacific rat (*Rattus exulans*), 23
Palagruža, 26
Paleo-Indian or Lithic age, 37, 128
  See Biche point, Trinidad
  Joboid-like, 37
Palm family (Arecaceae), 84, 94, 96, 97, 98, 100, 103, 104, 109, 110, 114, 116, 123, 124, 127, 130, 133, 134, 140, 142, 143, 145, 146, 148, 152, 153, 154, 168, 171, 177, 188, 198, 201, 213, 215, 216, 221, 224, 234, 236, 248, 257, 259, 260, 261, 268, 267, 269, 275, 277, 278, 280, 283, 287, 288, 289, 294, 296, 306, 307, 308, 309, 310, 311, 315, 351
Panicoid grasses, 71, 171, 177, 216, 221, 294, 295, 346
Particulate charcoal, 4, 7, 13, 14, 57, 59, 89, 106, 114, 116, 143, 148, 152, 177, 229, 234, 265, 268, 269, 277, 280, 282, 293, 296, 315, 318, 319, 334
Pavillon site, Marie-Galante, 228
Pearls site, Grenada, 44, 45, 132, 134, 135, 143, 150, 317, 334
Peccari, 38, 49
Pecten zic-zac, 52
Petroglyphs, 47
Phoenix Islands, 26, 28
Pilosocereus (tree cactus), 277–278
Pinctata radiata (oyster), 52
Pitcairn, 20, 26, 28
Plum Piece site, Saba, 41–42
Pointe de Grande Anse site, Basse-Terre, Guadeloupe, 50
Pointe du Cimetiere site, Marie-Galante, 228
Port St Charles site, Barbados, 190
Prickly ash (*Zanthoxylum*), 91, 123, 134, 140, 145, 146, 152, 169, 173, 202, 208, 212, 213, 237, 249, 258, 275, 284
Puerto Rico, xix, 4, 8, 10, 11, 12, 41, 43, 44, 45, 46, 47, 48, 154, 189, 190, 242, 285, 296, 303, 339, 347, 359, 364
  Laguna Tortuguero, 347

Pumpwood (*Cecropia*), 94, 96, 106, 108, 109, 116, 133, 145, 148, 168, 177, 180, 201, 213, 215, 234, 236, 249, 275, 283, 312, 313, 314, 315, 333
Put Bronswinkel site, Bonaire, 51

Rapa Nui, 16, 19, 23, 24, 360
Red mangrove (*Rhizophora*), 92, 109, 133, 144, 167, 169, 189, 193, 194, 200, 214, 229, 234, 236, 245, 248, 256, 265, 272, 274, 275, 277, 283, 306, 307, 308, 309, 310, 311, 312
Rooi Rincon site, Curaçao, 39, 318
Rosewood (*Machaerium*), 91, 133, 164, 169, 212, 213, 234, 237, 249
Rumex, 133, 168, 201, 249, 257, 309

Saba, 10, 35, 41, 42, 53, 54, 353, 358
Saccharum officinarum (sugarcane), 132, 191, 192, 202, 206, 225, 228, 229, 237, 243, 255, 258, 260, 261, 262, 269, 289, 303
Salines site, Martinique, 50
Samoa, 30
Sand box (*Hura*), 91, 123, 133, 142, 145, 212, 245, 249, 258, 262, 275, 284, 287
San Juan site, Curaçao, 51
Santa Barbara site, Curaçao, 51
Santa Cruz and Savaneta ceramic styles, 52
Santa Cruz II site, Aruba, 46
Santorini, Greece, 356
Sapodilla, 35
Sapote family (Sapotaceae), 36, 95, 108, 109, 134, 140, 145, 150, 153, 168, 201, 212, 215, 228, 234, 236, 237, 249, 257, 275, 283, 288, 289, 305, 306, 307, 308, 309, 310, 311, 337, 372
Sardinia, 16, 22, 30
Savanne Suazey site, Grenada, 132, 143
Sawgrass (*Cladium*), 92, 133, 144, 146, 150, 167, 201, 207, 212, 213, 214, 228, 256, 275, 277, 281, 283, 313, 314

sea grape (*Coccoloba*), 94, 96, 109, 133, 134, 140, 145, 168, 173, 188, 215, 228, 234, 236, 237, 249, 257, 265, 275, 278, 280, 282, 283, 287, 306, 307, 308, 309, 310, 311, 337
seagrass beds, 35, 38, 265
Seaview site, Barbuda, 272
Sebastiana, 95, 168, 173, 249, 275, 306, 308
Sedge family (Cyperaceae), 89, 92, 97, 124, 133, 144, 150, 164, 167, 177, 194, 198, 201, 202, 212, 213, 214, 234, 236, 249, 256, 261, 267, 275, 277, 283, 312, 313, 314, 317
Secondary products, 25
Serpentinite, 44
Seru Boca Rockshelter site, Curaçao, 39, 318
Sicily, 22, 30
Silver Sands site, Barbados, 190
Simon Beach site, Grenada, 135
Site BA1, Barbuda, 272
Site BA5, Barbuda, 272
Site BA7, Barbuda, 272
Site BA16, Barbuda, 272
Smith Gut site, St. Eustatius, 42
Soapberry family (Sapindaceae), 95, 109, 123, 134, 168, 201, 213, 215, 249, 257, 306, 307, 308, 309, 315
Social networks, 34, 47, 48, 51, 55
Socionatural landscapes, xviii, 6, 56, 333, 338, 343, 346, 348, 352, 436
See anthropogenic landscapes
 as evolving system, xviii
Spaanse Water site, Curaçao, 38, 42, 55, 155, 157, 171–180, 318, 334
Starch grain analyses, 38, 43
St. Catherine's ceramic style, 46
St. Croix, 8, 10, 45, 57, 69, 70
 geology, 285–286
 soils, 286–287
St. Eustatius, 10, 42, 47, 303, 353, 358
St. John site, Trinidad, 37, 38, 83, 84, 98, 103, 287, 288, 300, 305, 333, 339
St. Kitts, 10, 41, 242, 353, 358, 365, 366
 Liamuga volcano on, 281, 354
 Mt. Misery volcano on, 354

St. Lucia, 49, 50, 55, 277
St. Martin, 10, 36, 41, 42, 43, 44, 45, 358
St. Michielsberg site, Curaçao, 39, 40
St. Thomas, 41, 42, 287, 288, 296
St. Vincent, 49, 53, 54, 129, 182, 185, 301, 353, 354
  Soufrière volcano on, 353
subsistence strategies/practices, 45, 47, 49, 51
  human behavioral strategies, 35
  slash-and-burn, 36
  slope cultivation, 36
Sufferers site, Barbuda, 272
Swamp bloodwood tree (*Pterocarpus*), 82, 91, 114, 127, 134, 169, 202, 212, 249, 275, 284
Symphonia, 95, 127, 306, 307

Taboüi, 53
Taíno, 53, 55
Talisseronde site, Marie-Galante, 228
Tanki Flip site, Aruba, 52
tobacco, 36, 77, 132, 191, 192, 225, 229, 242, 361
Tobago, 34, 38, 53, 69, 70, 79, 182, 188, 205, 300, 301, 302, 358
Tomasitu site, Curaçao, 39
Transported landscapes, 22, 35
Trants site, Montserrat, 44, 45, 356
Tremiti Islands, 26
Trinidad, 8, 10, 35, 37, 38, 46, 48, 51, 55, 57, 68, 69, 70
  climate, 79–81
  climate periods in the Holocene, 82
  connection to South America, 34, 37
  geology, 77–79
  savannas as refugia of dry climate periods in the Holocene, 82
  soils, 82–83
Tristan da Cunha, 19
  instances of asthma on, 20
Trunk Bay site, St. John, 36

Tsunami, 36
Turquoise, 44
Tutu site, St. Thomas, 288, 289, 296

Upper Blake's site, Montserrat, 41, 302, 358, 359
Urumaco and Los Médanos ceramic styles, 52

Vieux Fort 2 site, Marie-Galante, 228
Vita Levu, 26
Vivé site, Martinique, 45
volcanic ash, 45, 132, 185, 207, 209, 228, 237, 251, 253, 256, 278, 281, 354, 355
volcanic hazards, 352–357
  perception of volcanic risk, 356–357

Wanapa site, Bonaire, 51
Water-procurement and management systems, 36
  Ditches (*rooi*), 36, 38, 39, 52
  Pot-stacks, 36
  Rainwater containers, 37
White mangrove (Combretaceae), 92, 133, 134, 143, 144, 167, 173, 177, 200, 214, 228, 234, 236, 245, 246, 248, 255, 256, 258, 265, 267, 274, 275, 277, 278, 281, 283, 306, 307, 308, 309, 310, 311, 318, 319
White-on-red painting, pottery decoration, 40, 45
Wild avocado, 36
Wonotobo Falls site, Western Surinam, 46

Xeric environments, 35

Yautia-madera (*Montrichardia*), 133, 144

Zoned-incised crosshatched, pottery decoration, 45

www.ingramcontent.com/pod-product-compliance
Lightning Source LLC
Chambersburg PA
CBHW051522020426
42333CB00016B/1739